Dale & Camil

(503) 804-

HYMNS

ISBN 0-7363-1122-X

Published by

Living Stream Ministry
2431 W. La Palma Ave., Anaheim, CA 92801 U.S.A.
P.O. Box 2121, Anaheim, CA 92814 U.S.A.

Living Stream Ministry
Anaheim, California, U.S.A.

07 08 09 10 11 12 / 10 9 8 7 6 5 4

ISBN 0-7363-1122-X

Published by

Living Stream Ministry
2431 W. La Palma Ave., Anaheim, CA 92801 U.S.A.
P.O. Box 2121, Anaheim, CA 92814 U.S.A.

07   08   09   10   11   12   /   10   9   8   7   6   5   4

TABLE OF CONTENTS

HYMNS 1-1080

TABLE OF CONTENTS
HYMNS 1-1080

IV

TABLE OF CONTENTS
HYMNS 1-1080

TABLE OF CONTENTS
HYMNS 1-1080

TABLE OF CONTENTS
HYMNS 1-1080

TABLE OF CONTENTS

HYMNS 1081-1348

TABLE OF CONTENTS
HYMNS 1081-1348

8.5.8.3.

1 Glory be to God the Father,
 And to Christ the Son,
Glory to the Holy Spirit —
 Ever One.

2 As we view the vast creation,
 Planned with wondrous skill,
So our hearts would move to worship,
 And be still.

3 But, our God, how great Thy yearning
 To have sons who love
In the Son e'en now to praise Thee,
 Love to prove!

4 'Twas Thy thought in revelation,
 To present to men
Secrets of Thine own affections,
 Theirs to win.

5 So in Christ, through His redemption
 (Vanquished evil powers!)
Thou hast brought, in new creation,
 Worshippers!

6 Glory be to God the Father,
 And to Christ the Son,
Glory to the Holy Spirit —
 Ever One.

BLESSING OF THE TRINITY — HIS REVELATION

2

12.13.12.10.

1 Glory, glory, glory, praise and adoration!
Hear the anthems swelling out thro' all eternity!
Father, Son, and Spirit — God in revelation —
Prostrate each soul before the Deity!

2 Father, source of glory, naming every fam'ly;
And the Son upholding all by His almighty power;
Holy Spirit, filling the vast scene of glory —
O glorious Fulness, let our hearts adore!

3 God supreme, we worship now in holy splendour,
Head of the vast scene of bliss, before Thy face
we fall!
Majesty and greatness, glory, praise and power
To Thee belong, eternal Source of all!

BLESSING OF THE TRINITY — HIS REIGN

3

6.6.4.6.6.6.4.

1 Come, Thou Almighty King,
Help us Thy name to sing,
Help us to praise.
Father, all glorious,
O'er all victorious,
Come, and reign over us,
Ancient of Days.

2 Come, Thou incarnate Word,
Gird on Thy mighty sword,
Our prayer attend:
Come, and Thy people bless,
And give Thy word success;
Spirit of holiness,
On us descend.

3 Come, holy Comforter,
  Thy sacred witness bear
    In this glad hour:
  Thou who Almighty art,
  Now rule in every heart,
  And ne'er from us depart,
    Spirit of power.

4 To Thee, great One in Three,
  Eternal praises be
    Hence evermore.
  Thy sov'reign majesty
  May we in glory see,
  And to eternity
    Love and adore.

BLESSING OF THE TRINITY — HIS SALVATION

8.8.8.8.   **4**

1 Father of heav'n, whose love profound
  A ransom for our souls hath found,
  Before Thy throne we sinners bend;
  To us Thy pard'ning love extend.

2 Almighty Son, incarnate Word,
  Our Prophet, Priest, Redeemer, Lord,
  Before Thy throne we sinners bend;
  To us Thy saving grace extend.

3 Eternal Spirit, by whose breath
  The soul is raised from sin and death,
  Before Thy throne we sinners bend;
  To us Thy quickening power extend.

4 Thrice holy — Father, Spirit, Son;
  Mysterious Godhead, Three in One,
  Before Thy throne we sinners bend;
  Grace, pardon, life to us extend.

BLESSING OF THE TRINITY — HIS FATHERHOOD

8.7.8.7.D.

5

1 God, our Father, we adore Thee!
We, Thy children, bless Thy Name!
Chosen in the Christ before Thee,
We are "holy without blame."
We adore Thee! we adore Thee!
Abba's praises we proclaim!
We adore Thee! we adore Thee!
Abba's praises we proclaim!

2 Son Eternal, we adore Thee!
Lamb upon the throne on high!
Lamb of God, we bow before Thee,
Thou hast brought Thy people nigh!
We adore Thee! we adore Thee!
Son of God, Who came to die!
We adore Thee! we adore Thee!
Son of God, Who came to die!

3 Father, Son and Holy Spirit —
Three in One! we give Thee praise!
For the riches we inherit,
Heart and voice to Thee we raise!
We adore Thee! we adore Thee!
Thee we bless, through endless days!
We adore Thee! we adore Thee!
Thee we bless, through endless days!

BLESSING OF THE TRINITY — HIS WORSHIP

12.13.12.10.

6

1 Holy, Holy, Holy, Lord God Almighty!
Unto everlasting days our song shall rise to Thee;
Holy, Holy, Holy, Merciful and Mighty!
God in Three Persons, blessed Trinity!

2 Holy, Holy, Holy! all the saints adore Thee;   [sea;
Heaven's elders cast their crowns down by the glassy
Cherubim and seraphim worship too before Thee,
Who wert, and art, and evermore shalt be.

3 Holy, Holy, Holy! though the darkness hide Thee,
Though the eye of sinful man Thy glory may not see,
Only Thou art holy, there is none beside Thee
Perfect in power, in love, and purity.

BLESSING OF THE TRINITY — HIS PRAISE

8.7.8.7. with chorus.   **7**

1   Glory, glory to the Father!
    Glory, glory to the Son!
Glory, glory to the Spirit!
    Glory to the Three in One!
        Let us praise Him! Let us praise Him!
        Praise our God, the Three in One!
        Give Him glory; give Him glory!
        Wondrous things for us our God hath done!

2   Praise the Father who has purposed!
    Praise the Son who all has done!
Praise the Spirit who transmitteth!
    Praise the Three who work as one!

8.8.8.8.   **8**

1   Praise God, from whom all blessings flow;
    Praise Him, all creatures here below;
    Praise Him above, ye heav'nly host;
    Praise Father, Son, and Holy Ghost!

2   Praise God the Father who's the source;
    Praise God the Son who is the course;
    Praise God the Spirit who's the flow;
    Praise God, our portion here below!

8.7.8.7.8.7.   **9**

Glory be to God the Father,
    Glory be to God the Son,
Glory be to God the Spirit,
    Great Jehovah, Three in One!
As it was, is now, and shall be
    While the endless ages run.

10*

8.8.8.8.

1 O God, th' eternal Father, Thou,
The uncreated, great I AM!
More ancient than the ancients are,
Before the primal age began!

2 From everlasting Thou art God,
All time and space Thou dost transcend!
The fulness of eternity,
Without beginning, without end!

3 Th' eternal source of all Thou art,
Before the heavens were decreed!
Thou art the first of all the first,
And e'en the foremost dost precede!

4 Thou art the life that ever lasts,
From age to age Thou endest not!
More lasting than all that which lasts,
Beyond the ultimate Thou art!

5 Thou art the Alpha as the first,
Omega, as the last Thou art!
From start to end Thou hast no lack,
Complete and perfect, wanting not!

6 We praise Thee for Thine endless years,
Extol Thee for Thy boundlessness!
We praise Thee for Thy fulness vast,
Extol Thee for Thy perfectness!

* All hymns marked with an asterisk are written by us.
We desire all of them to be freely available to the
Lord's children; but for the sake of avoiding con-
fusion, we request consultation with us before usage.

— The Living Stream

8.6.8.6.

1 Thou, Father, who art Spirit true,
　　The holiest of all;
　We worship in the spirit now,
　　In truth upon Thee call.

2 A spirit Thou hast made for us
　　That we may worship Thee,
　That echoing in spirit thus
　　One spirit we will be.

3 The Father in the Son has come,
　　The Son the Spirit is,
　That to our spirit God may come.
　　O what a grace is this!

4 The Son is Thine eternal Word,
　　The Word is Spirit too;
　The Spirit as our life has come
　　Our spirit to renew.

5 Thy Spirit in our spirit is,
　　And thus in unity
　Thy Spirit witnesseth with ours
　　That we are born of Thee.

6 In everything Thy Spirit leads
　　That we may follow Him;
　We thus may spiritual become,
　　With life and peace within.

7 In spirit we would worship Thee,
　　In spirit Thee address,
　Until our spirit is released
　　Thine image to express.

8 Our Father, we would praise Thee now
　　That Thou the Spirit art;
　In spirit and in truth to Thee
　　True worship we impart.

8.6.8.6.

1 O God, Thou art the source of life,
    Divine, and rich and free!
  As living water flowing out
    Unto eternity!

2 In love Thou in the Son didst flow
    Among the human race;
  Thou dost as Spirit also flow
    Within us thru Thy grace.

3 Though we in sin and wickedness
    Went far from Thee apace,
  Yet in the Son Thou didst redeem,
    Bestowing life and grace.

4 Though we have often slighted Thee,
    Thy Spirit often grieved,
  Yet Thou dost still as Spirit come
    As life to be received.

5 Thou as the Spirit in the Son
    Hast mingled heretofore;
  Thou wilt thru fellowship anoint
    And increase more and more.

6 The love of God, the grace of Christ,
    The Spirit's flowing free,
  Enable us God's wealth to share
    Thru all eternity.

7 The Father, Son, and Spirit — one,
    So richly care for us;
  Thy love with one accord we sing
    And e'er would praise Thee thus.

8.7.8.7. with chorus.

1   Thou art love and Thou art light, Lord,
     In the Son as life Thou art;
  Love expressing, light illum'ning,
     Thou dost life to us impart.

     Thou art love! Thou art light!
       In the Son as life Thou art;
     Love expressing, light illum'ning
       Thou dost life to us impart.

2   Love bespeaks Thy very being,
     What Thou dost is shown by light;
  Love is inward, light is outward,
     Love accompanies the light.

3   Love by grace is manifested,
     And the light by truth is shown;
  By Thy love we may enjoy Thee;
     By Thy light Thou, Lord, art known.

4   Thru Thy love, which led to Calvary,
     We receive the life of God;
  Light our understanding opens,
     That we may apply the blood.

5   Thru Thy love, as life Thou enter'st
     Fellowship with Thee to give;
  Thru Thy light we take Thy cleansing
     And in fellowship may live.

6   By the light and blood which cleanses,
     The anointing we shall know;
  Then the life of love Thine essence,
     More and more in us will flow.

continued

9

WORSHIP OF THE FATHER — AS LOVE AND LIGHT

7 By Thy love we are Thy children,
 Abba Father calling Thee;
Light disperses all our darkness,
 Till, like Him, Thy Son, we see.

O what grace! O what truth!
 Love is seen and light is shown!
We would praise Thee never ceasing,
 Thou by love and light art known!

WORSHIP OF THE FATHER — HIS IMMORTALITY

14
        11.11.11.11.

1 Immortal, invisible, God only wise,
In light inaccessible hid from our eyes,
Most blessed, most glorious, the Ancient of Days,
Almighty, victorious, Thy great name we praise.

2 Unresting, unhasting, and silent as light,
Nor wanting, nor wasting, Thou rulest in might;
Thy justice like mountains high soaring above,
Thy clouds which are fountains of goodness and love.

3 To all life Thou givest, to both great and small;
In all life Thou livest, the true life of all;
We blossom and flourish as leaves on the tree,
And wither and perish, but nought changeth Thee.

4 Great Father of Glory, pure Father of Light,
Thine angels adore Thee, all veiling their sight;
All laud we would render, O help us to see:
'Tis only the splendor of light hideth Thee.

5 Immortal, invisible, God only wise,
In light inaccessible hid from our eyes,
Most blessed, most glorious, the Ancient of Days,
Almighty, victorious, Thy great name we praise.

7.6.7.6.D.

1 O God, Thou art transcendent,
   The Holy One Thou art!
None other is Thine equal,
   Incomp'rable Thou art!
The holiest of the holy
   The universe may call!
Thy power and Thy nature
   Do far exceed it all!

2 Distinct, unique, and holy,
   Not only right and pure;
Not only without defect,
   But with perfection more;
For nothing can approach Thee,
   Nor e'er Thine equal be;
If aught Thy place hath taken,
   'Tis insult unto Thee.

3 The excellent excelling,
   The fairest of the fair,
Yet differing from the finest,
   For none with Thee compare.
From all the righteous different,
   For Thine is absolute;
None beauteous with Thee vying,
   For Thine excels repute.

4 Thy holiness transcendent
   Thou hast for us prepared,
And this distinctive nature
   We have already shared.
We share in Thy transcendence,
   Since we Thy nature own;
Thy holy life we follow
   Till unto fulness grown.

continued

5 We give Thee praise and worship
For all Thy holiness,
For Thy transcendent nature,
Thine utter peerlessness.
We praise Thee that Thy nature —
Unique, distinct — we share;
This separating nature
Is ours now and fore'er.

WORSHIP OF THE FATHER — HIS NEWNESS

16*

8.6.8.6.D.

1 Our Father, as the evergreen,
Thou art forever new;
Thou art the ever living Lord,
Thy freshness as the dew.

O Father, Thou art unchanging,
Thou never hast grown old;
Thru countless ages, ever fresh,
Thy newness doth unfold.

2 O Thou art God, and Thou art "new";
Without Thee all is worn,
But all with Thee is ever fresh,
Though many years have gone.

3 Each blessing Thou hast given us
Thy newness doth contain;
Thy covenant, Thy ways are new,
And ever thus remain.

4 Now we Thy new creation are —
New spirit and new heart;
We're daily from the old renewed,
New life Thou dost impart.

5   The earth and heavens will be new
       And Thy new city share;
       New fruits each month will be supplied,
       For all is newness there.

6   O Father, Thou art ever new,
       And all is new in Thee;
       We sing the new eternal song,
       New praise we give to Thee.

WORSHIP OF THE FATHER — HIS GREATNESS

11.10.11.10. with chorus.   **17***

1   My Father God, when on Thy vast creation,
    The wonders of the heav'n and earth, I gaze,
    Things great and small, beyond enumeration,
    Which manifest Thy pow'r in untold ways;

      Then all my being sings in praise to Thee,
        How marvellous! How great Thou art!
      And this I'll sing through all eternity,
        How marvellous! How great Thou art!

2   As I enjoy the grace of Thy salvation
    And contemplate how Thou Thy Son hast sent,
    Who died that we might be Thy new creation,
    Thy life expressing to the full extent;

3   When in the church, in blest participation,
    I see how millions Thine own life possess,
    How they are built to form Thy habitation,
    Containing Thee, Thy fulness to express;

4   As I expect the coming age of fulness
    And hope to share the new Jerusalem,
    With all the heavens and the earth in newness
    And all Thou art expressed in all of them;

18*

8.6.8.6.D.

1 How faithful and trustworthy too,
   My Father God, art Thou;
The universe and all therein
   Thy faithfulness avow.

   How stedfast is Thy faithfulness!
      For this I worship Thee;
   It is established in the heav'n,
      And ever stands for me.

2 No turning shadow could there be,
   Nor any change with Thee;
As Thou hast been, and now Thou art,
   Forever Thou wilt be.

3 Thy word, as certain as Thyself,
   Can never pass away;
Though heav'n and earth shall disappear,
   Thy word abides for aye.

4 Thy gifts without repentance are,
   Thy calling is the same;
Thy grace forever lasting is,
   Thy mercy as Thy name.

5 Thy word with Thine own faithfulness
   A surety is to me;
By it, with Thy salvation true,
   I have the certainty.

6 If, due to self, I trust Thee not,
   Yet Thou art faithful still;
Thou never canst deny Thyself,
   Thy word Thou shalt fulfill.

7 As Thou art faithful to perform
   Thy promise and Thy call;
So, feeding on Thy faithfulness,
   I take Thyself withal.

8 The rainbow round about Thy throne
   Thy faithfulness declares;
This attribute forevermore
   The holy city bears.

19

11.10.11.10. with chorus.

1 "Great is Thy faithfulness," O God my Father,
There is no shadow of turning with Thee;
Thou changest not, Thy compassions, they fail not;
As Thou hast been Thou forever wilt be.

   "Great is Thy faithfulness!" "Great is Thy
     faithfulness!"
   Morning by morning new mercies I see;
   All I have needed Thy hand hath provided —
   "Great is Thy faithfulness," Lord, unto me!

2 Summer and winter, and springtime and harvest,
Sun, moon and stars in their courses above,
Join with all nature in manifold witness
To Thy great faithfulness, mercy and love.

3 Pardon for sin and a peace that endureth,
Thy own dear presence to cheer and to guide;
Strength for today and bright hope for tomorrow,
Blessings all mine, with ten thousand beside!

20*

8.7.8.7.D.

1 God our Father, we adore Thee,
    For the sake of righteousness;
Thou in Christ hast justified us,
    Who our conscience can depress?
Thou art righteous, and art faithful,
    On Thy righteousness we stand;
No unrighteousness is in Thee,
    None can turn Thy righteous hand.

2 Thou hast laid our sins on Jesus,
    By Thy justice He was killed;
All Thy holy law's requirements
    For Thy justice He fulfilled.
Recompense from Him receiving,
    Thou art fully satisfied;
How couldst Thou, O God most righteous,
    Claim it once more from our side?

3 Father God, Thou hast accepted
    Jesus as our Substitute;
Judged the Just One for the unjust,
    Couldst Thou change Thy attitude?
As a proof of perfect justice,
    At Thine own right hand He sits;
He, as Thy full satisfaction,
    Righteously Thy need befits.

4 Father, through the blood of Jesus
    We possess Thy righteousness;
By Thy righteousness protected,
    None can shake our stedfastness.
Righteousness of Thine Thou mad'st us,
    None can ever us condemn;
We'll forever testify this
    In the new Jerusalem.

8.8.6.8.8.6.

1 We praise Thee for Thy righteousness;
Thy justice, Father, we confess,
And fully testify.
Thou art the judge of all mankind,
In Thee injustice none can find,
Nor wrong to Thee apply.

2 O holy Father, righteous One,
Thy righteousness upholds Thy throne,
'Tis a foundation sure.
'Tis through this righteousness of Thine
That reigns in Christ the grace divine,
And peace we thus secure.

3 Thy righteousness has caused Thy Son
To die for us that we be won,
Redemption thus was bought;
Thy righteousness has justified
When Christ's redemption was applied,
Salvation thus was wrought.

4 That Thou might show Thy righteousness,
With Thy forgiveness Thou didst bless
Men in the ancient age;
For Thee Thy righteousness to show,
Remission Thou dost now bestow
On sinners in this age.

5 All people Thou wilt judge one day,
Thy righteousness to all display
By Christ, Thy Son, our Lord;
Yet fast we'll stand, for none can move,
Thy righteousness we'll ever prove,
With grace Thou wilt afford.

continued

6　With justice is Thy kingdom filled,
　　And peace upon it Thou dost build
　　　With all in harmony;
　　In the new heaven and new earth
　　Thy righteousness will be their worth,
　　　As promised, God, by Thee.

WORSHIP OF THE FATHER — HIS HOLINESS

22*

8.7.8.7.

1　Holy Father, we adore Thee,
　　　Rev'rent song to Thee we raise;
　　Thou art holy, Thou art lofty,
　　　"Holy is Thy Name," we praise.

2　Loving is Thy heart, dear Father,
　　　Righteous ever are Thy ways;
　　But how holy is Thy nature,
　　　Yet, to us Christ it conveys.

3　Thou hast ever sanctified us
　　　With the blood of Christ our Lord;
　　Thou hast separated sinners
　　　Thru the truth which is Thy Word.

4　Thou hast, by Thy Holy Spirit,
　　　Made us holy unto Thee;
　　And our spirit, soul, and body
　　　Wholly sanctified will be.

5　Oh! the holy life of Jesus
　　　Thru Thy grace we now possess;
　　Thou wilt make us e'en partakers
　　　Of Thy very holiness.

6　When within that holy city,
　　　Thy full holiness we'll share,
　　To the uttermost forever,
　　　"Thou art holy," we'll declare.

8.6.8.6.D.

1 In all Thy wisdom, Father God,
    According to Thy will,
Eternal purpose Thou hast made
    That all Thy Son might fill.

    How deep and rich Thy wisdom is,
        O who can search and trace?
    Yet, Father God, in it we find
        Thy mercy and Thy grace!

2 How wondrously Thou mad'st all things,
    O who can know Thy mind?
All are of Thee, thru Thee, to Thee,
    Thy wisdom here we find.

3 Thy wisdom shuts up all in sin,
    That mercy may be shown,
That none may boast in anything
    But in Thyself alone.

4 In wisdom, by the cross, Thou hast
    For us redemption made,
That in our spirit we may have
    Thyself, the treasure, laid.

5 Thy wisdom thru Thy Church is known
    By principalities,
Thru us Thy wisdom manifold
    Shown in the heavenlies.

6 When in the new Jerusalem
    In mercy we will boast,
Thy wisdom will be known for aye
    Unto the uttermost.

24*

8.6.8.6. with repeat.

1 O God, in Christ all focused is
  Thy wisdom with Thy grace;
As wisdom Thou mad'st Him to us,
  In Him Thy way we trace.

2 What Thou has planned is all in Him,
  Thy way of grace is He;
In Him, Thy Wisdom, we have all,
  That glory be to Thee.

3 In Him, who is our righteousness,
  Have we been justified;
In Him, who is our holiness,
  We're being sanctified.

4 Redemption too He is to us,
  According to Thy plan,
That we may fully be redeemed
  To be a perfect man.

5 He is Thy wisdom, Father God,
  In Thine economy;
For Him we offer praise to Thee
  With all humility.

6 Thy wisdom we have seen in Him,
  So rich and so profound;
Yet richer, deeper, in Thy way,
  By us will it be found.

10.4.10.4.10.10.

1 Father, to us Thy mercy Thou hast shown,
    In Thine own way;
Sinners like us as dear sons Thou wouldst own,
    In love for aye.
Vessels of mercy, Thou didst us prepare;
Vessels of honor, we Thyself declare.

2 "In mercy I delight, not sacrifice,"
    Thou hast declared;
Thru this Thy mercy, favor in Thine eyes
    We all have shared.
'Tis not of them that will nor them that run,
But of Thee showing mercy as was done.

3 Father, Thy mercy with Thy love and grace
    Did we obtain;
And in Thy mercy, with Thee face to face,
    We'll e'er remain;
And for Thy mercy we would worship Thee
Through all our days and through eternity.

26*

8.7.8.7.8.7.

1 God, we praise Thee for Thy mercy,
    'Tis so great and so profound!
In our weakness and our failures;
    With its greatness it abounds.
We adore Thee! we adore Thee!
    With such mercy we've been crowned!

continued

2 How we marvel at this mercy
      So far-reaching and so vast!
   It has reached us, e'en the sinners,
      And will ever hold us fast.
   From this mercy, from this mercy,
      What can cause us to be cast?

3 For Thy mercy we are grateful,
      'Tis so rich, so plenteous!
   Thru Thy mercy in redemption,
      Thou hast richly favored us.
   If without this, if without this,
      How could we be favored thus?

4 Oh, Thy mercy, so inspiring!
      Gentle, tender, dear and sweet!
   With Thy patience and Thy kindness,
      Us in all our need it meets.
   It we treasure, it we treasure,
      Nothing can with it compete.

5 Father, we enjoy Thy mercy,
      Ever fresh and ever new;
   Every morning shed upon us,
      It refreshes as the dew.
   How we taste it! how we taste it!
      Giving Thee the praises due.

6 We can never cease to praise Thee,
      As Thy mercy e'er endures;
   All Thy grace and all Thy favor,
      Ever for us it secures.
   Trusting in it, trusting in it,
      Thy sure mercy us assures.

8.6.8.6.8.8.8.6.

1 Come, let us all unite to sing,
   God is love, God is love.
Let heav'n and earth their praises bring;
   God is love, God is love.
Let ev'ry soul from sin awake,
Each in his heart sweet music make,
And sing with us, for Jesus' sake,
   God is love! God is love!

2 How happy is our portion here!
   God is love, God is love.
His promises our spirits cheer;
   God is love, God is love.
He is our sun and shield by day,
Our help, our hope, our strength, and stay,
He will be with us all the way:
   God is love! God is love!

3 In glory we shall sing again,
   God is love, God is love.
Yes, this shall be our lofty strain,
   God is love, God is love.
While endless ages roll along,
In concert with the heav'nly throng,
This shall be still our sweetest song,
   God is love! God is love!

28

F.M. Lehman   Peculiar Meter.

1 The love of God is greater far
   Than tongue or pen can ever tell.
 It goes beyond the highest star
   And reaches to the lowest hell.
 The guilty pair, bowed down with care,
   God gave His Son to win;
 His erring child He reconciled
   And pardoned from his sin.

   O love of God, how rich and pure!
     How measureless and strong!
   It shall forevermore endure
     The saints' and angels' song.

2 When hoary time shall pass away,
   And earthly thrones and kingdoms fall;
 When men who here refuse to pray,
   On rocks and hills and mountains call;
 God's love, so sure, shall still endure,
   All measureless and strong;
 Redeeming grace to Adam's race —
   The saints' and angels' song.

3 Could we with ink the ocean fill,
   And were the skies of parchment made;
 Were every stalk on earth a quill,
   And every man a scribe by trade;
 To write the love of God above
   Would drain the ocean dry;
 Nor could the scroll contain the whole,
   Though stretched from sky to sky.

6.6.6.6.8.8.

1   What was it, blessed God,
     Led Thee to give Thy Son,
     To yield Thy Well-beloved
     For us by sin undone?
     'Twas love unbounded led Thee thus,
     To give Thy Well-beloved for us.

2   What led Thy Son, O God,
     To leave Thy throne on high,
     To shed His precious blood,
     To suffer and to die?
     'Twas love — unbounded love to us
     Led Him to die and suffer thus.

3   What moved Thee to impart
     Thy Spirit from above,
     Therewith to fill our heart
     With heavenly peace and love?
     'Twas love — unbounded love to us
     Moved Thee to give Thy Spirit thus.

4   What love to Thee we owe,
     Our God, for all Thy grace!
     Our hearts may well o'erflow
     In everlasting praise!
     Make us, O God, to praise Thee thus
     For all Thy boundless love to us.

30*

8.6.8.6.

1 What love Thou hast bestowed on us,
 We thank Thee from our heart;
Our Father, we would worship Thee
 And praise for all Thou art.

2 Thy heart Thou hast revealed to us,
 Made known th' eternal will;
Within the Son Thou hast come forth,
 Thy purpose to fulfill.

3 Thou gavest Thy beloved Son
 In love to come and die,
That we may be Thy many sons,
 As heirs with Him, made nigh.

4 Through Him we have Thy very life
 And Thou our Father art;
Thy very nature, all Thyself,
 Thou dost to us impart.

5 Thy Spirit into ours has come
 That we may "Abba" cry;
Of Spirit born, with Spirit sealed,
 To be transformed thereby.

6 The many sons to glory brought
 Is Thine eternal goal,
And to Thy Son's own image wrought,
 Thou wilt conform the whole.

7 Throughout Thy transformation work
 Thou dost direct each one,
From glory unto glory bring
 Until the work is done.

8 What love Thou, Father, hast bestowed;
 We'll ever grateful be;
We'll worship Thee forevermore
 And praise unceasingly.

8.6.8.6.

1 All that we were — our sin, our guilt,
    Our death — was all our own:
  All that we are we owe to Thee,
    Thou God of grace alone.

2 Thy mercy found us in our sins,
    And gave us to believe;
  Then, in believing, peace we found,
    And in Thy Christ we live.

3 All that we are, as saints on earth,
    All that we hope to be,
  When Jesus comes and glory dawns,
    We owe it all to Thee.

4 O God, how rich, how vast Thy love,
    Whoe'er can Thee repay?
  Thy love is past man's finding out,
    Thy grace no man can say.

5 But Lord, to me I pray Thee grant,
    More clearly may I see,
  That I may e'er more fully know
    How much I owe to Thee.

6 But if man's heart should e'er suppose
    He could repay Thy love,
  It only means he nothing knows
    Of love, all loves above.

7 So may we never bargains make
    With that dear love of Thine:
  The love that made Thine heart once break,
    Whoe'er that love could win?

8 Then nevermore suggest return,
    His love is far too high;
  But let our hearts with rapture burn
    That He for us should die.

continued

9   O Father God, we owe Thee all!
    All that we are and have!
    With grateful thanks before Thee fall,
    'Tis all that we can give.

WORSHIP OF THE FATHER — HIS INTENT

32*

8.8.8.8.

1   We bow and worship, Father, here
    And marvel at Thy wondrous love.
    O what is man that Thou shouldst deign
    To him such boundless grace to prove!

2   We praise Thee for Thy heart's intent
    That man Thy likeness should possess,
    That with Thy life and nature filled
    Thine image he should manifest.

3   Man in Thine image Thou didst make,
    To him authority didst give;
    Thyself presenting as his life,
    That by Thy riches he might live.

4   To enter man Thou dost desire,
    With him to mingle thru Thy grace,
    That man may be transformed and built
    To be Thy worthy dwelling place.

5   Tho' man did fall, Thou didst not leave
    Thy heart's intent, but Thou didst move;
    Redeeming man to bring him back,
    Thou didst Thy love and wisdom prove.

6   In Christ Thou didst Thyself reveal,
    Who died and rose, redemption wrought;
    In Spirit Thou hast entered man
    And to him life and grace hast brought.

7   My spirit is Thy holiest place,
    Thy throne of grace is founded there;
    Thou wouldst that we in spirit come
    To burn the incense thru our prayer.

8   Such grace is like a river full
Which from the throne of grace doth come;
It floweth thru, transforming us,
And builds us up to be Thy home.

9   Receiving of Thy matchless grace,
We marvel at Thy gift so free;
With grateful hearts for Thy great love,
In spirit now we worship Thee.

WORSHIP OF THE FATHER — HIS ELECTION

8.7.8.7.8.7.

33

1   Father, long before creation,
    Thou hadst chosen us in love;
And that love, so deep, so moving,
    Draws us close to Christ above,
And will keep us, and will keep us,
    Firmly fixed in Christ alone,
    Firmly fixed in Christ alone.

2   Though the world may change its fashion,
    Yet our God is e'er the same;
His compassion and His cov'nant
    Through all ages will remain.
God's own children, God's own children,
    Must forever praise His name,
    Must forever praise His name.

3   God's compassion is my story,
    Is my boasting all the day;
Mercy free and never failing
    Moves my will, directs my way.
God so loved us, God so loved us,
    That His only Son He gave,
    That His only Son He gave.

continued

4 Loving Father, now before Thee
　　We will ever praise Thy love;
And our song will sound unceasing
　　Till we meet Thy Son above,
Giving glory, giving glory,
　　To our God and to the Lamb,
　　To our God and to the Lamb.

34

8.7.8.7.8.7.

1 Father, 'twas Thy love that knew us
　　Earth's foundation long before:
That same love to Jesus drew us
　　By its sweet constraining pow'r,
And will keep us, and will keep us,
　　Safely now, and evermore,
　　Safely now, and evermore.

2 Now that changeless love enfolds us,
　　All its wealth on us bestows;
While its pow'r unchanging holds us
　　In a holy calm repose.
God and Father, God and Father,
　　Unto Thee our worship flows,
　　Unto Thee our worship flows.

3 God of love, our souls adore Thee!
　　We would still Thy grace proclaim,
Till we cast our crowns before Thee,
　　And in glory praise Thy name;
Praise and worship, praise and worship
　　Be to God and to the Lamb!
　　Be to God and to the Lamb!

9.8.9.8.

35

1 Blest Father of glory, we worship:
Thy greatness surpasses our praise;
We bless Thee Thy Spirit within us
Gives pow'r to these heavenly lays.

2 We think of the Man in Thy presence,
Set down there, exalted as Head;
Once raised by the might of Thy power,
When numbered along with the dead.

3 We think of the glory that chose us,
'Twas Thine, blessed Father, the Source;
The glory of love that redeemed us
Through Jesus, the Man of Thy choice.

4 As marked out beforehand for sonship,
We praise now the glory of grace
And bow in Thy presence and worship,
As conscious, in Christ, of our place.

7.6.7.6.D.

36

1 We praise Thee, glorious Father,
As objects of Thy grace,
Who for Thine own heart's pleasure
Are now before Thy face:
Thy sons marked out for glory —
Known from eternity —
With Christ Thy Well-beloved,
Object supreme to Thee.

2 Who else but Thee, O Father,
Could in Thine only Son
So bless us with Thy Spirit,
And have us for Thine own?
Soon shall we be forever
With Christ in glory; then
We'll shine in His blest image
Eternally, Amen!

37   8.8.8.8.

1 O God! we see Thee in the Lamb
   To be our hope, our joy, our rest;
   The glories that compose Thy name
   Standing engaged to make us blest.

2 Thou great and good! Thou just and wise!
   Hail! as our Father and our God!
   For we are Thine by sacred ties,
   Thy sons and daughters — bought with blood.

3 Then, Oh! to us this grace afford,
   That far from Thee we ne'er may move;
   Our guard — the presence of the Lord;
   Our joy — Thy perfect present love.

4 This gives us ever to rejoice,
   Turning to light our darkest days;
   And lifts on high each feeble voice,
   While we have breath to pray or praise.

38   8.6.8.6.

1 Of all the gifts Thy love bestows,
      Thou Giver of all good!
   E'en heav'n itself no richer knows
      Than Jesus and His blood.

2 Faith, too, that trusts in Him through grace,
      From that same love we gain;
   Else, sweetly as it suits our case,
      The gift had been in vain.

3 We praise Thee, and would praise Thee more,
      To Thee our all we owe:
   The precious Savior, and the power
      That makes Him precious too.

11.11.11.11. with chorus.

39

1 To God be the glory, great things He hath done,
So loved He the world that He gave us His Son,
Who yielded His life our redemption to win,
And opened the life-gate that all may go in.

Praise the Lord, praise the Lord,
Let the earth hear His voice;
Praise the Lord, praise the Lord,
Let the people rejoice;
Oh, come to the Father, through Jesus the Son,
And give Him the glory; great things He hath done.

2 Oh, perfect redemption, the purchase of blood,
To every believer the promise of God;
The vilest offender who truly believes,
That moment from Jesus a pardon receives.

3 Great things He hath taught us, great things He
hath done,
And great our rejoicing through Jesus the Son;
But purer, and higher, and greater will be
Our wonder, our transport when Jesus we see.

Peculiar Meter.

40

1 We praise Thee, O God,
For the Son of Thy love,
For our Savior who died and
Is now gone above.

Hallelujah! Thine the glory,
Hallelujah! Amen;
Hallelujah! Thine the glory,
We praise Thee again.

2 We praise Thee, O God,
For Thy Spirit of light,
Who has shown us our Savior,
And scattered our night. *continued*

3 All glory and praise
   To Thee, Father of love,
   For through Jesus' redemption
   Thy heart we may prove.

4 We praise Thee again;
   We are filled with Thy love,
   And each heart is rekindled
   With fire from above.

41 13.8.13.8. with chorus.

1 We are never weary singing our eternal song:
   Glory to God, hallelujah!
We would sing His praise forever with our spirit strong:
   Glory to God, hallelujah!

O the children of the Lord have a wondrous
      song to sing,
For the Lord will by His grace many sons
      to glory bring.
We are going in that day to the presence of
      the King:
   Glory to God, hallelujah!

2 We are lost amid the rapture of redeeming love:
   Glory to God, hallelujah!
We are seeking every moment all its grace to prove:
   Glory to God, hallelujah!

3 We are going on to glory as the Lord has told:
   Glory to God, hallelujah!
Where the King in all His beauty we shall soon behold:
   Glory to God, hallelujah!

4 There we'll sing His grace and mercy in a glad new song:
   Glory to God, hallelujah!
There we'll praise our glorious Savior with the
      blessed throng:
   Glory to God, hallelujah!

7.6.7.6.D.

1 By Thee, O God, invited,
  We look unto the Son,
In whom Thy heart delighted,
  Who all Thy will hath done;
And by the one chief treasure
  Thy bosom freely gave,
Thine own pure love we measure,
  Thy willing mind to save.

2 O God of mercy — Father!
  The one unchanging claim,
The brightest hopes, we gather
  From Christ's most precious name:
What always sounds so sweetly
  In Thine unwearied ear,
Has freed our souls completely
  From all our guilt and fear.

3 The trembling sinner feareth
  That God can ne'er forget;
But one full payment cleareth
  His memory of all debt.
When nought beside could free us,
  Or set our souls at large,
The death of God's Beloved
  Secured a full discharge.

4 No wrath God's heart retaineth
  To usward who believe;
No dread in ours remaineth
  As we His love receive;
Returning sons He kisses,
  And with His robe invests;
His perfect love dismisses
  All terror from our breasts.

43

8.7.8.7.D.

1 "Abba, Father," we approach Thee
   In our Savior's precious name.
We, Thy children, here assembling,
   Now the promised blessing claim.
From our guilt His blood has washed us,
   'Tis through Him our souls draw nigh,
And Thy Spirit too has taught us
   "Abba, Father," thus to cry.

2 Once as prodigals we wandered,
   In our folly, far from Thee;
But Thy grace, o'er sin abounding,
   Rescued us from misery.
Clothed in garments of salvation
   At Thy table is our place;
We rejoice, and Thou rejoicest,
   In the riches of Thy grace.

3 Thou the prodigal hast pardoned,
   "Kissed us" with a Father's love;
"Killed the fatted calf," and made us
   Fit Thy purpose to approve.
"It is meet," we hear Thee saying,
   "We should merry be and glad;
I have found My once-lost children,
   Now they live who once were dead."

4 "Abba, Father," we adore Thee,
   While the hosts in heaven above
E'en in us now learn the wonders
   Of Thy wisdom, grace, and love.
Soon before Thy throne assembled,
   All Thy children shall proclaim
Abba's love shown in redemption,
   And how full is Abba's name!

10.10.10.10.10.10.

1 O Holy Father, who in tender love
    Didst give Thine only Son for us to die,
The while He pleads at Thy right hand above,
    We in one Spirit now with faith draw nigh;
And, as we eat this bread and drink this wine,
    Plead His once offered sacrifice Divine.

2 We are not worthy to be called Thy sons,
    Nor gather up the fragments of Thy feast;
Yet look on us, Thy sorrowing contrite ones,
    On us in Him our Advocate and Priest,
Whose robe is fringed with mercy's golden bells,
    Whose breastplate fathomless compassion tells.

3 Oh, hear us, for Thou always hearest Him;
    Behold us sprinkled with His precious blood;
And from between the shadowing cherubim
    Shine forth, and grant us by this heav'nly food
Foretastes of coming glory, and meanwhile
    A Father's blessing and a Father's smile.

4 And, Father, ere we leave Thy mercy-throne,
    Bound by these sacred pledges, yet most free,
We give our hearts, and not our hearts alone,
    But all we are and all we have to Thee;
Glad free-will offerings all our pilgrim days,
    Hereafter an eternity of praise.

Printed by permission of the CHURCH BOOK ROOM PRESS, LTD.

45

8.7.8.7.D.

1 Abba, Father! we adore Thee,
   Humbly now our homage pay;
'Tis Thy children's bliss to know Thee,
   None but children "Abba" say.
This high honor we inherit,
   Thy free gift through Jesus' blood;
God the Spirit, with our spirit,
   Witnesseth we're sons of God.

2 Thine own purpose gave us being,
   When in Christ, in that vast plan,
Thou in Christ didst choose Thy people
   E'en before the world began.
Oh, what love Thou, Father, bore us!
   Oh, how precious in Thy sight!
When to Thine own Son Thou gav'st us,
   To Thy Son, Thy soul's delight.

3 Though our nature's fall in Adam
   Shut us wholly out from God,
Thine eternal counsel brought us
   Nearer still, through Jesus' blood;
For in Him we found redemption,
   Grace and glory in Thy Son;
O the height and depth of mercy!
   Christ and His redeemed are one.

4 Hence, through all the changing seasons,
   Trouble, sickness, sorrow, woe,
Nothing changeth Thine affections,
   Love divine shall bring us through;
Soon shall all Thy blood-bought children
   Round the throne their anthems raise,
And, in songs of rich salvation,
   Shout to Thine eternal praise.

7.6.7.6.D.

46

1 O gracious God, Thy pleasure
　　Is in Thy Christ made known,
　And tells the boundless measure
　　Of blessing for Thine own.
　He has Thy presence entered,
　　As Man in heav'n is known;
　In Him Thy glory's centered,
　　In Him Thy purpose shown.

2 And O what love is beaming
　　Refulgent in that face!
　What blessed light is streaming
　　From that most glorious place!
　Both love and light proclaiming
　　What Thou, the Father, art,
　And wondrous grace revealing,
　　With Thine own Son, our part.

3 Thou source of every blessing!
　　Thou spring of all delight!
　Thy Name with joy confessing
　　Let all the saints unite!
　Each heart its praise outpouring
　　To Thee all praise above,
　Each voice in strains adoring
　　Re-echoes — "God is love."

8.6.8.6.

47

1 Father, Thy name our souls would bless,
　　As children taught by grace,
　Lift up our hearts in righteousness,
　　And joy before Thy face.

2 Sweet is the confidence Thou giv'st,
　　Though high above our praise;
　Our hearts resort to where Thou liv'st
　　In heaven's unclouded rays.

continued

3 Eternal ages shall declare
    The riches of Thy grace,
To those who with Thy Son shall share
    A son's eternal place.

4 Absent as yet, we rest in hope,
    Treading the desert path,
Waiting for Him who takes us up
    Beyond the pow'r of death.

5 We joy in Thee, Thy fulness shall
    Our endless portion be,
Like Thine own Son, with whom we'll dwell
    In bright eternity.

6 O Holy Father, keep us here
    In that blest name of love,
Walking before Thee without fear,
    Thy perfect will to prove.

48   7.6.7.6.D.

1 We bless Thee, God and Father,
    We joy before Thy face;
Beyond dark death for ever,
    We share Thy Son's blest place.
He lives a Man before Thee,
    In cloudless light above,
In Thine unbounded favor,
    Thine everlasting love.

2 His Father and our Father,
    His God and ours Thou art;
And He is Thy Beloved,
    The gladness of Thy heart.
We're His, in joy He brings us
    To share His part and place,
To know Thy love and favor,
    The shining of Thy face.

3   Thy love that now enfolds us
    Can ne'er wax cold or dim;
In Him that love doth center,
    And we are loved in Him.
In Him Thy love and glory
    Find their eternal rest;
The many sons — His brethren —
    In Him, how near, how blest!

7.7.7.6.   **49**

1   Gracious God, we worship Thee,
    Rev'rently we bow the knee;
Jesus Christ, our only plea:
    Father, we adore Thee.

2   Vast Thy love, how deep, how wide,
    In the gift of Him who died;
Righteous claims all satisfied:
    Father, we adore Thee.

3   Low we bow before Thy face,
    Sons of God, O wondrous place;
Great the riches of Thy grace:
    Father, we adore Thee.

4   By Thy Spirit grant that we
    Worshipers in truth may be;
Praise, as incense sweet to Thee:
    Father, we adore Thee.

5   Yet again our song we raise,
    Note of deep adoring praise;
Now, and soon through endless days:
    Father, we adore Thee.

50

10.10.10.10.

1 Father, Thy Son beloved leads our praise
   After the banquet feast is had and done;
   How dear, how sweet to Thee the praise He leads,
   And in His praises joining we are one.

2 Father, we need no goodness more than Thee,
   Nor do we seek a love that's less than Thine;
   How we adore Thee now that here we know
   Thy searchless, uncreated life divine.

3 Father, within Thy love our love to Thee
   Grows, far transcending all our earthly ties;
   Thine own dear love in power leads our hearts
   Where Thine own presence deeply satisfies.

4 Father, by joining with Thy Son beloved,
   We all with gladness praise Thee now again;
   Joyfully feasting on Thy holy love,
   Tasting, as sons, the sweetness of Thy name.

51

10.4.10.4.10.10.

1 Our God and Father, we respond to Thee
         As sons brought near,
   Suited, in love and holy liberty,
         To this blest sphere.
   O wondrous thought, that many there should be
   Like Christ, for Thy delight eternally!

2 He, Thy delight, in whom we have our part,
         Through grace to share
   Thy love for Him, the Object of Thy heart
         Beyond compare.
   His glory in Thy presence now we see,
   As with Him there in love's complacency.

3   'Tis here He sings — what joy His heart doth find,
        Thyself to praise,
While many sons are stirred in heart and mind
        One voice to raise
In worship, God and Father, unto Thee,
Supreme, Thou Source in love's economy!

52

10.4.10.4.10.10.

1   Father, to Thee a joyful song we raise
        With all Thine own;
And in Thy presence sound a note of praise
        To Thee alone;
Bro't nigh, bro't home to Thee — O wondrous grace,
That gives us now with Thine own Son our place.

2   How deep the holy joy that fills that scene,
        Where love is known!
Thy love, our God and Father, now is seen,
        In Him alone;
As, in the holy calm of Thine own rest,
He leads the praise of those Thy love has blessed.

3   He leads the praise! How precious to Thine ear
        The song He sings!
How precious, too, to Thee — how near, how dear
        Are those He brings
To share His place: 'twas thus that Thou didst plan;
Thou lovedst Him before the world began.

53

10.10.10.10.

1 Our God and Father, we respond anew
　　To love in Christ revealed, and praise Thy Name.
He did Thy will; and for the joy in view,
　　Endured the cross, despising all the shame.

2 He, midst His brethren, strikes the note of praise;
　　We hear His song, our hearts responsive swell;
And on this day when He His voice doth raise,
　　In spirit we do join and praise Thee well.

3 Chosen in Him, Thy well-beloved Son,
　　We have our part in joy before Thy face;
Predestined, ere this world had yet begun,
　　For that blest world, where all bespeaks Thy grace.

4 Sons loved and loving, whom Thy Spirit fills,
　　Our endless portion Christ in us to be;
Each with some trait of Him whose love us thrills,
　　For Thy delight and joy eternally.

54

10.10.10.10.

1 O God and Father, we our praises bring,
　　For who more worthy of our praise could be
Than Thou, who seekest worshipers who sing
　　In spirit and in truth adoringly!

2 All worlds Thou hast created by the Son,
　　All things are held by His unmeasured power;
Yet we approach Thee in that glorious One:
　　What cause for worship in this holy hour!

3   'Tis He who leads us in this blessed sphere,
In the assembly singing praise to Thee;
What joy to Him that we should thus be near
As suited and in perfect liberty!

4   Here we unite, our song of joy is one!
And Thou, O God, art fully satisfied.
Amidst the praises led by Christ, Thy Son,
Thou hast a dwelling ever to abide.

55

10.10.10.10.

1   O God our Father, we would come to Thee
In virtue of our Savior's precious blood;
All distance gone, our souls by grace set free,
We worship Thee, our Father and our God.

2   We would, O God, present before Thy face
The fragrant name of Thy beloved Son;
By faith we view Him through Thy boundless grace,
Which, by His dying, He for us has won.

3   Thy joy in Him who is with Thee we share;
Our hearts delight in Thy delight in Him;
Chiefest of thousands, fairer than the fair;
His glory nought can tarnish, nought can dim.

4   We bow in worship now before Thy throne,
By faith the Object of Thy love would see;
Who, in the midst, His brethren's song doth lead.
To Him, our Savior, shall the glory be!

56*

8.6.8.6.

1 Dear Lord, Thou art the Word of God,
   Thou art God's very Son;
   Thou art His holy image true,
   And with Him ever one.

2 Thou art Thyself the very God,
   Thou dost embody Him;
   In Thee is manifested God,
   And we see God therein.

3 Effulgence of God's glory, Thou,
   By Thee God shines on us;
   Expression of His substance, Thou,
   In Thee He's real to us.

4 In Thee God is the life to us,
   In Thee He is the light;
   In Thee His nature we partake
   And with Him we unite.

5 In Thee the grace of God subsists,
   God we enjoy in Thee;
   His truth in Thee is also found,
   His full reality.

6 In Thee God's fulness we receive,
   Which fills from grace to grace;
   In Thee with God we're mingled here,
   Till one in every phase.

7 O Lord our God, we worship Thee,
   In Thee we have our all;
   Thyself we treasure in our heart,
   Thy Name we love to call.

8.6.8.6.

1 The image of the Father God,
    Lord, we behold in Thee;
  The fulness of the Godhead true
    In Thee dwells bodily.

2 Lord, Thou art God's eternal Word
    With life divine in Thee;
  In Thee His grace we all receive
    With His reality.

3 Effulgence of God's glory true,
    The Son of God art Thou;
  The very substance of Himself
    In Thee we all avow.

4 Embodiment of God Thou art,
    And with Him ever one;
  In Thee is God expressed to us
    Beyond comparison.

5 God we enjoy in Thee, dear Lord,
    As life and everything;
  To Thee and God our heartfelt thanks
    And praise we'll ever bring.

58* 8.6.8.6.D.

1 Thou art the living Word, O Lord,
   Which ever was with God;
   His glory Thou hast fully shown
   When Thou on earth hast trod.

   We praise Thee, O Thou living Word,
   For God in Thee we see;
   His glory and His character
   Are all revealed by Thee.

2 The heavens do God's glory speak,
   Creation vast doth show
   The things of God, His character
   And pow'r for man to know.

3 The Word of God — how rich, profound,
   His testimony shown;
   Within the Word Thou art declared,
   That God should be made known.

4 Thou, living Word, didst flesh become,
   With man on earth hast trod;
   And all Thy words and conduct here
   Expression gave to God.

5 O living Word, Thou art the life,
   Thou art the living light;
   As life Thou dost illuminate
   The Father to our sight.

6 God's judgment Thou wilt yet perform,
   His righteousness make known;
   This also doth expression give
   That God be fully shown.

7 God's full expression, Lord, Thou art,
   Himself Thou hast revealed;
   Declaring all He is to man,
   No more is God concealed.

8.6.8.6.8.8.

1 Thou art the everlasting Word,
  The Father's only Son,
God manifestly seen and heard,
  And heav'n's beloved One:
Divine, O Son of God, art Thou,
In Thee God's fulness find we now.

2 In Thee most perfectly expressed
  The Father's glories shine;
Of the full Deity possessed,
  Eternally divine:
Divine, O Son of God, art Thou,
In Thee God's fulness find we now.

3 True image of the Infinite,
  Whose essence is concealed;
Brightness of uncreated light;
  The heart of God revealed:
Divine, O Son of God, art Thou,
In Thee God's fulness find we now.

4 But the high mysteries of Thy Name
  An angel's grasp transcend;
The Father only, glorious claim!
  The Son can comprehend:
Divine, O Son of God, art Thou,
In Thee God's fulness find we now.

5 Throughout the universe of bliss,
  The center, Thou, and sun;
Th' eternal theme of praise is this,
  To heav'n's beloved One:
Divine, O Son of God, art Thou,
In Thee God's fulness find we now.

8.7.8.7.8.7.

1 Of the Father's love begotten,
    Ere the worlds began to be,
He is Alpha and Omega,
    He the source, the ending He,
Of the things that are and have been,
    And that future years shall see,
      Evermore and evermore.

2 This is He whom they in old time
    Chanted of with one accord,
Whom the voices of the prophets
    Promised in their faithful word;
Now He shines, the long-expected;
    Let creation praise its Lord,
      Evermore and evermore.

3 O ye heights of heav'n, adore Him;
    Angel hosts, His praises sing;
All dominions, bow before Him,
    And extol our Lord and King.
Let no tongue on earth be silent,
    Every voice in concert ring,
      Evermore and evermore.

4 Christ, to Thee, with God the Father,
    And, with Holy Ghost, to Thee,
Hymn and chant and high thanksgiving,
    And unwearied praises be;
Honor, glory, and dominion,
    And eternal victory,
      Evermore and evermore.

8.8.8.8.

1 O Lord, Thou art the Son of man,
  Our human nature Thou didst take;
  Begotten of a virgin true,
  Of flesh and blood Thou didst partake.

2 In bondman's form, with lowliness,
  Thou walkedst on this earth of woe;
  The human living Thou didst have
  And all its suff'rings undergo.

3 Born in a manger as a babe,
  Thou wast a child among the poor;
  Thou as a carpenter didst work,
  And e'en an outlaw's death endure.

4 Then Thou wast raised up from the dead,
  Still with the human nature true;
  And as a man in form divine,
  Thou didst ascend to heaven too.

5 Now over all, and on the throne,
  Thou, still a man, art glorified;
  A man with God in light divine
  With whom our God is satisfied.

6 In glory Thou wilt come again,
  Still as a man appearing then;
  As King of kings, with pow'r divine,
  With human nature seen by men.

7 Thou, as the center of all things,
  In the new heav'n and earth shalt be,
  Forever as the One divine,
  Existing in humanity.

62*

8.7.8.7.D. with chorus.

1 Dear Lord Jesus, we adore Thee,
   "Seed of woman" Thou became;
Of the virgin wast begotten,
   Called e'en with a human name.
Taking thus the human nature,
   Thou as man the serpent trod;
By the Cross his head Thou bruisèd
   And fulfilled the plan of God.

   Lord, we see Thy glory,
   Shown in human beauty,
   Full of splendor, manifested
   In humanity.

2 As a man, by incarnation,
   Flesh and blood didst Thou partake
To destroy the devil, Satan,
   In our stead and for our sake.
With the name of Jesus given
   And Emmanuel callèd too,
Thou becam'st our precious Savior,
   Bringing us salvation true.

3 Thou, "Last Adam" wast entitled,
   And wast called the "second man",
Head of all the new creation,
   Better than the first man.
On this earth in life and conduct
   Thou indeed wast Son of man;
Now in heaven with this nature
   Thou dost still appear as man.

4 In the time which God appointed
   Thou wilt come, dear Lord, again,
With the glory of the Father,
   Still appearing as a man.

Even on the throne of judgment
Son of man Thou still wilt be;
And with this, our human nature,
Thou forevermore wilt be.

8.6.8.6.   **63**

1   Praise to the Holiest in the height,
    And in the depth be praise:
In all His words most wonderful;
    Most sure in all His ways.

2   O loving wisdom of our God,
    When all was sin and shame,
He, the last Adam, to the fight
    And to the rescue came.

3   O wisest love! that flesh and blood
    Which did in Adam fail,
Should strive afresh against the foe,
    Should strive and should prevail.

4   And that a higher gift than grace
    Should flesh and blood refine,
God's presence, and His very self
    And essence all-divine.

5   O generous love! that He, who smote
    In man for man the foe,
The double agony in man
    For man should undergo.

6   And in the garden secretly,
    And on the cross on high,
Should teach His brethren, and inspire
    To suffer and to die.

7   Praise to the Holiest in the height,
    And in the depth be praise:
In all His words most wonderful;
    Most sure in all His ways.

7.6.7.6.D.

1   O soul-inspiring story —
     God's majesty and grace
In lustrous strokes of glory
     Deep-carved in Jesus' face!
Hearts rapt in contemplation
     Of Godhead's Image bright,
Break forth in adoration,
     In wonder and delight!

2   There Manhood, all perfection,
     And Godhead-fulness shine;
God's love and Man's affection,
     The human, the divine;
A life, a death, transcendent,
     Revealing God as love:
Here, lowly Man, dependent —
     God over all, above!

3   Unsullied blaze of glory!
     O ever-radiant Face!
Thy rich, unfathomed story
     Transfigures us in grace!
Made like Thee, soon, completely,
     With love-lit eyes we'll scan
God's face unveiled so sweetly
     In Thine, Thou Son of man!

6.4.6.4.6.6.6.4.

1 Jesus! that name we love,
    Jesus, our Lord!
Jesus, all names above,
    Jesus, the Lord!
Thou, Lord, our all must be;
Nothing that's good have we,
Nothing apart from Thee,
    Jesus, our Lord!

2 As Son of Man it was,
    Jesus, the Lord!
Thou gav'st Thy life for us,
    Jesus, our Lord!
Great was indeed Thy love,
All other loves above,
Love Thou didst dearly prove,
    Jesus, our Lord!

3 Righteous alone in Thee,
    Jesus, the Lord!
Thou wilt a refuge be,
    Jesus, our Lord!
Whom, then, have we to fear,
What trouble, grief, or care,
Since Thou art ever near,
    Jesus, our Lord!

4 Soon Thou wilt come again,
    Jesus, the Lord!
We shall be happy then,
    Jesus, our Lord!
When Thine own face we see,
Then shall we like Thee be,
Then evermore with Thee,
    Jesus, our Lord!

66

8.6.8.6. with repeat.

1 How sweet the Name of Jesus sounds
   In a believer's ear!
   It soothes his sorrow, heals his wounds,
   And drives away his fear.

2 It makes the wounded spirit whole,
   And calms the troubled breast;
   'Tis manna to the hungry soul,
   And to the weary rest.

3 Dear Name! the Rock on which we build;
   Our shield and hiding-place;
   Our never-failing treasury, filled
   With boundless stores of grace.

4 Jesus, our Savior, Shepherd, Friend,
   Our Prophet, Priest, and King;
   Our Lord, our Life, our Way, our End,
   Accept the praise we bring.

5 Weak is the effort of our heart,
   And cold our warmest thought;
   But when we see Thee as Thou art,
   We'll praise Thee as we ought.

6 Till then we would Thy love proclaim
   With every fleeting breath;
   And triumph in that blessed Name
   Which quells the pow'r of death.

(Repeat the last two lines of each stanza)

8.8.8.7. with chorus.

1 The name of Jesus is so sweet,
I love its music to repeat;
It makes my joys full and complete,
The precious name of Jesus.

Jesus! oh, how sweet the name,
Jesus! every day the same;
Jesus! let all saints proclaim
Its worthy praise forever.

2 I love the name of Him whose heart
Knows all my griefs and bears a part;
Who bids all anxious fears depart,
I love the name of Jesus.

3 That name I fondly love to hear,
It never fails my heart to cheer,
Its music dries the falling tear;
Exalt the name of Jesus.

4 No word of man can ever tell
How sweet the name I love so well,
Oh, let its praises ever swell,
Oh, praise the name of Jesus.

68*

8.7.8.7.D.

1 Lord, Thy Name is callèd Jesus,
　　Wonderful is this dear Name;
　Thou wast brought forth of the virgin,
　　And the Son of man became.
　Thou art our Jehovah-Savior,
　　Saving us from all our sins;
　When as Savior we receive Thee,
　　Life divine in us begins.

2 Thou as "Christ" art also titled,
　　Title of Thy ministry;
　Thou art truly God's anointed,
　　Even from eternity.
　Thou, O Lord, art God's Messiah;
　　God appointed Thee in love,
　That Thou might fulfill His purpose
　　And to all His glory prove.

3 Thou art also called "Emmanuel";
　　"God with us" Thou cam'st to be;
　God in grace is wholly mingled
　　With our own humanity.
　God in flesh is manifested,
　　Full of grace and truth therein;
　We have seen in Thee God's glory,
　　And in faith partake of Him.

4 How we treasure all Thy names, Lord,
　　How much they to us unfold;
　All their worth and all their sweetness
　　We in love will ever hold.
　Precious Savior, we adore Thee,
　　Worship unto Thee we bring;
　Our Emmanuel we exalt Thee,
　　And Thy praise will ever sing.

7.7.8.7.D.

1 Thy name we love, Lord Jesus,
  And lowly bow before Thee;
And while we live, to Thee we give
  All blessing, worship, glory.
We sing aloud Thy praises,
  Our hearts and voices blending,
'Tis Thou alone we worthy own,
  Thy beauty's all-transcending.

2 Thy name we love, Lord Jesus;
  It tells God's love unbounded
To ruined man, ere time began,
  Or heav'n and earth were founded:
Thine is a love eternal,
  That found in us its pleasure,
That brought Thee low to bear our woe
  And make us Thine own treasure.

3 Thy name we love, Lord Jesus;
  It tells Thy birth so lowly,
Thy patience, grace, and gentleness,
  Thy lonely path, so holy;
Thou wast the "Man of Sorrows";
  Our grief, too, Thou didst bear it;
Our bitter cup Thou drankest up;
  The thorny crown, didst wear it.

4 Thy name we love, Lord Jesus;
  God's Lamb — Thou wast ordained,
To bear our sins (Thyself all clean)
  And hast our guilt sustained.
We see Thee crowned in glory,
  Above the heavens now seated,
The vict'ry won, Thy work well done,
  Our righteousness completed.

70

8.6.8.6. with chorus.

1 There is a name I love to hear,
   I love to sing its worth;
   It sounds like music in mine ear,
   The sweetest name on earth.

   Oh, how I love Jesus,
   Oh, how I love Jesus,
   Oh, how I love Jesus,
   Because He first loved me!

2 It tells me of a Savior's love,
   Who died to set me free;
   It tells me of His precious blood,
   The sinner's perfect plea.

3 It tells me what my Father hath,
   In store for every day,
   And though I tread a darksome path,
   Yields sunshine all the way.

4 It tells of One whose loving heart
   Can feel my deepest woe,
   Who in each sorrow bears a part
   That none can bear below.

71

8.6.8.6.

1 Jesus! how much Thy name unfolds
   To every opened ear;
   The pardoned sinner's mem'ry holds
   None other half so dear.

2 Thy name encircles every grace
   That God as man could show;
   There only could He fully trace
   A life divine below.

3   Jesus — it speaks a life of love,
      Of sorrows meekly borne;
    It tells of sympathy above,
      Whatever makes us mourn.

4   Jesus, the One who knew no sin,
      Made sin to make us just;
    Thou gav'st Thyself our love to win,
      Our full confiding trust.

5   The mention of Thy name shall bow
      Our hearts to worship Thee;
    The chiefest of ten thousand Thou,
      Whose love has set us free.

72

8.6.8.6.

1   Jesus, the name high over all,
      In hell, or earth, or sky:
    Angels and men before it fall,
      And devils fear and fly.

2   Jesus, the name to sinners dear,
      The name to sinners giv'n;
    It scatters all their guilty fear,
      It brings them peace of heav'n.

3   Jesus the prisoner's fetters breaks,
      And bruises Satan's head;
    Pow'r into strengthless souls He speaks,
      And life into the dead.

4   Oh, that the world might taste and see,
      The riches of His grace!
    The arms of love that compass me,
      Would all mankind embrace.

continued

5 Him as my righteousness I show,
     His saving truth proclaim:
    'Tis all my business here below,
     To cry, Behold the Lamb!

6 Happy, if with my latest breath
     I may but gasp His name:
    Preach Him to all, and cry in death,
     "Behold, behold the Lamb!"

73   8.7.8.7.

1 Glorious, mighty Name of Jesus,
     Into Thy dear Name I flee;
    "Set aloft," I praise and worship,
     For Thy Name is victory!

2 Blessed Jesus! Mighty Savior!
     In Thy Name is all I need;
    Just to breathe the Name of Jesus,
     Is to drink of Life indeed.

3 Glorious, mighty Name of Jesus,
     Heav'n and earth its pow'r proclaim;
    But forgiven sinners only,
     Know the balm of Jesus' Name.

4 Jesus! Jesus! Name most precious,
     Balm in pain or mighty sword;
    In Thy Name, we live and conquer,
     Blessed, glorious, coming Lord.

9.8.9.8.D.

1 There is a name to Jesus given,
   His matchless love its accents tell;
For it declares: He is my Brother,
   And this His name — Emmanuel!
The Lord, by angels worshiped yonder,
   Has stooped to earth with men to dwell,
Incarnate God, and man forever —
   Our own beloved Emmanuel.

2 There is a name that's still more precious,
   That stirs our hearts with fondest love:
It is the charming name of Jesus,
   The name all other names above.
It tells me that He is my Savior
   From sin and sickness and the grave.
I love the precious name of Jesus,
   For I am one He came to save!

3 Though dear to us the name of Jesus,
   The name of Christ is higher still!
It tells of Him who dwells within us,
   Our old heart to renew and fill.
It tells me of the Spirit's fullness,
   It brings the pow'r of Pentecost.
O blessed Christ, anoint me also,
   And fill me with the Holy Ghost!

75

8.7.8.7.

1 Jesus, Name of matchless splendor!
   Name all other names above!
Glorious Son of God incarnate,
   King of kings, and Lord of love!

2 Name that to our hearts is nearest,
   Here the stricken soul doth hide;
Name that to our hearts is dearest,
   As in Jesus we confide.

3 "Call Him Jesus!" He shall save us
   From the tyranny of sin;
From its condemnation save us,
   From iniquity within.

4 Thanks we give, and adoration,
   Every day and every hour,
For an uttermost salvation,
   Freedom from sin's guilt and power.

5 Jesus! sweetest note of any
   In the lowly pilgrim's song;
Jesus! the triumphant music
   Of the bright angelic throng.

6 Earth to Him her face upraises,
   Knows Him as the great I AM!
Heaven resounds with Jesus' praises,
   Glory to the bleeding Lamb!

6.5.6.5.D.

1 In the Name of Jesus
    Every knee shall bow,
Every tongue confess Him
    King of glory now;
'Tis the Father's pleasure
    We should call Him Lord,
Who from the beginning
    Was the Mighty Word.

2 At His voice creation
    Sprang at once to sight:
All the angel faces,
    All the hosts of light,
Thrones and dominations,
    Stars upon their way,
All the heav'nly orders,
    In their great array.

3 Humbled for a season,
    To receive a Name
From the lips of sinners
    Unto whom He came,
Faithfully He bore it
    Spotless to the last,
Brought it back victorious,
    When from death He passed;

4 Bore it up triumphant,
    With its human light,
Through all ranks of creatures,
    To the central height;
To the throne of Godhead,
    To the Father's breast,
Filled it with the glory
    Of that perfect rest.

continued

5 Name Him, brothers, name Him,
    With love strong as death,
But with awe and wonder,
    And with bated breath;
He is God the Savior,
    He is Christ the Lord,
Ever to be worshiped,
    Trusted, and adored.

6 In your hearts enthrone Him;
    There let Him subdue
All that is not holy,
    All that is not true;
Crown Him as your Captain
    In temptation's hour;
Let His will enfold you
    In its light and power.

7 Brothers, this Lord Jesus
    Shall return again,
With His Father's glory,
    With His angel train;
For all wreaths of empire
    Meet upon His brow,
And our hearts confess Him
    King of glory now.

8.8.8.8.

1   Lift that Name high! That glorious Name,
        Let heav'n and earth its pow'r proclaim;
    Our mighty, conqu'ring, coming King,
        Earth yet shall with His praises ring.

2   Lift that Name high! To that high tower
        We flee in every trial hour,
    Safe, sheltered, satisfied and free,
        For Jesus' Name is victory.

3   Lift that Name high! Until one day
        His mighty Name the earth shall sway,
    And sin and death, distress and pain
        Shall be no more, for Christ shall reign.

4   Lift that Name high! Jesus shall reign,
        And kings shall follow in His train;
    Lift that Name high, all names above,
        The Name of Him we own and love.

5   Lift that Name high! For every knee
        Shall bow to Him; Jesus shall see
    Fruit of His Cross, when earth shall bring
        Her tribute to her Lord and King.

78*

8.8.8.5.

1 Gracious Lord, Thy name "I AM" is,
Precious name, how rich and full 'tis,
All-inclusive, faithful too 'tis —
   All we need, Thou art!

2 Thou the Son, the Father in Thee,
As the Spirit now indwell me,
That the riches of Thyself we
   May experience.

3 Thou the Temple for God's dwelling,
Thou the Father's life e'er telling;
We in Thee with joy excelling
   Face to face see Him.

4 Thou the Lamb and Thou the Bridegroom,
For the bride Thou sufferedst sin's doom,
Wounded, crucified in our room;
   Thus we find our rest.

5 Thou art wisdom and the way, Lord,
Thou our lives dost plan each day, Lord,
Grace to us Thou dost convey, Lord,
   In Thy path to walk.

6 Pure and holy, righteous Thou art,
One with God, well-pleasing His heart,
Thou within to us dost impart
   Harmony with God.

7 Thou art life and Thou art light, Lord,
Death hast swallowed, banished night, Lord,
Thou hast quickened, given sight, Lord;
   We are now set free.

8   Thou art resurrection power,
Thou the conqu'ror in hell's hour;
Thou dost us with might empower
    Over all to reign.

9   Living water, food supply, Lord,
Thou Thyself art, and didst die, Lord,
All our want to satisfy, Lord;
    Now we feast on Thee.

10   Thou the Shepherd and Physician,
Thou hast healed our sick condition;
Comfort, guide, protect — Thy mission;
    Thou dost care for us.

11   Priest and King Thou art fore'er, Lord;
Into God we're brought, and there, Lord,
Thine authority we share, Lord;
    What an honored place!

12   Thou our Hope and our Redemption,
Thou wilt change our old creation,
Make of Thee a duplication,
    Thus Thyself express.

13   Thou our Joy, our Peace, our Glory;
Truth, and Grace, the Rock, the Life-tree,
Building, Mountain, Sun, and Shield — we
    Ne'er can tell it all.

14   What Thou art — eternal, boundless,
Full and perfect, rich, exhaustless —
Meets our need to utter fullness
    And from us o'erflows.

79

8.6.8.6. with chorus.

1 All praise to Him who reigns on high,
   In majesty supreme,
   Who gave His life for man to die,
   That He might man redeem.

   Blessed be the name,
   Blessed be the name,
   Blessed be the name of the Lord.
   Blessed be the name,
   Blessed be the name,
   Blessed be the name of the Lord.

2 His name above all names shall stand,
   Exalted more and more,
   At God the Father's own right hand,
   Where angel hosts adore.

3 Redeemer, Savior, Friend of man
   Once ruined by the fall,
   Thou hast devised salvation's plan,
   For Thou hast died for all.

4 His name shall be the Counsellor,
   The mighty Prince of Peace,
   Of all earth's kingdoms, Conqueror,
   Whose reign shall never cease.

6.6.6.6.8.8.

1   Join all the glorious names
       Of wisdom, love, and pow'r,
       That mortals ever knew,
       That angels ever bore;
   All are too mean to speak His worth,
   Too mean to set my Savior forth.

2   Great Prophet of my God,
       My tongue would bless Thy name;
       By Thee the joyful news
       Of our salvation came;
   The joyful news of sins forgiv'n,
   Of death annulled, and Thy life giv'n.

3   Jesus, my great High Priest,
       Offered His blood, and died;
       My guilty conscience seeks
       No sacrifice beside:
   His pow'rful blood did me redeem,
   'Tis worthy of my heart's esteem.

4   I love my Shepherd's voice:
       His watchful eye shall keep
       My wand'ring soul among
       The thousands of His sheep:
   He feeds His flock, He calls their names,
   His bosom bears the tender lambs.

5   My Savior and my Lord,
       My Conqu'ror and my King,
       Thy scepter and Thy sword,
       Thy reigning grace I sing:
   Thine is the pow'r; behold I sit
   In willing bonds beneath Thy feet.

81*

8.8.8.8.

1 O Lord, Thy being is of old,
Before th' eternal past began!
For Thou th' eternal Father art,
The uncreated, great I AM!

2 Although a man with men become,
Yet Thou with God eternal art!
The same completeness Thou dost share,
And infinite as God Thou art!

3 Thine origin, the same as God,
Before creation was decreed!
Before the foremost, Thou art first,
None other doth Thyself precede!

4 Thou never changest thru all time,
Thy years are to eternity!
None is as lasting as Thyself,
Nor is there any after Thee!

5 Just as the Father, diff'ring not,
The same perfection Thou too hast!
Thou art the Alpha and the First,
Thou art Omega and the Last!

6 We praise Thee for Thine endless years,
Extol Thee for Thy perfectness!
Admiring all Thy fulness vast,
We marvel at Thy boundlessness!

82

PRAISE OF THE LORD — HIS INCARNATION

Peculiar Meter.

1 Down from His glory,
Ever living story,
My God and Savior came,
And Jesus was His name.
Born in a manger,
To His own a stranger,
A Man of sorrows, tears and agony.

Chorus:

O how I love Him! How I adore Him!
My breath, my sunshine, my all in all!
The great Creator became my Savior,
And all God's fulness dwelleth in Him.

2 What condescension,
    Bringing us redemption;
That in the dead of night,
    Not one faint hope in sight,
God, gracious, tender,
    Laid aside His splendor,
Stooping to woo, to win, to save my soul.

3 Without reluctance,
    Flesh and blood His substance
He took the form of man,
    Revealed the hidden plan.
O glorious myst'ry,
    Sacrifice of Calv'ry,
And now I know Thou art the great "I AM."

8.7.8.7.   **83**

1 Hark! what mean those holy voices
    Sweetly sounding in the skies?
Lo! th' angelic host rejoices,
    Loudest hallelujahs rise.

2 Listen to the wondrous story
    Which they chant in hymns of joy:
"Glory in the highest, glory!
    Glory be to God most high!

3 "Peace on earth, good-will from heaven,
    Reaching far as man is found;
Souls redeemed and sins forgiven,
    Loud our golden harps shall sound.

continued

4 "Christ is born! the great Anointed!
    Heaven and earth His glory sing;
Oh, receive whom God appointed
    For your Prophet, Priest, and King!

5 "Hasten, mortals, to adore Him,
    Learn His name and taste His joy,
Till one day ye sing before Him
    Glory be to God most high!"

6 Let us learn the wondrous story
    Of our great Redeemer's birth;
Spread the brightness of His glory,
    Till it cover all the earth.

84
         7.7.7.7.D. with repeat.

1 Hark! the herald angels sing,
    "Glory to the new-born King;
Peace on earth, and mercy mild;
    God and sinners reconciled."
Joyful, all ye nations, rise,
    Join the triumph of the skies;
With angelic hosts proclaim,
    "Christ is born in Bethlehem."
    (Repeat the last two lines)

2 Christ, by highest heav'n adored,
    Christ, the everlasting Lord:
Late in time behold Him come,
    Offspring of a virgin's womb.
Veiled in flesh the Godhead see,
    Hail th' incarnate Deity!
Pleased as man with man to dwell,
    Jesus our Immanuel.

3   Hail the heav'n-born Prince of Peace!
       Hail the Sun of righteousness!
    Light and life to all He brings,
       Ris'n with healing in His wings:
    Mild He lays His glory by,
       Born that man no more may die;
    Born to raise the sons of earth;
       Born to give them second birth.

4   Come, Desire of nations, come!
       Fix in us Thy humble home:
    Rise, the woman's conqu'ring seed,
       Bruise in us the serpent's head;
    Adam's likeness now efface,
       Stamp Thine image in its place:
    Final Adam from above,
       Reinstate us in Thy love.

Peculiar Meter.   **85**

1   O come, all ye faithful! joyfully triumphant,
    To Bethlehem hasten now with glad accord;
    Lo! in a manger lies the God Almighty;

        O come, let us adore Him,
        O come, let us adore Him,
        O come, let us adore Him,
        Christ the Lord!

2   Raise, raise choirs of angels, songs of loudest triumph,
    Through heaven's high arches be your praises poured:
    Now to our God be glory in the highest;

3   Amen! Lord, we bless Thee, born for our salvation!
    O Jesus! forever be Thy Name adored;
    Word of the Father, late in flesh appearing;

86*

8.8.8.6.

1 Though Thou art God, most glorious, high,
Thou in the flesh to us came nigh,
A lowly man become thereby;
    Lord, I remember Thee!

2 Glory divine was put away
Under the tent of flesh to stay,
No outward beauty to display;
    Lord, I remember Thee!

3 Thou art a root from out dry ground,
Thou wast the Man of sorrows found,
Hated, despised by man around;
    Lord, I remember Thee!

4 Gentle and lowly is Thy heart,
Willing to suffer all Thou art,
To God and man complaining not;
    Lord, I remember Thee!

5 Thou as a man art tender, sweet,
Balanced in every way, complete,
Meal-offering to the Father meet;
    Lord, I remember Thee!

6 Doing the Father's will Thy prize,
Never accepting Satan's lies,
None like Thyself, so faithful, wise;
    Lord, I remember Thee!

7 For Thine obedience to God's will,
Willing to suffer deathly ill,
E'en on the Cross my place to fill,
    Lord, I remember Thee!

8 Therefore hath God exalted Thee,
Given Thee glory, majesty,
Heaven and earth will bow the knee;
    O Lord, I worship Thee!

8.6.8.6.

1 O Lord! When we the path retrace
    Which Thou on earth hast trod,
  To men Thy wondrous love and grace,
    Thy faithfulness to God;

2 Thy love, by man so sorely tried,
    Proved stronger than the grave;
  The very spear that pierced Thy side
    Drew forth the blood to save;

3 Though Thou didst pass through woes and grief,
    Thy works were ever good;
  Although midst sorrows all Thy life,
    Thou spak'st no murmuring word.

4 Faithful amidst unfaithfulness,
    'Mid darkness only light,
  Thou didst Thy Father's name confess,
    And in His will delight;

5 Unmoved by Satan's subtle wiles,
    Or suffering, shame, and loss,
  Thy path, uncheered by earthly smiles,
    Led only to the cross.

6 We wonder at Thy lowly mind,
    And fain would like Thee be,
  And all our rest and pleasure find
    In learning, Lord, of Thee.

88

8.8.8.8.

1 How beauteous were the marks divine,
That in Thy meekness used to shine,
That lit Thy lonely pathway, trod
In wondrous love, O Son of God!

2 O who like Thee, so mild, so bright,
Thou Son of man, Thou Light of light?
O who like Thee did ever go
So patient, through a world of woe?

3 O who like Thee so humbly bore
The scorn, the scoffs of men, before?
So meek, so lowly, yet so high,
So glorious in humility?

4 And death, that sets the prisoner free,
Was pang, and scoff, and scorn to Thee;
Yet love through all Thy torture glowed,
And mercy with Thy life-blood flowed.

5 O wondrous Lord, my soul would be
Still more and more conformed to Thee,
And learn of Thee, the lowly One,
And like Thee, all my journey run.

89

8.6.8.6.

1 What grace, O Lord, and beauty shone
    Around Thy steps below!
What patient love was seen in all
    Thy life and death of woe!

2 Forever on Thy burdened heart
    A weight of sorrow hung,
Yet no ungentle, murm'ring word
    Escaped Thy silent tongue.

3 Thy foes did hate, despise, revile,
    Thy friends unfaithful prove;
Unwearied in forgiveness still,
    Thy heart could only love!

7.7.7.7.

1 Lord, accept our feeble song!
Pow'r and praise to Thee belong;
We would all Thy grace record,
Holy, gracious, loving Lord!

2 Rich in glory, Thou didst stoop,
Thence is all Thy people's hope;
Thou wast poor, that we might be
Rich in glory, Lord, with Thee.

3 Wherefore Thou high heaven didst spurn?
Wherefore Thou to earth didst turn?
Why leave heav'n to come to earth
Lonely, scorned, e'en suffering death?

4 Thou in heav'n — the glorious One!
Thou on earth — the outcast Man!
Though this suffering Thou didst know,
Love would come to bear our woe.

5 When we think of love like this,
Joy and shame our hearts possess;
Joy, that Thou couldst pity thus;
Shame, for such returns from us.

6 Yet we hope the day to see
When from every hindrance free,
When to Thee, in glory, brought,
We shall serve Thee as we ought.

7 Now, O Lord, we wait for Thee,
Wait "the blessed hope" to see.
May we ever for Thee live,
Till Thy saints Thou dost receive.

91

ALONE

Benjamin H. Price   8.6.8.6. with chorus.

1 It was alone the Savior prayed
      In dark Gethsemane;
   Alone He drained the bitter cup
      And suffered there for me.

      Alone, alone,
      He bore it all alone;
      He gave Himself to save His own,
      He suffered, bled and died alone, alone.

2 It was alone the Savior stood
      In Pilate's judgment hall;
   Alone the crown of thorns He wore,
      Forsaken thus by all.

3 Alone upon the cross He hung
      That others He might save;
   Forsaken then by God and man.
      Alone, His life He gave.

4 Can you reject such matchless love?
      Can you His claim disown?
   Come, give your all in gratitude,
      Nor leave Him thus alone.

11.11.11.5.

1 O dearest Lord, what law hast Thou e'er broken
That such sharp sentence should on Thee be spoken?
Of what misdeed hast Thou to make confession —
What dark transgression?

2 They crown Thy head with thorns, they smite,
they scourge Thee;
With cruel mockings to the cross they urge Thee;
They give Thee gall to drink, they still decry Thee;
They crucify Thee.

3 What punishment so strange is suffered yonder?
The shepherd dies for sheep that loved to wander;
The Master pays the debt His servants owe Him,
Who would not know Him.

4 The sinless Son of God must die in sadness;
The sinful child of man may live in gladness;
Man forfeited His life and is acquitted —
God is committed.

5 O mighty King, no time can dim Thy glory!
How shall I spread abroad Thy wondrous story?
How shall I find some worthy gift to proffer?
What dare I offer?

6 I'll think upon Thy mercy without ceasing;
That earth's vain joys no more to me be pleasing;
To do Thy will shall be my sole endeavor
Henceforth forever.

93   8.7.8.7. with chorus.

1 Lord, we treasure with affection
   All Thy path of sorrow here,
And those closing scenes of anguish
   To our hearts Thyself endear.

> Praise Thee, Savior! Praise Thee, Savior!
>   Praise Thee, Lord, for sinners slain!
> Give Thee glory! Give Thee glory!
>   Give Thee glory for the life we gain!

2 Deep Thy sorrow then, Lord Jesus,
   Deeper far than thought can reach;
Grief intense and suff'rings holy,
   Far beyond all tongues to teach.

3 None could follow there, blest Savior,
   When redemption's work was done;
For those suff'rings, deep, unfathomed,
   Were, Lord Jesus, Thine alone!

4 Thou didst measure then sin's distance,
   Darkness, wrath and curse were Thine;
Man-betrayed, by God forsaken;
   Thus we learn Thy love divine!

94   8.6.8.6.8.6.

1 O Christ, what burdens bow'd Thy head!
   Our load was laid on Thee;
Thou stoodest in the sinner's stead,
   Didst bear all ill for me.
A victim led; Thy blood was shed;
   Now there's no load for me.

2 Death and the curse were in our cup,
   O Christ, 'twas full for Thee!
But Thou hast drained the last dark drop —
   'Tis empty now for me.
That bitter cup — love drank it up;
   Now blessings' draught for me.

3 Jehovah lifted up His rod,
   O Christ, it fell on Thee!
Thou wast sore stricken of Thy God;
   There's not one stroke for me.
Thy tears, Thy blood, beneath it flowed;
   Thy bruising healeth me.

4 The tempest's awful voice was heard,
   O Christ, it broke on Thee!
Thy open bosom was my ward,
   It braved the storm for me.
Thy form was scarred, Thy visage marred;
   Now cloudless peace for me.

5 Jehovah bade His sword awake,
   O Christ, it woke 'gainst Thee!
Thy blood the flaming blade must slake;
   Thy heart its sheath must be —
All for my sake, my peace to make;
   Now sleeps that sword for me.

6 For me, Lord Jesus, Thou hast died,
   And I have died in Thee;
Thou'rt ris'n: my bands are all untied,
   And now Thou liv'st in me.
When purified, made white, and tried,
   Thy glory then for me!

7.6.7.6.D.   **95**

1 O Head once full of bruises,
   So full of pain and scorn,
Mid other sore abuses,
   Mocked with a crown of thorn:
O Head e'en now surrounded
   With brightest majesty,
In death once bowed and wounded
   On the accursed tree:

continued

2 Thou Countenance transcendent!
  Thou life-creating Sun!
To worlds on Thee dependent —
  Yet bruised and spit upon:
O Lord, what Thee tormented
  Was our sins' heavy load,
We had the debt augmented
  Which Thou didst pay in blood.

3 We give Thee thanks unfeigned,
  O Savior, Friend in need,
For what Thy soul sustained
  When Thou for us didst bleed.
Grant us to lean unshaken
  Upon Thy faithfulness,
Until, to glory taken,
  We see Thee face to face.

96   6.6.6.6.8.8.

1 My song is love unknown,
  My Savior's love to me;
Love to the loveless shown,
  That they might lovely be.
   O who am I,
   That for my sake
   My Lord should take
   Frail flesh, and die?

2 He came from His blest throne
  Salvation to bestow;
But men made strange, and none
  The longed-for Christ would know:
   But oh, my Friend,
   My Friend indeed,
   Who at my need
   His life did spend.

3 Sometimes they strew His way,
   And His sweet praises sing;
Resounding all the day
   Hosannas to their King:
      Then "Crucify!"
      Is all their breath,
      And for His death
      They thirst and cry.

4 They rise and needs will have
   My dear Lord made away;
A murderer they save,
   The Prince of life they slay.
      Yet cheerful He
      To suffering goes,
      That He His foes
      From thence might free.

5 In life, no house, no home
   My Lord on earth might have;
In death, no friendly tomb,
   But what a stranger gave.
      What may I say?
      Heav'n was His home;
      But mine the tomb
      Wherein He lay.

6 Here might I stay and sing,
   No story so divine;
Never was love, dear King,
   Never was grief like Thine.
      This is my Friend,
      In whose sweet praise
      I all my days
      Could gladly spend.

8.8.8.8.

1 Thy sorrows, Savior, we retrace,
And tears of praise Thy griefs compel.
What love and grace illume Thy face
As Jesus, as Immanuel!

2 Amid Thy loneliness below,
What scorn and outrage Thee befell:
Deep shame and woe, rude blow on blow,
Endured for us, Immanuel!

3 But oh, what grief, what agony,
When wrathful judgment's awful spell
Burst over Thee on Calv'ry's tree,
God's Lamb for us, Immanuel!

4 Arisen radiant from the dead,
Thy sorrow's scars forever tell,
Creation's Head is He who bled —
Still Jesus, still Immanuel!

5 E'en now from saints, in concord sweet,
Celestial strains of worship well;
For, O, 'tis meet glad songs should greet
Thy heart of love, Immanuel!

6 But when Thy glorious face we see,
How shall the bursting paean swell!
Our souls shall be outpoured for Thee —
Outpoured for Thee, Immanuel!

8.7.8.7.8.8.7.7.

1   Jesus! Source of life eternal!
    Jesus, Author of our breath!
    Victor o'er the hosts infernal,
      By defeat, and shame, and death,
    Thou through deepest tribulation
      Deigned to pass for our salvation:
    Thousand, thousand praises be,
      Lord of glory, unto Thee!

2   Thou, O Son of God! wert bearing
      Cruel mockings, hatred, scorn;
    Thou, the King of glory, wearing,
      For our sake, the crown of thorn:
    Dying, Thou didst us deliver
      From the chains of sin for ever;
    Thousand, thousand praises be,
      Precious Savior, unto Thee!

3   All the shame men heaped upon Thee,
      Thou didst patiently endure;
    Not the pains of death too bitter,
      Our redemption to procure:
    Wondrous Thy humiliation
      To accomplish our salvation:
    Thousand, thousand praises be,
      Precious Savior, unto Thee!

4   Heart-felt praise and adoration,
      Savior, thus to Thee we give:
    For Thy life's humiliation,
      For Thy death, whereby we live;
    All the grief Thou wert enduring,
      All the bliss Thou wert securing,
    Evermore the theme shall be,
      Of thanksgivings, Lord, to Thee.

99   8.8.8.8.

1 'Tis midnight, and on Olive's brow
    The star is dimmed that lately shone;
'Tis midnight in the garden now,
    The suff'ring Savior prays alone.

2 'Tis midnight, and from all removed,
    The Savior wrestles lone with fears —
E'en that disciple whom He loved
    Heeds not his Master's grief and tears.

3 'Tis midnight, and for other's guilt
    The Man of Sorrows weeps in blood;
Yet He that hath in anguish knelt
    Is not forsaken by His God.

4 'Tis midnight, and from ether-plains
    Is borne the song that angels know —
Unheard by mortals are the strains
    That sweetly soothe the Savior's woe.

100   8.8.8.8.

1 The Maker of the universe
As Man, for man was made a curse.
The claims of law which He had made,
Unto the uttermost He paid.

2 His holy fingers made the bough
Which grew the thorns that crowned His brow.
The nails that pierced His hands were mined
In secret places He designed.

3 He made the forest whence there sprung
The tree on which His body hung.
He died upon a cross of wood,
Yet made the hill on which it stood.

4 The sky that darkened o'er His head
    By Him above the earth was spread.
    The sun that hid from Him its face
    By His decree was poised in space.

5 The spear which spilled His precious blood
    Was tempered in the fires of God.
    The grave in which His form was laid,
    Was hewn in rocks His hands had made.

6 The throne on which He now appears
    Was His from everlasting years,
    But a new glory crowns His brow,
    And every knee to Him shall bow.

8.8.8.8.   **101**

1 When we survey the wondrous cross
    On which the Lord of glory died,
    Our richest gain we count but loss,
    And pour contempt on all our pride.

2 Our God forbid that we should boast,
    Save in the death of Christ, our Lord;
    All the vain things that charm us most,
    We'd sacrifice them to His blood.

3 There from His head, His hands, His feet,
    Sorrow and love flowed mingled down;
    Did e'er such love and sorrow meet,
    Or thorns compose so rich a crown?

4 His dying crimson, from His head
    Spreads o'er His body on the tree;
    To all the world then am I dead,
    And all the world is dead to me.

5 Were the whole realm of nature ours,
    That were an offering far too small;
    Love that transcends our highest pow'rs,
    Demands our heart, our life, our all.

102

8.8.8.8.

1 We sing the praise of Him who died,
Of Him who died upon the Cross;
The sinner's hope let men deride,
For this we count the world but loss.

2 Inscribed upon the Cross we see
In shining letters, God is love!
He bears our sins upon the tree,
He brings us mercy from above.

3 The Cross: it takes our guilt away;
It holds the fainting spirit up;
It cheers with hope the gloomy day,
And sweetens every bitter cup.

4 The balm of life, the cure of woe,
The measure and the pledge of love,
The sinner's refuge here below,
The angels' theme in heav'n above.

PRAISE OF THE LORD — HIS REDEMPTION

103

8.6.8.6.8.8.8.6.

1 Behold! behold the Lamb of God,
On the cross! On the cross!
For us He shed His precious blood,
On the cross! On the cross!
O hear His all-important cry,
"Eli, lama sabachthani?"
Draw near and see the Savior die,
On the cross! On the cross!

2   Behold His arms extended wide,
      On the cross! On the cross!
    Behold His bleeding hands and side,
      On the cross! On the cross!
    The sun withholds its rays of light,
    The heav'ns are clothed in shades of night,
    While Jesus wins the glorious fight,
      On the cross! On the cross!

3   By faith we see Him lifted up,
      On the cross! On the cross!
    He drinks for us the bitter cup,
      On the cross! On the cross!
    The rocks do rend, the mountains quake,
    While Jesus all our sins doth take,
    While Jesus suffers for our sake,
      On the cross! On the cross!

4   And now the mighty deed is done,
      On the cross! On the cross!
    The battle fought, the vict'ry won,
      On the cross! On the cross!
    To heav'n He turns triumphant eyes;
    " 'Tis finished" now, the Conqu'ror cries,
    Then bows His sacred head and dies,
      On the cross! On the cross!

5   But now He's ris'n, ascended, crowned,
      On the throne! On the throne!
    Heav'n's highest place for Him is found,
      On the throne! On the throne!
    Our hearts we low in worship bow,
    And join, as one, to hail Him now:
    "Worthy, O Lamb of God, art Thou!"
      On the throne! On the throne!

104

8.6.8.6.

1 Alas! and did my Savior bleed?
   And did my Sov'reign die,
   Would He devote that sacred head
   For such a worm as I?

2 Was it for sins that I had done
   He groaned upon the tree?
   Amazing pity! grace unknown!
   And love beyond degree!

3 Well might the sun in darkness hide,
   And shut his glories in,
   When the incarnate Maker died
   For man, His creature's sin.

4 Thus might I hide my blushing face
   While His dear cross appears
   Dissolve my heart in thankfulness,
   And melt mine eyes to tears.

5 But drops of grief can ne'er repay
   The debt of love I owe;
   Here, Lord, I give myself away:
   'Tis all that I can do.

105

6.6.6.6.8.8.

1 Himself He could not save,
   He on the cross must die,
   Or mercy could not come
   To ruined sinners nigh;
   Yes, Christ, the Son of God, must bleed,
   That sinners might from sin be freed.

2   Himself He could not save,
    For justice must be done;
Our sins' full weight must fall
    Upon the sinless One;
For nothing less can God accept
In payment of that fearful debt.

3   Himself He could not save,
    For He the Surety stood
For all who now rely
    Upon His precious blood;
He bore the penalty of guilt
When on the cross His blood was spilt.

4   Himself He could not save,
    What wondrous love is this!
In love Himself He gave,
    There ne'er was love like His!
Such love should melt a heart of stone,
Till praise flows forth to Him alone!

6.6.8.6.10.12.

106

1   No blood, no altar now,
    The sacrifice is o'er!
No flame, no smoke ascends on high,
    The lamb is slain no more,
But richer blood has flowed from nobler veins,
To purge the soul from guilt, and cleanse the
    reddest stains.

2   We thank Thee for the blood,
    The blood of Christ, God's Son:
The blood by which our peace is made,
    Redemption great is won,
Delivering us from hell, and sin, and woe;
That His eternal life God may to us bestow.

107   6.6.8.6.

1   Not all the blood of beasts,
       On Jewish altars slain,
   Could give the guilty conscience peace,
       Or wash away its stain.

2   But Christ, the heavenly Lamb,
       Takes all our sins away;
   A sacrifice of nobler name,
       And richer blood than they.

3   My faith would lay her hand
       On that dear head of Thine,
   While like a penitent I stand,
       And there confess my sin.

4   My soul looks back to see
       The burdens Thou didst bear
   When hanging on the cursèd tree,
       And knows her guilt was there.

5   Believing, we rejoice
       To see the curse remove;
   We bless the Lamb with cheerful voice,
       And sing His bleeding love.

108   7.7.7.8.

1   "Man of Sorrows," what a name
   For the Son of God who came
   Ruined sinners to reclaim!
       Hallelujah! what a Savior!

2   Bearing shame and scoffing rude,
   In my place condemned He stood;
   Sealed my pardon with His blood;
       Hallelujah! what a Savior!

3 Guilty, vile, and helpless, we,
   Spotless Lamb of God was He;
   Full redemption — can it be?
     Hallelujah! what a Savior!

4 Lifted up was He to die,
   "It is finished!" was His cry;
   Now in heaven exalted high;
     Hallelujah! what a Savior!

5 When He comes, our glorious King,
   To His kingdom us to bring,
   Then anew this song we'll sing:
     Hallelujah! what a Savior!

8.6.8.6.   **109**

1 The veil is rent! Lo! Jesus stands
   Before the throne of grace;
   And clouds of incense from His hands
   Fill all that glorious place.

2 His precious blood is sprinkled there,
   Before and on the throne;
   And His own wounds in heav'n declare
   His work on earth is done.

3 " 'Tis finished!" on the cross He said,
   In agonies and blood;
   'Tis finished: now He lives to plead
   Before the face of God.

4 " 'Tis finished!" Here our souls can rest,
   His work can never fail;
   By Him, our Sacrifice and Priest,
   We enter through the veil.

8.6.8.8.6.8.8.

1 O solemn hour! O hour alone,
   In solitary night,
When God the Father's only Son,
As Man, for sinners lost, undone,
   Expires — amazing sight!
The Lord of glory crucified!
The Lord of Life has bled and died!

2 O mystery of mysteries!
   Of life and death the tree!
Center of two eternities,
Which look with rapt, adoring eyes,
   Onward, and back to Thee!
O cross of Christ, where all His pain
And death is our eternal gain.

3 O how our inmost hearts do move,
   While gazing on that cross!
The death of the incarnate Love!
What shame, what grief, what joy we prove,
   That He should die for us!
Our hearts were broken by that cry,
"Eli, lama sabachthani!"

4 Worthy of death, O Lord, we were;
   That vengeance was our due;
In grace Thou, spotless Lamb, didst bear
Thyself our sins, and guilt, and fear;
   Justice our Surety slew.
With Thee, our Surety, we have died;
With Thee, we there were crucified.

5   Quickened with Thee with life divine,
Raised with Thee from the dead;
Thine Own, now human and divine,
Shall with Thee in Thy glories shine,
The Church's living Head!
We, who were worthy but to die,
Now with Thee, "Abba Father," cry.

6.6.8.6.

111

1   Jesus, the sinner's Friend,
We hide ourselves in Thee;
God looks upon Thy sprinkled blood,
It is our only plea.

2   He hears Thy precious Name,
We claim it as our own;
The Father must accept and bless
His well-beloved Son.

3   Thou hast fulfilled the law,
And we are justified:
Ours is the blessing, Thine the curse;
We live, for Thou hast died.

4   Jesus, the sinner's Friend!
We cannot speak Thy praise;
No mortal voice can sing the song
That ransomed hearts would raise.

5   But when before the throne,
Thy face we all shall see,
Clothed in our blood-bought robes of white,
We'll stand complete in Thee.

6   Jesus, we'll give Thee then
Such praises as are meet,
And give ten thousand thanks to Thee,
Adoring, at Thy feet.

112

11.11.11.11. with chorus.

1 How sweet is the story of Christ's boundless love,
   That brought Him to suffer from glory above!
   He died in our stead upon Calvary's tree,
   Obtaining redemption that we might be free.

> Sound His praise! Sound His praise!
>   All the work has been done;
> Praise His name! Praise His name!
>   Jesus, God's blessed Son.
> We give Him the glory, our Savior and Friend;
> Our song is of Jesus and never will end.

2 How wondrous the story! the law's holy claims
   Were met by the blood which redemption proclaims.
   The judgment of sin has been borne by the Son,
   Who glorified God in the work He has done.

3 How brilliant the glory where Christ is enthroned
   How rightly His name above others is owned!
   Yes, Jesus, the Savior, the glory-crowned Lord,
   Is worthy by all to be ever adored.

8.8.8.8.

1 How pleasant is the sound of praise!
   It well becomes the saints of God;
   Should we refuse our songs to raise,
   The stones might tell our shame abroad.

2 For Him Who washed us in His blood,
   Let us our sweetest songs prepare;
   He sought us wandering far from God,
   And now preserves us by His care.

3 One string there is of sweetest tone,
   Reserved for sinners saved by grace;
   'Tis sacred to one class alone
   And touched by one peculiar race.

4 Though angels may with rapture see
   How mercy flows in Jesus' blood,
   It is not theirs to prove, as we,
   The cleansing virtue of this flood.

5 Though angels praise the heavenly King,
   And worship Him as God alone,
   We can with exultation sing,
   "He wears our nature on the throne."

6 Lord, we adore Thy wondrous love,
   Which brought Thee here to bleed and die
   That Thou lost sinners may restore
   And to the Father bring them nigh.

114

8.7.8.7.D.

1 Hail, Thou once despisèd Jesus!
   Hail, Thou still rejected King!
Thou didst suffer to release us,
   Thou didst free salvation bring;
Through Thy death and resurrection,
   Bearer of our sin and shame!
We enjoy divine protection,
   Life and glory through Thy name.

2 Paschal Lamb, by God appointed,
   All our sins on Thee were laid;
By our Father's love anointed,
   Thou redemption's price hast paid.
All who trust Thee are forgiven
   Through the virtue of Thy blood;
Opened are the things of heaven,
   Grace shines forth to man from God.

3 Savior, hail! enthroned in glory,
   Where for us Thou dost abide;
We, by faith, do now adore Thee,
   Seated at Thy Father's side.
There, for us Thou now art pleading,
   There Thou dost our sorrows share,
Ever for us interceding,
   Till in glory we appear.

4 Worship, honor, praise, and blessing,
   Thou art worthy to receive;
Loudest praises, without ceasing,
   Meet it is for us to give.
In that day Thy saints will meet Thee,
   Welcome Thee with grateful song;
Joyful hearts will ever greet Thee,
   Source of joy to all the throng!

6.5.6.5.

1 Glory be to Jesus,
   Who in bitter pains
   Poured for me the life-blood
   From His sacred veins.

2 Grace and life eternal
   In that Blood I find;
   Blest be His compassion,
   Infinitely kind.

3 Blest through endless ages
   Be the precious stream,
   Which from endless torments
   Did the world redeem.

4 Abel's blood for vengeance
   Pleaded to the skies;
   But the blood of Jesus
   For our pardon cries.

5 It the conscience sprinkles,
   Frees our guilty hearts;
   Satan in confusion
   Terror-struck departs.

6 Oft as earth exulting
   Wafts its praise on high,
   Angel-hosts rejoicing
   Make their glad reply.

7 Lift ye then your voices;
   Swell the mighty flood;
   Louder still and louder
   Praise the precious blood.

116*

8.6.8.6.D.

1 How wonderful redemption is,
   My gracious Lord, in Thee!
Not seen, nor heard, nor e'er conceived
   What Thou hast done for me!
Thou art divine, mysterious,
   Beyond my grandest phrase!
Redemption is so marvellous,
   Beyond all pow'r to praise!

2 For us Thou on the Cross wast pierced,
   And blood and water streamed;
That life divine be giv'n to us,
   That we may be redeemed.
Thy precious blood has made us clean,
   That we accepted be;
Regenerated by Thy life,
   We now are one with Thee.

3 Thou art the grain divine that died
   The many grains to bear,
Which, blent and formed, Thy Body are,
   And all Thy nature share.
We are the increase of Thyself,
   And Thou our content art;
Through us Thou livest and dost move
   And manifested art.

4 Since we're Thy Body, Thou may come
   And settle down in us;
In us Thou may obtain Thy home
   And we become Thy trust.
Thy heart to satisfy and please,
   We are Thy counterpart,
Now in one Body with Thyself,
   Enjoying all Thou art.

5 While in remembrance now we meet
     And here the symbols see,
   For Thy redemption great and full
     We're filled with praise to Thee.
   Since we are made Thy Body, Lord,
     Thy dwelling place and bride,
   We would give thanks and worship Thee
     And in Thy praise abide.

PRAISE OF THE LORD — HIS RESURRECTION

7.4.7.4.D.

117

1 Christ the Lord is ris'n indeed,
     Hallelujah!
   He has met His people's need,
     Hallelujah!
   Raise your joys and triumphs high,
     Hallelujah!
   Sing, ye heav'ns and earth, reply,
     Hallelujah!

2 Lives again our glorious King,
     Hallelujah!
   Where, O Death, is now thy sting?
     Hallelujah!
   Dying once He all doth save,
     Hallelujah!
   Where thy victory, O grave?
     Hallelujah!

3 Love's redeeming work is done,
     Hallelujah!
   Fought the fight, the battle won,
     Hallelujah!
   Death in vain forbade Him rise,
     Hallelujah!
   Christ ascended o'er the skies,
     Hallelujah!

continued

4   Soar we now where Christ hath led,
      Hallelujah!
Following our exalted Head,
      Hallelujah!
Made like Him, like Him we rise,
      Hallelujah!
Free from all the earthly ties,
      Hallelujah!

118   8.7.8.7.D. with chorus.

1   Christ is risen! Hallelujah!
Risen our victorious Head;
Sing His praises; Hallelujah!
Christ is risen from the dead.
Gratefully our hearts adore Him,
As His light once more appears;
Bowing down in joy before Him,
Rising up from griefs and tears.

    Christ is risen: Hallelujah!
    Risen our victorious Head;
    Sing His praises; Hallelujah!
    Christ is risen from the dead.

2   Christ is risen! All the sadness
Of His earthly life is o'er;
Through the open gates of gladness
He returns to life once more;
Death and hell before Him bending,
He doth rise the Victor now,
Angels on His steps attending,
Glory round His wounded brow.

3   Christ is risen! Henceforth never
Death nor hell shall us enthrall;
We are Christ's, in Him forever
We have triumphed over all;
All the doubting and dejection
Of our trembling hearts have ceased,
'Tis His day of resurrection;
Let us rise and keep the feast.

8.7.8.7.8.7.   **119**

1   Hallelujah, "He is risen!"
Jesus is gone up on high!
Burst the bars of death asunder;
Angels shout, and men reply:
He is risen, He is risen,
Living now, no more to die.

2   Hallelujah, He is risen!
Our exalted Head to be;
Sends the witness of the Spirit
That our Advocate is He:
He is risen, He is risen,
Justified in Him are we.

3   Hallelujah, He is risen!
Death for aye has lost his sting;
Christ, Himself the Resurrection,
From the grave "His own" will bring:
He is risen, He is risen,
Living Lord and coming King.

120

10.10.10.10.

1 The Lord is ris'n; and death's dark judgment flood
 Is passed, in Him who bought us with His blood.
 The Lord is ris'n: we stand beyond the doom
 Of all our sin, through Jesus' empty tomb.

2 The Lord is ris'n: with Him we also rose,
 And in His grave see vanquished all our foes.
 The Lord is ris'n: beyond the judgment land,
 In Him, in resurrection-life we stand.

3 The Lord is ris'n: and now redeemed to God,
 We tread the desert which His feet have trod.
 The Lord is ris'n: the sanctu'ry's our place,
 Where now we dwell before the Father's face.

4 The Lord is ris'n: the Lord is gone before.
 We long to see Him, and to sin no more.
 The Lord is ris'n: our triumph-shout shall be,
 "Thou hast prevailed! Thy people, Lord, are free!"

121

10.11.11.11. with chorus.

1 Thine be the glory, risen, conqu'ring Son,
 Endless is the vict'ry Thou o'er death hast won;
 Angels in bright raiment rolled the stone away,
 Kept the folded grave-clothes, where Thy body lay.

 Thine be the glory, risen, conqu'ring Son,
 Endless is the vict'ry Thou o'er death hast won.

2 Lo! Jesus meets us, risen from the tomb;
 Lovingly He greets us, scatters fear and gloom;
 Let the Church with gladness, hymns of triumph sing,
 For her Lord now liveth, death hath lost its sting.

6.4.6.4.6.6.6.4.

1   Thou, Lord, to death's domain
      Didst go alone.
Death had on Thee no claim,
      Thou sinless One!
He who had death's dread pow'r
Met Thee in that dark hour:
Vanquished by Thee his power,
      By Thee alone.

2   But Thou hast burst the grave,
      Risen art Thou;
Death could not Thee enslave,
      Death had to bow!
Victorious hast Thou come
Out of the darksome tomb,
Broken the bands of gloom:
      Beyond death now.

3   What mighty triumphs, Lord,
      Thou didst achieve!
What fruitfulness doth God
      From Thee receive!
Out of Thy death has sprung
A wondrous living throng:
All, all to Thee belong,
      And in Thee live.

4   Firstborn of all Thou art,
      Lowly we bow;
Chief in Thy Father's heart —
      Chief to us now.
Thou art indeed supreme,
Our great eternal theme,
Worthy of all esteem:
      Worthy art Thou!

Peculiar Meter.

1 Low in the grave He lay —
    Jesus my Savior!
Waiting the coming day —
    Jesus my Lord!

    Up from the grave He arose,
    With a mighty triumph o'er
        His foes;
    He arose a Victor from the
        dark domain,
    And He lives forever with His
        saints to reign.
        He arose! He arose!
        Hallelujah! Christ arose!

2 Vainly they watch His bed —
    Jesus, my Savior!
Vainly they seal the dead —
    Jesus, my Lord!

3 Death cannot keep his prey —
    Jesus, my Savior!
He tore the bars away —
    Jesus, my Lord!

8.7.8.7.8.7.

1 Praise Him! praise Him! Christ is Victor!
   He has won the victory!
   Sin is judged, old Adam finished,
   Full redemption now we see!
   Vanquished all the evil powers
   Thru the Cross triumphantly!

2 Praise Him! Christ is resurrected!
   God hath raised Him from the dead!
   All the pow'r of death is swallowed,
   Man from death to life is led!
   Broken through are hell and darkness
   And His pow'r exhibited!

3 Praise Him! Christ hath now ascended!
   God hath raised Him to the throne!
   Far above all rule and power,
   He the highest Name doth own!
   All authority receiving
   Till His foe is overthrown!

4 Hallelujah, Christ the Victor
   Triumphed on Mt. Calvary!
   Hallelujah, resurrected,
   He displays His victory!
   Hallelujah, now ascended,
   He shall reign eternally!

125

8.7.8.7.D.

1 Hallelujah! sing to Jesus,
  His the scepter, His the throne;
Hallelujah! His the triumph,
  His the victory alone.
Hark, the songs of His redeemed ones
  Thunder like a mighty flood:
Jesus out of every nation
  Hath redeemed us by His blood.

2 Hallelujah! not as orphans
  Are we left in sorrow now;
Hallelujah! He is near us,
  Faith believes, nor questions how.
Though the clouds from sight received Him
  When the forty days were o'er,
Shall our hearts forget His promise,
  "I am with you evermore"?

3 Hallelujah! Bread of heaven,
  Thou on earth our food, our stay;
Hallelujah! here the hungry
  Come to Thee from day to day.
Advocate and Intercessor,
  My Redeemer pleads for me,
On the throne of the Almighty
  Now and to eternity.

4 Hallelujah! sing to Jesus,
  His the scepter, His the throne;
Hallelujah! His the triumph,
  His the victory alone.
Hark, the songs of His redeemed ones
  Thunder like a mighty flood:
Jesus out of every nation,
  Hath redeemed us by His blood.

8.6.8.6.D.

1 To Thee, dear Lord, O Christ of God,
    We sing, we ever sing;
  For Thou hast shed Thy precious blood
    Our cup of joy to bring.
  Thy mighty arm the fight hath fought,
    Thou art enthroned above;
  We into glory will be brought
    Thy wondrous grace to prove.

2 To Thee, dear Lord, O Christ of God,
    We sing, we ever sing;
  Thou hast invaded death's abode
    And robbed him of his sting.
  The house of dust enthralls no more,
    For Thou, the strong to save,
  Thyself doth guard that silent door,
    Great Keeper of the grave.

3 To Thee, dear Lord, O Christ of God,
    We sing, we ever sing;
  For Thou hast crushed beneath Thy rod
    The world's proud rebel king,
  And plunged in Thine imperial strength
    To gulfs of darkness down,
  And brought Thy trophy up at length,
    The foiled usurper's crown.

4 To Thee, dear Lord, O Christ of God,
    We sing, we ever sing;
  Thou hast redeemed us with Thy blood
    From every evil thing.
  God's saving strength Thine arm upbore,
    The arm that set us free;
  Glory, O Christ, for evermore
    Be to Thy God and Thee.

127

8.7.8.7.

1 Hark! ten thousand voices crying,
   "Lamb of God!" with one accord;
Thousand thousand saints replying,
   Wake at once the echo'ng chord.

2 "Praise the Lamb!" the chorus waking,
   All in heav'n together throng;
Loud and far each tongue partaking
   Rolls around the endless song.

3 Grateful incense this, ascending
   Ever to the Father's throne;
Every knee to Jesus bending,
   All the mind in heav'n is one.

4 All the Father's counsels claiming
   Equal honors to the Son,
All the Son's effulgence beaming,
   Makes the Father's glory known.

5 By the Spirit all pervading,
   Hosts unnumbered round the Lamb,
Crowned with light and joy unfading,
   Hail Him as the great "I AM."

6 Joyful now the new creation
   Rests in undisturbed repose,
Blest in Jesus' full salvation,
   Sorrow now nor thraldom knows.

7 Hark! the heavenly notes again!
   Loudly swells the song of praise;
Through creation's vault, Amen!
   Amen! responsive joy doth raise.

10.10.10.10. with chorus.

1   Far above all is our Savior enthroned;
    Crown'd is the Lamb who by sinners is owned,
    Living forever to list to our call,
    God hath exalted Him far above all.

        Far above all! Far above all!
        Jesus the crucified far above all!
        High as His members upon Him we call,
        God hath exalted Him far above all!

2   When the fierce tempest, uplifting its waves,
    Seeks to engulf us, we cry and He saves;
    Looking to Jesus, upheld by His hand,
    Tread we the billows as safe as on land.

3   High are the cities that dare our assault,
    Strong are the barriers that call us to halt;
    March we on fearless, and down they must fall,
    Vanquish'd by faith in Him far above all.

4   His is the kingdom from pole unto pole,
    Far above all while the ages shall roll,
    With Him the victors, who follow'd His call,
    Share in His royalty far above all.

129

8.6.8.6.

1 Behold the Lamb with glory crowned,
   To Him all pow'r is giv'n:
No place too high for Him is found,
   No place too high in heav'n.

2 He fills the throne — the throne above;
   Its rights to Him belong;
The object of His Father's love,
   Theme of the ransomed's song.

3 Though high yet He accepts the praise
   His people offer here;
The faintest, feeblest note they raise
   Will reach the Savior's ear.

4 This song be ours, we join in one
   To celebrate the Name
Of Him that sits upon the throne,
   And to exalt the Lamb.

5 To Him whom men despise and slight,
   To Him be glory giv'n;
The crown is His, and His by right
   The highest place in heav'n.

8.7.8.7.D.

1 See the Conqu'ror mount in triumph,
    See the King in royal state
Riding on the clouds His chariot
    To His heav'nly palace gate;
Hark! The choirs of angel voices
    Joyful hallelujahs sing,
And the portals high are lifted
    To receive, to receive, to receive
    their heav'nly King.

2 Who is this that comes in glory,
    With the trump of jubilee?
Lord of battles, God of armies,
    He has gained the victory;
He who on the cross did suffer,
    He who from the grave arose,
He has vanquished sin and Satan,
    He by death, He by death, He by
    death has spoiled His foes.

3 While He lifts His hands in blessing
    He is parted from His friends;
While their eager eyes behold Him,
    He upon the clouds ascends;
He who walked with God and pleased Him,
    Preaching truth and doom to come,
He, our Enoch, is translated
    To His home, to His home, to His
    everlasting home.

4 Now our heavenly Aaron enters,
    With His blood, within the veil;
Joshua now is come to Canaan,
    And the kings before Him quail;

continued

Now He plants the tribes of Israel
In their promised resting-place;
Now our great Elijah offers
Of His grace, of His grace,
double portion of His grace.

5　He has raised our human nature
On the clouds to God's right hand;
There we sit in heav'nly places,
There with Him in glory stand.
Jesus reigns, adored by angels;
Man with God is on the throne;
Mighty Lord, in Thine ascension
We by faith, we by faith, we by
faith behold our own.

131　　　　　　　　　8.8.6.8.8.6.

1　O Jesus, Lord, 'tis joy to know
Thy path is o'er of shame and woe,
By Thee so meekly trod.
All finished is Thy work of toil,
Thou reapest now the fruit and spoil,
Exalted by our God.

2　Thy holy head, once bound with thorns,
The crown of glory now adorns;
Thy seat, the Father's throne.
O Lord, e'en now we sing Thy praise,
Ours the eternal song to raise,
Worthy the Lord alone!

3　We triumph in Thy triumphs, Lord,
Thy joys our deepest joys afford,
The fruit of love divine.
While sorrowing, suff'ring, toiling here,
How does the thought our spirits cheer,
The throne of glory's Thine!

8.7.8.7.

1 Lo! in heaven Jesus sitting,
 Christ the Lord is there enthroned;
 As the man by God exalted,
 With God's glory He is crowned.

2 He hath put on human nature,
 Died according to God's plan,
 Resurrected with a body,
 And ascended as a man.

3 God in Him on earth was humbled,
 God with man was domiciled;
 Man in Him in heav'n exalted,
 Man with God is reconciled.

4 He as God with man is mingled,
 God in man is testified;
 He as man with God is blended,
 Man in God is glorified.

5 From the Glorified in heaven
 The inclusive Spirit came;
 All of Jesus' work and Person
 Doth this Spirit here proclaim.

6 With the Glorified in heaven
 Is the Church identified;
 By the Spirit of this Jesus
 Are His members edified.

7 Lo! a man is now in heaven
 As the Lord of all enthroned;
 This is Jesus Christ our Savior,
 With God's glory ever crowned!

133*

8.6.8.6.

1 Lord Jesus, Thou art Lord of all,
   With glory ever crowned;
In power and in majesty
   Thou art to all renowned.

2 As God in man, on earth Thou wast,
   A slave-form Thou didst own;
As man in God, in heav'n Thou art,
   As Lord of all art known.

3 Thou art the Man in glory there,
   And there by God enthroned;
All pow'r in heaven and on earth
   Now by Thyself is owned.

4 Exalted highly to the heav'ns
   And giv'n the highest Name,
All shall confess Thee as the Lord
   And all bow at Thy Name.

5 God made Thee both the Lord and Christ,
   The Spirit hath declared;
In glory and in heav'n we see
   God's throne by Thee is shared.

6 As Lord of glory we adore,
   To Thee our song we raise;
We worship Thee as Lord of all,
   How worthy of our praise!

8.7.8.7.D.

1 Glory, everlasting glory
    Be to Christ, the thronèd Lamb.
  Glory, everlasting glory
    Be to His most precious Name;
  Name above all names in heaven,
    Name above all names on earth.
  Glory, everlasting glory
    Be to Him of peerless worth.

2 Throned in heav'n, the Prince of Glory,
    Equal God, with God on high;
  Form of lowest servant taking,
    On the cross of shame to die:
  In obedience, strong, unswerving,
    His blest Father's will to do;
  Death of shame, all undeservèd,
    E'en to that His love could go.

3 Heaven's crown of brightest glory
    Be to Him, the humbled One.
  Heaven's robe of brightest splendor
    Be to Him and Him alone.
  In the Name of Jesus bowing,
    Every tongue shall Him confess
  Lord of earth and Lord of heaven;
    Myriads shall this Monarch bless.

4 Glory, everlasting glory
    Be to Him of peerless worth.
  In the highest heav'n be glory,
    Glory be to Him on earth.
  Unto God, our God, be glory,
    Glory to the great I AM.
  Glory, everlasting glory
    Be to Christ, the thronèd Lamb.

135

7.7.7.7.

1 O my Savior, glorified!
  Now the heavens, opened wide,
Show to faith's exultant eye
  One in beauteous majesty.

2 Worthy of the sweetest praise
  That my ransomed heart can raise,
Is that Man in whom alone
  God Himself is fully known.

3 For those clust'ring glories prove
  That glad gospel, "God is Love,"
Whilst those wounds, in glory bright,
  Voice the solemn, "God is Light."

4 Hark, my soul! thy Savior sings;
  Catch the joy that music brings,
And, with that sweet flood of song,
  Pour thy whisp'ring praise along.

5 O my Savior, glorified,
  Turn my eye from all beside,
Let me but Thy beauty see,
  Other light is dark to me.

136

8.7.8.7.

1 Gazing on the Lord in glory,
  While our hearts in worship bow,
There we read the wondrous story
  Of the cross — its shame and woe.

2 *Every mark of dark* dishonor
  Heaped upon the thorn-crowned brow,
All the depths of Thy heart's sorrow
  Told in answ'ring glory now.

3 On that cross, alone, forsaken,
　　Where no pity'ng eye was found;
　Now, to God's right hand exalted,
　　With Thy praise the heavens resound.

4 Did Thy God e'en then forsake Thee,
　　Hide His face from Thy deep need?
　In Thy face once marred and smitten,
　　All His glory now we read.

5 Gazing on it we adore Thee,
　　Blessed, precious, holy Lord;
　Thou, the Lamb, alone art worthy —
　　This be earth's and heaven's accord.

6 Rise our hearts, and bless the Father,
　　Ceaseless song e'en here begun,
　Endless praise and adoration
　　To the Father and the Son.

8.6.8.6. with repeat.　　**137**

1 All hail the pow'r of Jesus' name!
　　Before Him prostrate fall;
　With one accord His praise proclaim,
　　And crown Him Lord of all!

2 Ye saints redeemed from Adam's race,
　　Ye ransomed from the fall,
　Hail Him who saves you by His grace,
　　And crown Him Lord of all.

3 Tell forth the only Name that's giv'n
　　On which we now may call,
　The Name adored by hosts in heav'n,
　　And crown Him Lord of all.

4 In glory all the ransomed throng
　　Soon at His feet shall fall;
　Join in the blest eternal song,
　　And crown Him Lord of all.

(Repeat the last two lines of each stanza)

138

8.6.8.6.

1 All hail the pow'r of Jesus' name!
   Let angels prostrate fall;
Bring forth the royal diadem,

   And crown Him, crown Him,
     crown Him,
   Crown Him Lord of all!

2 Crown Him, ye martyrs of your God
   Who from His altar call;
Extol the Stem of Jesse's rod,

3 Hail Him, ye heirs of David's line,
   Whom David Lord did call;
The God incarnate, Man Divine;

4 Ye chosen seed of Israel's race,
   Ye ransomed from the fall,
Hail Him who saves you by His grace,

5 Sinners, whose love can ne'er forget
   The wormwood and the gall,
Go, spread your trophies at His feet,

6 Let every kindred, every tribe,
   On this terrestrial ball,
To Him all majesty ascribe,

7 O that with yonder sacred throng
   We at His feet may fall!
We'll join the everlasting song,

8.6.8.6. with repeat.

1 All hail the pow'r of Jesus' name!
   Let angels prostrate fall,
   Let angels prostrate fall;
   Bring forth the royal diadem,

   And crown Him, crown Him,
      crown Him, crown Him;
   And crown Him Lord of all!

2 Ye chosen seed of Israel's race,
   Ye ransomed from the fall,
   Ye ransomed from the fall,
   Hail Him who saves you by His grace,

3 Sinners, whose love can ne'er forget
   The wormwood and the gall,
   The wormwood and the gall,
   Go, spread your trophies at His feet,

4 Let every kindred, every tribe,
   On this terrestrial ball,
   On this terrestrial ball,
   To Him all majesty ascribe,

5 O that with yonder sacred throng
   We at His feet may fall,
   We at His feet may fall!
   We'll join the everlasting song,

140

8.7.8.7.8.7.

1 Look, ye saints, the sight is glorious;
   See the Man of sorrows now;
From the fight returned victorious,
   Every knee to Him shall bow;
Crown Him! Crown Him!
   Crown Him! Crown Him!
   Crowns become the Victor's brow.

2 Crown the Savior! Angels, crown Him!
   Rich the trophies Jesus brings;
In the seat of pow'r enthrone Him,
   While the vault of heaven rings:
Crown Him! Crown Him!
   Crown Him! Crown Him!
   Crown the Savior King of kings.

3 Sinners in derision crowned Him,
   Mocking thus the Savior's claim;
Saints and angels crowd around Him,
   Own His title, praise His name:
Crown Him! Crown Him!
   Crown Him! Crown Him!
   Spread abroad the Victor's fame.

4 Hark! those bursts of acclamation!
   Hark! those loud triumphant chords!
Jesus takes the highest station;
   O what joy the sight affords!
Crown Him! Crown Him!
   Crown Him! Crown Him!
   King of kings, and Lord of lords!

8.6.8.6.

1   Jesus, Thy head, once crown'd with thorns,
    Is crown'd with glory now;
    Heaven's royal diadem adorns
    The mighty Victor's brow.

2   Thou glorious light of courts above,
    Joy of the saints below,
    To us still manifest Thy love,
    That we its depths may know.

3   To us Thy cross with all its shame,
    With all its grace be giv'n;
    Though earth disowns Thy lowly name,
    God honors it in heav'n.

4   Who suffer with Thee, Lord, today,
    Shall also with Thee reign:
    Then let it be our joy to pay
    The price, this goal attain.

5   To us Thy cross is life and health;
    'Twas shame and death to Thee;
    Our present glory, joy and wealth,
    Our everlasting stay.

142

6.6.8.6.D.

1   Crown Him with many crowns,
The Lamb upon His throne;
Hark! how the heav'nly anthem drowns
All music but its own!
Awake, my soul, and sing
Of Him who died for thee,
And hail Him as thy matchless King
Through all eternity.

2   Crown Him the Virgin's Son,
The God Incarnate born,
Whose arm those crimson trophies won
Which now His brow adorn:
Fruit of the mystic Tree,
As of that Tree the Stem;
The Root whence flows Thy mercy free,
The Babe of Bethlehem.

3   Crown Him the Lord of Love:
Behold His hands and side;
Rich wounds yet visible above
In beauty glorified:
No angel in the sky
Can fully bear that sight,
But downward bends his burning eye
At mysteries so bright.

4   Crown Him the Lord of peace,
Whose power a scepter sways
From pole to pole, that wars may cease,
And all be prayer and praise.
His reign shall know no end,
And round His piercèd feet
Fair flowers of glory now extend
Their fragrance ever sweet.

5   Crown Him the Lord of years,
      The Potentate of time,
   Creator of the rolling spheres,
      Ineffably sublime.
     All hail, Redeemer, hail!
     For Thou hast died for me;
  Thy praise shall never, never fail
      Throughout eternity.

8.7.8.7.8.7.   **143**

1 On His Father's throne is seated
   Christ the Lord, the living One!
   All His toil on earth completed,
   All His work for sinners done.
   In the glory, in the glory,
   See Him — God's eternal Son!

2 Every knee shall bow before Him,
   Every tongue confess His name,
   Ransomed myriads shall adore Him,
   Who endured the sinner's shame!
   From the glory, from the glory,
   God doth now His worth proclaim.

3 Man, the cross to Him awarded;
   Man, the Savior crucified;
   This world's judgment stands recorded,
   God's own justice satisfied!
   By the glory, by the glory,
   Christ was claimed on earth who died.

4 Son of Man, His incarnation
   Opened first the tale of grace;
   Son of Man, in new creation
   Leader of a chosen race!
   Well may glory, well may glory,
   Give to Him the honored place!

PRAISE OF THE LORD — HIS GLORY

8.7.8.7.7.7.

144

1 Lord of glory, we adore Thee!
   Christ of God, ascended high!
   Heart and soul we bow before Thee,
   Glorious now beyond the sky:
   Thee we worship, Thee we praise —
   Excellent in all Thy ways.

2 Anointed King, with glory crownèd,
   Rightful Heir and Lord of all!
   Once rejected, scorned, disownèd,
   E'en by those Thou cam'st to call:
   Thee we honor, Thee adore —
   Glorious now and evermore.

3 Lord of life! to death once subject;
   Blesser, yet a curse once made;
   Of Thy Father's heart the object,
   Yet in depths of anguish laid;
   Thee we gaze on, Thee recall —
   Bearing here our sorrows all.

4 Royal robes shall soon invest Thee,
   Royal splendors crown Thy brow;
   Christ of God, our souls confess Thee
   King and Sov'reign even now!
   Thee we rev'rence, Thee obey —
   Own Thee Lord and Christ alway.

PRAISE OF THE LORD — HIS KINGDOM

145

8.8.8.8.

1 Jesus shall reign where'er the sun
   Doth his successive journeys run;
   His Kingdom stretch from shore to shore,
   Till moons shall wax and wane no more.

2 To Him shall endless prayer be made,
   And princes throng to crown His head,
   His name like sweet perfume shall rise
   With every morning sacrifice.

3　People and realms of every tongue
　　Dwell on His love with sweetest song;
　　And infant voices shall proclaim
　　Their early blessings on His name.

4　Blessings abound where'er He reigns:
　　The prisoner leaps to lose his chains,
　　The weary find eternal rest,
　　And all the sons of want are blest.

5　Where He displays His healing power
　　Death and the curse are known no more;
　　In Him the tribes of Adam boast
　　More blessings than their father lost.

6　Let every creature rise and bring
　　Peculiar honors to our King;
　　Angels descend with songs again,
　　And earth repeat the loud Amen.

146

6.6.6.6.8.8.

1　Rejoice, the Lord is King,
　　　Your Lord and King adore;
　　Mortals, give thanks and sing,
　　　And triumph evermore:
　　　Lift up your heart, lift up your voice;
　　　Rejoice, again I say, rejoice.

2　His kingdom cannot fail;
　　　He rules o'er earth and heav'n;
　　The keys of death and hell
　　　Are to our Jesus giv'n:

3　Jesus, the Savior reigns,
　　　The God of truth and love:
　　When He had purged our stains,
　　　He took His seat above:

continued

4   He sits at God's right hand
        Till all His foes submit,
    And bow to His command,
        And fall beneath His feet:

147*   7.6.7.6.D.

1   Lord, Thou art God's anointed,
        Thou art of kings the King!
    Here in full adoration
        Our song to Thee we bring!
    Thy kingdom is forever,
        Established is Thy throne!
    Thy reign with love and justice
        In glory stands alone!

2   Upon the hill of Zion
        Hath God established Thee
    And all the nations given
        Thy heritage to be.
    To Thee hath God committed
        His full authority
    To rule with might the nations
        Unto eternity.

3   Before the time of fulness,
        While darkness still prevails,
    Ten thousands daily render
        To Thee their loyal hails!
    From shore to shore Thy people
        To Thee their praises sing;
    They worship, love, and serve Thee
        As their dear Savior-King!

4 When in the time appointed
  With glory Thou wilt come,
The earth with all its nations
  Thy kingdom will become.
In majesty and splendor
  Wilt Thou be served as King,
All kindreds and all peoples
  To Thee their praise shall ring!

7.7.7.7.7.7.   **148***

1 Lord, the King of kings art Thou,
In Thy presence here we bow;
God's anointed we adore,
Worship Thee in holy awe.
Unto Thee, of kings the King,
All the saints Thy praises sing!

2 Thine authority and pow'r
Shall prevail from shore to shore!
All shall serve and worship Thee
In Thy kingly majesty!
Unto Thee, of kings the King,
All Thy praise shall ever ring!

3 Lord, Thy kingdom stands alone,
And forever is Thy throne!
To Thy glory and Thy pow'r
We will sing forevermore!
Now to Thee, of kings the King,
All the saints Thy praises sing!

4 Gracious Lord, our sovereign King,
Thy dear name we love to sing!
O how sweet Thy reign and rule,
May Thy kingdom come in full!
Yet to Thee, of kings the King,
Here Thy praise we gladly sing!

149

8.7.8.7.7.7. with chorus.

1 Hark! Ten thousand heav'nly voices
Sound the note of praise above;
Jesus reigns and heav'n rejoices,
Jesus reigns, the God of love.
See, He sits on yonder throne;
Jesus rules the world alone.

Hallelujah, Hallelujah,
Hallelujah, Amen.

2 Sing how Jesus came from heaven,
How He bore the cross below,
How all power to Him is given,
How He reigns in glory now.
'Tis a great and endless theme —
Oh, 'tis sweet to sing of Him.

3 Jesus, hail! Thy glory brightens
All above and gives it worth;
Lord of life, Thy smile enlightens,
Cheers, and charms Thy saints on earth.
When we think of love like Thine,
Lord, we own it love divine.

4 King of glory, reign forever!
Thine an everlasting crown.
Nothing from Thy love shall sever
Those whom Thou hast made Thine own:
Happy objects of Thy grace,
Destined to behold Thy face.

5 Savior, hasten Thine appearing:
Bring, oh, bring the glorious day,
When, the awful summons hearing,
Heav'n and earth shall pass away.
Then with raptured hearts we'll sing,
"Glory, glory to our King!"

Peculiar Meter.

1 Praise, praise ye the name of our Savior and God;
Declare, oh, declare ye His glories abroad;
Proclaim ye His mercy, from nation to nation,
Till the uttermost islands have heard His salvation.

For His love floweth on, free and full as a river;
And His mercy endureth forever and ever.

2 Praise, praise ye the Lamb, who for sinners
was slain;
Who went down to the grave, and ascended again;
And who soon shall return, when these dark days
are o'er,
To set up His kingdom, in glory and power.

3 Then the heav'ns and the earth, and the sea shall
rejoice;
The field and the forest shall lift their glad voice;
The sands of the desert shall flourish in green,
And Lebanon's glory be shed o'er the scene.

4 Her bridal attire, and her festal array,
All nature shall see on that glorious day;
For her King cometh down with His people
to reign,
And His presence shall bless her with glory
in men.

151

10.10.10.10. with chorus.

1 Sing we the King who is coming to reign,
Glory to Jesus, the Lamb that was slain;
Righteousness, peace then His empire shall bring,
Joy to the nations when Jesus is King.

Come let us sing: Praise to our King,
Jesus our King, Jesus our King:
This is our song, who to Jesus belong:
Glory to Jesus, to Jesus our King.

2 All men shall dwell in His marvelous light,
Races long severed His love shall unite,
Justice and truth from His scepter shall spring,
Wrong shall be ended when Jesus is King.

3 All shall be well in His kingdom of peace,
Freedom shall flourish and wisdom increase,
Foe shall be friend when His triumph we sing,
Sword shall be sickle when Jesus is King.

4 Knowledge and fear of the Lord then shall be
As the deep waters that cover the sea;
All things shall be in the splendor of spring
And all harmonious when Jesus is King.

5 Kingdom of Christ, for thy coming we pray,
Hasten, O Father, the dawn of the day
When this new song Thy creation shall sing,
Satan is vanquished and Jesus is King.

8.7.8.7.D.

1 O how deep and how far-reaching
    Is Thy love, dear Lord, to me!
Far beyond my pow'r to fathom,
    Deeper than the deepest sea!
It has caused Thee death to suffer
    And to me Thyself impart,
That in Thee I might be grafted
    And become of Thee a part.

2 Who can tell of all the wonders
    Which Thy love for me has wrought,
Yet the greatest of these wonders
    Is that Thou to me art brought.
Oh! to me Thy love has given
    All Thou art as my supply;
As true life I now may share Thee
    And Thy riches e'er enjoy.

3 Lord, Thy love is the expression
    Of Thy loving self divine,
Making life so full of meaning,
    Harmonized with God's design.
Grace of life, how all-sufficient,
    Is my portion day by day;
I'm the object of Thy favor
    And Thy sweetness taste alway.

4 What from Thee can separate me?
    Thou wilt love me to the end!
Oh! Thy love is so prevailing,
    E'en Thyself with me to blend!
We two one will be for ever;
    I am Thine and Thou art mine!
This will be my testimony:
    In Thy love we'll ever twine!

8.6.8.6.

153

1 O blessèd Savior, is Thy love
   So great! so full! so free!
   Fain would we have our thoughts, our hearts,
   Our lives, engaged with Thee.

2 We love Thee for the glorious worth
   Which in Thyself we see;
   We love Thee for that shameful cross,
   Endured so patiently.

3 No man of greater love can boast
   Than for his friend to die;
   Thou for Thine enemies wast slain!
   What love with Thine can vie?

4 Though in the very form of God,
   With heav'nly glory crowned,
   Thou didst a servant's form assume,
   Beset with sorrow round.

5 Thou wouldst like wretched man be made
   In everything but sin,
   That we as like Thee might become
   As we unlike had been:

6 Like Thee in strength, in meekness, love,
   In life in ev'ry phase;
   From glory into glory changed,
   Till we behold Thy face.

7 O Lord, we treasure in our hearts
   The mem'ry of Thy love;
   And ever shall Thy name to us
   A grateful odor prove.

154

10.10.10.10.4.

1 It passeth knowledge, that dear love of Thine,
My Savior, Jesus; yet this soul of mine
Would of Thy love in all its breadth and length,
Its height and depth, its everlasting strength,
   Know more and more.

2 It passeth telling, that dear love of Thine,
My Savior, Jesus; yet these lips of mine
Would fain proclaim to sinners, far and near,
A love which can remove all guilty fear,
     And love beget.

3 It passeth praises, that dear love of Thine,
My Savior, Jesus; yet this heart of mine
Would sing that love, so full, so rich, so free,
Which brings a rebel sinner, such as me,
     Nigh unto God.

4 But though I cannot sing, or tell, or know
The fulness of Thy love, while here below,
My empty vessel I may freely bring;
O Thou, who art of love the living spring,
     My vessel fill.

5 I am an empty vessel — not one thought
Or look of love to Thee I've ever brought;
Yet I may come, and come again to Thee,
With this the empty sinner's only plea,
     Thou lovest me.

6 Oh, fill me, Jesus, Savior, with Thy love!
Lead, lead me to the living fount above;
Thither may I, in simple faith draw nigh,
And never to another fountain fly,
     But unto Thee.

7 Lord Jesus, when Thee face to face I see,
When on Thy lofty throne I sit with Thee,
Then of Thy love, in all its breadth and length,
Its height and depth, its everlasting strength,
     My soul shall sing.

155   7.7.7.7.

1   Christ delivered me when bound,
    And when bleeding, healed my wound;
    Sought me wand'ring, set me right,
    Turned my darkness into light.

2   Can a woman's tender care
    Cease towards the child she bare?
    Yes, she may forgetful be;
    Yet will He remember me.

3   His is an unchanging love,
    Higher than the heights above;
    Deeper than the depths beneath,
    Free and faithful, strong as death.

4   I shall see His glory soon,
    When the work of grace is done;
    Partner of His throne shall be;
    Such is His great love for me!

5   Lord, it is my chief complaint
    That my love is weak and faint;
    Yet I love Thee, and adore:
    Oh, for grace to love Thee more.

156   8.8.8.8.4.4.8.8.

1   I have a Friend, whose faithful love
    Is more than all the world to me:
    'Tis higher than the heights above,
    And deeper than the soundless sea;
        So old, so new,
        So strong, so true;
    Before the earth received its frame,
    He loved me — Blessed be His name!

2 He held the highest place above,
   Adored by all the sons of flame,
   Yet such His self-denying love,
   He laid aside His crown and came
           To seek the lost,
           And at the cost
   Of heavenly rank and earthly fame
   He sought me — Blessed be His name!

3 It was a lonely path He trod,
   From every human soul apart;
   Known only to Himself and God
   Was all the grief that filled His heart,
           Yet from the track
           He turned not back,
   Till where I lay in want and shame,
   He found me — Blessed be His name!

4 Then dawned at last that day of dread,
   When desolate, yet undismayed,
   With wearied frame and thorn-crowned head,
   He, God-forsaken, man-betrayed,
           Was then made sin
           On Calvary,
   And, dying there in grief and shame,
   He saved me — Blessed be His name!

5 Long as I live my song shall tell
   The wonders of His dying love;
   And when at last I go to dwell
   With Him His sovereign grace to prove,
           My joy shall be
           His face to see,
   And bowing there with loud acclaim
   I'll praise Him — Blessed be His name!

157

8.6.8.6.

1   Lord Jesus, are we one with Thee?
    O height, O depth of love!
Thou one with us on Calvary,
    We one with Thee above.

2   Such was Thy grace that for our sake
    Thou didst from heaven come down,
With us of flesh and blood partake,
    In all our misery one.

3   Our sins, our guilt, in love Divine
    Confessed and borne by Thee;
The gall, the curse, the wrath were Thine,
    To set Thy members free.

4   Ascended now, in glory bright,
    Head of the Church Thou art;
Nor life nor death, nor depth nor height,
    Thy saints and Thee can part.

5   Oh teach us, Lord, to know and own
    This wondrous mystery,
That Thou in heaven with us art one,
    And we are one with Thee.

6   Soon, soon shall come that glorious day
    When, seated on Thy throne,
Thou shalt to wondering worlds display
    That Thou with us art one.

8.7.8.7.7.7.

1 Lord, Thy love has sought and found us
   Wand'ring in this desert wide;
Thou hast thrown Thine arms around us,
   For us suffered, bled, and died.
Sing, my soul! He lovèd thee,
Jesus gave Himself for me.

2 Hark! what sounds of bitter weeping
   From yon lonesome garden sweep;
'Tis the Lord His vigil keeping,
   While His followers sink in sleep.
Ah, my soul, He lovèd thee,
Yes, He gave Himself for me.

3 He is speaking to His Father,
   Tasting deep that bitter cup,
Yet He takes it, willing rather
   For our sakes to drink it up.
Oh, what love! He lovèd me!
Gave Himself, my soul, for thee.

4 Then that closing scene of anguish:
   All God's waves and billows roll
Over Him, there left to languish
   On the cross, to save my soul.
Matchless love! how vast, how free,
Jesus gave Himself for me.

5 Hark again! His cries are waking
   Echoes on dark Calvary's hill;
God, my God, art Thou forsaking
   Him who always did Thy will?
Ah, my soul! it was for thee,
Yes! He gave Himself for me.

continued

6 Lord, we joy, Thy toils are ended,
  Glad Thy suff'ring time is o'er;
To Thy Father's throne ascended,
  There Thou liv'st, to die no more.
Yes, my soul, He lives for thee,
He who gave Himself for me.

7 Lord, we worship and adore Thee
  For Thy rich, Thy matchless grace;
Perfect soon in joy before Thee,
  We shall see Thee face to face.
Yet e'en now our song shall be,
Jesus gave Himself for me.

159   Peculiar Meter.

1 Give me a sight, O Savior,
Of Thy wondrous love to me,
Of the love that brought Thee down to earth,
To die on Calvary.

  Oh, make me understand it,
  Help me to take it in,
  What it meant to Thee, the Holy One,
  To bear away my sin.

2 Was it the nails, O Savior,
That bound Thee to the tree?
Nay, 'twas Thine everlasting love,
Thy love for me, for me.

3 Oh, wonder of all wonders,
That through Thy death for me,
My open sins, my secret sins,
Can all forgiven be.

4 Then melt my heart, O Savior,
Bend me, yea, break me down,
Until I own Thee Conqueror,
And Lord and Sov'reign crown.

Used by permission of National Young Life Campaign.

8.6.8.6.8.8.8.6.

1 King of my life, I crown Thee now,
    Thine shall the glory be;
  Lest I forget Thy thorn-crowned brow,
    Lead me to Calvary.

      Lest I forget Gethsemane;
      Lest I forget Thine agony;
      Lest I forget Thy love for me,
        Lead me to Calvary.

2 Show me the tomb where Thou wast laid,
    Tenderly mourned and wept;
  Angels in robes of light arrayed
    Guarded Thee while Thou slept.

3 Let me like Mary, through the gloom,
    Come with a gift to Thee;
  Show to me now the empty tomb,
    Lead me to Calvary.

4 May I be willing, Lord, to bear
    Daily my cross for Thee;
  Even Thy cup of grief to share,
    Thou hast borne all for me.

5 Fill me, O Lord, with Thy desire
    For all that know not Thee;
  Then touch my lips with holy fire,
    To speak of Calvary.

161

8.8.8.5.

1   Praise the Savior, ye who know Him!
Who can tell how much we owe Him?
Gladly let us render to Him
    All we are and have.

2   Jesus is the name that charms us;
He for conflicts fits and arms us;
Nothing moves and nothing harms us
    When we trust in Him.

3   Trust in Him, ye saints, forever;
He is faithful, changing never;
Neither force nor guile can sever
    Those He loves from Him.

4   Keep us, Lord, oh, keep us cleaving
To Thyself and still believing,
Till the hour of Thy receiving
    The victorious Bride.

5   Then we shall be where we would be;
Then we shall be what we should be;
Things which are not now, nor could be,
    Then shall be our own.

11.12.12.12.

1 With praise and thanksgiving there
stands a great throng
In the presence of Jesus and sing
this new song.

Unto Him Who hath loved us and
washed us from sin,
Unto Him be the glory forever!
Amen!

2 All these once were sinners, defiled
in His sight,
Now arrayed in pure garments, in
praise they unite.

3 He maketh the rebel a priest and a
king,
He hath bought us, and taught us
this new song to sing.

4 How helpless and hopeless we sinners
had been,
If He never had loved us till cleansed
from our sin.

5 Aloud in His praises our voices shall
ring,
So that others, believing, this new
song shall sing.

163

8.6.8.6.

1   O for a thousand tongues to sing
      My great Redeemer's praise,
  The glories of my God and King,
      The triumphs of His grace.

2   My gracious Master and my God,
      Assist me to proclaim,
  To spread through all the earth abroad,
      The honors of Thy name.

3   Jesus! the name that charms our fears,
      That bids our sorrows cease;
  'Tis music in the sinner's ears,
      'Tis life, and health, and peace.

4   His love my heart has captive made,
      His captive would I be,
  For He was bound, and scourged and died,
      My captive soul to free.

5   He breaks the power of canceled sin,
      He sets the prisoner free;
  His blood can make the foulest clean;
      His blood availed for me.

6   So now Thy blessed Name I love,
      Thy will would e'er be mine.
  Had I a thousand hearts to give,
      My Lord, they all were Thine!

164

10.9.10.9.

1   Let me sing, for the glory of heaven
  Like a sunbeam has swept o'er my heart;
  I would praise Thee for sins all forgiven,
  For Thy love, which shall never depart.

2   If Thy works praise Thee, Giver of good,
  If the sun shines his praise unto Thee,
  If the wind, as it sighs through the wood,
  Makes a murmur of song from each tree,

3 Then these lips, sure, a tribute shall bring,
   Though unworthy the praises must be;
   Shall all nature be vocal and sing,
   And no psalm of rejoicing from me?

4 O wonderful, glorious Redeemer!
   I would worship Thee, Savior Divine;
   And rejoice, though surrounded with praises,
   Thou wilt still hear a song such as mine.

PRAISE OF THE LORD — HIS GOODNESS

7.6.7.6.D.   **165**

1 My song shall be of Jesus;
     His mercy crowns my days,
   He fills my cup with blessings,
     And tunes my heart to praise.
   My song shall be of Jesus,
     The precious Lamb of God,
   Who gave Himself my ransom,
     And bought me with His blood.

2 My song shall be of Jesus
     When, sitting at His feet,
   I call to mind His goodness
     In meditation sweet:
   My song shall be of Jesus,
     Whatever ill betide;
   I'll sing the grace that saves me,
     And keeps me at His side.

3 My song shall be of Jesus
     While pressing on my way
   To reach the blissful kingdom
     Of pure and perfect day:
   And when my soul shall enter
     That realm of splendor fair,
   A song of praise to Jesus
     I'll sing forever there.

14.14.4.7.8.

166

1 Praise to the Lord, the Almighty, the
King of creation!
O my soul, praise Him, for He is thy
health and salvation!
All ye who hear,
Now to His temple draw near;
Sing now in glad adoration!

2 Praise to the Lord, who o'er all
things so wondrously reigneth,
Who, as on wings of an eagle,
uplifteth, sustaineth.
Hast thou not seen
How thy desires all have been
Granted in what He ordaineth?

3 Praise to the Lord, who hath fearfully,
wondrously, made thee!
Health hath vouchsafed and, when
heedlessly falling, hath stayed thee.
What need or grief
Ever hath failed of relief?
Wings of His mercy did shade thee.

4 Praise to the Lord, who doth prosper
thy work and defend thee,
Who from the heavens the streams of
His mercy doth send thee.
Ponder anew
What the Almighty can do,
Who with His love doth befriend thee.

5 Praise to the Lord! Oh, let all that
is in me adore Him!
All that hath life and breath, come
now with praises before Him!
Let the Amen
Sound from His people again;
Gladly for aye we adore Him.

167

8.8.8.8.(A)

1 How good is the Lord we adore,
Our faithful, unchangeable Friend;
His love is as great as His pow'r
And knows neither measure nor end.

2 'Tis Jesus the first and the last,
Who shall guide us through all to the throne;
We'll praise Him for all that is past,
We'll trust Him for all that's to come.

168

8.8.8.8.

1 Now in a song of grateful praise,
To Thee, O Lord, my voice I'll raise;
With all Thy saints I'll join to tell,
My Savior has done all things well.

And above the rest this note shall swell,
This note shall swell, this note shall swell,
And above the rest this note shall swell,
My Savior has done all things well.

2 How sov'reign, wonderful and free,
Has been Thy love to sinful me!
Thou sav'dst me from the jaws of hell;
My Savior has done all things well.

3 Since e'er my soul has known His love,
What mercies He has made me prove,
Mercies which do all praise excel,
My Savior has done all things well.

4 And when on that bright day I rise,
And join the anthems of the skies,
Above the rest this note shall swell,
My Savior has done all things well.

169*

7.6.7.6.D.

1 Thou, Lord, to God art precious,
 His chosen, His delight;
With oil of joy, anointed,
 How comely in His sight.

We treasure with affection
 Thy perfect comeliness,
Thy sweetness and Thy fragrance,
 And all Thy loveliness.

2 The altogether lovely,
 The fairest of the fair,
Thy mouth with grace o'erfloweth;
 Our hearts their love declare.

3 The wise men offered treasures
 And honored Thee at birth;
Thou wast by noble buried,
 Still lovable in death.

4 Thy head has been anointed,
 The lovely One Thou art;
Thy feet anointed also,
 Beloved in every part.

5 Thy death as myrrh in sweetness
 Man's spirit comforteth;
Thy resurrection fragrance
 God's longing answereth.

6 As henna flow'rs, Thy beauty
 In loveliness complete;
As apple trees that flourish,
 Thy fruit abundant, sweet.

7 Sweet wine Thy love surpasseth,
 Thy name an ointment is;
We take Thee as our love feast
 And taste the sweetest bliss.

PRAISE OF THE LORD — HIS SWEETNESS

8 As on Thyself we ponder
And all Thy beauty trace,
We taste to full Thy sweetness
And rest in Thine embrace.

PRAISE OF THE LORD — HIS BEAUTY
8.7.8.7.

170*

1 Lord, Thou art the lovely Bridegroom,
God appointed, dear to us;
Thy dear self is so attractive,
To our heart so beauteous!

2 Dear Beloved, we admire Thee,
Who can tell Thy preciousness;
All Thy love we deeply treasure
And Thine untold loveliness.

3 Thou art fairer than the fairest,
Thou art sweeter than the sweet;
Thou art meek and Thou art gracious,
None can e'er with Thee compete.

4 Full of myrrh are all Thy garments,
And Thy lips are filled with grace;
In the savor of Thy suffering,
We in love Thyself embrace.

5 It is with the oil of gladness
Thy God hath anointed Thee;
From the palaces of ivory
Praise shall ever rise to Thee.

6 God hath blessed Thee, Lord, forever,
Thou hast won the victory;
Now we see Thee throned in glory
With Thy pow'r and majesty.

7 Thou art the desire of nations,
All Thy worth they'll ever prove;
Thou, the chiefest of ten thousand,
Ever worthy of our love.

171*

8.6.8.6. with chorus.

1 Lord Jesus Christ, our heart feels sweet
   Whene'er we think on Thee,
And long that to Thy presence dear
   We soon might raptured be!

   Lord, like the pretty henna-flower,†
      In vineyards blossoming Thou art;
   Incomp'rable Thy beauty is,
      Admires and loves our heart!

2 There is no music adequate
   Thy grace in full to praise,
Nor there a heart which could enjoy
   Thy love in every phase.

3 Yet, what delights our heart the most
   Is not Thy love, Thy grace;
But it is Thine own loving Self
   That satisfies always.

4 Oh, Thou art fairer than the fair,
   And sweeter than the sweet;
Beside Thee, none in heaven or earth
   Our heart's desire could meet.

† An Old World plant, prized for its fragrant yellow and white flowers.
(Song of Sol. 1:14, A.S.V.)

8.6.8.8.6.

1 I cannot breathe enough of Thee,
    O gentle breeze of love;
More fragrant than the myrtle tree
The Henna-flower† is to me,
    The Balm of Heaven above.

2 I cannot gaze enough on Thee,
    Thou Fairest of the Fair;
My heart is filled with ecstasy,
As in Thy face of radiancy
    I see such beauty there.

3 I cannot yield enough to Thee,
    My Savior, Master, Friend;
I do not wish to go out free,
But ever, always, willingly,
    To serve Thee to the end.

4 I cannot sing enough of Thee,
    The sweetest name on earth;
A note so full of melody
Comes from my heart so joyously,
    And fills my soul with mirth.

5 I cannot speak enough of Thee,
    I have so much to tell;
Thy heart it beats so tenderly
As Thou dost draw me close to Thee,
    And whisper, "All is well."

† An Old World plant, prized for its fragrant yellow and white flowers.
(Song of Sol. 1:14, A.S.V.)

173

8.7.8.7. with chorus.

1 Thou art fairer than the morning,
  O my Savior and my King!
Of Thy grandeur and Thy beauty,
  How my soul delights to sing.

  Thou art fairer than the morning,
  Thou art brighter, brighter than the day;
  At the glory of Thy presence
  Clouds and darkness flee away.

2 Clothed in light as with a garment,
  Crowned with majesty divine,
Lo, the scepter of dominion
  Now and ever, Lord, is Thine.

3 O the greatness of Thy mercy,
  And the richness of Thy grace!
O the love that in Thy kingdom
  Is preparing me a place!

4 When at last I reach the kingdom,
  Win the crown, the battle o'er,
With ten thousand times ten thousand
  I shall sing forevermore.

174

Peculiar Meter.

1 O Morning Star, how fair and bright,
Thou beamest forth in truth and light!
  O Sov'reign meek and lowly,
Thou Root of Jesse, David's Son,
My Lord and Master, Thou hast won
  My heart to serve Thee solely!
    Thou art holy,
Fair and glorious, all-victorious,
    Rich in blessing,
Rule and might o'er all possessing.

2 Thou heav'nly Brightness, Light divine,
O deep within my heart now shine,
And make Thee there an altar.
Fill me with joy and strength to be
Thy member, ever joined to Thee
In love that cannot falter;
Toward Thee longing
Doth possess me; turn and bless me;
Here in sadness
Eye and heart long for Thy gladness.

5.6.8.5.5.8.

175

1 Fairest Lord Jesus!
Ruler of all nature!
O Thou of God and man the Son!
Thee will I cherish,
Thee will I honor,
Thou, my soul's glory, joy, and crown!

2 Fair are the meadows,
Fairer still the woodlands,
Robed in the blooming garb of spring;
Jesus is fairer,
Jesus is purer,
Who makes the woeful heart to sing!

3 Fair is the sunshine,
Fairer still the moonlight,
And all the twinkling starry host;
Jesus shines brighter,
Jesus shines purer,
Than all the angels heav'n can boast!

4 All fairest beauty,
Heavenly and earthly,
Wondrously, Jesus, is found in Thee;
None can be nearer,
Fairer, or dearer,
Than Thou my Savior art to me.

176

6.5.6.5.D.

1 Jesus, wondrous Savior!
    Christ, of kings the King!
Angels fall before Thee,
    Prostrate, worshipping;
Fairest they confess Thee
    In the heav'n above.
We would sing Thee fairest
    Here in hymns of love.

2 All earth's flowing pleasures
    Were a wintry sea;
Heav'n itself without Thee
    Dark as night would be.
Lamb of God! Thy glory
    Is the light above.
Lamb of God! Thy glory
    Is the life of love.

3 Life is death, if severed
    From Thy throbbing heart.
Death with life abundant
    At Thy touch would start.
Worlds and men and angels
    All consist in Thee,
Yet Thou camest to us
    In humility.

4 Jesus! all perfections
    Rise and end in Thee;
Brightness of God's glory
    Thou, eternally.
Favored beyond measure
    They Thy face who see;
May we, gracious Savior,
    Share this ecstasy.

The "McMaster Hymn"; by permission.

8.6.8.6. with repeat.

177

1 Majestic sweetness sits enthroned
   Upon the Savior's brow;
   His head with radiant glories crowned,
   His lips with grace o'erflow.

2 No mortal can with Him compare
   Among the sons of men;
   Fairer is He than all the fair
   That fill the heavenly train.

3 To Him I owe my life and breath,
   And all the joys I have;
   He makes me triumph over death,
   And saves me from the grave.

4 To God, the Father, my abode,
   He brings my weary feet;
   Shows me the glories of my God,
   And makes my joys complete.

5 Since from His bounty I receive
   Such proofs of love divine,
   Had I a thousand hearts to give,
   Lord, they should all be Thine.

8.8.8.8.8.8.

178

1 Our hearts are full of Christ and long
   Their glorious matter to declare!
   Of Him we make our loftier song,
   We cannot from His praise forbear:
   Our ready tongues make haste to sing
   The glories of the heav'nly King.

2 Fairer than all the earthborn race,
   Perfect in comeliness Thou art;
   Replenished are Thy lips with grace,
   And full of love Thy tender heart.
   God ever-blest! we bow the knee,
   And own all fulness dwells in Thee.

6.6.4.6.6.6.4.

1 Glory to Christ on high!
   Let praises fill the sky!
     Praise ye His name:
   He all our sorrows bore;
   Angels His name adore,
   And saints cry evermore,
     "Worthy the Lamb!"

2 All they around the throne
   Cheerfully join in one,
     Praising His name:
   We who have known His blood
   Sealing our peace with God,
   Spread His dear name abroad;
     Worthy the Lamb!

3 Join all the human race
   Our Lord, God's Christ, to bless,
     Praise ye His name:
   In Him we will rejoice,
   Making a cheerful noise,
   Saying with heart and voice,
     "Worthy the Lamb!"

4 Though we must change our place,
   Our hearts shall never cease
     Praising His name:
   To Him we'll tribute bring,
   Laud Him, our gracious King,
   And, without ceasing, sing,
     "Worthy the Lamb!"

11.10.11.10. with chorus..

1 Jesus, our Lord, with what joy we adore Thee,
  Chanting our praise to Thyself on the throne!
Blest in Thy presence, we worship before Thee,
  Own Thou art worthy, and worthy alone.

  Lord, Thou art worthy: Lord, Thou art worthy;
    Lord, Thou art worthy, and worthy alone!
  Blest in Thy presence, we worship before Thee,
    Own Thou art worthy, and worthy alone!

2 Verily God, yet become truly human,
  Lower than angels to die in our stead;
How has that long promised "Seed of the woman"
  Trod on the serpent and bruisèd his head!

3 How didst Thou humble Thyself to be taken,
  Led by Thy creatures and nailed to the cross,
Hated of men, and of God too forsaken,
  Shunning not darkness, the curse, and the loss.

4 How hast Thou triumphed, and triumphed
      with glory,
  Battled death's forces, rolled back every wave!
Can we refrain then from telling the story?
  Lord, Thou art Victor o'er death and the grave.

181

8.4.8.4.8.8.8.4.

1 'Tis the Church triumphant singing,
    Worthy the Lamb;
Heav'n throughout with praises ringing,
    Worthy the Lamb.
Thrones and pow'rs before Him bending,
Odors sweet with voice ascending
Swell the chorus never ending,
    Worthy the Lamb.

2 Every kindred, tongue and nation,
    Worthy the Lamb;
Join to sing the great salvation,
    Worthy the Lamb.
Loud as mighty thunders roaring,
Floods of mighty waters pouring,
Prostrate at His feet adoring,
    Worthy the Lamb.

3 Harps and songs forever sounding,
    Worthy the Lamb;
Mighty grace o'er sin abounding,
    Worthy the Lamb.
By His blood He dearly bought us;
Wand'ring from the fold He sought us,
And to glory safely brought us;
    Worthy the Lamb.

4 Sing with blest anticipation
    Worthy the Lamb;
Through the vale of tribulation,
    Worthy the Lamb.
Sweetest notes, all notes excelling,
On the theme forever dwelling,
Still untold, though ever telling,
    Worthy the Lamb.

8.7.8.7.   **182**

1 Jesus, Thou alone art worthy
   Ceaseless praises to receive;
   For Thy love and grace and goodness
   Rise o'er all our thoughts conceive.

2 With adoring heart, we render
   Honor to Thy precious name,
   Overflowing with Thy mercies,
   Far and wide Thy worth proclaim.

3 Praise Him! praise Him! praise the Savior!
   Saints, aloud your voices raise,
   Praise Him! praise Him! till in glory
   Perfected we'll sing His praise.

8.6.8.6.   **183**

1 Come, let us join our cheerful songs,
       And thus approach the throne;
   Had we ten thousand thousand tongues,
       Our theme of joy's but one:

2 "Worthy the Lamb that's gone on high,
       To be exalted thus!"
   "Worthy the Lamb that died!" we cry,
       "For He was slain for us."

3 Jesus is worthy to receive
       Honor and pow'r divine;
   And blessings more than we can give
       Be, Lord, forever Thine.

4 Soon shall the saints, exalted high,
       A glorious anthem raise,
   And all that dwell beneath the sky
       Speak forth Thine endless praise.

5 Redeemed creation join in one,
       T'adore the sacred name
   Of Him that sits upon the throne,
       And to exalt the Lamb.

184

8.8.8.8.

1 Come, let us sing the song of songs,
The saints of old began the strain,
The blessing which to Christ belongs:
Worthy the Lamb, for He was slain!

2 Slain to redeem us by His blood,
To cleanse from every sinful stain;
And make us kings and priests to God;
Worthy the Lamb, for He was slain!

3 Long as we live, and should we die,
And while in light with Him we reign,
This song our song of songs shall be:
Worthy the Lamb, for He was slain!

185

8.5.8.5.D.

1 Blessed Lord, our hallelujahs
Now to Thee we raise.
Never could we fully utter
All Thy worth and praise!

Praise the Lamb, for He is worthy!
Sweet eternal strain.
Hallelujah! Hallelujah!
Praise the Lord! Amen.

2 Praise the Lamb! Yes, Thou art worthy,
Who didst shed Thy blood
To redeem Thy saints, and make us
Kings and priests to God!

3 Hallelujah! Thou, Lord Jesus,
　　Canst not cease to love;
　　Thine we are and Thine forever,
　　One with Thee above.

4 Praise the Lord! Yes, hallelujah!
　　Who would hush the song?
　　Join with saints from every nation,
　　Every tribe and tongue.

8.7.8.7.8.7.　　　　　　　　**186**

1 Glory be to Him who loved us,
　　Washed us from each sinful stain;
　　Glory be to Him who made us
　　Priests and kings with Him to reign;
　　Glory, worship, laud and blessing
　　To the Lamb who once was slain.

2 Glory, worship, laud and blessing,
　　Thus the choir triumphant sings;
　　Honor, riches, power, dominion,
　　Thus its praise creation brings;
　　Thou art worthy, Thou art worthy,
　　Lord of lords, and King of kings.

3 Glory to the King of angels,
　　Glory to the Church's King,
　　Glory to the King of nations,
　　Heaven and earth His praises sing;
　　Glory ever and forever
　　To the King of Glory bring.

187*

This hymn may be used as five separate hymns as follows:

1. Verses 1 to 8 and 26
2. Verses 1 and 9 to 13 and 26
3. Verses 1 and 14 to 17 and 26
4. Verses 1 and 18 to 21 and 26
5. Verses 1 and 22 to 26

8.7.8.7.(I)

1   O Lord, how rich Thou art to us,
     Thy love reveals the measure!
    The boundless riches of Thyself,
     In spirit here we treasure.

2   Thou art the Word, e'en God Himself,
     With God in the beginning;
    Incarnate in the flesh with us,
     And God to us defining.

3   Thou art the tabernacle true,
     In Thee we see God's glory;
    For God Thou art the temple too,
     In Thee is God's full story.

4   Thou art the only Son of God,
     The Father e'er declaring,
    That we may have the life divine,
     God's very nature sharing.

5   Thou art the Son of Man like us,
     And truly share our nature,
    That we may be the sons of God
     And grow to Thy full stature.

6   Thou art the Christ, the Lord of all,
     By God Thou art anointed;
    The One who is the All in all,
     For God and us appointed.

7 Thou art the Savior crucified,
  Whence issued blood and water,
  That we might be redeemed to God,
  And life divine may enter.

8 Thou now art Jesus glorified,
  From whom descends the Spirit;
  The all-inclusive Spirit comes
  To us with all Thy merit.

9 Thou art the very light of life
  That shineth in the darkness;
  The light divine that shines with God
  Within our hearts in fulness.

10 Thou art the very life divine,
  Which all our spirits quickens;
  The life which brings us out of death
  And all our being strengthens.

11 Lord, Thou art God's reality,
  The truth that meets God's pleasure;
  The truth that brings Thyself to us,
  That we may know Thy measure.

12 Thou also art the way of life,
  Which unto glory leads us;
  The way of Thy reality,
  Which into vict'ry speeds us.

13 Thou art the resurrection too,
  All death Thy life doth swallow;
  'Tis by Thy resurrection pow'r,
  We bear the cross and follow.

14 Thou art the spotless Lamb of God,
  Who died for our redemption;
  Thou art the Spirit-giver too,
  For our regeneration.

continued

15 Thou art the serpent made of brass,
       Who saveth us from evil;
   Thou on the tree wast lifted up,
       To crush for us the devil.

16 Thou art the Shepherd and the door,
       For us to leave the sheepfold,
   By Thee we have full liberty
       And share the pasture freehold.

17 Thy washing keeps us always clean,
       In function like the laver;
   Thus we are kept in fellowship,
       Partaking of Thy favor.

18 Thou art the heav'nly riven rock,
       With living water flowing;
   We drink of this refreshing stream,
       Thy quenching power knowing.

19 Thou art the heav'nly well, in Thee
       Is living water ever;
   We drink of Thine eternal life,
       And thirst no more forever.

20 Thou art the heav'nly bread of life,
       Thy food divine doth flourish;
   With all Thy riches bountiful
       Our spirits Thou dost nourish.

21 Thou even art our breath of life
       Thyself we breathe in spirit;
   By Thee we live, in Thee we walk,
       Thy riches we inherit.

22 Thou art the grain of wheat divine,
       That died and rose with glory,
   To bring forth us as many grains
       To form Thy glorious Body.

23 Thou art the true and heav'nly vine,
    And we in Thee are branches;
    In Thee abiding, Thou in us,
    We share in all Thy riches.

24 Thou art the Bridegroom from above
    To take the Bride, Thy Body;
    That we may be with Thee as one,
    In life and love and glory.

25 Thou art the ladder Jacob saw,
    By Thee the heav'n is open;
    In Thee we are the house of God,
    And earth is joined to heaven.

26 O Lord, Thou art the great "I AM,"
    Who all our need doth furnish;
    Enjoying Thee as all in all,
    God's purpose we accomplish.

188*

This hymn may be shortened by singing only verses
1, 2, 7, 9, 11, 14, 17, 21 & 22, as marked with asterisks.

8.7.8.7.(I)

1* Dear Lord, Thou art the Son of God,
    His absolute expression;
    In Thee God speaks to us today,
    Thou art His definition.

2* The impress of God's substance true,
    Effulgence of His glory,
    Thou even art our God Himself,
    In Thee is His full story.

continued

188*

3 By Thee was made the universe,
    Subsisting by Thy merit;
  The heir, God hath appointed Thee,
    That all Thou may inherit.

4 Since Thou hast purged our sins by death,
    In heaven Thou art seated,
  Till all Thy foes will be subdued
    And all God's will completed.

5 A better name than angels have,
    From God Thou didst inherit;
  As Son of God to us as life,
    Thou now art in the Spirit.

6 Thy kingdom is of righteousness,
    Thy throne will stand forever;
  God hath in love anointed Thee,
    And Thou shalt wax old never.

7* Thou also art a man indeed,
    With all our human nature;
  By grace Thou tastedst death for us
    That we may have Thy stature.

8 With glory and with honor crowned,
    All things to Thee are subject;
  As Captain of salvation, full,
    Thou art thru sufferings perfect.

9* By death the devil Thou hast spoiled,
    And from death's bondage freed us;
  Thou sanctifiest us in life
    And dost to glory speed us.

10 To us, Thy brethren, Thou art here,
    The Father's Name declaring;
  Within the Church Thou singest hymns,
    God's praises with us sharing.

11* Superior Thou to Moses, Lord,
    As to the house the builder;
Thou, our Apostle sent from God,
    Art worthy of more splendor.

12 Thou art our real Joshua,
    By Thee the rest we enter;
Our full salvation is of Thee,
    Our faith on Thee doth center.

13 Thou art the heav'nly rest to us,
    Now dwelling in our spirit,
For us to enter as the land
    And all Thy good inherit.

14* Superior Thou to Aaron too —
    Thyself, the offering given,
Thou enteredst, as our Great High Priest,
    The holiest place in heaven.

15 Thou art our true Melchisedec,
    With endless life in power,
To minister the "bread and wine,"
    In every needful hour.

16 Thou art the better sacrifice,
    Thru the eternal Spirit,
Once offered unto God for us,
    That we may gain Thy merit.

17* A better covenant was made
    With Thy dear blood in heaven;
By Thee this sure new testament
    To Thy redeemed was given.

18 Thou art its Maker adequate,
    For Thou dost have the merit;
Thou art its Giver competent
    That we may all inherit;

continued

19 Its qualified Executor,
    By life of resurrection;
  Its potent Mediator too,
    Fulfilling God's election.

20 Lord, Thou art now within the veil,
    As our unique Forerunner,
  That by Thy life, without the camp,
    We'll in the race be runners.

21* Thou art the Finisher of faith,
    As well its Author perfect;
  By faith and love we follow Thee,
    And e'er to Thee are subject.

22* Unequaled is Thy worth, dear Lord,
    And all Thou art we treasure;
  Thou art so perfect and complete,
    Beyond all human measure.

189*   7.6.7.6.D.

1 Thou art the Son beloved,
    The image of our God;
  Thou art the saints' dear portion,
    Imparted thru Thy blood.
  Among all God's creation
    Thou art the firstborn One;
  By Thee all was created,
    All for Thyself to own.

2 Thou art before all creatures,
    In Thee all things consist;
  Of all Thou art the center,
    By Thee all things subsist.
  Thou art the sole beginning,
    The Firstborn from the dead;
  And for the Church, Thy Body,
    Thou art the glorious Head.

3 Because it pleased the Father,
  All fulness dwells in Thee,
 That Thou might have the first place
  In all we ever see.
 All things Thou reconciledst
  To God by Thy shed blood,
 To thus present us holy
  And blameless unto God.

4 In Thee God's fulness dwelleth,
  Thou art God's mystery;
 The treasures of all wisdom
  And knowledge are in Thee.
 Thou art the hope of glory,
  In us Thou dost abide;
 In Thee we are perfected
  And God is satisfied.

5 All things are but a shadow
  Which unto us reveal
 Thyself, in whom we're rooted,
  The only One that's real.
 Enjoying all Thy riches,
  Thy fulness we will be;
 We'll hold Thee, as Thy Body,
  And grow with God in Thee.

6 With Thee in God we're hidden,
  Thou art in us our life;
 Thy peace in us presiding,
  We rest from all our strife.
 In the new man, Thy Body,
  Thou art the all in all;
 Our all-inclusive Savior,
  Thyself we'll ever call.

190*

8.8.8.8.D.

1 O Lord, as we consider Thee,
We worship Thee for all Thou art;
Thou art so rich, so wonderful,
So dear and precious to our heart.

What Thou art meets our every need!
Our hearts o'erflow with praise to Thee!
All our desires Thou dost exceed
And satisfy continually.

2 Thou art the very God in truth,
The God who is both love and light;
The God who is to us our life,
The God in whom we all delight.

3 Thou also art a man indeed,
A man so fine, so good, so pure;
A man in whom our God delights,
A man who can our love secure.

4 Thou even art a lowly slave,
A slave of God to serve for us;
Obedient to the cross's death
That we might be delivered thus.

5 Thou art, beside all these, a King,
A King in life and love to reign,
By God anointed with His pow'r
To rule with us in His domain.

6 Dear Lord, as we remember Thee,
We thus partake of all Thou art;
As we enjoy Thyself in love,
We share Thee as Thy counterpart.

8.7.8.7.D.

1 Lord, Thou art the "Seed of woman,"
    Born to bruise the enemy;
Thou didst take the human nature,
    Die to win the victory.
As the very God incarnate,
    Flesh and blood Thou didst partake;
Thou thru death hast crushed the devil
    And his pow'r of death didst break.

2 "Seed of Abraham," Thou art, Lord,
    By God's promise Thou hast come,
That the blessing He hath promised
    On all people thus might come.
Abraham Thou hast preceded,
    For Thou art the great "I AM,"
Yet Thou cam'st to be his offspring
    And become God's promised "Lamb."

3 Lord, Thou art the "Seed of David,"
    For the kingdom Thou wast raised;
For God's glory and His building
    On the throne Thou hast been placed.
Truly Thou art "David's offspring,"
    Yet "my Lord" he calleth Thee,
For Thou art his "root" and fountain,
    "Lord of all" eternally.

4 Though "a child" born with our nature,
    Thou the "Mighty God" art called;
Thou, "a son" to us art given,
    "Everlasting Father" called.
All the blessings God hath promised,
    With our faith on Thee depend;
Thou art "Yea" and "Amen" for them,
    All the content and the end!

192   6.6.6.6.8.8.

1 We come, O Christ, to Thee,
    True Son of God and man,
By whom all things consist,
    In whom all life began:
In Thee alone we live and move
And have our being in Thy love.

2 Thou art the Way to God,
    Thy blood our ransom paid;
In Thee we face our Judge
    And Maker unafraid.
Before the Throne absolved we stand:
Thy love has met Thy law's demand.

3 Thou art the living Truth!
    All wisdom dwells in Thee,
Thou Source of every skill,
    Eternal Verity!
Thou great I Am! In Thee we rest,
True answer to our every quest.

4 Thou only art true Life,
    To know Thee is to live
The more abundant life
    That earth can never give:
O Risen Lord! We live in Thee
And Thou in us eternally!

5 We worship Thee Lord Christ,
    Our Savior and our King,
To Thee our youth and strength
    Adoringly we bring:
So fill our hearts that men may see
Thy life in us and turn to Thee!

8.6.8.6.D.

1 Dear Lord, Thou art so much to us,
   Thou art our all in all;
   What Thou art fully meets our needs,
   Though they be great or small.
   Our hearts appreciate what Thou art,
   Our spirits worship Thee;
   Our grateful praise to Thee we give
   As we Thy riches see.

2 Thou art the Prophet raised by God,
   With pow'r for God to speak;
   Like Moses, Thou God's plan hast shown,
   That we God's will may seek.
   Thou art like Jonah sent by God,
   To enter death and live,
   That by this sign of death and life,
   We may in Thee believe.

3 Thou art the Prophet raised from men,
   To speak with pow'r and light;
   Thou, like Elisha, filled with love,
   Thy miracles in might.
   Thou, like Isaiah, full of grace,
   God's Christ dost e'er reveal,
   That we may share this Christ of all
   As life both rich and real.

4 Thou art the Priest from us to God,
   The holy Priest for us,
   Like Aaron called of God from men,
   For us Thou servest thus.
   In love Thou bearest us to God,
   The great High Priest to serve;
   With love Thou intercedest there
   And dost with strength preserve.

continued

5 Thou art the Priest from God to us,
   The royal Priest of God;
Like Salem's King, Melchisedec,
   The minister of God.
With bread and wine Thou cam'st from God
   To us in time of need;
Thou cam'st with God that we in Him
   Might fully share indeed.

6 Thou art the King as David was,
   And God's desire dost seek;
The battle fought, the foe subdued,
   God's heart Thou dost bespeak.
Thou art empowered on the throne,
   Not with a human rod,
But with authority divine
   To reign for us and God.

7 Thou art the King like Solomon,
   Whose rule with peace was filled;
With wisdom Thou dost reign in pow'r
   And Thou God's house dost build.
As King unseen Thou reignest now
   Among Thy saints with love;
One day, when Thou shalt reign with us,
   Thou wilt Thy kingship prove.

8 As King and Priest and Prophet too,
   How precious, Lord, art Thou;
Thy worth to God, Thy worth to us,
   We all with love avow.
O how we treasure what Thou art,
   Our hearts are drawn by Thee;
To Thee we'll give our thanks and praise
   Throughout eternity.

8.6.8.6.D.

1 Thou art God's testimony, Lord,
   Much better than the law;
The law in letter was engraved,
   In it Thy type men saw.
A definition was the law,
   God's picture to provide;
But Thou art God's reality,
   In Thee doth God abide.

2 The ark of testimony too
   Was but a type of Thee;
In it the law of God was placed,
   But God in Thee we see.
The ark, in type, was made of wood
   And overlaid with gold;
It typifies Thee as a man,
   Who God in full doth hold.

3 Thou art the tabernacle too,
   God's holy dwelling place;
Incarnate in the flesh Thou art,
   And full of truth and grace.
God's glory we behold in Thee,
   Thou art the Word divine;
Thy words and deeds of love and light
   Do God in life define.

4 The temple was a type of Thee;
   The house of God Thou art;
God dwells in Thee, Himself to show,
   His fulness to impart.
Though Thou by Satan wast destroyed
   And numbered with the dead,
In resurrection Thou dost build
   A larger one instead.

continued

5 The city shows Thy fulness true,
   A figure of Thy Bride,
The increase of Thyself in full,
   In whom Thou dost abide.
In Thee is God, the light divine,
   The lamp in her art Thou;
With Thee God shines thru her on all,
   His glory to avow.

6 The tabernacle and the ark,
   The law within them stored,
The temple and the city too,
   Are all Thyself, dear Lord.
Thou art the hub, Thou art the rim,
   The all in all Thou art!
In Thee we see both God and man,
   How precious to our heart!

195*   7.6.7.6.D.

1 Lord, Thou art all the offerings
   Prepared by God for us;
They are so rich in meaning,
   So sweet and glorious.
They have fulfilled God's purpose
   And met His heart's desire;
They too have satisfied us,
   And faced what we require.

2 Thou art the burnt-oblation,
   Consumed by holy fire;
To God as a sweet savor,
   Fulfilling His desire.
Thou walkedst in God's presence,
   And all His will pursued;
Thyself the spotless offering,
   For us to God as food.

3 Thou art the meal-oblation,
    With "oil" and "frankincense";
  'Tis holy, fine, and perfect,
    And sweet to every sense.
  Thou art the peace-oblation,
    The peace for us to make,
  That we with God may share Thee,
    As food of Thee partake.

4 Thou art the sin-oblation,
    For us Thou sin wast made;
  By death for our redemption
    The ransom Thou hast paid.
  Thou art the trespass-offering,
    Thou all our sins didst bear
  To satisfy God's justice,
    That we His pardon share.

5 Thou art the wave-oblation,
    The resurrected One;
  O'er hades, death and darkness,
    The vict'ry Thou hast won.
  Thou art the heave-oblation,
    Thou didst ascend to God;
  As such in heav'nly places
    Thou art our holy food.

8.7.8.7.D.

196*

1 Lord, the ancient types and symbols
    As our all Thyself portrayed;
  As was shadowed in those figures,
    Real to us Thou now art made.
  Contemplating such a picture,
    As we on its wonders gaze,
  How we marvel at Thy riches
    And our song of worship raise.

continued

2   Lord, Thou art our true Passover,
     God passed over us thru Thee;
By Thyself and Thy redemption
     We with God have harmony.
Thou, the Lamb of God, redeemedst us
     With Thyself and with Thy blood;
We apply Thy blood, our ransom,
     Eating Thee, our real food.

3   Lord, Thou art the Bread from heaven,
     The unleavened Bread of life;
Eating Thee, with Thee we mingle,
     Ceasing from our sin and strife.
Lamb and Bread are both Thy figures,
     Showing Thou art life to us;
Feasting on Thee at Thy table,
     We enjoy Thy riches thus.

4   Lord, Thou art the Heav'nly Manna,
     As our daily food supply;
Strengthening and energizing,
     All our need to satisfy.
Living Rock Thou also art, Lord,
     Cleft for us with life to flow;
Drinking of this living water,
     Thirst is quenched, Thy life we know.

5   Lord, Thou art the Land of Canaan —
     Elevated, rich and good,
Flowing with both milk and honey
     In a glorious plenitude.
By Thy surplus God we worship,
     In Thy fellowship we move;
Thus in love we're joined together
     And God's building we will prove.

8.6.8.6.

1　How all-inclusive, Lord, Thou art;
　　　Of God we are in Thee —
　　The portion God prepared for us,
　　　Our all in all to be.

2　Thou art to us God's wisdom true,
　　　We all are saved through Thee;
　　Thou art God's only way to save,
　　　Thou art our only plea.

3　Thou art to us our righteousness,
　　　All God requires to meet;
　　In Thee we all are justified,
　　　In Thee we are complete.

4　Thou art to us our holiness
　　　That we may be transformed;
　　In Thee we all are sanctified,
　　　To Thee we'll be conformed.

5　Thou art to us redemption too,
　　　That we Thy likeness bear;
　　Transfigured will our bodies be
　　　Thy liberty to share.

6　Dear Lord, while we remember Thee,
　　　Enjoying all Thou art,
　　We thus would hasten Thy return
　　　And ne'er from Thee depart.

7　How sweet to have this foretaste here,
　　　A taste so wonderful,
　　Yet still we fain would be with Thee,
　　　And share Thyself in full.

198*

8.6.8.6.

1   Dear Lord, Thou art the Tree of Life,
    The very life supply;
  Thy fruits, replete with life divine,
    Our hunger satisfy.

2   Thou art the true and heav'nly Vine,
    Our very source of life;
  By Thee we live, in Thee abide,
    And rest from all our strife.

3   Dear Lord, Thou art the Apple Tree,
    Thyself we all enjoy;
  Thy fruits are sweet to all our taste,
    Thy shadow brings us joy.

4   Thou art to us the healing Tree;
    Our death Thou didst endure;
  Thou on a tree for us wast slain,
    That we may have Thy cure.

5   Thou art the very Branch of God,
    His fulness dwells in Thee;
  In Thee we take of Him as grace
    And the reality.

6   Lord, Thou art also David's Branch
    Incarnate here to be;
  In Thee we see and comprehend
    The true humanity.

7   Thou art the sprouting Rod with God,
    In Thee is endless life;
  Before Thy resurrection pow'r
    Death never can be rife.

8   Thou also art the swimming Stick,
    The fallen "ax" are we;
  By Thine uplifting pow'r of life,
    From death we're lifted free.

9 Lord, Thou art such a "Plant of Fame,"
   Of Thee we richly share;
   As we are here remembering Thee,
   Thyself we thus declare!

8.7.8.7.D. with chorus.   **199***

1 Thou art the Rock everlasting,
   Spiritual Rock cleft for me;
   Drinking of Thee as the Spirit,
   Thus I become one with Thee.
   Thou art the Rock never shaken,
   'Tis on this Rock we are built;
   Joined unto Thee thru redemption,
   Nothing can shake us thru guilt.

   Lord, how we treasure Thy value,
   All that Thou art is for us;
   While here in loving remembrance
   We share Thy wealth glorious.

2 Thou art the Stone tried by many,
   Precious to God, dear to us,
   Thou art so sure and trustworthy,
   Thy strength is so marvelous.
   Thou art the Stone that is living,
   Chosen of God, made our own;
   So energetic and pow'rful,
   With endless life to us known.

3 Thou art the Stone of Foundation
   Laid by our God, safe and sure;
   It is by this sure foundation
   Safety fore'er we secure.
   To us no other foundation
   Of any kind man can lay;
   Thou art the only foundation
   Which we have now and for aye.

continued

4   Lord, for God's spiritual building,
    Thou art the Chief Cornerstone;
Both of the Jews and the Gentiles
    By Thee are built into one.
Lord, Thou art also the Topstone,
    Brought forth in measureless grace;
Thou art our cover and glory,
    Moving our hearts in Thy praise.

200*

8.6.8.6.

1   Thou art the Sun of righteousness
    With healing in Thy wings;
The shining of Thy glorious face
    To us Thy riches brings.

2   The tender mercy of our God
    Caused Thee on us to dawn,
To those in darkness giving light
    That shades of death be gone.

3   Thou art the Morning without clouds,
    And as the Morning Light;
We are the tender grass on earth,
    Who in Thy rays delight.

4   Thy shining light with pleasant rays
    Increases all the way;
It shines within us more and more
    Until the perfect day.

5   It shines thru woe with clearest beams,
    As shining after rain;
And in Thy mercy with Thy love
    Thy shining e'er remains.

6   Thou also art the Morning Star
    To us as a reward;
While still 'tis dark it shines with light
    To those who love the Lord.

7   Lord, help us e'er to love Thy light
     And see things from afar;
     And look for Thee in watch and prayer
     As for the Morning Star.

8.6.8.6.   **201***

1   O Lord, Thou art our Paraclete,
     Our Comforter indeed,
     Our Patron with our God above,
     The Advocate we need.

2   Thou art our Counsel of defense,
     The Pleader of our case,
     Our Interceder for all things,
     Our Helper in all ways.

3   Lord, Thou dost manage all affairs
     For us in God's delight,
     Both in the heavens and in us
     With power in Thy right.

4   Thou intercedest all the time,
     Lord Spirit, with Thy grace,
     In heav'n to plead, in us to groan,
     Entreating in our place.

5   Thou helpest as the living One,
     And actest by God's plan
     In resurrection pow'r of life,
     Empow'ring our inner man.

6   Thou, as the Spirit giving life,
     In weakness dost sustain;
     And in our spirit with Thy strength,
     Our being dost maintain.

7   Thou servest ever with Thyself,
     In mercy and in love,
     That Thou may be our all in all,
     And we Thy fulness prove.

202*   7.6.7.6.D.

1 O Lord, Thou art the Alpha
   And the Omega too;
Thou art the First, before all,
   And art the Last so true.
Thou art the sole Beginning,
   The only End of all;
In Thee all is included,
   Creations great and small.

2 Lord, since Thou art the Alpha,
   All things commenced of Thee;
And as the sole Omega,
   All things will end in Thee;
As God's full Alphabet, Lord,
   All is of Thee composed;
Since Thou art all the letters,
   All is in Thee enclosed.

3 As First of all the creatures,
   Thou art the Head of all;
As Last in God's creation,
   Thou art the close of all.
As First of all the creatures,
   All things by Thee consist;
As Last in God's creation,
   All things for Thee subsist.

4 Since Thou art the Beginning,
   Thou hast preceded all;
And since Thou art the Ending,
   Thou wilt inherit all.
Thou, the unique Beginning,
   Didst all originate;
Thou, as the only Ending,
   Wilt all things terminate.

5 O Lord, how we adore Thee
   And treasure Thee with love;
As Alpha and Omega,
   Thou art all things above.
We praise Thee, the Beginning,
   The very First we call;
We worship Thee, the Ending,
   The only Last of all.

PRAISE OF THE LORD — HIS INCREASE

8.7.8.7.D.   **203***

1 In the bosom of the Father,
   Ere the ages had begun,
Thou wast in the Father's glory,
   God's unique begotten Son.
When to us the Father gave Thee,
   Thou in person wast the same,
All the fulness of the Father
   In the Spirit to proclaim.

2 By Thy death and resurrection,
   Thou wast made God's firstborn Son;
By Thy life to us imparting,
   Was Thy duplication done.
We, in Thee regenerated,
   Many sons to God became;
Truly as Thy many brethren,
   We are as Thyself the same.

3 Once Thou wast the only grain, Lord,
   Falling to the earth to die,
That thru death and resurrection
   Thou in life may multiply.
We were brought forth in Thy nature
   And the many grains became;
As one loaf we all are blended,
   All Thy fulness to proclaim.   *continued*

PRAISE OF THE LORD — HIS INCREASE

4 We're Thy total reproduction,
   Thy dear Body and Thy Bride,
Thine expression and Thy fulness,
   For Thee ever to abide.
We are Thy continuation,
   Thy life-increase and Thy spread,
Thy full growth and Thy rich surplus,
   One with Thee, our glorious Head.

PRAISE OF THE LORD — THE FATHER'S DELIGHT

204   8.7.8.7.

1 Gathered in Thy name, Lord Jesus,
   Losing sight of all but Thee,
O what joy Thy presence gives us,
   Calling up our hearts to Thee!

2 Loved with love which knows no measure,
   Save the Father's love to Thee,
Blessed Lord, our hearts would treasure
   All the Father's thoughts of Thee.

3 All His joy, His rest, His pleasure —
   All His deep delight in Thee —
Lord, Thy heart alone can measure
   What Thy Father found in Thee.

4 How He set His love upon Thee —
   Called Thee His beloved Son;
Yet for us He did not spare Thee,
   By Thy death our life was won.

5 O the joy, the wondrous singing,
   When we see Thee as Thou art!
Thy blest name, Lord Jesus, bringing
   Sweetest music to God's heart.

6 Notes of gladness, songs unceasing,
   Hymns of everlasting praise,
Psalms of glory, joy increasing,
   Through God's endless day of days.

8.8.8.8.　　　　　　　　　　**205**

1　Jesus, Thou Joy of loving hearts,
　　Thou Fount of life, Thou Light of men,
　　From the best bliss that earth imparts,
　　We turn unfilled to Thee again.

2　Thy truth unchanged hath ever stood;
　　Thou savest those that on Thee call;
　　To them that seek Thee, Thou art good,
　　To them that find Thee, all in all!

3　We taste Thee, O Thou living Bread,
　　And long to feast upon Thee still;
　　We drink of Thee, the Fountain-head,
　　And thirst our souls from Thee to fill!

4　Our restless spirits yearn for Thee,
　　Where'er our changeful lot is cast;
　　Glad when Thy gracious smile we see,
　　Blest, when our faith can hold Thee fast.

5　O Lord, be Thou our strength and stay!
　　Make all our moments calm and bright,
　　Chase all dark thoughts of sin away,
　　Shed o'er us here Thy holy light.

7.6.7.6.D.　　　　　　　　　　**206**

1　O Christ, He is the fountain,
　　　The deep, sweet well of life:
　　Its living streams I've tasted
　　　Which save from grief and strife.
　　And to an ocean fulness,
　　　His mercy doth expand;
　　His grace is all-sufficient
　　　As by His wisdom planned.

2　O I am my Beloved's,
　　　And my Beloved's mine;
　　He brings a poor vile sinner
　　　Into His house of wine!　　*continued*

I stand upon His merit;
  I know no other stand.
I'm hidden in His presence
  And held by His own hand.

3 The Bride eyes not her garment,
    But her dear Bridegroom's face;
  I will not gaze at glory,
    But on my King of grace:
  Not at the crown He giveth,
    But on His piercèd hand;
  The Lamb is all the glory,
    And my eternal stand!

207   8.6.8.6.

1 Lord Jesus! when we think of Thee,
    Of all Thy love and grace,
  Our spirits long and fain would see
    Thy beauty face to face.

2 And though the wilderness we tread,
    A barren, thirsty ground,
  With thorns and briars overspread,
    Where foes and snares abound;

3 Yet in Thy love such depths we see,
    Our hearts o'erflow with praise —
  Content ourselves, while, Lord to Thee
    A joyful song we raise.

4 Our Lord, our Life, our Rest, our Shield,
    Our Rock, our Food, our Light;
  Each thought of Thee doth constant yield
    Unchanging, fresh delight.

5 Blest Savior, keep our spirit stayed,
    Hard following after Thee,
  Till we, in victory displayed,
    Thy face in glory see.

8.6.8.6.8.8.8.6.

1   O Jesus, Jesus, dearest Lord!
    Forgive me if I say,
For very love, Thy sacred name
    A thousand times a day.

    O Jesus, Lord, with me abide;
    I rest in Thee, whate'er betide;
    Thy gracious smile is my reward;
    I love, I love Thee, Lord!

2   I love Thee so I know not how
    My transports to control;
Thy love is like a burning fire
    Within my very soul.

3   For Thou to me art all in all;
    My honor and my wealth;
My heart's desire, my body's strength,
    My soul's eternal health.

4   Burn, burn, O love, within my heart,
    Burn fiercely night and day,
Till all the dross of earthly loves
    Is burned, and burned away.

5   O light in darkness, joy in grief,
    O heaven's life on earth;
Jesus, my love, my treasure, who
    Can tell what Thou art worth?

6   What limit is there to this love?
    Thy flight, where wilt Thou stay?
On, on! our Lord is sweeter far
    Today than yesterday.

209

8.6.8.6.

1 Jesus, the very thought of Thee
   With sweetness fills my breast;
   But sweeter far Thy face to see,
   And in Thy presence rest.

2 Nor voice can sing, nor heart can frame,
   Nor can the memory find
   A sweeter sound than Thy blest Name,
   O Savior of mankind!

3 O Hope of every contrite heart,
   O Joy of all the meek,
   To those who fall, how kind Thou art!
   How good to those who seek!

4 But what to those who find? Ah, this
   Nor tongue nor pen can show;
   The love of Jesus, what it is
   None but His loved ones know.

5 O Jesus! light of all below!
   Thou fount of life and fire!
   Surpassing all the joys we know,
   And all we can desire.

6 No other source have we but Thee,
   Soul-thirst to satisfy.
   Exhaustless spring! the waters free!
   All other streams are dry.

7 Jesus, our only Joy be Thou,
   As Thou our Prize wilt be;
   Jesus, be Thou our Glory now,
   And through eternity.

Peculiar Meter.

1   I've found a friend in Jesus, He's everything to me,
     He's the fairest of ten thousand to my soul;
  The Apple-tree of trees, in Him alone I see
     All I need to cleanse and make me fully whole.
  In sorrow He's my comfort, in trouble He's my stay,
     He tells me every care on Him to roll:
  He's the Apple-tree of trees, the Bright and Morning
     Star,
     He's the fairest of ten thousand to my soul.

2   He all my griefs has taken, and all my sorrows borne;
     In temptation He's my strong and mighty tower;
  I've all for Him forsaken, and all my idols torn
     From my heart, and now He keeps me by His
     power.
  Though all the world forsake me, and Satan tempt
     me sore,
     Through Jesus I shall safely reach the goal:
  He's the Apple-tree of trees, the Bright and Morning
     Star,
     He's the fairest of ten thousand to my soul.

3   He'll never, never leave me, nor yet forsake me here,
     While I live by faith and do His blessed will;
  A wall of fire about me, I've nothing now to fear,
     With His manna He my hungry soul shall fill.
  Then sweeping up to glory to see His blessed face,
     Where rivers of delight shall ever roll:
  He's the Apple-tree of trees, the Bright and Morning
     Star,
     He's the fairest of ten thousand to my soul.

211

8.8.8.8.

1 Jesus, my Savior! Thou art mine,
The Father's gift of love divine;
All Thou hast done, and all Thou art,
Are now the portion of my heart.

2 Poor, feeble, wretched, as I am,
I now can glory in Thy name;
Now cleansed in Thy most precious blood
And made the righteousness of God.

3 All that Thou hast Thou hast for me,
All my fresh springs are hid in Thee;
In Thee I live; while I confess
I nothing am, yet all possess.

4 O Savior, teach me to abide
Close sheltered at Thy wounded side,
Each hour receiving "grace on grace,"
Until I see Thee face to face.

212

10.10.10.10.

1 Lord Jesus, gladly do our lips express
Our heart's deep sense of all Thy worthiness;
Thou risen One, the Holy and the True,
We give Thee now the praise so justly due.

2 Thou giv'st us, Lord, once more to taste down here
The joy Thy presence brings, its warmth and cheer;
With great delight we 'neath Thy shadow rest;
Thy fruit is sweet to those Thy love has blest.

3 Thou wast alone, till like the precious grain
In death Thou layest, but didst rise again;
And in Thy risen life a countless host
Are "all of one" with Thee, Thy joy and boast.

7.6.7.6.D.

1 On that same night, Lord Jesus,
      When all around Thee joined
   To cast its darkest shadow
      Across Thy holy mind,
   We hear Thy voice, blest Savior,
      "This do, remember me",
   With grateful hearts responding,
      We do remember Thee.

2 The depth of all Thy suffering
      No heart could e'er conceive,
   The cup of wrath o'erflowing
      For us Thou didst receive;
   And, oh, of God forsaken
      On the accursèd tree;
   With grateful hearts, Lord Jesus,
      We now remember Thee.

3 We think of all the darkness
      Which round Thy spirit pressed,
   Of all those waves and billows,
      Which rolled across Thy breast.
   Oh, there Thy grace unbounded
      And perfect love we see;
   With joy and sorrow mingling,
      We would remember Thee.

4 We know Thee now as risen,
      The Firstborn from the dead;
   We see Thee now ascended,
      The Church's glorious Head.
   In Thee by grace accepted,
      The heart and mind set free
   To think of all Thy sorrow,
      And thus remember Thee.

continued

5 Till Thou shalt come in glory,
   And call us hence away,
To rest in all the brightness
   Of that unclouded day,
We show Thy death, Lord Jesus,
   And here would seek to be
More to Thy death conformèd,
   While we remember Thee.

214
               8.6.8.6.

1 According to Thy gracious word,
   In meek humility,
This will I do, my dying Lord,
   I will remember Thee.

2 Thy body, broken for my sake,
   My bread from heaven shall be;
Thy testamental cup I take,
   And thus remember Thee.

3 Gethsemane can I forget?
   Or there Thy conflict see,
Thine agony and bloody sweat,
   And not remember Thee?

4 When to the cross I turn mine eyes
   And rest on Calvary,
O Lamb of God, my sacrifice,
   I must remember Thee —

5 Remember Thee and all Thy pains
   And all Thy love to me;
Yea, while a breath, a pulse remains,
   I will remember Thee.

6 And when these failing lips grow dumb
   And mind and memory flee,
When Thou shalt in Thy kingdom come,
   Jesus, remember me.

8.7.8.7.D.

1 Jesus, Lord, we know Thee present
    At Thy table freshly spread,
Seated at Thy priceless banquet
    With Thy banner overhead.
Precious moments at Thy table,
    From all fear and doubt set free;
Here to rest, so sweetly able,
    Occupied alone with Thee.

2 Here rejoicing in Thy nearness,
    Gladly by Thy Spirit led;
Calmly in the blest remembrance
    Of Thyself, Thy blood once shed.
Lord, we take each simple token
    In fond memory of Thee,
Muse upon Thy body broken
    And Thy blood shed on the tree.

3 Oh, what joy it is to see Thee,
    In these chosen emblems here;
In the bread and wine of blessing —
    Bread to strengthen, wine to cheer!
Lord, behold us met together,
    One in Thee, our risen Head,
Thus we take the cup of blessing,
    Thus we share the broken bread.

4 Lord, we know how true Thy promise
    To be with us where we meet,
When in Thy loved name we gather
    To enjoy communion sweet;
Dearer still that looked-for promise
    To each waiting, yearning heart,
That with Thee we soon shall be, Lord,
    Yes, "forever" where Thou art.

216   8.6.8.6.

1 Around Thy table, holy Lord,
 In fellowship we meet,
 Obedient to Thy gracious word,
 This feast of love to eat.

2 Here every one that loves Thy name,
 Our willing hearts embrace;
 Our source of life and hope the same,
 All debtors to Thy grace.

3 Commune with each at this blest hour,
 Thy peace, Thy joy impart;
 Thy thoughts of love, of truth, of pow'r,
 Impress upon each heart.

217   8.5.8.3.

1 On that night of nights most solemn,
 Jesus called His own
 'Round the table of remembrance,
 All alone.

2 Then this feast of feasts He ordered,
 Feast of grace Divine;
 Sacred symbols He appointed,
 Bread and wine.

3 Thus His death of deaths is shadowed
 In this simple way,
 Looking backward, pointing upward,
 To that day.

4 Till the morn of morns bright dawning,
 Earth's dark shadows passed;
 And the splendor of God's glory
 Breaks at last.

5 Thus the day of days shall open,
 Deathless, cloudless, fair;
 In that day, the Savior's glories
 We shall share!

8.6.8.6.   **218**

1 As gathered in Thy precious name,
     This table we surround,
   Thy death, Lord Jesus, to proclaim,
     O may our praise abound.

2 We give what from Thee we receive,
     For all we have is Thine —
   O may each heart with joy believe,
     And echo "Thine is mine!"

3 Grace, grace it was that brought Thee down;
     Love shone in all Thy ways;
   Through death Thine is the Victor's crown,
     And Thine the endless praise.

4 We, here, in silence, or in song,
     Together worship Thee;
   Before our God we shall ere long
     Give praise eternally.

5 Lord Jesus Christ, Thou comest soon —
     Today Thy death we show;
   In light, eclipsing sun at noon,
     Its myst'ry we shall know.

10.10.10.10.   **219**

1 Lord Jesus Christ, we would remember Thee,
   As, on the table, we the emblems see;
   Thy holy body shadowed in the bread,
   Thy precious blood is in the cup portrayed.

2 Lord, we adore Thee for Thy matchless grace,
   That Thou, for us, didst take the servant's place;
   From Godhead's glory to the shameful tree,
   From wealth, so vast, to abject poverty!

3 O Lamb of God, we join to bless Thy name,
   That Thou, on Calv'ry, bore our sin and shame;
   And, by Thy death, didst put our guilt away,
   Triumphant rose, our night to turn to day.

continued

4 We see Thee now, at God's right hand enthroned,
   Vested with honor and with glory crowned;
   Blessed Redeemer, Savior, Lord, to Thee
   Be all the glory, pow'r and majesty!

220*   8.6.8.6.

1 When on Thy table, Lord, we gaze,
     We marvel at the signs:
   A loaf of bread, a cup of wine,
     Displayed as God designs.

2 The loaf portrays the bread of life
     As heav'nly food to us,
   Imparted by Thy mystic death
     That we may share Thee thus.

3 The portion is the cup divine,
     Composed of Jesus' blood;
   This cup of blessing we receive
     And gain what is of God.

4 We eat of Thee, the Bread of life,
     By sharing here this bread;
   Thus we remember Thee in love
     And with Thyself are fed.

5 We all enjoy the blessings gained
     By drinking of this cup;
   Thus we remember Thee with joy,
     Till we are taken up.

6 By feasting on this bread and cup
     Thy death we now declare,
   And testify Thou art our life
     And all we daily share.

7 We're waiting for that glorious hour,
     When in the fullest way
   We'll feed on Thee and feast with Thee
     And worship Thee for aye.

8.7.8.7.D. with chorus.

1 Lord, we thank Thee for the table,
   With the bread and with the wine;
At this table we enjoy Thee
   As the feast of love divine.
We partake the bread, the emblem
   Of Thy body giv'n for us;
And we share the wine, the symbol
   Of Thy blood Thou shedd'st for us.

   Lo, the holy table!
   With the sacred symbols;
   Its significance in figure
   Is unsearchable!

2 By the death of Thy redemption,
   That Thy life Thou may impart,
E'en Thyself to us Thou gavest
   That we share in all Thou art.
By the bread and wine partaking,
   We Thy death display and prove;
Eating, drinking of Thyself, Lord,
   We remember Thee with love.

3 By this bread which signifieth
   Thy one body mystical,
We commune with all Thy members
   In one bond identical.
By this holy cup of blessing,
   Cup of wine which now we bless,
Of Thy blood we have communion
   With all those who faith possess.

continued

4 Thou art our eternal portion,
   Here we take a sweet foretaste;
We are waiting for Thy kingdom,
   And Thy coming now we haste.
At Thy coming, in Thy kingdom,
   With all saints that overcome,
We anew will feast upon Thee
   And Thy loving Bride become.

222*
          8.6.8.6.

1 Dear Lord, we thank Thee for this bread,
   It is a sign divine;
In it we see the mysteries
   Of God's unique design.

2 This bread Thy body signifies,
   Which Thou hast giv'n for us,
That we may share Thy life divine,
   Partaking of Thee thus.

3 For us Thy body Thou didst break
   That Thou may thus impart
Thyself as life to us that we
   May be Thy counterpart.

4 This bread thus also signifies
   Thy body mystical,
Of which we living members are,
   With Thee identical.

5 Though we are many grains of wheat,
   Yet all one loaf, one bread;
Remembering Thee in such a way,
   With Thee we all are fed.

6 As of this bread we all commune,
   Thou, Lord, dost satisfy;
With all the saints we fellowship,
   And Thee we testify.

7.7.7.7.D.

1 On the table of Thy love,
    With the bread, the cup is spread.
By partaking of these signs,
    We with Thee are richly fed.
How we thank Thee for this cup,
    For the cup of blessing, Lord,
Cup of Thy Salvation full,
    Cup of all Thou dost afford.

2 'Tis the blood Thou shedd'st for us,
    That our sins may be forgiv'n;
'Tis the cov'nant made for us,
    That Thy blessings may be giv'n.
Thou didst drink the cup of wrath,
    Thou hast tasted death for us,
Thus the cup of blessing bought,
    As the portion gained for us.

3 In this portion we have God,
    Whom we lost thru Adam's fall;
By the shedding of Thy blood,
    God becomes our all in all.
In this portion all we have —
    Life and peace, redemption sure;
All that God has planned and willed,
    In this portion we secure.

4 An eternal portion, 'tis,
    Overflowing cup divine;
Heav'nly taste do we enjoy
    In this cup of God's design.
Here in love we drink this cup
    In remembrance, Lord, of Thee;
Thus in spirit we partake
    All Thy work on Calvary.

224*

7.7.7.7.D.

1 As we're sharing of the cup,
    How can we restrain our praise;
For the blood Thou shedd'st for us,
    Worth of which none can appraise.
O how precious is Thy blood!
    All our problems it resolves;
In Thine efficacious blood
    All our care and fear dissolves.

2 It is by this blood of worth
    The new testament was made;
For this better covenant,
    'Tis a sure foundation laid.
We have been redeemed by God,
    Not with silver or with gold,
But, Lord, with Thy precious blood,
    Which Thy love doth e'er unfold.

3 For remission of our sins
    Thou hast shed Thy cleansing blood,
Which for us has fully met
    All the righteous claims of God.
Thou hast washed us from our sins
    In Thy pow'rful purging blood;
And our conscience purged by it,
    Thus to serve the living God.

4 By Thy separating blood,
    We have all been sanctified;
'Tis by Thy preserving blood
    Holiness is testified.

By Thy propitiating blood,
  We have all been justified;
'Tis by Thy redeeming blood
  God is fully satisfied.

5 Thru Thy blood shed on the cross,
  We are reconciled to God,
That the way to contact Him
  May in peace by us be trod.
By partaking of Thy blood,
  We have Thine eternal life;
In Thy blood and life received,
  We have rest, free from all strife.

6 Now, in heav'n Thy sprinkled blood
  Speaks for us of better things;
Under its defending pow'r
  We are kept from Satan's stings.
By Thine overcoming blood,
  We defeat the enemy;
Over our accuser thus,
  We will have the victory.

7 Of Thy blood, for fellowship,
  We commune with all Thy saints;
Under its full covering,
  Our freed spirit never faints.
How can we exhaust, in words,
  The account of Thy dear blood;
We will need eternity
  To declare its boundless good.

225

10.10.10.10.

1 Here, O my Lord, I see Thee face to face;
   Here faith can touch and handle things unseen;
   Here would I grasp with firmer hand Thy grace,
   And all my weariness upon Thee lean.

2 Here would I feed upon the Bread of God;
   Here drink with Thee the royal wine of heav'n;
   Here would I lay aside each earthly load;
   Here taste afresh the calm of sin forgiv'n.

3 I have no help but Thine; nor do I need
   Another arm save Thine to lean upon;
   It is enough, my Lord, enough indeed;
   My strength is in Thy might, Thy might alone.

4 This is the hour of banquet and of song;
   This is the heav'nly table spread for me;
   Here let me feast, and, feasting, still prolong
   The brief bright hour of fellowship with Thee.

5 Too soon we rise; the symbols disappear;
   The feast, though not the love, is past and gone;
   The bread and wine remove, but Thou art here,
   Nearer than ever still our Shield and Sun.

6 Feast after feast thus comes and passes by,
   Yet passing, points to the glad feast above,
   Giving sweet foretastes of the festal joy,
   The Lamb's great bridal-feast of bliss and love.

7.7.7.6.

1 For the bread and for the wine,
For the pledge that seals Him mine,
For the words of love divine,
We give Thee thanks, O Lord.

2 Only bread and only wine,
Yet to faith, the solemn sign
Of the heav'nly and divine!
We give Thee thanks, O Lord.

3 For the words that turn our eye
To the cross of Calvary,
Bidding us in faith draw nigh,
We give Thee thanks, O Lord.

4 For the words that fragrance breathe
These plain symbols underneath,
Words that His own peace bequeath,
We give Thee thanks, O Lord.

5 For Thy words in Spirit shown,
For Thy will to us made known,
"Do ye this until I come,"
We give Thee thanks, O Lord.

6 Till He come we take the bread,
Type of Him on whom we feed,
Him who liveth and was dead!
We give Thee thanks, O Lord.

7 Till He come we take the cup;
As we at His table sup,
Eye and heart are lifted up!
We give Thee thanks, O Lord.

8 For that coming, here foreshown,
For that day to man unknown,
For the glory and the throne,
We give Thee thanks, O Lord.

227*

8.7.8.7.D. with chorus.

1 Through the bread and cup, Lord Jesus,
   We Thy death exhibit here;
What Thy love has done reviewing,
   All Thy suff'ring we revere.
Bread and cup in separation,
   Show that Thou thru death hast gone;
Grateful now, our spirit worships,
   And to Thee we give our song.

> Thine the cup of suff'ring,
> Mine the cup of blessing;
> For Thy love in Thy redemption,
> Praise we ever sing!

2 Thou, in love, hast shed Thy blood, Lord,
   Bringing us to God in grace,
That from God, no longer severed,
   We may ever see His face.
All God's righteousness and glory
   Have been fully satisfied;
Thru Thy death's abundant merit
   We may now with God abide.

3 By Thy death the veil was riven,
   Opened was the holiest place,
All the barriers have been broken;
   We approach the throne of grace,
There receiving grace and mercy,
   Thus the timely need to meet,
Drinking as of living water,
   Tasting God Himself replete.

4 Thou in grace hast so redeemed us,
   We the priests may be fore'er
To fulfill that holy office,
   All God's sweetness thus to share.

Such a blessing, such a mercy,
From Thy death for us ensue;
We would ever Thee remember
Till with Thee we drink anew.

228

6.6.8.6.

1 Sweet feast of love divine!
'Tis grace that makes us free
To feed upon this bread and wine,
In mem'ry, Lord, of Thee.

2 Here every welcome guest
Waits, Lord, from Thee to learn
The secrets of Thy Father's breast,
And all Thy grace discern.

3 Here conscience ends its strife,
And faith delights to prove
The sweetness of the Bread of Life,
The fulness of Thy love.

4 That blood that flowed for sin
In symbol here we see,
And feel the blessed pledge within
That we are loved of Thee.

5 O if this glimpse of love
Is so divinely sweet,
What will it be, O Lord, above,
Thy gladd'ning smile to meet!

6 To see Thee face to face,
Thy perfect likeness wear,
And all Thy ways of wondrous grace
Through endless years declare.

229

8.5.8.3.

1 Gathered round Thyself, Lord Jesus,
   We now seek Thy face;
   May we know Thy presence with us,
   Lord of grace!

2 Love divine first drew us to Thee,
   In our sin and need;
   For our sin, in deep compassion,
   Thou didst bleed.

3 Risen Lord, in glory seated,
   We are one with Thee;
   Thou hast snapt the chains that bound us,
   We are free.

4 Gratefully we Thee remember
   As we break the bread,
   Symbol of Thy body given
   In our stead.

5 Drink we too "the cup of blessing"
   Which Thy love has filled;
   Through Thy blood we have redemption
   Fears are stilled.

6 Backward look we, drawn to Calv'ry,
   Musing while we sing;
   Forward haste we to Thy coming,
   Lord and King!

230

8.6.8.6.

1 Lord Jesus, in Thy precious name,
   And in that name alone;
   At Thy request we gladly meet,
   Thy Lordship here would own.

2 As on that dark betrayal night,
  Thou didst this feast ordain;
  We too, the bread and cup would take,
  Thy death, Lord, thus proclaim.

3 The bread, Thy body doth portray;
  The cup, Thy precious blood;
  By which our sin was put away,
  Our peace was made with God.

4 The Host art Thou, O blessed Lord,
  Thy honored guests are we;
  With grateful and adoring hearts
  We would remember Thee!

5 Lord Jesus, whom unseen we love,
  As thus we muse on Thee;
  We none would see, save Thee alone,
  Thou Man of Calvary!

8.8.8.8.   **231**

1 Amidst us our Beloved stands,
  And bids us view His piercèd hands;
  Points to the wounded feet and side,
  Blest emblems of the Crucified.

2 What food luxurious loads the board
  When, at His table, sits the Lord!
  The wine how rich, the bread how sweet,
  When Jesus deigns the guests to meet!

3 If now, with eyes defiled and dim,
  We see the signs, but see not Him;
  Oh, may His love the scales displace,
  And bid us see Him face to face!

4 Thou glorious Bridegroom of our hearts,
  Thy present smile Thy grace imparts!
  Oh, lift the veil, if veil there be,
  Let every saint Thy glory see!

8.8.8.4.

1 By Christ redeemed, in Christ restored,
   We keep the memory adored,
   And show the death of our dear Lord
       Until He come.

2 His body broken in our stead
   Is seen in this memorial bread,
   And so our feeble love is fed
       Until He come.

3 The drops of His dread agony,
   His life-blood shed for us, we see;
   The wine shall tell the mystery
       Until He come.

4 And thus that dark betrayal-night
   With the last advent we unite,
   By one blest chain of loving rite,
       Until He come.

5 Until the trump of God be heard,
   Until the ancient graves be stirred,
   And with the great commanding word
       The Lord shall come.

6 O blessed hope! with this elate;
   Let not our heart be desolate,
   But, strong in faith, in patience wait
       Until He come.

8.8.8.8.

1 O what a miracle, my Lord,
   That I'm in Thee and Thou in me,
   That Thou and I are really one;
   O what a wondrous mystery!

2 For me Thy body Thou didst give,
   That I may ever share in Thee;
   For me Thy precious blood was shed,
   That from my sins I might be free.

3 By resurrection Thou didst change
   Thy form and as the Spirit come;
   Thou wouldst that I be filled with Thee
   That all Thy riches mine become.

4 Now as the symbols we behold,
   Thy loving self we see anew;
   We thank Thee for Thy heart's desire
   As all Thy travail we review.

5 We eat the bread and drink the wine,
   And to Thy sweetness we are led;
   In spirit each receiving Thee,
   Our spirits with Thyself are fed.

6 We long to eat and drink e'en more,
   To take Thyself in spirit thus,
   Till Thou shalt all our being fill
   And true remembrance have from us.

7.7.8.8.7.7.

1 Who is He in yonder stall,
At whose feet the shepherds fall?

'Tis the Lord! oh wondrous story!
'Tis the Lord! the King of glory!
At His feet we humbly fall,
Crown Him! crown Him, Lord of all!

2 Who is He in deep distress,
Fasting in the wilderness?

3 Who is He the people bless
For His words of gentleness?

4 Who is He to whom they bring
All the sick and sorrowing?

5 Who is He that stands and weeps
At the grave where Lazarus sleeps?

6 Who is He the gathering throng
Greet with loud triumphant song?

7 Lo! at midnight, who is He
Prays in dark Gethsemane?

8 Who is He on yonder tree
Dies in grief and agony?

9 Who is He who from the grave
Comes to succor, help, and save?

10 Who is He who from His throne
Rules through all the worlds alone?

Peculiar Meter.

1 Praise Him! praise Him! Jesus, our blessed Redeemer!
  Sing, ye saints! His wonderful love proclaim!
Hail Him! hail Him! mightiest angels in glory;
  Strength and honor give to His holy name!
Like a shepherd, Jesus will feed His people,
  In His arms He carries them all day long;
O ye saints that live in the light of His presence,
  Praise Him! praise Him! ever in joyful song!

2 Praise Him! praise Him! Jesus, our blessed Redeemer,
  For our sins He suffered and bled and died;
He, our Rock, our Hope of eternal salvation,
  Hail Him! hail Him! Jesus, the Crucified;
Loving Savior, meekly enduring sorrow,
  Crowned with thorns that cruelly pierced His brow;
Once for us rejected, despised, and forsaken,
  Prince of Glory, ever triumphant now.

3 Praise Him! praise Him! Jesus, our blessed Redeemer,
  Heavenly portals, loud with hosannahs ring!
Jesus, Savior, reigneth for ever and ever;
  Crown Him! crown Him! Prophet and Priest
    and King!
Death is vanquished! Tell it with joy, ye faithful,
  Where is now thy victory, boasting grave?
Jesus lives! No longer thy portals are cheerless;
  Jesus lives, the mighty and strong to save.

236

8.7.8.7.D.

1 Lamb of God! our souls adore Thee,
   While upon Thy face we gaze;
There the Father's love and glory
   Shine in all their brightest rays;
Thine Almighty pow'r and wisdom
   All creation's works proclaim;
Heav'n and earth alike confess Thee
   As the ever great "I AM."

2 Lamb of God! Thy Father's bosom
   Ever was Thy dwelling place;
His delight, in Him rejoicing,
   One with Him in pow'r and grace;
O what wondrous love and mercy!
   Thou didst lay Thy glory by;
And for us didst come from heaven
   As the Lamb of God to die.

3 Lamb of God! When we behold Thee
   Lowly in the manger laid,
Wand'ring as a homeless stranger
   In the world Thy hands had made;
When we see Thee in the garden
   In Thine agony of blood,
At Thy grace we are confounded,
   Holy, spotless Lamb of God!

4 When we see Thee, as the victim,
   Bound to the accursèd tree,
For our guilt and folly stricken,
   All our judgment borne by Thee,
Lord, we own, with hearts adoring,
   Thou hast loved us unto blood;
Glory, glory everlasting
   Be to Thee, Thou Lamb of God.

5 Lamb of God, Thou soon in glory
Wilt to this sad earth return;
All Thy foes shall quake before Thee,
All that now despise Thee mourn;
Then Thy saints all gathered to Thee,
With Thee in Thy kingdom reign;
Thine the praise and Thine the glory,
Lamb of God, for sinners slain!

237

10.10.10.10.

1 Amazing words! — He 'gave Himself for me,'
For me — rebellious, sinful, guilty me.
For me the Savior bore the cross and shame;
Rejoice, my soul, and bless His sacred name.

2 For me He left His glorious throne above,
For me revealed His Father's wondrous love,
For me He tabernacled here below,
For me He drank the bitter cup of woe.

3 For me He was reviled, despised, betrayed;
For me was scourged, condemned and crucified;
For me He suffered on th' accursèd tree,
For me — lost, wretched, vile, unworthy me.

4 For me in agony He groaned and died,
For me God's righteous law He satisfied,
For me His precious blood He shed to save,
For me He rose triumphant from the grave.

238

6.6.6.6.6.6.

1 When morning gilds the skies,
My heart awaking cries:
May Jesus Christ be praised!
Alike at work and prayer
To Jesus I repair:
May Jesus Christ be praised!

2 To Thee, my God above,
I cry with glowing love,
May Jesus Christ be praised!
The fairest graces spring
In hearts that ever sing,
May Jesus Christ be praised!

3 Does sadness fill my mind?
A solace here I find,
May Jesus Christ be praised!
Or fades my earthly bliss?
My comfort still is this,
May Jesus Christ be praised!

4 When evil thoughts molest,
With this I shield my breast,
May Jesus Christ be praised!
The powers of darkness fear,
When this sweet chant they hear,
May Jesus Christ be praised!

5 When sleep her balm denies,
My silent spirit sighs,
May Jesus Christ be praised!
The night becomes as day,
When from the heart we say,
May Jesus Christ be praised!

6 Be this, while life is mine,
My canticle divine,
May Jesus Christ be praised!
Be this th' eternal song
Through all the ages long,
May Jesus Christ be praised!

239

7.6.7.6.D. with chorus.

1 Ten thousand thanks to Jesus,
Whose life our ransom paid,
Whose blood a full redemption
For all the world has made:
Let every heart adore Him;
Let every creature sing
Ten thousand thanks to Jesus,
Our Savior and our King.

Ten thousand thanks, ten thousand thanks,
We'll praise Him o'er and o'er;
And for the life with Him to live,
Ten thousand thousand more.

2 Ten thousand hearts to Jesus
How gladly would we give;
Ten thousand lives to Jesus,
Had we so long to live;
Ten thousand tongues shall praise Him,
Ten thousand songs ascend
To Him, our blest Redeemer,
To Him, our dearest Friend.

continued

3 Ten thousand thanks to Jesus
   For blessings every hour;
Ten thousand times ten thousand,
   For love's redeeming pow'r;
And when He comes in glory
   His blessed face we'll see,
His love through endless ages
   Our sweetest song shall be.

240 8.8.8.8.8.8.

Glory, honor, praise and power,
Be unto the Lamb forever!
Jesus Christ is our Redeemer,
Hallelujah! Hallelujah!
Hallelujah! Praise ye the Lord!

241 Peculiar Meter.

Blessing and honor and glory be Thine,
   And glory be Thine,
   And glory be Thine.
Blessing and honor and glory be Thine,
   Both now and evermore.
   Praise Him! Praise Him!
   All ye saints adore Him.
   Praise Him! Praise Him!
   Both now and evermore.
     Hallelujah!
Blessing and honor and glory be Thine,
   And glory be Thine,
   And glory be Thine.
Blessing and honor and glory be Thine,
   Both now and evermore.

Peculiar Meter.

1 The Spirit of God today
  The Spirit of Jesus is,
  The God-man who died and rose,
  Ascending to glory His.

2 'Tis from such a Jesus came
  The Spirit of Jesus to us,
  To make His reality
  Experience unto us.

3 The Spirit of Jesus has
  All elements human, divine,
  The living of man in Him
  And glory of God combine.

4 The suff'ring of human life,
  Effectiveness of His death,
  His rising and reigning too
  Are all in the Spirit's breath.

5 With all these components true
  His Spirit in us doth move,
  And by His anointing full
  The riches of Christ we prove.

6 This Spirit of Jesus doth
  Encompass both great and small;
  Inclusively He doth work
  In us, making God our all.

8.8.8.8.

1 God's Spirit is of Christ today,
　　The Spirit of reality,
　He dwells in me with Christ as life
　　To make this Christ so real to me.

2 As Christ is God's embodiment,
　　Expressing God as life divine;
　So is the Spirit unto Christ,
　　Revealing Him in life sublime.

3 The fulness of the Father God
　　In Christ the Son dwells bodily;
　And all the riches of the Son
　　Are Spirit, our reality.

4 Oh in the Son the Father is,
　　And now the Spirit is the Son;
　The Father with the Son is joined,
　　The Spirit with the Son is one.

5 'Tis when the Spirit strengthens us
　　And Christ His home makes in our hearts,
　The Father's fulness with His love
　　Will fill us in our inward parts.

6 In Christ, the Father we possess,
　　Receiving Him for all our need;
　In Spirit we experience Christ
　　As life and everything indeed.

7 With Thy divine reality,
　　Lord, fill us by Thy Spirit now,
　That we may all be full of Thee,
　　And all Thy riches thus avow.

8.8.8.8.

1 The Holy Spirit is today
The Spirit of the life divine;
He quickens us and gives us life,
And makes us fit for God's design.

2 As living water quenching thirst
The stream of life He e'er supplies;
Imparting Christ as life divine,
My hungry heart He satisfies.

3 Enlight'ning with the light of life,
He chases darkness far away;
Imparting Christ as light divine,
He turns for us the night to day.

4 He strengthens with the pow'r of life
To energize our inner man;
Imparting Christ as strength divine,
He moves within us for God's plan.

5 By law of life He liberates,
And frees us from the law of sin;
And with the nature all divine
He regulates us from within.

6 As Spirit of the life divine,
Thru us abundant fruit He bears;
Expressing God-like attributes,
To others Christ in life He shares.

7 The Spirit ever giving life
Transforms me thus with life divine;
Renewing all my inward parts,
In life He makes Christ's image mine.

8 Oh, by Thy Spirit, fill me, Lord,
The Spirit of Thy life divine,
And saturate me thoroughly
Till all my life is filled with Thine.

245

12.12.12.6. with chorus.

1 Oh, spread the tidings 'round, wherever man is found,
Wherever human hearts and human woes abound;
Let every Christian tongue proclaim the joyful sound:
    The Comforter has come!

    The Comforter has come,
    The Comforter has come!
    The Holy Ghost from heav'n,
    The Lord's dear promise giv'n;
    Oh, spread the tidings 'round,
    Wherever man is found —
    The Comforter has come!

2 The long, long night is past, the morning breaks at last;
And hushed the dreadful wail and fury of the blast,
As o'er the golden hills the day advances fast!
    The Comforter has come!

3 Lo, the great King of kings, with healing in His wings,
To every captive soul a full deliv'rance brings;
And through the vacant cells the song of triumph rings:
    The Comforter has come!

4 O boundless love divine! how shall this tongue of mine
To wond'ring mortals tell the matchless grace divine —
That I, a child of hell, should in His image shine!
    The Comforter has come!

8.7.8.7. with chorus.

1 Joys are flowing like a river,
Since the Comforter has come;
He abides with us forever,
Makes the trusting heart His home.

Blessed quietness, holy quietness —
What assurance in my soul!
On the stormy sea He speaks peace
to me.
How the billows cease to roll!

2 Bringing life and health and gladness
All around, this heavenly Guest
Banished unbelief and sadness,
Changed our weariness to rest.

3 Like the rain that falls from heaven,
Like the sunlight from the sky,
So the Holy Ghost is given,
Coming to us from on high.

4 See a fruitful field is growing
Blessed fruits of righteousness,
And the streams of life are flowing
In the lonely wilderness.

5 What a wonderful salvation
Where we always see His face!
What a perfect habitation!
What a quiet resting place!

247

8.6.8.4.

1 Our blest Redeemer ere He breathed
    His tender last farewell,
A guide, a comforter, bequeathed
    With us to dwell.

2 He came sweet influence to impart,
    A gracious, willing guest,
While He can find one humble heart
    Wherein to rest.

3 And His that gentle voice we hear,
    Soft as the breath of even,
That checks each fault, that calms each fear
    With peace of heav'n.

4 And every virtue we possess,
    And every victory won,
And every thought of holiness,
    Are His alone.

5 Lord, in Thy purity and grace,
    Our weakness pitying see;
Oh, make our heart Thy dwelling place,
    And worthier Thee.

FULNESS OF THE SPIRIT — AS THE LIVING WATER

248

Peculiar Meter.

1 Fainting in the desert,
    Israel's thousands stand
    At the rock of Kadesh.
    Hark! the Lord's command,
    Speak to the Rock,
    Bid the waters flow,
    Strike not its bosom
    Opened long ago,
    Speak to the Rock,
    Till the waters flow.

Chorus:
Speak to the Rock,
Bid the waters flow,
Doubt not the Spirit,
Given long ago;
Take what He waiteth,
Freely to bestow,
Drink till its fulness
All Thy being know.

2 Blessed Rock of Ages,
Thou art open still;
Thy blest Holy Spirit
All our being fill;
Still Thou dost say,
Wherefore struggle so?
Call for the Spirit,
Whisper soft and low,
Speak to the Rock
Bid the waters flow.

3 Oh, for trust more simple,
Fully to believe;
Oh, for hearts more childlike,
Freely to receive;
E'en as a babe,
On its mother's breast,
So on Thy bosom
Let my spirit rest,
Filled with Thy life,
With Thy blessing blest.

249

11.10.11.10.

1 Flow through me, Lord, a weak and earthly vessel,
　Cleansed by Thy blood, and quickened at Thy call.
Flow through me, Lord, all utterly abandoned,
　To Thy dear service, great, or high, or small.

2 Flow through me, Lord, with overflowing fulness,
　Make me to know Thine own deep love for souls.
Work in me, Lord, the faith that moveth mountains,
　As power, Almighty power, my being holds.

3 Flow through me, Lord, till sin in all its blackness
　To captives bound by Satan is revealed.
Flow through me, Lord, till hearts are stricken, broken,
　And in Thy cleansing fountain saved and healed.

4 Flow through me, Lord, till lagging souls are
　　quickened,
　Till lives of failure sing the victory song,
Till praise from lips long dumb and silent, open,
　And join with rapture earth's glad, cleansèd throng.

5 Flow through me, Lord, till waters from Thy fountain
　Shall slake the thirst of souls in deserts drear.
Flow through me, Lord, till arid places blossom
　With roses fresh and sweet, and wondrous fair.

6 Flow through me, Lord, set all my heart-strings
　　thrilling,
　With Thine own love, so matchless, perfect, free.
Flow through me, Lord, till naught in earth or heaven,
　Can satisfy my being, Lord, but Thee.

250*

6.6.6.6. (T)

1 Spring up, well, with water;
Dig Thou, Lord, completely;
Dig away all barriers
That Thy stream flow through me.

2 Christ, the Rock, is riven;
Living water's flowing;
But within my heart now
It is blocked from going.

3 I will dig by praying,
Dig the dirt entirely,
Thus release the Spirit,
Let the stream flow freely.

4 There's no need again that
Christ, the Rock, be riven,
But unto the digging
That I should be given.

5 What I need most deeply
Is the Spirit's filling,
That the living water
From my heart be welling.

6 Dig till there is nothing
Left to block the passage;
Dig until the stream flows
With the living message.

7 Spring up, well, with water;
Dig Thou, Lord, completely;
Dig away all barriers
That Thy stream flow through me.

7.7.8.7. with chorus.

1 Rivers of living water,
　　Rivers that flow from the throne,
　Rivers o'erflowing with blessing,
　　Coming from Jesus alone.

　　　Rivers of living water,
　　　　Rivers of life so free,
　　　Flowing from Thee, my Savior,
　　　　Send now the rivers through me.

2 Whoso is thirsty come hither,
　　Here is abundant supply;
　Water transparent as crystal,
　　Come without money and buy.

3 Cleanse me, oh, cleanse me, my Savior,
　　Make me a channel today;
　Empty me, fill me and use me,
　　Teach me to trust and obey.

4 Then, and then only, Lord Jesus,
　　Through me the rivers can flow;
　Thus and thus only will others
　　Learn Thy great fulness to know.

5 Now I surrender to Jesus,
　　Here I lay all at His feet;
　Anything, anywhere only,
　　Just for His service made meet!

Used by permission of the South Africa General Mission.

FULNESS OF THE SPIRIT — AS THE BREATH

8.8.8.8.8.8.

252

1 Thou Breath from still eternity
   Breathe o'er my spirit's barren land —
The pine tree and the myrtle tree
   Shall spring amid the desert sand;
And where Thy living water flows
   The waste shall blossom as the rose.

2 May I in will and deed and word
   Obey Thee as a little child;
And keep me in Thy love, my Lord,
   For ever holy, undefiled;
Within me teach, and strive, and pray,
   Lest I should choose my own wild way.

3 Thy Spirit, Stream by Thee, the Son,
   Is opened to us crystal pure,
Forth flowing from the heavenly throne
   To waiting hearts and spirits poor;
Athirst and weary do I sink
   Beside Thy waters, there to drink.

4 My spirit turns to Thee and clings,
   All else forsaking, unto Thee;
Forgetting all created things,
   Remembering only "God in me."
Thy living Stream, Thy gracious Rain,
   None wait for these, and wait in vain.

6.6.8.6.

253

1 Breathe on us, Lord of life,
   Fill us with life anew,
That we may love what Thou dost love,
   And do what Thou wouldst do.

2 Breathe on us, Lord of life,
   Until our hearts are pure,
Until with Thee we will one will,
   To do or to endure.

continued

3   Breathe on us, Lord of life,
    Till we are wholly Thine,
    Till all this earthly part of us
    Glows with Thy fire divine.

4   Breathe on us, Lord of life,
    So shall we never die,
    But live with Thee the perfect life
    Of Thine eternity.

254   8.8.8.8.

1   O Lord of life, breathe on us now,
    And move within us while we pray;
    The spring of our new life art Thou,
    The very light of our new day.

2   O strangely art Thou with us, Lord,
    Neither in height nor depth to seek;
    In nearness shall Thy voice be heard;
    Spirit to spirit Thou dost speak.

3   Thou art our Advocate on high;
    He is our Advocate within;
    O plead the truth, and make reply
    To every argument of sin.

4   But ah, this faithless heart of mine!
    The way I know, I know my guide;
    Forgive me, O my Friend divine,
    That I so often turn aside.

5   Be with me when no other friend
    The myst'ry of my heart can share;
    And be Thou known, when fears transcend,
    By Thy best name of Comforter.

Used and altered by permission of Mrs. Alice Tempest.

8.7.8.7. with chorus.

255

1   O Lord, breathe Thy Spirit on me,
    Teach me how to breathe Thee in;
  Help me pour into Thy bosom
    All my life of self and sin.

      I am breathing out my sorrow,
        Breathing out my sin;
      I am breathing, breathing, breathing,
        All Thy fulness in.

2   I am breathing out my own life,
    That I may be filled with Thine;
  Letting go my strength and weakness,
    Breathing in Thy life divine.

3   Breathing out my sinful nature,
    Thou hast borne it all for me;
  Breathing in Thy cleansing fulness,
    Finding all my life in Thee.

4   I am breathing out my sorrow,
    On Thy kind and gentle breast;
  Breathing in Thy joy and comfort,
    Breathing in Thy peace and rest.

5   I am breathing out my sickness,
    Thou hast borne its burden too;
  I am breathing in Thy healing,
    Ever promised, ever new.

6   I am breathing out my longings
    In Thy listening, loving ear;
  I am breathing in Thy answers,
    Stilling every doubt and fear.

7   I am breathing every moment,
    Drawing all my life from Thee;
  Breath by breath I live upon Thee,
    Lord, Thy Spirit breathe in me.

256*

12.12.12.8. with chorus.

1 Oh, blow upon us, Lord, while here we wait on Thee;
Oh, blow with mighty wind and bring us liberty;
Oh, blow till in our midst revival we shall see;
   Oh, blow upon us, Lord, we pray!

   Oh, blow upon us, Lord, today!
   Oh, blow all sloth and sleep away!
     Oh, may Thy wind descend,
     All our backsliding end!
   Oh, blow upon us, Lord, we pray!

2 Oh, blow with love divine and stir up our cold heart;
Oh, blow and to our soul the breath of heav'n impart;
Oh, blow till from each one indifference shall depart;
   Oh, blow upon us, Lord, we pray!

3 Oh, blow with pow'r from heav'n our spirit to inspire;
Oh, blow and quicken us and fill with Thy desire;
Oh, blow till all of us be wholly set on fire;
   Oh, blow upon us, Lord, we pray!

257*

8.6.8.6.D.

1 Lord, may Thy Wind of heaven blow
   Upon us here today!
With stirring and reviving might,
   To us Thy pow'r display.

   Oh, mighty Lord, on us descend,
     Oh, may Thy Spirit blow!
   With power cause us to transcend,
     Grant us the living flow!

FULNESS OF THE SPIRIT — AS THE WIND

2 With Thy empow'ring Spirit blow
   And all the barriers break;
   With Thy life-giving Spirit breathe,
   That we of Thee partake.

3 Thy Spirit is of sevenfold wealth,
   For us to share of Thee;
   Grant us the full experience of
   The God in persons Three.

FULNESS OF THE SPIRIT — AS THE LATTER RAIN

10.10.10.10.   **258**

1 "With one accord" within an upper room
   The faithful followers of Jesus met:
   One was the hope of every waiting soul,
   And on one object great each heart was set.

2 "With one accord," until the mighty gift
   Of pentecostal power was outpoured;
   Then forth as witnesses possessed of God,
   To preach the resurrection of the Lord!

3 "With one accord" within the house of God
   A hallelujah song is daily raised,
   As with the voice of one, from vocal hearts
   Christ Jesus' name is glorified and praised.

4 Pour down Thy Spirit once again, dear Lord;
   Our cry goes up to Thee for "latter rain";
   Unite Thy people as the "heart of one,"
   And pentecostal days shall come again!

Used by permission of Marshall, Morgan & Scott, Ltd.

8.7.8.7. with chorus.

1 Lord, I hear of show'rs of blessing
   Thou art scatt'ring full and free,
   Show'rs the thirsty land refreshing;
   Let some drops now fall on me.

       Even me, even me,
       Let some drops now fall on me.

2 Pass me not, O gracious Father!
   Sinful though my heart may be;
   Thou might'st leave me, but the rather
   Let Thy mercy fall on me.

3 Pass me not, O tender Savior!
   Let me love and cling to Thee;
   I am longing for Thy favor;
   While Thou'rt calling, call for me.

4 Pass me not, O Lord, the Spirit!
   Thou canst make the blind to see;
   By the Witness of Thy merit,
   Speak the word of power to me.

5 Love of God, so pure and changeless!
   Blood of Christ, so rich and free!
   Grace of God, so strong and boundless!
   Magnify them all in me.

6 Pass me not! Thy lost one bringing,
   Bind my heart, O Lord, to Thee;
   While the streams of life are springing,
   Blessing others, oh, bless me.

8.7.8.7. with chorus.

1 There shall be showers of blessing:
This is the promise of love;
There shall be seasons refreshing,
Sent from the Savior above.

Showers of blessing,
Showers of blessing we need;
Mercy-drops round us are falling,
But for the showers we plead.

2 There shall be showers of blessing —
Precious reviving again;
Over the hills and the valleys,
Sound of abundance of rain.

3 There shall be showers of blessing;
Send them upon us, O Lord!
Grant to us now a refreshing;
Come, and now honor Thy Word.

4 There shall be showers of blessing;
O that today they might fall,
Now as to God we're confessing,
Now as on Jesus we call!

5 There shall be showers of blessing,
If we but trust and obey;
There shall be seasons refreshing,
If we let God have His way.

261

8.6.8.6.D.

1 Praise waiteth Thee in mercy's court,
    Where Thy beloved dwell;
Ransomed, released from Satan's thrall,
    Their Hallelujahs swell.
Come, as the Spirit, Lord, today,
    Our songs of praise inspire;
Purge the iniquity, and touch
    Our lips with living fire.

2 Praise for what Thou our God hast wrought;
    For promised blessings ours;
The cloud on faith's horizon seen,
    The pentecostal showers.
Praise for Thine own right way, dear Lord,
    We did not understand,
But as Thy plans unfolded lie,
    We see Thy guiding hand.

3 Enlarge our soul's capacity,
    Cut deeper channels, Lord;
Room for the floods of blessing now,
    According to Thy Word.
E'en while we praise, the heavens rend,
    In power come from on high;
Make this another Pentecost,
    Answer our spirit's cry.

7.7.7.7. with chorus.

1 Come, Lord, as the Spirit come,
Lo! we stretch our hands to Thee;
From the Father to the Son,
Let us now Thy glory see.

> Come, oh Lord, Great Spirit, come!
> Let the mighty deed be done!
> Satisfy our soul's desire,
> See us waiting for the fire,
> Waiting, waiting,
> See us waiting for the fire.

2 On the altar now we lay
Soul and body, mind and will;
All the evil passions slay,
Come, and every corner fill.

3 Now the sacrifice we make,
Though as dear as a right eye,
For our blessed Savior's sake,
Who for us did bleed and die.

4 Now, by faith, the gift I claim,
Bought for me by blood divine:
Through the all-prevailing Name
All the promises are mine.

263

6.6.6.6.D. with chorus.

1 God sent His mighty pow'r
  To this poor, sinful heart,
To keep me every hour,
  And needful grace impart;
And since His Spirit came,
  To take supreme control,
The love-enkindled flame
  Is burning in my soul.

  'Tis burning in my soul,
  'Tis burning in my soul;
  The fire of heav'nly love is
    burning in my soul;
  The Holy Spirit came,
  All glory to His name!
  The fire of heav'nly love is
    burning in my soul.

2 Before the cross I bow,
  Upon the altar lay
A willing off'ring now,
  My all from day to day.
My Savior paid the price,
  My name He sweetly calls;
Upon the sacrifice
  The fire from heaven falls.

3 No good that I have done,
  His promise I embrace;
Accepted in the Son,
  He saves me by His grace.
All glory be to God!
  Let hallelujahs roll;
His love is shed abroad,
  The fire is in my soul.

8.6.8.6. with repeat.

1 Jesus, Thine all-victorious love
    Shed in my soul abroad;
  Then shall my heart no longer rove,
    Rooted and fixed in God,
    Rooted and fixed in God.

2 Oh, that in me the sacred fire
    Might now begin to glow;
  Burn up the dross of base desire,
    And make the mountains flow,
    And make the mountains flow.

3 He, who at Pentecost didst fall,
    May He my sins consume;
  Thy Holy Ghost, for Him I call;
    Thy burning Spirit, come,
    Thy burning Spirit, come.

4 Refining fire, go through my heart,
    Illuminate my soul;
  Scatter Thy life through every part,
    And sanctify the whole,
    And sanctify the whole.

5 My steadfast soul, from falling free,
    Shall then no longer move,
  While Christ is all the world to me,
    And all my heart is love,
    And all my heart is love.

8.7.8.7.

1 Where the sprinkling of the blood is,
   There the ointment doth remain;
Man in touch with God thus bringing,
   These the fellowship maintain.

2 Blood, the emblem of redemption,
   Cleansing all the sins away;
Ointment, symbol of the Spirit,
   Bringing God to man for aye.

3 Blood doth speak of what God worketh,
   Ointment, what He is for us;
By His work and by His person
   God Himself is blent with us.

4 By the blood of Christ's redemption
   We are cleansed from all alloy;
By th' anointing of the Spirit
   God Himself we may enjoy.

5 By the cleansing and anointing
   We with God are kept in one;
By the blood and by the ointment
   God, our portion full, is won.

6 We in faith must claim the cleansing
   When we need the precious blood,
Ever to obey th' anointing,
   Thus to live and walk with God.

7 God as light we'll then be knowing,
   God experience as love,
And in God as life e'er growing,
   God as power we will prove.

Peculiar Meter.

1 Divine anointing in me dwelleth,
  And it teaches me all things;
  It ever leads me in the Lord to live
  And to me His presence brings.

  In my spirit the anointing dwells,
    O the anointing dwells and
      teaches everything;
  In my spirit the anointing dwells
    And ever teaches everything.

2 It is the moving of the Spirit
    Gracious as the ointment pure;
  'Tis based upon the sprinkling of the blood,
    And it ever shall endure.

3 With God's own essence it anoints me,
    God to know subjectively,
  That I may have His very element
    Fully saturating me.

4 'Tis by this inner life-anointing
    I in fellowship may move;
  In God, the light of truth, I'm walking,
    And the love of grace I prove.

8.7.8.7. with chorus.

1 Fill me with Thy gracious Spirit,
    Fill my longing spirit now;
Fill me with Thy hallowed presence,
    Come, dear Lord, and fill me now!

    Fill me now! Fill me now!
        Fill me with Thy Spirit now!
    Strip me wholly, empty throughly,
        Fill me with Thy Spirit now!

2 Thou can'st fill me with Thy Spirit,
    Though I cannot tell Thee how;
But I need Thee, greatly need Thee;
    Come, dear Lord, and fill me now!

3 I am weakness, full of weakness;
    At Thy sacred feet I bow;
By Thy blest, eternal Spirit,
    Fill with strength, and fill me now!

4 Cleanse and comfort, bless and save me;
    Fill my broken spirit now!
Thou art comforting and saving,
    Thou art sweetly filling now.

FULNESS OF THE SPIRIT — THE FILLING

8.7.8.7.D.

1 How I praise Thee, precious Savior,
That Thy love laid hold of me;
Thou hast saved and cleansed and filled me,
That I might Thy channel be.

Channels only, blessed Master,
But with all Thy wondrous grace,
Flowing through us, Thou canst use us
Every hour in every place.

2 Just a channel, full of blessing,
To the thirsty hearts around;
To tell out Thy full salvation,
All Thy loving message sound.

3 Emptied that Thou shouldest fill me,
A clean vessel in Thine hand;
With no strength but as Thou givest
Graciously with each command.

4 Witnessing Thy grace to save me,
Setting free from self and sin;
Thou hast bought me to possess me,
In Thy fulness, Lord, come in.

5 O Lord, fill now with Thy Spirit
Hearts that full surrender know;
That the streams of living water
From our inner man may flow.

269

7.7.7.7.7.7.

1 O Lord, with Thy Holy Ghost,
Fill me to the uttermost;
Let my life Thy channel be,
Just a channel, Lord, for Thee;
Through me all Thy riches pour,
Give me ever more and more.

2 O Lord, with Thy Holy Ghost,
Fill me to the uttermost;
Be it unto me, O Lord,
Now, according to Thy word;
Let the life of Jesus be,
Ever filling, even me.

3 O Lord, with Thy Holy Ghost,
Fill me to the uttermost;
Cleansed and holy, pure and clean,
Let the life of Christ be seen;
Hold o'er me Thy gracious sway,
Every hour of every day.

4 O Lord, with Thy Holy Ghost,
Fill me to the uttermost;
For Thy love, Thy light, Thy grace,
Just a channel all my days;
Till my Savior's face I see,
Fill me, Lord, fill even me.

10.10.10.10.

1 Lord, in Thy Spirit, take and fill my heart;
Wean it from earth, through all its pulses move;
Into my spirit all Thy grace impart,
And make me love Thee as I ought to love.

2 I ask no dream, no prophet ecstasies,
No sudden rending of the veil of clay,
No angel visitant, no opening skies;
But take the dimness of my soul away.

3 Hast Thou not bid us love Thee, God and King?
All, all Thine own — soul, heart and strength
    and mind.
I see Thy cross — there teach my heart to cling.
Oh, let me seek Thee, and, oh, let me find.

4 Teach me to feel that Thou art always nigh;
Teach me the struggles of the soul to bear,
To check the rising doubt, the rebel sigh;
Teach me the patience of unanswered prayer.

5 Teach me to love Thee with a virgin love,
One holy passion filling all my frame;
Thus all the riches of Thyself to prove,
My heart an altar, and Thy love the flame.

271*

8.7.8.7.D.

1 Of the Spirit born in spirit,
　　As the sons of God indeed,
We possess the Holy Spirit,
　　Dwelling in us for all need.
Yet we still need more of Him, Lord,
　　That we may be full of Thee;
May Thou fill us with Thy Spirit,
　　Give us life abundantly.

2 Lord, we know the Spirit in us,
　　But of life Thy Spirit is,
That the riches of Thy fulness
　　We may share thru what He is.
Yet we still require Thy Spirit
　　As the power from on high,
That for all Thy work and service,
　　We may be equipped thereby.

3 Lord, baptize us with Thy Spirit,
　　Clothe us with Thy pow'r of might;
With this "mantle" of Thy power,
　　We may then the battle fight.
May Thy wind now blow upon us,
　　Giving us the tongues of fire,
That, as witnesses anointed,
　　We'll fulfill Thy heart's desire.

4 With the power of Thy Spirit,
　　Still we need the gifts to share,
That as members we may function
　　And Thy testimony bear.
By Thy Spirit's full outpouring,
　　Lord, impart the gifts we need,
That the building of Thy Body
　　With Thy blessing might proceed.

5 For Thy glory and Thy kingdom,
   May Thou hear Thy Body's cry!
Now fulfill Thy holy purpose,
   All our hunger satisfy.
May we all partake Thy Spirit,
   Him apply in many ways;
His infilling, His outpouring,
   And His gifts to share always.

8.7.8.7.D.

272*

1 Christ indeed was born of Spirit
   When He came a man to be;
And before His service started,
   With the Spirit filled was He.
Yet He still received the baptism
   Of the Spirit from on high
When He came to start His service
   And was clothed with pow'r thereby.

2 Peter and the Lord's disciples
   All were Spirit born and filled,
Breathing in the Holy Spirit
   As on them Christ breathed and willed.
Yet they still received the baptism
   Of the Spirit from on high
When they were equipped for service,
   And were clothed with pow'r thereby.

3 Saul of Tarsus, the Ephesians,
   And Samaritans believed;
Thus by Spirit generated,
   Of His fulness they received.
Yet they still received the baptism
   Of the Spirit from on high
When some laid their hands upon them,
   And were clothed with pow'r thereby.

continued

4 We are also born of Spirit
　　On the day when we believe,
And of Him we now are drinking
　　As we daily Him receive.
Yet we also must be baptized
　　With the Spirit from on high,
Thus to be equipped for service,
　　And be clothed with pow'r thereby.

5 Lord, baptize us with Thy Spirit!
　　This is what we need today;
Clothe us with Thy heav'nly power,
　　Bring us under its full sway.
Oh, baptize us in this hour!
　　This is all our earnest cry;
Now on us repeat Thine answer,
　　Clothe with power from on high.

273*　　　　Peculiar Meter.

1 Lord, we come to Thee, and with liberty
　　Claim we now from Thee pow'r of might;
For Thy kingdom's sake, may we pow'r partake,
　　Sitting in the heavenlies to fight.

　　Power! power! clothe us with Thy power!
　　With Thy mighty power from on high!
　　Power! power! clothe us with Thy power!
　　Boldly, as Thy Body, now we cry!

2 Lord, we look to Thee and with certainty
　　Claim we now from Thee show'r divine.
For Thy Body's sake, may we show'r partake,
　　Thus be fitted for the work of Thine.

　　Shower! shower! pour on us Thy shower!
　　Pour Thy heav'nly shower from on high!
　　Shower! shower! pour on us Thy shower!
　　Boldly, as Thy Body, now we cry!

3 Lord, we wait on Thee, and with surety
    Claim we now from Thee fire divine.
For Thy gospel's sake, may we fire partake,
    That the people's heart Thou may refine.

      Fire! fire! give us tongues of fire!
      To proclaim Thy message from on high!
      Fire! fire! give us tongues of fire!
      Boldly, as Thy Body, now we cry!

274*

9.9.9.6. with chorus.

1 O Lord, we seek the power we need;
    We are so weak in word and in deed
And in Thy service cannot proceed,
    Clothe us with pow'r we pray!

    We are waiting, and to Thee we bow,
      In Thy presence all our need avow;
    Give us Thy power, give even now,
      Clothe us with pow'r today.

2 Lord, come and visit us at this place,
    Grant to Thy Church the gifts of Thy grace,
Fully with might our service embrace,
    Clothe us with pow'r we pray!

3 Send us Thy power with its full sway,
    As Thou didst send on Pentecost day;
Answer our prayer and make no delay,
    Clothe us with pow'r we pray!

4 Here, as Thy Body, Thy pow'r we claim;
    Claiming by faith in Thy mighty Name,
Thy heav'nly show'r with Thy heav'nly flame;
    Clothe us with pow'r we pray!

8.6.8.6. with chorus.

1 Thy Holy Spirit, Lord, alone
  Can meet our need today;
  His might alone empow'ring us
  Can bring us neath Thy sway.

  Thy Spirit of pow'r with might,
    Send in our midst, we pray,
  And come upon each seeking soul;
    Baptize us with power today.

2 Thy Holy Spirit, Lord, alone
  Can grant us Thy desire;
  His power alone can turn our heart
  And light the sacred fire.

3 Thy Holy Spirit, Lord, can give
  The gifts we seek to share;
  His pow'r can signs and wonders work
  And stir up holy fear.

4 Thy Holy Spirit, Lord, can bring
  The show'r we need this hour;
  And while we seek, Lord Jesus, come
  In motivating power.

  Thy Spirit of pow'r with might,
    Send in our midst, we pray,
  And like a rushing, mighty wind
    Sweep over our souls today.

1 What a blessed fact! What a tiding glad!
   In the Spirit we have been baptized;
Take this settled fact, nothing need we add,
   In the Spirit we have been baptized.

      Take it! take it!
   Take now this fact by living faith;
      Take it! take it!
   Take now this accomplished fact by faith.

2 In the testament it is clearly told,
   In the Spirit we have been baptized;
It is so complete, we need only hold,
   In the Spirit we have been baptized.

      Hold it! hold it!
   Hold now this fact by living faith;
      Hold it! hold it!
   Hold now this accomplished fact by faith.

3 Christ upon the Church hath His Spirit poured,
   In the Spirit we have been baptized;
Share her portion now, share in full accord,
   In the Spirit we have been baptized.

      Share it! share it!
   Share now this fact by living faith;
      Share it! share it!
   Share now this accomplished fact by faith.

4 With the Body right, on the Body ground,
   Move and act on this accomplished fact;
Sins and doubts condemn, wait no more around,
   But by living faith now move and act.

      Act now! act now!
   Act on this fact by living faith;
      Act now! act now!
   Act on this accomplished fact by faith.

277*

8.7.8.7.8.7.

1 Christ the Savior hath ascended
   To the heavens far above,
 Crowned with glory and with honor
   By the Father God in love;
 He hath made Him Head of all things,
   His supremacy to prove.

2 From this Christ to God ascended
   Hath the Spirit been outpoured,
 Poured upon the Church, His Body,
   That His members be empow'red;
 Thus the Lord of all in heaven
   Thru His Church will be adored.

3 In the flesh by incarnation,
   Into man He God hath brought;
 By His death and resurrection,
   Into God He man hath brought;
 God and man together mingled,
   In Himself is fully wrought.

4 Now in heaven by ascension
   He is seated on the throne;
 All the lordship, all the headship,
   He Himself doth fully own;
 And by pouring out His Spirit,
   He as such might be made known.

5 By this outpour, His descension
   On the Church was realized;
 'Tis by this, that in His Spirit
   All the Church He hath baptized;
 Thus the baptism of the Spirit
   Was forever actualized.

6   Hallelujah, 'tis accomplished,
    And accomplished once for all!
  Hallelujah, we're included,
    All included, great or small!
  Praise Him, He hath sent the Spirit
    And baptized the Church withal!

FULNESS OF THE SPIRIT — THE TWO ASPECTS

11.11.11.11.   **278***

1   The Spirit of life is within us today,
    Who's likened to water our thirst to allay;
    Of Him we may drink and be filled thus with Him,
    Until as a river He flows from within.

2   The Spirit of pow'r comes upon us today,
    Who's likened to clothing ourselves to array;
    In Him we are baptized, with Him we are dressed,
    For service equipping with power possessed.

3   The Spirit of life is as breath glorious,
    As spirit of life it is breathed into us;
    The Spirit of pow'r doth the wind typify,
    Which bloweth upon us with pow'r from on high.

4   Into His disciples the risen Lord breathed,
    The Spirit of life thus to them He bequeathed;
    Th' ascended Lord poured at the Pentecost hour
    Upon His disciples the Spirit of pow'r.

5   The Spirit of life is within as the life,
    The Spirit of power is giv'n for this life;
    As blowing of wind brings the fresh air to breathe,
    The Spirit of power to life doth bequeath.

continued

6   These are not two spirits apart and afar,
But of the one Spirit the two functions are,
To clothe us with God and to fill us within,
That we may be thoroughly mingled with Him.

7   Lord, fill with Thy Spirit of life every part,
That we may grow up in Thy life as Thou art;
And clothe us without with Thy Spirit of pow'r
Thy will to fulfill in Thy service each hour.

FULNESS OF THE SPIRIT — BY THE CROSS

279 †   8.7.8.7.D. with chorus.

1   First the blood, and then the ointment,
Cleansing, then anointing comes;
If we pass not thru Golgotha,
Ne'er to Pentecost we'll come.
If the blood has never cleansed us,
Ne'er the Spirit's pow'r we'll know,
If for Christ we'd truly witness,
Self-life to the Cross must go.

Through the Cross, O Lord, I pray,
Put my soul-life all away;
Make me any price to pay,
Full anointing to receive.

2   Christ, the Rock, must first be smitten,
That the living water flow;
Without death the Spirit's fulness
Ne'er could dwell in man below.
If with Christ we die completely,
Willing thus our all to lose,
He will clothe us with His power
And to win the world will use.

† All hymns marked with a dagger have been translated by us from
the writings of others. We desire all of them to be freely available to
the Lord's children; but for the sake of avoiding confusion, we request
consultation with us before usage. — The Living Stream

3   First the altar, then the fire,
     If no loss, there'll be no gain;
If our all has not been offered,
     To the throne we'll ne'er attain.
If to sacrifice we're willing,
     All forsaking, God t'obey,
He to us will be committed
     And thru us His pow'r display.

4   First we must prepare the vessels
     That the Oil they may contain;
Dig the valley full of ditches
     That they may be filled with Rain.
First we must go thru the Jordan
     Ere anointed from above;
First in death we must be baptized,
     Then experience the Dove.

5   When we see the ripened harvest
     Of the golden countryside,
We may know that many seeds have
     Fallen to the earth and died.
Ere the fruit of life may blossom,
     We must surely suffer death;
If with Christ we've not been buried,
     We'll not feel the Spirit's breath.

6   Since it must be thus, I pray, Lord,
     Help me go the narrow way;
Deal with pride and make me willing
     Thus to suffer, Thee t'obey.
I for greater power pray not,
     Deeper death is what I need;
All the meaning of the Cross, Lord,
     Work in me — for this I plead.

280†

7.6.7.6.D. with chorus.

1 Lord, may Thy blood now cleanse me,
Wash all my sins away,
That with Thy Holy Spirit
Thou may anoint, I pray.
My service, I confess, Lord,
Is failure-full and weak;
The filling of Thy Spirit
To live for Thee I seek.

Oh, from myself deliver,
From all its misery;
I'd henceforth be forever
Completely filled with Thee.

2 Oh, Lord, how dry my heart is,
It yearns and pants for Thee;
The filling of Thy Spirit
Is now my fervent plea.
Within the smitten Rock, Lord,
I would entirely hide;
Pour thru Thy living water,
Till I am satisfied.

3 How cold my heart has been, Lord,
How slow obeying Thee;
So fill me with Thy Spirit,
I'll ne'er rebellious be.
I lie upon Thy altar
And dare not move away;
Oh, may Thy flame descending
Consume my all, I pray.

4 Oh, may Thy Cross within me
Deepen its work and burn,
In me enlarge Thy measure,
And me to ashes turn.

FULNESS OF THE SPIRIT — BY THE CROSS

Oh, may Thy Spirit fill me
Each day more than before,
And may Thy living water
On me and thru me pour.

FULNESS OF THE SPIRIT — GENERAL

281

7.7.7.7. with repeat.

1 Lord, the Spirit, Truth divine,
Dawn upon this heart of mine;
Word of God, and inward light,
Wake my spirit, clear my sight.

2 Lord, the Spirit, Love divine,
Glow within this heart of mine,
Kindle every high desire,
Perish self in Thy pure fire.

3 Lord, the Spirit, Power divine,
Fill and nerve this will of mine;
By Thee may I strongly live,
Bravely bear, and nobly strive.

4 Lord, the Spirit, Peace divine,
Still this restless heart of mine,
Speak to calm this tossing sea,
Stayed in Thy tranquillity.

5 Lord, the Spirit, Joy divine,
Gladden Thou this heart of mine;
In the desert ways I'll sing:
Spring, O Well, forever spring!

(Repeat the last line of each stanza)

282

7.7.7.7.

1 Lord of light, with light divine,
   Shine upon this heart of mine;
   Chase the shades of night away,
   Turn the darkness into day.

2 Lord of power, with power divine,
   Cleanse this guilty heart of mine;
   Long has sin without control
   Held dominion o'er my soul.

3 Lord of joy, with joy divine,
   Cheer this saddened heart of mine;
   Bid my many woes depart,
   Heal my wounded, bleeding heart.

4 Lord, the Spirit, all divine,
   Dwell within this heart of mine;
   Cast down every idol throne,
   Reign supreme, and reign alone.

283

8.7.8.7. with chorus.

1 Lord, Thou knowest all the hunger
   Of the heart that seeks Thee now;
   How my soul hath long been craving
   What Thou only canst bestow.

   Seeking now, seeking now,
   Let Thy Spirit meet me now.

2   Failure in my walk and witness,
     Failure in my work I see;
  Fruitless toil, un-Christlike living,
     Calling forth no praise to Thee.

3   Now to Thee my soul confesses
     All its failure, all its sin;
  All the pride, the self-contentment,
     All the "secret faults" within.

4   Save me from myself, my Father,
     From each subtle form of pride;
  Lead me now with Christ to Calvary,
     Show me I with Him have died.

5   No more let it be my working,
     Nor my wisdom, love, or power,
  But the life of Jesus only,
     Passing through me hour by hour.

6   Let the fulness of Thy Spirit
     Resting on Him cover me,
  That the witness borne to others,
     May bring glory, Lord, to Thee.

7   Father, in Thy Son's Name, pleading,
     I believe my prayer is heard;
  And I praise Thee for the answer,
     Resting simply on Thy word.

    Praising now, praising now,
    Thou hast answered, Lord, I know.

7.7.7.7.D.

1 Loved with everlasting love,
Led by grace that love to know;
Spirit, breathing from above,
Thou hast taught me it is so.
Oh, this full and perfect peace!
Oh, this transport all divine!
In a love which cannot cease,
I am His, and He is mine.

2 Heaven above is softer blue,
Earth around is sweeter green;
Something lives in every hue
Christless eyes have never seen:
Birds with gladder songs o'erflow,
Flow'rs with deeper beauties shine,
Since I know, as now I know,
I am His, and He is mine.

3 Things that once were wild alarms
Cannot now disturb my rest;
Closed in everlasting arms,
Pillowed on the loving breast.
Oh, to lie forever here,
Doubt and care and self resign,
While He whispers in my ear,
I am His, and He is mine.

4 His forever, only His:
Who the Lord and me shall part?
Ah, with what a rest of bliss
Christ can fill the loving heart.
Heaven and earth may fade and flee,
Firstborn light in gloom decline;
But, while God and I shall be,
I am His, and He is mine.

1 Come and rejoice with me!
For once my heart was poor,
And I have found a treasury
Of love, a boundless store.

2 Come and rejoice with me!
I, once so sick at heart,
Have met with One who knows my case,
And knows the healing art.

3 Come and rejoice with me!
For I was wearied sore,
And I have found a mighty arm
Which holds me evermore.

4 Come and rejoice with me!
My feet so wide did roam,
And One has brought me from afar,
To find in Him my home.

5 Come and rejoice with me!
For I have found a Friend
Who knows my heart's most secret depths,
Yet loves me without end.

6 I knew not of His love;
And He had loved so long,
With love so faithful and so deep,
So tender and so strong.

7 And now I know it all,
Have heard and known His voice,
And hear it still from day to day.
Can I enough rejoice?

7.6.7.6.D with chorus.

1 Of Jesus' love that sought me,
    When I was lost in sin;
Of wondrous grace that brought me
    Back to His fold again;
Of heights and depths of mercy,
    Far deeper than the sea,
And higher than the heavens,
    My theme shall ever be.

    Sweeter as the years go by,
    Sweeter as the years go by;
    Richer, fuller, deeper,
    Jesus' love is sweeter,
    Sweeter as the years go by.

2 He trod in old Judea
    Life's pathway long ago;
The people thronged about Him,
    His saving grace to know.
He healed the broken-hearted,
    And caused the blind to see;
And still His great heart yearneth
    In love for even me.

6.5.6.5.

1 Jesus, Jesus, Jesus!
Sweetest Name on earth,
How can I, a sinner,
Come to know its worth?

2 Oh! the sinful sorrow,
Oh! the strangest shame,
That I saw no beauty
In that sacred Name.

3 Never felt the sweetness!
Never knew the grace,
Never saw the love-pain
In that wounded face!

4 Never found the mystery
In that simple word —
Jesus, Jesus, Jesus,
Savior, Lover, Lord.

5 Now 'tis past and over.
Gone my guilt and shame;
Jesus, Jesus did it,
Glory to His Name!

6 Wonderful compassion,
Reaching even me;
Bows my humbled spirit
In captivity.

7 Jesus! Jesus! Jesus!
Loved me in my shame.
Oh! the joy and rapture
Of that sacred Name.

288

8.7.8.7.D. (I)

1 I've found a Friend, oh, such a Friend!
  He loved me ere I knew Him;
He drew me with the cords of love,
  And thus He bound me to Him.
And round my heart still closely twine
  Those ties which naught can sever,
For I am His, and He is mine,
  Forever and forever.

2 I've found a Friend, oh, such a Friend!
  He bled, He died to save me;
And not alone the gift of life,
  But His own self He gave me.
Naught that I have my own I call,
  I hold it for the Giver;
My heart, my strength, my life, my all,
  Are His, and His forever.

3 I've found a Friend, oh, such a Friend!
  So kind, and true, and tender,
So wise a Counsellor and Guide,
  So mighty a Defender!
From Him who loves me now so well,
  What power my soul can sever?
Shall life or death, or earth or hell?
  No, I am His forever.

289   13.13.13.13. with chorus.

1 I stand all amazed at the love Jesus offers me,
  Confused at the grace that so fully He proffers me;
I tremble to know that for me He was crucified,
  That for me, a sinner, He suffered, He bled and died.

Chorus:
> O it is wonderful that He should care for me
> Enough to die for me!
> O it is wonderful, wonderful to me!

2 I marvel that He would descend from His throne divine
To rescue a soul so rebellious and proud as mine;
That He should extend His great love unto such as I,
Sufficient to own, to redeem, and to justify.

3 I think of His side, pierced and bleeding to pay the debt,
Such mercy, such love and devotion can I forget?
No, no! I will praise and adore at the mercy seat,
And testify all my desires He doth fully meet.

290

8.7.8.7. with chorus.

1   I stand amazed in the presence
        Of Jesus the Nazarene,
    And wonder how He could love me,
        A sinner condemned, unclean.

        How marvelous! How wonderful!
            And my song shall ever be:
        How marvelous! How wonderful!
            Is my Savior's love for me!

2   For me it was in the garden,
        He prayed: "Not my will, but Thine."
    He had no tears for His own griefs,
        But sweat-drops of blood for mine.

3   In pity angels beheld Him,
        And came from the world of light
    To strengthen Him in the sorrows
        He bore for my soul that night.

continued

4   He took my sins and my sorrows,
        He made them His very own;
    He bore the burden to Calv'ry,
        And suffered, and died alone.

5   When with the ransomed in glory
        His face I at last shall see,
    'Twill be my joy through the ages
        To sing of His love for me.

291   10.10.10.10. with chorus.

1   I am so glad that our Father in heav'n
    Tells of His love in the Book He has giv'n;
    Wonderful things in the Bible I see:
    This is the dearest, that Jesus loves me.

        I am so glad that Jesus loves me,
            Jesus loves me, Jesus loves me;
        I am so glad that Jesus loves me,
            Jesus loves even me.

2   Though I forget Him and wander away,
    Still He doth love me whenever I stray;
    Back to His dear loving arms would I flee,
    When I remember that Jesus loves me.

3   Oh, if there's only one song I can sing,
    When in His beauty I see the great King,
    This shall my song in eternity be:
    "Oh, what a wonder that Jesus loves me."

8.8.8.8.D. (A)

1 A debtor to mercy alone,
Of covenant mercy I sing,
Nor fear, with God's righteousness on,
My person and off'rings to bring.
The terrors of law and of God
With me can have nothing to do;
My Savior's obedience and blood
Hide all my transgressions from view.

2 The work which His goodness began,
The arm of His strength will complete;
His promise is Yea and Amen,
And never was forfeited yet.
Things future, nor things that are now,
Not all things below or above,
Can make Him His purpose forego,
Or sever my soul from His love.

3 My name from the palms of His hands
Eternity will not erase;
Imprest on His heart, it remains
In marks of indelible grace.
Yes! I to the end shall endure,
As sure as the earnest is giv'n;
More happy, but not more secure,
When all earthly ties have been riv'n.

293

8.8.8.8.

1 Cleansed in our Savior's precious Blood,
Filled with the fulness of our God,
Walking by faith the path He trod,
Hallelujah! Hallelujah!

2 Leaning our heads on Jesus' breast,
Knowing the joy of that sweet rest,
Finding in Him the chief, the best,
Hallelujah! Hallelujah!

3 Kept by His pow'r from day to day,
Held by His hand, we cannot stray,
Glory to glory all the way,
Hallelujah! Hallelujah!

4 Living in us His own pure life,
Giving us rest from inward strife,
From strength to strength, from death to life,
Hallelujah! Hallelujah!

5 O what a Savior we have found;
Well may we make the world resound
With one continual joyous sound,
Hallelujah! Hallelujah!

294

10.10.10.12. with chorus.

1 Gone from my heart the world and all its charms;
Now through the blood I'm saved from all alarms;
Down at the cross my heart is bending low;
The precious blood of Jesus cleanses white as snow.

I love Him, I love Him,
Because He first loved me,
And purchased my salvation on Calv'ry's tree.

2 Once I was lost, and fallen deep in sin;
Once was a slave to passions fierce within,
Once was afraid to meet an angry God,   [blood.
But now I'm cleansed from every stain thro' Jesus'

3 Once I was bound, but now I am set free;
Once I was blind, but now the light I see;
Once I was dead, but now in Christ I live, [give.
To tell the world around the peace that He doth

JUSTIFIED IN CHRIST

8.8.8.8.

295

1 God's Christ, who is my righteousness,
My beauty is, my glorious dress;
Midst flaming worlds, in this arrayed,
With joy shall I lift up my head.

2 Lord, I believe Thy precious blood,
Which, at the mercy seat of God,
Forever doth for sinners plead,
For me, e'en for my soul, was shed.

3 Lord, I believe were sinners more
Than sands upon the ocean shore,
Thou hast for all a ransom paid,
For all a full redemption made.

4 Bold can I stand in every way,
For who aught to my charge shall lay?
Fully, by Thee, absolved I am
From sin and fear, from guilt and shame.

5 This spotless robe the same appears,
When ruined nature sinks in years;
No age can change its glorious hue,
Its glory is forever new.

6 Thou God of power, Thou God of love,
Let all Thy saints Thy mercy prove;
Our beauty this, our glorious dress,
Jesus the Lord, our Righteousness.

296

8.8.8.8.8.8. with repeat.

1 And can it be that I should gain
An int'rest in the Savior's blood?
Died He for me, who caused His pain?
For me, who Him to death pursued?
Amazing love! how can it be
That Thou, my God, shouldst die for me?
Amazing love! how can it be
That Thou, my God, shouldst die for me?

2 'Tis mystery all! The Immortal dies!
Who can explore His strange design?
In vain the firstborn seraph tries
To sound the depths of love Divine!
'Tis mercy all! let earth adore,
Let angel minds inquire no more.
'Tis mercy all! let earth adore,
Let angel minds inquire no more.

3 He left His Father's throne above,
So free, so infinite His grace;
Emptied Himself of all but love,
And bled for Adam's helpless race:
'Tis mercy all, immense and free;
For, O my God, it found out me.
'Tis mercy all, immense and free;
For, O my God, it found out me.

4 Long my imprisoned spirit lay
Fast bound in sin and nature's night;
Thine eye diffused a quickening ray,
I woke, the dungeon flamed with light;
My chains fell off, my heart was free,
I rose, went forth, and followed Thee.
My chains fell off, my heart was free,
I rose, went forth, and followed Thee.

5 No condemnation now I dread;
   Jesus, and all in Him, is mine!
   Alive in Him, my living Head,
   And clothed in righteousness Divine,
   Bold I approach the eternal throne,
   And claim the crown, through Christ my own.
   Bold I approach the eternal throne,
   And claim the crown, through Christ my own.

297

8.6.8.6.

1 "No condemnation!" precious word!
      Consider it, my soul!
   Thy sins were all on Jesus laid,
      His stripes have made thee whole.

2 In God's own presence now for us
      The Savior doth appear;
   The saints, as jewels on His heart,
      Jesus doth ever bear.

3 "No condemnation!" O my soul,
      'Tis God that speaks the word;
   Perfect in comeliness art thou
      In Christ, the risen Lord.

4 Teach me, O God, to fix mine eyes
      On Christ, the spotless Lamb,
   So shall I love Thy precious will,
      And glorify His name.

8.8.8.8. with chorus.

1 My hope is built on nothing less
Than Jesus Christ, my righteousness;
I dare not trust the sweetest frame,
But wholly lean on Jesus' name.

On Christ, the solid Rock, I stand;
All other ground is sinking sand,
All other ground is sinking sand.

2 When darkness veils His lovely face,
I rest on His unchanging grace;
In every high and stormy gale,
My anchor holds within the veil.

3 His oath, His covenant, His blood,
Support me in the whelming flood;
When all around my soul gives way,
He then is all my hope and stay.

4 When He shall come with trumpet sound,
Oh, may I then in Him be found;
In Him, my righteousness, alone,
Faultless to stand before the throne.

8.6.8.6.

1 A mind at perfect peace with God;
    O what a word is this!
  A sinner reconciled through blood;
    This, this indeed is peace.

2 By nature and by practice far,
    How very far from God;
  Yet now by grace brought nigh to Him,
    Through faith in Jesus' blood.

3 So nigh, so very nigh to God,
    I cannot nearer be;
  For in the person of His Son
    I am as near as He.

4 So dear, so very dear to God,
    More dear I cannot be;
  The love wherewith He loves the Son,
    Such is His love to me.

5 Why should I ever anxious be,
    Since such a God is mine?
  He watches o'er me night and day,
    And tells me "Mine is thine."

300

6.6.6.6.8.8.

1 Arise, my soul, arise!
Shake off thy guilty fears;
The bleeding Sacrifice
In my behalf appears.
Before the throne my Surety stands;
My name is written on His hands.

2 He ever lives above
For me to intercede,
His all-redeeming love,
His precious blood to plead.
His blood was shed for all our race,
And sprinkles now the throne of grace.

3 Five bleeding wounds He bears,
Received on Calvary;
They pour effectual prayers;
They strongly speak for me.
Forgive him, O forgive, they cry,
Nor let that ransomed sinner die!

4 The Father hears Him pray,
His dear anointed One;
He cannot turn away
The presence of His Son.
His Spirit answers to the blood,
And tells me I am born of God.

5 To God I'm reconciled,
His pardoning voice I hear;
He owns me for His child,
I can no longer fear.
With confidence I now draw nigh,
And Father, Abba, Father, cry.

9.8.9.8. with chorus.

1 Redeemed — how I love to proclaim it!
Redeemed by the blood of the Lamb;
Redeemed through His infinite mercy,
His child, and forever, I am.

Redeemed, redeemed,
Redeemed by the blood of the Lamb;
Redeemed, redeemed,
His child, and forever, I am.

2 Redeemed and so happy in Jesus,
No language my rapture can tell;
I know that the light of His presence
With me doth continually dwell.

3 I think of my blessed Redeemer,
I think of Him all the day long;
I sing, for I cannot be silent;
His love is the theme of my song.

4 I know I shall see in His beauty
The King in whose way I delight;
Who lovingly guardeth my footsteps,
And giveth me songs in the night.

8.6.8.6. with chorus.

1 I have a song I love to sing,
    Since I have been redeemed,
Of my Redeemer, Savior, King —
    Since I have been redeemed.

    Since I have been redeemed,
    Since I have been redeemed,
    I will glory in His name;
    Since I have been redeemed,
    I will glory in the Savior's name.

2 I have a Christ that satisfies,
    Since I have been redeemed,
To do His will my highest prize —
    Since I have been redeemed.

3 I have a witness bright and clear,
    Since I have been redeemed,
Dispelling every doubt and fear —
    Since I have been redeemed.

4 I have a joy I can't express,
    Since I have been redeemed,
All through the Lord, my righteousness —
    Since I have been redeemed.

5 I have a God who is for me,
    Since I have been redeemed,
With whom I'll dwell eternally —
    Since I have been redeemed.

12.11.12.11. with chorus.

1 Nor silver nor gold hath obtained my redemption;
No riches of earth could have saved my poor soul.
The blood of the cross is my only foundation;
The death of my Savior now maketh me whole.

I am redeemed, but not with silver;
I am bought, but not with gold;
Bought with a price — the blood of Jesus,
Precious price of love untold.

2 Nor silver nor gold hath obtained my redemption;
The guilt on my conscience too heavy had grown.
The blood of the cross is my only foundation;
The death of my Savior I only can own.

3 Nor silver nor gold hath obtained my redemption;
The holy commandment forbade me draw near.
The blood of the cross is my only foundation;
The death of my Savior removeth my fear.

4 Nor silver nor gold hath obtained my redemption;
The way to God's kingdom could not thus be bought.
The blood of the cross is my only foundation;
The death of my Savior redemption hath wrought.

304

10.10.10.10.10.10.

1 How should the Lord keep back His sword from blood?
"The soul that sinneth it shall surely die:"
But ah, can Justice make His counsels good?
Can Law bring in the glory from on high?
Grace must provide a Lamb — a Ransom find;
Redeem by One whom death no more may bind.

2 "One poor wise man" hath cried, O God, to Thee;
His blood is counted precious in Thy sight.
He liveth, and His name shall ever be
Thy praise, Thy glory, Thy supreme delight.
By Jesus' blood — that new and living way —
God's priests shall now within the holiest stay.

3 The blood of bulls and goats for ages failed
To purge the conscience, burdened sore with sins;
Thy precious blood, O Lamb of God, prevailed —
Through Thee, sweet Peace her endless reign begins.
Thy blood hath made redemption e'en for me;
Complete I stand, O risen Christ, in Thee.

4 The precious blood of Christ, it speaketh peace
To guilty sinners, groaning 'neath their load;
To captive spirits it proclaims release,
And Pharaoh's slaves become the "hosts of God."
His flesh is meat — His blood is drink indeed;
He died, He rose, His people's cause to plead.

5 Oh, precious blood! poured freely forth for me,
My sins are sunk beneath thy crimson tide.
No more before th' Avenger's sword I flee!
Christ is the Refuge-City, where I hide.
My life's dark page, blood-sprinkled, gleameth white;
My name shines forth in heaven in words of light.

Used by permission of The Overcomer Literature Trust, Ltd.

8.7.8.7. with chorus.

1 I will sing of my Redeemer,
    And His wondrous love to me;
  On the cruel cross He suffered,
    From the curse to set me free.

  Sing, oh, sing of my Redeemer,
    With His blood He purchased me,
  On the cross He sealed my pardon,
    Paid the debt, and made me free.

2 I will tell the wondrous story,
    How my lost estate to save,
  In His boundless love and mercy,
    He the ransom freely gave.

3 I will praise my dear Redeemer,
    His triumphant pow'r I'll tell,
  How the victory He giveth
    Over sin, and death, and hell.

4 I will sing of my Redeemer,
    And His heav'nly love to me;
  He from death to life hath brought me,
    Son of God with Him to be.

306

6.5.7.5.

1 I belong to Jesus;
I am not my own;
All I have and all I am
Shall be His alone.

2 I belong to Jesus;
He is Lord and King,
Reigning in my inmost heart
Over everything.

3 I belong to Jesus;
What can hurt or harm,
When He folds around my soul
His almighty Arm?

4 I belong to Jesus;
Blessed, blessed thought!
With His own most precious blood
Has my soul been bought.

5 I belong to Jesus;
He has died for me;
I am His and He is mine
Through eternity.

6 I belong to Jesus;
He will keep my soul,
If the deathly waters dark
Round about me roll.

7 I belong to Jesus;
And ere long I'll be
With my precious Savior there
In His royalty.

307

8.8.8.8.D.

1 On Calvary's brow my Savior died
'Twas there my Lord was crucified;
'Twas on the cross He bled for me,
And purchased there my pardon free.

Chorus:
O Calvary! dark Calvary!
Where Jesus shed His blood for me;
O Calvary! blest Calvary!
'Twas there my Savior died for me.

2 'Mid rending rocks and darkening skies
My Savior bows His head and dies;
The opening veil reveals the way
To life divine and endless day.

3 O Jesus, Lord, how can it be
That Thou shouldst give Thy life for me,
To bear the cross and agony
In that dread hour on Calvary!

BORN OF THE SPIRIT

308

9.10.9.9. with chorus.

1 Blessed assurance, Jesus is mine;
Oh, what a foretaste of glory divine!
Heir of salvation, purchase of God,
Born of His Spirit, washed in His blood.

This is my story, this is my song,
Praising my Savior all the day long.
This is my story, this is my song,
Praising my Savior all the day long.

2 Perfect submission, perfect delight,
Visions of rapture now burst on my sight;
Angels descending, bring from above
Echoes of mercy, whispers of love.

3 Perfect submission, all is at rest,
I in my Savior am happy and blest;
Watching and waiting, looking above,
Filled with His goodness, lost in His love.

309

12.8.12.8. with chorus.

1 What a wonderful change in my life has been wrought
  Since Jesus came into my heart!
I have light in my soul for which long I had sought,
  Since Jesus came into my heart!

     Since Jesus came into my heart!
     Since Jesus came into my heart!
  Floods of joy o'er my soul like the sea billows roll,
     Since Jesus came into my heart!

2 I have ceased from my wand'ring and going astray,
  Since Jesus came into my heart!
And my sins which were many are all washed away,
  Since Jesus came into my heart!

3 I'm possessed of a hope that is steadfast and sure,
  Since Jesus came into my heart!
And no dark clouds of doubt now my pathway obscure,
  Since Jesus came into my heart!

4 There's a light in the valley of death now for me,
  Since Jesus came into my heart!
And the gates of the City beyond I can see,
  Since Jesus came into my heart!

5 I shall go there to dwell in that City I know,
  Since Jesus came into my heart!
And I'm happy, so happy as onward I go,
  Since Jesus came into my heart!

ASSURANCE AND JOY OF SALVATION —
FREED BY THE LORD

Haldor Lillenas   10.9.10.9.D.

1   Once I was bound by sin's galling fetters,
    Chained like a slave I struggled in vain;
    But I received a glorious freedom,
    When Jesus broke my fetters in twain.

      Glorious freedom, wonderful freedom,
      No more in chains of sin I repine!
      Jesus the glorious Emancipator,
      Now and forever He shall be mine.

2   Freedom from all the carnal affections,
    Freedom from envy, hatred and strife;
    Freedom from vain and worldly ambitions,
    Freedom from all that saddened my life.

3   Freedom from pride and all sinful follies,
    Freedom from love and glitter of gold;
    Freedom from evil temper and anger,
    Glorious freedom, rapture untold.

4   Freedom from fear with all of its torments,
    Freedom from care with all of its pain;
    Freedom in Christ my blessed Redeemer,
    He who has rent my fetters in twain.

311

10.10.9.9. with chorus.

1 Naught have I gotten but what I received;
Grace hath bestowed it since I have believed;
Boasting excluded, pride I abase;
I'm only a sinner saved by grace!

　　Only a sinner saved by grace!
　　Only a sinner saved by grace!
　　This is my story, to God be the glory,
　　I'm only a sinner saved by grace!

2 Once I was foolish, and sin ruled my heart,
Causing my footsteps from God to depart;
Jesus hath found me, happy my case;
I now am a sinner saved by grace!

3 Tears unavailing, no merit had I;
Mercy had saved me, or else I must die;
Sin had alarmed me, fearing God's face;
But now I'm a sinner saved by grace!

4 Suffer a sinner whose heart overflows,
Loving his Savior to tell what he knows;
Once more to tell it, would I embrace —
I'm only a sinner saved by grace!

6.6.8.6. with chorus.

1   Grace! 'tis a charming sound,
      Harmonious to the ear;
   Heav'n with the echo shall resound,
      And all the earth shall hear.

         All sufficient grace!
            Never powerless!
         It is Christ who lives in me,
            In His exhaustlessness.

2   'Twas grace that wrote my name
      In life's eternal book;
   'Twas grace that gave me to the Lamb,
      Who all my sorrows took.

3   Grace taught my wandering feet
      To tread the pilgrim road;
   And new supplies each hour I meet
      While pressing on to God.

4   Grace taught my heart to pray,
      And made my eyes o'erflow;
   'Tis grace which kept me to this day,
      And will not let me go.

5   Grace all the work shall crown
      Through everlasting days;
   It lays in love the topmost stone,
      And well deserves the praise.

6   Oh, let that grace inspire
      My heart with strength divine;
   May all my powers to Thee aspire,
      And all my days be Thine.

313

8.6.8.6.

1 Amazing grace! how sweet the sound,
   That saved a wretch like me!
I once was lost, but now am found,
   Was blind, but now I see.

2 'Twas grace that taught my heart to fear,
   And grace my fears relieved;
How precious did that grace appear
   The hour I first believed!

3 The Lord hath promised good to me,
   His word my hope secures;
He will my shield and portion be
   As long as life endures.

4 When we've been there ten thousand years,
   Bright shining as the sun,
We've no less days to sing God's praise
   Than when we first begun.

314

8.7.8.7.D.

1 Sov'reign grace o'er sin abounding,
   Ransomed souls, the tidings swell;
'Tis a deep that knows no sounding,
   Who its breadth or length can tell?
On its glories, on its glories,
   Let my soul forever dwell!
On its glories, on its glories,
   Let my soul forever dwell!

2 What from Christ the soul can sever,
    Bound by everlasting bands?
  Once in Him, in Him forever,
    Thus th' eternal cov'nant stands.
  None shall pluck thee, none shall pluck thee
    From the Savior's mighty hands!
  None shall pluck thee, none shall pluck thee
    From the Savior's mighty hands!

3 Heirs of God, joint-heirs with Jesus,
    Long ere time its race begun;
  To His name eternal praises,
    O what wonders love has done!
  One with Jesus, one with Jesus,
    By eternal union one.
  One with Jesus, one with Jesus,
    By eternal union one.

4 On such love, my soul, still ponder,
    Love, so great, so rich, so free;
  Say, while lost in holy wonder,
    Why, O Lord, such love to me?
  Hallelujah! Hallelujah!
    Grace shall reign eternally!
  Hallelujah! Hallelujah!
    Grace shall reign eternally!

315

10.10.10.10. with chorus.

1 Saved to the uttermost, I am the Lord's;
Jesus my Savior salvation affords;
Gives me His Spirit a witness within,
Whisp'ring of pardon, and saving from sin.

Saved, saved, saved to the uttermost:
Saved, saved by power divine;
Saved, saved, I'm saved to the uttermost;
Jesus the Savior is mine!

2 Saved to the uttermost; Jesus is near;
Keeping me safely, He casteth out fear;
Trusting His promises, how I am blest;
Leaning upon Him, how sweet is my rest.

3 Saved to the uttermost: this I can say,
"Once all was darkness, but now it is day."
Beautiful visions of glory I see;
Jesus in brightness revealed unto me.

4 Saved to the uttermost: cheerfully sing
Loud hallelujahs to Jesus my King!
Ransomed and pardoned, redeemed by His blood,
Cleansed from unrighteousness, glory to God!

316

8.8.8.8.D.

1 Some day the silver cord will break,
And I no more as now shall sing;
But, O the joy when I shall wake
Within the presence of the King!

And I shall see Him face to face,
And tell the story, saved by grace:
And I shall see Him face to face,
And tell the story, saved by grace.

2   Some day my earthly house will fall,
I cannot tell how soon 'twill be,
But this I know — my All in all
Has now a place with Him for me.

3   Or some day when my Lord will come,
And called to meet Him I'll be blest,
He then will say to me, "Well done,"
And I shall enter into rest.

4   Some day, till then I'll watch and wait,
My lamp all trimmed and burning bright,
That when my Savior I will greet,
My faith will then be changed to sight.

6.6.6.6. with chorus.

317

1   Dear Savior, Thou art mine,
How sweet the thought to me;
Let me repeat Thy name,
And lift my heart to Thee.

Mine! Mine! Mine!
I know Thou art mine;
Savior, dear Savior,
I know Thou art mine.

2   Thou art the sinner's friend,
So I Thy friendship claim,
A sinner saved by grace,
When Thy sweet message came.

3   My hardened heart was touched;
Thy pard'ning voice I heard;
And joy and peace came in
While list'ning to Thy word.

4   So let me sing Thy praise,
So let me call Thee mine.
I cannot doubt Thy word,
I know that I am Thine.

8.7.8.7.D.

1 Precious Savior, Thou hast saved me;
Thine, and only Thine, I am:
Oh, the cleansing blood has reached me!
Glory, glory to the Lamb!

Glory, glory, hallelujah!
Glory, glory to the Lamb!
Oh, the cleansing blood has reached me!
Glory, glory to the Lamb!

2 Long my yearning heart was striving
To obtain this precious rest;
But, when all my struggles ended,
Simply trusting, I was blessed.

3 Trusting, trusting every moment;
Feeling now the blood applied;
Lying in the cleansing fountain,
Dwelling in my Savior's side.

4 Consecrated to Thy service,
I will live and die to Thee;
I will witness to Thy glory,
Of salvation, full and free.

5 Yes, I will stand up for Jesus,
He has sweetly saved my soul,
Cleansed my soul from sin's corruption,
Sanctified, and made me whole.

6 Glory to the Lord who bought me,
Glory for His saving power;
Glory to the Lord who keeps me,
Glory, glory evermore!

8.7.8.7.D.

1 Come, Thou Fount of every blessing,
　Tune my heart to sing Thy grace;
Streams of mercy, never ceasing,
　Call for songs of loudest praise.
Jesus sought me when a stranger,
　Wand'ring from the face of God;
He, to save my soul from danger,
　Interposed His precious blood.

2 O to grace how great a debtor
　Daily I'm constrained to be!
Let that grace, Lord, like a fetter,
　Bind my wand'ring heart to Thee.
Teach me, Lord, some rapturous measure,
　Meet for me Thy grace to prove,
While I sing the countless treasure
　Of my God's unchanging love.

3 Prone to wander, Lord, I feel it;
　Prone to leave the God I love:
Take my heart, oh, take and seal it
　With Thy Spirit from above.
Rescued thus from sin and danger,
　Purchased by the Savior's blood,
May I walk on earth a stranger,
　As a son and heir of God.

8.8.8.6. with chorus.

1 In loving-kindness Jesus came
   My soul in mercy to reclaim,
   And from the depths of sin and shame
   Through grace He lifted me.

   From sinking sand He lifted me,
   With tender hand He lifted me,
   From shades of night to plains of light,
   Oh, praise His name, He lifted me!

2 He called me long before I heard,
   Before my sinful heart was stirred,
   But when I took Him at His word,
   Forgiv'n, He lifted me.

3 His brow was pierced with many a thorn,
   His hands by cruel nails were torn,
   When from my guilt and grief, forlorn,
   In love He lifted me.

4 Now on a higher plane I dwell,
   And with my soul I know 'tis well;
   Yet how or why, I cannot tell,
   He should have lifted me.

8.7.8.7.8.7.

1 Full salvation! Full salvation!
    Lo, the fountain opened wide,
Streams through every land and nation
    From the Savior's wounded side.
Full salvation! Full salvation!
    Streams an endless crimson tide.

2 Oh, the glorious revelation!
    See the cleansing current flow,
Washing stains of condemnation
    Whiter than the driven snow:
Full salvation! Full salvation!
    Oh, the rapturous bliss to know.

3 Love's resistless current sweeping
    All the regions deep within;
Thought, and wish, and senses keeping
    Now, and every instant, clean:
Full salvation! Full salvation!
    From the guilt and power of sin.

4 Life immortal, Christ descending,
    Lo! my heart the Spirit's shrine:
God and man in oneness blending,
    Oh, what fellowship is mine!
Full salvation! Full salvation!
    Raised in Christ to life divine!

5 Care and doubting, gloom and sorrow,
    Fear and shame are mine no more;
Faith knows naught of dark tomorrow,
    For my Savior goes before:
Full salvation! Full salvation!
    Full and free for evermore!

11.7.11.7. with chorus.

1 Many weary years I vainly sought a spring,
　　One that never would run dry;
Unavailing all that earth to me could bring,
　　Nothing seemed to satisfy.

　　Drinking at the Fountain that never runs dry,
　　Drinking at the Fountain of life am I;
　　　Finding joy and pleasure
　　　In abounding measure,
　　I am drinking at the Fountain of life.

2 Through the desert land of sin I roam no more,
　　For I find a living Spring,
And my cup of gladness now is running o'er,
　　Jesus is my Lord and King.

3 Here is sweet contentment as the days go by,
　　Here is holy peace and rest;
Here is consolation as the moments fly,
　　Here my heart is always blest.

4 Here I find a never ending, sure supply,
　　While the endless ages roll;
To this healing Fountain I would ever fly,
　　There to bathe my weary soul.

8.6.8.6.D.

1 I heard the voice of Jesus say,
   "Come unto Me, and rest;
Lay down, thou weary one, lay down
   Thy head upon My breast."
I came to Jesus as I was,
   Weary, and worn, and sad;
I found in Him a resting-place,
   And He has made me glad.

2 I heard the voice of Jesus say,
   "Behold, I freely give
The living water: thirsty one,
   Stoop down, and drink, and live."
I came to Jesus, and I drank
   Of that life-giving stream;
My thirst was quenched, my soul revived,
   And now I live in Him.

3 I heard the voice of Jesus say,
   "I am this dark world's Light;
Look unto Me, thy morn shall rise,
   And all thy day be bright."
I looked to Jesus, and I found
   In Him my Star, my Sun;
And in that Light of life I'll walk
   Till trav'lling days are done.

ASSURANCE AND JOY OF SALVATION —
SATISFIED WITH CHRIST

324

Peculiar Meter.

1 Far away the noise of strife upon my ear
    is falling,
Then I know the sins of earth beset on every hand;
Doubt and fear and things of earth in vain to me
    are calling,
    None of these shall move me from Beulah Land.

I'm living on the mountain, underneath
    a cloudless sky,
I'm drinking at the fountain that never
    shall run dry;
O yes, I'm feasting on the manna from a
    bountiful supply,
    For I am dwelling in Beulah Land.

2 Far below the storm of doubt upon the world
    is beating,
Sons of men in battle long the enemy withstand;
Safe am I within the castle of God's word
    retreating,
    Nothing then can reach me, 'tis Beulah Land.

3 Let the stormy breezes blow, their cry cannot
    alarm me,
I am safely sheltered here, protected by God's hand;
Here the sun is always shining, here there's naught
    can harm me,
    I am safe forever in Beulah Land.

4 Viewing here the works of God, I sink in
    contemplation,
Hearing now His blessed voice, I see the way
    is planned;
Dwelling in the spirit, here I learn of full salvation,
    Gladly will I tarry in Beulah Land.

8.7.8.7.D.

325

1 All my life long I had panted
   For a draught from some cool spring,
That I hoped would quench the burning
   Of the thirst I felt within.

   Hallelujah! I have found Him
   Whom my soul so long has craved!
   Jesus satisfies my longings;
   Through His life I now am saved.

2 Feeding on the husks around me,
   Till my strength was almost gone,
Longed my soul for something better,
   Only still to hunger on.

3 Poor I was, and sought for riches,
   Something that would satisfy,
But the dust I gathered round me
   Only mocked my soul's sad cry.

4 Well of water, ever springing,
   Bread of life, so rich and free,
Untold wealth that never faileth,
   My Redeemer is to me.

SECURED BY DIVINE PROVISIONS

8.8.8.8.

326

1 He lives, the great Redeemer lives,
   What joy the blest assurance gives!
And now, before His Father, God,
   Pleads the full merits of His blood.

2 Repeated crimes awake our fears,
   And Justice armed with frowns appears;
But in the Savior's lovely face
   Sweet Mercy smiles, and all is peace.

continued

3 Hence, then, ye black, despairing thoughts;
Above our fears, above our faults,
His mighty intercessions rise,
And guilt recedes, and terror dies.

4 In every dark, distressful hour,
When sin and Satan join their power,
Let this dear hope repel the dart,
That Jesus bears us on His heart.

5 Great Advocate, almighty Friend!
On Him our humble hopes depend;
Our cause can never, never fail,
For Jesus pleads, and must prevail.

327   8.8.8.8.

1 Before the throne of God above
I have a strong, a perfect plea;
A great High Priest, whose Name is Love,
Who ever lives and pleads for me.

2 My name is graven on His hands,
My name is written on His heart;
I know that while with God He stands
No tongue can bid me thence depart.

3 When Satan tempts me to despair,
And tells me of the guilt within,
Upward I look, and see Him there
Who made an end of all my sin.

4 Because the sinless Savior died,
My sinful soul is counted free;
For God, the Just, is satisfied
To look on Him and pardon me.

5 Behold Him there, the risen Lamb!
My perfect, spotless Righteousness,
The great unchangeable I AM,
The King of glory and of grace.

6 One with Himself, I cannot die;
My soul is purchased by His blood;
My life is hid with Christ on high,
With Christ, my Savior and my God.

328

8.8.8.8.D.

1 Complete in Thee! no work of mine
May take, dear Lord, the place of Thine;
Thy blood hath pardon bought for me,
And I am now complete in Thee.

Yea, justified! O blessed thought!
And sanctified! Salvation wrought!
Thy blood hath pardon bought for me,
And glorified, I too, shall be!

2 Complete in Thee — no more shall sin,
Thy grace hath conquered, reign within;
Thy voice shall bid the tempter flee,
And I shall stand complete in Thee.

3 Complete in Thee — each want supplied,
And no good thing to me denied;
Since Thou my portion, Lord, wilt be,
I ask no more, complete in Thee.

4 Dear Savior! when before Thy bar
All tribes and tongues assembled are,
Among Thy chosen will I be,
At Thy right hand — complete in Thee.

329

6.10.10.6.

1   Blessed be God, our God,
Who gave for us His well-beloved Son,
The gift of gifts, all other gifts in one;
    Blessed be God, our God!

2   What will He not bestow!
Who freely gave this mighty gift unbought,
Unmerited, unheeded, and unsought,
    What will He not bestow?

3   He sparèd not His Son!
'Tis this that silences each rising fear,
'Tis this that bids the hard thought disappear;
    He sparèd not His Son!

4   Who shall condemn us now?
Since Christ has died, and ris'n, and gone above,
For us to plead at the right hand of Love;
    Who shall condemn us now?

5   'Tis God that justifies!
Who shall recall His pardon or His grace?
Or who the broken chain of guilt replace?
    'Tis God that justifies!

6   The victory is ours!
For us in might came forth the mighty One;
For us He fought the fight, the triumph won:
    The victory is ours!

8.6.8.6.D.

1 My faith has found a resting place,
   Not in device nor creed;
   I trust the Ever-living One,
   His wounds for me shall plead.

   I need no other argument,
   I need no other plea;
   It is enough that Jesus died,
   And that He died for me.

2 Enough for me that Jesus saves,
   This ends my fear and doubt;
   A sinful soul I come to Him,
   He'll never cast me out.

3 My heart is leaning on the Word,
   The written Word of God,
   Salvation by my Savior's name,
   Salvation through His blood.

4 My great Physician heals the sick,
   The lost He came to save;
   For me His precious blood He shed,
   For me His life He gave.

10.9.10.9. with chorus.

1 Will your anchor hold in the storms of life,
When the clouds unfold their wings of strife?
When the strong tides lift, and the cables strain,
Will your anchor drift or firm remain?

We have an anchor that keeps the soul
Stedfast and sure while the billows roll,
Fastened to the Rock which cannot move,
Grounded firm and deep in the Savior's love.

2 It is safely moored, 'twill the storm withstand,
For 'tis well secured by the Savior's hand;
And the cables passed from His heart to mine,
Can defy the blast, through strength divine.

3 It will firmly hold in the straits of fear,
When the breakers have told the reef is near;
Though the tempest rave and the wild winds blow,
Not an angry wave shall our bark o'erflow.

4 It will surely hold in the floods of death,
When the waters cold chill our latest breath;
On the rising tide it can never fail,
While our hopes abide within the veil.

6.6.8.6.

1   I hear the words of love,
     I gaze upon the blood,
     I see the mighty sacrifice,
     And I have peace with God.

2   'Tis everlasting peace!
     Sure as Jehovah's Name,
     'Tis stable as His steadfast throne,
     For evermore the same.

3   The clouds may go and come,
     And storms may sweep my sky;
     This blood-sealed friendship changes not,
     The Cross is ever nigh.

4   My love is ofttimes low,
     My joy still ebbs and flows,
     But peace with Him remains the same,
     No change my Savior knows.

5   I change, He changes not;
     The Christ can never die;
     His love, not mine, the resting-place,
     His truth, not mine, the tie.

6   The Cross still stands unchanged,
     Though heaven is now His home;
     The mighty stone is rolled away,
     But yonder is His tomb!

7   And yonder is my peace,
     The grave of all my woes!
     I know the Son of God has come,
     I know He died and rose.

8   I know He liveth now
     At God's right hand above;
     I know the throne on which He sits,
     I know His truth and love!

8.6.8.6. with chorus.

1 I know not why God's wondrous grace
   To me He hath made known,
   Nor why, unworthy, Christ in love
   Redeemed me for His own.

   But "I know Whom I have believèd
   And am persuaded that He is able
   To keep that which I've committed
   Unto Him against that day."

2 I know not how this saving faith
   To me He did impart,
   Nor how believing in His word
   Wrought peace within my heart.

3 I know not how the Spirit moves,
   Convincing men of sin,
   Revealing Jesus through the Word,
   Creating faith in Him.

4 I know not what of good or ill
   May be reserved for me,
   Of weary ways or golden days,
   Before His face I see.

5 I know not when my Lord may come,
   At night or noon-day fair,
   Nor if I'll walk the vale with Him,
   Or "meet Him in the air."

11.8.11.8. with chorus.

1 A wonderful Savior is Jesus my Lord,
   A wonderful Savior to me;
He hideth my soul in the cleft of the rock,
   Where rivers of pleasure I see.

   He hideth my soul in the cleft of the rock
      That shadows a dry, thirsty land;
   He hideth my life in the depths of His love,
      And covers me there with His hand,
      And covers me there with His hand.

2 A wonderful Savior is Jesus my Lord,
   He taketh my burden away;
He holdeth me up and I shall not be moved,
   He giveth me strength as my day.

3 With numberless blessings each moment He crowns,
   And, filled with His fulness divine,
I sing in my rapture, oh, glory to God,
   For such a Redeemer as mine!

4 When clothed in His brightness, transported I rise
   To meet Him in clouds of the sky,
His perfect salvation, His wonderful love,
   I'll shout with the millions on high.

HE'S A WONDERFUL SAVIOUR TO ME

Virgil P. Brock   11.9.11.9. with chorus.

1 I was lost in sin but Jesus rescued me,
   He's a wonderful Savior to me;
I was bound by fear but Jesus set me free,
   He's a wonderful Savior to me.

   For He's a wonderful Savior to me,
     He's a wonderful Savior to me;
   I was lost in sin, but Jesus took me in,
     He's a wonderful Savior to me.

2 He's a Friend so true, so patient and so kind,
   He's a wonderful Savior to me;
Everything I need in Him I always find,
   He's a wonderful Savior to me.

3 He is always near to comfort and to cheer,
   He's a wonderful Savior to me;
He forgives my sins, He dries my every tear,
   He's a wonderful Savior to me.

4 Dearer grows the love of Jesus day by day,
   He's a wonderful Savior to me;
Sweeter is His grace while pressing on my way,
   He's a wonderful Savior to me.

10.10.10.10.

1 Jesus has loved me, wonderful Savior!
Jesus has loved me, I cannot tell why;
Came He to rescue sinners all worthless;
My heart He conquered, for Him I would die.

Glory to Jesus, wonderful Savior!
Glory to Jesus, the One I adore;
Glory to Jesus, wonderful Savior!
Glory to Jesus, and praise evermore.

2 Jesus has saved me, wonderful Savior!
Jesus has saved me, I cannot tell how;
All that I know is He was my ransom,
Dying on Calv'ry with thorns on His brow.

3 Jesus will lead me, wonderful Savior!
Jesus will lead me, I cannot tell where;
But I will follow, through joy or sorrow,
Sunshine or tempest, sweet peace or despair.

4 Jesus will crown me, wonderful Savior!
Jesus will crown me, I cannot tell when;
His throne of splendor hail I with gladness,
Crowned with the glory of God among men.

337

8.7.8.7.D.

1 I will sing the wondrous story
   Of the Christ who died for me,
How He left His home in glory
   For the cross of Calvary.

   Yes, I'll sing the wondrous story
      Of the Christ who died for me,
   Sing it in the light of glory,
      Sing it through eternity.

2 I was lost, but Jesus found me,
      Found the sheep that went astray,
   Threw His loving arms around me,
      Drew me back into His way.

3 I was bruised, but Jesus healed me;
      Faint was I from many a fall;
   Sight was gone, and fears possessed me,
      But He freed me from them all.

4 Days of darkness still come o'er me,
      Sorrow's paths I often tread,
   But the Savior still is with me;
      By His hand I'm safely led.

5 He will keep me till the rapture,
      Day by day He'll wash my feet,
   And will transform all my nature
      That in glory we may meet.

8.10.10.10.

1   Wounded for me, wounded for me,
There on the cross He was wounded for me;
Gone my transgressions, and now I am free,
All because Jesus was wounded for me.

2   Dying for me, dying for me,
There on the cross He was dying for me;
Now in His death my redemption I see,
All because Jesus was dying for me.

3   Risen for me, risen for me,
Up from the grave He has risen for me;
Now evermore from death's sting I am free,
All because Jesus has risen for me.

4   Living for me, living for me,
Up in the skies He is living for me;
Daily He's pleading and praying for me,
All because Jesus is living for me.

5   Coming for me, coming for me,
Soon in the air He is coming for me;
Then with what joy His dear face I shall see,
Oh, how I praise Him! He's coming for me.

11.11.11.11.

1 How firm a foundation, ye saints of the Lord,
Is laid for your faith in His excellent word!
What more can He say than to you He hath said,
To you who for refuge to Jesus have fled?

2 "Fear not, I am with thee, O be not dismayed,
For I am thy God, and will still give thee aid;
I'll strengthen thee, help thee, and cause thee to
stand,
Upheld by My righteous, omnipotent hand.

3 "When through the deep waters I call thee to go,
The rivers of sorrow shall not overflow;
For I will be with thee, thy troubles to bless,
And sanctify to thee thy deepest distress.

4 "When through fiery trials thy pathway shall lie,
My grace, all sufficient, shall be thy supply;
The flame shall not hurt thee; I only design
Thy dross to consume, and thy gold to refine.

5 "E'en down to old age all My people shall prove
My sovereign, eternal, unchangeable love;
And then, when grey hairs shall their temples adorn,
Like lambs they shall still in My bosom be borne.

6 "The soul that on Jesus hath leaned for repose,
I will not, I will not desert to his foes;
That soul, though all hell should endeavor to shake,
I'll never, no, never, no, never forsake!"

11.11.11.9. with chorus.

1 Standing on the promises of Christ my King,
Through eternal ages let His praises ring,
Glory in the highest, I will shout and sing,
   Standing on the promises of God.

   Standing, standing,
   Standing on the promises of God my Savior;
   Standing, standing,
   I'm standing on the promises of God.

2 Standing on the promises that cannot fail,
When the howling storms of doubt and fear assail,
By the living Word of God I shall prevail,
   Standing on the promises of God.

3 Standing on the promises I now can see
Perfect, present cleansing in the blood for me;
Standing in the liberty where Christ makes free,
   Standing on the promises of God.

4 Standing on the promises of Christ the Lord,
Bound to Him eternally by love's strong cord,
Overcoming daily with the Spirit's sword,
   Standing on the promises of God.

5 Standing on the promises I shall not fall,
List'ning every moment to the Spirit's call.
Resting in my Savior as my All in all,
   Standing on the promises of God.

341

11.8.11.9. with chorus.

1 When peace like a river attendeth my way,
   When sorrows like sea billows roll;
Whatever my lot Thou hast taught me to say,
   "It is well, it is well with my soul!"

      It is well with my soul!
      It is well, it is well with my soul!

2 Though Satan should buffet, though trials should come,
   Let this blest assurance control,
That Christ hath regarded my helpless estate,
   And hath shed His own blood for my soul.

3 My sin — oh, the bliss of this glorious thought —
   My sin, not in part, but the whole,
Is nailed to His Cross, and I bear it no more;
   Praise the Lord, praise the Lord, O my soul!

4 For me, be it Christ, be it Christ hence to live;
   If dark hours about me shall roll,
No pang shall be mine, for in death as in life
   Thou wilt whisper Thy peace to my soul.

342

9.9.9.4. with chorus.

1   Years I spent in vanity and pride,
      Caring not my Lord was crucified,
      Knowing not it was for me He died
            On Calvary.

         Mercy there was great, and grace was free;
         Pardon there was multiplied to me;
         There my burdened soul found liberty,
               At Calvary.

2   By God's Word at last my sin I learned;
      Then I trembled at the law I'd spurned,
      Till my guilty soul imploring turned
            To Calvary.

3 Now I've giv'n to Jesus everything,
   Now I gladly own Him as my King,
   Now my raptured soul can only sing
      Of Calvary.

4 Oh, the love that drew salvation's plan!
   Oh, the grace that brought it down to man!
   Oh, the mighty gulf that God did span
      At Calvary!

9.6.8.6. with chorus.   **343**

1 There is sunshine in my soul today,
      More glorious and bright
   Than glows in any earthly sky,
      For Jesus is my light.

   O there's sunshine, blessed sunshine,
   While the peaceful, happy moments roll;
   When Jesus shows His smiling face
   There is sunshine in my soul.

2 There is music in my soul today,
      A carol to my King;
   And Jesus, listening, can hear
      The song I cannot sing.

3 There is springtime in my soul today,
      For when the Lord is near
   The dove of peace sings in my heart,
      The flowers of grace appear.

4 There is gladness in my soul today,
      And hope, and praise, and love,
   For blessings which He gives me now,
      For joys laid up above.

344

9.9.9.4.

Grace there is my every debt to pay,
Blood to wash my every sin away,
Pow'r to keep me spotless day by day,
In Christ for me.

Used by permission of The Salvation Army Musical Board.

345

8.6.8.6. with chorus.

1 I wandered in the shades of night,
Till Jesus came to me,
And with the sunlight of His love
Bid all my darkness flee.

Sunlight, sunlight, in my soul today,
Sunlight, sunlight, all along the way,
Since the Savior found me, took away my sin,
I have had the sunlight of His love within.

2 Though clouds may gather in the sky,
And billows 'round me roll,
However dark the world may be,
I've sunlight in my soul.

3 While walking in the light of God,
I sweet communion find;
I press with holy vigor on
And leave the world behind.

4 Soon I shall see Him as He is,
The Light that came to me;
Behold the brightness of His face,
Throughout eternity.

8.8.8.7.

1 I am not skilled to understand
What God hath willed, what God hath planned;
I only know at His right hand
     Stands One who is my Savior.

2 I take Him at His word indeed:
"Christ died for sinners" — this I read;
For in my heart I find a need
     Of Him to be my Savior!

3 That He should leave His place on high
And come for sinful man to die,
You count it strange? So once did I
     Before I knew my Savior!

4 And, oh, that He fulfilled may see
The travail of His soul in me,
And with His work contented be,
     As I with my dear Savior!

5 Yes, living, dying, let me bring
My strength, my solace from this spring —
That He who lives to be my King
     Once died to be my Savior!

347 8.8.8.8. with chorus.

1 O happy day that fixed my choice
On Thee, my Savior and my God!
Well may this glowing heart rejoice,
And tell its raptures all abroad.

Happy day, happy day,
When Jesus washed my sins away!
He taught me how to watch and pray,
And live rejoicing every day;
Happy day, happy day,
When Jesus washed my sins away!

2 'Tis done — the great transaction's done;
I am my Lord's, and He is mine;
He drew me and I followed on,
Rejoiced to own the call divine.

3 Now rest, my long-divided heart,
Fixed on this blissful center, rest;
Here have I found a nobler part,
Here heav'nly pleasures fill my breast.

4 High heav'n that hears the solemn vow,
That vow renewed shall daily hear!
Till in life's latest hour I bow,
And bless, in death, a bond so dear.

348 8.8.8.8.D.

1 Since Christ my soul from sin set free,
This life has been a joy to me;
And 'mid earth's sorrows and its woe,
'Tis joy my Jesus here to know.

O hallelujah, yes, 'tis joy!
For it is Christ that I enjoy!
On land or sea, what matters where?
Where Jesus is, my joy is there.

2 The earth was once a bitter place
Till Jesus showed His smiling face;
Now joy's begun within my soul,
'Twill last while endless ages roll.

3 What matters where on earth we dwell?
On mountain top, or in the dell,
In cottage, or a mansion fair,
Where Jesus is, my joy is there.

LONGINGS — FOR GOD

8.6.8.6. **349**

1 As pants the hart for cooling streams
When heated in the chase,
So longs my soul, O God, for Thee,
And Thy refreshing grace.

2 Why restless, why cast down, my soul?
Trust God, who will employ
His aid for thee, and change these sighs
To thankful hymns of joy.

3 For Thee, my God, the living God,
My thirsty soul doth pine;
Oh, when shall I behold Thy face,
Thou Majesty Divine?

4 God of my strength, how long shall I,
Like one forgotten, mourn,
Forlorn, forsaken, and exposed
To my oppressor's scorn?

5 Why restless, why cast down, my soul?
Hope still, and thou shalt sing
The praise of Him who is thy God,
Thy health's eternal spring.

LONGINGS — FOR GOD

350

10.10.10.10.

1 My goal is God Himself, not joy, nor peace,
Nor even blessing, but Himself, my God;
'Tis His to lead me there — not mine, but His —
At any cost, dear Lord, by any road.

2 So faith bounds forward to its goal in God,
And love can trust her Lord to lead her there;
Upheld by Him, my soul is following hard
Till God hath full fulfilled my deepest prayer.

3 No matter if the way be sometimes dark,
No matter though the cost be oft-times great,
He knoweth how I best shall reach the mark,
The way that leads to Him must needs be strait.

4 One thing I know, I cannot say Him nay;
One thing I do, I press towards my Lord;
My God my glory here, from day to day,
And in the glory there my great Reward.

LONGINGS — FOR GOD AS LIFE

351

10.10.10.10.

1 God the Almighty, Uncreated Life,
List to my cry as I lie in the dust,
Fathomless glory all about Thee is;
Life Giver, my Creator, know Thee I must.

2 Oh, by the Cross, the passion of Thy Christ,
Oh, by the death of my Lord crucified,
From pow'r of darkness translate me today
Into the kingdom of Thy light to abide.

3 Fill from the center with Thine utmost filling,
Fill to circumf'rence, fill right to the brim;
Blaze forth, the light, the glory of Thy being
About and 'round me to the uttermost rim.

4 Life Uncreated, Thou most holy God,
Life-giving Spirit, oh, create in me
Something that speaks of Thee and of Thy glory,
Something compelling that will draw to Thee.

5 Father, I thank Thee that my quest is ended.
I reign in life with Christ upon the throne,
How satisfied to triumph now in Him,
The Cross the touchstone that makes me His own.

7.7.7.7.   **352**

1 In the wilderness for God!
Just a common bush aflame!
Thus may I be, blessed Lord,
For the glory of Thy Name.

2 Just a common bush to be,
Something in which God can dwell,
Something thru which God can speak,
Something thru which God can tell,

3 All His yearning over men,
All His purposes of love,
Flaming with no light of earth,
But with glory from above:

4 God Himself within the bush,
Nothing seen but just the flame;
Make me that, just that, O God,
For the glory of Thy Name.

353 I NEED JESUS

George O. Webster   Peculiar Meter.

1 I need Jesus, my need I now confess;
No friend like Him in times of deep distress;
I need Jesus, the need I gladly own;
Though some may bear their load alone,
    Yet I need Jesus.

    I need Jesus, I need Jesus,
      I need Jesus every day;
    Need Him in the sunshine hour,
    Need Him when the storm-clouds low'r;
    Every day along my way,
      Yes, I need Jesus.

2 I need Jesus, I need a friend like Him,
A friend to guide when paths of life are dim;
I need Jesus, when foes my soul assail;
Alone I know I can but fail,
    So I need Jesus.

3 I need Jesus, I need Him to the end;
No one like Him, He is the sinner's friend;
I need Jesus, no other friend will do;
So constant, kind, so strong and true,
    Yes, I need Jesus.

354   10.10.10.10.

1 Come in, O come! the door stands open now;
I knew Thy voice; Lord Jesus, it was Thou.
The sun has set long since; the storms begin;
'Tis time for Thee, my Savior, O come in!

2 Alas, ill-ordered shows the dreary room;
The household stuff lies heaped amidst the gloom,
The table empty stands, the couch undressed;
Ah, what a welcome for th' Eternal Guest!

3   Yet welcome, and tonight; this doleful scene
    Is e'en itself my cause to hail Thee in;
    This dark confusion e'en at once demands
    Thine own bright presence, Lord, and ord'ring hands.

4   I seek no more to alter things, or mend,
    Before the coming of so great a Friend;
    All were at best unseemly; and 'twere ill
    Beyond all else to keep Thee waiting still.

5   Come, not to find, but make this troubled heart
    A dwelling worthy of Thee as Thou art;
    To chase the gloom, the terror, and the sin:
    Come, all Thyself, yea come, Lord Jesus, in!

6.6.8.6.   **355**

1   O blessed, living Lord,
      Engage our hearts with Thee,
   And strike within some answ'ring chord
      To love so rich and free!

2   To know Thy loving heart!
      To cleave to Thy blest side!
   To gaze upon Thee where Thou art,
      And in Thy love abide!

3   To walk with Thee below!
      To learn Thy holy ways!
   And more to Thine own stature grow,
      To Thine eternal praise!

4   Thyself our one Desire!
      Thyself our Object here!
   The goal to which our hearts aspire —
      To meet Thee in the air!

6.6.8.6.

1 Thou Magnet of my soul!
   Let me come nearer, till
The life of self pulsates no more,
   But is forever still.

2 Thou Sunshine of my heart!
   Fill Thou each crevice there,
And let Thy garden yield to Thee
   A fragrance sweet and rare.

3 Thou Ransomer from death!
   Possess Thy ransomed one:
Appropriate to Thine Own use
   The spoil that Thou hast won.

4 Thou Lord of Life and Light!
   I bow beneath Thy sway,
And count it holy privilege
   Thy precepts to obey.

5 Thou Gift unspeakable!
   Straight from God's heart of love;
I break my heart to give Thee room
   And thus Thy sweetness prove.

8.8.6.8.8.6.

1 Come, Jesus, Lord, with holy fire,
  Come, and my quickened heart inspire,
    My conscience purged by blood;
  Now to my soul Thyself reveal,
  Thy mighty working let me feel,
    Since I am born of God.

2 Let nothing now my heart divide,
  Since with Thee I am crucified,
    And live to God in Thee.
  Dead to the world and all its toys,
  Its idle pomp and fading joys,
    Jesus, my glory be.

3 Now with a quenchless thirst inspire,
  A longing, infinite desire,
    And fill my craving heart.
  Less than Thyself, oh, do not give,
  In might Thyself within me live;
    Come, all Thou hast and art.

4 My will be swallowed up in Thee,
  Light in Thy light still may I see
    In Thine unclouded face:
  Called the full strength of trust to prove,
  Let all my quickened heart be love,
    My spotless life be praise.

358

8.7.8.7.D.

1 Love Divine, all love excelling,
   Joy of heav'n, to earth come down;
Fix in us Thy humble dwelling,
   All Thy faithful mercies crown.
Jesus, Thou art all compassion;
   Pure, unbounded love Thou art;
Visit us with Thy salvation,
   Enter every trembling heart.

2 Breathe, O breathe Thy loving Spirit
   Into every troubled breast;
Let us all in Thee inherit,
   Let us find the promised rest.
Take away the love of sinning;
   Alpha and Omega be;
End of faith, as its beginning,
   Set our hearts at liberty.

3 Come, Almighty, to deliver,
   Let us all Thy life receive;
May Thy presence e'er be with us,
   Never more Thy temples leave.
Thee we would be always blessing,
   Serve Thee as Thou wouldst approve,
Pray, and praise Thee without ceasing,
   Glory in Thy perfect love.

4 Finish, then, Thy new creation;
   Pure and spotless let us be;
Let us see Thy great salvation
   Perfectly restored in Thee;
Changed from glory into glory
   Till with Thee we take our place,
Till we cast our crowns before Thee,
   Lost in wonder, love and praise.

6.6.6.6. with chorus.

1 O Light of light, shine in!
  Cast out this night of sin,
Create true day within:
  O Light of light, shine in!

  O Light, all light excelling,
    Make my heart Thy dwelling;
  O Joy, all grief dispelling,
    To my poor heart come in!

2 O Joy of joys, come in!
  End Thou this grief of sin,
Create calm peace within:
  O Joy of joys, come in!

3 O Life of life, pour in!
  Expel this death of sin,
Awake true life within:
  O Life of life, pour in!

4 O Love of love, flow in!
  This hateful root of sin
Deal with, renew, within:
  O Love of love, flow in!

5 O Heaven of heavens, descend!
  This cloudy curtain rend,
And all earth's turmoil end:
  O Heaven of heavens, descend!

6 My God and Lord, O come!
  Of joys the Joy and Sum,
Make in this heart Thy home:
  My God and Lord, O come!

360

6.6.8.6.

1 O Everlasting Light,
  Shine graciously within;
 Brightest of all on earth that's bright,
  Come, shine away my sin.

2 O Everlasting Truth,
  Truest of all that's true,
 Sure guide of erring age or youth,
  Lead me, and teach me too.

3 O Everlasting Strength,
  Uphold me in the way;
 Bring me, in spite of foes, at length
  To joy and light of day.

4 O Everlasting Love,
  Wellspring of grace and peace,
 Pour down Thy fulness from above,
  Bid doubt and trouble cease.

5 O Everlasting Rest,
  Lift off life's load of care;
 Relieve, revive this burdened breast
  And every sorrow bear.

6 Thou art in heaven our all,
  Our all on earth art Thou;
 Upon Thy glorious Name we call,
  Lord Jesus, bless us now.

8.8.8.8.

1 O Love divine, by Christ revealed,
Incarnate Love that died for me,
To Thee myself I gladly yield,
I consecrate my all to Thee.

2 O Light divine, by Christ displayed,
Source of all light, who flesh became,
Shed Thy bright beams upon my head,
Burn in my heart a constant flame.

3 O Truth divine, by Christ made known,
All truth must Thy reflection be;
Within my heart set up Thy throne,
And in Thy freedom make me free.

4 O Cross divine, by Christ endured,
Thou cross on which He groaned and died,
And man's redemption thus secured,
In Thy blest shadow let me hide.

5 O Peace divine, by Christ bestowed,
Thy heavenly dove to earth come down,
May He within make His abode,
My life with His dear presence crown.

6 O Joy divine, by Christ possessed,
For which He did the cross endure,
Fill with Thyself and make me blest,
Contented, restful and secure.

362

8.6.8.6. with chorus.

1 He died for me that I might live;
   I live for Him who died,
My life, my love to Him I give —
   Jesus, the Crucified.

   O Jesus, my Lord and Savior,
   Help me to fully follow Thee
   In life and death and loving service,
   As Thou hast lived and died for me.

2 He died for me that I might die
   To Satan, self, and sin;
O death so deep! O life so high!
   Help me to enter in.

3 He lives for me that I may live
   As spotless e'en as He;
Savior, to me Thy nature give,
   And live Thy life in me.

4 He lives for me that I may give
   His love to hearts that pine;
Let me like Him for others live,
   And trace His steps divine.

Used by permission of Christian Publications, Inc., Harrisburg, Pa.

363

11.10.11.10.D.

1 Lord, I would have Thyself in all Thy beauty,
Take Thou control of all my life just now;
In Thee to live, and move, and have my being,
With full abandon, Lord, to Thee I bow.

   Thy blood was shed to cleanse from sin, Lord Jesus,
   Thy risen life transforms the old to new;
   I take my stand upon Thy word of promise:
   Sin shall not have dominion over you!

2 Show me the things of which I am unconscious,
Lord, put Thy finger now upon my heart;
Whisper to me, through Thy blest Holy Spirit,
Tell me what grieves Him, that it may depart.

3 Thou art my Victor over keen temptation,
Thou art my Shield, to meet the darts of sin;
Lord Jesus, Thou alone can keep me trusting,
And living out Thy glorious life within.

8.6.8.6. **364**

1 Jesus, my life, Thyself apply;
Thy Holy Spirit breathe;
My vile affections crucify;
Conform me to Thy death.

2 Conqu'ror of hell and earth and sin,
Still with the rebel strive;
Enter my soul and work within,
And kill and make alive.

3 More of Thy life, and more I have,
As the old Adam dies;
Bury me, Savior, in Thy grave,
That I with Thee may rise.

4 Reign in me, Lord; Thy foes control,
Who would not own Thy sway;
Diffuse Thine image through my soul;
Shine to the perfect day.

5 Scatter the last remains of sin,
And seal me Thine abode;
O make me glorious all within,
A temple built by God!

6.6.4.6.4.

1 Jesus, Thy life is mine,
   Dwell evermore in me;
      And let me see
   That nothing can untwine
      Thy life from mine.

2 Thy life in me be shown,
   Lord, I would henceforth seek
      To think and speak
   Thy thoughts, Thy words alone,
      No more my own.

3 Thy love, Thy joy, Thy peace,
   Continuously impart
      Unto my heart,
   Fresh springs that never cease,
      But still increase.

4 The blest reality
   Of resurrection power,
      Thy Church's dower,
   Life more abundantly,
      Lord, give to me.

5 Thy fullest gift, O Lord,
   Now at Thy word I claim,
      Through Thy dear Name,
   And touch the rapturous chord
      Of praise forth-poured.

6   Jesus, my life is Thine,
    And evermore shall be
    Hidden in Thee,
    For nothing can untwine
    Thy life from mine.

7.7.7.7.7.7.   **366**

1   Christ, whose glory fills the skies
    Christ, the true, the only Light,
    Sun of Righteousness, arise,
    Triumph o'er the shades of night;
    Dayspring from on high, be near,
    Daystar, in my heart appear.

2   Dark and cheerless is the morn
    Unaccompanied by Thee;
    Joyless is the day's return,
    Till Thy mercy's beams I see,
    Till Thou inward light impart,
    Glad my eyes, and warm my heart.

3   Visit then this soul of mine,
    Pierce the gloom of sin and grief;
    Fill me, Radiancy divine,
    Scatter all my unbelief;
    More and more Thyself display,
    Shining to the perfect day.

367

8.6.8.6.

1 Be Thou supreme, O Jesus Christ,
    Nor creed, nor form, nor word,
Nor holy Church, nor human love,
    Compare with Thee, my Lord!

2 Be Thou supreme, O Jesus Christ,
    Thy love has conquered me;
Beneath Thy Cross I die to self,
    And live alone to Thee.

3 Be Thou supreme, O Jesus Christ,
    My inmost being fill;
So shall I think as Thou dost think,
    And will as Thou dost will.

4 Be Thou supreme, O Jesus Christ,
    Thy life transfigure mine;
And through this veil of mortal flesh,
    Lord, let Thy splendor shine.

5 Be Thou supreme, O Jesus Christ,
    My soul exults in Thee;
To be Thy slave, to do Thy will,
    Is my felicity.

6.4.6.4.6.6.4.4.

1 More love to Thee, O Lord,
    More love to Thee!
  Hear Thou the prayer I make
    On bended knee;
  This is my earnest plea:
    More love, O Lord, to Thee,
  More love to Thee,
    More love to Thee!

2 Once earthly joy I craved,
    Sought peace and rest;
  Now Thee alone I seek,
    Give what is best;
  This all my prayer shall be:
    More love, O Lord, to Thee,
  More love to Thee,
    More love to Thee!

3 Let sorrow do its work,
    Send grief and pain;
  Sweet are Thy messengers,
    Sweet their refrain,
  When they can sing with me,
    More love, O Lord, to Thee,
  More love to Thee,
    More love to Thee!

4 Then shall my latest breath
    Whisper Thy praise;
  This be the parting cry
    My heart shall raise;
  This still its prayer shall be:
    More love, O Lord, to Thee,
  More love to Thee,
    More love to Thee!

369

8.7.8.7.D. with chorus.

1 Let me love Thee, Thou art claiming
Every feeling of my soul;
Let that love in pow'r prevailing,
Render Thee my life, my all;
For life's burdens they are easy,
And life's sorrows lose their sting,
If they're carried, Lord, to please Thee,
If their pain Thy smile should win.

Let me love Thee, Savior,
Take my heart forever;
Nothing but Thy favor
My soul can satisfy.

2 Let me love Thee, come revealing
All Thy love has done for me;
Help my heart, so unbelieving,
By the sight of Calvary:
Let me see Thy love despising
All the shame my sins had brought;
By Thy torments realizing
What a price my pardon bought.

3 Let me love Thee, I am gladdest
When I'm loving Thee, the best;
For in sunshine or in sadness
I can find in Thee a rest;
But without Thee life is fading,
Treasureless its choicest flowers;
Taken are its gifts eternal;
Left, its empty passing hours.

4 Let me love Thee, love is mighty,
Swaying realms of deed and thought;
By it I shall walk uprightly,
I shall serve Thee as I ought:

LONGINGS — FOR LOVE TO CHRIST

Love will soften every sorrow,
Love will lighten every care,
Love unquestioning will follow,
Love will triumph, love will dare.

LONGINGS — FOR FELLOWSHIP WITH CHRIST

10.10.10.10.   **370**

1 Abide with me! fast falls the eventide;
   The darkness deepens; Lord, with me abide!
   When other helpers fail and comforts flee,
   Help of the helpless, oh, abide with me.

2 Swift to its close ebbs out life's little day;
   Earth's joys grow dim, its glories pass away;
   Change and decay in all around I see;
   O Thou who changest not, abide with me.

3 Come not in terrors, as the King of kings;
   But kind and good, with healing in Thy wings:
   Tears for all woes, a heart for every plea;
   Come, Friend of sinners, thus abide with me.

4 I need Thy presence every passing hour:
   What but Thy grace can foil the tempter's power?
   Who like Thyself my guide and stay can be?
   Through cloud and sunshine, oh, abide with me.

5 I fear no foe, with Thee at hand to bless:
   Ills have no weight, and tears no bitterness:
   Where is death's sting? where, grave, thy victory?
   I triumph still, if Thou abide with me.

371

6.4.6.4. with chorus.

1 I need Thee every hour,
   Most gracious Lord;
   No tender voice like Thine
   Can peace afford.

   I need Thee, oh, I need Thee;
   Every hour I need Thee;
   Oh, bless me now, my Savior!
   I come to Thee.

2 I need Thee every hour,
   Stay Thou near by;
   Temptations lose their power
   When Thou art nigh.

3 I need Thee every hour,
   In joy or pain;
   Come quickly and abide,
   Or life is vain.

4 I need Thee every hour,
   Teach me Thy will;
   And Thy rich promises
   In me fulfill.

5 I need Thee every hour,
   Most Holy One;
   Oh, make me Thine indeed,
   Thou blessed Son.

Peculiar Meter.

1 Nothing between my soul and the Savior,
Naught of this world's delusive dream;
I have renounced all sinful pleasure;
Jesus is mine, there's nothing between.

Nothing between my soul and the Savior,
So that His blessed face may be seen;
Nothing preventing the least of His favor,
Keep the way clear! Let nothing between.

2 Nothing between, like worldly pleasure;
Habits of life, though harmless they seem,
Must not my heart from Him e'er sever;
He is my all, there's nothing between.

3 Nothing between, like pride or station;
Self-life or friends shall not intervene;
Though it may cost me much tribulation,
I am resolved; there's nothing between.

4 Nothing between, e'en many hard trials,
Though the whole world against me convene;
Watching with prayer and much self-denial,
I'll triumph at last, with nothing between.

Peculiar Meter.

1 Nothing between, Lord, nothing between;
   Let me Thy glory see,
   Draw my soul close to Thee,
   Then speak in love to me —
   Nothing between.

2 Nothing between, Lord, nothing between;
   Let not earth's din and noise
   Stifle Thy still small voice;
   In it let me rejoice —
   Nothing between.

3 Nothing between, Lord, nothing between;
   Nothing of earthly care,
   Nothing of tear or prayer,
   No robe that self may wear —
   Nothing between.

4 Nothing between, Lord, nothing between;
   Unbelief disappear,
   Vanish each doubt and fear,
   Fading when Thou art near —
   Nothing between.

5 Nothing between, Lord, nothing between;
   Shine with unclouded ray,
   Chasing each mist away,
   O'er my whole heart bear sway —
   Nothing between.

6 Nothing between, Lord, nothing between;
   Thus may I walk with Thee,
   Thee only may I see,
   Thine only let me be —
   Nothing between.

7   Nothing between, Lord, nothing between;
      Till Thine eternal light,
      Rising on earth's dark night,
      Bursts on my open sight —
        Nothing between.

By permission of Marshall, Morgan and Scott, Ltd.

8.8.8.8.   **374**

1   Sun of my soul, Thou Savior dear,
      It is not night if Thou be near;
      Oh, may no earthborn cloud arise
      To hide Thee from Thy servant's eyes.

2   When the soft dews of kindly sleep
      My wearied eyelids gently steep,
      Be my last thought how sweet to rest
      Forever on my Savior's breast.

3   Abide with me from morn till eve,
      For without Thee I cannot live;
      Abide with me when night is nigh,
      For without Thee I dare not die.

4   Come near, and bless us when we wake,
      Ere through the world our way we take;
      Till in the ocean of Thy love
      We lose ourselves in Thee above.

375   8.6.8.6. with chorus.

1   There is a place of quiet rest,
      Near to the heart of God,
    A place where sin cannot molest,
      Near to the heart of God.

      O Jesus, blest Redeemer,
        Sent from the heart of God,
      Hold us, who wait before Thee,
        Near to the heart of God.

2   There is a place of comfort sweet,
      Near to the heart of God,
    A place where we our Savior meet,
      Near to the heart of God.

3   There is a place of full release,
      Near to the heart of God,
    A place where all is joy and peace,
      Near to the heart of God.

376   8.6.8.6.

1   Fill Thou my life, O Lord my God,
      In every part with praise,
    That my whole being may proclaim
      Thy being and Thy ways.

2   Not for the lip of praise alone,
      Nor e'en the praising heart,
    I ask, but for a life made up
      Of praise in every part:

3   Praise in the common things of life,
      Its goings out and in;
    Praise in each duty and each deed,
      However small and mean.

4 Fill every part of me with praise;
　　Let all my being speak
Of Thee and of Thy love, O Lord,
　　Poor though I be and weak.

5 So shall no part of day or night
　　From sacredness be free,
But all my life, in every step,
　　Be fellowship with Thee.

6.5.6.5.D. **377**

1 If the path I travel
　　Lead me to the cross,
If the way Thou choosest
　　Lead to pain and loss,
Let the compensation
　　Daily, hourly, be
Shadowless communion,
　　Blessed Lord, with Thee.

2 If there's less of earth joy,
　　Give, Lord, more of heaven.
Let the spirit praise Thee,
　　Though the heart be riven;
If sweet earthly ties, Lord,
　　Break at Thy decree,
Let the tie that binds us,
　　Closer, sweeter, be.

3 Lonely though the pathway,
　　Cheer it with Thy smile;
Be Thou my companion
　　Through earth's little while;
Selfless may I live, Lord,
　　By Thy grace to be
Just a cleansèd channel
　　For Thy life through me.

378   8.7.8.7.D.

1 Savior, lead me up the mountain,
   Where the Lord alone is seen,
Where we hear the voice from heaven,
   Where the air is pure and clean.

   Lead me higher up the mountain,
      Give me fellowship with Thee;
   In Thy light I see the fountain,
      And the blood it cleanses me.

2 Higher up where light increases,
      Far above all earthly strife,
   Where the strain of effort ceases,
      Where in Christ we reign in Life.

3 Savior, keep me up the mountain
      Pressing on toward the goal,
   Till, as one, we share Thine image,
      And Thy love and grace extol.

LONGINGS — FOR FEEDING ON CHRIST

379   6.6.6.6.

1 I hunger and I thirst;
      Jesus, my manna be;
   Ye living waters, burst
      Out of the rock for me.

2 Thou bruised and broken Bread,
      My lifelong wants supply;
   As living souls are fed,
      O feed me, or I die.

3 Thou true life-giving Vine,
      Let me Thy sweetness prove;
   Renew my life with Thine,
      Refresh my soul with love.

4 For still the desert lies
 My thirsting soul before;
O living waters, rise
 Within me evermore.

7.6.7.6.D.   **380**

1 O Bread to pilgrims given,
 O Food for saints to eat,
O Manna sent from heaven,
 For heav'n-born natures meet;
Give us, for Thee long pining,
 To eat till richly filled;
Till, earth's delights resigning,
 Our every wish is stilled.

2 O Water, life bestowing,
 From out the Savior's heart,
A fountain purely flowing,
 A fount of love Thou art.
Oh, let us, freely tasting,
 Our burning thirst assuage;
Thy sweetness, never wasting,
 Avails from age to age.

3 Jesus, this feast receiving,
 We Thee unseen adore;
Thy faithful word believing,
 We take, and doubt no more.
Give us, Thou true and loving,
 On earth to live in Thee;
Then, God the veil removing,
 Thy glorious face to see.

LONGINGS — FOR VISION OF CHRIST

381

9.9.9.10. with chorus.

1 Fill all my vision, Savior, I pray,
Let me see only Jesus today;
Though through the valley Thou leadest me,
Thy fadeless glory encompasseth me.

Fill all my vision, Savior divine,
Till with Thy glory my spirit shall shine.
Fill all my vision, that all may see
Thy Holy Image reflected in me.

2 Fill all my vision, every desire
Keep for Thy glory; my soul inspire
With Thy perfection, Thy holy love,
Flooding my pathway with light from above.

3 Fill all my vision, let naught of sin
Shadow the brightness shining within.
Let me see only Thy blessed face,
Feasting my soul on Thy infinite grace.

LONGINGS — FOR KNOWLEDGE OF CHRIST

382

8.8.8.8. with chorus.

1 More about Jesus would I know,
More of His grace to others show;
More of His saving fulness see,
More of His love who died for me.

More, more about Jesus,
More, more about Jesus;
More of His saving fulness see,
More of His love who died for me.

2 More about Jesus let me learn,
More of His holy will discern;
Spirit of God my teacher be,
Showing the things of Christ to me.

3   More about Jesus; in His Word,
    Holding communion with my Lord;
    Hearing His voice in every line,
    Making each faithful saying mine.

4   More about Jesus; on His throne,
    Riches in glory all His own;
    More of His kingdom's sure increase;
    More of His coming, Prince of Peace.

LONGINGS — FOR OBEDIENCE TO CHRIST

9.8.9.8.D.   **383**

1   My stubborn will at last hath yielded;
    I would be Thine, and Thine alone,
    And this the prayer my lips are bringing,
    "Lord, let in me Thy will be done."

        Sweet will of God, still fold me closer,
        Till I am wholly lost in Thee;
        Sweet will of God, still fold me closer,
        Till I am wholly lost in Thee.

2   I'm tired of sin, footsore and weary,
    The darksome path hath dreary grown,
    But now a light has ris'n to cheer me;
    I find in Thee my Star, my Sun.

3   Thy precious will, O conqu'ring Savior,
    Doth now embrace and compass me;
    All discords hushed, my peace a river,
    My soul a prisoned bird set free.

4   Shut in with Thee, O Lord, forever,
    My wayward feet no more to roam;
    What pow'r from Thee my soul can sever?
    The center of God's will my home.

384

6.6.6.6.D.

1 My Jesus, as Thou wilt!
Oh, may Thy will be mine!
Into Thy hand of love
I would my all resign;
Through sorrow, or through joy,
Conduct me as Thine own,
And help me still to say,
My Lord, Thy will be done!

2 My Jesus, as Thou wilt!
Though seen through many a tear,
Let not my star of hope
Grow dim or disappear;
Since Thou on earth hast wept,
And sorrowed oft alone,
If I must weep with Thee,
My Lord, Thy will be done!

3 My Jesus, as Thou wilt!
All shall be well for me;
Each changing future scene
I gladly trust with Thee.
Straight to Thy rest above
I travel calmly on,
And sing, in life or death,
My Lord, Thy will be done!

10.4.10.4.10.10.

1   Oh, tame me, Lord! rebellious nature calm,
      Oh, tame me, Lord!
  This heart, so tossed and filled with wild alarm,
      Oh, tame me, Lord!
  These human longings, let them end in Thee,
  And let me be Thy bondslave, even me!

2   I will not ask Thee to account to me
      For aught Thou dost;
  For crosses sore, or paths I cannot see:
      But I will trust.
  No second causes shall perplex my soul,
  Or stay from yielding all to Thy control.

3   The raging storm I dare not fight alone,
      Ah, show Thy face!
  Say, "It is I!" Thyself to me make known,
      Ah, show Thy face!
  Then what care I for darkest depths of woe?
  Thine arms, O Christ, shall fold me close, I know!

4   Oh, save me, Lord! Subdue this stubborn will;
      Oh, save me, Lord!
  In spite of all, Thy purposes fulfil
      In me, Oh, Lord;
  I yield my self, and all I have and am,
  To follow Thee, Thou all redeeming Lamb!

5   How can I fear? Thou art so near to me;
      How can I fear?
  I hear Thee say, "Believe, and thou shalt see!"
      How can I fear?
  I now believe, and trust Thy mighty power,
  To save, to heal, to keep this very hour!

8.7.8.7. with chorus.

1 Thou my everlasting Portion,
   More than friend or life to me,
   All along my pilgrim journey,
   Savior, let me walk with Thee.

   Close to Thee, close to Thee,
   Close to Thee, close to Thee;
   All along my pilgrim journey,
   Savior, let me walk with Thee.

2 Not for ease or worldly pleasure,
   Not for fame my prayer shall be;
   Gladly will I toil and suffer,
   Only let me walk with Thee.

   Close to Thee, close to Thee,
   Close to Thee, close to Thee;
   Gladly will I toil and suffer,
   Only let me walk with Thee.

3 Lead me through the vale of shadows,
   Bear me o'er life's fitful sea;
   Then the gate of life eternal
   May I enter, Lord, with Thee.

   Close to Thee, close to Thee,
   Close to Thee, close to Thee;
   Then the gate of life eternal
   May I enter, Lord, with Thee.

10.7.10.7. with chorus. **387**

1 I am Thine, O Lord, I have heard Thy voice,
    And it told Thy love to me;
But I long to rise in the arms of faith,
    And be closer drawn to Thee.

> Draw me nearer, nearer, blessed Lord,
>   To the cross where Thou hast died;
> Draw me nearer, nearer, nearer, blessed Lord,
>   To Thy precious, bleeding side.

2 Consecrate me now to Thy service, Lord,
    By the pow'r of grace divine;
Let my soul look up with a steadfast hope,
    And my will be lost in Thine.

3 O the pure delight of a single hour
    That before Thy throne I spend,
When I kneel in prayer, and with Thee, my God,
    I commune as friend with friend!

4 There are depths of love that I yet may know
    Ere Thee face to face I see;
There are heights of joy that I yet may reach
    Ere I rest in peace with Thee.

11.10.11.10. **388**

1 Hold Thou my hand: so weak I am, and helpless;
I dare not take one step without Thy aid.
Hold Thou my hand: for then, O Loving Savior,
No dread of ill shall make my soul afraid.

2 Hold Thou my hand: and closer, closer draw me
To Thy dear self, my hope, my joy, my all;
Hold Thou my hand: lest haply I should wander,
And missing Thee, my trembling feet should fall.

3 Hold Thou my hand: the way is dark before me
Without the sunlight of Thy face divine;
But when by faith I catch its radiant glory,
What heights of joy, what rapturous songs are mine.

389†

11.11.11.11.D.

1 Lord Jesus, I long in Thy presence to live,
From morning to evening my one world Thou art;
O let not my heart be contented or rest
When loving or seeking what with Thee doth part.
Each moment, each day, throughout suff'ring and pain,
When nought in the world can give comfort or cheer,
When sighing and weeping encompasses me,
Lord, still all my sighing and wipe every tear.

2 Each time when I dream of the goodness of life,
I pray Thee, dear Lord, that Thou in it may be;
O do not allow me to choose by myself,
Nor seek any pleasure that's other than Thee.
Each night when alone in the stillness I lie,
I pray Thee, Lord Jesus, that Thou wilt be near;
Each morning ere dawn comes, while still in my sleep,
Then whispering call me and open my ear.

3 Each time, Lord, when reading in Thy holy Word,
I pray that Thy glory may shine on each line,
That clearly I'll see what a Savior I have
And how great salvation that Thou hast made mine.
When helpless I come, Lord, to kneel at Thy throne,
I pray Thee to hear me and grant me Thy grace;
If thru my shortcomings Thou hear not my prayer,
Withdraw not Thy presence, O hide not Thy face.

4 Each time when of heavenly blessings I think,
O let my heart long to be raptured to Thee;
My only hope here is Thy coming again,
My only joy there, Lord, Thy presence will be.
Lord, teach me each day in Thy presence to live,
From morning to evening my one world Thou art;
O let not my heart be contented or rest
When loving or seeking what with Thee doth part.

7.7.7.7. with chorus.

1 Savior, lead me, this I pray,
  In the Spirit all the day;
  Walking in the light of life,
  I would cease from all my strife.

> Lead me, lead me,
> Savior, lead me, this I pray;
> Deeply in the stream of life,
> Lead me, Savior, in Thy way.

2 Thou as life in me indeed,
  By the law of life dost lead;
  When Thou reignest in Thy might,
  All my darkness turns to light.

3 Liberating Spirit, Thou,
  Wholly regulate me now;
  Thus my mind Thou wilt renew
  And Thy will I'll fully know.

391

8.7.8.7.4.7. with repeat.

1 Guide me, O Thou gracious Savior,
  Pilgrim through this barren land;
  I am weak, but Thou art mighty,
  Hold me with Thy pow'rful hand;
  > Bread of heaven,
  Feed me till I want no more;
  > Bread of heaven,
  Feed me till I want no more.

continued

2   Open now the crystal fountain,
Whence the healing waters flow;
Let the fiery, cloudy pillar
Lead me all my journey through;
    Strong Deliv'rer,
Be Thou still my strength and shield;
    Strong Deliv'rer,
Be Thou still my strength and shield.

392   7.7.7.7.7.7.

1   Jesus, Savior, pilot me
Over life's tempestuous sea;
Unknown waves before me roll,
Hiding rock and treach'rous shoal;
Chart and compass come from Thee;
    Jesus, Savior, pilot me.

2   As a mother stills her child,
Thou canst hush the ocean wild;
Boist'rous waves obey Thy will
When Thou say'st to them, "Be still."
Wondrous Sov'reign of the sea,
    Jesus, Savior, pilot me.

3   Though death's valley I may pass,
Still Thy grace will fear surpass;
In Thy presence I will rest,
And, while leaning on Thy breast,
I will hear Thee say to me,
    "Fear not, I will pilot thee."

6.6.6.6.

1 Thy way, not mine, O Lord,
  However dark it be;
Lead me by Thine own hand,
  Choose out the path for me.

2 Smooth let it be, or rough,
  It will be still the best;
Winding or straight it leads
  Right onward to Thy rest.

3 I dare not choose my lot;
  I would not if I might:
Choose Thou for me, my God,
  So shall I walk aright.

4 Take Thou my cup, and it
  With joy or sorrow fill,
As best to Thee may seem;
  Choose Thou my good and ill.

5 Choose Thou for me my friends,
  My sickness or my health.
Choose Thou my cares for me,
  My poverty or wealth.

6 Not mine, not mine the choice,
  In things both great and small;
Be Thou my guide, my strength,
  My wisdom and my all.

394

8.7.8.7.7.7.

1 Unto him that hath Thou givest
   Ever more abundantly;
   Lord, I live because Thou livest,
   Therefore give more life to me,
   Therefore speed me in the race,
   Therefore let me grow in grace.

2 Deepen all Thy work, O Master,
   Strengthen every downward root;
   Only do Thou ripen faster,
   More and more Thy pleasant fruit;
   Purge me, prune me, self abase;
   Only let me grow in grace.

3 Let me grow by sun and shower,
   Every moment water me;
   Make me really, hour by hour,
   More and more conformed to Thee,
   That Thy loving eye may trace
   Day by day my growth in grace.

4 From Thy fulness grace outpouring,
   Show me ever greater things;
   Raise me higher, sunward soaring,
   Mounting as on eagle-wings.
   By the brightness of Thy face,
   Ever let me grow in grace.

5 Let me, then, be always growing,
   Never, never standing still,
   Listening, learning, better knowing
   Thee and Thy most blessed will.
   Till I win the glorious race,
   Daily let me grow in grace.

8.6.8.6.D.

1 O Jesus Christ, grow Thou in me,
     And all things else recede;
   My heart be daily nearer Thee,
     From sin be daily freed.

     Each day let Thy supporting might
       My weakness still embrace;
     My darkness vanish in Thy light,
       Thy life my death efface.

2 In Thy bright beams which on me fall,
     Fade every evil thought;
   That I am nothing, Thou art all,
     I would be daily taught.

3 More of Thy glory let me see,
     Thou Holy, Wise, and True;
   I would Thy living image be,
     In joy and sorrow too.

4 Fill me with gladness from above,
     Hold me by strength divine;
   Lord, let the glow of Thy great love
     Through all my being shine.

5 Make this poor self grow less and less,
     Be Thou my life and aim;
   Oh, make me daily through Thy grace
     More meet to bear Thy name.

396

8.8.8.8.D.

1 I'm pressing on the upward way,
New heights I'm gaining every day;
Still praying as I onward bound,
"Lord, plant my feet on higher ground."

Lord, lift me up, and let me stand
By faith on Canaan's tableland;
A higher plane than I have found,
Lord, plant my feet on higher ground.

2 My heart has no desire to stay
Where doubts arise and fears dismay;
Though some may dwell where these abound,
My prayer, my aim, is higher ground.

3 I want to live above the world,
Though Satan's darts at me are hurled;
For faith has caught the joyful sound,
The song of saints on higher ground.

4 I want to scale the utmost height
And catch a gleam of glory bright;
But still I'll pray till rest I've found,
"Lord, lead me on to higher ground."

6.5.6.5.D. with chorus.

1 More holiness give me,
More sweetness within,
More patience in suff'ring,
More sorrow for sin,
More faith in my Savior,
More sense of His care,
More joy in His service,
More freedom in prayer.

Come, my Savior, and help me,
Comfort, strengthen and keep me;
Thou each moment wilt save me,
Thou art saving me now.

2 More gratitude give me,
More trust in the Lord,
More zeal for His glory,
More hope in His Word,
More tears for His sorrows,
More pain at His grief,
More meekness in trial,
More praise for relief.

3 More victory give me,
More strength to o'ercome,
More freedom from earth-stains,
More quest for the throne,
More fit for the kingdom,
More useful I'd be,
More blessed and holy,
More, Savior, like Thee.

398

10.9.10.9.D.

1 O to be like Thee! blessed Redeemer;
This is my constant longing and prayer;
Gladly I'll forfeit all of earth's treasures,
Jesus, Thy perfect likeness to wear.

O to be like Thee! O to be like Thee!
Blessed Redeemer, pure as Thou art;
Come in Thy sweetness, come in Thy fullness;
Stamp Thine own image deep on my heart.

2 O to be like Thee! full of compassion,
Loving, forgiving, tender and kind,
Helping the helpless, cheering the fainting,
Seeking the wand'ring sinners to find.

3 O to be like Thee! lowly in spirit,
Holy and harmless, patient and brave;
Meekly enduring cruel reproaches,
Willing to suffer, others to save.

4 O to be like Thee! Lord, I am coming,
Now to receive th' anointing divine;
All that I am and have I am bringing;
Lord, from this moment all shall be Thine.

5 O to be like Thee! While I am pleading
Pour out Thy Spirit, fill with Thy love.
Make me a temple meet for Thy dwelling,
Fit for a life which Thou wouldst approve.

6.5.6.5.

1 Changed into His likeness!
  This my heart's desire!
May the Lord fulfill it,
  All my soul inspire.

2 Changed into His likeness!
  He the Spirit is!
If the Spirit governs,
  He'll fulfill my wish.

3 As a glass, beholding
  With uncovered face,
I can see His glory
  And reflect His grace.

4 O that no more covering
  May the Lord obscure,
That I may reflect Him
  With a heart made pure.

5 Gazing on His glory,
  Face to face to see;
Constantly beholding,
  Ever would I be.

6 Changed into His likeness!
  This my heart's one quest!
From my heart reflected,
  He will be expressed.

7 Changed into His likeness
  And reflecting more
Glory unto glory,
  Boundless evermore.

400   I WOULD BE LIKE JESUS

James Rowe   8.6.8.6. with chorus.

1 Earthly pleasures vainly call me,
      I would be like Jesus;
   Nothing worldly shall enthrall me,
      I would be like Jesus.

      Be like Jesus, this my song,
         In the home and in the throng;
      Be like Jesus, all day long!
         I would be like Jesus.

2 He has broken every fetter,
      I would be like Jesus;
   That my soul may serve Him better,
      I would be like Jesus.

3 All the way from earth to glory,
      I would be like Jesus;
   Telling o'er and o'er the story,
      I would be like Jesus.

401   8.7.8.5.

1 May the mind of Christ my Savior
   Live in me from day to day,
   By His love and pow'r controlling
      All I do and say.

2 May the Word of Christ dwell richly
   In my heart from hour to hour,
   So that all may see I triumph
      Only through His pow'r.

3 May the peace of Christ my Savior
   Rule my life in every thing,
   That I may be calm to comfort
      Sick and sorrowing.

4   May the love of Jesus fill me,
As the waters fill the sea;
Him exalting, self abasing,
This is victory.

5   May I run the race before me,
Strong and brave to face the foe,
Looking only unto Jesus
As I onward go.

6   May His beauty rest upon me
As I seek the lost to win,
And may they forget the channel,
Seeing only Him.

Used and altered by permission of Miss E.W.M. Gould.

Peculiar Meter.   **402**

1 I want that adorning divine,
Thou only, my Lord, canst bestow;
I want in those beautiful garments to shine,
Which mark out Thy beauty below.

2 I want every moment to feel
Thy Spirit indwelling my heart,
His pow'r ever present to cleanse and to heal,
And newness of life to impart.

3 I want, oh, I want to attain
Some likeness, my Savior, to Thee;
That longed-for resemblance once more to regain;
Thy comeliness put upon me.

4 I want to be marked for Thine own,
Thy seal on my forehead to wear;
And have that new name on the mystic white stone,
Which none but Thyself can declare.

5 I want, and this sums up my prayer,
To glorify Thee till I die;
Then calmly to yield up my soul to Thy care,
And breathe out in faith my last sigh!

403 †

8.7.8.7.D.

1 Live Thyself, Lord Jesus, through me,
    For my very life art Thou;
Thee I take to all my problems
    As the full solution now.
Live Thyself, Lord Jesus, through me,
    In all things Thy will be done;
I but a transparent vessel
    To make visible the Son.

2 Consecrated is Thy temple,
    Purged from every stain and sin;
May Thy flame of glory now be
    Manifested from within.
Let the earth in solemn wonder
    See my body willingly
Offered as Thy slave obedient,
    Energized alone by Thee.

3 Every moment, every member,
    Girded, waiting Thy command;
Underneath the yoke to labor
    Or be laid aside as planned.
When restricted in pursuing,
    No disquiet will beset;
Underneath Thy faithful dealing
    Not a murmur or regret.

4 Ever tender, quiet, restful,
    Inclinations put away,
That Thou may for me choose freely
    As Thy finger points the way.
Live Thyself, Lord Jesus, through me,
    For my very life art Thou;
Thee I take to all my problems
    As the full solution now.

10.6.10.6.

1 Let me come closer to Thee, Lord Jesus,
   Oh, closer day by day;
   Let me lean harder on Thee, Lord Jesus,
   Yes, harder, all the way.

2 Let me show forth Thy beauty, Lord Jesus,
   Like sunshine on the hills;
   Oh, let my lips pour forth all Thy sweetness
   In joyous sparkling rills.

3 Yes, like a channel, precious Lord Jesus,
   Make me and let me be;
   Keep me and use me daily, Lord Jesus,
   For Thee, for only Thee.

4 In all my heart and will, O Lord Jesus,
   Be altogether king;
   Make me a loyal subject, Lord Jesus,
   To Thee in everything.

5 Thirsting and hungering for Thee, Lord Jesus,
   With blessed hunger here.
   Longing for New Jerusalem's fullness —
   No thirst, no hunger there.

LONGINGS — FOR THE LORD'S DELIGHT

405 †

This hymn was written shortly after its author,
who had been born blind, gained her sight.

8.7.8.7.D.

1 Having seen the world's fair beauty,
  Lord, I would be blind once more,
Lest I lose the loving Presence
And Delight I knew before.

Having seen the world's fair beauty,
Lord, I would be blind once more,
Lest I lose the loving Presence
And Delight I knew before.

2 Dawn and sunset, star and moonlight,
  I can see in paradise,
But while here on earth His mercy
For my blindness will suffice.

3 I no more would be delivered
  From my thorn, but look for grace,
While within the veil His glory
Shineth brightly on my face.

4 In the deep dark night, His beauty
  I by faith, not sight, may trace;
He was ridiculed and hated,
Yet I see His glorious face.

5 Sun and moonlight far surpassing,
  Clouds and Milky Way o'erspread,
Is the glory all transcending
Shining from His thorn-crowned head.

6.4.6.4.6.6.6.4.

1 Teach me Thy way, O Lord,
   Teach me Thy way;
Thy gracious aid afford,
   Teach me Thy way.
Help me to walk aright;
More by faith, less by sight;
Lead me with heav'nly light,
   Teach me Thy way.

2 When doubts and fears arise,
   Teach me Thy way;
When storms o'erspread the skies,
   Teach me Thy way.
Shine through the cloud and rain,
Through sorrow, toil, and pain;
Make Thou my pathway plain,
   Teach me Thy way.

3 Long as my life shall last,
   Teach me Thy way;
Where'er my lot be cast,
   Teach me Thy way.
Until the race is run,
Until the journey's done,
Until the crown is won,
   Teach me Thy way.

407

8.6.8.6.

1 Search me, O God, my actions try,
  And let my life appear
  As seen by Thine all-searching eye —
  To mine my ways make clear.

2 Search all my sense, and know my heart
  Who only canst make known,
  And let the deep, the hidden part
  To me be fully shown.

3 Throw light into the darkened cells,
  Where passion reigns within;
  Quicken my conscience till it feels
  The loathsomeness of sin.

4 Search all my thoughts, the secret springs,
  The motives that control;
  The chambers where polluted things
  Hold empire o'er the soul.

5 Search, till Thy fiery glance has cast
  Its holy light through all,
  And I by grace am brought at last
  Before Thy face to fall.

6 Thus prostrate I shall learn of Thee,
  What now I feebly prove,
  That God alone in Christ can be
  Unutterable love.

11.11.11.11. with chorus.

1 Lord Jesus, I long to be perfectly whole,
I want Thee forever to live in my soul;
Break down every idol, cast out every foe;
Now wash me, and I shall be whiter than snow.

Whiter than snow; yes, whiter than snow;
Now wash me and I shall be whiter than snow.

2 Lord Jesus, let nothing unholy remain,
Apply Thine own blood and extract every stain;
To get this blest cleansing I all things forego;
Now wash me, and I shall be whiter than snow.

3 Lord Jesus, look down from Thy throne in the skies,
And help me to make a complete sacrifice;
I give up myself and whatever I know;
Now wash me, and I shall be whiter than snow.

4 Lord Jesus, for this I most humbly entreat;
I wait, blessed Lord, at Thy crucified feet;
By faith, for my cleansing I see Thy blood flow;
Now wash me, and I shall be whiter than snow.

5 Lord Jesus, Thou seest I patiently wait;
Come now, and within me a new heart create;
To those who have sought Thee Thou never
saidst, No;
Now wash me, and I shall be whiter than snow.

409   8.8.8.8.D.

1 One thing I of the Lord desire,
   For all my path hath miry been:
   Be it by water or by fire,
   Oh, make me clean, oh, make me clean!

     So wash me, Thou, without, within,
     Or purge with fire, if that must be;
     No matter how, if only sin
     Die out in me, die out in me.

2 I watch to shun the miry way,
   And staunch the springs of guilty thought;
   But, watch and struggle as I may,
   Pure I am not, pure I am not.

3 If clearer vision Thou impart,
   Grateful and glad my soul shall be,
   But yet to have a purer heart
   Is more to me, is more to me.

4 Yea, only as this heart is clean
   May larger vision yet be mine,
   For mirrored in the depths are seen
   The things divine, the things divine.

LONGINGS — FOR A RENEWED HEART

410   8.6.8.6.

1 Oh, for a heart to praise my God,
     A heart from sin set free,
   With conscience sprinkled by the blood
     So freely shed for me.

2 A heart resigned, submissive, meek,
     My dear Redeemer's throne;
   Where only Christ is heard to speak,
     Where Jesus reigns alone.

3 A humble, lowly, contrite heart,
 Believing, true, and clean,
Which neither death nor life can part
 From Him that dwells within.

4 A heart in every thought renewed,
 And filled with love divine;
Perfect and right, and pure and good,
 A copy, Lord, of Thine.

5 Thy nature, gracious Lord, impart,
 Come quickly from above;
Write Thy new name upon my heart,
 Thy new, best name of Love.

6.6.8.6.   **411**

1 Bless'd are the pure in heart,
 For they shall see our God;
The secret of the Lord is theirs,
 Their heart is Christ's abode.

2 The Lord, who left the heavens,
 Our life and peace to bring,
To dwell in lowliness with men,
 Their pattern and their King.

3 He to the lowly soul
 Doth still Himself impart,
And for His dwelling and His throne
 Chooseth the pure in heart.

4 Lord, we Thy presence seek;
 May ours this blessing be;
Give us a pure and lowly heart,
 A temple meet for Thee.

412†

7.7.7.7.D.

1 Lord, reveal Thyself to me,
That the flesh I'll fully know;
May Thy grace so work in me,
That in dust I'll lowly bow.
How I long for victory,
Yet, thru all my life, how weak!
Evil things I cannot leave,
Nor can do the good I seek.

2 Inwardly I want the Lord,
But my conduct hateful is;
Though I would, I cannot change,
O what real bondage 'tis!
By God's law my sin's revealed,
But the law of sin doth bind;
Though I struggle to be free,
No release my soul can find.

3 Many times I fall and rise,
Oft resolve, and often fail;
Craving vict'ry, I retreat,
And my sad defeat bewail.
Truly I am sold to sin
And completely powerless;
There's no good within my flesh,
All is dark and sinfulness.

4 Now I know myself in part,
And confess my helplessness;
All my temperament is odd,
All my life corrupted is.

Subtle self I cannot trust,
Nor to fleshly strength can cling;
All my trust and all my hope
Is in Jesus Christ my King.

5 May the Cross put me to death
That on Christ I may rely;
May His Holy Spirit fill,
That Himself I may apply.
May His death so work in me
Daily deeper than before,
That my self may be destroyed
And His life thru me may pour.

6 O how bitter is my case!
Who this wretched slave can free,
Who deliver from this death,
To a life of victory?
Jesus shed His blood for me,
Christ is now my holiness;
I receive Him as my life
And my portion measureless.

7 Now I'm wholly sanctified,
Selfless, I obey His word;
Nevermore to feel ashamed
When I come before the Lord.
How transcendent is this life!
Grace thru faith He gives to me!
Praise the Lord, He heard my cry
And has made me wholly free.

413

7.7.7.7.

1 Jesus, cast a look on me;
Give me sweet simplicity;
Make me poor, and keep me low,
Seeking only Thee to know.

2 Weaned from all my lordly self,
Weaned from all the miser's pelf,
Weaned from all the scorner's ways,
Weaned from all the lust of praise.

3 All that feeds my busy pride,
Cast it evermore aside;
Bid my will to Thine submit,
Lay me humbly at Thy feet.

4 Make me like a little child,
Of my strength and wisdom spoiled;
Seeing only in Thy light,
Walking only in Thy might;

5 Leaning on Thy loving breast,
Where a weary soul may rest;
Feeling well the peace of God
Flowing from Thy precious blood.

6 In this posture let me live,
And hosannas daily give;
In this temper let me die,
And hosannas ever cry.

8.6.8.6.

1 My Savior, Thou hast offered rest:
    Oh, give it then to me;
The rest of ceasing from myself,
    To find my all in Thee.

2 This cruel self, oh, how it strives
    And works within my breast,
To come between Thee and my soul,
    And keep me back from rest.

3 How many subtle forms it takes
    Of seeming verity,
As if it were not safe to rest
    And venture all on Thee.

4 O Lord, I seek a holy rest,
    A victory over sin;
I seek that Thou alone shouldst reign
    O'er all without, within.

5 In Thy strong hand I lay me down,
    So shall the work be done;
For who can work so wondrously
    As the Almighty One?

6 Work on, then, Lord, till on my soul
    Eternal light shall break,
And, in Thy likeness perfected,
    I "satisfied" shall wake.

415

8.6.8.6.D.

1   There is a foe whose hidden pow'r
     The Christian well may fear,
  More subtle far than inbred sin,
     And to the heart more dear.
  It is the pow'r of selfishness,
     It is the wilful I,
  And ere my Lord can live in me,
     My very self must die.

2   There is, like Anak's sons of old,
     A race of giants still:
  Self-glorying, self-confidence,
     Self-seeking and self-will.
  Still must these haughty Anakims
     By Caleb's sword be slain,
  Ere Hebron's heights of heav'nly love,
     Our conqu'ring feet can gain.

3   Oh, save me from self-will, dear Lord,
     Which claims Thy sacred throne;
  Oh! let my will be lost in Thine,
     And let Thy will be done.
  Oh, keep me from self-confidence,
     And self-sufficiency;
  Let me exchange my strength for Thine,
     And lean alone on Thee.

4   Oh, save me from self-seeking, Lord,
     Let me not be my own;
  A living sacrifice I come,
     Lord, keep me Thine alone.
  From proud vain glory save me, Lord,
     From pride of praise and fame;
  To Christ be all the honor given,
     The glory to His name.

5 Oh, Savior, slay the self in me
   By Thy consuming breath;
Show me Thy heart, Thy wounds, Thy shame,
   That self be put to death.
When the Shekinah flame came down,
   E'en Moses could not stay;
So let Thy glory fill me now,
   And self forever slay.

10.10.10.10. with chorus.

416

1 Lower and lower, dear Lord, at Thy feet,
Seeking Thy Spirit, Thy mercy so sweet;
Down in our need, blessed Master, we fall,
Lower and lower; be Thou all in all.

   Lower and lower, down at Thy cross,
   All the world's treasure counting but dross;
   Down at Thy feet, blessed Savior, we fall,
   Lower, still lower, Christ all in all!

2 Lower and lower, dear Savior, we pray,
Losing the self-life still more every day;
Weak and unworthy, we're looking above;
Empty us wholly; then fill us with love.

3 Lower and lower; yet higher we rise,
Lifted in Christ, freed from all the earth ties;
Humbly we follow the way of the cross,
Then, crowns of glory, and gain for all loss.

10.10.10.6.

417

1 Deep in me, Lord, mark Thou Thy holy Cross,
On motives, choices, private dear desires.
Let all that self in any form inspires
   Be unto me as dross.

2 And when Thy touch of death is here and there
Laid on a thing most precious in mine eyes,
Let me not wonder, let me recognize
   The answer to my prayer.

418

8.8.8.8.8.8.

1 From pray'r that asks that I may be
Sheltered from winds that beat on Thee,
From fearing when I should aspire,
From falt'ring when I should climb high'r
From silken self, O Captain, free
Thy soldier who would follow Thee.

2 From subtle love of softening things,
From easy choices, weakenings,
(Not thus are spirits fortified,
Not this way went the Crucified),
From all that dims Thy Calvary,
O Lamb of God, deliver me.

3 Give me the love that leads the way,
The faith that nothing can dismay,
The hope no disappointments tire,
The passion that will burn like fire,
Let me not sink to be a clod:
Make me Thy fuel, O flame of God.

Used by permission of Dohnavur Fellowship.

LONGINGS — **FOR BREAKING**

419

8.8.8.8.9.9.

1 O God, unblessing and unblest,
A withered plant, but not at rest,
A useless cumberer I'm found
Upon Thy field, Thy purchased ground;
And yet I pray — "Do not forsake me,
But in Thy hand, O Savior, take me.

2   As women take unbroken flax,
    As molders take unshapen wax,
    As smith, the iron, rough and cold,
    A useful instrument to mold,
    So in Thy skillful hands, O take me,
    And never let Thy love forsake me."

3   Like rock uncrushed, the stubborn will,
    Though bearing gold is barren still;
    Like marble in the quarry rough,
    The natural heart is useless stuff;
    And so, I pray — "Do not forsake me,
    But with Thy hand, O Savior, break me.

4   As mortars crush the hardest rock,
    As hammers break the stony block,
    As millstones bruise the finest wheat,
    As nuts are broken for their meat,
    So with Thy mighty hand, O break me,
    And never let Thy love forsake me."

5   Though crushed and broken, yet I'm nought
    But fragments to the furnace brought;
    Though bruised, I have no worth to feed
    The multitudes that die in need;
    And so, I pray — "Do not forsake me,
    But meet for service, Savior, make me.

6   As into useful forms the ore
    From molten scraps the molders' pour;
    As fire doth make the bruisèd wheat,
    When mixed and molded, fit to eat;
    So, fit for use by fire, O make me,
    And never let Thy love forsake me."

420

11.10.11.10.

1 Jesus, Redeemer and my one Inspirer,
   Heat in my coldness, set my life aglow.
Break down my barriers; draw, yea, draw me nigher.
   Thee would I know, whom it is life to know.

2 Deepen me, rid me of the superficial;
   From pale delusion set my spirit free;
All the entangled in me quick unravel;
   Pluck forth each thread of insincerity.

3 Thy vows are on me, oh to serve Thee truly —
   Love perfectly, in purity obey —
Burn, burn, O Fire, O Wind, now winnow throughly;
   O Sword, awake against the flesh and slay.

421

6.5.6.5.

1 Jesus, meek and gentle,
   Son of God most High,
Pitying, loving Savior,
   Hear Thy children's cry.

2 Pardon our offences,
   Loose our captive chains,
Break down every idol
   Which our soul detains.

3 Give us holy freedom,
   Fill our heart with grace;
Lead us on our journey,
   Till we win the race.

4 Jesus, meek and gentle,
   Son of God most high,
Pitying, loving Savior,
   Hear Thy children's cry.

6.6.8.6.D.

1   Make me a captive, Lord,
And then I shall be free;
Force me to render up my sword,
And I shall conq'ror be.
I sink in life's alarms
When by myself I stand,
Imprison me within Thine arms,
And strong shall be my hand.

2   My heart is weak and poor
Until it master find:
It has no spring of action sure,
It varies with the wind;
It cannot freely move
Till Thou hast wrought its chain;
Enslave it with Thy matchless love,
And deathless it shall reign.

3   My power is faint and low
Till I have learned to serve:
It wants the needed fire to glow,
It wants the breeze to nerve;
It cannot drive the world
Until itself be driven;
Its flag can only be unfurled
When Thou shalt breathe from heaven.

4   My will is not my own
Till Thou hast made it Thine;
If it would reach the monarch's throne
It must its crown resign;
It only stands unbent
Amid the clashing strife,
When on Thy bosom it has leant,
And found in Thee its life.

423

8.8.8.8.8.8.

1 Thou hidden love of God, whose height,
Whose depth unfathomed no man knows,
I see from far Thy beauteous light,
Inly I sigh for Thy repose;
My heart is pained, nor can it be
At rest, till it finds rest in Thee.

2 Thy secret voice invites me still
The sweetness of Thy yoke to prove;
And fain I would: but though my will
Seems fixed, yet wide my passions rove;
Yet hindrances strew all the way;
I aim at Thee, yet from Thee stray.

3 'Tis mercy all, that Thou hast brought
My mind to seek her peace in Thee;
Yet, while I seek but find Thee not,
No peace my wand'ring soul shall see.
Oh, when shall all my wand'rings end,
And all my steps to Thee-ward tend!

4 Is there a thing beneath the sun
That strives with Thee my heart to share?
Ah! tear it thence, and reign alone,
The Lord of every motion there.
Then shall my heart from earth be free,
When it has found repose in Thee.

5 Oh, hide this self from me, that I
No more, but Christ in me may live;
My vile affections mortify,
Nor let one darling sin survive.
In all things nothing may I see,
Nothing desire or seek but Thee.

6 O Lord, Thy sovereign aid impart,
   To save me from low-thoughted care;
   Chase this self-will through all my heart,
   Through all its latent mazes there.
   Make me Thy duteous child, that I
   Ceaseless may Abba, Father, cry.

7 Each moment draw from earth away
   My heart which lowly waits Thy call;
   Speak to my inmost soul and say,
   "I am Thy Love, Thy God, Thy All."
   To feel Thy power, to hear Thy voice,
   To taste Thy love, be all my choice.

8.6.8.6.   **424**

1 Lord, I believe a rest remains
   To all Thy people known;
  A rest where pure enjoyment reigns,
   And Thou art loved alone.

2 A rest, where all our soul's desire
   Is fixed on things above;
  Where fear and sin and grief expire,
   Cast out by perfect love.

3 Oh, that I now the rest might know,
   Believe, and enter in;
  Now, Savior, now the power bestow,
   And let me cease from sin.

4 Remove this hardness from my heart,
   This unbelief remove;
  To me the rest of faith impart,
   The Sabbath of Thy love.

5 I would be Thine, Thou know'st I would,
   And have Thee all my own;
  Thee, O my all-sufficient Good,
   I want, and Thee alone.

425

7.7.7.7.

1 Prince of peace, control my will;
   Bid this struggling heart be still:
   Bid my fears and doubtings cease:
   Hush my spirit into peace.

2 Thou hast bought me with Thy blood,
   Opened wide the gate to God;
   Peace I ask, but peace must be,
   Lord, in being one with Thee.

3 May Thy will, not mine be done;
   May Thy will and mine be one;
   Chase these doubtings from my heart,
   Now Thy perfect peace impart.

4 Savior, at Thy feet I fall,
   Thou, my life, my God, my all;
   Let Thy happy servant be
   One forevermore with Thee.

LONGINGS — FOR LIGHT

426*

6.6.6.6. with chorus.

1 Remove my covering, Lord,
   That I may see Thy light,
   And be deceived no more,
   But all things see aright.

   Oh, may Thy living light, Lord,
   Scatter all my night, Lord,
   And everything make bright, Lord,
   For this I pray to Thee.

2   I hardly know myself;
Deceived so much by pride,
I often think I'm right
And am self-satisfied.

3   I know Thee even less;
In doctrine, shallowly;
True revelation lack
Of Thy reality.

4   As for Thy life within,
In darkness I mistake —
If spirit or the flesh,
One for the other take.

5   As for Thy way, O Lord,
I often am not clear;
I toward seclusion tend
And from the pathway veer.

6   As for Thy will for me,
I do not know it well;
I substitute my own
And often would rebel.

7   As for the church, I need
Thy revelation more,
The Body-life to know,
Thy wisdom to explore.

8   I long to be unveiled,
In everything made clear,
No more to be deceived
Or to my pride adhere.

8.8.6.8.8.6.

1 O Love divine, how sweet Thou art,
When shall I find my willing heart
    All taken up by Thee?
My thirsty spirit faints to prove
The greatness of redeeming love,
    The love of Christ to me.

2 Stronger His love than death and hell,
Its riches are unsearchable:
    The first-born sons of light
Desire in vain its depths to see;
They cannot reach the mystery,
    The length, and breadth, and height.

3 God only knows the love of God;
Oh, that it now were shed abroad
    In this poor stony heart;
For love I sigh, for love I pine;
This only portion, Lord, be mine,
    Be mine this better part.

4 Oh, that I could forever sit
Like Mary, at the Master's feet;
    Be this my happy choice;
My only care, delight, and bliss,
My joy, my rest on earth be this,
    To hear the Bridegroom's voice.

8.8.8.8.8.8.

1 O Lord, Thy boundless love to me
No thought can reach, no tongue declare;
Oh, knit my thankful heart to Thee,
And reign without a rival there;
Thine wholly, Thine alone I am;
Lord, with Thy love my heart inflame.

2 Oh, grant that nothing in my soul
May dwell but Thy pure love alone;
Oh, may Thy love possess me whole,
My joy, my treasure, and my crown;
All coldness from my heart remove;
May every act, word, thought, be love.

3 O Love, how cheering is Thy ray,
All pain before Thy presence flies;
Care, anguish, sorrow, melt away,
Where'er Thy healing beams arise;
Lord Jesus, nothing may I see,
And naught desire, or seek, but Thee.

1 My faith looks up to Thee,
Thou Lamb of Calvary,
Savior Divine;
Now hear me while I pray;
Take all my guilt away;
Oh, let me from this day
Be wholly Thine.

2 May Thy rich grace impart
Strength to my fainting heart,
My zeal inspire;
As Thou hast died for me,
Oh, may my love to Thee
Pure, warm, and changeless be,
A living fire.

3 While life's dark maze I tread,
And griefs around me spread,
Be Thou my Guide;
Bid darkness turn to day,
Wipe sorrow's tears away,
Nor let me ever stray
From Thee aside.

4 All thru life's transient dream,
Until death's sullen stream
Shall o'er me roll,
Blest Savior, with Thy love,
Fear and distrust remove;
Make me Thy grace to prove,
Transform my soul.

LONGINGS — FOR MERCY

430 †

8.8.8.4.

1 When I am in the natural man,
How very strong I feel I am,
I do not know, I cannot scan
How weak I am.

2 When in the world I have my life,
  I cannot sense my failure rife,
  But boasting in my earnest strife,
      I forward press.

3 When I within the darkness dwell,
  My shallow state I cannot tell,
  I only think how I excel,
      And proudly dream.

4 But when at last I come to Thee,
  Thy searching light uncovers me,
  I see what I could never see —
      My self exposed.

5 I wither 'neath Thy piercing ray,
  And all my strength dissolves away,
  My self-esteem in dust I lay,
      And lowly bow.

6 How blind and foolish is the pride
  With which my soul was fortified;
  From my dark heart, self-satisfied,
      It issued forth.

7 There's not a thing that pride can claim,
  There's not a member but is lame,
  There's only deep regret and shame,
      How can I pray?

8 Thy blood from judgment saveth me,
  Thy life from wrath delivers me,
  How filthy yet in poverty
      I really am.

9 I want to pray, but faith have not,
  I fain would seek Thee as Thou art.
  Oh, canst Thou e'er renew my heart,
      Have mercy, Lord!

431

10.10.10.10.

1 Thy mighty love, O God, constraineth me,
As some strong tide it presseth on its way,
Seeking a channel in my self-bound soul,
Yearning to sweep all barriers away.

2 Shall I not yield to that constraining power?
Shall I not say, O tide of love, flow in?
My God, Thy gentleness hath conquered me,
Life cannot be as it hath hither been.

3 Break through my nature, mighty, heavenly love,
Clear every avenue of thought and brain,
Flood my affections, purify my will,
Let nothing but Thine own pure life remain.

4 Thus wholly mastered and possessed by God,
Forth from my life, spontaneous and free,
Shall flow a stream of tenderness and grace,
Loving, because God loved, eternally.

Used by permission of Marshall, Morgan & Scott, Ltd.

432

8.8.8.8.6.

1 O Love, that wilt not let me go,
I rest my weary soul in Thee;
I give Thee back the life I owe,
That in Thine ocean depths its flow
    May richer, fuller be.

2 O Light, that followest all my way,
I yield my flickering torch to Thee;
My heart restores its borrowed ray,
That in Thy sunshine's blaze its day
    May brighter, fairer be.

3 O Joy, that seekest me through pain,
   I cannot close my heart to Thee;
   I trace the rainbow through the rain,
   And feel the promise is not vain
      That morn shall tearless be.

4 O Cross, that liftest up my head,
   I dare not ask to fly from Thee;
   I lay in dust life's glory dead,
   And from the ground there blossoms red
      Life that shall endless be.

11.10.11.10.   **433**

1 I am the Lord's! O joy beyond expression,
      O sweet response to voice of love Divine;
   Faith's joyous "Yes" to the assuring whisper,
      "Fear not! I have redeemed thee; thou art Mine."

2 I am the Lord's! It is the glad confession
      Wherewith the Bride recalls the happy day,
   When love's "I will" accepted Him forever,
      "The Lord's," to love, to honor and obey.

3 I am the Lord's! Yet teach me all it meaneth,
      All it involves of love and loyalty,
   Of holy service, absolute surrender,
      And unreserved obedience unto Thee.

4 I am the Lord's! Yes; body, soul, and spirit,
      O seal them irrecoverably Thine;
   As Thou, Beloved, in Thy grace and fulness
      Forever and forevermore art mine.

434

8.8.6.8.8.6.

1 Lord, Thou hast won, at length I yield;
My heart by mighty grace compelled
Surrenders all to Thee;
Against Thy terrors long I strove,
But who can stand against Thy love?
Love conquers even me.

2 If Thou hadst bid Thy thunders roll,
And light'nings flash, to blast my soul,
I still had stubborn been;
But mercy has my heart subdued,
A bleeding Savior I have viewed,
And now I hate my sin.

3 Now, Lord, I would be Thine alone,
Come, take possession of Thine own,
For Thou hast set me free;
Released from Satan's hard command,
See all my powers waiting stand,
To be employed by Thee.

435

8.7.8.8.7. with repeat.

1 Oh, the bitter shame and sorrow,
That a time could ever be,
When I let the Savior's pity
Plead in vain, and proudly answered,
All of self, and none of Thee,
All of self, and none of Thee.

2   Yet He found me; I beheld Him
     Bleeding on the cursèd tree;
  Heard Him pray, Forgive them, Father,
  And my wistful heart said faintly,
     Some of self, and some of Thee,
     Some of self, and some of Thee.

3   Day by day His tender mercy,
     Healing, helping, full and free,
  Sweet and strong, and ah! so patient,
  Brought me lower while I whispered,
     Less of self, and more of Thee,
     Less of self, and more of Thee.

4   Higher than the highest heavens,
     Deeper than the deepest sea,
  Lord, Thy love at last hath conquered;
  Grant me now my heart's petition,
     None of self, and all of Thee,
     None of self, and all of Thee.

6.6.6.6.8.6.   **436**

1   Thy Life was giv'n for me,
    Thy blood, O Lord, was shed,
    That I might ransomed be,
    And quickened from the dead;
    Thy Life was giv'n for me, for me;
    What have I giv'n for Thee?

continued

2 Long years were spent for me
In weariness and woe,
That through eternity
Thy glory I might know;
Long years were spent for me,
    for me;
Have I spent one for Thee?

3 Thy Father's home of light,
Thy rainbow-circled throne,
Were left for earthly night,
For wanderings sad and lone;
Yea, all was left for me, for me;
Have I left aught for Thee?

4 Thou, Lord, hast borne for me
More than my tongue can tell
Of bitterest agony,
To rescue me from hell;
Thou suff'redst all for me, for me;
What have I borne for Thee?

5 And Thou hast brought to me
Down from Thy home above
Salvation full and free,
Thy pardon and Thy love;
Great gifts, great gifts Thou
    broughtest me;
What have I brought to Thee?

6 Oh, let my life be given,
My years for Thee be spent;
World-fetters all be riven,
And joy with suff'ring blent;
Thou gav'st Thyself for me, for me,
I give myself to Thee.

8.7.8.7.D.   **437**

1   Hast thou heard Him, seen Him, known Him?
    Is not thine a captured heart?
    Chief among ten thousand own Him;
    Joyful choose the better part.

    Captivated by His beauty,
    Worthy tribute haste to bring;
    Let His peerless worth constrain thee,
    Crown Him now unrivaled King.

2   Idols once they won thee, charmed thee,
    Lovely things of time and sense;
    Gilded thus does sin disarm thee,
    Honeyed lest thou turn thee thence.

3   What has stripped the seeming beauty
    From the idols of the earth?
    Not a sense of right or duty,
    But the sight of peerless worth.

4   Not the crushing of those idols,
    With its bitter void and smart;
    But the beaming of His beauty,
    The unveiling of His heart.

5   Who extinguishes their taper
    Till they hail the rising sun?
    Who discards the garb of winter
    Till the summer has begun?

6   'Tis that look that melted Peter,
    'Tis that face that Stephen saw,
    'Tis that heart that wept with Mary,
    Can alone from idols draw:

7   Draw and win and fill completely,
    Till the cup o'erflow the brim;
    What have we to do with idols
    Who have companied with Him?

438

8.7.8.7.D. with chorus.

1 I've turned my back upon the world
   With all its idle pleasures,
And set my heart on better things,
   On higher, holier treasures;
No more its glitter and its glare,
   And vanity shall blind me;
I've crossed the separating line,
   And left the world behind me.

> Far, far behind me!
> Far, far behind me!
> I've crossed the separating line,
>   And left the world behind me.

2 I've left the old sad life of sin,
   Its follies all forsaken;
My standing place is now in Christ,
   His holy vows I've taken;
Beneath the standard of the cross
   The world henceforth shall find me;
I've passed in Christ from death to life,
   And left the world behind me.

> Far, far behind me!
> Far, far behind me!
> I've passed in Christ from death to life,
>   And left the world behind me.

3 My soul shall ne'er return again
    Back to its former station,
  For here alone is perfect peace,
    And rest from condemnation;
  I've made exchange of masters now,
    The vows of glory bind me,
  And once for all I've left the world,
    Yes, left the world behind me.

      Far, far behind me!
      Far, far behind me!
  And once for all I've left the world,
    Yes, left the world behind me.

4 My choice is made forevermore,
    I want no other Savior;
  I ask no purer happiness
    Than His sweet love and favor;
  My heart is fixed on Jesus Christ,
    No more the world shall blind me;
  I've crossed the Red Sea of His death,
    And left the world behind me.

      Far, far behind me!
      Far, far behind me!
  I've crossed the Red Sea of His death,
    And left the world behind me.

6.5.6.5.D. with chorus.

1 Utterly abandoned
     To the Holy Ghost!
Seeking all His fulness
     At whatever cost;
Cutting all the shorelines,
     Launching in the deep
Of His mighty power,
     Strong to save and keep.

Utterly abandoned
     To the Lord of all,
Seeking all His fulness,
     Answ'ring His dear call.

2 Utterly abandoned
     To the Holy Ghost!
Oh! the sinking, sinking,
     Till the self is lost!
Till the vessel's emptied
     Broken at His feet;
Waiting till His filling
     Makes the work complete.

3 Utterly abandoned
     To the will of God;
Walking in the pathway
     That my Master trod;
Leaving ease and pleasure;
     Making Him my choice,
Waiting for His guidance,
     Listening for His voice.

4 Utterly abandoned!
     Through eternity;
   My will never choosing,
     His it e'er shall be;
   All my plans and longings
     Lost in His sweet will,
   Having nothing, owning
     All things in Him still.

5 Utterly abandoned!
     'Tis so sweet to be
   Captive in His love-bonds,
     Yet so wondrous free;
   Free from sin's dominion,
     Free from doubt and fear,
   Free from every worry,
     Burden, grief or care.

6 Utterly abandoned!
     Oh, the rest is sweet,
   Waiting in His presence
     At His blessed feet;
   Waiting for the filling
     Of the Host divine,
   Who my inward parts shall
     Perfectly refine.

7 Lo! His Spirit fills me,
     With His presence sweet!
   I, in Him, am blessed!
     I, in Him, complete!
   Now the light within me
     Never shall grow dim
   While abandoned ever,
     Living unto Him!

440

8.7.8.8.7. with repeat.

1 Holy, happy separation!
They alone are truly blest
Who from all besides retiring,
And Himself alone desiring
Find in Jesus only rest,
Find in Jesus only rest.

2 Jesus calls to separation,
And Himself hath led the way;
His own life the explanation,
His own life the illustration
Who is ready to obey?
Who is ready to obey?

3 Blessed Jesus, make us willing,
Thus without the camp to go
Unto Thee in glad subjection,
Unto Thee in Thy rejection,
Unto Thee from all below,
Unto Thee from all below!

4 Separate from all that grieves Thee,
Separate from sinners too;
Yet, like Thee, for sinners caring,
And, like Thee, with sinners bearing,
Asking, "What would Jesus do?"
Asking, "What would Jesus do?"

5 Unto Thee! Beloved Master,
Nearer, nearer let us be:
Unto Thee in consecration,
Unto Thee in separation,
Ever, only, unto Thee,
Ever, only, unto Thee!

8.7.8.7. with chorus.

1 All to Jesus I surrender,
All to Him I freely give;
I will ever love and trust Him,
In His presence daily live.

I surrender all,
I surrender all.
All to Thee, my blessed Savior,
I surrender all.

2 All to Jesus I surrender,
Humbly at His feet I bow,
Worldly pleasures all forsaken;
Take me, Jesus, take me now.

3 All to Jesus I surrender,
Make me, Savior, wholly Thine;
Let me feel Thy Holy Spirit,
Truly know that Thou art mine.

4 All to Jesus I surrender,
Lord, I give myself to Thee;
Fill me with Thy love and power,
Let Thy blessing fall on me.

5 All to Jesus I surrender,
Now I feel the sacred flame.
Oh, the joy of full salvation!
Glory, glory to His name!

442

9.9.6.6.6.4.

1 Fully surrendered — Lord, I would be,
Fully surrendered, dear Lord, to Thee.
  All on the altar laid,
  Surrender fully made,
  Thou hast my ransom paid;
    I yield to Thee.

2 Fully surrendered — life, time, and all,
All Thou hast given me held at Thy call.
  Speak but the word to me,
  Gladly I'll follow Thee,
  Now and eternally
    Obey my Lord.

3 Fully surrendered — silver and gold,
His, who hath given me riches untold.
  All, all belong to Thee,
  For Thou didst purchase me,
  Thine evermore to be,
    Jesus, my Lord.

4 Fully surrendered — Lord, I am Thine;
Fully surrendered, Savior divine!
  Live Thou Thy life in me;
  All fullness dwells in Thee;
  Not I, but Christ in me,
    Christ all in all.

7.6.7.6.

1 In full and glad surrender,
    I give myself to Thee,
Thine utterly and only
    And evermore to be.

2 O Son of God, who lov'st me,
    I will be Thine alone;
And all I have and am, Lord,
    Shall henceforth be Thine own!

3 Reign over me, Lord Jesus;
    Oh, make my heart Thy throne;
It shall be Thine, dear Savior,
    It shall be Thine alone.

4 Oh, come and reign, Lord Jesus,
    Rule over everything!
And keep me always loyal,
    And true to Thee, my King.

8.7.8.7.D.   **444**

1 All for Jesus! All for Jesus!
All my being's ransomed pow'rs;
All my thoughts and words and doings,
All my days and all my hours.
    All for Jesus! All for Jesus!
    All my days and all my hours.
    All for Jesus! All for Jesus!
    All my days and all my hours.

continued

2 Let my hands perform His bidding;
Let my feet run in His ways;
Let mine eyes see Jesus only;
Let my lips speak forth His praise.
    All for Jesus! All for Jesus!
    Let my lips speak forth His praise.
    All for Jesus! All for Jesus!
    Let my lips speak forth His praise.

3 Worldlings prize their gems of beauty,
Cling to gilded toys of dust;
Boast of wealth, and fame, and pleasure;
Only Jesus will I trust.
    All for Jesus! All for Jesus!
    Only Jesus will I trust.
    All for Jesus! All for Jesus!
    Only Jesus will I trust.

4 Since mine eyes were fixed on Jesus,
I've lost sight of all beside —
So enchained my spirit's vision,
Looking at the Crucified.
    All for Jesus! All for Jesus!
    Looking at the Crucified.
    All for Jesus! All for Jesus!
    Looking at the Crucified.

5 Oh, what wonder! how amazing!
Jesus, glorious King of kings,
Deigns to call me His beloved,
Lets me rest beneath His wings.
    All for Jesus! All for Jesus!
    Resting now beneath His wings.
    All for Jesus! All for Jesus!
    Resting now beneath His wings.

7.7.7.7. with repeat.

1 Take my life, and let it be
Consecrated, Lord, to Thee;
Take my moments and my days,
Let them flow in ceaseless praise,
Let them flow in ceaseless praise.

2 Take my hands, and let them move
At the impulse of Thy love;
Take my feet and let them be
Swift and beautiful for Thee,
Swift and beautiful for Thee.

3 Take my voice, and let me sing
Always, only, for my King;
Take my lips, and let them be
Filled with messages from Thee,
Filled with messages from Thee.

4 Take my silver and my gold;
Not a mite would I withhold;
Take my intellect, and use
Every power as Thou shalt choose,
Every power as Thou shalt choose.

5 Take my will, and make it Thine;
It shall be no longer mine.
Take my heart; it is Thine own;
It shall be Thy royal throne,
It shall be Thy royal throne.

6 Take my love; my Lord, I pour
At Thy feet its treasure-store.
Take myself, and I will be
Ever, only, all for Thee,
Ever, only, all for Thee.

446

Peculiar Meter.

1   What shall I give Thee, Master?
    Thou who didst die for me.
  Shall I give less of what I possess,
    Or shall I give all to Thee?

    Jesus, my Lord and Savior;
      Thou hast giv'n all for me;
    Thou didst leave Thy home above
      To die on Calvary.
    What shall I give Thee, Master?
      Thou hast giv'n all for me;
    Not just a part or half of my heart,
      I will give all to Thee.

2   What shall I give Thee, Master?
    Thou hast redeemed my soul;
  My gift is small but it is my all —
    Surrendered to Thy control.

3   What shall I give Thee, Master?
    Giver of gifts divine!
  I will not hold time, talents or gold —
    For everything shall be Thine.

7.6.7.6.D.

1 My spirit, soul, and body,
   Dear Lord, I give to Thee,
   A consecrated offering,
   Thine evermore to be.

   My all is on the altar;
   Lord, I am all Thine own;
   Oh, may my faith ne'er falter!
   Lord, keep me Thine alone.

2 Lord Jesus, mighty Savior,
   I trust in Thy great name;
   I look for Thy salvation,
   Thy promise now I claim.

3 Now, Lord, I yield my members,
   From sin's dominion free,
   For warfare and for triumph,
   As weapons unto Thee.

4 Oh, blissful self-surrender,
   To live, my Lord, by Thee;
   Now, Son of God, my Savior,
   Live out Thy life in me.

5 I'm Thine, O dear Lord Jesus,
   Washed in Thy precious blood,
   Sealed by Thy Holy Spirit,
   A sacrifice to God.

   My all is on the altar;
   I'm waiting for the fire;
   I'm waiting, waiting, waiting;
   I'm waiting for the fire.

448

12.9.12.9. with chorus.

1   You have longed for sweet peace, and for faith
       to increase,
    And have earnestly, fervently prayed;
  But you cannot have rest, or be perfectly blest,
    Until all on the altar is laid.

    Is your all on the altar of sacrifice laid?
      Your heart, does the Spirit control?
    You can only be blest and have peace and
      sweet rest,
      As you yield Him your body and soul.

2   Would you walk with the Lord in the light
      of His Word,
    And have peace and contentment alway;
  You must do His sweet will to be free from
      all ill;
    On the altar your all you must lay.

3   Oh, we never can know what the Lord will
      bestow
    Of the blessings for which we have prayed,
  Till our body and soul He doth fully control,
    And our all on the altar is laid.

4   Who can tell all the love He will send from
      above!
    Oh, how happy our heart will be made!
  Oh, what fellowship sweet we shall share at
      His feet,
    When our all on the altar is laid!

5.4.5.4.D.

449

1 Have Thine own way, Lord,
   Have Thine own way;
Thou art the Potter,
   I am the clay.
Mould me and make me
   After Thy will,
While I am waiting,
   Yielded and still.

2 Have Thine own way. Lord.
   Have Thine own way;
Search me and try me,
   Master, today.
Whiter than snow, Lord,
   Wash me just now,
As in Thy presence
   Humbly I bow.

3 Have Thine own way, Lord,
   Have Thine own way;
Wounded and weary,
   Help me, I pray.
Power, all power,
   Surely is Thine,
Touch me and heal me,
   Savior divine.

4 Have Thine own way, Lord,
   Have Thine own way;
Hold o'er my being
   Absolute sway.
Fill with Thy Spirit
   Till all shall see
Christ only, always,
   Living in me.

450

7.6.7.6. with chorus.

1 Lie still, and let Him mould thee!
   Oh, Lord, I would obey;
Be Thou the skillful Potter,
   And I the yielding clay.

   Bend me, oh, bend me to Thy will,
   While in Thy hand I'm lying still.

2 In Thy dear hand I'm resting,
   Oh, hold me quiet there;
Then soften me and mould me,
   And for Thy will prepare.

3 I need not fear to trust Thee,
   Thy love and skill are such,
New lessons Thou wilt teach me,
   While yielding to Thy touch.

4 Impress Thine image on me,
   Fulfil Thy blest design,
Till others see upon me
   That beauteous face of Thine.

451

8.5.8.5.

1 Not by wrestling, but by clinging
   Shall we be most blest;
Wrestling only brings us sorrow;
   Clinging brings us rest.

2 When we stay our feeble efforts,
   And from struggling cease,
Unconditional surrender
   Brings us God's own peace.

3 Lean we all our weight on Jesus,
   Who alone can save;
He by might of love hath triumphed
   O'er His willing slave.

4 Yielding, we shall know true conquest;
   Dying, we shall live;
"Not my will, but Thine" prevaileth,
   Victory to give.

CONSECRATION — BELONGING TO THE LORD

8.7.8.7.D. with chorus.   **452**

1 Tell me not of earthly pleasures,
   Tempt me not with sordid gain;
Mock me not with earth's illusions,
   Vex me not with honors vain.
I am weaned from sinful idols;
   I am henceforth not my own;
I have given my heart to Jesus,
   I belong to Him alone.

     I am not my own,
     I am not my own.
     I belong to Jesus,
     And I am not my own.

2 Oh, the blessed rest it brings us
   To belong to Christ alone;
We can draw on all His fulness
   When we've nothing of our own.
Blessed Jesus, take me, own me,
   Make me, keep me wholly Thine.
Deign to find in me Thy portion,
   While I joy to call Thee mine.
                  continued

3 Weary soul, give up the struggle,
   Cease at length thyself to own;
Give yourself away to Jesus,
   And belong to Him alone.
Once He gave His all to win thee,
   Now He asks as much of thee;
All He has He fully gives thee;
   Let thy love His portion be.

453   6.6.6.4.

1 Under an eastern sky,
   Amid a rabble's cry,
   A Man went forth to die,
     For me! for me!

2 Thorn-crowned His blessed head,
   Blood-stained His every tread;
   Cross-laden He was led,
     For me! for me!

3 Pierced His hands and feet,
   Three hours o'er Him beat
   Fierce rays of noon-tide heat,
     For me! for me!

4 Thus wert Thou made all mine;
   Lord, make me wholly Thine;
   Grant grace and strength divine
     To me! to me!

5 In thought and word and deed,
   Thy will to do, O lead
   My soul, e'en though it bleed,
     To Thee, to Thee.

10.10.10.10.

1 I lift my heart to Thee,
  Savior Divine,
 For Thou art all to me,
  And I am Thine;
Is there on earth a closer bond than this,
That my Beloved's mine, and I am His?

2 Thine am I by all ties,
  And chiefly Thine,
 For through Thy sacrifice
  Thou, Lord, art mine;
By Thine own cords of love, so sweetly wound
Around me, closely I to Thee am bound.

3 To Thee, Thou Bleeding Lamb,
  I all things owe,
 All that I have and am,
  And all I know;
All that I have is now no longer mine,
And I am not my own: Lord, I am Thine.

4 How can I, Lord, withhold
  Life's brightest hour
 From Thee; or gathered gold,
  Or any power?
Why should I keep one precious thing from Thee,
When Thou hast given Thine own dear Self for me?

5 I pray Thee, Savior, keep
  Me in Thy love,
 Until the world Thou sweep
  And me remove
To that fair realm, where, sin and sorrow o'er,
Thou and Thine own are one for evermore.

455

7.7.7.7.8.8.

1 Every thread I wind this day,
Every footstep on life's way,
Every clod I shall unearth,
Every task, whate'er its worth:
Only for God's glory living,
Blessing, praise and honor giving!

2 All the burdens of the day,
All the words which I shall say,
All the works my God may send,
All the hours in rest I spend:
Ever for His glory living,
Blessing, praise and honor giving!

3 Every blood-drop in the heart,
Every grief and aching smart,
Every bitter pulse of pain,
Every hour of joy again:
Only for God's glory living,
Blessing, praise and honor giving!

4 As I take my daily food,
Greet another on life's road,
Pluck a flower beside the way,
Stoop to lift a wisp of hay:
Ever for God's glory living,
Blessing, praise and honor giving!

5 All, from deeds of little worth,
To the greatest things on earth;
Mine to build some world to be,
Or to lie and gaze on Thee:
For Thy glory daily living,
Blessing, praise and honor giving!

LIVING FOR JESUS

456

Thomas O. Chisholm   10.10.10.10. with chorus.

1 Living for Jesus a life that is true,
   Striving to please Him in all that I do;
   Yielding allegiance, glad-hearted and free,
   This is the pathway of blessing for me.

      O Jesus, Lord and Savior,
      I give myself to Thee,
      For Thou, in Thy atonement,*
      Didst give Thyself for me;
      I own no other Master,
      My heart shall be Thy throne,
      My life I give, henceforth to live,
      O Christ, for Thee alone.

2 Living for Jesus who died in my place,
   Bearing on Calv'ry my sin and disgrace;
   Such love constrains me to answer His call,
   Follow His leading and give Him my all.

3 Living for Jesus wherever I am,
   Doing each duty in His holy name;
   Willing to suffer affliction and loss,
   Deeming each trial a part of my cross.

4 Living for Jesus through earth's little while,
   My dearest treasure, the light of His smile;
   Seeking the lost ones He died to redeem,
   Bringing the weary to find rest in Him.

*The Compilers prefer that the New Testament word, "redemption,"
be used and sung instead of "atonement."

457

8.8.8.6.

1 My life, my love, I give to Thee,
Thou Lamb of God who died for me;
Oh, may I ever faithful be,
  My Savior and my God!

I'll live for Him who died for me,
How happy then my life shall be!
I'll live for Him who died for me,
  My Savior and my God!

2 The world and all its joys I leave;
My life, O Lord, Thou wilt receive;
Henceforth no more Thyself I'll grieve,
  My Savior and my God!

3 O Thou who died on Calvary,
To save my soul and make me free,
That I may ever live for Thee
  My Savior and my God!

458

8.8.8.8.D.

1 Living for Jesus, oh, what peace!
Rivers of pleasure never cease;
Trials may come, yet I'll not fear,
Living for Jesus, He is near.

Help me to serve Thee more and more,
Help me to praise Thee o'er and o'er;
Live in Thy presence day by day,
Never to turn from Thee away.

2 Living for Jesus, oh, what rest!
Pleasing my Savior, I am blest;
Only to live for Him alone,
Doing His will till life is done.

3 Living for Jesus, everywhere,
   All of my burdens He doth bear;
   Friends may forsake me, He'll be true;
   Trusting in Him, He'll guide me through.

4 Living for Jesus, till at last
   Into His glory I have passed;
   There to behold Him on His throne,
   Hear from His lips, "My child, well done!"

6.6.8.6.   **459**

1   Not to ourselves again,
       Not to the flesh we live;
     Not to the world henceforth shall we
       Our strength, our being give.

2   The time past of our lives
       Sufficeth to have wrought
     The fleshly will, which only ill
       Hath to us ever brought.

3   No longer is our life
       A thing unused or vain;
     To us e'en here to live is Christ,
       To us to die is gain.

4   Our life is hid with Christ,
       With Christ in God above,
     Upward our heart would go to Him,
       Whom, seeing not, we love.

5   He liveth, and we live!
       His life for us prevails;
     His fulness fills our mighty void,
       His strength for us avails.

460 (1)

8.7.8.7.D.

1 Jesus, I my cross have taken,
   All to leave and follow Thee;
Destitute, despised, forsaken,
   Thou, from hence, my all shalt be.
Perish every fond ambition,
   All I've sought, and hoped, and known;
Yet how rich is my condition,
   God and Christ are still my own!

2 Let the world despise and leave me,
   They have left my Savior, too;
Human hearts and looks deceive me;
   Thou art not, like man, untrue;
And, while Thou shalt smile upon me,
   God of wisdom, love, and might,
Foes may hate, and friends disown me;
   Show Thy face, and all is bright.

3 Man may trouble and distress me,
   'Twill but drive me to Thy breast;
Life with trials hard may press me,
   Christ will bring me sweeter rest.
O 'tis not in grief to harm me,
   While Thy love is left to me;
O 'twere not in joy to charm me,
   Were that joy unmixed with Thee.

4 Haste thee on from grace to glory,
   Armed by faith and winged by prayer;
God's eternal day's before thee,
   God's own hand shall guide thee there.
Soon shall close thy earthly mission,
   Swift shall pass thy pilgrim days,
Hope shall change to glad fruition,
   Faith to sight, and prayer to praise.

8.7.8.7.D.   **460** (2)

1   Jesus, I my cross have taken,
      All to leave and follow Thee;
  Destitute, despised, forsaken,
      Thou, from hence, my all shalt be.

      I will follow Thee, my Savior,
        Thou didst shed Thy blood for me,
      And though all the world forsake Thee,
        By Thy grace I'll follow Thee.

2   Perish every fond ambition,
      All I've sought, and hoped, and known;
  Yet how rich is my condition,
      God and Christ are still mine own.

3   Let the world despise and leave me,
      They have left my Savior too;
  Human hearts and looks deceive me;
      Thou art not, like man, untrue.

4   And, while Thou shalt smile upon me,
      God of wisdom, love, and might,
  Foes may hate, and friends disown me;
      Show Thy face, and all is bright.

5   Man may trouble and distress me,
      'Twill but drive me to Thy breast;
  Life with trials hard may press me,
      Christ will bring me sweeter rest.

6   Oh! 'tis not in grief to harm me,
      While Thy love is left to me;
  Oh! 'twere not in joy to charm me,
      Were that joy unmixed with Thee.

7   Haste thee on from grace to glory,
      Armed by faith and winged by prayer;
  God's eternal day's before thee,
      God's own hand shall guide thee there.

                                    continued

8 Soon shall close thy earthly mission,
　　Swift shall pass thy pilgrim days,
　Hope shall change to glad fruition,
　　Faith to sight, and prayer to praise.

461

Peculiar Meter.

1 Down in the valley with my Savior I would go,
　Where the flowers are blooming and the sweet
　　　waters flow;
　Everywhere He leads me I would follow, follow on,
　Walking in His footsteps till the crown be won.

　Follow! follow! I would follow Jesus!
　Anywhere, everywhere, I would follow on!
　Follow! follow! I would follow Jesus!
　Everywhere He leads me I would follow on!

2 Down in the valley with my Savior I would go,
　Where the storms are sweeping and the dark
　　　waters flow;
　With His hand to lead me I will never, never fear,
　Dangers cannot fright me if my Lord is near.

3 Down in the valley, or upon the mountain steep,
　Close beside my Savior would my heart ever keep;
　He will lead me safely in the path that He has trod,
　Up to where they gather in the rest of God.

8.8.8.8.   **462**

1   How shall I follow Him I serve?
    How shall I copy Him I love?
    Nor from those blessed footsteps swerve,
    Which lead me to His seat above?

2   Privations, sorrows, bitter scorn,
    The life of toil, the mean abode,
    The faithless kiss, the crown of thorn —
    Are these the consecrated road?

3   Lord, should my path through suff'ring lie,
    Forbid it I should e'er repine;
    Still let me turn to Calvary,
    Nor heed my griefs, rememb'ring Thine.

4   O let me think how Thou didst leave
    Untasted every pure delight,
    To fast, to faint, to watch, to grieve,
    The toilsome day, the homeless night:

5   To faint, to grieve, to die for me!
    Thou camest, not Thyself to please;
    And, dear as earthly comforts be,
    Shall I not love Thee more than these?

CONSECRATION — SERVING THE LORD

7.6.7.6.D.   **463**

1   I love, I love my Master,
        I will not go out free,
    For He is my Redeemer;
        He paid the price for me.
    I would not leave His service,
        It is so sweet and blest;
    And in the weariest moments
        He gives the truest rest.

continued

2 My Master shed His life-blood
   My vassal life to win,
And save me from the bondage
   Of tyrant self and sin.
He chose me for His service,
   And gave me power to choose
That blessed, perfect freedom,
   Which I shall never lose.

3 I would not halve my service,
   His only it must be!
His only, who so loved me,
   And gave Himself for me.
Rejoicing and adoring,
   Henceforth my song shall be,
I love, I love my Master,
   I will not go out free.

464   8.8.8.8.

1 My glorious Victor, Prince Divine,
   Clasp these surrendered hands in Thine;
At length my will is all Thine own,
   Glad vassal of a Savior's throne.

2 My Master, lead me to Thy door;
   Pierce this now willing ear once more;
Thy bonds are freedom; let me stay
   With Thee, to toil, endure, obey.

3 Yes, ear and hand, and thought and will,
   Use all in Thy dear slav'ry still!
Self's weary liberties I cast
   Beneath Thy feet; there keep them fast.

4 Tread them still down; and then I know,
   These hands shall with Thy gifts o'erflow;
And piercèd ears shall hear the tone
   Which tells me Thou and I are one.

7.6.7.6.D.

1 O Jesus, I have promised
     To serve Thee to the end;
   Be Thou forever near me,
     My Master and my Friend;
   I shall not fear the battle
     If Thou art by my side,
   Nor wander from the pathway
     If Thou wilt be my Guide.

2 Oh, let me feel Thee near me;
     The world is ever near;
   I see the sights that dazzle,
     The tempting sounds I hear;
   My foes are ever near me,
     Around me and within;
   But, Jesus, draw Thou nearer,
     And shield my soul from sin.

3 Oh, let me hear Thee speaking,
     In accents clear and still,
   Above the storms of passion,
     The murmurs of self-will;
   Oh, speak to reassure me,
     To hasten, or control;
   Oh, speak, and make me listen,
     Thou Guardian of my soul.

4 O Jesus, Thou hast promised
     To all who follow Thee
   That where Thou art in glory
     There shall Thy servant be;
   And, Jesus, I have promised
     To serve Thee to the end;
   Oh, give me grace to follow,
     My Master and my Friend.

continued

5 Oh, let me see Thy footmarks,
And in them plant mine own;
My hope to follow duly
Is in Thy strength alone.
Oh, guide me, call me, draw me,
Uphold me to the end;
And then to rest receive me,
My Savior and my Friend.

CONSECRATION —
ACKNOWLEDGING THE LORD'S REIGN

466

8.7.8.7.

1 He has entered! He has entered!
Every guest may now depart;
He has taken all the chamber
Of my once divided heart.

2 He has entered! He has entered!
Vanish every doubt and sin;
He has taken full possession,
He is Lord of all within.

3 Long at my poor heart He tarried,
Knocking with His wounded hand;
Wide at last to Him I opened,
Yielding all to His command.

4 He has entered! He has entered!
Every sorrow now must flee;
Where He reigns as King and Master,
There no grief can ever be.

7.6.7.6

1 This day the Lord has spoken,
    This day my choice is made:
  I will be all for Jesus,
    Who all for me has paid.

2 Now His shall be the empire,
    In all things over me;
  And I will be His bond slave,
    Yet gloriously free.

3 From henceforth, owning nothing,
    I cannot lose at all;
  I cannot well be poorer,
    Whatever may befall.

4 Yet could I not be richer,
    If I the world should gain;
  For heav'n and earth shall perish,
    But Jesus will remain.

5 And He will be my treasure,
    And He my boundless store;
  And those who live on Jesus,
    Will never hunger more.

6 Though I am utter weakness,
    In Him I shall prevail;
  And though my love may falter,
    Yet His will never fail.

468

8.6.8.6. with chorus.

1 Am I a soldier of the Cross —
   A follower of the Lamb?
And shall I fear to own His cause,
   Or blush to speak His name?

In the name, the precious name,
   Of Him who died for me,
Through grace I'll win the promised crown,
   Whate'er my cross may be.

2 Must I be carried to the skies
   On flowery beds of ease,
While others fought to win the prize
   And sailed through bloody seas?

3 Are there no foes for me to face?
   Must I not stem the flood?
Is this vile world a friend to grace,
   To help me on to God?

4 Since I must fight if I would reign,
   Increase my courage, Lord!
I'll bear the toil, endure the pain,
   Supported by Thy Word.

469

6.5.6.5.D. with chorus.

1 Who is on the Lord's side?
   Who will serve the King?
Who will be His helpers,
   Other lives to bring?
Who will leave the world's side?
   Who will face the foe?
Who is on the Lord's side?
   Who for Him will go?

By Thy grand redemption,
   By Thy grace divine,
We are on the Lord's side;
   Savior, we are Thine.

2   Not for weight of glory,
     Not for crown and palm,
   Enter we the army,
     Raise the warrior psalm;
   But for love that claimeth
     Lives for whom He died;
   He whom Jesus nameth
     Must be on His side.

3   Jesus, Thou hast bought us,
     Not with gold or gem,
   But with Thine own life-blood,
     For Thy diadem;
   With Thy blessing filling
     Each who comes to Thee,
   Thou hast made us willing,
     Thou hast made us free.

4   Fierce may be the conflict,
     Strong may be the foe,
   But the King's own army
     None can overthrow.
   Round His standard ranging
     Victory is secure,
   For His truth unchanging
     Makes the triumph sure.

5   Chosen to be soldiers
     In an alien land:
   Chosen, called, and faithful,
     For our Captain's band;
   In the service royal
     Let us not grow cold;
   Let us be right loyal,
     Noble, true, and bold.

470

7.7.7.7.7.7.

1 Father, Son and Holy Ghost,
  One in Three, and Three in One,
  As by the celestial host,
  Let Thy will on earth be done;
  Praise by all to Thee be giv'n,
  Glorious Lord of earth and heav'n!

2 Vilest of the sinful race,
  Lo, I answer to Thy call:
  Meanest vessel of Thy grace,
  Grace divinely free for all;
  Lo, I come to do Thy will,
  All Thy counsel to fulfil.

3 If so poor a worm as I,
  May to Thy great glory live,
  All my actions sanctify,
  All my words and thoughts receive;
  Claim me for Thy service, claim
  All I have, and all I am.

4 Take my soul and body's powers,
  Take my mem'ry, mind, and will;
  All my goods and all my hours,
  All I know, and all I feel;
  All I think, or speak, or do;
  Take my heart, but make it new.

5 Now, O God, Thine own I am,
  Now I give Thee back Thine own:
  Freedom, friends, and health, and fame,
  Consecrate to Thee alone;
  Thine I live, thrice happy I;
  Happier still when Thine I die.

8.8.6.8.8.6.

1 How can I ever stay away
And grieve Thy Spirit all the day
　　While Thou dost wait for me?
I now am willing to return,
And wait no longer, for I yearn
　　Henceforth to follow Thee.

2 I offer now without reserve
All that I am and all I have
　　Thy purpose to fulfill.
Oh, may the Lord accept and keep,
That henceforth I may only seek
　　To do the Father's will.

3 When I look back, what grief and shame
That I've brought none to trust Thy name,
　　Thy word I've locked within.
Oh, may the Lord anointing give
And richly through my being live,
　　That I may speak of Him.

4 My gracious Lord has giv'n much grace,
Exceeding e'en a friend my place;
　　I fain would be His bride.
I'd share His life and suffer loss,
Accepting willingly the cross,
　　With Him identified.

472

8.5.8.5.D.

1 Many crowd the Savior's kingdom,
　Few receive His cross;
Many seek His consolation,
　Few will suffer loss.
For the dear sake of the Master,
　Counting all but dross,
For the dear sake of the Master,
　Counting all but dross.

2 Many sit at Jesus' table,
　Few will fast with Him,
When the sorrow-cup of anguish
　Trembles to the brim.
Few watch with Him in the garden,
　Who have sung the hymn,
Few watch with Him in the garden,
　Who have sung the hymn.

3 Many will confess His wisdom,
　Few embrace His shame.
Many, should He smile upon them,
　Will His praise proclaim;
Then, if for a while He leave them,
　They desert His name,
Then, if for a while He leave them,
　They desert His name.

4 But the souls who love Him truly,
　Let woe come or bliss,
These will count their dearest hearts' blood
　Not their own, but His.
Savior, Thou who thus hast loved me,
　Give me love like this,
Savior, Thou who thus hast loved me,
　Give me love like this.

8.6.8.6.D.

1 No mortal tongue can e'er describe
   The freedom of the soul,
When passed beyond all earthly bribe
   To God's complete control.
All things are his, yes, life, and death,
   Things present or to come;
In Christ he draws in peace each breath,
   In Christ he finds his home.

2 When such as we the King can choose,
   To share with Him His throne,
'Tis passing strange that we refuse
   To be our Lord's alone.
O never speak of sacrifice!
   A privilege untold
Is to be His at any price,
   In Calv'ry's hosts enrolled.

3 Arise! the holy bargain strike —
   The fragment for the whole —
All men and all events alike
   Must serve the ransomed soul.
All things are yours when you are His,
   And He and you are one;
A boundless life in Him there is,
   Whence doubt and fear are gone.

474

8.7.8.7. with chorus.

1 I am one with Thee, Lord Jesus,
  One in spirit now with Thee;
All Thyself I now possess, Lord,
  All Thou art now lives in me.

    One with Thee, one with Thee,
      One with Thee, one with Thee;
    Day by day I share Thy riches,
      Thou art everything to me.

2 Now I share Thy human life, Lord,
    Filled with Thy humanity,
  All of Thy complete obedience
    Is available to me.

3 One with Thee in crucifixion,
    On the cross I died in Thee;
  I am dead unto the world, Lord,
    And the world is dead to me.

4 One with Thee in resurrection,
    Risen now to live in Thee,
  With that life which is Thyself, Lord,
    Now in me, Lord, even me.

5 One with Thee in Thine ascension,
    In the heavens now with Thee;
  Here a pilgrim and a stranger,
    My true life is hid in Thee.

6 One with Thee in Thine enthronement,
    Sharing Thine authority,
  Even as I share Thy life, Lord,
    I in Thee and Thou in me.

8.7.8.7.D.

1 One with Thee, Thou Son eternal,
    Joined by faith in spirit one,
Share we in Thy death inclusive
    And Thy life, O God the Son.
One with Thee, Thou Son beloved,
    Part of Thee become thru grace,
Heirs with Thee of our one Father,
    We're Thy Spirit's dwelling place.

2 One with Thee, Thou Son incarnate,
    Born with Thee, the Man of worth,
We, the members of Thy body,
    Sojourn with Thee here on earth.
One with Thee, Thou Son anointed,
    Sharing too the Spirit's power,
We in full cooperation
    Labor with Thee hour by hour.

3 One with Thee, Thou Son forsaken,
    Judgment and the curse we've passed;
We to sin are dead forever,
    Hell beneath our feet is cast.
One with Thee in resurrection,
    Death can never us oppress;
Live we in Thy new creation,
    Bearing fruits of righteousness.

4 One with Thee, Thou Son ascended,
    Seated with Thee on the throne,
Thine authority we share and
    Rule with Thee, Thy rank our own.
One with Thee, Thou Son returning,
    Glorified with Thee we'll be,
E'er to manifest Thy beauty,
    One with Thee eternally.

476

10.10.10.10.

1 Oh, sacred union with the Perfect Mind,
Transcendent bliss which Thou alone canst give;
How blest are they this Peerless One who find,
And, dead to earth, have learned in Thee to live.

2 Thus in Thine arms of love, O Christ, I live,
Lost, and forever lost to all but Thee.
My happy soul, since it hath learned to die,
Hath found new life in Thine Infinity.

3 Go, then, and learn this lesson of the Cross,
And tread the way that saints and prophets trod:
Who, counting life and self and all things loss,
Have found in inward death the life of God.

477

6.6.6.6.D. with chorus.

1 Though Christ a thousand times
In Bethlehem be born,
If He's not born in thee
Thy soul is still forlorn.
The Cross on Golgotha,
Will never save thy soul;
The Cross in thine own heart,
Alone can make thee whole.

O, Cross of Christ, I take thee
Into this heart of mine,
That I to my own self may die
And rise to thy life Divine.

2 What e'er thou lovest, man,
That too become thou must;
God, if thou lovest God,
Dust, if thou lovest dust.

Go out, God will come in;
Die thou and let Him live;
Be not and He will be;
Wait and He'll all things give.

3 To bring thee to thy God,
Love takes the shortest route;
The way which knowledge leads,
Is but a roundabout.
Drive out from thee the world,
And then thy heart shall be
Filled with the love of God,
And holy like as He.

478

8.7.8.7.D. with repeat.

1 Once I stood in condemnation,
Waiting thus the sinner's doom;
Christ in death has wrought salvation,
God has raised Him from the tomb.
Once I was to God a stranger,
Filled with enmity and fear;
He has rescued me from danger,
Love revealed and brought me near.
He has rescued me from danger,
Love revealed and brought me near.

2 Now I see in Christ's acceptance
But the measure of my own;
He who lay beneath my sentence,
Seated high upon the Throne.

continued

Quickened, raised, and in Him seated,
I a full deliverance know;
Every foe has been defeated,
Every enemy laid low,
Every foe has been defeated,
Every enemy laid low.

3 Now I have a life in union
With the risen Lord above;
Now I drink in sweet communion
Some rich foretaste of His love.
Soon, O Lord! in highest glory,
All its vastness I'll explore;
Soon I'll cast my crown before Thee,
While I worship and adore,
Soon I'll cast my crown before Thee,
While I worship and adore.

479 7.7.7.7.D. with chorus.

1 Oh, what a wonderful place
Jesus has given to me!
Saved by His glorious grace,
I may be even as He.
When with my Lord I appear,
Like Him I know I shall be;
But while I walk with Him here,
I may be even as He.

Even as He, even as He,
Wonderful words that even we,
Saved by His marvelous grace may be
One with the Savior, even as He.

2 One in His death on the tree,
   One as He rose from the dead;
I from the curse am as free
   E'en as my glorious head.
One on the throne by His side,
   One in His sonship divine;
One as the bride-groom and bride,
   One as the branch and the vine.

3 One in His merits I stand,
   One as I pray in His name;
All that His worth can command,
   I can with confidence claim.
One in His faith and His love,
   One in His life I may be.
Sealed by the heavenly Dove,
   I may be holy as He.

8.6.8.6   **480**

1 Joined unto Christ the Conqueror,
   His Calv'ry triumph, too,
Assures me in the darkest hour
   That He will take me through.

2 Joined unto Christ the risen Lord,
   Triumphant now above;
The glory of His cross reveals
   Magnificence of love.

3 Joined unto Christ's full victory,
   Magnificently free;
Declare it in the conquering name,
   And powers of darkness flee.

4 Joined unto Christ! Magnificent!
   His wondrous Calvary plan,
Draws us through ages to adore;
   For "Worthy is the Lamb."

481

8.7.8.7.D. with chorus.

1 Crucified with Christ my Savior,
To the world and self and sin;
To the death-born life of Jesus
I am sweetly ent'ring in:
In His fellowship of suff'ring,
To His death conformed to be,
I am going with my Savior
All the way to Calvary.

All the way to Calvary,
Where my Savior went for me,
Help me, Lord, to go with Thee,
All the way to Calvary.

2 'Tis not hard to die with Christ
When His risen life we know;
'Tis not hard to share His suff'rings
When our hearts with joy o'erflow.
In His resurrection power
He has come to dwell in me,
And my heart is gladly going
All the way to Calvary.

3 If we die we'll live with Christ,
If we suffer we shall reign;
Only thus the prize of glory
Can the conqueror attain.
Oh, how sweet, on that glad morning
Should the Master say to thee,
"Yes, my child, thou didst go with me
All the way to Calvary."

8.7.8.7. with chorus.

1   I am crucified with Christ,
And the cross hath set me free;
I have ris'n again with Christ,
And He lives and reigns in me.

Oh! it is so sweet to die with Christ,
To the world, and self, and sin;
Oh! it is so sweet to live with Christ,
As He lives and reigns within.

2   Mystery hid from ancient ages!
But at length to faith made plain:
Christ in me the Hope of Glory,
Tell it o'er and o'er again.

3   This the secret nature hideth,
Harvest grows from buried grain;
A poor tree with better grafted,
Richer, sweeter life doth gain.

4   This the secret of the holy,
Not our holiness, but Him;
O Lord! empty us and fill us,
With Thy fulness to the brim.

5   This the balm for pain and sickness,
Just to all our strength to die,
And to find His life and fulness,
All our being's need supply.

6   This the story of the Master,
Thru the Cross, He reached the Throne,
And like Him our path to glory,
Ever leads through death alone.

9.8.9.9.5.

1 Buried with Christ, and raised with Him too;
What is there left for me to do?
Simply to cease from struggling and strife,
Simply to walk in newness of life.
Glory be to God!

2 Risen with Christ, my glorious Head,
Holiness now the pathway I tread,
Beautiful thought, while walking therein:
He that is dead is freed from sin.
Glory be to God!

3 Living with Christ, who dieth no more,
Following Christ, who goeth before;
I am from bondage utterly freed,
Reckoning self as dead indeed.
Glory be to God!

4 Living for Christ, my members I yield,
Servants to God, for evermore sealed,
Not under law, I'm now under grace,
Sin is dethroned, and Christ takes its place.
Glory be to God!

5 Growing in Christ; no more shall be named
Things of which now I'm truly ashamed,
Fruit unto holiness will I bear,
Life evermore, the end I shall share.
Glory be to God!

8.4.8.8.4. with chorus.

1 When Christ once died on Calvary,
   I too was there;
   'Twas in my place He stood for me,
   And now accepted e'en as He,
   His name I bear.

   I am crucified with Christ, nevertheless I live,
   Yet, not I, but Christ who liveth in me;
   And the life I live in the flesh,
   I live by the faith of the Son of God,
   Who loved, and gave Himself for me.

2 When Christ once rose with life divine,
   I too was there;
   His resurrection pow'r is mine,
   And as the branches and the vine
   His life I share.

3 When Christ will come some day for me,
   I shall be there;
   With Him and like Him I shall be,
   And all His glorious majesty
   I too shall share.

4 O blessed life so deep, so high,
   Lord, keep me there;
   Help me with Christ to live, to die,
   And let me with Him, bye and bye
   His glory share.

485

8.8.8.8.

1 What great provision God has made
   In Jesus' death on Calvary!
   I hung with Him upon the tree,
   And in His tomb I too was laid.

2 I rose with Him from out the grave —
   And how shall I who died to sin
   Continue still to live therein,
   The victor living as the slave?

3 At God's right hand He took His place,
   And while for saints my Savior pleads,
   My heart for sinners intercedes
   That they might know His saving grace.

4 Oh, what a name to me is given —
   A son of God, by second birth!
   I represent Him on the earth,
   He represents me now in heaven.

5 As Jesus dwells beyond the skies,
   I dwell within this world of strife;
   And as He lives within my life,
   In Him I'm in the heavenlies!

486

10.10.10.10.D.

1 Dying with Jesus, by death reckoned mine;
   Living with Jesus a new life divine;
   Looking to Jesus till glory doth shine,
   Moment by moment, O Lord, I am Thine.

UNION WITH CHRIST — IDENTIFIED WITH HIS DEATH AND RESURRECTION

Chorus:

> Moment by moment I'm kept in His love,
> Moment by moment I've life from above;
> Looking to Jesus till glory doth shine;
> Moment by moment, O Lord, I am Thine.

2 Never a battle with wrong for the right,
Never a contest that He doth not fight;
Lifting above us His banner so white;
Moment by moment I'm kept in His sight.

3 Never a trial that He is not there,
Never a burden that He doth not bear;
Never a sorrow that He doth not share,
Moment by moment, I'm under His care.

4 Never a heartache, and never a groan,
Never a teardrop, and never a moan;
Never a danger but there on the throne
Moment by moment He thinks of His own.

5 Never a weakness that He doth not feel,
Never a sickness that He cannot heal;
Moment by moment, in woe or in weal,
Jesus, my Savior, abides with me still.

487*

11.9.11.9. with chorus.

What a wondrous fact, I'm crucified with Christ;
  Of my flesh and passion I'm relieved;
What a glorious fact, with Christ, the Lord, I live,
  Resurrection life in Him received.

> On the Cross of Calvary the Lord and I
>   Were crucified, were crucified;
> Now in resurrection life with Him I live
>   And in Him e'er abide.

488 †

8.8.8.8.

1 Lord, Thou hast shown the mystery,
How on the Cross I died with Thee;
I need no other pow'r or way
That I may triumph day by day.

2 That cross of Thine is also mine,
Into my life its light doth shine;
When I believe I'm dead with Thee,
The world has lost its pow'r o'er me.

3 Since I am crucified with Thee,
From sin and self I am set free;
How can I still enjoy the world
Or seek its vanities unfurled?

4 I take my place, dear Lord, with Thee
Upon the cross of Calvary.
Thy life and power then are mine,
Since Thou and I in oneness twine.

5 Since Thou didst come to slay the foe,
His work and power to overthrow,
I too can overcome in Thee
And prove Thy mighty pow'r in me.

6 Yet, for the vict'ry we rely
Upon the death which Thou didst die;
We tread the path which Thou hast trod
Until we reach the goal in God.

7 My death with Thee I now believe
And all its meaning would receive.
Thy death more deeply show to me,
That from my flesh I may be free.

8 I long to win as Thou hast won,
To reign with Thee when Thou dost come.
If we the cross will gladly bear,
Then in Thy glory we will share.

8.8.8.8.

1 Oh, Jesus, Lord, when Thou on earth
Accompanied Thy faithful band,
It seemed they knew, but knew Thee not,
Thyself they did not understand.

2 They heard Thy voice, beheld Thy form,
Thy beauteous stature unforgot;
They crowded 'round Thee, met Thy gaze,
But who Thou art, they knew it not.

3 As they of old we too are veiled;
We've known Thee long apparently;
Yet if we say we know, at best
We know Thee not transparently.

4 But as the Spirit now Thou art,
Another Comforter become;
Reveal Thyself within my heart,
Since to Thy temple Thou hast come.

5 With Thy blest Spirit, Lord, fill me,
Fill every corner of my soul;
May Thou inspire my every part,
Oh may Thou touch, renew the whole.

6 The Spirit then revealing make
Thyself more real within my heart,
That ear not hear, nor eye may see
How very real to me Thou art.

7 When Thou in mercy dost reveal
And give Thyself as Spirit thus,
What in the world can be more real,
More true than what Thou art to us?

8 Thy Spirit, Lord, in mine, I pray,
O'erflow my being as a flood,
That every part with glory shine
And everywhere be Thee and God.

continued

9   How close we are in such a life,
     In one is blended earth with heav'n;
     Thy presence sweetly fills our souls;
     Our hearts are to Thy praises giv'n.

490 †   8.8.8.8.

1   Lord, when the Father ne'er was known,
     The Father came through Thee below,
     That we who lived in ignorance
     Might through Thyself the Father know.

2   But, Lord, when Thou wast here on earth,
     How scarce were those Thyself who knew;
     A veil there was 'twixt Thee and them;
     They crowded 'round, but saw not through.

3   Now as the Spirit Thou hast come
     E'en as the Father came in Thee;
     As we through Thee the Father know,
     Now through the Spirit we know Thee.

4   Not with the flesh Thou now art clothed —
     Then must Thou walk with toil around;
     But as the Spirit in our heart
     Thou dost supply Thyself unbound.

5   Thou, Lord, the Father once wast called,
     But now the Holy Spirit art;
     The Spirit is Thine other form,
     Thyself to dwell within our heart.

6   By knowing Thee as Spirit, Lord,
     We realize Thy life's outflow,
     Thy glory and Thy character,
     And all Thy being's wonders know.

7   Praise to Thy Name now floods our heart;
     There is no one as dear as Thee;
     For since we know how real Thou art,
     No other one could lovelier be.

8.8.8.8.

1 Lord, Thou didst know when in the flesh,
As such I'd know Thee shallowly;
Then as the Spirit Thou didst come
Within my spirit, known to be.

2 In flesh Redeemer mine Thou art;
As Spirit now my Comforter.
The outward touch has passed away
For inward union worthier.

3 Because Thou art the Spirit now,
Thyself revealing ceaselessly,
Within my spirit I may know
Thy presence and reality.

4 I know Thy life surpassing far
The knowledge Thy disciples had,
Although they walked and lived with Thee,
When Thou on earth in flesh wast clad.

5 Because Thy Spirit dwells within,
How real, O Lord, Thou art to me;
Not touched, yet more reliable,
Not seen, yet loved more fervently.

6 Thy Holy Spirit deep within
Supplies Thyself as righteousness,
As holiness, redemption full,
As wisdom and as fruitfulness.

7 Thy Spirit in my spirit now
Supplies Thyself, unites with me,
Thus I am all the time myself
And constantly am also Thee.

492†

8.8.8.8

1 In all thy work, O Lord, Thou didst
 At Calv'ry's cross once come to rest;
 Yet Thou art working still today,
 But in another form expressed.

2 Thy saving pow'r Thou still dost show;
 Thou still dost speak, enlighten, guide;
 Thou and the Spirit in one stream
 Sweep many in Thy living tide.

3 Through Him Thy power's not withheld;
 Through Him Thy working does not cease;
 Thou still dost comfort and command,
 Encourage, strengthen, and release.

4 Since Thou art with the Spirit one
 His coming means that Thou hast come,
 And His indwelling is Thine own,
 Since Thou the Spirit hast become.

5 He executes within my heart
 All Thy desires and Thy demands,
 As for the Father here on earth
 Thou hast performed all His commands.

6 By knowing Him we know Thyself;
 Obeying Him we Thee obey;
 Allowing Him ourselves to fill,
 We're filled with Thee, O wondrous way!

7 Thou art not far away in heav'n,
 Leaving us here alone, apart;
 But Thou art still on earth; how grand!
 Thou livest right within my heart.

493*

8.8.8.8.

1 O Lord, Thou art the Spirit now
That gives us life and quickens us,
With all Thy riches strengthening,
O how divine and glorious!

2 O Lord, Thou art the Spirit now
That with Thy power liberates;
And by Thy liberation true
The law of life now regulates.

3 O Lord, Thou art the Spirit now
That transforms us and saturates,
And to Thine image true conforms
And with Thy light illuminates.

4 O Lord, Thou art the Spirit now
Who in my spirit makes His home;
He mingles with my spirit too,
And both one spirit thus become.

5 Lord, teach me how to exercise
My spirit now to contact Thee,
That in Thy Spirit I may walk
And live by Thy reality.

494*　　　　　　　8.8.8.8.

1　Christ is the testimony true
　　Of God in essence and in deed;
　　God's glory He has fully shown,
　　And we in Him God's nature read.

2　His testimony is more full
　　Than was the witness of the law,
　　Which only God in letter showed,
　　And not in endless living pow'r.

3　The fulness of the Godhead dwells
　　In Him, His very element;
　　God's full embodiment is He —
　　A vessel, God the resident.

4　The Father God He manifests;
　　God's glorious features He displays;
　　In Him consummately are seen
　　The Father's heart and all His ways.

5　Christ as the Spirit now has come
　　That He our portion be fore'er;
　　In spirit we partake of Him
　　And all God's being fully share.

AS GOD'S CENTRALITY AND UNIVERSALITY

495*　　　　　　　7.7.7.7.

1　Christ is God's centrality
　　And His universality;
　　He is God's delight and joy
　　Throughout all eternity.

2　He's th' embodiment of God,
　　In Him all God's fulness dwells;
　　His unique supremacy
　　And His Godhead none excels.

3   All God's purpose is for Him,
    That He might be all in all;
    All the things in heav'n and earth
    With Himself are made withal.

4   All creation is for Christ,
    Everything was made by Him;
    'Tis by Him all things subsist,
    He's the hub and He's the rim.

5   In redemption He is all,
    All through Him is reconciled;
    By His blood all things with God
    Now in peace are domiciled.

6   He the great beginning is,
    And the Church's living Head;
    He her life and content too,
    And the firstborn from the dead.

7   In God's Kingdom He's the King,
    All the pow'r to Him is giv'n;
    In His glory He shall rule
    Over all in earth and heav'n.

8   In new heaven and new earth
    Center of all things He'll be,
    For the Godhead and for man
    Throughout all eternity.

9   God intends in everything
    Christ should have preeminence,
    And that such a Christ of all
    We should now experience.

496*

10.10.10.10.

1   Christ is the one reality of all,
    Of Godhead and of man and all things else;
    No man without Him ever findeth God,
    Without Him man and everything is false.

2   All types and figures of the ancient time,
    All things we ever need, both great and small,
    Only are shadows of the Christ of God,
    Showing that He must be our all in all.

3   All things are vanity of vanities,
    Christ, the reality all things to fill;
    Though everything we may enjoy and own,
    If we're devoid of Christ we're empty still.

4   Christ is our real God, our real Lord,
    Christ is our real life, our real light;
    Christ is our real food, our real drink,
    Our real clothing, and our real might.

5   Christ also is the one reality
    Of all our doctrine and theology;
    And all our scriptural knowledge without Him
    Is just in letter and is vanity.

6   Christ, the reality of time and space,
    Christ, the reality of every stage;
    Christ is the one reality of all
    Thru all eternity from age to age.

10.10.10.10.

1 Grace in its highest definition is
God in the Son to be enjoyed by us;
It is not only something done or giv'n,
But God Himself, our portion glorious.

2 God is incarnate in the flesh that we
Him may receive, experience ourself;
This is the grace which we receive of God,
Which comes thru Christ and which is
   Christ Himself.

3 Paul the Apostle counted all as dung,
'Twas only God in Christ he counted grace;
'Tis by this grace — the Lord experienced —
That he surpassed the others in the race.

4 It is this grace — Christ as our inward strength —
Which with His all-sufficiency doth fill;
It is this grace which in our spirit is,
There energizing, working out God's will.

5 This grace, which is the living Christ Himself,
Is what we need and must experience;
Lord, may we know this grace and by it live,
Thyself increasingly as grace to sense.

498

8.6.8.6. with chorus.

1 This is my wonderful story,
   Christ to my heart has come;
Jesus, the King of Glory,
   Finds in my heart a home.

      Christ in me, Christ in me,
      Christ in me, O wonderful story,
      Christ in me, Christ in me,
      Christ in me, the hope of glory.

2 Was there e'er story so moving,
   Story of love and pain;
Was there e'er Bridegroom so loving,
   Seeking our hearts to gain.

3 I am so glad I received Him,
   Jesus my heart's dear King;
I who so often have grieved Him,
   All to His feet would bring.

4 How can I ever be lonely,
   How can I ever fall;
What can I want, if only
   Christ is my all in all?

5 Now in His bosom confiding,
   This my glad song shall be;
I am in Christ abiding,
   And Christ abides in me.

8.8.8.8.8.8. with repeat.

499*

1 Oh, what a life! Oh, what a peace!
The Christ who's all within me lives.
With Him I have been crucified;
This glorious fact to me He gives.
Now it's no longer I that live,
But Christ the Lord within me lives.

2 Oh, what a joy! Oh, what a rest!
Christ now is being formed in me.
His very nature and life divine
In my whole being inwrought shall be.
All that I am came to an end,
And all of Christ is all to me.

3 Oh, what a thought! Oh, what a boast!
Christ shall in me be magnified.
In nothing shall I be ashamed,
For He in all shall be applied.
In woe or blessing, death or life,
Through me shall Christ be testified.

4 Oh, what a prize! Oh, what a gain!
Christ is the goal toward which I press.
Nothing I treasure, nor aught desire,
But Christ of all-inclusiveness.
My hope, my glory, and my crown
Is Christ, the One of peerlessness.

(Repeat the last two lines of each stanza)

8.8.8.8.8.8. with repeat.

500*

1 Oh, what a might! Oh, what a strength!
God wrought to raise Christ from the dead.
Far above all at His right hand,
O'er all to us He is the Head.
All this great pow'r is to the Church
That she o'er all her foes may tread.

(Repeat the last two lines of each stanza) *continued*

2 Oh, what a fact! Oh, what a bliss!
   That I of Christ a member am.
   With all the saints I blend as one
   And share the life of the new man.
   Joined to our great ascended Head,
   We'll be the Church of His own plan.

3 Oh, what a breadth! Oh, what a length!
   The height, the depth unsearchable!
   Christ the Lord is unlimited,
   So vast, immense, immeas'rable.
   All that He is and all He has
   Is now our life unspeakable.

501* 8.8.8.8. with chorus.

1 O glorious Christ, Savior mine,
   Thou art truly radiance divine;
   God infinite, in eternity,
   Yet man in time, finite to be.

        Oh! Christ, expression of God, the Great,
        Inexhaustible, rich, and sweet!
        God mingled with humanity
        Lives in me my all to be.

2 The fulness of God dwells in Thee;
   Thou dost manifest God's glory;
   In flesh Thou hast redemption wrought;
   As Spirit, oneness with me sought.

3 All things of the Father are Thine;
   All Thou art in Spirit is mine;
   The Spirit makes Thee real to me,
   That Thou experienced might be.

4 The Spirit of life causes Thee
   By Thy Word to transfer to me.
   Thy Spirit touched, Thy word received,
   Thy life in me is thus conceived.

5 In spirit while gazing on Thee,
   As a glass reflecting Thy glory,
   Like to Thyself transformed I'll be,
   That Thou might be expressed thru me.

6 In no other way could we be
   Sanctified and share Thy vict'ry;
   Thus only spiritual we'll be
   And touch the life of glory.

7 Thy Spirit will me saturate,
   Every part will God permeate,
   Deliv'ring me from the old man,
   With all saints building for His plan.

6.6.6.6.8.6.   **502**

1 Once I was dead in sin,
      And hope within me died;
   But now I'm dead to sin,
      With Christ I'm crucified.

      And can it be that "He loved me,
         And gave Himself for me"?

2 O height I cannot reach!
      O depth I cannot sound!
   O love, O boundless love,
      In my Redeemer found!

3 I live — and yet not I,
      But Christ that lives in me,
   Who from the law of sin
      And death has made me free.

HE LIVES

503

Alfred H. Ackley   Peculiar Meter.

1 I serve a risen Savior;
   He's in the world today.
I know that He is living,
   Whatever men may say.
I see His hand of mercy;
   I hear His voice of cheer;
And just the time I need Him
   He's always near.

He lives, He lives, Christ Jesus
   lives today!
He walks with me and talks with
   me along life's narrow way.
He lives, He lives, salvation to
   impart!
You ask me how I know He lives?
   He lives within my heart.

2 In all the world around me
   I see His loving care,
And though my heart grows weary,
   I never will despair;
I know that He is leading,
   Through all the stormy blast;
The day of His appearing
   Will come at last.

3 Rejoice, rejoice, O Christian,
   Lift up your voice and sing
Eternal hallelujahs
   To Jesus Christ the King!
The Hope of all who seek Him,
   The Help of all who find,
None other is so loving,
   So good and kind.

504

6.6.8.6.

1 Jesus, I live to Thee,
The Loveliest and Best;
My life in Thee, Thy life in me,
In Thy blest love I rest.

2 Jesus, I die to Thee,
Whenever death shall come;
To die in Thee is life to me,
With Thee I'm ever one!

3 Whether to live or die,
I know not which is best;
To live in Thee is bliss to me,
To die is endless rest.

4 Living or dying, Lord,
I ask but to be Thine;
My life in Thee, Thy life in me,
Makes Thee forever mine.

Peculiar Meter.

505

1 There's a Man in the
glory
Whose Life is for me.
He's pure and He's holy,
Triumphant and free.
He's wise and He's loving,
How tender is He!
His Life in the glory,
My life must be;
His Life in the glory,
My life must be.

2 There's a Man in the
glory
Whose Life is for me.
He overcame Satan;
From bondage He's free.
In Life He is reigning;
How kingly is He!
His Life in the glory,
My life must be;
His Life in the glory,
My life must be.

continued

3 There's a Man in the
    glory
  Whose Life is for me.
  In Him is no sickness;
  No weakness has He.
  He's strong and in vigor,
  How buoyant is He!
  His Life in the glory
  My life may be;
  His Life in the glory
  My life may be.

4 There's a Man in the
    glory
  Whose Life is for me.
  His peace is abiding;
  How patient is He!
  He's joyful and radiant,
  Expecting to see
  His Life in the glory
  Lived out in me;
  His Life in the glory
  Lived out in me.

506   7.8.7.8.4.

1 Jesus lives! thy terrors now
   Can, O Death, no more appall us;
   Jesus lives! by this we know
   Thou, O Grave, canst not enthrall us.
     Hallelujah!

2 Jesus lives! henceforth is death
   But the gate of Life immortal;
   This shall calm our trembling breath,
   When we pass its gloomy portal.
     Hallelujah!

3 Jesus lives! for us He died;
   Then alone to Jesus living,
   Pure in heart may we abide,
   Glory to our Savior giving.
     Hallelujah!

4 Jesus lives! our hearts know well
   Naught from us His love shall sever;
   Life, nor death, nor powers of hell
   Tear us from His keeping ever.
     Hallelujah!

5   Jesus lives! to Him the Throne
    Over all the world is given;
    We, in spirit with Him one,
    Rest and reign with Him in heaven.
    Hallelujah!

8.6.8.6. with chorus.   **507**

1   Once far from God and dead in sin,
    No light my heart could see;
    But in God's Word the light I found,
    Now Christ liveth in me.

      Christ liveth in me,
      Christ liveth in me;
      Oh! what a salvation this,
      That Christ liveth in me.

2   As rays of light from yonder sun,
    The flow'rs of earth set free,
    So life and light and love come forth
    From Christ living in me.

3   As lives the flow'r within the seed,
    As in the cone the tree,
    So, praise the Christ of truth and grace,
    His Spirit dwelleth in me.

4   With longing all my heart is filled,
    That like Him I may be,
    As on the wondrous thought I dwell
    That Christ liveth in me.

508

7.6.7.6.D.

1 Made free! Made free! O captive!
   Bound by the law of sin,
The law of life in Spirit
   Will quicken you within.
And counting on the Spirit,
   His life shall now control
The members of your body,
   The portals of your soul.

2 Made free! Made free in Jesus:
   For crucified with Him,
From center to circumf'rence,
   He breaks the power of sin.
No longer act in body
   As if it had no "law";
His "law of life" must govern
   All that ran wild before.

3 Made free! Made free in Jesus:
   Deep planted in His death,
He liberates His life pow'r,
   And breathes His Spirit's breath.
Then waxing strong in spirit,
   With force of quickening life;
The soul and body governed,
   Its members cease from strife!

4 Made free! Made free in Jesus:
   Joined to the Risen One,
By conflict prayer you triumph,
   And claim His victory won.
Freed with His glorious freedom,
   Above the darkness rife;
For now the law of sin and death
   Is conquered by His life.

8.8.8.6. with chorus.

1 A flowing river and a tree,
   Eden's outstanding features are,
   Man to supply with food and drink
   That he may live fore'er.

   God is in Christ to be my supply,
   God as the Spirit nourisheth me;
   If upon Christ in spirit I feed,
   Filled with His life I'll be.

2 The tree the glorious Christ does show,
   As living food to man supplied,
   That he God's riches may enjoy,
   Thus to be satisfied.

3 The river does the Spirit show,
   Coming man's spirit to supply,
   That with God's riches he be filled,
   Holy to be thereby.

4 The Christ of glory is my life,
   He as the Spirit lives in mine,
   That I with God be fully blent
   And in His image shine.

5 I would exalt this glorious Christ,
   Ever the Spirit I'd obey,
   Making His glory fully known,
   Filled with His grace for aye.

510*

8.6.8.6.

1 I've found the One of peerless worth,
My heart doth sing for joy;
And sing I must, for Christ I have:
Oh, what a Christ have I!

2 My Christ, He is the Lamb of God,
Who full salvation brings;
He is the Sun of Righteousness,
With healing in His wings.

3 My Christ, He is the Tree of Life
With fruit abundant, sweet;
My hunger He doth satisfy;
Of Him I daily eat.

4 My Christ, He is the smitten Rock
Whence living waters burst;
He is the fountain in my heart
Which quenches all my thirst.

5 Christ is my life, my light, my way,
My comfort and my health,
My peace, my rest, my joy, my hope,
My glory and my wealth.

6 Christ is my wisdom and my pow'r,
My boast and righteousness,
My vict'ry and redemption sure,
My truth and holiness.

7 Christ is my Savior, Shepherd, Lord,
My Advocate above,
My Counsellor, my Father, God,
My Brother, Friend, and Love.

8　Christ is my Captain and my Guard,
　　My Teacher and my Guide,
　　My Bridegroom, Master and my Head;
　　In me doth He reside.

9　Christ is my Prophet, Priest, and King;
　　My Prophet full of sight;
　　My Priest that stands 'twixt me and God,
　　My King that rules with might.

10　Christ is the Author of my faith,
　　And its Perfecter too,
　　My Mediator, Guarantee,
　　And faithful Witness true.

11　Christ is my everlasting home,
　　My all-sufficient land;
　　My fortress, tower, hiding-place,
　　And my eternal stand.

12　Christ is my sabbath and new moon,
　　My morning and my day,
　　My age and my eternity
　　That ne'er will pass away.

13　Christ is my trust and my desire,
　　In comeliness replete,
　　My satisfaction and delight,
　　Who all my need doth meet.

14　My Christ, the all-inclusive One,
　　My Christ what shall I call?
　　He is the first, He is the last,
　　My Christ is All in all.

15　Since such a treasure I possess,
　　My heart doth sing for joy;
　　And I must sing, and sing again;
　　Oh, what a Christ have I!

511   8.7.8.7.D.

1 Jesus only is our message,
  Jesus all our theme shall be;
  We will lift up Jesus ever,
  Jesus only will we see.

    Jesus only, Jesus ever,
    Jesus all in all we sing,
    Savior, Sanctifier, and Healer,
    Glorious Lord and coming King.

2 Jesus only is our Savior,
  All our guilt He bore away,
  He, our righteousness forever,
  All our strength from day to day.

3 Jesus is our Sanctifier,
  Saving us from self and sin,
  And with all His Spirit's fulness,
  Filling all our hearts within.

4 Jesus only is our Healer,
  All our sicknesses He bare,
  And His risen life and fulness,
  All His members still may share.

5 Jesus only is our Power,
  He the gift of Pentecost;
  Jesus, breathe Thy pow'r upon us,
  Fill us with the Holy Ghost.

6 And for Jesus we are waiting,
  List'ning for the Advent Call;
  But 'twill still be Jesus only,
  Jesus ever, all in all.

7.6.7.6.7.7.

1 Jesus, Sun and Shield art Thou,
   Sun and Shield forever.
   Never canst Thou cease to shine,
   Cease to guard us, never.
   Cheer our steps as on we go,
   Come between us and the foe.

2 Jesus, Bread and Wine art Thou,
   Wine and Bread forever.
   Never canst Thou cease to feed
   Or refresh us, never.
   Feed us still on bread divine,
   Drink we still of heavenly wine.

3 Jesus, Love and Life art Thou,
   Life and Love forever.
   Ne'er to quicken shalt Thou cease,
   Or to love us, never.
   All of life and love we need
   Is in Thee, in Thee indeed.

4 Jesus, Peace and Joy art Thou,
   Joy and Peace forever.
   Joy that fades not, changes not,
   Peace that leaves us never.
   Joy and Peace we have in Thee
   Now and through eternity.

5 Jesus, Song and Strength art Thou,
   Strength and Song forever.
   Strength that never can decay,
   Song that ceaseth never.
   Still to us this strength and song,
   Through eternal days prolong.

6.5.6.5.D. with chorus.

1 Once it was the blessing,
　　Now it is the Lord;
　Once it was the feeling,
　　Now it is His Word;
　Once His gift I wanted,
　　Now, the Giver own;
　Once I sought for healing,
　　Now Himself alone.

　　All in all forever,
　　　Only Christ I'll sing;
　　Everything is in Christ,
　　　And Christ is everything.

2 Once 'twas painful trying,
　　Now 'tis perfect trust;
　Once a half salvation,
　　Now the uttermost;
　Once 'twas ceaseless holding,
　　Now He holds me fast;
　Once 'twas constant drifting,
　　Now my anchor's cast.

3 Once 'twas busy planning,
　　Now 'tis trustful prayer;
　Once 'twas anxious caring,
　　Now He has the care;
　Once 'twas what I wanted,
　　Now what Jesus says;
　Once 'twas constant asking,
　　Now 'tis ceaseless praise.

4   Once it was my working,
    His it hence shall be;
Once I tried to use Him,
    Now He uses me;
Once the pow'r I wanted,
    Now the Mighty One;
Once for self I labored,
    Now for Him alone.

5   Once I hoped in Jesus,
    Now I know He's mine;
Once my lamps were dying,
    Now they brightly shine;
Once for death I waited,
    Now His coming hail;
And my hopes are anchored
    Safe within the veil.

514

Peculiar Meter.

1   There is One amid all changes
    Who standeth ever fast,
One who covers all the future,
    The present and the past;
It is Christ the Rock of Ages,
    The first and the last,
    The first and the last.

continued

514

Chorus:

> Jesus is the first,
> Jesus is the last,
> Trust Him for thy future,
> Leave with Him the past;
> Jesus is the first,
> Jesus is the last,
> Christ the Rock of Ages,
> The first and the last.

2 There is One whose arms upholdeth
   This whole creation vast,
Yet He bids us on His bosom
   Our cares and sorrows cast;
Let us bring them all to Jesus,
   The first and the last,
   The first and the last.

3 There is One whose love has kept us
   Through every stormy blast,
And His hand will guard and guide us
   Till all the storms are past;
Jesus, we will trust Thee ever,
   The first and the last,
   The first and the last.

4 First and last, O Christ, we crown Thee,
   Our fondest love Thou hast;
Lord of lords, before Thy footstool
   Let every crown be cast;
Haste the day when all shall crown Thee,
   The first and the last,
   The first and the last.

Peculiar Meter.

1 All is in Christ;
   God's dear Son is Lord of all.
Jesus Christ is life's perfection,
   Perfect love and perfect light.
Son of God, the true reflection
   Of the Father's radiance bright.
All the treasures of God's riches,
   All the secrets of His wisdom,
All in Christ are hid away.
   Let His name be praised today!

2 All is in Christ;
   God's dear Son is Lord of all.
Blessings are imparted to us
   By the shameful cross He bore.
By His suffering inglorious
   We have peace forevermore.
By the Cross we have forgiveness,
   Life eternal, endless mercy.
By God's Son is freely giv'n
   Everything in earth and heav'n.

3 All is in Christ;
   God's dear Son is Lord of all.
In me there is naught but weakness,
   I am worthless, full of sin,
Stricken by its mortal sickness,
   Lacking light and hope within.
Now in Christ I find abundant
   Victory and strength and power.
Savior, come and live in me,
   Come and make me rich in Thee.

4 All is in Christ;
   God's dear Son is Lord of all.

continued

Savior, pardon my transgressions,
    For my love is still so small;
Though I gave all my possessions,
    This would profit scarce at all.
'Tis myself that Thou desirest;
    So I give myself, dear Master;
No thing hast Thou kept from me —
    Nor will I keep aught from Thee.

5   All is in Christ;
        Your whole self present to Him.
    Vain your quest for lasting pleasure,
        Wealth, success, and worldly fame;
    Christ alone must be your treasure,
        His resource your only claim.
    Come, let Him disperse the famine
        Of your arid, waste existence.
    Let God's Son, th' Immortal King
        Freely give you everything.

With kind permission of La Ligue pour la lecture
de la Bible, Vennes-Lausanne.

516   8.8.8.8.

1   Lord of all being, throned afar,
    Thy glory flames from sun and star;
    Center and light of every sphere,
    Yet to each loving heart how near.

2   Sun of our life, Thy quickening ray
    Sheds on our path the glow of day;
    Star of our hope, Thy softened light
    Cheers the long watches of the night.

3   Our midnight is Thy smile withdrawn,
    Our noontide is Thy gracious dawn,
    Our rainbow arch Thy mercy's sign;
    All, save the clouds of sin, are Thine.

4 Lord of all life, below, above,
Whose light is truth, whose warmth is love,
Before Thy ever-blazing throne
We ask no luster of our own.

5 Grant us Thy truth to make us free,
And kindling hearts that burn for Thee,
Till all Thy living altars claim
One holy light, one heavenly flame.

10.10.10.9. with chorus.   **517**

1 Jesus, my Savior, is all things to me;
Oh, what a wonderful Savior is He,
Guiding, protecting, o'er life's rolling sea,
Mighty Deliv'rer — Jesus for me.

Jesus for me,
Jesus for me,
All the time everywhere,
Jesus for me.

2 Jesus in sickness, and Jesus in health,
Jesus in poverty, comfort or wealth;
Sunshine or tempest, whatever it be,
He is my safety — Jesus for me.

3 He is my Refuge, my Rock, and my Tower,
He is my Fortress, my Strength and my Pow'r;
Life everlasting, my Daysman is He,
Blessed Redeemer — Jesus for me.

4 He is my Prophet, my Priest and my King,
He is my Bread of Life, Fountain and Spring;
Bright Sun of Righteousness, Daystar is He,
Horn of Salvation — Jesus for me.

5 Jesus in sorrow, in joy, or in pain,
Jesus my Treasure in loss or in gain;
Constant Companion where'er I may be,
Living or dying — Jesus for me.

518

8.6.8.6.8.8.8.6.

1 Whom have I, Lord, in heav'n but Thee?
   None but Thee! None but Thee!
And this my song through life shall be:
   Christ for me! Christ for me!
He hath for me the serpent trod,
   He hath redeemed me "by His blood,"
And reconciled my soul to God:
   Christ for me! Christ for me!

2 I envy not the rich their joys:
   Christ for me! Christ for me!
I covet not earth's glitt'ring toys:
   Christ for me! Christ for me!
Earth can no lasting bliss bestow,
   "Fading" is stamped on all below;
Mine is a joy no end can know:
   Christ for me! Christ for me!

3 Though with the poor be cast my lot:
   Christ for me! Christ for me!
"He knoweth best," I murmur not:
   Christ for me! Christ for me!
Though "vine" and "fig-tree" blight assail,
   The "labor of the olive fail,"
And death o'er flock and herd prevail,
   Christ for me! Christ for me!

4 Though I am now on hostile ground,
   Christ for me! Christ for me!
And sin beset me all around,
   Christ for me! Christ for me!
Let earth her fiercest battles wage,
   And foes against my soul engage,
Strong in His strength I scorn their rage:
   Christ for me! Christ for me!

5 And when my life draws to its close,
   Christ for me! Christ for me!
Safe in His arms I shall repose,
   Christ for me! Christ for me!
When sharpest pains my frame pervade,
   And all the powers of nature fade,
Still will I sing through death's cold shade;
   Christ for me! Christ for me!

8.6.8.6.8.8.8.6.   519

1 My heart is fixed, eternal God,
   Fixed on Thee, fixed on Thee;
And my immortal choice is made,
   Christ for me, Christ for me;
He is my prophet, priest, and king,
Who did for me salvation bring,
And while I've breath I mean to sing,
   Christ for me, Christ for me.

2 In Him I see the Godhead shine,
   Christ for me, Christ for me;
He is the majesty divine,
   Christ for me, Christ for me;
The Father's well-beloved Son,
Co-partner of His royal throne,
Who bore the guilt of man alone,
   Christ for me, Christ for me.

3 Let others boast of heaps of gold,
   Christ for me, Christ for me;
His riches never can be told,
   Christ for me, Christ for me;
Your gold will waste and wear away,
Your honors perish in a day;
My portion never can decay,
   Christ for me, Christ for me.

continued

4   In pining sickness, or in health,
        Christ for me, Christ for me;
    In deepest poverty or wealth,
        Christ for me, Christ for me;
    And in that all-important day,
    When I the summons must obey,
    And pass from this dark world away,
        Christ for me, Christ for me.

520   8.10.10.4.

1   None other Lamb, none other Name,
    None other hope in heav'n or earth or sea,
    None other hiding-place from guilt and shame,
        None beside Thee.

2   My faith burns low, my hope burns low;
    Only my heart's desire cries out in me
    By the deep thunder of its want and woe,
        Cries out to Thee.

3   Lord, Thou art Life, though I be dead;
    Love's fire Thou art, however cold I be;
    Nor heaven have I, nor place to lay my head,
        Nor home but Thee.

521   8.6.8.6.8.8.

1   I thank Thee, Lord, that Thou hast shown,
        And I begin to see,
    What Thou canst be to all Thine own,
        What they may be to Thee;
    If only they will yield Thee all,
    And trustingly obey Thy call.

2 How wonderful! I never knew
   That I might trust Thee so;
   That Thou wouldst be so much to me,
   In all the way I go,
   That every need Thou wouldst supply,
   And all my longings satisfy.

3 I take Thee as my keeper now,
   And I commit to Thee
   My soul, my way, my works, my cause,
   In Thy sole charge to be;
   And my deposit, Thou, I know
   Wilt guard secure from every foe.

4 I take Thee for my peace, O Lord,
   My heart to keep and fill,
   Thine own great calm, amid earth's storms
   Shall keep me always still;
   And as Thy kingdom doth increase,
   So shall Thine ever-deep'ning peace.

5 I take Thee as my wisdom too,
   For wisdom's sum Thou art;
   Thou, who dost choose the foolish things,
   Set me henceforth apart,
   That I may speak and work for Thee
   As Thou shalt work and speak in me.

6 I take Thee, Lord, to be my all,
   Since all Thou art is mine;
   I nothing have, and nothing am;
   That nothing, Lord, is Thine.
   Thou shalt be everything to me,
   In all things my sufficiency.

522

8.6.8.6.D.

1 O Christ, in Thee my soul hath found,
And found in Thee alone,
The peace, the joy I sought so long,
The bliss till now unknown.

Now none but Christ can satisfy,
None other name for me;
There's love and life and lasting joy,
Lord Jesus, found in Thee.

2 I sighed for rest and happiness,
I yearned for them, not Thee;
But, while I passed my Savior by,
His love laid hold on me.

3 I tried the broken cisterns, Lord,
But, ah, the waters failed!
E'en as I stooped to drink they fled,
And mocked me as I wailed.

4 The pleasures lost I sadly mourned,
But never wept for Thee,
Till grace the sightless eyes received,
Thy loveliness to see.

523

9.8.9.8.D. with chorus.

1 I have come to the Fountain of Life,
A fountain that flows from above;
I have passed from the waters of strife
And come to the Elim of love;
I have drunk of the heavenly well,
In the depths of my being it springs.
No mortal can measure or tell
The gladness the Comforter brings.

Chorus:

Oh, come to the Fountain of Life,
The fountain that never runs dry;
Oh, drink of the boundless supply,
For Christ is the Fountain of Life.

2 I have come to the Fountain of Blood
That for guilt and uncleanness doth flow;
I have washed in its sin-cleansing flood
And my garments are whiter than snow.
I count not my righteousness mine —
'Tis Jesus that lives in my soul.
I partake of His nature divine,
And in Him I am perfectly whole.

3 I have come to the Fountain of Health,
A boundless and endless supply;
'Tis a secret man's wisdom or wealth
Can never discover or buy.
But the secret my Lord hath revealed
In the fountain that flows from His side,
In the stripes by whose pain we are healed,
In Himself as He comes to abide.

4 I have come to the Fountain of Joy;
His joy is the strength of my heart.
My delight is unmixed with alloy,
My sunshine can never depart.
The fig tree may wither and die,
Earth's pleasures and prospects decline;
But my fountains can never be dry —
My portion, my joy is divine.

524　　　　　　Peculiar Meter.

1　I have found, I have found the way
　　　Which leads to heav'nly rest;
　　I have found, I have found the peace
　　　Which filled my Savior's breast.
　　O friends in the desert past,
　　　Come, join in prayer and praise;
　　E'en now He waits our cry,
　　　The Savior who saves always.

2　He hath taken our sins away,
　　　When on Calv'ry's cross He bled;
　　The disease of our soul He heals
　　　By His Spirit freely shed;
　　Though Satan hath pierced us deep,
　　　And great the grace each prays;
　　The more we prove His might,
　　　The Savior who saves always.

3　Long, alas! in the gloom I fought,
　　　'Mid strife of wind and waves;
　　Jesus seemed only this to me:
　　　A Savior who sometimes saves.
　　But sweet are the light and calm
　　　That fill my happy days,
　　Since now I fully trust
　　　The Savior who saves always.

4　O my Sun and my Shield art Thou!
　　　Lead on where Thou hast trod;
　　My Salvation, my Joy, my Song,
　　　My Brother, and yet my God.
　　Whate'er then my life betide,
　　　I now can trust and praise;
　　Each moment Thou wilt save,
　　　O Savior, who sav'st always.

7.7.7.7.7.7. **525**

1 Jesus, Fountain of my days,
    Well-spring of my heart's delight,
  Brightness of my morning rays,
    Solace of my hours of night;
  When I see Thee, I arise
  To the hope of cloudless skies.

2 Oh, how weary were the years
    Ere Thy form to me was known;
  Oh, how gloomy were the fears
    When I seemed to be alone;
  I despaired the storm to brave
  Till Thy footprints touched the wave.

3 But Thy presence on the deep
    Calmed the pulses of the sea,
  And the waters sank to sleep
    In the rest of seeing Thee;
  And my once rebellious will
  Heard the mandate, Peace, be still!

4 Now Thy will and mine are one,
    Heart in heart, and hand in hand;
  All the clouds have touched the sun,
    And the ships have reached the land;
  For Thy love has said to me,
  No more night! and No more sea!

526

8.8.8.8.8.8.

1 Lord, Thou hast made Thyself to me
  A living, bright reality,
  More present to faith's vision keen
  Than any earthly object seen;
  More dear, more intimately nigh
  Than e'en the closest earthly tie.

2 And Thou, blest vision of my soul,
  Hast made my broken nature whole;
  Hast purified my base desires,
  And kindled passion's holiest fires;
  My nature Thou hast lifted up,
  And filled me with a glorious hope.

3 Nearer and dearer still to me,
  Thou living, loving Savior be;
  Brighter the vision of Thy face,
  More charming still Thy words of grace;
  So, life shall be transformed to love,
  Thy grace and mercy more to prove.

527

8.6.8.6

1 The Lord's my Shepherd, I'll not want;
  He makes me down to lie
  In pastures green; He leadeth me
  The quiet waters by.

2 My soul He doth restore again,
  And me to walk doth make
  Within the paths of righteousness,
  E'en for His own name's sake.

3 Yea, though I walk in death's dark vale,
  Yet will I fear no ill;
  For Thou art with me, and Thy rod
  And staff me comfort still.

4   My table Thou hast furnishèd
     In presence of my foes;
     My head Thou dost with oil anoint,
     And my cup overflows.

5   Goodness and mercy all my life
     Shall surely follow me,
     And in God's house forevermore
     My dwelling-place shall be.

8.7.8.7. (I)   **528**

1   The King of love my Shepherd is,
     Whose goodness faileth never;
     I nothing lack if I am His,
     And He is mine forever.

2   Where streams of living water flow
     My ransomed soul He leadeth,
     And, where the verdant pastures grow,
     With food celestial feedeth.

3   Perverse and foolish oft I strayed,
     But yet in love He sought me,
     And on His shoulder gently laid,
     And home rejoicing brought me.

4   In death's dark vale I fear no ill
     With Thee, dear Lord, beside me;
     Thy rod and staff my comfort still,
     Thy Cross before to guide me.

5   Thou spread'st a table in my sight;
     Thy unction grace bestoweth;
     And oh, what transport of delight
     From Thy pure chalice floweth!

6   And so through all the length of days
     Thy goodness faileth never;
     Good Shepherd, may I sing Thy praise
     Within Thy house forever.

529

8.8.8.8.D. (A)

1 How tedious and tasteless the hours
  When Jesus no longer I see!
  Sweet prospects, sweet birds and sweet flow'rs,
  Have all lost their sweetness to me.
  The midsummer sun shines but dim,
  The fields strive in vain to look gay;
  But when I am happy in Him
  December's as pleasant as May.

2 His name yields the richest perfume,
  And sweeter than music His voice;
  His presence disperses my gloom,
  And makes all within me rejoice.
  I should, were He always thus nigh,
  Have nothing to wish or to fear;
  No mortal so happy as I;
  My summer would last all the year.

3 Content with beholding His face,
  My all to His pleasure resigned;
  No changes of season or place,
  Would make any change in my mind.
  While blessed with a sense of His love,
  A palace a toy would appear;
  And prisons would palaces prove,
  If Jesus would dwell with me there.

4 My Lord, if indeed I am Thine,
  If Thou art my sun and my song,
  Say, why do I languish and pine?
  And why are my winters so long?
  Oh, drive these dark clouds from the sky,
  Thy soul-cheering presence restore;
  Or take me to Thee up on high,
  Where winter and clouds are no more.

Peculiar Meter.

1 Jesus is all the world to me:
   My life, my joy, my all.
He is my strength from day to day;
   Without Him I would fall.
When I am sad, to Him I go;
No other one can cheer me so.
When I am sad, He makes me glad;
   He's my Friend.

2 Jesus is all the world to me,
   My Friend in trials sore.
I go to Him for blessings, and
   He gives them o'er and o'er.
He sends the sunshine and the rain;
He sends the harvest's golden grain:
Sunshine and rain, harvest of grain —
   He's my Friend.

3 Jesus is all the world to me,
   And true to Him I'll be.
Oh, how could I this Friend deny
   When He's so true to me?
Following Him I know I'm right;
He watches o'er me day and night.
Following Him by day and night,
   He's my Friend.

4 Jesus is all the world to me,
   I want no better friend.
I trust Him now; I'll trust Him when
   Life's fleeting days shall end.
Beautiful life with such a Friend;
Beautiful life that has no end!
Eternal life, eternal joy,
   He's my Friend.

531

6.4.6.4.6.6.6.4.

1 Fade, fade each earthly joy;
   Jesus is mine.
   Break every tender tie;
   Jesus is mine.
   Dark is the wilderness,
   Earth has no resting place,
   Jesus alone can bless;
   Jesus is mine.

2 Tempt not my soul away;
   Jesus is mine.
   Here would I ever stay;
   Jesus is mine.
   Perishing things of clay,
   Born but for one brief day,
   Pass from my heart away;
   Jesus is mine.

3 Farewell, ye dreams of night;
   Jesus is mine.
   Lost in this dawning bright;
   Jesus is mine.
   All that my soul has tried
   Left but a dismal void;
   Jesus has satisfied;
   Jesus is mine.

4 Farewell, mortality;
   Jesus is mine.
   Welcome, eternity;
   Jesus is mine.

Welcome, O Loved and Blest,
Welcome, sweet scenes of rest,
Welcome, my Savior's breast;
   Jesus is mine.

532

8.8.8.8.8.8.

1 Thou hidden source of calm repose,
    Thou all-sufficient love divine;
    My help and refuge from my foes,
    Secure I am, if Thou art mine;
    From sin and grief, from guilt and shame,
    I hide me, Jesus, in Thy name.

2 Jesus, my All in all Thou art,
    My rest in toil, mine ease in pain;
    The med'cine of my broken heart;
    In war, my peace; in loss, my gain;
    My smile beneath the tyrant's frown;
    In shame, my glory and my crown.

3 In want, my plentiful supply;
    In weakness, mine almighty power;
    In bonds, my perfect liberty;
    My light in Satan's darkest hour;
    In grief, my joy unspeakable;
    My life in death; my Lord, my all.

8.8.8.6.

1 For every sin however deep,
For every path however steep,
For all the weary ones who weep,
Thou art sufficient, Lord.

2 For every trial great or small,
For every care that would appall,
For all the stumbling feet that fall,
Thou art sufficient, Lord.

3 When earthly things bring sweet delight,
When all is well, and skies are bright,
When ease would cloud the heavenly light,
Thou art sufficient, Lord.

4 When sorrow darkens all the day,
When disappointments bar the way,
When hearts are numb and cannot pray,
Thou art sufficient, Lord.

5 Whate'er my circumstances be,
Help me in all Thy hand to see,
So wilt Thou then be unto me,
My all-sufficient Lord.

Oswald J. Smith   9.8.9.8. with chorus.

1 The Savior can lift every burden,
    The heavy as well as the light;
    His strength is made perfect in weakness,
    In Him there is power and might.

    The Savior can solve every problem,
    The tangles of life can undo;
    There is nothing too hard for Jesus,
    There is nothing that He cannot do.

2 The Savior can bear every sorrow,
    In Him there is comfort and rest;
    No matter how great the affliction,
    He only permits what is best.

3 The Savior can strengthen the weary,
    His grace is sufficient for all;
    He knows every step of the pathway
    And listens to hear when we call.

4 The Savior can break sin's dominion,
    The vict'ry He won long ago;
    In Him there is freedom from bondage,
    He's able to conquer the foe.

5 The Savior can satisfy fully
    The heart that the world cannot fill;
    His Spirit will sanctify wholly
    The soul that is yielded and still.

EXPERIENCE OF CHRIST —
AS THE ALL-SUFFICIENT ONE

8.8.8.8.8.8.

1 All things are possible to him
That can in Jesus' name believe;
Lord, I no more Thy name blaspheme,
Thy truth I lovingly receive.
I can, I do believe in Thee;
All things are possible to me.

2 'Twas most impossible of all
That here sin's reign in me should cease;
Yet shall it be, I know it shall;
Jesus, I trust Thy faithfulness.
If nothing is too hard for Thee,
All things are possible to me.

3 Though earth and hell the Word gainsay,
The Word of God shall never fail;
The Lord can break sin's iron sway;
'Tis certain, though impossible.
The thing impossible shall be,
All things are possible to me.

4 All things are possible to God;
To Christ, the power of God in man;
To me when I am all renewed,
In Christ am fully formed again,
And from the reign of sin set free,
All things are possible to me.

5 All things are possible to God;
To Christ, the power of God in me;
Now shed Thy mighty Self abroad,
Let me no longer live, but Thee;
Give me this hour in Thee to prove
The sweet omnipotence of love.

11.11.11.11.

1   Objective and subjective Christ is to us,
    In heaven He's pleading objectively thus;
    Subjectively now in His members He lives
    And inwardly to them His being He gives.

2   In heaven He sits at the right hand of God,
    Where as the High Priest He presented His blood;
    Our Advocate, bearing our burdens above,
    Our Surety, He careth for us in His love.

3   He now is the Spirit, our spirit within;
    He's there as our life, all things bringing with Him;
    He's there as our strength and our grace every hour,
    Our Paraclete in us, sustaining with pow'r.

4   In heaven for us He's the glorified man,
    The Forerunner entered, fulfilling God's plan;
    Man into God bringing and making him one
    With God in the heav'nlies, in Him as the Son.

5   In us all the fulness of God dwells in Him;
    As Spirit He brings God Himself thus within
    Revealing and making God real unto us,
    God one with us building in life glorious.

6   The Savior ascended in heaven now dwells,
    And soon He's returning for us His Word tells;
    Deliverer indwelling, He now in us lives,
    And soon will transfigure, His glory to give.

7   The day soon is coming when heaven and earth
    Will mingle in one in that city of worth;
    Objective and subjective will in that day
    Be mingled within us in glory for aye.

537*   8.7.8.7. with chorus.

1   Christ to me is so subjective,
     In my spirit dwelleth He;
  Christ to me is all-inclusive,
     As the Spirit one with me.

    So subjective is my Christ to me!
     Real in me, and rich and sweet!
    All-inclusive is my Christ to me!
     All my needs He fully meets.

2   Christ to me is so subjective,
     Life imparting all the way;
  As the Spirit He revives me
     And refreshes day by day.

3   Christ to me is so subjective,
     All my being He transforms;
  By the mind and will renewing
     To His image He conforms.

4   Christ to me is so subjective,
     Liberating pow'r is He,
  By the law of life and power
     As the Spirit setting free.

5   Christ to me is so subjective,
     Regulating all the day;
  He corrects and rules and guides me,
     And adjusts in every way.

6   Christ to me is so subjective,
     All my thirst He satisfies;
  With His riches He supplies me,
     Thus God's fulness testifies.

8.7.8.7.D.   **538***

1   It is God's intent and pleasure
      To have Christ revealed in me,
    Nothing outward as religion,
      But His Christ within to be.

      It is God's intent and pleasure
        That His Christ be wrought in me;
      Nothing outwardly performing,
        But His Christ my all to be.

2   It is God's intent and pleasure
      That His Christ may live in me;
    Nothing as an outward practise,
      But Christ working inwardly.

3   It is God's intent and pleasure
      That His Christ be formed in me;
    Not the outward forms to follow,
      But Christ growing inwardly.

4   It is God's intent and pleasure
      That His Christ make home in me;
    Not just outwardly to serve Him,
      But Christ dwelling inwardly.

5   It is God's intent and pleasure
      That His Christ my hope may be;
    It is not objective glory,
      But 'tis Christ subjectively.

6   It is God's intent and pleasure
      That His Christ be all in me;
    Nothing outwardly possessing,
      But His Christ eternally.

539*

8.6.8.6.D.

1 O Lord, Thou art in me as life
　　And everything to me!
　Subjective and available,
　　Thus I experience Thee.

　　　O Lord, Thou art the Spirit!
　　　　How dear and near to me!
　　　How I admire Thy marvelous
　　　　Availability!

2 To all my needs both great and small
　　Thou art the rich supply;
　So ready and sufficient too
　　For me now to apply.

3 Thy sweet anointing with Thy might
　　In weakness doth sustain;
　By Thy supply of energy
　　My strength Thou dost maintain.

4 Thy law of life in heart and mind
　　My conduct regulates;
　The wealth of Thy reality
　　My being saturates.

5 O Thou art ever one with me,
　　Unrivaled unity!
　One spirit with me all the time
　　For all eternity!

8.7.8.7.D.

1 What release the Savior gave me!
   Christ indeed has set me free!
All the pow'r of sin is broken,
   All death's sting is passed from me!

      Christ has made me more than conqu'ror,
         By His mighty victory,
      Now His resurrection power
         From my spirit strengthens me!

2 From the law Christ has delivered,
   To its claims I'm ever dead;
Nevermore the law shall bind me,
   But by grace I'll live instead.

3 Christ has sin condemned at Calv'ry
   And its power done away;
Now it has no ground within me,
   I am freed from all its sway.

4 Death by Him has been abolished,
   Incorrupted life is shown;
Death's enthralling bonds are broken,
   Resurrection life is known.

5 Christ through death has crushed the devil,
   World and demons by His might,
From the pow'r of darkness brought me
   To the realm of life and light.

6 All-sufficient grace He giveth,
   With His pow'r He covers me,
Makes me glory in my weakness
   And in weakness strengthens me.

541*

6.5.6.5.D.

1 Not the law of letters,
But the Christ of life
God desires to give us,
Saving us from strife;
It is not some doctrine,
But 'tis Christ Himself
Who alone releases
From our sinful self.

2 Any kind of teaching,
Any kind of form,
Cannot quicken spirits
Or our souls transform;
It is Christ as Spirit
Gives us life divine,
Thus thru us to live the
Life of God's design.

3 Not philosophy nor
Any element
Can to Christ conform us
As His complement;
But 'tis Christ Himself who
All our nature takes
And in resurrection
Us His members makes.

4 Not religion, even
Christianity,
Can fulfill God's purpose
Or economy;
But 'tis Christ within us
As our all in all
Satisfies God's wishes,
And His plan withal.

5 All the gifts we're given
By the Lord in grace,
All the different functions
Cannot Christ replace.
Only Christ Himself must
Be our all in all!
Only Christ Himself in
All things, great or small!

8.7.8.7.D.

1 O the riches of my Savior,
     So unsearchable, immense;
  All the fulness of the Godhead
     I may now experience.

        O the riches, O the riches,
           Christ my Savior has for me!
        How unsearchable their measure,
           Yet my full reality!

2 O the riches of my Savior,
     All-embracing: life and light,
  Wisdom, power, healing, comfort,
     Treasures rich of God's delight;

3 God's redemption, full salvation,
     And His resurrection pow'r,
  Sanctifying, glorifying,
     All transcending every hour!

4 O the riches of my Savior —
     Nothing less than God as all!
  All His person and possessions,
     Now my spirit doth enthrall.

5 O the riches of my Savior!
     Who can know their breadth and length,
  Or their depth and height unmeasured,
     Yet they are my joy and strength.

6 May I know these boundless riches,
     Christ experience in full;
  And with others may I share them
     In their content bountiful.

543

6.6.8.6.

1 I give my heart to Thee,
O Jesus most desired;
And heart for heart the gift shall be,
For Thou my heart hast fired.

2 Thou hearts alone wouldst move,
Thou only hearts dost love;
I would love Thee as Thou lov'st me,
O Jesus most desired.

3 What off'ring can I make,
Dear Lord, to love like Thine;
That Thou, the Word, didst stoop to take
A human form like mine?

4 "Give Me thy heart, my son":
Lord, Thou my heart hast won;
I would love Thee as Thou lov'st me,
O Jesus most desired.

5 Thy heart is opened wide,
Its offered love most free,
That heart to heart I may abide,
And hide myself in Thee.

6 Ah, how Thy love doth burn,
Till I that love return!
I would love Thee as Thou lov'st me,
O Jesus most desired.

7 Here finds my heart its rest,
Repose that knows no shock,
The strength of love that keeps it blest
In Thee, the riven Rock.

8 My heart, as girt around,
Her citadel hath found;
I would love Thee as Thou lov'st me,
O Jesus most desired.

11.11.11.11.

544

1 Lord Jesus, I love Thee, I know Thou art mine;
For Thee all the pleasures of sin I resign;
My gracious Redeemer, my Savior art Thou,
If ever I loved Thee, Lord Jesus, 'tis now.

2 I love Thee, because Thou hast first lovèd me,
And purchased my pardon on Calvary's tree;
I love Thee for wearing the thorns on Thy brow;
If ever I loved Thee, Lord Jesus, 'tis now.

3 I'll love Thee in life, I will love Thee in death,
And praise Thee as long as Thou lendest me breath;
And say when the death-dew lies cold on my brow,
If ever I loved Thee, Lord Jesus, 'tis now.

4 In ages eternal of endless delight
I'll ever adore Thee in glory so bright;
I'll sing with the glittering crown on my brow,
If ever I loved Thee, Lord Jesus, 'tis now.

7.7.7.7.7.7.

545

1 When this passing world is done,
When has sunk yon glaring sun,
When we stand with Christ on high,
Looking o'er life's history;
Then, Lord, shall I fully know,
Not till then, how much I owe.

2 When I stand before the throne
Dressed in beauty not my own,
When I see Thee as Thou art,
Love Thee with unsinning heart;
Then, Lord, shall I fully know,
Not till then, how much I owe.

3 E'en on earth, as through a glass
Darkly, let Thy glory pass;
Make forgiveness feel so sweet;
Make Thy Spirit's help so meet:
E'en on earth, Lord, make me know
Something of how much I owe.

546

10.6.10.6.10.10.

1 I love my Lord, but with no love of mine,
  For I have none to give;
I love Thee, Lord, but all the love is Thine,
  For by Thy love I live.
I am as nothing, and rejoice to be
Emptied, and lost, and swallowed up in Thee.

2 Thou, Lord, alone, art all Thy children need,
  And there is none beside;
From Thee the streams of blessedness proceed,
  In Thee the bless'd abide.
Fountain of life, and all-abounding grace,
Our source, our center, and our dwelling-place.

547

8.7.8.7.

1 Something every heart is loving:
  If not Jesus, none can rest;
Lord, my heart to Thee is given;
  Take it, for it loves Thee best.

2 Thus I cast the world behind me;
  Jesus most beloved shall be;
Beauteous more than all things beauteous,
  He alone is joy to me.

3 Bright with all eternal radiance
  Is the glory of Thy face;
Thou art loving, sweet, and tender,
  Full of pity, full of grace.

4 When I hated, Thou didst love me,
  Shedd'st for me Thy precious blood;
Still Thou lovest, lovest ever,
  Shall I not love Thee, my God?

5 Keep my heart still faithful to Thee,
   That my earthly life may be
   But a shadow to that glory
   Of my hidden life in Thee.

EXPERIENCE OF CHRIST — CONTAINING HIM

7.7.7.7.   **548***

1 Earthen vessel I was made,
   Christ in me the treasure laid;
   His container I must be,
   As the content He in me.

2 In His image I was made,
   Fit that Christ should all pervade;
   Thus the vessel God did form
   With the content uniform.

3 In my spirit He remains,
   With His power He sustains;
   As the Spirit one with me,
   He is my reality.

4 Moving in me day by day,
   Mingling with me all the way,
   All my steps He regulates,
   Every part He saturates.

5 Him expressing from within,
   Making Him to others seen,
   I transparent have to be
   That He may be shown thru me.

6 Transformation is my need,
   To be broken more indeed,
   That the clay may change in form,
   To the treasure to conform.

549*

10.10.10.10.

1 Enter the veil and go without the camp,
  Taste heaven's sweetness, thus the earth forsake;
  If by the Holiest I am satisfied,
  How can I of earth's vanities partake?

2 Enter the veil and go without the camp,
  By heaven's presence will the earth depart;
  If heaven's glory doth my spirit charm,
  How can earth's happiness possess my heart?

3 Enter the veil, behold the glorious Christ,
  Go out the camp to Jesus, let Him lead;
  If throne and crown my spirit here enthrall,
  Manger and cross cannot my steps impede.

4 Enter the veil for resurrection pow'r,
  Go out the camp to bear the cross and woe,
  If I His radiant face in heaven see,
  His footsteps I will follow here below.

5 Enter the veil, on heaven's fatness feast,
  Without the camp, in hardship persevere;
  Though earthly trials sorely pain my heart,
  Heaven's communion doth my spirit cheer.

6 Enter the veil, Christ's riches there enjoy,
  Without the camp, the needs of men supply;
  The life of heaven living out thru me
  The souls of earth will bless and satisfy.

7 Enter the veil till it exists no more,
  Go out the camp till all the camps are gone;
  Until the heavens and the earth unite,
  Till God and man together dwell in one.

8.4.8.4.8.8.8.4.

1 Through Thy precious body broken —
    Inside the veil;
Oh! what words to sinners spoken —
    Inside the veil.
Precious as the blood that bought us;
Perfect, as the love that sought us;
Holy, as the Lamb that brought us —
    Inside the veil.

2 When we see Thy love unshaken —
    Outside the camp.
Scorned by man, by God forsaken —
    Outside the camp.
Thy loved cross alone can charm us;
Shame need now no more alarm us;
Glad we follow, nought can harm us —
    Outside the camp.

3 Lamb of God, through Thee we enter —
    Inside the veil.
Cleansed by Thee, we boldly venture —
    Inside the veil.
Not a stain; a new creation:
Ours is such a full salvation;
Low we bow in adoration —
    Inside the veil.

4 Unto Thee, the homeless stranger —
    Outside the camp,
Forth we hasten, fear no danger —
    Outside the camp.
Thy reproach, far richer treasure
Than all Egypt's boasted pleasure;
Drawn by love that knows no measure —
    Outside the camp.

continued

5 Soon Thy saints shall all be gathered —
    Inside the veil.
All with Thee — no more be scattered —
    Inside the veil.
Nought from Thee, our hearts shall sever;
We shall see Thee; grieve Thee never;
"Praise the Lamb!" shall sound forever —
    Inside the veil.

551   Peculiar Meter.

1 I've believed the true report,
    Hallelujah to the Lamb!
I have passed the outer court,
    O glory be to God!
I am all on Jesus' side,
On the altar sanctified,
To the world and sin I've died,
    Hallelujah to the Lamb!

Hallelujah! Hallelujah!
I have passed the riven veil,
Here the glories never fail,
Hallelujah! Hallelujah!
I am living in the presence
    of the King.

2 I'm a king and priest to God,
    Hallelujah to the Lamb!
By the cleansing of the blood,
    O glory be to God!
By the Spirit's pow'r and light,
I am living day and night,
In the holiest place so bright,
    Hallelujah to the Lamb!

3 I have passed the outer veil,
    Hallelujah to the Lamb!
  Which did once God's light conceal,
    O glory be to God!
  But the blood has brought me in
  To God's holiness so clean,
  Where there's death to self and sin,
    Hallelujah to the Lamb!

4 I'm within the holiest pale,
    Hallelujah to the Lamb!
  I have passed the inner veil,
    O glory be to God!
  I am sanctified to God
  By the power of the blood,
  Now the Lord is my abode,
    Hallelujah to the Lamb!

8.7.8.7.D.   **552**

1 Marvel not that Christ in glory
    All my inmost heart hath won;
  Not a star to cheer my darkness,
    But a light beyond the sun.
  All below lies dark and shadowed,
    Nothing here to claim my heart,
  Save the lonely track of sorrow
    Where of old He walked apart.

2 Others in the earthly sunshine
    Wearily may journey on,
  I have seen a light from heaven
    Past the brightness of the sun —
  Light that knows no cloud, no waning,
    Light wherein I see His face,
  All His love's uncounted treasures,
    All the riches of His grace:

continued

3 All the wonders of His glory,
  Deeper wonders of His love —
How for me He won, He keepeth
  That high standing all above;
Not a glimpse — the veil uplifted —
  But within the veil to dwell,
Gazing on His face forever,
  Hearing words unspeakable.

4 I have seen the face of Jesus —
  Tell me not of aught beside;
I have heard the voice of Jesus —
  All my soul is satisfied.
In the radiance of the glory
  First I saw His blessed face,
And forever shall that glory
  Be my home, my dwelling-place.

553   8.7.8.7.D. with repeat.

1 In the secret of His presence
  How my soul delights to hide!
Oh, how precious are the lessons
  Which I learn at Jesus' side!
Earthly cares can never vex me,
  Neither trials lay me low;
For when Satan comes to tempt me,
  To the secret place I go.
  (Repeat the last line of each stanza)

2 When my soul is faint and thirsty,
  'Neath the shadow of His wing
There is cool and pleasant shelter,
  And a fresh and crystal spring;

And my Savior rests beside me,
    As we hold communion sweet;
If I tried, I could not utter
    What He says when thus we meet.

3 Only this I know: I tell Him
    All my doubts and griefs and fears;
Oh, how patiently He listens!
    And my drooping soul He cheers;
Do you think He ne'er reproves me?
    What a false friend He would be,
If He never, never told me
    Of the sins which He must see.

4 Would you like to know that sweetness
    Of the secret of the Lord?
Go and hide beneath His shadow;
    This shall then be your reward;
And whene'er you leave the silence
    Of that happy meeting-place,
By the Spirit bear the image
    Of the Master in your face.

Peculiar Meter.   **554***

1 I come to His presence afresh
    Ere the night has passed into morning;
And His face I see as it shines on me —
    The Lord within is dawning.
And He speaks to me and reveals to me
    All His riches for me today;
And with sweet delight I partake of Him,
    My hunger has passed away.

2 As Spirit He speaks thru the Word
    Till my heart in echo is singing,
And the fount of life with His grace and pow'r
    Within my soul is springing.

continued

And He speaks to me and reveals to me
    All His riches for me today;
And I drink of Him for my every need,
    My thirsting has passed away.

3 In tenderness He deals with me,
    While I stay with joy in His presence;
And He saturates and supplies my soul
    With all His precious essence.
And He speaks to me and reveals to me
    All His riches for me today;
And in every way I partake of Him,
    My problems all passed away.

555   11.10.11.10.

1 Still, still with Thee, when purple morning breaketh,
When the bird waketh, and the shadows flee;
Fairer than morning, lovelier than daylight,
Dawns the sweet consciousness, I am with Thee.

2 As in the dawning, o'er the waveless ocean,
The image of the morning star doth rest,
So in this stillness Thou beholdest only
Thine image in the waters of my breast.

3 When sinks the soul, subdued by toil, to slumber,
Its closing eye looks up to Thee in prayer;
Sweet the repose, beneath Thy wings o'ershadowing,
But sweeter still to wake and find Thee there.

4 So shall it be at last, in that bright morning
When the soul waketh, and life's shadows flee;
Oh, in that hour, fairer than daylight's dawning,
Shall rise the glorious thought, I am with Thee!

10.10.10.10.   **556***

1 Thy name is sweet as ointment pourèd forth;
   Better Thy love than wine, O draw Thou me!
   If we the footsteps follow of the flock,
   Entered Thy fellowship of love we'll be.

2 He's my Beloved, I am His own love;
   He draweth me, pursue I after Him.
   Fragrant as myrrh, I'd hide Him in my heart;
   Beauteous as henna,† I'd be clothed with Him;

3 Bathe in His love, and of His fatness taste,
   Lie on His breast, His sweetness there enjoy;
   His love the banner, His affection shown
   Tenderly soothes my heart to purest joy.

4 Oh, my Beloved's mine, and I am His;
   I am a lily and my Shepherd He;
   May daybreak come, the shadows flee away,
   Him on the mountains as a hart I'd see.

5 Myrrh of the death with Him and frankincense,
   The resurrection, permeate my heart;
   North wind awake, and let the south wind blow,
   Make my heart's garden pleasure to His heart.

6 I'd be to Him a dove that's undefiled,
   As a pure lily in His presence be,
   His, wholly His, the joy of all His joys,
   He wholly mine, the Song of songs to me.

7 Fair as the moon, conformed to Him I'd be,
   Clear as the sun, unto His stature grown;
   For my Beloved, all to please His heart,
   For mv Beloved, that His life be shown.

8 Thou art my life, and I Thine image real;
   Love in such union is as death most strong,
   Ne'er can it be destroyed or e'er replaced
   Till Thou on spices mountains come ere long.

† An Old World plant, prized for its fragrant yellow and
white flowers. (Song of Sol. 1:14, A.S.V.)

557

6.6.8.6.4.

1 Jesus Himself drew near,
  And joined them as they walked,
  And soon their hearts began to burn,
  As of Himself He talked:
    Draw near, O Lord.

2 Jesus Himself drew near,
  They were no longer sad;
  When He was walking at their side,
  How could they but be glad?
    Draw near, O Lord.

3 Jesus Himself drew near,
  And all their doubts were solved;
  He showed them why Christ came to die,
  And what that death involved:
    Draw near, O Lord.

4 Jesus Himself drew near,
  And at the journey's end
  They could not let Him leave them thus,
  The Stranger was their Friend:
    Draw near, O Lord.

558

10.9.10.9. with chorus.

1 What a fellowship, what a joy divine,
  Leaning on the Everlasting Arms!
  What a blessedness, what a peace is mine,
  Leaning on the Everlasting Arms!

    Leaning, leaning,
  Safe and secure from all alarms;
    Leaning, leaning,
  Leaning on the Everlasting Arms.

2 O how sweet to walk in this pilgrim way,
  Leaning on the Everlasting Arms!
  O how bright the path grows from day to day,
  Leaning on the Everlasting Arms!

3 What have I to dread, what have I to fear,
   Leaning on the Everlasting Arms!
I have peace complete with my Lord so near,
   Leaning on the Everlasting Arms!

8.7.8.7.D.   **559**

1 Savior, I by faith am touching
   Thee, the source of every good;
Virtue now, by faith am claiming,
   Through the cleansing of Thy blood.

   Touching Thee, new life is glowing
     By Thy Spirit's burning flame;
   Cleansing, purging, Spirit filling,
     Glory to Thy Holy Name!

2 Touching Thee in faith, I take Thee
   In Thy riches full and free;
All I am I open to Thee,
   All Thou art Thou giv'st to me.

3 Touching now Thine outstretched scepter,
   O most mighty King of kings;
Of Thy fulness now receiving,
   High I mount on eagle wings.

4 Grace and virtue, strength and wisdom,
   All my need, by Thee supplied;
Keep me touching, keep me claiming,
   Keep me ever at Thy side.

8.8.8.8.8.8.   **560**

1 Come, O Thou Traveler unknown,
   Whom still I hold but cannot see;
My company before is gone,
   And I am left alone with Thee;
With Thee all night I mean to stay,
And wrestle till the break of day.

continued

2   I need not tell Thee who I am,
    My sin and misery declare;
    Thyself hast called me by my name,
    Look on Thy hands, and read it there;
    But who, I ask Thee, who art Thou?
    Tell me Thy name, and tell me now.

3   In vain Thou strugglest to get free;
    I never will unloose my hold;
    Art Thou the Man that died for me?
    The secret of Thy love unfold;
    Wrestling, I will not let Thee go,
    Till I Thy name, Thy nature know.

4   Yield to me now, for I am weak,
    But confident in self-despair;
    Speak to my heart, in blessings speak,
    Be conquered by my instant prayer;
    Speak, or Thou never hence shalt move,
    And tell me if Thy name be Love.

5   'Tis Love! 'tis Love! Thou diedst for me;
    I hear Thy whisper in my heart;
    The morning breaks, the shadows flee:
    Pure, universal Love Thou art;
    To me, to all Thy mercies move;
    Thy nature and Thy name is Love.

6   Lame as I am, I take the prey;
    Hell, earth and sin, with ease o'ercome.
    I leap for joy, pursue my way,
    And, as a bounding hart, I run,
    Through all eternity to prove
    Thy nature and Thy name is Love.

8.7.8.7.

1 Thou hast said Thou art the Vine, Lord,
   And that I'm a branch in Thee,
But I do not know the reason
   Why I should so barren be.

2 Bearing fruit is my deep longing,
   More Thy life to manifest,
To Thy throne to bring more glory,
   That Thy will may be expressed.

3 But I fail to understand, Lord,
   What it means — "abide in me"
For the more I seek "abiding,"
   More I feel I'm not in Thee.

4 How I feel I'm not abiding;
   Though I pray and strongly will,
Yet from me Thou seemest distant
   And my life is barren still.

5 Yet Thou art the Vine, Thou saidst it,
   And I am a branch in Thee;
When I take Thee as my Savior,
   Then this fact is wrought in me.

6 Now I'm in Thee and I need not
   Seek into Thyself to come,
For I'm joined to Thee already,
   With Thy flesh and bones I'm one.

7 Not to "go in" is the secret,
   But that I'm "already in"!
That I ne'er may leave I'd ask Thee,
   Not how I may get within.

8 I am in, already in Thee!
   What a place to which I'm brought!
There's no need for prayer or struggling,
   God Himself the work has wrought.

continued

9 Since I'm in, why ask to enter;
    O how ignorant I've been!
    Now with praise and much rejoicing
    For Thy Word, I dwell therein.

10 Now in Thee I rest completely,
    With myself I gladly part;
    Thou art life and Thou art power,
    All in all to me Thou art.

562   8.8.8.8. with chorus.

1 Abiding, oh, so wondrous sweet,
    I'm resting at the Savior's feet;
    I trust in Him, I'm satisfied,
    I'm resting in the Crucified.

        Abiding, abiding,
        Oh! so wondrous sweet;
        I'm resting, resting
        At the Savior's feet.

2 He speaks, and by His word is giv'n
    His peace, a blessed gift of heav'n;
    Not as the world He peace doth give,
    'Tis through this hope my soul shall live.

3 I live; not I; 'tis He alone
    By whom the mighty work is done;
    Dead to myself, alive to Him,
    I count all loss His rest to gain.

4 Now rest, my heart, the work is done,
    I'm saved through the Eternal Son;
    Let all my pow'rs my soul employ,
    To tell the world my peace and joy.

563

10.10.10.10.

1 Abide in Thee! in that deep love of Thine,
My Jesus, Lord, Thou Lamb of God divine,
Down, closely down, as living branch with tree,
I would abide, my Lord, my Christ, in Thee.

2 Abide in Thee! my Savior God, I know
How love of Thine so vast in me may flow,
My empty vessel, running o'er with joy,
Must overflow to Thee without alloy.

3 Abide in Thee! nor doubt, nor self, nor sin,
Can e'er prevail with Thy blest life within;
Joined to Thyself, communing deep, my soul
Knows naught besides its motions to control.

4 Abide in Thee! 'tis thus I only know
The secrets of Thy mind e'en while below —
All joy and peace, and knowledge of Thy word,
All pow'r and fruit, and service for the Lord.

8.7.8.7.D. with chorus.

564

1 I have learned the wondrous secret
Of abiding in the Lord;
I have tasted life's pure fountain,
I am drinking of His word;
I have found the strength and sweetness
Of abiding 'neath the blood;
I have lost myself in Jesus,
I am sinking into God.

continued

564

Chorus:

I'm abiding in the Lord
And confiding in His word;
I am hiding in the bosom of His love.
Yes, abiding in the Lord
And confiding in His word,
I am hiding in the bosom of His love.

2 I am crucified with Jesus,
And He lives and dwells with me;
I have ceased from all my struggling,
'Tis no longer I, but He.
All my will is yielding to Him,
And His Spirit reigns within;
And His precious blood each moment
Keeps me cleansed and free from sin.

3 All my sicknesses I bring Him,
And He bears them all away;
All my fears and griefs I tell Him,
All my cares from day to day,
All my strength I draw from Jesus,
By His breath I live and move;
E'en His very mind He gives me,
And His faith, and life, and love.

4 For my words I take His wisdom,
For my works His Spirit's power;
For my ways His ceaseless presence
Guards and guides me every hour.
Of my heart, He is the portion,
Of my joy the boundless spring;
Savior, Sanctifier, Healer,
Glorious Lord, and coming King.

11.10.11.10. with chorus.

1 Under His wings I am safely abiding;
   Though the night deepens and tempests are wild.
Still I can trust Him, I know He will keep me;
   He has redeemed me, and I am His child.

   Under His wings, under His wings,
      Who from His love can sever?
   Under His wings my soul shall abide,
      Safely abide forever.

2 Under His wings — what a refuge in sorrow!
   How the heart yearningly turns to His rest!
Often when earth has no balm for my healing,
   There I find comfort, and there I am blest.

3 Under His wings — oh, what precious enjoyment!
   There will I hide till life's trials are o'er;
Sheltered, protected, no evil can harm me;
   Resting in Jesus I'm safe evermore.

11.11.11.11. with chorus.

566

1 Oh, safe to the Rock that is higher than I,
   My soul in its conflicts and sorrows would fly,
So sinful, so weary, Thine, Thine would I be,
   Thou blest Rock of Ages, I'm hiding in Thee.

   Hiding in Thee, hiding in Thee,
   Thou blest Rock of Ages, I'm hiding in Thee.

2 In the calm of the noontide, in sorrow's lone hour,
   In times when temptation casts o'er me its power;
In the tempests of life, on its wide, heaving sea,
   Thou blest Rock of Ages, I'm hiding in Thee.

3 How oft in the conflict, when pressed by the foe,
   I have fled to my Refuge and breathed out my woe;
How often, when trials like sea-billows roll,
   Have I hidden in Thee, O Thou Rock of my soul.

567

7.6.7.6.

1 O Lamb of God, still keep me
   Close to Thy wounded side;
   'Tis only there in safety
   And peace I can abide.

2 What foes and snares surround me,
   What lusts and fears within;
   The grace that sought and found me
   Alone can keep me clean.

3 'Tis only in Thee hiding
   I feel myself secure;
   Only in Thee abiding,
   The conflict can endure;

4 Thine arm the victory gaineth
   O'er every hateful foe;
   Thy love my heart sustaineth
   In all its care and woe.

5 Soon shall my eyes behold Thee,
   With rapture face to face;
   One half hath not been told me
   Of all Thy power and grace;

6 Thy beauty, Lord, and glory,
   The wonders of Thy love,
   Shall be the endless story
   Of all Thy saints above.

8.7.8.7.D.

1 'Tis so sweet to trust in Jesus,
   Just to take Him at His word;
   Just to rest upon His promise;
   Just to know, Thus saith the Lord.

   Jesus, Jesus, how I trust Him,
   How I've proved Him o'er and o'er,
   Jesus, Jesus, Precious Jesus!
   O for grace to trust Him more.

2 O how sweet to trust in Jesus,
   Just to trust His cleansing blood;
   Just in simple faith to plunge me,
   'Neath the healing, cleansing flood.

3 Yes, 'tis sweet to trust in Jesus,
   Just from sin and self to cease;
   Just from Jesus simply taking
   Life, and rest, and joy, and peace.

4 I'm so glad I learned to trust Thee,
   Precious Jesus, Savior, Friend;
   And I know that Thou art with me,
   Wilt be with me to the end.

569

7.7.7.7.D.

1 Simply trusting every day;
Trusting through a stormy way;
Even when my faith is small,
Trusting Jesus, that is all.

Trusting as the moments fly,
Trusting as the days go by,
Trusting Him, whate'er befall,
Trusting Jesus, that is all.

2 Brightly doth His Spirit shine
Into this poor heart of mine;
While He leads I cannot fall,
Trusting Jesus, that is all.

3 Singing if my way be clear,
Praying if the path be drear;
If in danger, for Him call,
Trusting Jesus, that is all.

4 Trusting Him while life shall last,
Trusting Him till earth is past,
Till His gracious advent call,
Trusting Jesus, that is all.

570

8.7.8.7.D.

1 All my doubts I give to Jesus;
I've His gracious promise heard:
I shall never be confounded,
I am trusting in that word.

Chorus:

I am trusting, fully trusting,
Sweetly trusting in His word;
I am trusting, fully trusting,
Sweetly trusting in His word.

2 All my sins I lay on Jesus,
He doth wash me in His blood,
He will keep me pure and holy,
He will keep me close to God.

3 All my fears I give to Jesus,
Rests my weary soul on Him;
Though my way be hid in darkness,
Never can His light grow dim.

4 All my joys I give to Jesus,
He is all I want of bliss;
He of all the worlds is Master;
He has all I need in this.

5 All I am I give to Jesus;
All my body, all my soul;
All I have, and all I hope for,
While eternal ages roll.

8.7.8.7.7.7.   **571**

1 Thou whose name is callèd Jesus,
Risen Lord of life and pow'r,
Oh, it is so sweet to trust Thee,
Every day and every hour;
Of Thy wondrous grace I sing,
Savior, Counsellor, and King.

continued

2 Thou canst keep my feet from falling,
  Even my poor wayward feet;
Thou who dost present me faultless
  In Thee — Righteousness complete;
Jesus, Lord, in knowing Thee,
  Oh, what strength and victory.

3 All the sin in me, my Savior,
  Thou canst conquer and subdue;
With Thy sanctifying power
  Permeate my spirit through;
Let Thy government increase,
  Risen, crownèd, Prince of Peace.

4 Thou canst keep me upward looking,
  Ever upward in Thy face;
Thou canst make me stand, upholden
  By the greatness of Thy grace;
Every promise of Thy word
  Now I claim from Thee, dear Lord.

5 Oh! what joy to trust Thee, Jesus,
  Mighty Victor o'er the grave,
And to learn amid earth's shadows
  Thine unceasing power to save!
Only those who prove Thee know
  What the grace Thou dost bestow.

6 Make my life a bright outshining
  Of Thy life, that all may see
Thine own resurrection power
  Mightily put forth in me;
Ever let my heart become
  Yet more consciously Thy home.

Peculiar Meter.

1 Jesus hath died and hath risen again,
  Pardon and peace to bestow;
  Fully I trust Him; from sin's guilty stain,
  Jesus saves me now.

    Jesus saves me now,
    Jesus saves me now;
    Yes, Jesus saves me all the time;
    Jesus saves me now.

2 Sin's condemnation is over and gone,
  Jesus alone knoweth how;
  Life and salvation my soul hath put on:
  Jesus saves me now.

3 Satan may tempt, but he never shall reign,
  That Christ will never allow;
  Doubts I have buried, and this is my strain,
  Jesus saves me now.

4 Resting in Jesus, abiding in Him,
  Gladly my faith can avow,
  Never again need my pathway be dim:
  Jesus saves me now.

5 Jesus is stronger than Satan and sin,
  Satan to Jesus must bow;
  Therefore I triumph without and within:
  Jesus saves me now.

6 Sorrow and pain may beset me about,
  Nothing can darken my brow;
  Battling in faith, I can joyfully shout:
  "Jesus saves me now."

573   8.7.8.7. with chorus.

1 Once I thought I walked with Jesus,
     Yet such changeful feelings had;
   Sometimes trusting, sometimes doubting,
     Sometimes joyful, sometimes sad.

     Oh, the peace the Savior gives!
       Peace I never knew before;
     And my way has brighter grown
       Since I've learned to trust Him more.

2 But He call'd me closer to Him,
     Bade my doubting, fearing, cease;
   And when I had fully yielded,
     Filled my soul with perfect peace.

3 Now I'm trusting every moment,
     Nothing less can be enough;
   And the Savior bears me gently
     O'er those places once so rough.

4 Day by day my soul He's keeping
     By His wondrous power within;
   And my heart is full of singing
     To my Savior from all sin.

574   8.8.6.8.8.6.

1 Lord Jesus, Thou dost keep Thy child
   Thru sunshine or thru tempests wild;
     Jesus, I trust in Thee:
   Thine is such wondrous pow'r to save;
   Thine is the mighty love that gave
     Its all on Calvary.

2 O glorious Savior, Thee I praise;
   To Thee my new glad song I raise,
     And tell of what Thou art.
   Thy grace is boundless in its store;
   Thy face of love shines evermore;
     Thou givest me Thy heart.

3 Upon Thy promises I stand,
Trusting in Thee: Thine own right hand
  Doth keep and comfort me;
My soul doth triumph in Thy word;
Thine, Thine be all the praise, dear Lord,
  As Thine the victory.

4 Love perfecteth what it begins;
Thy power doth save me from my sins;
  Thy grace upholdeth me.
This life of trust, how glad, how sweet;
My need and Thy great fulness meet,
  And I have all in Thee.

10.10.10.10.   **575**

1 I take Thy promise, Lord, in all its length,
And breadth and fulness, as my daily strength;
Into life's future fearless I may gaze,
For, Savior, Thou art with me all the days.

2 Days may be coming fraught with loss and change,
New scenes surround my life and fancies strange;
I thank Thee that no day can ever break,
Savior, when Thou wilt leave me or forsake.

3 There may be days of darkness and distress,
When sin has power to tempt, and care to press,
Yet in the darkest day I will not fear,
For, 'mid the shadows, Thou wilt still be near.

4 Days there may be of joy and deep delight,
When earth seems fairest, and her skies most bright,
Then draw me closer to Thee, lest I rest
Elsewhere, my Savior, than upon Thy breast.

continued

5 And all the other days that make my life,
Marked by no special joy or grief or strife,
Days filled with quiet duties, trivial care,
Burdens too small for other hearts to share;

6 Spend Thou these days with me, all shall be Thine,
So shall the darkest hour with glory shine.
Then when these earthly years have passed away,
Let me be with Thee in the perfect day.

Used by permission of Miss Elsie Deck.

576   8.8.8.6. with chorus.

1 I clasp the hand of Love divine,
I claim the gracious promise mine,
And add to His my countersign,
   "I take" — "He undertakes."

   I take Thee, blessed Lord,
   I give myself to Thee,
   And Thou, according to Thy word,
   Dost undertake for me.

2 I take salvation full and free,
Through Him who gave His life for me,
He undertakes my all to be,
   "I take" — "He undertakes."

3 I take Him as my holiness,
My spirit's spotless, heavenly dress,
I take the Lord, my righteousness,
   "I take" — "He undertakes."

4 I take the promised Holy Ghost,
I take the power of Pentecost,
To fill me to the uttermost,
   "I take" — "He undertakes."

5 I take Him for this mortal frame,
   I take my healing through His Name,
   And all His risen life I claim,
   "I take" — "He undertakes."

6 I simply take Him at His word,
   I praise Him that my prayer is heard,
   And claim my answer from the Lord,
   "I take" — "He undertakes."

7.5.7.5. with chorus.

577

1 When I fear my faith will fail,
      Christ will hold me fast;
   When the tempter would prevail,
      He can hold me fast.

      He will hold me fast,
      He will hold me fast;
   For my Savior loves me so,
      He will hold me fast.

2 I could never keep my hold,
      He will hold me fast;
   For my love is often cold,
      He must hold me fast.

3 I am precious in His sight,
      He will hold me fast;
   Those He saves are His delight,
      He will hold me fast.

4 He'll not let my soul be lost,
      Christ will hold me fast;
   Bought by Him at such a cost,
      He will hold me fast.

578 †

8.8.8.8.

1 My will is weak, my strength is frail,
And all my hope is nearly gone;
I can but trust Thy working true
To gently hold and lead me on.

2 I've tried my best, but still have failed,
E'en as before I've failed and erred;
Thy patience is my only trust
To hold and keep me to Thy word.

3 Whene'er my heart is lifted up,
How very near I am to fall;
I dare not do, I dare not think,
I need Thyself in great or small.

4 Thou art my Savior, strength and stay,
O Lord, I come to seek Thy face;
Though I'm the weakest of the weak,
My strength is nothing but Thy grace.

EXPERIENCE OF CHRIST — RESTING ON HIM

579

8.7.8.5.D.

1 Jesus! I am resting, resting
In the joy of what Thou art;
I am finding out the greatness
Of Thy loving heart.
Thou hast bid me gaze upon Thee,
And Thy beauty fills my soul,
For, by Thy transforming power,
Thou hast made me whole.

Chorus:

> Jesus! I am resting, resting
> In the joy of what Thou art;
> I am finding out the greatness
> Of Thy loving heart.

2 Oh, how great Thy loving kindness,
> Vaster, broader than the sea:
> Oh, how marvelous Thy goodness,
> Lavished all on me!
> Yes, I rest in Thee, Beloved,
> Know what wealth of grace is Thine,
> Know Thy certainty of promise,
> And have made it mine.

3 Simply trusting Thee, Lord Jesus,
> I behold Thee as Thou art,
> And Thy love, so pure, so changeless,
> Satisfies my heart,
> Satisfies its deepest longings,
> Meets, supplies its every need,
> Compasseth me round with blessings,
> Thine is love indeed.

4 Ever lift Thy face upon me,
> As I work and wait for Thee;
> Resting 'neath Thy smile, Lord Jesus,
> Earth's dark shadows flee.
> Brightness of my Father's glory,
> Sunshine of my Father's face,
> Keep me ever trusting, resting,
> Fill me with Thy grace.

580   11.11.11.11.

1 Resting on the faithfulness of Christ our Lord,
Resting on the fulness of His own sure word,
Resting on His wisdom, on His love and pow'r,
Resting on His covenant from hour to hour.

2 Resting 'neath His guiding hand for untrack'd days,
Resting 'neath His shadow from the noontide rays,
Resting at the eventide beneath His wing,
In the glorious presence of our Savior King.

3 Resting in the fortress while the foe is nigh,
Resting in the lifeboat while the waves roll high,
Resting in His chariot for the swift, glad race,
Resting, always resting, in His boundless grace.

4 Resting in the pastures and beneath the Rock,
Resting by the waters where He leads His flock,
Resting, while we listen, at His glorious feet,
Resting in His very arms, oh, rest complete!

5 Resting and believing, let us onward press;
Resting on Himself, the Lord our righteousness;
Resting and rejoicing, let His saved ones sing,
Glory, glory, glory be to Christ our King!

581   7.6.7.6.D. with chorus.

1   On Thee my heart is resting,
       Ah, this is rest indeed:
    What else, Almighty Savior,
       Can a poor sinner need?
    Thy light is all my wisdom,
       Thy love is all my stay;
    Thy coming back in glory,
       Draws nearer every day.

    On Thee my heart is resting,
       Ah, this is rest indeed:
    What else, Almighty Savior,
       Can a poor sinner need?

2 My guilt is great, but greater
   The mercy Thou dost give;
Thyself, a spotless Off'ring,
   Hast died that I should live.
With Thee, my soul unfettered
   Has risen from the dust;
Thy blood is all my treasure,
   Thy word is all my trust.

3 Through me, Thou gentle Master,
   Thy purposes fulfil;
I yield myself forever
   To Thy most holy will.
What though I be but weakness?
   My strength is not in me;
The poorest of Thy people
   Has all things, having Thee.

4 When clouds are darkest round me,
   Thou, Lord, art then most near,
My drooping faith to quicken,
   My weary soul to cheer.
Safe nestling in Thy bosom,
   I gaze upon Thy face;
In vain my foes would drive me
   From Thee, my hiding-place.

5 'Tis Thou hast made me happy,
   'Tis Thou hast set me free;
To whom shall I give glory
   Forever, but to Thee?
Of earthly love and blessing
   Should every stream run dry,
Thy grace shall still be with me,
   Thy grace, to live and die.

6.6.9.6.6.9. with chorus.

582

1   When we walk with the Lord
In the light of His Word,
What a glory He sheds on our way;
While we do His good will,
He abides with us still,
And with all who will trust and obey.

     Trust and obey,
For there's no other way
To be happy in Jesus,
But to trust and obey.

2   Not a shadow can rise,
Not a cloud in the skies,
But His smile quickly drives it away;
Not a doubt or a fear,
Not a sigh or a tear,
Can abide while we trust and obey.

3   Not a burden we bear,
Not a sorrow we share,
But our toil He doth richly repay;
Not a grief or a loss,
Not a frown or a cross,
But is blest if we trust and obey.

4   But we never can prove
The delights of His love,
Until all on the altar we lay;
For the favor He shows,
And the joy He bestows,
Are for them who will trust and obey.

5   Then in fellowship sweet
We will sit at His feet,
Or we'll walk by His side in the way;
What He says we will do;
Where He sends, we will go,
Never fear, only trust and obey.

7.7.7.7.

1 Go to Him "without the camp,"
His reproach to gladly bear.
Suffered He without the gate,
How can I in comfort share?

2 Go to Him "without the camp,"
Willing e'en to bear the cross;
He has trod the narrow way,
I will follow, suff'ring loss.

3 Go to Him "without the camp,"
Dear ones, relatives forsake;
He the Father's will did mind,
In His passion I partake.

4 Go to Him "without the camp,"
His companion I will be;
Never join religion's ranks
Or the world's society.

5 Go to Him "without the camp,"
Though the path be lone and grim;
Let all human friends desert,
I am satisfied with Him.

6 Go to Him "without the camp,"
There to walk with Him, how blest!
E'er to see His smiling face
Ever in His presence rest.

7 Go to Him "without the camp,"
Till the dawning of the day;
Then I'll see Him and rejoice,
With Him in His kingdom stay.

584   11.11.11.11. with chorus.

1 Anywhere with Jesus I can safely go,
   Anywhere He leads me in this world below.
   Anywhere without Him, dearest joys would fade;
   Anywhere with Jesus I am not afraid.

   Anywhere! anywhere! Fear I cannot know.
   Anywhere with Jesus I can safely go.

2 Anywhere with Jesus I am not alone,
   Other friends may fail me, He is still my own.
   Though His hand may lead me over dreary ways,
   Anywhere with Jesus is a house of praise.

3 Anywhere with Jesus I can go to sleep,
   When the darkling shadows round about me creep;
   Knowing I shall waken never more to roam,
   Anywhere with Jesus will be home, sweet home.

585   8.8.8.8.D.

1 He leadeth me! O blessed thought,
   O words with heav'nly comfort fraught;
   Whate'er I do, where'er I be,
   Still 'tis Christ's hand that leadeth me.

   He leadeth me! He leadeth me!
   By His own hand He leadeth me;
   His faithful follower I would be,
   For by His hand He leadeth me.

2 Sometimes 'mid scenes of deepest gloom,
   Sometimes where Eden's bowers bloom,
   By waters still, o'er troubled sea,
   Still 'tis His hand that leadeth me.

3 Lord, I would clasp Thy hand in mine,
   Nor ever murmur or repine;
   Content, whatever lot I see,
   Since it is Thou that leadest me.

4 And when my task on earth is done,
   When, by Thy grace, the vict'ry's won,
   E'en death's cold wave I will not flee,
   Since Thou in triumph leadest me.

8.8.8.9.D.

586

1 I can hear my Savior calling,
   In the tend'rest accents calling;
   On my ear these words are falling,
   "Take thy cross, and daily follow me."

    I will take my cross and follow,
    My dear Savior I will follow,
    Where He leads me I will follow,
    I'll go with Him, with Him all the way.

2 Though the way be dark and dreary,
   Though my feet be worn and weary,
   Yet my heart keeps bright and cheery
   As I follow, follow all the way.

3 Savior, ever go before me,
   Shining heaven's sunlight o'er me,
   And when weak, by grace restore me
   As I follow, follow all the way.

4 Through the valley safely lead me,
   Heav'nly manna daily feed me;
   Every hour, dear Lord, I need Thee
   As I follow, follow all the way.

5 In Thy heart's affection hold me,
   In Thy arms of love enfold me,
   And with Thine own grace uphold me,
   As I follow, follow all the way.

6 I would never leave Thee, never;
   Faithful I would be forever;
   Nothing from Thy love can sever
   As I follow, follow all the way.

587

8.7.8.7. with chorus.

1 'Tis so sweet to walk with Jesus,
   Step by step and day by day;
Stepping in His very footprints,
   Walking with Him all the way.

   Step by step, step by step,
   I would walk with Jesus,
   All the day, all the way,
   Keeping step with Jesus.

2 'Tis so safe to walk with Jesus,
   Leaning hard upon His arm,
Following closely where He leads us,
   None can hurt and naught can harm.

3 Step by step I'll walk with Jesus,
   Just a moment at a time,
Heights I have not wings to soar to,
   Step by step my feet can climb.

4 All the way I'll walk with Jesus,
   Through the sunshine, through the gloom,
Though His blood-marked steps may lead me
   To the garden, to the tomb.

5 Here a while we walk with Jesus,
   But the time will not be long
Till the night shall change to morning,
   And the sorrow into song.

6 Then, with all who walked with Jesus,
   We shall walk with Him in white,
While He turns our grief to gladness,
   And our darkness into light.

7 Jesus, keep me closer — closer,
   Step by step, and day by day;
   Stepping in Thy very footprints,
   Walking with Thee all the way.

EXPERIENCE OF CHRIST — LIVING IN HIM

8.8.8.8.

588

1 O blessed life — the heart at rest
   When all without tumultuous seems,
   That trusts a higher will, and deems
   That higher will, not mine, the best.

2 O blessed life, the mind that sees,
   Whatever change the years may bring,
   A mercy still in everything,
   And shining through all mysteries.

3 O blessed life, as spirit soars,
   When sense of mortal sight is dim,
   Beyond the sense, beyond to Him,
   Whose love unlocks the glorious doors.

4 O blessed life, heart, mind, and soul,
   From self-born aims and wishes free,
   In all at one with Deity,
   And loyal to the Lord's control.

5 O life, how blessed, how divine,
   High life, the earnest of a higher;
   Savior, fulfil my deep desire,
   And let this blessed life be mine.

589

8.7.8.7.D.

1 God in heaven hath a treasure,
    Riches none may count or tell;
 Hath a deep eternal pleasure,
    Christ the Son, He loveth well.
 God hath here on earth a treasure,
    None but He its price may know —
 Deep, unfathomable pleasure,
    Christ revealed in saints below.

2 God in tongues of fire descending,
    Chosen vessels thus to fill
 With the treasure never ending,
    Ever spent — unfailing still.
 God's own hand the vessel filling
    From the glory far above,
 Longing hearts forever stilling
    With the riches of His love.

3 Thus though worn, and tried, and tempted,
    Glorious calling, saint, is thine;
 Let the Lord but find thee emptied,
    Living branch in Christ the Vine!
 Vessels of the world's despising,
    Vessels weak and poor and base,
 Bearing wealth God's heart is prizing,
    Glory from Christ's blessed face.

4 Oh to be but emptier, lowlier,
    Mean, unnoticed — and unknown,
 And to God a vessel holier,
    Filled with Christ and Christ alone!
 Naught of earth to cloud the glory,
    Naught of self the light to dim,
 Telling forth His wondrous story,
    Emptied to be filled with Him.

8.7.8.7.

1 Lo, from vessels, earthen only,
    Shining forth in ceaseless grace,
   Reaching weary hearts, and lonely,
    Beams the light from Jesus' face!

2 Christ, the light that fills the heavens
    Shining forth on earth beneath,
   Through His Spirit freely given
    Light of life 'midst shades of death;

3 Down from heaven's unclouded glory
    God Himself the treasure brought,
   Closing thus His love's sweet story
    With His sweetest, deepest thought.

4 Earthen vessels, marred, unsightly,
    But the treasure as of old,
   Fresh from glory, gleaming brightly,
    Heaven's undimmed, unchanging gold.

5 Vessels, broken, frail, yet bearing
    Through the hungry ages on
   Riches giv'n with hand unsparing —
    God's great Gift, His precious Son!

591   11.10.11.10. with chorus.

1 Not I, but Christ be honored, loved, exalted,
Not I, but Christ be seen, be known and heard;
Not I, but Christ in every look and action,
Not I, but Christ in every thought and word.

Oh, to be saved from myself, dear Lord,
Oh, to be lost in Thee,
Oh, that it may be no more I,
But Christ that lives in me.

2 Not I, but Christ to gently soothe in sorrow,
Not I, but Christ to wipe the falling tear;
Not I, but Christ to lift the weary burden,
Not I, but Christ to hush away all fear.

3 Christ, only Christ, no idle word e'er falling,
Christ, only Christ, no needless bustling sound;
Christ, only Christ, no self-important bearing,
Christ, only Christ, no trace of I be found.

4 Not I, but Christ my every need supplying,
Not I, but Christ my strength and health to be;
Christ, only Christ, for spirit, soul, and body,
Christ, only Christ, live then Thy life in me.

5 Christ, only Christ, ere long will fill my vision,
Glory excelling soon, full soon I'll see;
Christ, only Christ, my every wish fulfilling,
Christ, only Christ, my all in all to be.

EXPERIENCE OF CHRIST — REFLECTING HIM

592   10.10.10.10.

1 The earth absorbs the soft, refreshing rain,
And sends it back in flow'rs and fruits again;
So we receive Thy life so rich and free,
And live it out for joy and praise to Thee.

2 The moon receives the sun's bright, golden light,
And gives it forth to cheer the darksome night;
So we receive the rays of light Divine,
And with them on this darkened world we shine.

3 'Tis by Thy love that I can love and bless
The foes who seek to blast my happiness;
Can e'en rejoice, when bearing wrong and shame,
Thou deem'st me meet to suffer for Thy name.

4 Naught but Thyself can satisfy my heart,
Constrain my will from self and sin to part:
In love so great Thou giv'st Thyself to me;
That I may Thee express eternally.

EXPERIENCE OF CHRIST — BY MINDING THE SPIRIT

11.11.11.11.   **593***

1 All I have in Adam is but sin and death,
I in Christ inherit life and righteousness;
When in flesh abiding, Adam I express,
But when in the spirit Christ is manifest.

2 When I am in Adam, though I may not sin,
Unto death, a sinner, sentenced I have been;
When in Christ I need not righteously to act,
I'm already righteous, justified in fact.

3 In the flesh I need no effort to express
Marks of Adam's nature and its sinfulness;
In the spirit I need not to strive or strain,
I can live as He is and in spirit reign.

4 Thru my death with Christ, from Adam I am free,
Thru my life with Christ, new life is given me!
Minding not the flesh, old Adam cannot move,
Minding just the spirit, life divine I prove.

continued

5   Minding just the spirit is God's saving way,
Minding just the spirit, Christ we will display;
Minding just the spirit, we can overcome,
Minding just the spirit, we the race may run.

6   Minding just the spirit, we the cross will know,
And His resurrection pow'r thru us will flow;
Minding just the spirit, Christ will live thru me,
And His life within will reach maturity.

7   In the spirit Christ is life and all to me,
Strengthening and blessing all-inclusively;
Living in the spirit, holiness I prove,
And the triune God within my heart doth move.

EXPERIENCE OF CHRIST —
BY FOLLOWING THE SPIRIT

594*   6.5.6.5.D.

1 Christ my very peace is
And my life within;
Sharing in the spirit
I unite with Him.

Following the Spirit,
Living in the Lord,
Life He doth supply me
And His peace afford.

2 To the Lord belonging,
Bound I'll never be,
For the law of life now
Sets me wholly free.

3 Minding flesh no longer,
I'll the spirit mind;
Self-will never follow,
But the Spirit's find.

4 Christ within empow'rs me
Spiritual to be!
E'en my body quick'ning
By His pow'r in me.

5 Spirit with the spirit
Witnesseth in one,
I'm of God begotten,
Heir with Christ the Son.

8.7.8.7.D. with repeat.

1 There is always something over,
   When we taste our gracious Lord;
Every cup He fills o'erfloweth,
   Rich supply He doth afford.
Nothing narrow, nothing stinted,
   Ever issued from His store;
To His own He gives full measure,
   Running over, evermore,
To His own He gives full measure,
   Running over, evermore.

2 There is always something over,
   When we, from the Father's hand,
Take our portion with thanksgiving,
   Praising for the things He planned.
Satisfaction, full and deepening,
   All our need He doth supply,
When the heart has tasted Jesus
   Its desires to satisfy,
When the heart has tasted Jesus
   Its desires to satisfy.

3 There is always something over,
   When we share in all His love;
Unplumbed depths still lie beneath us,
   Unscaled heights rise far above.
Human lips can never utter
   All His wondrous tenderness.
We can only praise and wonder
   And His Name forever bless,
We can only praise and wonder
   And His Name forever bless.

596

11.10.11.10.

1 Mine is the earth, the worlds in all their fulness;
   Mine, every ocean, river, plain, and hill;
Mine are the stars within the heaven's stillness,
   Mine are the clouds that wander at their will.

2 Mine is the spring, when blossoms sweet are blowing,
   Wakened from slumb'ring neath the winter snow;
Mine, summer's wealth, with her bright colors glowing;
   Mine is the fruit rich autumn doth bestow.

3 Mine, all the things created: praise the Giver!
   Fish, and all beasts, the birds upon the wing,
Sun-loving butterflies — now and forever;
   Beauty and grace of every living thing.

4 Mine, all things lovely, blessing every hour,
   Wealth of creation, over and around;
Mine is the sun, with its life-giving power,
   Mine is the music wonderful of sound.

5 Mine are the pillars which cannot be shaken —
   Truth in the Word, the Word that cannot fall.
Mine is the wisdom which great thoughts awaken
   In a man's soul, that this life is not all.

6 Knowledge as needed, skill in all the doing,
   Mine, when kept closely for my Lord above;
Beauty and wisdom, living streams e'er flowing
   Fresh from the springs of God, the God of love.

7 Mine are the battles, triumph-shouts e'er ringing —
   Joy of the warriors for the truth and right;
Mine are the trophies God's brave ones are bringing,
   Heroes of faith and overcoming might.

8 Mine, mercies granted, and each new awaking,
   Every experience, and each soul that's won;
Mine, the confessions sinners poor are making,
   Yea, I am joined with them, one in God's Son.

9 One Lord in all, and all one in His Spirit,
    Heavenly fellowship earth has not known;
    Faith sees the riches we shall yet inherit,
    Glorious treasure laid up for His own.

10 All in the bounds of earth and sea and heaven,
    Creation's wonders and Thy grace are stored:
    Praise to Thee, Christ, for all the wealth Thou'st given!
    Poor in myself, but wealthy in my Lord!

8.6.8.6.   **597**

1 I know that my Redeemer lives
    And ever prays for me;
    A token of His love He gives,
    A pledge of liberty.

2 I know that my Redeemer lives,
    A quick'ning Spirit He;
    I know eternal life He gives —
    Amazing grace — to me.

3 I find Him lifting up my head;
    He brings salvation near;
    His presence makes me free indeed,
    And He will soon appear.

4 He wills that I should holy be:
    What can withstand His will?
    The counsel of His grace in me
    He surely shall fulfill.

5 Jesus, I hang upon Thy word:
    I steadfastly believe
    Thou wilt return and claim me, Lord,
    And to Thyself receive.

598

10.10.10.10.8.8.8.8.

1 All fair within those children of the light,
Though dark their brows beneath the desert sun;
Mysterious joys, far hidden from all sight,
The King of Glory giveth to each one;
    No thought of man has pictured them,
    No hand may touch that diadem;
    Within God's light His own abide
    With hidden glory glorified.

2 To earthly eyes they are as Adam's race —
They wear the earthly form, and scars of pain
On them as on all sinners leave their trace;
Their outward needs are those of other men.
    And theirs the forms of earthly life,
    Theirs sleeping, waking, want, and strife,
    Yet this they have that they despise
    What fairest seems to earthly eyes.

3 And inwardly their life is from above,
The Lord's Almighty Word hath quickened them;
Flames kindled from the everlasting Love,
The children of the New Jerusalem;
    Their brethren are the saints in light,
    And songs of sweetness infinite
    They sing with them to God Most High,
    A deep and wondrous melody.

4 They walk upon the earth, and dwell in heaven,
Though pow'rless, guard the world with arms unseen;
Deep peace to them in midst of strife is given,
And all they wish they have, though poor and mean.
    Storms beat them, but may not destroy,
    Fast rooted in eternal joy;
    They walk as in the shade of death,
    Yet living on in silent faith.

5 When Christ their Life shall be made manifest,
   When He shall come with all His pow'r to rule,
   Their glory, hidden long, shall be confessed;
   Arise and shine! O bright and beautiful!
    With Christ ye shall ascend on high,
    Victorious in His victory —
    The hidden light shall shine afar,
    Each saint an everlasting star.

8.8.8.8.   **599**

1 Lord, I was blind; I could not see
   In Thy marred visage any grace,
   But now the beauty of Thy face
   In radiant vision dawns on me.

2 Lord, I was deaf; I could not hear
   The thrilling music of Thy voice;
   But now I hear Thee and rejoice,
   And all Thine uttered words are dear!

3 Lord, I was dumb; I could not speak
   The grace and glory of Thy name;
   But now, as touched with living flame,
   My lips Thine eager praises wake.

4 Lord, I was dead; I could not stir
   My lifeless soul to come to Thee;
   But now, since Thou hast quickened me,
   I rise from sin's dark sepulcher.

5 For Thou hast made the blind to see,
   The deaf to hear, the dumb to speak,
   The dead to live; and, lo, I break
   The chains of my captivity.

8.6.8.6. with repeat.

1 My God, my Portion, and my Love,
  My everlasting All,
I've none but Thee in heav'n above,
  Or on this earthly ball,
  Or on this earthly ball.

2 What empty things are all the skies,
  And this inferior clod!
There's nothing here deserves my joys,
  There's nothing like my God,
  There's nothing like my God.

3 To Thee I owe my wealth, and friends,
  And health, and safe abode;
Thanks to Thy name for meaner things,
  But they are not my God,
  But they are not my God.

4 How vain a toy is glittering wealth,
  If once compared to Thee!
Or what's my safety, or my health,
  Or all my friends to me,
  Or all my friends to me.

5 Were I possessor of the earth,
  And called the stars my own,
Without Thy graces and Thyself,
  I were a wretch undone,
  I were a wretch undone.

6 Let others stretch their arms like seas,
  And grasp in all the shore;
Grant me the visits of Thy grace,
  And I desire no more,
  And I desire no more.

8.6.8.6.D.

1 My heart is resting, O my God,
   I will give thanks and sing;
My heart is at the secret source
   Of every precious thing.

   Oh, peace of God that passeth thought,
      I daily, hourly sing;
   My heart is at the secret source
      Of every precious thing.

2 Now this frail vessel Thou hast made,
   No hand but Thine shall fill;
The waters of the earth have failed,
   And I am thirsty still.

3 I thirst for springs of heavenly life,
   And here all day they rise;
I seek the treasure of Thy love,
   And close at hand it lies.

4 A glad, new song is in my mouth,
   To long-loved music set,
A song of praise for all the grace
   I have not tasted yet.

5 I have a heritage of joy
   That yet I must not see;
The hand that bled to make it mine
   Is keeping it for me.

6 There is a certainty of love
   That sets my heart at rest;
A calm assurance for today
   That to be poor is best.

7 A prayer reposing on His truth,
   Who hath made all things mine;
That draws my captive will to Him,
   And makes it one with Thine.

602*

8.7.8.7.8.7.

1 O how glorious! O how holy!
     God is the eternal life!
  Full, unlimited, and pow'rful,
     Pure, and merciful, and bright!
  In this life are all His riches,
     All His nature, love and light.

2 O how loving! O how gracious!
     God Himself is life to man!
  He in man hath made a spirit
     That He might fulfill His plan.
  'Tis His heart's delight and longing
     E'er to be received by man.

3 O what love and grace unbounded!
     God as life to man doth flow!
  He no more is hid in secret
     But Himself to man doth show,
  First in flesh and then as Spirit
     That His life all men may know.

4 How approachable! How near us!
     God in Christ our life to be!
  Christ is God in flesh incarnate,
     Manifest for man to see.
  Died and risen, now He enters
     Into man, his life to be.

5 O what wonder! As the Spirit
     God as life to man is shown!
  'Tis His other transformation,
     He as Spirit thus is known;
  Men convicting and inspiring,
     He within them makes His home.

6   O how glorious! O how precious!
      Thus the triune God to know!
    First the Father in the Son came,
      Now the Son as Spirit flows.
    When in man the Spirit enters
      God as life He doth bestow.

7   How mysterious, yet how real!
      God Himself now flows in me!
    In my heart, with me in oneness,
      He has come my life to be.
    Hallelujah! Hallelujah!
      I will praise unceasingly!

EXPERIENCE OF GOD — AS LIGHT

8.6.8.8.6.   **603**

1   Eternal Light! Eternal Light!
      How pure the soul must be
    When, placed within Thy searching sight,
    It shrinks not, but with calm delight
      Can live and look on Thee.

2   The spirits that surround Thy throne
      May bear the burning bliss;
    But that is surely theirs alone,
    Since they have never, never known
      A fallen world like this.

3   Oh, how shall I, whose native sphere
      Is dark, whose mind is dim,
    Before th' Ineffable appear,
    And on my natural spirit bear
      The uncreated beam?

continued

EXPERIENCE OF GOD — AS LIGHT

4 There is a way for man to rise
   To Thee, sublime Abode;
An Offering and a Sacrifice,
A Holy Spirit's energies,
   An Advocate with God:

5 These, these prepare us for the sight
   Of holiness above;
The sons of ignorance and night
May dwell in the eternal Light,
   Through the eternal Love.

EXPERIENCE OF GOD — AS HELP

604   10.4.10.4.10.10.

1 Unto the hills around do I lift up
   My longing eyes;
O whence for me shall my salvation come,
   From whence arise?
From God the Lord doth come my certain aid,
From God the Lord, who heaven and earth hath made.

2 He will not suffer that thy foot be moved:
   Safe shalt thou be.
No careless slumber shall His eyelids close,
   Who keepeth thee.
Behold, He sleepeth not, He slumbereth ne'er,
Who keepeth Israel in His holy care.

3 Jehovah is Himself thy keeper true,
   Thy changeless shade;
Jehovah thy defense on thy right hand
   Himself hath made.
And thee no sun by day shall ever smite;
No moon shall harm thee in the silent night.

4 From every evil shall He keep thy soul,
   From every sin;
Jehovah shall preserve thy going out,
   Thy coming in.
Above thee, watching, He whom we adore
Shall keep thee henceforth, yea, for evermore.

EXPERIENCE OF GOD — AS THE DWELLING PLACE

10.10.10.10.10.10.   **605**

1 My home is God Himself; Christ brought me there,
   And bade me dwell in Him, rejoicing there;
   He bore me where no foot but His hath trod,
   Within the holiest at home with God.
   O holy place! O home divinely fair!
   And we, God's little ones, abiding there.

2 A long, long road I traveled night and day,
   And sought to find within myself some way,
   Aught I could do, or feel to bring me near;
   Self effort failed, and I was filled with fear,
   And then I found Christ was the only way
   That I must come to Him and in Him stay.

3 O wondrous place! O home divinely fair!
   And I, God's little one, safe hidden there.
   Lord, as I dwell in Thee and Thou in me,
   So make me dead to everything but Thee;
   That as I rest within my home most fair,
   I'll share my God in all and everywhere.

606

8.6.8.6.

1 Oh, how the thought of God attracts
   And draws the heart from earth,
   And sickens it of passing shows
   And dissipating mirth!

2 'Tis not enough to save our souls,
   To shun th' eternal fires;
   The thought of God will rouse the heart
   To more sublime desires.

3 God only is the creature's home,
   Though rough and straight the road;
   Yet nothing less can satisfy
   The love that longs for God.

4 Oh, utter but the Name of God
   Down in your heart of hearts,
   And see how from the world at once
   All tempting light departs.

5 A trusting heart, a yearning eye,
   Can win their way above;
   If mountains can be moved by faith,
   Is there less power in love?

6 How little of that road, my soul!
   How little hast thou gone!
   Take heart, and let the thought of God
   Allure thee further on.

7 The freedom from all willful sin,
   The Christian's daily task;
   Oh! these are graces far below
   What longing love would ask!

8 The perfect way is hard to flesh;
   It is not hard to love;
   If thou wert sick for want of God,
   How swiftly wouldst thou move!

9   Then keep thy conscience sensitive;
     No inward token miss:
     And go where grace entices thee —
     Perfection lies in this.

8.6.8.6.   **607**

1   O God, our help in ages past,
     Our hope for years to come,
     Our shelter from the stormy blast,
     And our eternal home.

2   Under the shadow of Thy throne
     Thy saints have dwelt secure;
     Sufficient is Thine arm alone,
     And our defence is sure.

3   Before the hills in order stood,
     Or earth received her frame,
     From everlasting Thou art God,
     To endless years the same.

4   A thousand ages in Thy sight
     Are like an evening gone;
     Short as the watch that ends the night
     Before the rising sun.

5   Time, like an ever-rolling stream,
     Bears all its sons away;
     They fly forgotten, as a dream
     Dies at the opening day.

6   O God, our help in ages past,
     Our hope for years to come,
     Be Thou our guard while life shall last,
     And our eternal home.

608*   11.10.11.10. with chorus.

1 What mystery, the Father, Son, and Spirit,
  In person three, in substance all are one.
How glorious, this God our being enters
  To be our all, thru Spirit in the Son!

  The Triune God has now become our all!
    How wonderful! How glorious!
  This Gift divine we never can exhaust!
    How excellent! How marvelous!

2 How rich the source, the Father as the fountain,
  And all this wealth He wants man to enjoy!
O blessed fact, this vast exhaustless portion
  Is now for us forever to employ!

3 How wonderful, the Son is God's expression
  Come in the flesh to dwell with all mankind!
Redemption's work, how perfectly effective,
  That sinners we with God might oneness find.

4 The Spirit is the Son's transfiguration
  Come into us as life the full supply.
Amazing fact, our spirit with the Spirit
  Now mingles and in oneness joins thereby!

5 How real it is that God is now the Spirit
  For us to touch, experience day by day!
Astounding fact, with God we are one spirit,
  And differ not in life in any way!

609*   8.8.8.8.

1 I praise Thee for Thy mystery,
  That I may truly contact Thee;
  In unapproachable light Thou wast
  But now as Spirit nigh to me.

2 The Father, Son, and Spirit, Thou,
  The triune God, my life fore'er;
  In me Thou art the full supply
  That I Thy holy nature share.

3 The triune God the Spirit is,
    And comes as breath and wind to me;
    'Tis thus I may experience
    The Godhead's wondrous mystery.

4 All that the Father is and has
    In His beloved Son doth rest,
    And all the riches of the Son
    Are by the Spirit now possessed.

5 The Spirit doth descend on me
    And to my spirit enters in,
    That He, the Father in the Son,
    My blessed portion be within.

6 The Father is the fountainhead,
    The Son expression gives to Him;
    The Spirit is His very flow,
    As my reality within.

7 The Father in the Son has come
    That God to man Himself may show;
    The Son as Spirit enters me
    That God I inwardly may know.

8 The Father purposed that the Son
    Should be the first in everything;
    The Son the Father takes as Head
    And over all His headship brings.

9 The Spirit perfectly desires
    That Christ, the Son, be glorified,
    And He reveals Him unto me,
    That He be fully testified.

10 Thy final form the Spirit is,
    Our worship to receive within;
    If I Thy riches would enjoy,
    In spirit I must contact Him.

continued

11 If I in spirit worship Thee,
In spirit live, in spirit pray,
The Holy Spirit I will touch
And Thee enjoy in every way.

EXPERIENCE OF GOD —
BY THE SPIRIT AS THE TRANSMISSION

610*   8.8.8.8.

1 God's Spirit His transmission is,
In Him God enters into us;
It is in Him that God in Christ
May be experienced by us.

2 God as the Father is the source,
And God the Son doth Him express;
God as the Spirit enters us,
That God as all we may possess.

3 The Father, who is veiled in light,
The Son to man hath fully shown;
The Spirit then transmitteth Him
That He may inwardly be known.

4 The Son within the Father is,
And now the Spirit is the Son.
The Spirit, Son, and Father God
Are now in us and with us one.

5 God as the Father in the Son
Has been embodied and expressed,
And God the Spirit is the Son's
Reality to be possessed.

6 May God the Father's love to us
In God the Son as grace be known,
Thru God the Spirit's fellowship,
That God our portion we may own.

8.8.8.8.

611*

1 God's glorious substance Spirit is,
His essence, holy and divine;
To contact God and Him enjoy,
His Spirit I must touch with mine.

2 The spirit is the innermost,
The part of man most deep and real;
If he would contact God in life,
'Tis with the spirit he must deal.

3 The worship which the Father seeks
Is in the spirit's strength alone;
His Spirit into man's would come,
That His and man's may thus be one.

4 When Spirit unto spirit calls
The two commingle and are one;
Man's spirit is the Spirit's home,
The Spirit doth man's life become.

5 Man's spirit must God's Spirit touch
If in God's fulness he would live;
'Tis only with the spirit thus
That he to God may worship give.

6 In ministry and fellowship
Man to the spirit we must bring;
All ministry should turn to prayer,
Spirit to spirit answering.

7 In spirit we must pray and serve,
In spirit touch the life divine,
In spirit grow, in spirit build,
That Christ thru us may fully shine.

8 Lord, to the spirit I would turn
And learn to truly contact Thee;
Thy Spirit thus will flow with mine
And overflow eternally.

612*

8.5.8.3.D.

1 God intends that all His being
  Be my full supply;
  With Him I must be united,
    In spirit nigh.

  All God's being, all His riches
    In the Spirit flow;
  I must exercise my spirit
    Him to know.

2 All the riches of His nature
    He has given me;
  I must touch Him in the spirit,
    These to see.

3 With the mind we understand Him,
    With the spirit touch;
  Those who never use the spirit
    Lack very much.

4 When to messages I listen,
    I must pray them in;
  Thus the word will be digested
    From within.

5 When the Word of God I study,
    I must touch the Lord;
  If in mind and not in spirit,
    Dead is the Word.

6 O what riches, O what glory
    In the Spirit shine!
  When I exercise my spirit,
    All are mine.

8.6.8.6. with repeat.

1 I would commune with Thee, my God;
      E'en to Thy seat I come;
   I leave my joys, I leave my sins,
      And seek in Thee my home.

2 I stand upon the mount of God,
      With sunlight in my soul;
   I see the storms in vales beneath,
      I hear the thunder's roll.

3 But I am calm with Thee, my God,
      Beneath these glorious skies;
   And to the height on which I stand
      Nor storms nor clouds can rise.

4 Oh, this is life! oh, this is joy,
      My God, to find Thee so;
   Thy face to see, Thy voice to hear,
      And all Thy love to know.

(Repeat the last line of each stanza)

6.4.6.4.6.6.6.4.

1 Nearer, my God, to Thee,
      Nearer to Thee;
   E'en though it be a cross
      That raiseth me,
   Still all my song shall be
   Nearer, my God, to Thee,
   Nearer, my God, to Thee,
      Nearer to Thee.

2 Though, like a wanderer,
      The sun gone down,
   Darkness comes over me,
      My rest a stone;

continued

Yet in my dreams I'd be
Nearer, my God, to Thee,
Nearer, my God, to Thee,
  Nearer to Thee.

3 There let me see the sight,
    An open heaven;
All that Thou sendest me,
    In mercy given;
Angels to beckon me
Nearer, my God, to Thee,
Nearer, my God, to Thee,
  Nearer to Thee.

4 Then, with my waking thoughts
    Bright with Thy praise,
Out of my stony griefs
    Bethel I'll raise,
So by my woes to be
Nearer, my God, to Thee,
Nearer, my God, to Thee,
  Nearer to Thee.

615   6.6.8.6.

1 Begin the day with God!
    He is thy Sun and Day!
His is the radiance of thy dawn;
    To Him address thy lay.

2 Sing a new song at morn!
    Join the glad woods and hills;
Join the fresh winds and seas and plains,
    Join the bright flowers and rills.

3 Sing thy first song to God!
    Not to thy fellow men;
Not to the creatures of His hand,
    But to the glorious One.

4 Take thy first walk with God!
Let Him go forth with thee;
By stream, or sea, or mountain path,
Seek still His company.

5 Thy first transaction be
With God Himself above;
So shall thy business prosper well
And all the day be love.

7.7.7.7.4. with chorus. **616**

1 Day is dying in the west,
Heav'n is touching earth with rest,
Wait and worship while the night
Sets her evening lamps alight
Through all the sky.

Holy, holy, holy,
Lord God of Hosts!
Heav'n and earth are full of Thee!
Heav'n and earth are praising Thee,
O Lord, most high!

2 Lord of life, beneath the dome
Of the universe, Thy home,
Gather us, who seek Thy face,
To the fold of Thy embrace,
For Thou art nigh.

3 While the deepening shadows fall,
Heart of love, enfolding all,
Through the glory and the grace
Of the stars that veil Thy face,
Our hearts ascend.

617

8.8.8.8.

1 Thou sweet, beloved will of God,
  My anchor ground, my fortress hill,
My spirit's silent, fair abode,
  In Thee I hide me and am still.

2 O Will, that willest good alone,
  Lead Thou the way, Thou guidest best;
A little child, I follow on,
  And, trusting, lean upon Thy breast.

3 God's will doth make the bitter sweet,
  And all is well when it is done;
Unless His will doth hallow it,
  The glory of all joy is gone.

4 Thy beautiful sweet will, my God,
  Holds fast in its sublime embrace
My captive will, a gladsome bird,
  Prisoned in such a realm of grace.

5 Within this place of certain good
  Love evermore expands her wings,
Or nestling in Thy perfect choice,
  Abides content with what it brings.

6 Oh, lightest burden, sweetest yoke;
  It lifts, it bears my happy soul,
It giveth wings to this poor heart;
  My freedom is Thy grand control.

7 Upon God's will I lay me down,
  As child upon its mother's breast;
No silken couch, nor softest bed,
  Could ever give me such deep rest.

8 Thy wonderful grand will, my God,
  With triumph now I make it mine;
And faith shall cry a joyous Yes
  To every dear command of Thine.

THE OLD RUGGED CROSS

618

George Bennard   12.8.12.8. with chorus.

1 On a hill far away stood an old rugged cross,
     The emblem of suff'ring and shame,
   And I love that old cross where the Dearest and Best
     For a world of lost sinners was slain.

     So I'll cherish the old rugged cross,
     Till my trophies at last I lay down;
     I will cling to the old rugged cross,
     And exchange it some day for a crown.

2 Oh, that old rugged cross, so despised by the world,
     Has a wondrous attraction for me;
   For the dear Lamb of God left His glory above,
     To bear it to dark Calvary.

3 In the old rugged cross, stained with blood so divine,
     A wondrous beauty I see;
   For 'twas on that old cross Jesus suffered and died,
     To pardon and sanctify me.

GLORYING IN THE CROSS — TOWERING OVER ALL

8.7.8.7.   **619**

1 In the cross of Christ I glory,
     Tow'ring o'er the wrecks of time;
   All the light of sacred story
     Gathers round its head sublime.

2 When the woes of life o'ertake me,
     Hopes deceive, and fears annoy,
   Never shall the cross forsake me,
     Lo! It glows with peace and joy.

3 When the sun of bliss is beaming
     Light and love upon my way,
   From the cross the radiance streaming
     Adds more luster to the day.   *continued*

4 Bane and blessing, pain and pleasure,
 By the cross are sanctified;
Peace is there that knows no measure,
 Joys that through all time abide.

DEFYING EVERY BLAST

620

Peculiar Meter.

1 The cross it standeth fast,
 Hallelujah! hallelujah!
Defying every blast,
 Hallelujah! hallelujah!
The winds of hell have blown,
The world its hate hath shown,
Yet it is not overthrown,
 Hallelujah for the cross!

 Hallelujah, hallelujah,
  Hallelujah for the cross;
 Hallelujah, hallelujah,
  It shall never suffer loss.

2 It is the old cross still,
 Hallelujah! hallelujah!
Its triumph let us tell,
 Hallelujah! hallelujah!
The grace of God here shone,
Through Christ the blessed Son,
Who hath redemption won,
 Hallelujah for the cross!

3 'Twas here the debt was paid,
 Hallelujah! hallelujah!
Our sins on Jesus laid,
 Hallelujah! hallelujah!
So round the cross we sing
Of Christ, our offering,
Of Christ, our living King,
 Hallelujah for the cross!

7.6.8.6.8.6.8.6.

1 Beneath the cross of Jesus
   I fain would take my stand,
The shadow of a mighty Rock
   Within a weary land;
A home within the wilderness,
   A rest upon the way,
From the burning of the noontide heat,
   And the burden of the day.

2 Oh, safe and happy shelter!
   Oh, refuge tried and sweet!
Oh, trysting place where heaven's love
   And heaven's justice meet.
As to the holy patriarch
   That wondrous dream was given,
So is my Savior by the cross
   A ladder up to heaven.

3 There lies beneath its shadow,
   But on the farther side,
The darkness of an awful grave
   That gapes both deep and wide;
And there between us stands the cross,
   Two arms outstretched to save,
Like a watchman set to guard the way
   From that eternal grave.

4 Upon that cross of Jesus
   Mine eye at times can see
The very dying form of One,
   Who suffered there for me;
And from my smitten heart, with tears,
   Two wonders I confess,
The wonders of His glorious love,
   And my own worthlessness.

continued

5   I take, O cross, thy shadow
       For my abiding place;
    I ask no other sunshine than
       The sunshine of His face;
    Content to let the world go by,
       To know no gain nor loss,
    My sinful self my only shame,
       My glory all the cross.

THE WAY OF THE CROSS —
THE MEANING OF THE CROSS

622*

12.12.12.12.

1 If we take up the cross, will we but suffer pain?
  Nay, if we bear the cross, be sure that we will die!
  The meaning of the cross is that we may be slain;
  The cross experienced the self will crucify.

2 Divine deliverance e'er slays man by the cross;
  Though cruel it may seem, it is a grand release.
  Christ ne'er will be our life if we escape the cross;
  Christ ne'er will be expressed but by our sure decease.

3 The cross's final goal, that God's will be fulfilled;
  His will's arch enemy is but the self of man.
  If self be done away and all the soul-life killed,
  God's will shall then prevail and prospered be His plan.

8.8.8.8.D.

1 There is no gain but by a loss;
   We cannot save but by the cross,
   The corn of wheat to multiply
   Must fall into the ground and die;
   O should a soul alone remain
   When it a hundredfold can gain?
   O should a soul alone remain
   When it a hundredfold can gain?

2 Our souls are held by all they hold;
   Slaves still are slaves in chains of gold;
   To whatsoever we may cling,
   We make it a soul-chaining thing.
   Whether it be a life or land,
   And dear as our right eye or hand.
   Whether it be a life or land,
   And dear as our right eye or hand.

3 Wherever you ripe fields behold,
   Waving to God their sheaves of gold,
   Be sure some corn of wheat has died,
   Some saintly soul been crucified;
   Someone has suffered, wept and prayed,
   And fought hell's legions undismayed.
   Someone has suffered, wept and prayed,
   And fought hell's legions undismayed.

Used by permission of Victoria Booth-Clibborn Demarest.

624

8.8.8.8.8.8.

1 The heavier the cross, the nearer God;
No cross without, no God within!
The prince of darkness thus is trod,
Amid the world's false glare and din.
Oh, happy he, with all his loss,
Whom God hath set beneath the cross.

2 The heavier the cross, the better saint;
This is the touchstone God applies.
The gardens many would be faint,
Unwet by showers from weeping eyes!
The gold by fire is purified;
The saint is by much trouble tried.

3 The heavier the cross, the stronger faith:
The loaded palm strikes deeper root;
The vine juice sweetly issueth
When men have pressed the clustered fruit;
And courage grows where dangers come,
Like pearls beneath the salty foam.

4 The heavier the cross, the deeper prayer;
The bruisèd herbs most fragrant are.
If sky and wind were always fair,
The sailor would not watch the star;
And David's Psalms had ne'er been sung
If grief his heart had never wrung.

5 The heavier the cross, the more inspired;
From vales to climb to mountain crest;
The pilgrim, of the desert tired,
Longs for the Canaan of his rest.
The dove has here no rest in sight,
And to the ark she wings her flight.

6 The heavier the cross, the easier to die;
Death is a kinder face to see;
Our life's decay we dare defy,
From life's distress we then are free.
The cross sublimely lifts our faith
To Him who triumphed over death.

7 Thou Crucified! the cross I bear.
The longer, may it dearer be;
And lest I faint while ling'ring here,
Implant Thou such a heart in me
That faith and love may flourish e'er,
Till for the cross the crown I wear.

7.7.7.7.

625

1 'Tis my happiness below
Not to live without the cross;
But the Savior's pow'r to know
Sanctifying every loss.

2 Trials must and will befall;
But with humble faith to see
Love inscribed upon them all —
This is happiness to me.

3 Did I meet no trials here,
No chastisement by the way,
Might I not with reason fear
I should prove a castaway?

4 Trials make the promise sweet;
Trials give new life to prayer;
Bring me to my Savior's feet,
Lay me low and keep me there.

626 †   8.5.8.7.D. with chorus.

1   Olives that have known no pressure
     No oil can bestow;
  If the grapes escape the winepress,
     Cheering wine can never flow;
  Spikenard only through the crushing,
     Fragrance can diffuse.
  Shall I then, Lord, shrink from suff'ring
     Which Thy love for me would choose?

      Each blow I suffer
      Is true gain to me.
      In the place of what Thou takest
      Thou dost give Thyself to me.

2   Do my heart-strings need Thy stretching,
     Songs divine to prove?
  Do I need for sweetest music
     Cruel treatment of Thy love?
  Lord, I fear no deprivation
     If it draws to Thee;
  I would yield in full surrender
     All Thy heart of love to see.

3   I'm ashamed, my Lord, for seeking
     Self to guard alway;
  Though Thy love has done its stripping,
     Yet I've been compelled this way.
  Lord, according to Thy pleasure
     Fully work on me;
  Heeding not my human feelings,
     Only do what pleases Thee.

4   If Thy mind and mine should differ,
     Still pursue Thy way;
  If Thy pleasure means my sorrow,
     Still my heart shall answer, "Yea!"

'Tis my deep desire to please Thee,
    Though I suffer loss;
E'en though Thy delight and glory
    Mean that I endure the cross.

5 Oh, I'll praise Thee, e'en if weeping
    Mingle with my song.
Thine increasing sweetness calls forth
    Grateful praises all day long.
Thou hast made Thyself more precious
    Than all else to me:
Thou increase and I decrease, Lord —
    This is now my only plea.

10.4.10.4.   **627**

1 Lord, day by day I view Thy wondrous Cross
    On Calvary!
And day by day I stretch my hands thereon
    And die with Thee.

2 I "glory in the Cross" most loving Lord,
    Because I know
It is the power to save and satisfy,
    Where'er I go.

3 The daily Cross becomes the deepest joy,
    For just beyond
The Cross, I clearly see how Cross and Crown
    Do correspond.

4 Oh, gracious Lord, how sweet to take from Thee
    The daily Cross!
And know that I can never separate
    Its gain and loss.

5 The daily Cross is daily loss to all
    That keeps from Thee;
The daily Cross is daily gain of all
    Thou art for me.

THE WAY OF THE CROSS —
THE WAY OF FOLLOWING THE LORD

628

8.7.8.7.D.

1 Via Bethlehem we journey,
We whose hearts on God are set;
Babelike souls of Jesus learning,
While our cheeks with tears are wet;
For the manger and the stable
Are not pleasant to our eyes,
But our feet must follow Jesus,
If our hands would grasp the prize.

2 Via Nazareth! the pathway
Narrows still as on we go,
Years of toil none understanding,
Yet God teaches us to know
That the servant is not greater
Than the Lord, who through long years
Hid Himself from this world's glory,
Follow Him! Count not the tears.

3 Via Galilee, we see Him!
Stones are hurled, and curses hissed
By the men who gather round Him,
Has He not the pathway missed?
No! unharmed the Savior passes,
And this rough bit of the way
We must travel, since like Jesus,
Nothing can our purpose stay.

4 Via too, the awful anguish
Of the hours beneath the trees,
Where the hosts of Satan linger,
Awful hours of anguish these!
Yet we fail not, for God's angels
Minister to us, and say,
"Look, beloved, at the glory,
Conflict is but for a day!"

5   Then the Cross! for via Calvary
Every royal soul must go;
Here we draw the veil, for Jesus
Only can the pathway show;
"If we suffer with Him," listen,
Just a little, little while,
And the memory will have faded
In the glory of His smile!

6   Then the grave, with dear ones weeping,
Knowing that all life has fled;
(Fellow-pilgrims, art thou numbered
With the men the world calls dead?)
Thence we rise, and live with Jesus,
Throned above the world's mad strife,
Gladly forfeiting forever,
All that worldlings count as life.

7   On we press! and yonder gleaming,
Nearing every day, we see
The great walls of that fair city,
God has built for such as we;
And we catch the tender music
Of the choirs that sing of One
Who once died to have us with Him
In His kingdom, on the throne.

8   Just a few more miles, beloved!
And our feet shall ache no more;
No more sin, and no more sorrow,
Hush thee, Jesus went before;
And I hear Him sweetly whispering,
"Faint not, fear not, still press on,
For it may be ere tomorrow,
The long journey will be done."

THE WAY OF THE CROSS —
THE WAY OF FOLLOWING THE LORD

4.10.8.8.6.

1 Hast thou no scar?
No hidden scar on foot, or side, or hand?
I hear thee sung throughout the land,
I hear them hail thy shining star,
Hast thou no scar? no scar?

2 Hast thou no wound?
Yet I was wounded by the archers, spent,
Leaned Me against a tree; and rent
By ravening beasts 'round Me, I swooned:
Hast thou no wound? no wound?

3 No wound? no scar?
Yet, as the Master shall the servant be,
And pierced the feet that follow Me;
But whole? can he have followed far
Who has no wound nor scar?

Used by permission of the Dohnavur Fellowship.

THE WAY OF THE CROSS — THE WAY OF LIFE

Peculiar Meter.

1 The way of the Cross means sacrifice,
As to God you yield your all
To be laid on the altar, the place of death,
Where fire will surely fall.

'Tis the way of the Cross, are you willing for this?
What does bearing the Cross mean to you?
You who've given yourself, your all to God!
To God are you wholly true?

THE WAY OF THE CROSS — THE WAY OF LIFE

2 As the voice of song and prayer we raise,
 How easy to say, We give all;
Till some rougher cross lies just before,
 And sterner is duty's call.

3 Do you falter then, or, true to death,
 Just die on the cross in the way,
Till the fulness of life from the Living One
 Is filling you day by day?

4 'Tis the plan of life, for you die to live,
 One with Jesus crucified;
With the life alone to be lived through you,
 Of the Risen, the Glorified.

8.7.8.7. with chorus.

631*

1 If I'd know Christ's risen power,
 I must ever love the Cross;
Life from death alone arises;
 There's no gain except by loss.

  If no death, no life,
  If no death, no life;
 Life from death alone arises;
  If no death, no life.

2 If I'd have Christ formed within me,
 I must breathe my final breath,
Live within the Cross's shadow,
 Put my soul-life e'er to death.

3 If God thru th' Eternal Spirit
 Nail me ever with the Lord;
Only then as death is working
 Will His life thru me be poured.

THE WAY OF THE CROSS —
THE WAY OF DELIVERANCE

7.7.7.7.

1 Never further than Thy Cross,
Never higher than Thy feet,
Here earth's precious things seem dross,
Here earth's bitter things grow sweet.

2 Gazing thus our sin we see,
Learn Thy love while gazing thus;
Sin which laid the Cross on Thee;
Love which bore the Cross for us.

3 Here we learn to serve and give,
And rejoicing, self deny;
Here we gather love to live;
Here we gather faith to die.

4 Symbols of our liberty
And our service here unite;
Captives, by Thy Cross set free;
Soldiers of Thy Cross, we fight.

5 Pressing onwards as we can,
Still to this our hearts must tend;
Where our earliest hopes began,
There our last aspirings end.

6 Till amid the hosts of light
We in Thee redeemed, complete,
Through Thy Cross made pure and white,
Cast our crowns before Thy feet.

633

1 And wouldst thou live on earth as "more than
    conqu'ror"?
  Victorious o'er the worldly life around?
  Mark well the pathway that thy Lord hath trodden,
  Since here alone the secret can be found.

2 He died, and by His death He dealt the death-blow
  To sin and Satan's power for evermore,
  And they, who die with Him, shall rise victorious,
  And "in this sign" shall triumph more and more.

3 The Cross henceforth their mark of perfect freedom,
  What can they lose, who have surrendered all?
  What can they fear, who have no reputation?
  What shall they shrink from, when His voice doth call?

4 "In this sign," therefore, go henceforth and conquer,
  Finding the place of death the gate of life,
  "Life more abundant," life in all its fulness,
  In the deep calm of God, set free from strife.

634

1   Cross of Christ! lead onward,
        Through the holy war;
     In this sign we conquer
        Now and evermore.
     Not of man the power,
        Not to man the fame;
     We are victors only
        In our Leader's name.

        Cross of Christ! lead onward,
           Through the holy war;
        In this sign we conquer
           Now and evermore.

continued

2 Not with pomp and pageant,
    Not in earthly pride;
We must fight our battles
    Like the Crucified.
Overcome by suff'ring,
    Conquer through defeat;
Tried and tested daily
    In the furnace heat.

3 Kind, yet we are fighting,
    Bold, yet humbly meek;
Resting while we're working,
    Strong, but ever weak.
Timid, though courageous,
    Gaining as we give;
Crucified with Jesus,
    Yet, in Him, we live.

4 By a cloud encompassed,
    Witnesses to prove,
Saints, apostles, prophets,
    Precious ones we love;
While "advance!" is sounding,
    Mounts the battle thrill.
Cross of Christ! lead onward
    Where the Captain will.

5 Marching in the pathway
    That the Master trod,
Walks One daily with us
    Like the Son of God.
To the end enduring,
    Armor ne'er laid down,
Till the Cross leads upward
    To the blood-bought crown.

635†

8.7.8.7.D.

1 Let us contemplate the grape vine,
　　From its life now let us learn,
　How its growth is fraught with suff'ring,
　　Midst environment so stern;
　How unlike the untamed flowers
　　Growing in the wilderness
　In a maze of wild confusion,
　　Making patterns numberless.

2 But the blossoms of the grape vine
　　Without glory are and small;
　Though they do have some expression,
　　They are hardly seen withal.
　But a day since they have flowered
　　Into fruit the blooms have grown;
　Never may they wave corollas
　　With luxuriant beauty shown.

3 To a post the vine is fastened;
　　Thus it cannot freely grow;
　When its branches are extended,
　　To the trellis tied they go.
　To the stony soil committed,
　　Drawing thence its food supply;
　It can never choose its own way,
　　Or from difficulty fly.

4 Oh, how beautiful its verdure,
　　Which in spring spreads o'er the field.
　From life's energy and fulness
　　Growth abundant doth it yield.
　Till it's full of tender branches
　　Twining freely everywhere,
　Stretching 'gainst the sky's deep azure
　　Tasting sweetly of the air.

continued

5   But the master of the vineyard
     Not in lenience doth abide,
But with knife and pruning scissors
     Then would strip it of its pride.
Caring not the vine is tender,
     But with deep, precision stroke
All the pretty, excess branches
     From the vine are neatly broke.

6   In this time of loss and ruin,
     Dare the vine self-pity show?
Nay, it gives itself more fully
     To the one who wounds it so,
To the hand that strips its branches,
     Till of beauty destitute,
That its life may not be wasted,
     But preserved for bearing fruit.

7   Into hard wood slowly hardens
     Every stump of bleeding shoot,
Each remaining branch becoming
     Clusters of abundant fruit.
Then, beneath the scorching sunshine,
     Leaves are dried and from it drop;
Thus the fruit more richly ripens
     Till the harvest of the crop.

8   Bowed beneath its fruitful burden,
     Loaded branches are brought low —
Labor of its growth thru suff'ring
     Many a purposed, cutting blow.
Now its fruit is fully ripened,
     Comforted the vine would be;
But the harvest soon is coming,
     And its days of comfort flee.

9 Hands will pick and feet will trample
    All the riches of the vine,
Till from out the reddened wine-press
    Flows a river full of wine.
All the day its flow continues,
    Bloody-red, without alloy,
Gushing freely, richly, sweetly,
    Filling all the earth with joy.

10 In appearance now the grape vine
    Barren is and pitiful;
Having given all, it enters
    Into night inscrutable.
No one offers to repay it
    For the cheering wine that's drunk,
But 'tis stripped and cut e'en further
    To a bare and branchless trunk.

11 Yet its wine throughout the winter
    Warmth and sweetness ever bears
Unto those in coldness shiv'ring,
    Pressed with sorrow, pain, and cares.
Yet without, alone, the grape vine
    Midst the ice and snow doth stand,
Steadfastly its lot enduring,
    Though 'tis hard to understand.

12 Winter o'er, the vine prepareth
    Fruit again itself to bear;
Budding forth and growing branches,
    Beauteous green again to wear;
Never murmuring or complaining
    For the winter's sore abuse,
Or for all its loss desiring
    Its fresh off'ring to reduce.

continued

13 Breathing air, untainted, heavenly,
   As it lifts its arms on high,
Earth's impure, defiled affections
   Ne'er the vine may occupy.
Facing sacrifice, yet smiling,
   And while love doth prune once more,
Strokes it bears as if it never
   Suffered loss and pain before.

14 From the branches of the grape vine
   Sap and blood and wine doth flow.
Does the vine, for all it suffered,
   Lost, and yielded, poorer grow?
Drunkards of the earth and wanderers,
   From it drink and merry make.
From their pleasure and enjoyment
   Do they richer thereby wake?

15 Not by gain our life is measured,
   But by what we've lost 'tis scored;
'Tis not how much wine is drunken,
   But how much has been outpoured.
For the strength of love e'er standeth
   In the sacrifice we bear;
He who has the greatest suff'ring
   Ever has the most to share.

16 He who treats himself severely
   Is the best for God to gain;
He who hurts himself most dearly
   Most can comfort those in pain.
He who suffering never beareth
   Is but empty "sounding brass";
He who self-life never spareth
   Has the joys which all surpass.

8.5.8.5.

1 "If it die," oh, hear the message
   Falling from thy Lord,
"If it die," much fruit it beareth,
   'Tis thy Savior's word.

2 Would'st thou see life work in others,
   Thou thyself must die.
Fall into the ground, be buried,
   Low in darkness lie.

3 But He leaves thee not in darkness,
   Light shall greet thine eyes,
And in glad new life and glory
   He shall bid thee rise.

4 Dost thou crave to tread the pathway
   And His life to share?
As thou passest thru death's gateway
   He will meet thee there.

5 Thou shalt learn the blessed secret,
   He shall live that dies;
From a life poured out in secret
   Shall a harvest rise.

THE WAY OF THE CROSS — THE WAY OF REST

7.7.7.7.7.7.

1 "Wrecked outright on Jesus' breast":
Only "wrecked" souls thus can sing;
Little boats that hug the shore,
Fearing what the storm may bring,
Never find on Jesus' breast,
All that "wrecked" souls mean by rest.

continued

2 "Wrecked outright!" So we lament;
But when storms have done their worst,
Then the soul, surviving all,
In Eternal arms is nursed;
There to find that nought can move
One, embosomed in such love.

3 "Wrecked outright!" No more to own
E'en a craft to sail the sea;
Still a voyager, yet now
Anchored to Infinity;
Nothing left to do but fling
Care aside, and simply cling.

4 "Wrecked outright!" 'Twas purest gain,
Henceforth other craft can see
That the storm may be a boon,
That, however rough the sea,
God Himself doth watchful stand,
For the "wreck" is in His hand.

THE WAY OF THE CROSS — TURNING TO THE CROSS

638   8.8.8.8.

1 To Calv'ry let our eyes be turned,
With Calv'ry love our hearts be burned;
For there in Calv'ry's awful hour,
Love conquered sin and Satan's pow'r.

2 Lord, turn our gaze upon Thy Cross,
Counting all else not gain but loss;
For this we pray, this is our plea —
Lord, keep our eyes on Calvary.

From WINGS, Part I, S.P.C.K., London, 1960.
Used by permission of The Dohnavur Fellowship.

THE RESURRECTION LIFE — CHRIST HIMSELF

10.10.10.10.

639*

1 Death cannot hold the resurrection life,
   The life of God eternal manifest;
   'Tis uncreated, indestructible,
   'Tis Christ Himself, unconqu'rable, expressed.

2 Death cannot hold the resurrection life,
   Though all its force against it may combine;
   Death only gives it opportunity
   To show the boundless pow'r of life divine.

3 Death cannot hold the resurrection life,
   The more interred, the more it multiplies;
   All kinds of suff'ring only help it grow
   And fruits of life abundant realize.

4 Death cannot hold the resurrection life,
   Thru every block and barrier it breaks;
   Conqu'ring the pow'r of darkness and of hell,
   It swallows death and victory partakes.

5 Death cannot hold the resurrection life,
   All of God's fulness it will manifest;
   God's righteousness and holiness it yields,
   His glorious image by it is expressed.

6 Oh, may I know this resurrection life,
   In every kind of death its pow'r outpoured,
   In my experience ever realize
   This life is nought but Christ my living Lord.

THE RESURRECTION LIFE — LIFE OUT OF DEATH

11.10.11.10.

640

1 Life out of death — dear Master, is it spoken
   Of the life here, or in the better land?
   Nay, wherefore wait? The vessel marred and broken,
   Shall now be moulded by the Potter's hand.

continued

2 Life out of death — oh, wondrous resurrection!
   Seed sown in conscious weakness, raised in power;
   Thy life lived out in days of toil and friction,
   "Not I, but Christ" in me from hour to hour.

3 Life out of death — a pilgrim path and lonely,
   Trodden by those who glory in the Cross.
   They live in fellowship with "Jesus only,"
   And for His sake count earthly gain but loss.

4 Life out of death — blest mission to be ever
   Bearing the living water brimming o'er.
   With life abundant from the clear, pure river,
   Telling that thirsty souls need thirst no more.

ENCOURAGEMENT — FOR EXPERIENCING CHRIST AS LIFE

641   8.7.8.7.D.

1 Art thou hung'ring for the fulness
      Of the blessing Christ doth give?
   Longing now to learn the secret
      Of the life He bids thee live?
   In His word thine answer standeth,
      "Christ who is our Life" it saith;
   Open now thy heart, and trust Him,
      There to dwell, henceforth, by faith.

2 Christ, the Lord's Anointed, reigning
      O'er the life He died to win,
   Daily shall reveal more fully
      His great power, without, within.
   What thou never could'st accomplish
      Shall His Spirit work through thee,
   While thy soul this witness beareth,
      'Tis not I, but Christ in me.

3   In Him dwelleth all God's fulness,
      In Him thou art made complete;
   Rise, and claim thy heavenly birthright,
      Kneeling at thy Father's feet.
   He will never disappoint thee,
      Praise Him that the gift is thine;
   Then go forth to live each moment
      On sufficiency divine.

4   Lord, I come, and simply resting
      On Thy faithful, changeless word,
   I believe the blood doth cleanse me,
      And that Christ is crownèd Lord.
   Grant henceforth a ceaseless outflow
      Of Thy life and love through me;
   Reaching those who sit in darkness,
      Winning priceless souls to Thee.

ENCOURAGEMENT — FOR FELLOWSHIP WITH THE LORD

11.10.11.10.   **642**

1   "Within the Veil": be this, belov'd, thy portion,
     Within the secret of thy Lord to dwell;
  Beholding Him, until thy face His glory,
     Thy life His love, thy lips His praise shall tell.

2   "Within the Veil," for only as thou gazest
     Upon the matchless beauty of His face,
  Canst thou become a living revelation
     Of His great heart of love, His untold grace.

3   "Within the Veil," His fragrance poured upon thee,
     Without the Veil, that fragrance shed abroad;
  "Within the Veil," His hand shall tune the music
     Which sounds on earth the praises of Thy Lord.

continued

4 "Within the Veil," thy spirit deeply anchored,
   Thou walkest calm above a world of strife;
"Within the Veil," thy soul with Him united,
   Shall live on earth His resurrection life.

643   6.5.6.5.D.

1 Take time to behold Him,
      Speak oft with Thy Lord,
   Abide in Him always,
      And feed on His Word.
   Wait thou in His presence,
      Submissive and meek,
   Forgetting in nothing
      His blessing to seek.

2 Take time to behold Him,
      The world rushes on;
   Spend much time in secret
      With Jesus alone.
   By looking to Jesus
      Like Him thou shalt be;
   Thy friends, in thy conduct,
      His likeness shall see.

3 Take time to behold Him,
      Let Him be thy guide;
   And run not before Him
      Whatever betide;
   In joy or in sorrow
      Still follow thy Lord,
   And, looking to Jesus,
      Still trust in His Word.

4 Take time to behold Him,
      Be calm in thy soul,
   Each thought and each temper
      Beneath His control.

Thus led by His Spirit
To fountains of love,
Thou then shalt be fitted
His mercy to prove.

6.5.6.5.D. with chorus.   **644**

1   Looking unto Jesus,
        Never need we yield!
    Over all the armor,
        Faith the battle-shield!
    Standard of salvation,
        In our hearts unfurled,
    Let its elevation
        Overcome the world.

        Looking unto Jesus,
        Never need we yield!
        Over all the armor,
        Faith the battle-shield!

2   Look away to Jesus,
        Look away from all!
    Then we need not stumble,
        Then we shall not fall.
    From each snare that lureth,
        Foe or phantom grim,
    Safety this ensureth,
        Look away to Him.

3   Looking into Jesus,
        Wond'ringly we trace
    Heights of power and glory,
        Depths of love and grace.
    Vistas far unfolding
        Ever stretch before,
    As we gaze, beholding,
        Ever more and more.

continued

4 Looking up to Jesus
  On the emerald throne,
Faith shall pierce the heavens,
  Where our King is gone.
Lord, on Thee depending,
  Now, continually,
Heart and mind ascending,
  Let us dwell with Thee.

645 9.8.9.8. with chorus.

1 O soul, are you weary and troubled?
No light in the darkness you see?
There's light for a look at the Savior,
And life more abundant and free.

  Turn your eyes upon Jesus,
  Look full in His wonderful face,
  And the things of earth will grow strangely dim,
  In the light of His glory and grace.

2 Through death into life everlasting
He passed, and we follow Him there;
O'er us sin no more hath dominion
For more than conqu'rors we are!

3 His Word shall not fail you, He promised;
Believe Him and all will be well;
Then go to a world that is dying,
His perfect salvation to tell!

7.6.7.6.D.

1 Oh, trust thyself to Jesus
　　When conscious of thy sin,
Its heavy weight upon thee,
　　Its mighty pow'r within:
Then is the hour for pleading
　　His finished work for thee:
Then is the time for singing,
　　His blood was shed for me.

2 Oh, trust thyself to Jesus
　　When tempted to transgress,
By word or look of anger,
　　Or thought of bitterness:
Then is the hour for claiming
　　Thy Lord to fight for thee:
Then is the time for singing,
　　He doth deliver me.

3 Oh, trust thyself to Jesus
　　When daily cares perplex,
And trifles seem so mighty
　　Thy inner soul to vex:
Then is the hour for grasping
　　His hand who walked the sea:
Then is the time for singing,
　　He makes it calm for me.

4 Oh, trust thyself to Jesus
　　When thou art wearied sore,
When head or hand refuses
　　To think or labor more:
Then is the hour for leaning
　　Upon the Master's breast:
Then is the time for singing,
　　My Savior gives me rest.

647

8.7.8.7.

1   Trust Him when thy wants are many;
    Trust Him when thy friends are few;
And the time of swift temptation
    Is the time to trust Him too.

2   Trust Him when thy soul is burdened
    With the sense of all its sin;
He will speak the word of pardon,
    He will make thee clean within.

3   Trust Him for the grace sufficient,
    Ever equal to thy need;
Trust Him always for the answer,
    When in His dear name you plead.

4   Trust Him for the grace to conquer,
    He is able to subdue;
Trust Him for the power for service;
    Trust Him for the blessing too.

5   Trust Him when dark doubts assail thee,
    Trust Him when thy strength is small,
Trust Him when to simply trust Him
    Seems the hardest thing of all.

6   Trust Him; He is ever faithful;
    Trust Him, for His will is best;
Trust Him, for the heart of Jesus
    Is the only place of rest.

7   Trust Him, then, through cloud or sunshine,
    All thy cares upon Him cast,
Till the storm of life is over,
    And the trusting days are past.

Peculiar Meter.

648

1 Soldier, soldier, fighting in the world's great strife,
On thyself relying, battling for thy life;
    Trust thyself no longer,
    Trust to Christ — He's stronger;
I can all things, all things do
Through Christ, which strengtheneth me.

2 In your daily duty, standing up for right,
Are you sometimes weary — heart not always light?
    Doubt your Savior never,
    This your motto ever:
I can all things, all things do
Through Christ, which strengtheneth me.

3 If your way be weary He will help you through —
Help you in your troubles and your pleasures too;
    Say, when Satan's by you;
    Say, when all things try you:
I can all things, all things do
Through Christ, which strengtheneth me.

4 In a world of trouble, tempted oft to stray,
You need never stumble, Satan cannot stay,
    Will but tempt you vainly,
    If you tell him plainly:
I can all things, all things do
Through Christ, which strengtheneth me.

5 Jesus' power is boundless, boundless as the sea;
He is always able, able to keep me,
    Power bring from my weakness,
    Glory from my meekness:
I can all things, all things do
Through Christ, which strengtheneth me.

Used by permission of the South Africa General Mission.

649

ONLY BELIEVE

Paul Rader   11.11.11.11. with chorus.

1   Fear not, little flock, from the cross to the throne,
From death into life He went for His own;
All power in earth, all power above,
Is given to Him for the flock of His love.

    Only believe, only believe;
All things are possible, only believe;
Only believe, only believe;
All things are possible, only believe.

2   Fear not, little flock, He goeth ahead,
Your Shepherd selecteth the path you must tread;
The waters of Marah He'll sweeten for thee,
He drank all the bitter in Gethsemane.

3   Fear not, little flock, whatever your lot,
He enters all rooms, "the doors being shut";
He never forsakes, He never is gone,
So count on His presence in darkness and dawn.

650

7.6.7.6. with chorus.

1   O doubting, struggling Christian,
Why thus in anguish pray?
O cease to doubt and struggle,
There is a better way.

    O settle it all with Jesus,
O settle it all today;
O cease to doubt and struggle,
O cease to plead and pray;
O rest in His word forever,
And settle it all today.

2　Give up thy will to Jesus,
　　And trust Him though He slay;
　　Hush all thy fears and questions,
　　And settle it today.

3　O soul so tossed with tempest,
　　Upon His promise stay;
　　Cast out faith's strong sheet anchor,
　　And settle it today.

4　Lord, I give up the struggle,
　　To Thee commit my way;
　　I trust Thy word forever,
　　And settle it today.

Used by permission of Christian Publications, Inc., Harrisburg, Pa.

6.6.6.6.D.　　　　　　**651**

1　When is the time to trust?
　　Is it when all is calm,
　　When waves the victor's palm,
　　And life is one glad psalm?
　　Nay! but the time to trust
　　Is when the waves beat high,
　　When storm clouds fill the sky,
　　And pray'r is one long cry.

2　When is the time to trust?
　　Is it when friends are true?
　　Is it when comforts woo
　　In all we say and do?
　　Nay! but the time to trust
　　Is when we stand alone,
　　And summer birds have flown,
　　And every prop is gone.

3　When is the time to trust?
　　Is it some future day,
　　When you have tried your way,
　　And learned to trust and pray?

continued

Nay! but the time to trust
Is in this moment's need,
Poor, broken, bruisèd reed.
Poor, troubled soul, make speed!

4 When is the time to trust?
Is it when hopes beat high,
When sunshine gilds the sky
With joy and ecstasy?
Nay! but the time to trust
Is when our joy has fled,
When sorrow bows the head,
And all is cold and dead.

ENCOURAGEMENT—FOR RESTING ON THE LORD

652   8.8.8.8. with chorus.

1 O troubled soul, beneath the rod
Thy Father speaks — be still, be still;
Learn to be silent unto God,
And let Him mold thee to His will.

Be still, O troubled soul, be still;
Fear not, thy Father's arms enfold thee.
Take up thy cross, lay down thy will;
Be silent unto God, and let Him mold thee.

2 O anxious soul, lay down thy load,
Oh, hear His voice, He speaks to thee,
"Be still and know that I am God,
And cast thy every care on Me."

3 O fearful soul, be still, be still,
Be of good cheer; has He not said,
"I will be with you, fear no ill,
'Tis I, 'tis I, be not afraid"?

4 O praying soul, be still, be still,
    He cannot break His plighted word;
    Sink down into His blessed will,
    And wait in patience on the Lord.

5 O waiting soul, be still, be strong,
    And though He tarry, trust and wait;
    Doubt not, He will not wait too long,
    Fear not, He will not come too late.

653

6.6.6.6.

1 Rest, rest thee, weary heart,
    Let toil and anguish cease;
    Take from Thy Savior's hands
    Thine heritage of peace.

2 Lie low before His feet,
    Too low thou canst not be,
    For sacred calm is here,
    And here is liberty.

3 Submit, lay down thine arms,
    Nor question, nor rebel;
    So shalt thou hear erewhile
    His whisper, It is well.

4 No secret wound of thine,
    Though it be great or small,
    Presume to hide from Him;
    Confess, confess it all;

5 Nor merit of thine own
    Upon His altar place;
    All is of Christ alone,
    And of His perfect grace.

continued

6 Rest, rest thee, weary heart,
   Let care and anguish cease;
   Take from thy Savior's hands
   Thine heritage of peace.

654

11.10.11.10.

1 "Be all at rest, my soul!" Oh! blessed secret
   Of the true life that glorifies thy Lord;
Not always doth the busiest soul best serve Him,
   But he who resteth on His faithful word.

2 "Be all at rest!" for rest is highest service;
   To the still heart God doth His secrets tell;
Thus shalt thou learn to wait, and watch, and labor
   Strengthened to bear, since Christ in thee
     doth dwell.

3 "Be all at rest!" for rest alone becometh
   The soul that casts on Him its every care;
"Be all at rest!" so shall thy life proclaim Him
   A God who worketh and who heareth prayer.

4 "Be all at rest!" so shalt thou be an answer
   To those who question, "Who is God, and where?"
For God is rest, and where He dwells is stillness,
   And they who dwell in Him that rest shall share.

8.6.8.6.6.6.8.6.

1 Feed on His faithfulness, my soul,
  Who chose thee for His own,
  Who bears thy name in Love's pure flame
  Before the heav'nly throne;
  Lay at His feet thy fear,
  Thy burdens, thy distress,
  Prostrate embrace thy Fount of Grace —
  Feed on His faithfulness.

2 Feed on His faithfulness, my soul,
  Who suffered Calvary,
  Who Victor rose o'er all thy foes,
  Who lives, who prays, for thee!
  Not thine the battle is,
  Though close the conflict press;
  'Tis His alone who wears the crown —
  Feed on His faithfulness.

3 Feed on His faithfulness, my soul,
  Then naught shall thee affright;
  His perfect will all fear shall still,
  His wisdom guide aright.
  He slumbers not nor sleeps,
  But waits His saints to bless;
  Th' eternal Throne is His alone —
  Feed on His faithfulness.

4 Feed on His faithfulness, my soul;
  So shalt thou see His face,
  Transforming thee till all shall see
  The glory of His grace;
  Closer to His great heart
  In glad abandon press;
  Fling thy soul down upon His own —
  Feed on His faithfulness.

From CLEAR SHINING AFTER RAIN, by E. Margaret Clarkson
Published by Eerdmans Publishing Co. Used by permission.

656

10.10.10.10.

1   "Consider Him," let Christ thy pattern be,
    And know that He hath apprehended thee
    To share His very life, His pow'r divine,
    And in the likeness of thy Lord to shine.

2   "Consider Him"; so shalt thou, day by day,
    Seek out the lowliest place, and therein stay,
    Content to pass away, a thing of nought,
    That glory to the Father's name be brought.

3   Shrink not, O child of God, but fearless go
    Down into death with Jesus; thou shalt know
    The power of an endless life begin,
    With glorious liberty from self and sin.

4   "Consider Him," and thus thy life shall be
    Filled with self-sacrifice and purity;
    God will work out in thee the pattern true,
    And Christ's example ever keep in view.

5   "Consider Him," and as you run the race,
    Keep ever upward looking in His face;
    And thus transformed, illumined thou shalt be,
    And Christ's own image shall be seen in thee.

Used by permission of the South Africa General Mission.

6.5.6.5.D.

1 Can you be obedient
   To the Lord of all,
Though the earth should totter,
   Though the heav'ns should fall?
Face e'en a disaster
   With a faith-filled heart,
Knowing naught can harm him
   Who with Christ will start?

2 Can you be obedient
   To the Lord you serve,
Never even flinch, friend,
   Never even swerve;
Though your next step onward
   Seem to lead to death?
Can you then obey Him
   Without bated breath?

3 Can you trust your Leader
   When He bids you go
Right into a battle
   With a mighty foe?
Can you step up briskly
   And with joy obey?
Can you fight the battle,
   Till the end of day?

4 Can you? Then beloved,
   Christ just waits for you;
Listen for His orders,
   Glad His will to do;
Then when soldiers muster
   At the set of sun,
And your name is mentioned,
   Christ will say, "Well done."

658

8.6.8.6.

1 Walk in the light, and thou shalt know
That fellowship of love
His Spirit only can bestow,
Who reigns in light above.

2 Walk in the light, and thou shalt find
Thy heart made truly His;
Who dwells in cloudless light enshrined,
In whom no darkness is.

3 Walk in the light, and sin abhorred
Shall ne'er defile again;
The blood of Jesus Christ the Lord
Shall cleanse from every stain.

4 Walk in the light, and e'en the tomb
No fearful shade shall wear;
The glory shall dispel the gloom,
For Christ hath conquered there.

5 Walk in the light, and thou shalt own
Thy darkness passed away,
Because that light hath on thee shone
In which is perfect day.

6 Walk in the light, thy path shall be
Serene and clear and bright;
For God, by grace, shall dwell in thee,
And *God* Himself is Light.

11.8.11.8. with chorus.

1 Rejoice in the Lord! Oh, let His mercy cheer:
    He sunders the bands that enthrall;
    Redeemed by His blood, why should we ever fear.
    Since Jesus is our all in all?

    If God be for us, if God be for us,
        if God be for us,
      Who can be against us?
   Who? who? who?
      Who can be against us, against us?

2 Be strong in the Lord! rejoicing in His might.
    Be loyal and true day by day;
    When evils assail, be valiant for the right.
    And He will be our strength and stay.

3 Confide in His Word, His promises so sure;
    In Christ they are yea and amen;
    Though earth pass away, they ever shall endure,
    'Tis written o'er and o'er again.

4 Abide in the Lord, secure in His control,
    'Tis life everlasting begun;
    To pluck from His hand the weakest, trembling soul,
    It never, never can be done!

660   11.11.11.11.

1 In nothing be anxious; the Lord is at hand.
In peace and in vict'ry triumphantly stand;
Let nothing affright thee and nothing dismay,
For Jesus is coming! It may be today.

2 In nothing be anxious; on Him roll thy care.
Thy sins were laid on Him, thy sorrows He'll bear;
Care free and triumphant press on, still to prove
The strength of His arm and the balm of His love.

3 In nothing be anxious; should Jesus delay
His strength will be thine till the end of the day.
His arm thou canst lean on; His Spirit will cheer;
Then wherefore be anxious, press on without fear.

661   8.6.8.6.8.6.

1 Master, how shall I bless Thy name
  For love so great to me,
For sweet enablings of Thy grace,
  So sov'reign, yet so free,
That taught me to obey Thy word,
  And cast my care on Thee?

2 No anxious thought upon thy brow
  The watching world should see;
No carefulness! O child of God,
  For nothing careful be!
But cast thou all thy care on Him
  Who always cares for thee.

3 How shall I praise Thee, Savior dear,
  For this new life so sweet,
For taking all the care I laid
  At Thy beloved feet,
Keeping Thy hand upon my heart
  To still each anxious beat?

4 I long to praise Thee more, and yet
　　This is no care to me;
If Thou shalt fill my mouth with songs
　　Then I shall sing to Thee;
And if my silence praise Thee best,
　　Then silent I will be.

5 Yet if it be Thy will, dear Lord,
　　Oh, send me forth to be
Thy messenger to careful hearts,
　　To bid them taste, and see
How good Thou art to those who cast
　　All, all their care on Thee.

ENCOURAGEMENT — FOR PRESSINC ON

6.6.8.6.

662

1 "On toward the goal!" Press on!
　　Alone, yet unafraid;
He cut the path, who beckons thee,
　　On then, and undismayed.

2 "On toward the goal!" Press on!
　　The eyes that are a flame
Are watching thee, what then are men?
　　What matter praise, or blame?

3 "On toward the goal!" Press on!
　　Look not behind thee now,
When just ahead lies His "Well done,"
　　And crowns await thy brow.

4 "On toward the goal!" Press on!
　　Blind, deaf and sometimes dumb
Along the blood-marked, uphill way,
　　Hard after Christ, press on!

663

6.5.6.5.D. with chorus.

1 "Forward!" be our watchword,
   Steps and voices joined;
Seek the things before us,
   Not a look behind;
Burns the fiery pillar
   At our army's head;
Who shall dream of shrinking,
   By our Captain led?
Forward through the desert,
   Through the toil and fight;
Heaven's Kingdom waits us,
   Forward into light.

2 Glories upon glories
   Hath our God prepared,
By the souls that love Him,
   One day to be shared:
Eye hath not beheld them,
   Ear hath never heard;
Nor of these hath uttered
   Thought or speech or word;
Forward, marching forward
   Where the kindgom's bright,
Till the veil be lifted,
   Till our faith be sight!

664

8.7.8.7.

1 Rise, my soul, thy God directs thee;
   Stranger hands no more impede;
Pass thou on, His strength protects thee,
   Strength that has the captive freed.

2 *Is the wilderness* before thee,
   Desert lands where drought abides?
Heavenly springs shall there restore thee,
   Fresh from God's exhaustless tides.

3   Light divine surrounds thy going,
     God Himself shall mark thy way;
  Secret blessings, richly flowing,
     Lead to everlasting day.

4   God, thine everlasting portion,
     Feeds thee with the Mighty's meat;
  Saved from Egypt's hard extortion,
     Egypt's food no more to eat.

5   Art thou weaned from Egypt's pleasures?
     God in secret shall thee keep;
  There unfold His hidden treasures,
     There His love's exhaustless deep.

6   In the desert God will teach thee
     What the God that thou hast found —
  Patient, gracious, powerful, holy;
     All His grace shall there abound.

7   On to Canaan's rest still wending,
     E'en thy wants and woes shall bring
  Suited grace from high descending;
     Thou shalt taste of mercy's spring.

8   Though thy way be long and dreary,
     Eagle strength He'll still renew;
  Garments fresh, and feet unweary,
     Tell how God hath brought thee through.

9   When to Canaan's long-loved dwelling
     Love divine thy feet shall bring,
  Thou, with shouts of triumph swelling,
     Zion's songs in rest shall sing.

665

8.6.8.6.

1 Come, let us to the Lord our God
  With contrite heart return;
  Our God is gracious, nor will leave
  The desolate to mourn.

2 His voice commands the tempest forth,
  And stills the stormy wave;
  And though His arm be strong to smite,
  'Tis also strong to save.

3 Long hath the night of sorrow reigned;
  The dawn shall bring us light;
  God shall appear, and we shall rise
  With gladness in His sight.

4 Our heart, if God we seek to know,
  Shall know Him, and rejoice;
  His coming like the morn shall be,
  Like morning songs His voice.

5 As dew upon the tender herb,
  Diffusing fragrance round,
  As showers that usher in the spring,
  And cheer the thirsty ground;

6 So shall His presence bless our souls,
  And shed a joyful light;
  That hallowed morn shall chase away
  The sorrows of the night.

7.6.7.5.D.

1 Watch, for the night is ending!
  Watch, and the world not seek;
Watch, for the day is dawning!
  Watch, sink not in sleep.
Watch, for the Lord is coming!
  Watch for the foe's attack:
Watch, for the Lord is waiting!
  Watch, be never slack.

2 Watch, and arise in service!
  Watch, though the day be drear;
Watch, and go forth to labor!
  Watch, the end is near.
Watch and put on thy armor!
  Watch with thy spirit strong;
Watch to resist the devil!
  Watch, Christ comes ere long.

3 Watch for the Savior's coming!
  Watch for the Morning Star;
Watch and pursue the Kingdom!
  Watch with many a scar.
Watch, and be ever watchful!
  Watch, till the night is done;
Watch till the dawn of glory!
  Watch till the Lord shall come.

667

8.8.8.3. with repeat.

1 Seek ye first, not earthly pleasure,
Fading joy and failing treasure,
But the love that knows no measure
   Seek ye first.

2 Seek ye first, not earth's aspirings,
Ceaseless longings, vain desirings,
But your precious soul's requirings
   Seek ye first.

3 Seek ye first God's peace and blessing;
Ye have all if this possessing;
Come, your need and sin confessing,
   Seek Him first.

4 Seek Him first, then when forgiven,
Pardoned, with the peace of heaven,
Let your life to Him be given:
   Seek this first.

5 Seek this first — Be pure and holy;
Like the Master, meek and lowly;
Yielded to His service wholly:
   Seek this first.

6 Seek the coming of His kingdom;
Seek the souls around to win them,
Seek to Jesus Christ to bring them:
   Seek this first.

7 Seek this first, His promise trying;
It is sure, all need supplying.
Heavenly things, on Him relying,
   Seek ye first.

7.6.7.6.D. with chorus.

1 Have you felt the Father's love?
    Still there's more to follow;
And His mercy have you proved?
    Still there's more to follow.
Oh, the love the Father shows,
    Still there's more to follow;
Freely He His love bestows,
    Still there's more to follow.

    More and more, more and more,
        Always more to follow;
    Oh, His matchless, boundless love,
        Still there's more to follow.

2 Have you felt the Savior near?
    Still there's more to follow;
Does His blessed presence cheer?
    Still there's more to follow.
Oh, the grace that Jesus shows,
    Still there's more to follow;
Freely He His grace bestows,
    Still there's more to follow.

3 Have you felt the Spirit's power?
    Still there's more to follow;
Falling like the gentle shower?
    Still there's more to follow.
Oh, the power the Spirit shows,
    Still there's more to follow;
Freely He His power bestows,
    Still there's more to follow.

669

6.5.6.5.D.

1 In the heart of Jesus
   There is love for you,
Love most pure and tender,
   Love most deep and true;
Why should you be lonely,
   Why for friendship sigh,
When the heart of Jesus
   Has a full supply?

2 In the mind of Jesus
   There is thought for you,
Warm as summer sunshine,
   Sweet as morning dew;
Why should you be fearful,
   Why take anxious thought,
Since the mind of Jesus
   Cares for those He bought?

3 In the field of Jesus
   There is work for you;
Such as even angels
   Might rejoice to do;
Why stand idly sighing
   For some life-work grand,
While the field of Jesus
   Seeks your reaping hand?

4 In the Church of Jesus
   There's a place for you;
Glorious, bright, and joyous,
   Right and peaceful too;
Why then, like a wand'rer,
   Roam with weary pace,
If the Church of Jesus
   Holds for you a place?

8.7.8.7. with chorus.

670

1 Take the name of Jesus with you,
   Child of sorrow and of woe;
   It will joy and comfort give you,
   Take it then where'er you go.

   Precious name! Oh, how sweet!
   Hope of earth and joy of heav'n;
   Precious name! Oh, how sweet!
   Hope of earth and joy of heav'n.

2 Take the name of Jesus ever,
   As a shield from every snare.
   If temptations round you gather,
   Breathe that holy name in prayer.

3 Oh, the precious name of Jesus,
   How it thrills our souls with joy;
   All the favor of the Father
   In this name we may enjoy.

4 At the name of Jesus bowing,
   Falling prostrate at His feet,
   Claim His vict'ry over evil
   And the enemy defeat.

10.10.10.10.

671

1 Deep down into the depths of this Thy Name,
   My God, I sink and dwell in calm delight;
   Thou art enough however long the day,
   Thou art enough however dark the night.

2 Thou art my God — the All-Sufficient One,
   Thou canst create for me whate'er I lack;
   Thy mighty hand has strewn the lonely track
   With miracles of love and tender care

3 For me Thy trusting one. My God I dare
   Once more to fling myself upon Thy breast,
   And there adore Thy ways in faith's deep rest,
   And there adore Thy ways in faith's quiet rest.

672

10.10.10.10.

1 Not what I am, O Lord, but what Thou art;
That, that alone, can be my soul's true rest;
Thy love, not mine, bids fear and doubt depart,
And stills the tempest of my tossing breast.

2 It is Thy perfect love that casts out fear;
I know the voice that speaks the It is I,
And in these well-known words of heavenly cheer
I hear the joy that bids each sorrow fly.

3 Thy Name is Love! I hear it from yon Cross;
Thy Name is Love! I read it in yon tomb:
All meaner love is perishable dross,
But this shall light me through time's thickest gloom.

4 It blesses now, and shall for ever bless;
It saves me now, and shall for ever save;
It holds me up in days of helplessness,
It bears me safely o'er each swelling wave.

5 'Tis what I know of Thee, my Lord and God,
That fills my soul with peace, my lips with song;
Thou art my health, my joy, my staff, my rod;
Leaning on Thee, in weakness I am strong.

6 More of Thyself, Oh, show me, hour by hour;
More of Thy glory, O my God and Lord;
More of Thyself in all Thy grace and power;
More of Thy love and truth, Incarnate Word.

8.8.8.8.D.

1 I take my portion from Thy hand,
And do not seek to understand;
For I am blind, while Thou dost see,
Thy will is mine, whate'er it be.

Whate'er it be! whate'er it be!
I do not fear, whate'er it be!
Thy love divine sustaineth me;
Thy will is mine, whate'er it be.

2 When darkness doth Thy face obscure,
And many sorrows I endure,
I think of Christ's Gethsemane;
Thy will is mine, whate'er it be.

3 When tender joys to me are known,
I render thanks to Thee alone;
I know my cup is filled by Thee;
Thy will is mine, whate'er it be.

4 Thus calmly do I face my lot,
Accept it, Lord, and doubt Thee not;
Lo! all things work for good to me;
Thy will is mine, whate'er it be.

674

9.8.8.8.

1 The Lord will silently plan for thee,
Thou object of omniscient care;
God undertakes Himself to be
Thy Pilot through each subtle snare.

2 The Lord will silently plan for thee,
So certainly, He cannot fail!
Rest on the faithfulness of God,
In Him thou surely shalt prevail.

3 The Lord will silently plan for thee
Some wonderful surprise of love.
Eye hath not seen, nor ear hath heard,
But it is kept for thee to prove.

4 The Lord will silently plan for thee,
His purpose He'll to thee unfold;
The tangled skein shall shine at last,
A masterpiece of skill untold.

5 The Lord will silently plan for thee,
A happy child kept in His care
As though no other claimed His love,
But thou alone to Him wert dear.

675

8.6.8.6.

1 God moves in a mysterious way
His wonders to perform:
He plants His footsteps in the sea,
And rides upon the storm.

2 Deep in unfathomable mines
Of never-failing skill,
He treasures up His bright designs,
And works His sovereign will.

3 Ye fearful saints, fresh courage take;
　　The clouds ye so much dread
Are big with mercy, and shall break
　　In blessings on your head.

4 Judge not the Lord by feeble sense,
　　But trust Him for His grace;
Behind a frowning providence
　　He hides a smiling face.

5 His purposes will ripen fast,
　　Unfolding every hour:
The bud may have a bitter taste,
　　But sweet will be the flower.

6 Blind unbelief is sure to err,
　　And scan His work in vain;
God is His own Interpreter,
　　And He will make it plain.

8.7.8.7.D.　　　　　　**676**

1 All thy griefs by Him are ordered,
　　Needful is each one for thee;
All thy tears by Him are counted,
　　One too much there cannot be;
And if while they fall so quickly
　　Thou canst own His way is right,
Then each bitter tear of anguish
　　Precious is in Jesus' sight.

2 Far too well thy Savior loves thee
　　To allow thy life to be
One long, calm, unbroken summer —
　　One unruffled, stormless sea;
He would have thee fondly nestling
　　Closer to His loving breast,
He would have that day seem brighter
　　When alone is perfect rest.

677

8.7.8.7.D. with chorus.

1 Art thou sunk in depths of sorrow
Where no arm can reach so low?
There is One whose arms almighty
Reach beyond thy deepest woe.
God th' Eternal is thy refuge,
Let it still thy wild alarms;
Underneath thy deepest sorrow,
Are the everlasting arms.

Underneath thee, underneath thee,
Are the everlasting arms,
Everlasting, everlasting,
Are the everlasting arms.

2 Other arms grow faint and weary,
These can never faint, nor fail;
Others reach our mounts of blessing,
These our lowest loneliest vale.
O that all might know His friendship!
O that all might see His charms!
O that all might have beneath them
Jesus' everlasting arms.

3 Underneath us, O how easy;
We have not to mount on high,
But to sink into His fulness,
And in trustful weakness lie.
And we find our humbling failures
Save us from the strength that harms!
We may fail, but underneath us
Are the everlasting arms.

4 Arms of Jesus! fold me closer,
To Thy strong and loving breast,
Till my spirit on Thy bosom
Finds its everlasting rest;

And when time's last sands are sinking,
Shield my heart from all alarms,
Softly whispering, "Underneath thee,
Are the everlasting arms."

Peculiar Meter. **678**

1 I will not be afraid;
I will not be afraid;
I will look upward,
And travel onward,
And not be afraid.

2 He says He will be with me;
He says He will be with me;
He goes before me,
And is beside me,
So I'm not afraid.

3 His arms are underneath me;
His arms are underneath me;
His hand upholds me,
His love enfolds me,
So I'm not afraid.

4 His Word will stand for ever;
His Word will stand for ever;
His truth it shall be
My shield and buckler,
So I'm not afraid.

5 He will give grace and glory;
He will give grace and glory;
His cross before me,
His banner o'er me,
So I'm not afraid.

6 So we go singing onward;
So we go singing onward;
We're pressing forward,
We're marching upward,
To Him unafraid.

7.6.7.6.D. with chorus.

1 Safe in the arms of Jesus,
  Safe on His gentle breast,
There by His love o'ershaded,
  Sweetly my soul doth rest.
Hark! 'tis a song of heaven
  Borne in the sweetest voice,
Echoed by saints in spirit,
  Making my heart rejoice.

  Safe in the arms of Jesus,
    Safe on His gentle breast,
  There by His love o'ershaded,
    Sweetly my soul doth rest.

2 Safe in the arms of Jesus,
  Safe from corroding care,
Safe from the world's temptations,
  Sin cannot harm me there.
Free from the blight of sorrow,
  Free from my doubts and fears;
Only a few more trials,
  Only a few more tears.

3 Jesus, my heart's dear Refuge,
  Jesus has died for me;
Firm on the Rock of Ages
  Ever my trust shall be.
Here let me wait with patience,
  Wait till the night is o'er,
Wait till I see the morning
  Break on the golden shore.

680

1 "All in His hands" — what confidence it brings
To tested hearts, to know that all the things
That make up life and circumstance, He holds
In His strong hands, and patiently unfolds
Th' eternal purpose of His sovereign Will —
That all things shall His grace and glory fill.

2 "All in His hands"? Then life with purpose moves
Within the circle of His will, and proves
It good, acceptable. The hands of man
Or Satan cannot mar or foil the plan
Which God ordained — to manifest His Son
In earthen vessels, to a world undone.

681

1 Our times are in Thy hand;
　　O God, we wish them there;
　Our lives, our souls, our all, we leave
　　Entirely to Thy care.

2 Our times are in Thy hand:
　　Whatever they may be;
　Pleasing or painful, dark or bright,
　　As best may seem to Thee.

3 Our times are in Thy hand;
　　Why should we doubt or fear?
　A father's hand will never cause
　　His child a needless tear.

4 Our times are in Thy hand;
　　Jesus, the Crucified,
　Whose hand our many sins have pierced,
　　Is now our guard and guide.

5 Our times are in Thy hand;
　　We'll always trust to Thee,
　Till we possess the promised crown,
　　And all Thy glory see.

8.6.8.6.

1 When I survey life's varied scene,
   Amid the darkest hours
Sweet rays of comfort shine between
   And thorns are mixed with flowers.

2 Lord, teach me to adore Thy hand,
   From whence my comforts flow,
And let me in this desert land
   A glimpse of glory know.

3 Father, whate'er of earthly bliss
   Thy sovereign hand denies,
Accepted at Thy throne of grace,
   Let this petition rise:

4 Give me a calm, a thankful heart,
   From every murmur free;
The blessings of Thy grace impart,
   And let me live to Thee.

5 Let the sweet hope that Thou art mine
   My life and death attend,
Thy presence through my journey shine,
   And crown my journey's end.

8.4.8.8.4.

1 God holds the key of all unknown,
   And I am glad;
   If other hands should hold the key,
   Or if He trusted it to me,
   I might be sad.

2 What if tomorrow's cares were here,
   Without its rest?
   I'd rather He unlocked the day,
   And, as the hours swing open, say,
   My will is best.

3 The very dimness of my sight
   Makes me secure;
   For, groping in my misty way,
   I feel His hand; I hear Him say,
   My help is sure.

4 I cannot read His future plans;
   But this I know:
   I have the smiling of His face,
   And all the refuge of His grace
   While here below.

5 Enough; this covers all my wants;
   And so I rest;
   For what I cannot, He can see,
   And in His care I saved shall be,
   Forever blest.

684   11.10.11.10.

1 Come, ye disconsolate, where'er ye languish;
  Come to the mercy-seat, fervently kneel;
  Here bring your wounded hearts, here tell
       your anguish,
  Earth has no sorrow that heaven cannot heal.

2 Joy of the comfortless, light of the straying,
  Hope of the penitent, fadeless and pure;
  Here speaks the Comforter, tenderly saying —
  Earth has no sorrow that heaven cannot cure.

3 Here see the Bread of Life; see waters flowing
  Forth from the throne of God, pure from above;
  Come to the feast of love; come, ever knowing
  Earth has no sorrow but heaven can remove.

COMFORT IN TRIALS — BY THE LORD'S PRESENCE

685   5.4.5.4.D.

1 Lord, Thou art with me!
      Whom shall I fear?
  Who then can harm me
      While Thou art near?
  Under Thy shadow
      Is my retreat;
  There to my taste,
      Lord, Thy fruit is sweet.

2 Lord, Thou art with me,
      And Thou dost give
  Strength for the journey,
      Grace now to live.

Mercies each morning
    Thou dost renew;
And for my prospect,
    Thy rest in view.

3 Lord, Thou art with me;
      Onward I move;
  Each day I'm proving
      More of Thy love.
  Now Thou art training,
      Setting me free
  From all that hinders,
      To dwell with Thee.

Peculiar Meter.

1 "Fear not, I am with thee";
Blessed golden ray,
Like a star of glory,
Lighting up my way!
Through the clouds of midnight,
This bright promise shone,
"I will never leave thee,
Never will leave thee alone."

No, never alone,
No, never alone;
He promised never to leave me,
Never to leave me alone;
No, never alone,
No, never alone;
He promised never to leave me,
Never to leave me alone.

2 Roses fade around me,
Lilies bloom and die,
Earthly sunbeams vanish —
Radiant still the sky!
Jesus, Henna-flower,*
Blooming for His own,
Jesus, heaven's sunshine,
Never will leave me alone.

3 Steps unseen before me,
Hidden dangers near;
Nearer still my Savior,
Whispering, "Be of cheer";
Joys, like birds of springtime,
To my heart have flown,
Singing all so sweetly,
"He will not leave me alone."

* An Old World plant, prized for its fragrant yellow and
white flowers. (Song of Sol. 1:14, A.S.V.)

687

11.8.11.8.

1 O Thou, in whose presence my soul takes delight,
   On whom in affliction I call,
My comfort by day and my song in the night,
   My hope, my salvation, my all!

2 Where dost Thou, dear Shepherd, resort with
     Thy sheep,
   To feed them in pastures of love;
Say, why in the valley of death should I weep,
   Or alone in this wilderness rove?

3 Oh, why should I wander, an alien from Thee,
   Or cry in the desert for bread?
Thy foes will rejoice when my sorrows they see,
   And smile at the tears I have shed.

4 Ye daughters of Zion, declare, have you seen
   The Star that on Israel shone?
Say, if in your tents my Beloved has been,
   And where with His flocks He is gone.

5 Dear Shepherd! I hear, and will follow Thy call;
   I know the sweet sound of Thy voice;
Restore and defend me, for Thou art my all,
   And in Thee I'll ever rejoice.

688

Peculiar Meter.

1 I've seen the lightning flashing,
   And heard the thunder roll;
I've felt sin's breakers dashing,
   Trying to conquer my soul;
I've heard the voice of Jesus,
   Telling me still to fight on;
He promised never to leave me,
   Never to leave me alone.

Chorus: **688**

No, never alone,
No, never alone,
He promised never to leave me,
Never to leave me alone;
No, never alone,
No, never alone,
He promised never to leave me,
Never to leave me alone.

2 The world's fierce winds are blowing,
Temptations are sharp and keen;
I feel a peace in knowing
My Savior stands between;
He stands to shield me from danger,
When earthly friends are gone,
He promised never to leave me,
Never to leave me alone.

3 When in affliction's valley,
I'm treading the road of care,
My Savior helps me to carry
My cross when heavy to bear;
My feet entangled with briars,
Ready to cast me down;
My Savior whispered His promise,
Never to leave me alone.

4 He died for me on the mountain,
For me they pierced His side,
For me He opened that fountain,
The crimson, cleansing tide;
For me He waiteth in glory,
Seated upon His throne;
He promised never to leave me,
Never to leave me alone.

689

11.11.11.11. with chorus.

1 O child of the Kingdom in doubt and distress!
Why linger — thy Father is waiting to bless?
Assured of the mercy and love of thy Lord,
Claim each precious promise, take God at His Word!

> Take God at His Word,
> Take God at His Word!
> Believe every promise,
> Take God at His Word!

2 Thy pathway through sorrows and trials may go,
Though deep be the waters, they will not o'erflow;
Oh, trust in the Savior, His name be adored!
Confide in His promise, take God at His Word!

3 He says He will guide thee through sunshine
and gloom;
His presence shall brighten thy path to the throne;
And down in death's valley His voice shall be heard:
Fear not, tempted Christian, take God at His Word!

4 An heir to a kingdom, and promised a crown;
With God thy protector — oh, why be cast down?
Oh, think of the triumphs of faith thou hast heard;
Be not unbelieving, take God at His Word!

COMFORT IN TRIALS — BY THE LORD'S WORD

8.3.8.3. with chorus.

690

1 Hark! a voice from heav'n proclaiming,
    "It is done."
Faith repeats the echo claiming,
    "It is done."

    Hear the message from the throne,
    Claim the promise, doubting one;
    God hath spoken, "It is done."
    Faith has answered, "It is done."
    Prayer is over, praise begun.
    Hallelujah, "It is done."

2 Hear the bleeding Savior crying,
    "It is done."
Claim His finished work, replying,
    "It is done."

3 Yield thyself in consecration,
    "It is done."
Take the Lord for full salvation,
    "It is done."

4 Claim the promise of His healing,
    "It is done."
Trust without a sign or feeling,
    "It is done."

5 Say of every promised blessing,
    "It is done."
Rest upon His word, confessing,
    "It is done."

6 This the secret of receiving,
    "It is done."
Take Him at His word believing,
    "It is done."

691

8.7.8.7.8.7.

1 Hark! the voice of love and mercy
 Sounds aloud from Calvary;
See, it rends the rocks asunder,
 Shakes the earth, and veils the sky:
"It is finished!" "It is finished!"
 Hear the dying Savior cry.

2 "It is finished!" Oh, what pleasure
 Do these charming words afford!
Heavenly blessings without measure
 Flow to us from Christ, the Lord:
"It is finished!" "It is finished!"
 Saints, the dying words record.

3 Finished all the types and shadows
 Of the ceremonial law!
Finished all that God had promised;
 Death and hell no more shall awe:
"It is finished!" "It is finished!"
 Saints, from hence your comfort draw.

4 Tune your harps anew, ye seraphs,
 Join to sing the pleasing theme;
All on earth and all in heaven
 Join to praise Immanuel's name:
Hallelujah! Hallelujah!
 Glory to the bleeding Lamb!

COMFORT IN TRIALS — BY THE LORD'S WORD

Peculiar Meter.

1 There's a little word that the Lord has giv'n
    For our help in the hour of need:
Let us reckon ourselves to be dead to sin,
    To be dead and dead indeed.

    Let us reckon, reckon, reckon,
    Let us reckon, rather than feel;
    Let us be true to the reck'ning,
    And He will make it real.

2 There's another word that the Lord has giv'n,
    In the very same verse we read,
Let us reckon ourselves as alive in Him,
    As alive and alive indeed.

3 While we trust in feeling or inward frames
    We shall always be tossed about,
Let us anchor fast to the Word of God,
    And reckon away our doubt.

4 As the mariner, when the skies are dim,
    Sails on by his compass true;
So our faith would cling to the promise firm,
    And reckon the journey through.

5 O how sweet it is to be anchored fast
    To a hope that can never fail;
Let us reckon on with a firmer trust,
    Till we anchor within the veil.

6 You may claim the promise from every pain,
    You may know His power to heal;
But your faith must rest in His word alone,
    And reckon, rather than feel.

693

8.8.8.8.

1 He faileth not, for He is God;
He faileth not, His grace how good!
He faileth not, His Word is clear;
If we have God, whom need we fear?

2 The highest mount, He can make plain;
The wildest flood, He can restrain!
God of Impossibilities!
Poor puny man, now learn His ways.

3 The axe did swim on Jordan's wave!
Our God the Red Sea's waters clave!
He stopped the sun! made long the day!
This is the God to whom we pray.

4 He bars the sea with feeble sand!
The proud waves bow at His command!
If God is thine, what more your need?
Can He not work for you indeed?

5 Our God is love; your needs are known;
His promises He'll fully own.
Our gracious God bows down His ear
The feeblest, weakest cry to hear.

6 Our God is light, and never yet,
One promise did He e'er forget.
His promises in Christ the Son
Are fully pledged, Yea and Amen.

7 Our faithful God, faith cannot break,
Nor death, nor hell, His promise shake!
Who ask in faith, He'll not deny;
His Word is sure, He must reply.

8 He faileth not, let all men hear;
He faileth not, His Word is clear.
He faileth not, His grace how good;
He faileth not, for He is God!

8.6.8.6. with chorus.

1 Be not dismayed whate'er betide,
    God will take care of you!
Beneath His wings of love abide,
    God will take care of you!

    God will take care of you,
    Through every day o'er all the way;
    He will take care of you;
    God will take care of you!

2 Through days of toil when heart doth fail,
    God will take care of you!
When dangers fierce your path assail,
    God will take care of you!

3 All you may need He will provide,
    God will take care of you!
Trust Him, and you will be satisfied,
    God will take care of you!

4 Lonely and sad, from friends apart,
    God will take care of you!
He will give peace to your aching heart,
    God will take care of you!

5 No matter what may be the test,
    God will take care of you!
Lean, weary one, upon His breast,
    God will take care of you!

695

Peculiar Meter.

1 Does Jesus care when my heart is pained
Too deeply for mirth or song,
As the burdens press,
And the cares distress,
And the way grows weary and long?

O yes, He cares, I know He cares,
His heart is touched with my grief;
When the days are weary,
The long night dreary,
I know my Savior cares.

2 Does Jesus care when my way is dark
With a nameless dread and fear?
As the daylight fades
Into deep night shades,
Does He care enough to be near?

3 Does Jesus care when I've tried and failed
To resist some temptation strong;
When for my deep grief
There is no relief,
Though my tears flow all the night long?

4 Does Jesus care when I've said "goodbye"
To the dearest on earth to me,
And my sad heart aches
Till it nearly breaks,
Is it aught to Him? Does He see?

696

8.6.8.6.

1 Cast thou thy care upon the Lord,
The care that loads thy heart;
Take Him this moment at His word,
And let Him do His part.

2   The need is deep, the care is great,
     The burden hard to bear;
     Roll it on Him with all its weight,
     And leave it resting there.

3   This heavy thing, it is His gift,
     His portion, thee to bless;
     Give it Him back; what He shall lift
     No more on thee shall press.

4   Cast all thy care, and not a part,
     The great things and the small;
     The Lord's all-loving, mighty heart
     Has room and thought for all.

5   Yes, He will ponder every care,
     Consider each detail;
     Thyself, thy burden, let Him bear;
     He will not, cannot, fail.

8.7.8.7. with chorus.   **697**

1   Weary pilgrim on life's pathway —
     Struggling on beneath thy load —
     Hear these words of consolation,
     "Cast thy burden on the Lord."

     Cast thy burden on the Lord!
     Cast thy burden on the Lord,
     And He will strengthen thee,
        sustain and comfort thee —
     Cast thy burden on the Lord.

2   Are thy tired feet unsteady?
     Does thy lamp no light afford?
     Is thy cross too great and heavy?
     "Cast thy burden on the Lord."

continued

3 Are the ties of friendship severed?
   Hushed the voices fondly heard?
   Breaks thy heart with weight of anguish?
     "Cast thy burden on the Lord."

4 Does thy heart with faintness falter?
   Does thy mind forget His word?
   Does thy strength succumb to weakness?
     "Cast thy burden on the Lord."

5 He will hold thee up from falling;
   He will guide thy steps aright;
   He will strengthen each endeavor;
     He will keep thee by His might.

698   8.8.8.6. with chorus.

1 Amid the trials that I meet,
   Amid the thorns that pierce my feet,
   One thought remains supremely sweet —
     Thou thinkest, Lord, of me!

     Thou thinkest, Lord, of me!
     Thou thinkest, Lord, of me!
     What need I fear when Thou art near,
     And thinkest, Lord, of me!

2 The cares of life come thronging fast,
   Upon my soul their shadows cast;
   Their gloom reminds my heart at last
     Thou thinkest, Lord, of me!

3 Let shadows come, let shadows go,
   Let life be bright, or dark with woe,
   I am content, for this I know
     Thou thinkest, Lord, of me!

6.5.6.5.D.

1 In the hour of trial,
   Jesus, plead for me,
Lest by base denial,
   I depart from Thee;
When Thou seest me waver,
   With a look recall,
Nor for fear or favor
   Suffer me to fall.

2 Should Thy mercy send me
   Sorrow, toil, and woe;
Or should pain attend me
   On my path below;
Grant that I may never
   Fail Thy hand to see;
Grant that I may ever
   Cast my care on Thee.

3 When the last hour cometh,
   Fraught with strife and pain,
When Thou, Lord, returneth
   To the earth again;
On Thy truth relying
   As that hour draws near,
Jesus, take me, waiting,
   To Thy presence dear.

8.3.8.3.8.7.

700

1 "Be not anxious for the morrow,"
   Jesus said;
Why should we its trials borrow?
   Trust instead!
For each hour of need or sorrow,
   Grace He gives, and daily bread.

continued

2   Thus our treasures safe investing
       In His care,
   Kept in His pavilion resting,
       May we dare
   Still to trust, thru faith's deep testing,
   Sure, God will His ways declare.

COMFORT IN TRIALS — BY THE LORD'S LEADING

701   8.7.8.7.D. with repeat.

1   All the way my Savior leads me;
       What have I to ask beside?
   Can I doubt His tender mercy,
       Who through life has been my Guide?
   Heav'nly peace, divinest comfort,
       Here by faith in Him to dwell!
   For I know, whate'er befall me,
       Jesus doeth all things well,
   For I know, whate'er befall me,
       Jesus doeth all things well.

2   All the way my Savior leads me,
       Cheers each winding path I tread,
   Gives me grace for every trial,
       Feeds me with the living bread.
   Though my weary steps may falter,
       And my soul athirst may be,
   Gushing from the Rock before me,
       Lo! a spring of joy I see,
   Gushing from the Rock before me,
       Lo! a spring of joy I see.

3   All the way my Savior leads me;
       Oh, the fullness of His grace!
   Perfect rest to me is promised
       In my Father's blest embrace.

When my spirit, clothed immortal,
Wings its flight to realms of day,
This my song through endless ages:
Jesus led me all the way,
This my song through endless ages:
Jesus led me all the way.

8.8.8.8.D.   **702**

1 'Tis now in part I know His grace;
I catch sweet glimpses of His face,
But in that better world of His,
I shall behold Him as He is.

Then shall I know as I am known,
And sing His praise before the throne;
Then shall I know as I am known,
And sing His praise before the throne.

2 'Tis now in part I know His love;
Bright sunbeams shine from skies above;
But glories more exceeding far,
Shall rise beyond life's evening star.

3 'Tis now in part I understand
The leadings of my Father's hand;
But I shall own His ways were right,
When welcomed to His presence bright.

4 'Tis now in part, but O how sweet
To rest by faith at His dear feet;
Though now we see as through a glass,
The veil will lift, the shadows pass.

COMFORT IN TRIALS — BY THE LORD'S LEADING

703   8.7.8.7.D.

1 Precious promise God doth give thee,
   Thou, the weary passerby,
On the way from earth to glory:
   "I will guide thee with Mine eye."

   I will guide thee, I will guide thee,
      I will guide thee with Mine eye;
   On the way from earth to glory,
      I will guide thee with Mine eye.

2 When temptations fierce assail thee,
   When thy trusted helpers fly,
Let this promise ring within thee,
   "I will guide thee with Mine eye."

3 When thy secret hopes have perished
   In the grave of years gone by,
Let this promise still be cherished,
   "I will guide thee with Mine eye."

4 When the shades of life are falling,
   And the hour has come to die,
Hear thy faithful Pilot calling,
   "I will guide thee with Mine eye."

COMFORT IN TRIALS — BY THE LORD'S PROVIDING

704   5.5.5.5.6.5.6.5.

1 Though troubles assail,
   And dangers affright;
Though friends should all fail,
   And foes all unite,
Yet one thing secures us,
   Whatever betide:
The Scripture assures us,
   "The Lord will provide."

2 The birds, without barn
Or storehouse, are fed;
From them let us learn
To trust for our bread;
His saints what is fitting
Shall ne'er be denied,
So long as 'tis written,
"The Lord will provide."

3 His call we obey,
Like Abram of old,
Not knowing our way,
But faith makes us bold;
For though we are strangers,
We have a good Guide;
And trust in all dangers:
"The Lord will provide."

4 When Satan appears
To stop up our path,
And fills us with fears,
We triumph by faith;
He cannot take from us,
Though oft he has tried,
The heart-cheering promise,
"The Lord will provide."

5 He tells us we're weak,
Our hope is in vain;
The good that we seek
We ne'er shall obtain;
But when such suggestions
Our faith thus have tried,
This answers all questions,
"The Lord will provide."

continued

6 No strength of our own,
   Nor goodness we claim;
   Our trust is all thrown
   On Jesus' dear name.
   In this our strong tower
   For safety we hide;
   The Lord is our power,
   "The Lord will provide."

7 When life sinks apace,
   And death is in view,
   The word of His grace
   Shall comfort us through;
   Not fearing or doubting,
   With Christ on our side,
   We hope to die shouting,
   "The Lord will provide."

705   11.12.11.11.11.

1 In some way or other the Lord will provide:
   It may not be my way, it may not be thy way;
   And yet in His own way, "the Lord will provide."

   Then we'll trust in the Lord, and He will provide;
   Yes, we'll trust in the Lord, and He will provide.

2 At some time or other the Lord will provide:
   It may not be my time, it may not be thy time;
   And yet in His own time, "the Lord will provide."

3 Despond then no longer; the Lord will provide:
   And this be the token — no word He hath spoken
   Was ever yet broken: "The Lord will provide."

4 *March on then right boldly: the sea shall divide;*
   The pathway made glorious, with shoutings victorious,
   We'll join in the chorus, "The Lord will provide."

7.6.7.6.D.

1 Sometimes a light surprises
   The Christian while he sings;
It is the Lord who rises
   With healing in His wings;
When comforts are declining,
   He grants the soul again
A season of clear shining,
   To cheer it after rain.

2 In holy contemplation
   We sweetly then pursue
The theme of God's salvation,
   And find it ever new;
Set free from present sorrow,
   We cheerfully can say —
E'en let the unknown morrow
   Bring with it what it may.

3 It can bring with it nothing,
   But He will bear us through;
Who gives the lilies clothing,
   Will clothe His people too:
Beneath the spreading heavens
   No creature but is fed;
And He, who feeds the ravens,
   Will give His children bread.

4 Though vine nor fig tree neither
   Their wonted fruit shall bear;
Though all the fields should wither
   Nor flocks nor herds be there;
Yet God the same abiding,
   His praise shall tune my voice,
For, while in Him confiding,
   I cannot but rejoice.

COMFORT IN TRIALS — BY THE LORD'S BLESSINGS

707   11.11.11.11. with chorus.

1 When upon life's billows you are tempest tossed,
When you are discouraged, thinking all is lost,
Count your many blessings name them one by one,
And it will surprise you what the Lord hath done.

Count your blessings, name them one by one;
Count your blessings, see what God hath done;
Count your blessings, name them one by one,
And it will surprise you what the Lord hath done.

2 Are you ever burdened with a load of care?
Does the cross seem heavy you are called to bear?
Count your many blessings, every doubt will fly,
And you will be singing as the days go by.

3 When you look at others with their lands and gold,
Think that Christ has promised you His wealth untold.
Count your many blessings, money cannot buy
Your reward in heaven, nor your Lord on high.

4 So amid the conflict, whether great or small,
Do not be discouraged, God is over all;
Count your many blessings, angels will attend,
Help and comfort give you to your journey's end.

COMFORT IN TRIALS — BY THE LORD OF HOPE

708*   8.7.8.7.D. with chorus.

1 Fresh as the dew of the morning,
Bringing a sweet rest unheard,
Christ, in the gentle anointing,
Whispers His comforting word:
Stand till the trial is over,
Stand till the tempest is gone,
Stand for the glory of Jesus,
Stand till the kingdom is won.

COMFORT IN TRIALS — BY THE LORD OF HOPE

Chorus:
> Lord of all hope, O how
>   sweet is Thy voice,
> Making my heart in Thy
>   presence rejoice.

2 If in the test of my trouble,
>   Faint be my spirit and heart,
> Faith, with the star of hope glimm'ring,
>   Shall all be taken apart,
> May then Thy faith with Thy life-pow'r
>   Over me hold its full sway
> That all Thy riches of glory
>   Now I may share and for aye.

3 Lord, as the morning sun dawning,
>   Chase all my darkness away,
> And with Thy kind wings of healing
>   Turn all my night into day.
> Come Thou, O come, Lord of comfort,
>   Come to my sad, weary heart,
> Come, O Thou blest hope of glory,
>   Never, O never depart.

COMFORT IN TRIALS — BY THE LORD'S TRIUMPH

10.10.10.10.   **709**

1 Jesus triumphant when the storm-clouds break,
   And the loud thunder bids the soul awake;
   When biting blasts lay earthly projects low,
   And one by one the fondest treasures go.

2 Jesus triumphant, through the fleeting years;
   Jesus triumphant, spite of blinding tears;
   High over all, to hear Thy loving voice,
   Which bids the heart look upward and rejoice.

continued

3   Jesus triumphant, when in work for Thee,
Sad and disheartened, no results we see;
When gathered force of evil seems to win,
And work for Christ seems lost in work of sin.

4   Jesus triumphant all along the line;
Triumphant Savior, all Thy triumph mine;
For since I am a partner in Thy love,
My life on earth is lived through Thee above.

5   Jesus triumphant when the spirit wings
Onward and upward to the King of kings;
And through the last great triumph of Thy grace
Triumphant saints shall see Thee face to face.

COMFORT IN TRIALS —
BY CLOSER FELLOWSHIP WITH THE LORD

710   7.6.7.6.D.

1   The days may yet grow darker,
The nights more weary grow,
And Jesus may still tarry,
But this one thing I know:
The Lord will still grow dearer,
And fellowship will be
The closer and the sweeter
Between my Lord and me.

2   'Tis our dear Lord we wait for,
Our Hope! our Joy! our Friend!
Himself we long to welcome,
And just beyond the bend
Hidden, perchance to meet us
Before the day is done,
The waiting will be over
And rest will have begun.

Peculiar Meter.

1 I know not what awaits me,
  God kindly veils my eyes,
And o'er each step of my onward way
  He makes new scenes to rise;
And every joy He sends me comes
  A sweet and glad surprise.

  Where He may lead I'll follow,
    My trust in Him repose;
  And every hour in perfect peace,
    I'll sing, "He knows, He knows";
  And every hour in perfect peace,
    I'll sing, "He knows, He knows."

2 One step I see before me,
    'Tis all I need to see,
  The light of heaven more brightly shines
    When earth's illusions flee;
  And sweetly through the silence comes,
    His loving, "Trust in Me!"

3 Oh, blissful lack of wisdom,
    'Tis blessed not to know;
  He holds me with His own right hand,
    And will not let me go,
  And lulls my troubled soul to rest
    In Him who loves me so.

4 So on I go not knowing;
    I would not if I might;
  I'd rather walk in the dark with God
    Than go alone in the light;
  I'd rather walk by faith with Him
    Than go alone by sight.

8.8.8.8.

1 Be still, my heart! these anxious cares
To thee are burdens, thorns and snares;
They cast dishonor on the Lord,
And contradict His gracious word.

2 Brought safely by His hand thus far,
Why wilt thou now give place to fear?
How canst thou want if He provide,
Or lose thy way with such a Guide?

3 When first before His mercy-seat
Thou didst to Him thine all commit;
He gave thee warrant from that hour
To trust His wisdom, love, and power.

4 Did ever trouble yet befall,
And He refuse to hear thy call?
And has He not His promise passed,
That thou shalt overcome at last?

5 He who has helped me hitherto
Will help me all my journey through,
And give me daily cause to raise
New Ebenezers to His praise.

6 Though rough and thorny be the road,
It leads thee on, apace, to God;
Then count thy present trials small,
For God will make amends for all.

COMFORT IN TRIALS — BY TRUSTING THE LORD

10.9.10.9.D.

1 Day by day, and with each passing moment,
Strength I find to meet my trials here;
Trusting in my Father's wise bestowment,
I've no cause for worry or for fear.
He, whose heart is kind beyond all measure,
Gives unto each day what He deems best,
Lovingly its part of pain and pleasure,
Mingling toil with peace and rest.

2 Every day the Lord Himself is near me,
With a special mercy for each hour;
All my cares He fain would bear and cheer me,
He whose name is Counsellor and Pow'r.
The protection of His child and treasure
Is a charge that on Himself He laid;
"As thy days, thy strength shall be in measure,"
This the pledge to me He made.

3 Help me then, in every tribulation,
So to trust Thy promises, O Lord,
That I lose not faith's sweet consolation,
Offered me within Thy holy Word.
Help me, Lord, when toil and trouble meeting,
E'er to take, as from a father's hand,
One by one, the days, the moments fleeting,
Till with Christ the Lord I stand.

714

8.6.8.6.

1 Through all the changing scenes of life,
   In trouble and in joy,
The praises of my God shall still
   My heart and tongue employ.

2 Oh, magnify the Lord with me,
   With me exalt His name;
When in distress to Him I called,
   He to my rescue came.

3 The hosts of God encamp around
   The dwellings of the just;
Deliverance He affords to all
   Who on His succor trust.

4 Oh, make but trial of His love,
   Experience will decide
How blest they are, and only they,
   Who in His truth confide.

5 Fear Him, ye saints, and you will then
   Have nothing else to fear;
Make you His service your delight,
   Your wants shall be His care.

715

8.8.8.8.D.

1 Not now, but in the coming years,
   It may be when with Christ we stand,
We'll read the meaning of our tears,
   And there, sometime, we'll understand.

   Then trust in God through all thy days;
   Fear not, for He doth hold thy hand;
   Though dark thy way, still sing and praise,
   Sometime, sometime, we'll understand.

2 We'll catch the broken thread again,
   And finish what we here began;
   God will the mysteries explain,
   And then, ah, then, we'll understand.

3 We'll know why clouds instead of sun
   Were over many a cherished plan;
   Why song has ceased when scarce begun;
   'Tis then, sometime, we'll understand.

4 Why what we long for most of all,
   Eludes so oft our eager hand;
   Why hopes are crushed and castles fall,
   Till then, sometime, we'll understand.

5 God knows the way, He holds the key,
   He guides us with unerring hand;
   Sometime with tearless eyes we'll see;
   Yes, then, 'tis then, we'll understand.

5.5.5.5.6.5.6.5.   **716**

1 Begone, unbelief,
      My Savior is near,
   And for my relief
      Will surely appear;
   By prayer let me wrestle,
      And He will perform;
   With Christ in the vessel,
      I smile at the storm.

2 Though dark be my way,
      Since He is my Guide,
   'Tis mine to obey,
      'Tis His to provide;
   Though cisterns be broken,
      And creatures all fail,
   The word He hath spoken
      Shall surely prevail.   *continued*

3 His love, in time past,
    Forbids me to think
He'll leave me at last
    In trouble to sink:
Each sweet Ebenezer
    I have in review
Confirms His good pleasure
    To help me quite through.

4 Why should I complain
    Of want or distress,
Temptation or pain?
    He told me no less;
The heirs of salvation,
    I know from His Word,
Through much tribulation
    Must follow their Lord.

5 How bitter that cup
    No heart can conceive,
Which He drank quite up,
    That sinners might live!
His way was much rougher
    And darker than mine;
Did Christ, my Lord, suffer,
    And shall I repine?

6 Since all that I meet
    Shall work for my good,
The bitter is sweet,
    The medicine, food;
Though painful at present,
    'Twill cease before long,
And then, oh, how pleasant
    The conqueror's song!

COMFORT IN TRIALS — BY REJOICING IN THE LORD

11.9.11.9. with chorus.

717

1   O let us rejoice in the Lord evermore,
Though all things around us be trying,
Though floods of affliction like sea billows roar,
It's better to sing than be sighing.

Then rejoice evermore, rejoice evermore,
It is better to sing than be sighing:
It is better to live than be dying;
So let us rejoice evermore.

2   O let us rejoice in the Lord evermore,
When the darts of the tempter are flying,
For Satan still dreads, as he oft did of yore,
Our singing much more than our sighing.

3   O let us rejoice in the Lord evermore,
When sickness upon us is stealing,
No cordial like gladness our strength can restore,
For joy is the fountain of healing.

COMFORT IN TRIALS — BY PEACE IN THE LORD

10.10.

718

1   Peace, perfect peace, in this dark world of sin?
The blood of Jesus whispers peace within.

2   Peace, perfect peace, by thronging duties pressed?
To do the will of Jesus — this is rest.

3   Peace, perfect peace, with sorrows surging round?
On Jesus' bosom naught but calm is found.

4   Peace, perfect peace, with loved ones far away?
In Jesus' keeping we are safe, and they.

5   Peace, perfect peace, our future all unknown?
Jesus we know, and He is on the throne.

6.5.6.5.D.

1 Like a river, glorious
   Is God's perfect peace,
Over all victorious
   In its bright increase;
Perfect, yet it floweth
   Fuller every day,
Perfect, yet it groweth
   Deeper all the way.

   Stayed upon Christ Jesus,
      Hearts are fully blest;
   Finding, as He promised,
      Perfect peace and rest.

2 Hidden in the hollow
   Of His blessed hand,
Never foe can follow,
   Never traitor stand;
Not a surge of worry,
   Not a shade of care,
Not a blast of hurry
   Touch the spirit there.

3 Every joy or trial
   Falleth from above,
Traced upon our dial
   By the Sun of Love.
We may trust Him fully
   All for us to do;
They who trust Him wholly
   Find Him wholly true.

9.9.9.9. with chorus.

720

1　God hath not promised skies always blue,
　　Flower-strewn pathways all our lives through;
　　God hath not promised sun without rain,
　　Joy without sorrow, peace without pain.

　　　But God hath promised strength for the day,
　　　Rest for the labor, light for the way,
　　　Grace for the trials, help from above,
　　　Unfailing sympathy, undying love.

2　God hath not promised we shall not know
　　Toil and temptation, trouble and woe;
　　He hath not told us we shall not bear
　　Many a burden, many a care.

3　God hath not promised smooth roads and wide,
　　Swift, easy travel, needing no guide;
　　Never a mountain, rocky and steep,
　　Never a river, turbid and deep.

9.8.9.8.D. with chorus.

721

1　I'll sing of the wonderful promise
　　That Jesus has given to me;
　　"My strength is made perfect in weakness,
　　My grace is sufficient for thee."
　　And lest my poor heart should forget it,
　　Or ever forgetful should be,
　　He still keeps repeating the promise,
　　My grace is sufficient for thee.

　　　Yes, over and over and over,
　　　My Savior keeps saying to me;
　　　My strength is made perfect in weakness,
　　　My grace is sufficient for thee.

continued

2 His grace is sufficient to save me,
And cleanse me from guilt and from sin;
Sufficient to sanctify wholly,
And give me His Spirit within.
His grace is sufficient for trials,
No matter how hard they may be,
This promise stands over against them,
My grace is sufficient for thee.

3 His grace is sufficient for sickness,
Sustaining and making me whole;
His grace is sufficient when sorrows
Like billows roll over the soul.
His grace is sufficient for service,
It sets us from selfishness free,
And sends us to tell to the tried ones,
His grace is sufficient for thee.

4 His grace is sufficient to live by,
And should we be summoned to die
'Twill light up the valley of shadows,
And bear us away to Him nigh.
Or when we shall stand in His vict'ry,
And Christ in His glory shall see,
We'll fall at His footstool confessing,
Thy grace was sufficient for me.

5 It is not our grace that's sufficient,
But His grace, it ever must be:
Our graces are transient and changing;
His grace is unfailing as He.
And so I am ever repeating
His wonderful promise to me,
My strength is made perfect in weakness,
My grace is sufficient for thee.

COMFORT IN TRIALS — BY GRACE FOR SUFFERING

722

9.7.9.7. with chorus.

1 The cross that He gave may be heavy,
  But it ne'er outweighs His grace;
 The storm that I feared may surround me,
  But it ne'er excludes His face.
   The cross is not greater than His grace,
   The storm cannot hide His blessed face;
    I am satisfied to know
    That with Jesus here below,
    I can conquer every foe.

2 The thorns in my path are not sharper
  Than composed His crown for me;
 The cup that I drink not more bitter
  Than He drank in Gethsemane.

3 The light of His love shineth brighter,
  As it falls on paths of woe;
 The toil of my work groweth lighter,
  As I stoop to raise the low.

4 His will I have joy in fulfilling,
  As I'm walking in His sight;
 My trials more blessings are bringing,
  Christ in them is my delight.

12.11.12.11.

723

1 He giveth more grace when the burdens grow greater,
He sendeth more strength when the labors increase,
To added affliction He addeth His mercy,
To multiplied trials, His multiplied peace.

2 When we have exhausted our store of endurance,
When our strength has failed ere the day is half-done,
When we reach the end of our hoarded resources,
Our Father's full giving is only begun.

3 His love has no limit, His grace has no measure,
His power no boundary known unto men,
For out of His infinite riches in Jesus,
He giveth and giveth and giveth again.

724

6.6.8.6.8.8.

1   A little bird I am,
    Shut from the fields of air,
And in my cage I sit and sing
    To Him who placed me there;
Well pleased a prisoner to be,
Because, my God, it pleaseth Thee.

2   Nought have I else to do,
    I sing the whole day long;
And He whom most I love to please
    Doth listen to my song;
He caught and bound my wandering wing;
But still He bends to hear me sing.

3   Thou hast an ear to hear
    A heart to love and bless;
And though my notes were e'er so rude,
    Thou wouldst not hear the less;
Because Thou knowest as they fall,
That love, sweet love, inspires them all.

4   My cage confines me round;
    Abroad I cannot fly;
But though my wing is closely bound,
    My heart's at liberty;
For prison walls cannot control
The flight, the freedom of the soul.

5   O it is good to soar
    These bolts and bars above!
To Him whose purpose I adore,
    Whose providence I love;
And in Thy mighty will to find
The joy, the freedom of the mind.

7.6.7.6.8.8.

725

1 Strong are the walls around me,
    That hold me all the day;
But they who thus have bound me,
    Cannot keep God away:
My very dungeon walls are dear,
Because the God I love is here.

2 They know, who thus oppress me,
    'Tis hard to be alone;
But know not One can bless me,
    Who comes through bars and stone;
He makes my dungeon's darkness bright,
And fills my bosom with delight.

3 Thy love, O God, restores me
    From sighs and tears to praise;
And deep my soul adores Thee,
    Nor thinks of time or place:
I ask no more, in good or ill,
But union with Thy holy will.

4 'Tis that which makes my treasure,
    'Tis that which brings my gain;
Converting woe to pleasure,
    And reaping joy from pain.
Oh, 'tis enough, whate'er befall,
To know that God is All in all..

8.8.6.8.8.6.

726

1 Long plunged in sorrow, I resign
    My soul to that dear hand of Thine,
      Without reserve or fear;
That hand shall wipe my streaming eyes,
Or into smiles of glad surprise
      Transform the falling tear.

continued

2   Adieu! ye vain delights of earth;
    Insipid sports, and childish mirth,
      I taste no sweets in you;
    Unknown delights are in the cross,
    All joy beside to me is dross;
      And Jesus thought so too.

3   The Cross! O ravishment and bliss —
    How grateful e'en its anguish is;
      Its bitterness how sweet!
    There every sense, and all the mind,
    In all her faculties refined,
      Taste happiness complete.

4   Self-love no grace in sorrow sees,
    Consults her own peculiar ease:
      'Tis all the bliss she knows;
    But nobler aims true love employ.
    In self-denial is her joy,
      In suffering her repose.

5   Thy choice and mine shall be the same,
    Inspirer of that holy flame
      Which must forever blaze!
    To take the cross and follow Thee,
    Where love and duty lead, shall be
      My portion and my praise.

COMFORT IN TRIALS — BY GAIN FROM SUFFERING

727   5.4.5.4.D.

1   Light after darkness,
    Gain after loss,
  Strength after weakness,
    Crown after cross;
  Sweet after bitter,
    Hope after fears,
  Home after wand'ring,
    Praise after tears.

2   Sheaves after sowing,
    Sun after rain,
  Sight after mystery,
    Peace after pain;
  Joy after sorrow,
    Calm after blast,
  Rest after weariness,
    Sweet rest at last.

COMFORT IN TRIALS — BY GAIN FROM SUFFERING

3 Near after distant,   After long agony,
    Gleam after gloom,   Rapture of bliss,
    Love after loneliness,   Right was the pathway,
    Life after tomb;   Leading to this.

13.8.13.8.

728

1 I have been through the valley of sorrow and weeping,
    The valley of trouble and pain;
  But the "God of all comfort," the "God of all comfort,"
  Was with me to hold and sustain.

2 As the earth needs the clouds and the rain with the
       sunshine,
    Our souls need both sorrow and joy,
  So He places us oft in the fire of affliction
  The dross from the gold to destroy.

3 When He leads thru the valleys of trouble and sorrow,
    His mercy and love there we trace;
  For the trials and sorrows He sends us in wisdom
  Are part of His lessons in grace.

4 Yet how often we shrink from the purging and pruning,
    Forgetting the Husbandman knows
  That the deeper and closer the cutting and paring,
  The richer the cluster that grows.

5 O how well does He know that afflictions are needed;
    He has a wise purpose in view,
  And within the dark valley He whispers to comfort,
  "Hereafter thou'lt know what I do."

6 As we travel the pathway thru life's shadowed valleys,
    Fresh springs of His love ever rise;
  And we learn that our troubles, our sorrows and losses,
  Are blessings just sent in disguise.

7 So we'll follow Him faithfully where'er He leadeth,
    The pathway be dreary or bright;   [fort,"
  For we've proved that our God is the "God of all com-
  The God who gives songs in the night.

729

7.5.7.5.7.7.

1 Is it raining, little flower?
   Oh, be glad of rain!
Too much sun would wither thee;
   Soon 'twill shine again.
Though the sky is black, 'tis true,
Yet behind it shines the blue.

2 Art thou weary, tender heart?
   Oh, be glad of pain;
Sweetest things in sorrow grow
   As the flow'rs in rain.
God is watching, thou'lt have sun
When the clouds their work have done.

730

10.10.10.10. with chorus.

1 Pressed out of measure, pressed beyond all length;
Pressed so intensely, seeming beyond strength;
Pressed in the body, pressed within the soul,
Pressed in the mind till darksome surges roll.

   God is my hope and God is my joy;
   He is the resurrection life I enjoy.

2 Pressure by foes, and pressure from our friends;
Pressure on pressure, till life nearly ends;
Pressed into knowing none to help but God,
Pressed into loving both the staff and rod.

3 Pressed into liberty where nothing clings,
Pressed into faith for hard and hopeless things;
Pressed into life, a life in Christ the Lord,
Pressed into life, the life of Christ outpoured.

8.8.8.

1 Why should I fear the darkest hour,
  Or tremble at the tempter's power?
  Jesus vouchsafes to be my tower.

2 Though hot the fight, why quit the field?
  Why must I either fly or yield,
  Since Jesus is my mighty shield?

3 When creature comforts fade and die,
  Worldlings may weep, but why should I?
  Jesus still lives, and still is nigh.

4 Though all the flocks and herds were dead,
  My soul a famine need not dread,
  For Jesus is my living bread.

5 I know not what may soon betide,
  Or how my wants shall be supplied;
  But Jesus knows, and will provide.

6 Though sin would fill me with distress,
  The throne of grace I dare address,
  For Jesus is my righteousness.

7 Though faint my prayers and cold my love,
  My steadfast hope shall not remove,
  While Jesus intercedes above.

8 Against me earth and hell combine;
  But on my side is power divine;
  Jesus is all, and He is mine!

732

10.11.10.11. with chorus.

1 My Father is rich in houses and lands,
He holdeth the wealth of the world in His hands!
Of rubies and diamonds, of silver and gold,
His coffers are full, He has riches untold.

    I'm a child of the King,
    A child of the King:
    With Jesus my Savior,
    I'm a child of the King.

2 My Father's own Son, the Savior of men,
Once wandered on earth as the poorest of them.
But now He is pleading our pardon on high,
That we may be His when He comes by and by.

3 I once was an out-cast stranger on earth,
A sinner by choice, and an alien by birth;
But I've been adopted, my name's written down,
An heir of salvation, the kingdom and crown.

4 Though poor on this earth, oh, why should I care?
Since glorious things for me God doth prepare;
Though trials abound, yet, still I may sing:
All glory to God, I'm a child of the King.

8.8.8.8.

1 In Eden's garden fair we see
  That God before two trees placed man,
  The trees of life, and knowledge too,
  Which for the Lord and Satan stand.

2 The tree of life the center is
  Of God's eternal, perfect plan,
  Denoting God in Christ as life
  To be received as all by man.

3 The tree of knowledge standing there,
  Bespeaks a sure and warning voice:
  Outside of God there is a source
  Of death to all who make this choice.

4 If man would eat the tree of life,
  Then God as life he will receive,
  And be transformed to precious stones,
  God's will and purpose to achieve.

5 If man the tree of knowledge takes,
  Then Satan enters into man
  As sin, which brings him into death,
  That he may not fulfill God's plan.

6 This signifies that only God
  Is our full source of life and breath;
  To touch ought else is but to touch
  The source of knowledge and of death.

7 For knowledge only bringeth death,
  Though evil or though good it seem;
  For any thing apart from God,
  Is but the fruit of Satan's scheme.

continued

8   Not only evil, but the good
    Is contradictory to Christ;
    Not only knowledge of the bad,
    But even good is versus Christ.

9   Lord, teach us only Thee to touch,
    That with Thy life we filled may be,
    And not to touch the good or bad,
    Or anything apart from Thee.

THE FOUR LAWS
8.8.8.8.

734*

1   The law of God is holy, good,
    To practise good it doth command;
    Its purpose is to clearly show
    That we cannot meet God's demand.

2   Yet in our mind there is a law
    Which always tries the good to do;
    But in our members is a law
    Which always doth this law subdue.

3   The law within our mind is good,
    'Tis of our human life obtained
    At our creation from the Lord,
    That good behavior be maintained.

4   The law within our members is
    The evil of satanic life;
    Into our members at the fall
    It came thru Satan's subtle strife.

5   This evil law of Satan is
The law of sin, in us its seat;
'Tis stronger than the law of good
And always brings it to defeat.

6   But in our spirit is a law,
Which is the Spirit's law of life;
'Tis of the very life of God
Which we from our rebirth derive.

7   This law divine the strongest is,
Transcending all the others o'er;
From sin's law freeing, it fulfills
The full requirement of God's law.

8   We then must always set our mind
Upon the spirit deep within,
And not upon the things of flesh,
The body ruined by the sin.

9   To set the mind upon the flesh
Is sin and death and darkest night;
The mind upon the spirit set
Is life and peace and full of light.

10   This is the way of true release!
This is the way of victory!
Lord, may we in the spirit live,
And by the Spirit walk with Thee.

735*

8.8.8.8.

1 The law of letters God defines,
It is His testimony true;
It shows how loving, holy, just,
Is God, with whom we have to do.

2 According to His nature shown
God's law requires that we must live,
That He our souls may justify
And unto us His blessing give.

3 The law can never give us life,
Nor any strength to us supply,
But doth its full demands exact
And all our weakness show thereby.

4 It was not for God's final plan,
But for man's sin was introduced,
That man by breaking it might know
Himself, his sin to him adduced.

5 'Tis by the law all mouths are stopped
And all are shut up under sin;
It brings us to the Christ of God
That God may bless us all in Him.

6 The law is but a type of Christ,
Who God's full testimony is,
Who fully has expressed His love,
His holiness and righteousness.

7 'Tis Christ, God's testimony real,
Who doth with life divine supply,
That with the law's demands we may
Be more than able to comply.

8 God's living testimony, He;
By whom God's potent life we share;
Thru Him we're dead unto the law,
And in His Spirit fruit we bear.

8.8.8.8.

1 In ancient times the law of God
In letter was engraved on stone;
But now it is a law of life,
Which in our heart is written down.

2 The law in letters good demands
And thus our utter weakness shows;
But now the law of life sustains,
And strength for God to please bestows.

3 The law in letters brings to us
God's knowledge only outwardly;
But now the law of life supplies
A deeper knowledge inwardly.

4 The law in letters can but rule
By dead commandments outwardly;
But now the law of life controls
By living knowledge inwardly.

5 This living law is moving now
In all of our experience,
To regulate us from within
And check us by our inner sense.

6 How deep its regulation is
Within the inmost part of us,
A living consciousness to give,
And God Himself impart to us.

7 'Tis by this living law of life
We need no teaching outwardly,
For all God's living knowledge now
This law will teach us inwardly.

8 Lord, teach us by this law to walk,
Its inner ruling to obey,
That we may of Thyself partake
And know Thee in a living way.

6.5.6.5.

1 Life eternal brings us
     Fellowship of life,
   Fellowship in Spirit,
     Saving us from strife.

2 Life eternal gives us
     Fellowship divine;
   Thus the Lord as Spirit
     May with us combine.

3 It is life in Spirit
     Brings this fellowship;
   Fellowship in Spirit
     Doth with grace equip.

4 We, by life's enabling,
     Fellowship aright;
   Fellowship in Spirit
     Brings us into light.

5 By the outward cleansing,
     Fellowship we keep;
   Inwardly anointed,
     Fellowship we reap.

6 Fellowship is deepened
     Thru the cross of death;
   Fellowship is lifted
     By the Spirit's breath.

7 Fellowship will free us
     From our sinful self;
   Fellowship will bring us
     Into God Himself.

8.6.8.6.

1 There is a certain sense of life
   With life of every kind;
   And in th' eternal life in us
   It is a sense divine.

2 The higher any life may be,
   The better is its sense;
   The life divine the highest is
   And has the highest sense.

3 It is the sense of life in us,
   It is the sense of God;
   'Tis in our spirit made alive,
   And more than sense of good.

4 It is the inner sense in us,
   The inmost consciousness,
   Discerning matters inwardly,
   God's will to thus express.

5 'Tis by this sense that God we know,
   The sense of inner life;
   'Tis pow'rful and spontaneous,
   And not of any strife.

6 The greater is our growth in life,
   The keener is this sense;
   The more we walk and act in life,
   The more it is intense.

7 The sense of life when exercised
   Will make our spirit bold,
   And by this inner sense of God
   True fellowship we hold.

739*

10.10.10.10.

1 In those regenerated by the Lord
There is an inner knowledge bountiful;
Thus we the outward teachings do not need,
But God we inwardly may know in full.

2 Eternal life, the highest and the best,
Possesses full divine capacity,
That by this life God's knowledge we may have
More than by knowledge given outwardly.

3 The law of life is put within our mind
And on our heart 'tis written sovereignly,
Inwardly ruling us that God we know
More than by teachings given outwardly.

4 Holy anointing in our spirit dwells,
Showing the things of God to mind and heart;
By this anointing we God's knowledge have
More than man's teachings can to us impart.

5 We have the triune God indwelling us,
Living and acting, working all the time,
That by the inner sense we have of Him
God we may know in magnitude sublime.

6 This inner knowledge obviates the need
Of outward knowledge, human eloquence,
But in the spirit we must ever live
And walk according to the inner sense.

7 The more we live in Christ, the life divine,
And by the inner consciousness behave,
The more we'll have the inward knowledge true,
And on our heart God will His Son engrave.

8 'Tis by this living inward knowledge gained
That fellowship with God in life we hold;
'Tis by this hidden knowledge thus obtained
God unto us His fulness doth unfold.

9.8.9.8.

1 The principle of incarnation
    Is but the blend of God and man,
Both acting in cooperation
    To thus fulfill th' eternal plan.

2 To God, the man is His expression,
    And man is of God's life possessed;
The man is wholly God's possession,
    And God thru man is thus expressed.

3 Redemption is accomplished fully
    In man, God's wisdom thus to show;
Salvation is expounded wholly
    By man, that all creation know.

4 God's service in this dispensation
    Requires that man should work with Him;
Thus God and man in close relation
    And joint dependence work therein.

5 It is not God Himself to labor,
    Nor man to try to serve alone,
But God and man to work together
    Each moment that His plan be shown.

6 The principle of incarnation
    To all our work we must apply,
To all our gift and operation,
    That we as one may serve thereby.

VARIOUS ASPECTS OF THE INNER LIFE
THE ADOPTION

741*

8.7.8.7.D.

1 God ordained us unto sonship,
　　Ere creation's work was done,
To conform us by His Spirit
　　To the image of His Son;
That His only dear Begotten
　　Might become the firstborn One,
And by Him with many brethren
　　His expression full be won.

2 By divine regeneration
　　We the sons of God became,
But we must mature to fullness,
　　Thus the birthright to obtain.
Born and fully grown to manhood,
　　God's adoption we may share;
By the measure of full stature,
　　We God's sonship will declare.

3 All our spirit, soul and body
　　Unto Christ conformed must be;
This will be accomplished fully
　　When our glorious Lord we see.
By our body's full redemption
　　Shall adoption be complete;
By the final transformation
　　All God's purpose we shall meet.

4 By that final transformation,
　　We'll be fully sanctified;
God will bring us into glory,
　　With His Son identified.
All creation is expecting
　　Sons of God revealed to be,
That they might be freed from bondage
　　Into glorious liberty.

8.8.8.8.

742*

1 Man is a being of three parts,
  The body, soul, and spirit too,
  Th' eternal purpose to fulfill
  With God's inheritance in view.

2 The body is the outward part
  That man a world-sense may possess;
  Thus he may touch the outward things
  And bodily himself express.

3 The soul within — the inward part —
  Is but the very self of man;
  The sense of self it gives to him
  To touch the psychic world of man.

4 The spirit is the inmost part
  With which the Lord he may receive;
  The sense of God it gives to man
  That he the spirit-world perceive.

5 Within the soul of man there are
  The mind, emotion, and the will;
  These are the functions for the man
  His human nature to fulfill.

6 Within the spirit of the man
  Are found the conscience, fellowship,
  And intuition, which thereby
  The man to worship God equip.

7 The man must exercise his soul
  To choose that God he may possess,
  And by his spirit God partake,
  And thru his body God express.

8 Man's spirit has to be reborn
  With life divine to him conveyed;
  His soul must be transformed by God,
  His body like Christ's body made.

continued

9   'Tis by these steps of work divine
In each of man's three separate parts
That man is mingled with the Lord
And His expression full imparts.

THE NEW HEART AND THE NEW SPIRIT

743*   8.7.8.7.

1   God created us His vessels
His expression to achieve;
Thus He made a heart to love Him
And a spirit to receive.

2   With our heart we have to love Him,
With our spirit Him possess
As our life, of Him partaking,
That Himself we may express.

3   Satan has our heart corrupted,
To our spirit death did give,
That the Lord we should not contact
But by self attempt to live.

4   Thus the Lord in His salvation
Heart and spirit has renewed
To recover our receiving
And our loving aptitude.

5   It is by our heart's renewal
We may God in love pursue,
And in newness of the spirit
We may contact God anew.

6   Ever true and pure and single
To the Lord our heart must be,
Poor in spirit, ever seeking
God to contact constantly.

7   Keep our heart, Lord, in love's freshness,
    And our spirit strengthen more,
That in newness of the spirit
    We may touch Thee o'er and o'er.

THE PROPER HEART

8.6.8.6.

744*

1   In dealings with the Lord as life
    We need a proper heart,
That of His riches, in His grace,
    We fully may take part.

2   We need a heart in all things pure,
    With mind both sound and clear,
To understand His mind and heart
    In trembling and in fear.

3   We need a fervent, loving heart,
    A heart on fire with love,
With an emotion filled with zeal
    For Him, all else above.

4   We need a true, obedient heart,
    With a submissive will,
A will made pliable, yet strong,
    God's purpose to fulfill.

5   We need a heart condemning not,
    In all things right with God;
A heart which has a conscience purged
    And covered with the blood.

6   Lord, grant us such a heart as this,
    Forever fixed on Thee,
That of Thyself we may partake
    And Thy true fulness be.

VARIOUS ASPECTS OF THE INNER LIFE
THE TWO SPIRITS AS ONE

745*

8.6.8.6.

1   O Lord, Thou art the Spirit now
     Who in our spirit lives;
  One spirit have the two become,
     Which oneness to us gives.

2   Thy Spirit with our spirit, Lord,
     The witness ever bears
  That we the Father's children are
     And of God's glory heirs.

3   'Tis in our spirit Thee we touch
     Thy riches to enjoy,
  And as the Spirit Thou dost give
     Thyself without alloy.

4   'Tis in our spirit we may walk
     And follow Thee alway,
  While, as the Spirit, Thou dost lead
     And light impart each day.

5   In spirit, by Thy Spirit, Lord,
     We live and worship Thee;
  Thou, in our spirit, thru Thine own
     Strengtheneth constantly.

6   In spirit, with Thy Spirit, Lord,
     We offer prayer to Thee,
  While, as the Spirit, Thou in us
     Groanest unutterably.

7   We to our spirit would return
     And there would contact Thine;
  'Tis in the spirit we may share
     Our heritage divine.

8   What oneness, O my Lord, is this —
     Two spirits intertwine!
  Thy Spirit in our spirit lives,
     And ours abides in Thine!

VARIOUS ASPECTS OF THE INNER LIFE
DISCERNING THE SPIRIT

9.8.9.8.

1 Lord, teach us to discern the spirit
    From soul that we Thyself may know;
Thou art the Spirit in our spirit,
    In oneness mingled with us so.

2 Lord, teach us to discern the spirit,
    The soul-life ever to deny,
And ever follow Thee in spirit,
    Thyself, the Spirit, to apply.

3 Lord, teach us to discern the spirit
    That we may never set our mind
Upon the flesh but on the spirit,
    That sin and self no more may bind.

4 Lord, teach us to discern the spirit
    That we may never soulish be,
But truly spiritual, in spirit
    To know all things discernibly.

5 Lord, teach us to discern the spirit
    That subtle self exposed might be,
That by the cross to it applying
    We'll live not by ourselves but Thee.

6 Lord, teach us to discern the spirit
    That we may be transformed in soul,
Till we're conformed to Thine own image,
    Till we're matured and reach the goal.

7 Lord, teach us to discern the spirit,
    To us Thy living Word so give
That soul from spirit be divided
    And in the holiest place we'll live.

747*

8.8.8.8.

1 The holiest of God's temple is
  The inmost part; the mercy seat,
  God's presence and the ark are there,
  And there the priests the Lord may meet.

2 Now we're God's temple in three parts;
  Our inmost part the spirit is;
  There God and Christ as Spirit dwell,
  The holiest place of holy 'tis.

3 'Tis here within our inmost part
  That God in Christ is all to us;
  'Tis here the Holy Spirit makes
  The Lord reality to us.

4 'Tis here within the spirit-part
  We contact Christ and dwell with Him;
  'Tis by our spirit we with God
  Have fellowship and worship Him.

5 'Tis here that Christ is like the land
  Where we may dwell, its wealth enjoy;
  'Tis here that we must fight the foe,
  And Christ's authority employ.

6 The spirit we must seek to know,
  Discerning spirit from the soul,
  And live within this holiest place,
  To worship God and reach His goal.

7 The soul we ever must forsake,
  Press on, God's rest to enter in,
  That Christ we may possess in full
  And all God's plan fulfill therein.

8.7.8.7.

1   By the cross discern the spirit,
    Put the soul to death alway;
Bear the cross, deny the self-life,
    Walk in spirit day by day.

2   By the cross discern the spirit,
    Through the living Word of God,
Separating soul from spirit,
    That the right path may be trod.

3   By the cross discern the spirit,
    With the mind by light renewed,
All emotion consecrated,
    And the will in love subdued.

4   By the cross discern the spirit;
    Passing thru the riven veil,
Flesh and soul are wholly broken,
    And the spirit doth prevail.

5   By the cross discern the spirit,
    'Tis the holiest place divine;
There commune with God in spirit
    And His presence will be thine.

6   By the cross discern the spirit
    And the Jordan River cross;
Enter then the Land of Canaan,
    And enjoy Christ thru the cross.

7   By the cross discern the spirit
    And within the spirit move;
As good land, on Christ e'er labor,
    And His riches thou wilt prove.

749*

8.8.8.8.

1 The Spirit of the triune God
Within our spirit now doth rest;
He ever seeks thru us to flow,
That God in Christ may be expressed.

2 But by the outward, natural man
The Spirit is confined within;
Instead of giving Him a home,
A prison we've become to Him.

3 He's like a treasure of great worth
Contained in vessels earthen-made;
The vessel must be broken through
And thus the treasure be displayed.

4 Oh, how the Lord our self must break,
Our outward man does so impede!
It must be broken thoroughly,
And thus the Spirit will be freed.

5 This is the reason why the Lord
For us a certain measure makes
Of circumstantial suffering;
'Tis thus our outward man He breaks.

6 The outward man, the self, the soul,
Must be consumed, must be decreased;
The inner man, our spirit, then
Shall with the Spirit be released.

7 Lord, grant Thy holy brokenness,
Deliver me from being whole;
And make me willing to receive
The wounds that Thou wouldst give my soul.

8 Oh, cause me to appreciate
Thy breaking, never to complain;
And grant that I may value more
All kinds of loss instead of gain.

8.7.8.7.D.

1 God's intention is to have us
All conformed to His dear Son;
Thus a work of transformation
By the Spirit must be done.

Lord, transform us to Thine image
In emotion, mind, and will;
Saturate us with Thy Spirit,
All our being wholly fill.

2 God hath us regenerated
In our spirit with His life;
But He must transform us further —
In our soul by His own life.

3 Spreading outward from our spirit
Doth the Lord transform our soul,
By the inward parts renewing,
Till within His full control.

4 By the power of His Spirit
In His pattern He transforms;
From His glory to His glory
To His image He conforms.

5 He transforms, all sanctifying,
Till like Him we are matured;
He transforms, our soul possessing,
Till His stature is secured.

751*

6.5.6.5.D.

1 It is not by struggling,
But by yielding all,
I may rest from labor,
All my burden fall.
It is not resolving,
But Thyself to heed,
I'm from sin delivered
And from bondage freed.

2 It is not by letter,
But by Spirit 'tis,
I will be approvèd,
Share Thy life of bliss.
It is not man's teaching,
But anointing Thine,
Which imparts Thy light and
Fellowship divine.

3 It is not resolving
Now to run the race,
But 'tis by Thy mercy
I receive Thy grace.
It is not by knowledge,
But by grace alone,
I can pass thru suff'ring
To Thine image grown.

4 Not by lofty phrases,
But by power Thine,
I the lost can pilot
Unto life divine.
It is not my wisdom,
But Thy Spirit, Lord,
Which alone can fit me
To fulfill Thy Word.

8.8.8.9.

1 I am the Lord that healeth thee,
   I am the Lord that healeth thee;
   Jehovah-Rapha is My Name:
   For I am the Lord that healeth thee.

2 I am the Lord that healeth thee,
   I am the Lord that healeth thee;
   Sickness must flee at My command:
   For I am the Lord that healeth thee.

3 I am the Lord that healeth thee,
   I am the Lord that healeth thee;
   The prayer of faith shall banish disease:
   For I am the Lord that healeth thee.

4 I am the Lord that healeth thee,
   I am the Lord that healeth thee;
   My Name is still as ointment poured forth:
   For I am the Lord that healeth thee.

5 I am the Lord that healeth thee,
   I am the Lord that healeth thee;
   Come and be free from all your pains:
   For I am the Lord that healeth thee.

8.8.8.8.

1 There is a healing branch that grows
   Where every bitter Marah flows;
   This is our health-renewing tree.
   "I am the Lord that healeth thee."

2 There is an old appointed way
   For those who hearken and obey;
   Above the gate these words we see:
   "I am the Lord that healeth thee."

continued

3 There is an ordinance that has stood
Since Israel crossed the parted flood;
It stands today for you and me —
"I am the Lord that healeth thee."

4 There is a great Physician still
Whose hand has all its ancient skill;
At His command our pains will flee —
"I am the Lord that healeth thee."

DIVINE HEALING — THE HEALING WINGS

754   8.8.8.6.

1 To those who fear Jehovah's name
How sweet the word the prophet brings:
The Sun of Righteousness shall rise
With healing in His wings.

2 It is to those that fear His name
His healing power the Savior brings;
Oh, let us hide with contrite hearts
Beneath His healing wings.

3 He is the Sun of Righteousness;
And while to sin our being clings
We cannot know His healing touch
Or rest beneath His wings.

4 It is His wings that heal our pains
And soothe the serpent's poisoned stings;
Close to His bosom we must press
To feel His healing wings.

5 Beneath those healing wings I rest,
While all my heart with rapture sings:
The Sun of Righteousness has risen
With healing in His wings.

8.8.8.8.D.

1 He healeth me, oh, bless His name!
I want to spread abroad His fame;
From dread disease He sets me free,
The Lord my healer, strong is He!

He healeth me, He healeth me!
By power divine He healeth me;
He healed the sick in Galilee,
And now by faith He healeth me!

2 He healeth me! my simple faith
Believes the word that Jesus saith,
And takes the place of ardent hope,
Believes the Lord will raise me up.

3 He healeth me! I touch for cure
The border of His garment pure,
And virtue through my being flows,
A healing balm for nature's woes.

4 He healeth me, as when of yore,
Their sins and sicknesses He bore;
Nor has He lost His power and skill —
Our blessed Christ is living still.

5 He healeth me! how oft I sought
This healing power, but found it not:
But now I trust with all my soul,
And now through faith He makes me whole.

756

8.8.8.8.D. with chorus.

1 When Christ of old with healing pow'r
Went forth through all the suffering land,
His word so oft was wont to be,
"Stretch forth thy hand, stretch forth thy hand!"
And though the palsied arm might shrink
And tremble at the strange command,
The healing touch was only felt
While stretching forth the withered hand.

O suffering one, stretch forth your hand,
Upon His promise take your stand.
At His command stretch forth your hand,
And Christ shall make you whole.

2 That changeless Christ is still as near
And just as kind and strong to save;
He came to lift our fallen race
From sin and sickness and the grave.
As in the days of Galilee,
Disease still flees at His command;
But ere His touch your frame can feel,
You, too, must still stretch forth your hand.

3 What though you feel so weak and faint?
He can your will with strength endue,
New faith and courage breathe within
And work in you to will and do.
Reach out to meet His quickening touch;
Take up your bed, arise and stand;
And pressing through to meet your Lord,
Stretch forth your hand, stretch forth your hand.

8.8.8.8.   **757**

1 At even when the sun was set,
   The sick, O Lord, around Thee lay;
   O in what divers pains they met!
   O with what joy they went away!

2 Once more 'tis eventide, and we
   Oppressed with various ills draw near;
   What if Thy form we cannot see?
   We know and feel that Thou art here.

3 O Savior Christ, our woes dispel;
   For some are sick, and some are sad,
   And some have never loved Thee well
   And some have lost the love they had;

4* And some have found the world is vain,
   Yet from the world they break not free;
   And some have friends who give them pain,
   Yet have not sought a friend in Thee;

5* And none, O Lord, have perfect rest,
   For none are wholly free from sin;
   And they who fain would serve Thee best
   Are conscious most of wrong within.

6 O Savior Christ, Thou too art Man;
   Thou hast been troubled, tempted, tried;
   Thy kind but searching glance can scan
   The very wounds that shame would hide.

7 Thy touch has still its ancient power;
   No word from Thee can fruitless fall;
   Hear in this solemn evening hour,
   And in Thy mercy heal us all.

*Vv. 4 and 5 may be omitted if hymn is sung for physical healing.

758

8.7.8.7.D. with chorus.

1 Have you found the great Physician,
   Jesus Christ of Galilee?
He who bore our pain and sorrow,
   On the shameful, cruel tree?
Still He heals the sick and suff'ring,
   As before He went away;
For His word most plainly tells us,
   "He is just the same today."

He is just the same today;
As before He went away.
Look to Him, believe and pray;
Trust His word and then obey.
"Praise God, He is just the same today."

2 Consecrate your life to Jesus,
   Spirit, soul, and body too;
For "the Lord is for the body,"
   Every pow'r He gave to you.
Let there be no reservation,
   Give the Lord full right of way;
He will come and heal His temple,
   For He is the same today.

3 Do you doubt God's will to heal you?
   Take His word and ask for light;
If you seek in deep contrition,
   He will guide your heart aright.
Do not fear to claim His promise,
   He will not your trust betray;
When on earth He gladly healed them,
   And He is the same today.

4 *Oh! I'm glad to tell you, suff'rer,*
   Christ has more than healing too;
Life abundant overflowing,
   He will gladly give to you.

DIVINE HEALING — CHRIST THE SAME AS OF OLD

Step out boldly, claim His fulness,
　Let your sadness flee away;
When on earth He made them joyful,
　And He is the same today.

DIVINE HEALING — BY A TOUCH

8.8.8.7. with chorus.

759

1　Just one touch as He moves along,
　Pushed and pressed by the jostling throng,
　Just one touch and the weak was strong,
　　Cured by the Healer divine.

　　Just one touch as He passes by,
　　He will list to the faintest cry.
　　Come and be cured while the Lord is nigh,
　　　Christ is the Healer divine.

2　Just one touch! and He makes me whole,
　Speaks sweet peace to my sin-sick soul,
　At His feet all my burdens roll,
　　Cured by the Healer divine.

3　Just one touch! and the work is done,
　I am cured by the blessed Son,
　I will sing while the ages run,
　　Cured by the Healer divine.

4　Just one touch! and He turns to me,
　O the love in His eyes I see!
　I am His for He hears my plea,
　　Cured by the Healer divine.

5　Just one touch! by His mighty power
　He can heal thee this very hour,
　Thou canst hear though the tempests low'r,
　　Cured by the Healer divine.

DIVINE HEALING — BY A TOUCH

760

10.6.10.6. with chorus.

1 She only touched the hem of His garment
    As to His side she stole,
  Amid the crowd that gathered around Him;
    And straightway she was whole.

  Oh, touch the hem of His garment,
    And thou, too, shalt be free!
  His healing pow'r this very hour
    Shall give new life to thee!

2 She came in fear and trembling before Him,
    She knew her Lord had come,
  She felt that from Him virtue had healed her,
    The mighty deed was done.

3 He turned with "Daughter, be of good comfort,
    Thy faith hath made thee whole";
  And peace that passeth all understanding
    With gladness filled her soul.

PRAYER — THE MEANING

761

8.6.8.6.

1 Prayer is the soul's sincere desire,
    Uttered, or unexpressed;
  The motion of a hidden fire
    That trembles in the breast.

2 Prayer is the burden of a sigh,
    The falling of a tear;
  The upward glancing of an eye
    When none but God is near.

3 Prayer is the simplest form of speech
    That infant lips can try;
  Prayer the sublimest strains that reach
    The Majesty on high.

4   Prayer is the Christian's vital breath,
     The Christian's native air;
     His watchword at the gates of death;
     He enters rest with prayer.

5   The saints in prayer appear as one,
     In word, and deed, and mind;
     While with the Father and the Son
     Sweet fellowship they find.

6   O Thou, by whom we come to God,
     The Life, the Truth, the Way,
     The path of prayer Thyself hast trod —
     Lord, teach us how to pray.

10.10.10.10.   **762**

Prayer is the incense of a holy heart
Rising to God from bruised and broken things,
When kindled by the Spirit's burning breath
And upward borne by faith's ascending wings.

Prayer is the perfume of the plants of grace,
The flowers of patience, faith, and suffering love;
Treasured in "vials full of odors sweet,"
God breathes their fragrance in His courts above.

Prayer is th' ascending vapor which supplies
The showers of blessing, and the stream that flows
Through earth's dry places, till on every side
"The wilderness shall blossom as the rose."

Prayer is the heavenly telephone that brings
The distant near, till heaven to earth comes down,
And in our Father's ear and heart we may
Our burdens tell and all our sorrows drown.

Prayer is the wireless telegraph that sends
Its heart throbs on the ether waves of heaven;
It finds the heart of God, and back to earth
The answering thrill to faith and love are given.

continued

6 Prayer is the golden pipes the Spirit fills,
Which feed the lamps of God with oil divine,
And, as with one accord we wait and pray,
The Spirit fills, the lamps with brightness shine.

7 Prayer is the mightiest force of earth and heaven,
Prayer is the very dynamite of God;
It moves the hand that all things moves, and turns
The living wheels that sweep through earth abroad.

8 Teach us to pray! Move on our hearts, O Lord,
Till Thine own passion all our being move!
Teach us! Pray in us, till our prayer shall be
Christ in us praying to the Christ above!

9 Teach us to pray! Reveal Thy will to us,
Till Thine own purpose all our being move!
Teach us! Pray in us, till our prayer shall be
God in us answering to the God above!

763   8.6.8.6.

1 Christ is the Alpha of our prayers;
We know not how to pray
Save as His Spirit in our hearts
Shall teach us what to say.

2 Christ is the Omega of prayer,
The Father's great Amen
That rounds our halting periods
To sense beyond our ken.

3 But in the little space between
He lets us make the links,
And with our slow and stammering speech
Interpret what He thinks.

4 O First and Last, take Thou the prayers
Of every trusting soul,
And weld them to Thine own desire
To make a perfect whole.

5 Thou great Beginning of that Word
   We cannot speak or spell,
Of the short syllable we lisp
   Be Thou the End as well!

10.10.10.10.   **764***

1 Lord, in Thy presence silent I would be,
   That in the inmost I to Thee may come;
   I would not in my own way pray to Thee,
   But let Thy prayer in me my prayer become.

2 It seems Thou art in heaven hearing me,
   But right within my spirit Thou dost dwell;
   It seems that I am praying unto Thee,
   But really from Thyself the prayers do well.

3 When, Lord, no words my burden can express,
   My spirit with Thy Spirit deeply groans;
   Not verbally I then my plea address,
   But Thou dost pray within with words unknown.

4 I would inhale Thee, Lord, e'en as I breathe,
   And eat and drink Thee as my life supply.
   A deeper fellowship with Thee bequeath
   That Thou express Thyself through me thereby.

5 Here in this fellowship Thy light doth shine,
   Thy precious blood doth cleanse and make me clean;
   May I not only, Lord, Thy light enshrine,
   But may Thou be expressed and clearly seen.

6 Thy oil anoints me here in every way,
   Anointing Thee within unceasingly;
   I more decrease, Thou more increase each day,
   Thus full expression Thou shalt have through me.

7 Myself I open that Thou may flow in;
   Op'ning myself to others, Lord, flow out;
   By such a stream, the fellowship within,
   Thou, Lord, expressed will be my life throughout.

765

7.7.7.3.

1 Christian, seek not yet repose,
   Hear thy gracious Savior say;
   Thou art in the midst of foes:
     Watch and pray.

2 Principalities and powers,
   Mustering their unseen array,
   Wait for thy unguarded hours:
     Watch and pray.

3 Gird thy heavenly armor on,
   Wear it ever night and day;
   Ambushed lies the evil one:
     Watch and pray.

4 Hear the victors who o'ercame,
   Still they mark each warrior's way;
   All with one sweet voice exclaim,
     Watch and pray.

5 Hear, above all, hear thy Lord,
   Him thou lovest to obey;
   Hide within thy heart His word:
     Watch and pray.

6 Watch, as if on that alone
   Hung the issue of the day;
   Pray, that help may be sent down:
     Watch and pray.

PRAYER — THE TEACHING

766

9.9.9.9. with chorus.

1 Teach me to pray, Lord, teach me to pray;
   This is my heart-cry day unto day;
   I long to know Thy will and Thy way;
   Teach me to pray, Lord, teach me to pray.

PRAYER — THE TEACHING

Chorus:

Living in Thee, Lord, and Thou in me,
Constant abiding, this is my plea;
Grant me Thy power, boundless and free,
Power with men and power with Thee.

2 Power in prayer, Lord, power in prayer!
Here 'mid earth's sin and sorrow and care,
Men lost and dying, souls in despair;
O give me power, power in prayer!

3 My weakened will, Lord, Thou canst renew;
My sinful nature Thou canst subdue;
Fill me just now with power anew;
Power to pray and power to do!

4 Teach me to pray, Lord, teach me to pray;
Thou art my pattern day unto day;
Thou art my surety, now and for aye;
Teach me to pray, Lord, teach me to pray.

767 †

8.6.8.6.

1 Teach us to pray that we may cause
The enemy to flee,
That we his evil pow'r may bind,
His prisoners to free.

2 Teach us to pray and firmly stand
Upon the battleground,
To fight and break the stronghold down,
The enemy confound.

3 Teach us to pray and use Thy rod
In strong, prevailing prayer,
Beneath Thy blood to shake the earth
And powers of the air.

4 By prayer and faith, O may we learn
To labor, Lord, with Thee,
To know the victory is ours
And Thine authority.

PRAYER — THE TEACHING

768

6.6.6.6.

1 Lord, teach us to use
The intercessor's rod,
As Moses did of old
Upon the hill of God.

2 Before the upstayed arm
The ranks of darkness quailed!
In great Jehovah's Name
The hosts of light prevailed!

3 Teach us to bind the foe
With iron chains of prayer,
That all Thy Church may move
To victory everywhere.

4 Give us the steady arm,
Until the sun go down,
That we in Christ may win
The overcomer's crown.

PRAYER — IN THE HOLIEST

769*

7.7.7.7.

1 To the holiest place I'd come,
There within the veil to be;
There to touch the throne of grace,
Let life's water flow thru me.

2 Now the holiest place of all
Right within my spirit is;
Here the Lord in me abides,
And my spirit joins with His.

3 To my spirit I'd return,
For 'tis here the Lord I'll meet;
O how marvellous it is!
He's within, in me complete.

4 Fragrance of the risen Christ
   Thru my spirit may be spread;
   If in spirit I will pray
   Christ will be exhibited.

5 If in spirit Him I touch,
   With His riches filled I'll be;
   Life and light and love and grace
   As a stream will flow thru me.

6 Touching deeply, richly I
   Of Himself experience,
   Thus the law of life I touch
   And His clear anointing sense.

7 In my spirit deeper still
   I would touch the Lord I love,
   Touch Him in His hidden depth
   And His hidden manna prove.

8 When the resurrection life
   Is made real in pow'r to me,
   As the rod with sprouting buds,
   I will then accepted be.

9 Here I find the throne of grace,
   Where the living water flows
   As a river full of grace
   Into me grace to bestow.

10 Then whene'er we meet to pray,
    All our spirits we'll release;
    Mingled will our spirits be,
    And we'll serve the Lord as priests.

11 This the holiest place is too,
    Where we all may touch the Lord,
    Touch His throne in many ways
    Till His grace on us is poured.

770*

Peculiar Meter.

1 In the holiest place, touch the throne of grace,
    Grace as a river shall flow;
  In the holiest place, touch the throne of grace,
    Grace as a river shall flow.

    Hallelujah! Hallelujah!
  Grace as a river shall flow;
    Hallelujah! Hallelujah!
  Grace as a river shall flow.

2 In the holiest place, live before His face,
    Light of glory thru me will shine;
  In the holiest place, live before His face,
    Light of glory thru me will shine.

    Hallelujah! Hallelujah!
  Light of glory thru me will shine;
    Hallelujah! Hallelujah!
  Light of glory thru me will shine.

3 To the spirit turn, and the incense burn,
    Touch the living fountain of life;
  To the spirit turn, and the incense burn,
    Touch the living fountain of life.

    Hallelujah! Hallelujah!
  Touch the living fountain of life;
    Hallelujah! Hallelujah!
  Touch the living fountain of life.

PRAYER — IN THE HOLIEST

8.6.8.6.

1 The veil is rent and opened is
　　A new and living way;
　With boldness thru the precious blood,
　　We come to Thee to pray.

2 By Thy redemption we may come
　　Into the holiest place;
　Thy Spirit now anointing us,
　　We touch the throne of grace.

3 In spirit only we would pray,
　　Ourselves by Thee possessed,
　That from our spirit Christ the Lord
　　As incense be expressed.

4 Thy grace and mercy as a stream
　　From out the throne does flow,
　Refreshing in the hour of need —
　　How rich, how sweet to know!

5 Though for our needs we do not ask
　　But by Thy Spirit pray,
　Our every need is known to Thee,
　　We're in Thy care alway.

6 Though griefs and trials on us press,
　　We will not anxious be,
　But all our care upon Thee cast
　　And set our spirit free.

7 O may I concentrated be
　　In fellowship with Thee,
　My prayer and incense offering,
　　Thy Spirit leading me.

772*

7.7.7.7.D.

1 Lord, we meet to seek Thy face
  And in one accord to pray;
  We a holy priesthood are,
  Waiting on Thee here today.

  Here together we would pray,
  Touch the highest and the best,
  Till our spirits mingled are
  And Thy Church is built and blest.

2 As true priests we long to be,
  With our spirit sense Thy will,
  Thus to serve before Thee here
  That Thy plan Thou may fulfill.

3 To the holiest place we come,
  Now to touch Thy throne of grace,
  By the inner sense to pray
  And Thy Spirit's flow to trace.

4 From Thy throne of grace to me
  Rivers of Thy grace proceed;
  Thus my spirit is refreshed,
  Helping me in time of need.

5 May our prayers expression give
  To Thy Spirit's mind alone;
  Praying not by our desire,
  But according to Thine own.

6 Though with temporal matters pressed,
  Which we fain would bring to Thee,
  Rather than Thy care to seek,
  We would here Thy channel be.

7 Here we seek Thy list'ning ear,
   May Thy living water flow;
   When Thy grace does satisfy,
   Only then Thy work we'll know.

8.8.8.8.   **773**

1 Lord Jesus Christ, we seek Thy face;
   Within the veil we bow the knee;
   Oh, let Thy glory fill the place,
   And bless us while we wait on Thee.

2 We thank Thee for the precious blood
   That purged our sins and brought us nigh;
   All cleansed and sanctified to God,
   Thy holy name to magnify.

3 Shut in with Thee far, far above
   The restless world that wars below;
   We seek to learn and prove Thy love,
   Thy wisdom and Thy grace to know.

4 The brow that once with thorns was bound,
   Thy hands, Thy side, we fain would see;
   Draw near, Lord Jesus, glory crowned,
   And bless us while we wait on Thee.

Used by permission of Pickering & Inglis, Ltd.

PRAYER — AROUND THE MERCY SEAT

774

8.8.8.8.

1 From every stormy wind that blows,
From every swelling tide of woes,
There is a calm, a sure retreat —
'Tis found beneath the mercy seat.

2 There is a place where Jesus sheds
The oil of gladness on our heads,
A place than all besides more sweet —
It is the blood-bought mercy seat.

3 There is a scene where spirits blend,
Where friend holds fellowship with friend;
Though sundered far, by faith they meet
Around one common mercy seat.

4 There, there on eagle's wings we soar,
And time and sense seem all no more,
And heaven comes down our souls to greet,
And glory crowns the mercy seat.

PRAYER — IN THE LORD'S NAME

775

8.7.8.7. with chorus.

1 In the mighty Name of Jesus,
When we bow before the throne,
Many deadly foes are vanquished,
Many victories are won.

Mighty Name! Mighty Name!
In that Name alone we win.
Mighty Name! Mighty Name!
Conquering Satan, death and sin.

2   When we plead the Name of Jesus,
    Satan and his hosts must flee.
    Jesus! Jesus! Precious Jesus!
    In Thy Name is victory.

3   Soon shall come the blessed moment
    When the battle shall be won,
    When the Mighty Name of Jesus
    Shall exalt us to the throne.

PRAYER — IN FAITH

8.7.8.7.

776

1   "Ask in faith," the Name of Jesus
    All your plea before the throne;
    As you trust, the Lord will whisper,
    "See, my child, the work is done."

2   "Ask in faith," God waits to answer
    Each petition, Spirit-wrought;
    He will work in wondrous power,
    Far beyond your highest thought.

3   "Ask in faith," 'tis just the asking,
    In a faith that dares to stand,
    Full of joyful expectation,
    With an open, outstretched hand.

4   "Ask in faith," for God is waiting
    For thy faith-filled, earnest prayer.
    Faith delights Him; faith can touch Him,
    Every moment, everywhere.

777

6.6.6.6.8.8.

1   Say to this mountain, "Go,
Be cast into the sea!"
And doubt not in thine heart
That it shall be to thee.
It shall be done, doubt not His Word,
Command thy mountain in the Lord!

2   Claim thy redemption right,
Purchased by precious blood;
The Trinity unite
To make it true and good.
It shall be done, obey the Word,
Command thy mountain in the Lord!

3   Self, sickness, sorrow, sin,
The Lord did meet that day
On His beloved One,
And thou art "loosed away."
It shall be done, rest on His Word!
Command thy mountain in the Lord!

4   Compass the frowning wall
With silent prayer, then raise —
Before its ramparts fall —
The victor's shout of praise.
It shall be done, faith rests assured,
Command thy mountain in the Lord!

5   The two-leaved gates of brass,
The bars of iron yield,
To let the faithful pass,
Conquerors in every field.
It shall be done, the foe ignored,
Command thy mountain in the Lord!

6   Take then the faith of God,
       Free from the taint of doubt;
       The wonder-working rod
       That casts all reasoning out.
    It shall be done, stand on the Word.
    Command thy mountain in the Lord!

6.6.8.6.

778

1   Keep up the song of faith,
       However dark the night;
    And as you praise, the Lord will work
       To change your faith to sight.

2   Keep up the song of faith,
       And let your heart be strong,
    For God delights when faith can praise
       Though dark the night and long.

3   Keep up the song of faith,
       The foe will hear and flee;
    Oh, let not Satan hush your song,
       For praise is victory.

4   Keep up the song of faith,
       The dawn will break ere long,
    And we shall go to meet the Lord,
       And join the endless song.

(Repeat the last line of each stanza)

PRAYER — WITH ONE ACCORD

779*

8.7.8.7.D.

1 Pray with one accord in spirit,
  Not according to our thought,
But alone by the anointing,
  As the Lord has ever sought.

  Pray with one accord in spirit,
    Not according to our thought,
  But alone by the anointing,
    As the Lord has ever sought.

2 Pray with one accord in spirit,
  By the cross deny the soul;
All desires and all intentions
  Let the Spirit now control.

3 Pray with one accord in spirit,
  Pray as in the heavenlies;
All the earthly interests treading,
  Fight the principalities.

4 Pray with one accord in spirit,
  Supplicate relatedly;
Seek the Lord, His mind, His leading,
  In the Spirit's harmony.

5 Pray with one accord in spirit,
  Pray and watch persistently;
For God's kingdom and His glory,
  Pray and watch in harmony.

6 Pray with one accord in spirit
  Seeking God in unity;
In the Spirit of the Body
  Ever pray in harmony.

780*

8.7.8.7.D.

1 Praying always in the spirit,
   Never in the flesh or mind!
If this secret we will practise,
   God's full presence we will find.

    Praying always in the spirit
      Is the secret we are told!
    In the spirit, God to contact,
      Is the secret we must hold!

2 Praying always in the spirit,
   Never by our human thought!
Fellowship with God the Spirit
   Only thus to us is brought.

3 Praying always in the spirit,
   Thus expressing God's desire;
Staying with the Lord in spirit,
   We'll be wholly set afire.

4 Praying always in the spirit,
   Even groaning from within,
Thus we utter God's intention
   By the Spirit's discipline.

5 Praying always in the spirit,
   In the holiest place divine;
It is only in the spirit
   God and we in oneness twine.

6 Praying always in the spirit,
   'Tis the only way of prayer;
All the fulness of the Godhead
   By this secret we may share.

PRAYER — EXERCISING THE SPIRIT

781*

6.5.6.5.D.

1 Exercise the spirit,
Pray in every way!
I have prayed too little,
Keen my spirit, nay.
Even when I prayed, my
Spirit seldom proved
Ever just to follow
As Thy Spirit moved.

2 Now I'd pray in spirit
As Thy Spirit groans;
Pray by the anointing,
Not as memory owns.
Not the mind applying,
But with spirit pray,
Praising or beseeching,
Spirit-led alway.

3 Not just by myself my
Spirit exercise,
But with others praying
I would do likewise;
Praying in the spirit,
As the spirit wants,
For 'tis in the inmost
Spirits have response.

4 When we serve together,
We thru prayer would move,
Fellowship in spirit,
Not in word to prove.
Never pray together,
Shouting, crying much,
Yet the fellowship in
Spirit never touch.

5 Exercise the spirit
Here and everywhere,
Few or many present,
Caring not who's there.
Not a place or person
Will influence me,
In all kinds of meetings
I'll my spirit free.

6 Thus my spirit lifted
Gives the Lord His way;
Thus, my spirit strengthened,
I'll be used each day.
In the spirit's flowing
Living water see;
Thus the saints are mingled,
Built the church will be.

7.7.7.7.

1 How mysterious, O Lord,
That Thy Spirit dwells in mine;
O how marvelous it is,
Into one, two spirits twine.

2 By the spirit I can walk,
Spiritual in spirit be;
By the spirit I can serve,
And in spirit worship Thee.

3 Thru Thy Word and by my prayer
In the spirit touching Thee,
Lifted high my spirit is,
Strengthened shall my spirit be.

4 Make my spirit strong I pray
Others' spirits to revive;
Lift my spirit high and free,
Others' spirits then may thrive.

5 Every time I speak, O Lord,
May my spirit actuate;
And whatever I may do,
Let my spirit motivate.

6 Every time my spirit acts
Others' spirits opened be,
Every time my spirit moves
Others' lifted unto Thee.

7 Lord, have mercy, from above
May Thy Spirit breathe on me;
Then my spirit will be rich,
Strengthened and refreshed by Thee.

783*

7.7.7.7.

1   Pray to touch the throne of God,
    Touch the throne of grace divine,
    Grace to find and mercy too
    Which will meet the need of thine.

2   Pray to touch the throne of God,
    Deeply sense thy need of grace;
    In the spirit stay with God,
    Fellowshipping face to face.

3   Pray to touch the throne of God,
    Learning all the wealth of grace;
    Ever take and ever taste,
    Giving God the thanks and praise.

4   Pray to touch the throne of God,
    Touch the throne of power too;
    In the name of Jesus Christ
    Deal with what you have to do.

5   Pray to touch the throne of God
    By the hand of living faith;
    Exercise authority
    Over all the pow'r of death.

6   Pray to touch the throne of God,
    Pray to shake the evil pow'r;
    Pray with kingship on the throne,
    Pray with Christ this very hour.

8.7.8.7.D.

1 Pray to fellowship with Jesus,
   In the spirit seek His face;
Ask and listen in His presence,
   Waiting in the secret place.

   Pray to fellowship with Jesus,
      In the spirit seek His face;
   Ask and listen in His presence,
      Waiting in the secret place.

2 Pray to fellowship with Jesus,
   Fully opened from within,
With thy face unveiled, beholding,
   Single, pure, and genuine.

3 Pray to fellowship with Jesus,
   Seeking Him in confidence;
Learn to touch Him as the Spirit,
   Looking up in reverence.

4 Pray to fellowship with Jesus,
   Speaking nothing in pretense;
Ask according to the spirit,
   Praying by the inner sense.

5 Pray to fellowship with Jesus,
   List'ning earnestly to Him;
Be impressed with His intentions,
   Yielding to Him from within.

6 Pray to fellowship with Jesus,
   Bathing in His countenance;
Saturated with His beauty,
   Radiate His excellence.

PRAYER — EXPRESSING THE LORD

785*

7.7.7.7.

1 Praying to express the Lord,
We must not ourselves express,
But let Christ reveal Himself,
His desire in us impress.

2 Praying to express the Lord,
We must utter His intent,
Quieting our human thoughts
That with His our mind be blent.

3 Praying to express the Lord,
Ever looking unto Him
As a mirror to reflect
All His glory from within.

4 Praying to express the Lord,
Letting Him beseech in us;
Christ indwelling prays within
To the Christ in heaven thus.

5 Praying to express the Lord,
Learning not to pray by self,
Praying wholly with the Lord,
Praying only by Himself.

PRAYER — LABORING WITH THE LORD

786*

7.7.7.7.

1 Pray to labor with the Lord,
Pray to pave the way for Him;
Pray to move Him and be moved
From the center to the rim.

2 Pray to labor with the Lord,
Be identified with Him
In His purpose and His aim
Till His blessing floodeth in.

PRAYER — LABORING WITH THE LORD

3   Pray to labor with the Lord;
      Self-ambition and self-will
      We must ever cast away,
      All His purpose to fulfill.

4   Pray to labor with the Lord;
      Let the Lord initiate
      All the plan and all the work;
      Then thru us He'll operate.

5   Pray to labor with the Lord
      Till the wheel begins to move;
      Pray together with the Lord
      Till the Church His pow'r shall prove.

PRAYER — TELLING THE LORD

787

10.9.10.9. with chorus.

1   I must tell Jesus all of my trials;
      I cannot bear these burdens alone;
      In my distress He kindly will help me;
      He ever loves and cares for His own.

      I must tell Jesus! I must tell Jesus!
      I cannot bear my burdens alone;
      I must tell Jesus! I must tell Jesus!
      Jesus can help me, Jesus alone.

2   I must tell Jesus all of my troubles;
      He is a kind, compassionate Friend;
      If I but ask Him, He will deliver,
      And in my griefs with me He will blend.

3   Tempted and tried I need a great Savior,
      One who can help my burdens to bear;
      I must tell Jesus, I must tell Jesus;
      He all my cares and sorrows will share.

continued

4   O how the world to evil allures me!
O how my heart is tempted to sin!
I must tell Jesus; He will enable
Over the world the vic'try to win.

788

8.7.8.7.D.

1   When thou wakest in the morning
     Ere thou tread'st the untried way
Of the lot that lies before thee
     Through the coming busy day;
Whether sunbeams promise brightness,
     Whether dim forebodings fall,
Be thy dawning glad or gloomy,
     Go to Jesus, tell Him all.

2   In the calm of sweet communion
     Let thy daily work be done;
In the peace of soul-outpouring
     Care be banished, patience won;
And if earth with its enchantments
     Seek thy spirit to enthrall,
Ere thou listen, ere thou answer,
     Turn to Jesus, tell Him all.

3   Then, as hour by hour glides by thee,
     Thou wilt blessed guidance know,
Thine own burdens being lightened,
     Thou canst bear another's woe;
Thou canst help the weak ones onward,
     Thou canst raise up those that fall:
But remember, while thou servest,
     Still tell Jesus, tell Him all.

4 And if weariness creeps o'er thee
      As the day wears to its close,
   Or if sudden fierce temptation
      Bring thee face to face with foes;
   In thy weakness, in thy peril,
      Raise to heaven a truthful call;
   Strength and calm for every crisis
      Come, in telling Jesus all.

8.7.8.7.D.   **789**

1 What a Friend we have in Jesus,
      All our sins and griefs to bear!
   What a privilege to carry
      Everything to God in prayer!
   O what peace we often forfeit,
      O what needless pain we bear,
   All because we do not carry
      Everything to God in prayer!

2 Have we trials and temptations?
      Is there trouble anywhere?
   We should never be discouraged,
      Take it to the Lord in prayer.
   Can we find a friend so faithful
      Who will all our sorrows share?
   Jesus knows our every weakness,
      Take it to the Lord in prayer.

3 Are we weak and heavy-laden,
      Cumbered with a load of care?
   Precious Savior, still our refuge —
      Take it to the Lord in prayer;
   Do thy friends despise, forsake thee?
      Take it to the Lord in prayer;
   In His arms He'll take and shield thee,
      Thou wilt find a solace there.

790

6.5.6.5.D.

1 "Keep the incense burning"
      On the altar fire;
Let thy heart's petition,
      Let thy deep desire,
Be a cloud of incense
      Wreathing God's own throne,
Till His will among us
      Shall be fully done.

2 "Keep the incense burning"
      On the altar fire;
Feed the flame, Lord Jesus,
      Till Thy whole desire
Shall in us, Thy children,
      Find free course, and be
Breathed through lips anointed
      For this ministry.

3 "Keep the incense burning"
      Though thy faith be weak;
Though in words thou canst not
      All thy longing speak;
Silent heart-petitions,
      Spirit-taught, will be
Gloriously answered;
      Wrought by God for thee.

4 "Keep the incense burning,"
      Hourly let it rise,
Till from opened heavens,
      Till from flame-swept skies,
Fire shall fall and kindle
      All hearts to a flame;
Making us a glory
      To our Savior's name.

PRAYER — BURNING THE INCENSE

8.8.8.6. with chorus.

791*

1 The priest's position holy is;
He sacrifices e'er to God,
Beholds His beauty, incense burns
    Of prayer before the Lord.

    Let us the incense burn
    Of prayer before the Lord;
    The lamp we'd light, through day and night
    Our praise to Him outpoured.

2 No natural light, but just the lamp
Within the holy place gives sight;
Whene'er the priest the incense burns,
    The lamp he too must light.

3 The grace of God let us extol
And stir our heart sweet praise to sing;
For priests not only light the lamp,
    But constant praises bring.

4 I'll offer prayers as incense burns,
Christ's resurrection bring therein,
God's wish thus meet, His heart give joy,
    And I'll rejoice with Him.

5 I'll read His Word, His light receive,
E'en as the lamp before Him lit,
His holy light illum'ning me
    To others I'll transmit.

6 Unto the Lord His praise I'll sing
As holy priests their songs did raise;
O may my heart be filled with Him
    His love and grace to praise.

7 I'll offer Christ to God in prayer,
I'll read the Word, His light to know,
For all His grace I'll sing His praise,
    The Spirit then may flow.

792*

Peculiar Meter.

1 Waiting on Thee, Lord, waiting on Thee;
   Let me now rest in Thee;
   Make Thy will clear to me,
   This is my earnest plea —
Waiting on Thee, waiting on Thee.

2 Waiting on Thee, Lord, waiting on Thee;
   While here with Thee I stay,
   Show me Thy glorious way,
   Ever by Thee to pray —
Waiting on Thee, waiting on Thee.

3 Waiting on Thee, Lord, waiting on Thee;
   Mingle Thyself with me,
   Till truly one with Thee
   Thine image I will be —
Waiting on Thee, waiting on Thee.

4 Waiting on Thee, Lord, waiting on Thee;
   Make me Thy will to know,
   Help me Thy way to go,
   That life thru me may flow —
Waiting on Thee, waiting on Thee.

5 Waiting on Thee, Lord, waiting on Thee;
   Make all my prayer to Thee
   Thyself expressed thru me,
   Give me Thy secret key —
Waiting on Thee, waiting on Thee.

10.10.10.10.

1 My soul, be silent, wait upon the Lord!
First let Him speak to thee, then speak to Him;
True prayer in thee the Lord initiates,
Thou but a channel art expressing Him.

2 My soul, be silent, wait upon the Lord!
Learn to deny thy thought and all thy will.
Learn to let God anoint thee with Himself
And thru thy prayer His purposes fulfill.

3 My soul, be silent, wait upon the Lord!
Silent to all thy wishes and thy plans,
Silent to all thy earthly cares and calls,
That God may work in thee all His demands.

4 My soul, be silent, wait upon the Lord!
Yield to the spirit all thy heart and mind;
Here let the spirit show what God reveals,
Thee its obedient servant thus to find.

5 My soul, be silent, wait upon the Lord!
Learn thus to let the Spirit pray thru thee;
All of thy being with the Spirit move,
Thy prayer will thus God's own expression be.

6 My soul, be silent, wait upon the Lord!
Till in the spirit thou with God art one,
Till thru the spirit God possesses all
And thus transforms each part unto His Son.

7 My soul, be silent, wait upon the Lord!
Till God may freely, fully flow thru thee,
Till all thy words and actions hour by hour
Are the fulfillment of God's will thru thee.

PRAYER — FOR THE WHOLE WORLD

794   10.10.10.10.10.10.

1 Stir me, oh, stir me, Lord, I care not how,
But stir my heart in passion for the world,
Stir me to give, to go, but most to pray;
Stir till the blood-red banner be unfurled
O'er lands that still in heathen darkness lie,
O'er deserts where no cross is lifted high.

2 Stir me, oh, stir me, Lord, till all my heart
Is filled with strong compassion for these souls;
Till Thy compelling word drives me to pray;
Till Thy constraining love reach to the poles
Far north and south, in burning deep desire,
Till east and west are caught in love's great fire.

3 Stir me, oh, stir me, Lord, till prayer is pain,
Till prayer is joy, till prayer turns into praise;
Stir me, till heart and will and mind, yea, all
Is wholly Thine to use through all the days.
Stir, till I learn to pray exceedingly;
Stir, till I learn to wait expectantly.

4 Stir me, oh, stir me, Lord, Thy heart was stirred
By love's intensest fire, till Thou didst give
Thine only Son, Thy best beloved One,
E'en to the dreadful cross, that I might live.
Stir me to give myself so back to Thee,
That Thou canst give Thyself again through me.

5 Stir me, oh, stir me, Lord, for I can see
Thy glorious triumph-day begin to break;
The dawn already gilds the eastern sky;
Oh, *Church of Christ*, arise, awake, awake.
Oh! stir us, Lord, as heralds of that day.
For night is past, our King is on His way.

7.7.7.7.

1 Father, let Thy kingdom come,
Let it come with living power;
Speak at length the final word,
Usher in the triumph hour.

2 As it came in days of old,
In the deepest hearts of men,
When Thy martyrs died for Thee,
Let it come, O God, again.

3 Tyrant thrones and idol shrines,
Let them from their place be hurled;
Enter on Thy better reign,
Wear the crown of this poor world.

4 Oh, what long, sad years have gone,
Since Thy Church was taught this prayer;
Oh, what eyes have watched and wept
For the dawning everywhere.

5 Break, triumphant day of God!
Break at last our hearts to cheer;
Throbbing souls and holy songs
Wait to hail Thy dawning here.

6 Empires, temples, scepters, thrones,
May they all for God be won;
And, in every human heart,
Father, let Thy kingdom come.

796

7.7.7.7.

1 Christ, from whom all blessings flow,
   Perfecting the saints below,
   Hear us, who Thy nature share,
   Who Thy mystic body are.

2 Join us, in one spirit join,
   Let us still receive of Thine;
   Still for more on Thee we call,
   Thou who fillest all in all.

3 Move, and actuate, and guide:
   Divers gifts to each divide;
   Placed according to Thy will,
   Let us all our work fulfil.

4 Sweetly may we all agree,
   Touched with loving sympathy;
   Kindly for each other care,
   Every member feel its share.

5 Love, like death, hath all destroyed,
   Rendered all distinctions void;
   Names, and sects, and parties fall:
   Thou, O Christ, art all in all.

6.6.8.6.D.

1   Revive Thy work, O Lord!
Now to Thy saints appear!
Oh, speak with power to every soul,
And let Thy people hear!

Revive Thy work, O Lord!
While here to Thee we bow;
Descend, O gracious Lord, descend!
Oh, come, and bless us now!

2   Revive Thy work, O Lord!
And every soul inspire;
Oh, kindle in each heart, we pray,
The Pentecostal fire!

3   Revive Thy work, O Lord!
Exalt Thy precious name!
And may Thy love in every heart
Be kindled to a flame!

4   Revive Thy work, O Lord!
And bless to all Thy Word!
And may its pure and sacred truth
In living faith be heard!

5   Revive Thy work, O Lord!
And make Thy servants bold;
Convict of sin and work once more
As in the days of old.

6   Revive Thy work, O Lord!
Give Pentecostal showers!
Be Thine the glory, Thine alone!
The blessing, Lord, be ours!

798

6.6.8.6.D.

1   Revive Thy work, dear Lord!
    Thy mighty arm make bare;
Move in the hearts and wake the souls,
    And make Thy presence dear.

        Revive Thy work, dear Lord!
        And manifest Thy power;
    O come upon Thy church as in
        The Pentecostal hour.

2   Revive Thy work, dear Lord!
    Disturb this sleep of death;
Quicken the smouldering embers now
    By Thine almighty breath.

3   Revive Thy work, dear Lord!
    Create soul-thirst for Thee;
And hungering for the Bread of Life,
    O may our spirits be!

4   Revive Thy work, dear Lord!
    And give abounding joy;
O fill our hearts with perfect love,
    And burn out all alloy!

5   Revive Thy work, dear Lord!
    Repeat Thy deeds of grace;
Thy mighty name be magnified,
    To Thee be all the praise.

10.10.10.10.

1 All Scripture is the very breath of God,
And by His Spirit into words was breathed;
By godly men the words were written down,
With all God's fulness unto man bequeathed.

2 It is the breath of God as light to man,
With rays divine man to illuminate;
It shines in darkness and to man reveals
What is his truest need and actual state.

3 It is the breath of God as life to man,
Nature divine to man it doth impart;
The dead it quickens and regenerates,
Transforms the soul-life and renews the heart.

4 It is the breath of God as wisdom too,
Knowledge divine to man it has to teach;
Th' eternal purpose of the Lord it shows,
And leadeth man God's final goal to reach.

5 It is the breath of God as strength to man,
Power divine to man it doth transmit,
Strength'ning the weak, empowering the faint,
Enabling man God's purpose full to fit.

6 It is the breath of God for us to breathe,
That as our portion God we may enjoy;
Receiving it by spirits exercised,
Our need is met, His wealth we may employ.

800*

11.11.11.11.(T)

1 God the Lord has spoken, God has been unveiled;
   All His character and persons are expressed;
   Unto Adam's sons His mystery is revealed,
   Fully illustrated and made manifest.

2 God the Lord has spoken, and His heart disclosed,
   That His Son should have pre-eminence in all,
   That in His dear Son He might be glorified
   Midst all His creation, either great or small.

3 God the Lord has spoken, Christ has been revealed:
   He is very God and yet is truly man;
   He is all in all, in Him all things subsist,
   Center and circumference of th' eternal plan.

4 God the Lord has spoken, and His mystery shown,
   Christ and His expression has His counsel willed:
   Christ with all God's fulness as the glorious Head,
   And the Church His Body, with His riches filled.

5 God the Lord has spoken, and from heaven shown
   That the triune God would blend with creature-man:
   Father in the Son, the Son the Spirit is,
   Dwelling in the Body to fulfill His plan.

6 God the Lord has spoken, revelation giv'n
   Of His vast creation and His lowly birth,
   Of His great redemption and salvation full;
   May His adoration ever fill the earth.

10.10.10.10.

1 O living Word of God, God's image true,
   Thou art the content of God's written word;
   God in Thee we have met, God's fulness found,
   And in the Scripture we Thyself have heard.

2 No man has e'er seen God, apart from Thee,
   Without the Scripture Thee we'd hardly see;
   Thou to the human race God hast declared,
   And thru the Scripture Thou art shown to me.

3 Perfect embodiment Thou art of God,
   A portrait full the Scripture gives of Thee;
   In Thee we comprehend God's image true,
   And thru the Scripture Thou art real to me.

4 Life-giving Spirit Thou, as well as Word,
   Now e'en the Spirit in the Word Thou art;
   When thru the Spirit giv'n, I touch the Word,
   Fulness divine to me Thou dost impart.

5 In Thee I may with God have fellowship,
   And thru the Scripture I on Thee may feed;
   Thru study of the Word with prayer to God
   Thy glorious riches fully meet my need.

6 Teach me to exercise my spirit, Lord,
   Thy Word to study, so to contact Thee,
   That Thou, the living Word, with Scripture, too,
   As one my daily manna e'er may be.

802*

8.8.8.8.

1 Thou art the Word and Spirit, Lord;
    Now in one spirit worship we;
    'Tis by the Word we understand,
    And in the Spirit contact Thee.

2 Since Thou with me hast joined in one,
    Thou art my all, O Lord, thereby;
    And as the Spirit and the Word
    Thou cam'st to me as my supply.

3 If Thou art Lord, yet not the Word,
    How couldest Thou be known to me?
    If Thou art God yet Spirit not,
    How could I ever contact Thee?

4 The Word reveals Thyself to me
    And knowledge of Thyself imparts;
    The Spirit is Thy substance true
    Whereby I touch Thee as Thou art.

5 Thou art my life, my light, my way,
    My food, my strength and guaranty;
    By Word made known, as Spirit these
    Become experience to me.

6 Thy Word in Scripture is expressed,
    Thy Spirit, the Indwelling One;
    Thy Word is spirit and is life
    When to my spirit it doth come.

7 If I Thy Word would understand,
    I must Thy Holy Spirit touch;
    Not only grasp it with my mind,
    But with my spirit, praying much.

8 Thy precious Word my heart doth love,
    My spirit fellowships with Thine;
    My heart rejoices in Thy Word,
    My spirit praises sings in Thine.

7.6.7.6.D.

1 O Word of God incarnate,
   O Wisdom from on high,
O Truth unchanged, unchanging,
   O Light of our dark sky,
We praise Thee for the radiance
   That from the hallowed page,
A lantern to our footsteps,
   Shines on from age to age.

2 The Church from her dear Master
   Received the gift divine,
And still that light she lifteth
   O'er all the earth to shine:
It is the golden treasure
   Where gems of truth are stored;
It is the heaven-drawn picture
   Of Christ, the living Word.

3 It floateth like a banner
   Before God's host unfurled;
It shineth like a beacon
   Above the darkling world;
It is the chart and compass
   That, o'er life's surging sea,
'Mid mists and rocks and quicksands
   Still guide, O Christ, to Thee.

4 O make Thy Church, dear Savior,
   A lampstand of pure gold,
To bear before the nations
   Thy light, that all behold;
O teach Thy wandering pilgrims
   By this their path to trace,
Till, clouds and darkness ended,
   They see Thee face to face.

804

8.6.8.6.D.

1 Thy Word is like a storehouse, Lord,
With full provision there,
And everyone who seeks may come,
Its glorious wealth to share.
Thy Word is like a deep, deep mine,
And jewels rich and rare
Are hidden in its mighty depths
For every searcher there.

2 Thy Word is like a starry host:
A thousand rays of light
Are seen to guide the traveler,
And make his pathway bright.
Thy Word is like an armory,
Where soldiers may repair,
And find, for life's long battle day,
All needful weapons there.

3 O may I love Thy precious Word,
May I explore the mine,
May I its glorious riches take,
May light upon me shine.
O may I find my armor there,
Thy Word my trusty sword;
I'll learn to fight with every foe
The battle of the Lord.

4 Word of the ever living God,
Will of His glorious Son;
Without Thee how could earth be trod,
Or God and Christ be won?
Lord, grant us all aright to learn
The wisdom it imparts,
And to its heav'nly teaching turn,
With simple, child-like hearts.

8.8.8.8.

805

1 Oh, how I love this blessed Book!
  The story of redeeming grace,
Love letter of my Bridegroom's heart
  And mirror of my Savior's face.

2 Oh, how I love this blessed Book!
  My checkbook on the bank above,
Deed of my heavenly heritage
  And dying will of Him I love.

3 Oh, how I love this blessed Book!
  Bright telescope through which I view
The wonders of the world to come
  And gaze on glories ever new.

4 Oh, how I love this blessed Book!
  My Guide Book all my earthly way,
The lamp that cheers my darkest night,
  The sunshine of my brightest day.

SEEKING FOR THE WORD

6.4.6.4.D.

806

1 Break Thou the Bread of Life,
    Dear Lord, to me,
  As Thou didst break the loaves
    Beside the sea;
  Beyond the sacred page
    I seek Thee, Lord;
  My spirit pants for Thee,
    O Living Word.

2 Thou art the Bread of Life,
    O Lord, to me,
  Thy holy Word the truth
    That saveth me;
  Give me to eat and live
    With Thee above;
  Teach me to love Thy truth,
    For Thou art Love. *continued*

735

3 Oh, send Thy Spirit, Lord,
   Now unto me,
That He may touch my eyes,
   And make me see;
Show me the truth concealed
   Within Thy Word,
And in Thy Book revealed
   I see the Lord.

4 Bless Thou the truth, dear Lord,
   To me, to me,
As Thou didst bless the bread
   By Galilee;
Then shall all bondage cease,
   All fetters fall,
And I shall find my peace,
   My All in all.

807
8.8.9.8. with chorus.

1 Open my eyes that I may see
Glimpses of truth Thou hast for me;
Place in my hands the wonderful key
That shall unclasp and set me free.

   Silently now I wait for Thee,
   Ready, my God, Thy will to see;
   Open my eyes, illumine me,
      Spirit Divine!

2 Open my ears that I may hear
Voices of truth Thou sendest clear;
And while the wave notes fall on my ear,
Everything false will disappear.

3 Open my mouth and let me bear
Tidings of mercy everywhere;
Open my heart and let me prepare
Love with Thy children thus to share.

4 Open my mind that I may read
  More of Thy love in word and deed;
What shall I fear while yet Thou dost lead?
Only for light from Thee I plead.

8.7.8.7.7.7.

808

1 Master, speak! Thy servant heareth,
  Waiting for Thy gracious word,
Longing for Thy voice that cheereth,
  Master, let it now be heard.
I am list'ning, Lord, for Thee;
What hast Thou to say to me?

2 Often through my heart is pealing
  Many another voice than Thine,
Many an unwilled echo stealing
  From the walls of this Thy shrine.
Let Thy longed-for accents fall;
Master, speak! and silence all.

3 Master, speak! though least and lowest,
  Let me not unheard depart;
Master, speak! for oh, Thou knowest
  All the yearning of my heart.
Knowest all its truest need;
Speak! and make me blest indeed.

4 Master, speak! and make me ready,
  When Thy voice is truly heard,
With obedience glad and steady,
  Still to follow every word,
I am listening, Lord, for Thee:
Master, speak, oh, speak to me!

continued

5 Speak to me by name, O Master,
    Let me know it is to me;
  Speak, that I may follow faster,
    With a step more firm and free,
  Where the Shepherd leads the flock,
  In the shadow of the Rock!

809   6.5.6.5.

1 Speak, Lord, in the stillness,
    While I wait on Thee;
  Hushed my heart to listen,
    In expectancy.

2 Speak, O blessed Master,
    In this quiet hour;
  Let me see Thy face, Lord,
    Feel Thy touch of power.

3 For the words Thou speakest,
    They are life indeed;
  Living bread from heaven,
    Now my spirit feed!

4 All to Thee is yielded,
    I am not my own;
  Blissful, glad surrender,
    I am Thine alone.

5 Speak, Thy servant heareth,
    Be not silent, Lord;
  Waits my soul upon Thee
    For the quickening word.

6 Fill me with the knowledge
    Of Thy glorious will;
  All Thine own good pleasure
    In Thy child fulfill.

7   Like a watered garden,
     Full of fragrance rare,
     Lingering in Thy presence,
     Let my life appear.

Used by permission of the South Africa General Mission.

8.8.8.8.   **810**

1   Lord, hast Thou not one word for me
     To bind my soul more close to Thee,
     That every evil I may flee;
     One word, O Lord! one word from Thee?

2   One word, to show how weak am I
     When in my strength alone I try,
     In vain I toil, in vain I sigh;
     One word, O Lord! one word from Thee.

3   One word, to show how near Thou art,
     For Thou dost dwell within my heart;
     And of Thy life I share a part;
     One word, O Lord! one word from Thee.

4   One word of power, oh, let me hear,
     Above the heart's most anxious fear,
     Thy still, small voice, yet deep and clear;
     One word, O Lord! one word from Thee.

5   One word of final triumph, Lord;
     Sweet hope Thy promises afford,
     To dwell with Thee in sweet accord;
     One word, O Lord! one word from Thee.

811*

10.10.10.10. with chorus.

1 My heart is hungry, my spirit doth thirst;
   I come to Thee, Lord, to seek Thy supply;
   All that I need is none other but Thee,
   Thou canst my hunger and thirst satisfy.

   Feed me, Lord Jesus, give me to drink,
   Fill all my hunger, quench all my thirst;
   Flood me with joy, be the strength of my life,
   Fill all my hunger, quench all my thirst.

2 Thou art the food and the water of life,
   Thou canst revive me, my spirit upbear;
   I long to eat and to drink here of Thee,
   Thyself enjoy through my reading and prayer.

3 Thou art the Word with God's fulness in Thee,
   Thou too the Spirit that God my life be;
   Thee in the Word I enjoy as my food,
   Thou as the Spirit art water to me.

4 Thou from the heavens as food camest down,
   Thou to be drink hast been smitten for me;
   Thou as the food, my exhaustless supply,
   Thou as the water, a stream unto me.

5 Thou in the Word art the Spirit and life,
   Thus by the Word I may feed upon Thee;
   Thou dost as Spirit in my spirit live,
   Thus I may drink in the spirit of Thee.

6 Now to enjoy Thee I come to Thy Word,
   On Thee to feed till my hunger is o'er.
   Now in my spirit I turn unto Thee,
   Of Thee to drink till I'm thirsty no more.

7   Feeding and drinking, Lord Jesus, of Thee,
     Feeding by reading, and drinking by prayer;
     Reading and praying, I eat and I drink,
     Praying and reading — Lord, Thou art my fare.

8   Here, O my Lord, may I feast upon Thee;
     Flood with Thy Spirit and fill by Thy Word;
     May, Lord, Thou be such a feast unto me
     As man hath never enjoyed nor e'er heard.

812*

6.6.8.6.

1   I come to Thee, dear Lord,
     My heart doth thirst for Thee;
  Of Thee I'd eat, of Thee I'd drink,
     Enjoy Thee thoroughly.

2   Just to behold Thy face,
     For this my heart doth cry;
  I deeply long to drink of Thee
     My thirst to satisfy.

3   Thy glorious, radiant face
     My heart delights to see;
  Here I'd abide and ne'er depart,
     Beholding constantly.

4   In such a fellowship
     Thou, Lord, art grace to me;
  My heart and spirit gladdened, filled,
     I enter rest in Thee.

5   Lord, I would linger here,
     Still seeking after Thee,
  Continue in the Word and prayer
     Till Thou dost flow thru me.

813*

8.8.8.8.

1 I come before Thy throne of grace
With hungry heart on Thee to feed,
Thy grace and mercy to receive
To help me in this hour of need.

2 Here I behold Thy radiant face,
Its light upon my heart doth shine
With healing rays consuming all
The weaknesses and faults of mine.

3 'Tis here Thy light illuminates
My true condition unto me;
'Tis here Thy blood's effectiveness
To cleanse from sin I gladly see.

4 Thy Spirit too anoints me here
And makes Thy very substance mine;
Thy very self I thus enjoy
And know Thy very heart's design.

5 Thy Word I read before Thee here
E'en as the priests the lamp did light;
Thy Spirit is as oil to me
To light Thy Word and give me sight.

6 E'en as the priests the incense burned,
In prayer to Thee I persevere;
As incense Thou the Spirit art
Mixed with the prayer I offer here.

7 Thy Word is light, Thy Word is food;
Which doth enlighten and supply;
I long to read and feed much more,
For light and food to satisfy.

8 Thou art the living water too
　Which full revival doth bestow;
　I wish to pray and drink e'en more
　That through me living rivers flow.

9 Thou art the incense unto God,
　In Thee acceptance is complete;
　I want to pray yet more and more,
　To offer up this fragrance sweet.

10 By reading I'm enlightened, filled,
　By prayer my thirst is quenched indeed;
　Thus Thou to me may be supplied,
　And Thou through me may meet the need.

11 I long to have such fellowship,
　To read and pray and blend with Thee;
　I long that Thou wouldst saturate
　Till Thou may overflow from me.

814*

8.8.8.8.

1 "Man shall not live by bread alone,
　But by each word which doth proceed
　From God's own mouth"; these we must eat
　And let them be our life indeed.

2 Not just a body we were made,
　But body, soul, and spirit too;
　The inmost part the spirit is
　To contact God and Him pursue.

continued

814*

3   Just as we need the earthly food
Our body's need to satisfy,
We need the food for spirit too —
Thyself, Thy Word, its true supply.

4   Thou art the Spirit, and Thy Word
Thy very Self expressed doth make;
Thus, it is Spirit as Thyself,
Which by our spirit we must take.

5   Thus, to receive Thy Word is not
To read it only with our eyes
And understand it in our mind,
But 'tis the spirit's exercise.

6   Thy Word in spirit we must eat
And to our inmost part receive;
'Tis by our spirit's exercise
To pray with what our minds perceive.

7   Thy Word remaining in our mind
Is only knowledge burdensome,
But when it to the spirit goes
Then life and spirit it becomes.

8   'Tis only when our spirit acts
To take Thy Word and contact Thee,
We truly feed upon Thy Word
And touch Thyself most inwardly.

9   Lord, teach us how to exercise
Our spirit when Thy Word we read;
Then will our spirit nourished be
As thus upon Thyself we feed.

8.8.8.8.

1 Christ is the Word and Spirit too,
   And as the Spirit in the Word;
   And all the words He speaks to us
   Are life and spirit thus conferred.

2 The Holy Word we have without,
   The Holy Spirit is within;
   The greatest gifts divine are these,
   That we may God enjoy therein.

3 The Word the Spirit doth express,
   The Spirit its reality;
   They're but two aspects of one thing
   And should not separated be.

4 Whene'er the Spirit lights the Word
   The Word becometh life to us;
   When Word from Spirit is divorced,
   'Tis empty mental stimulus.

5 When we the Word in spirit touch,
   As life the Spirit it becomes;
   The Spirit, when expressed from us,
   As words of life to others comes.

6 Our spirit we must exercise
   To take the Word most inwardly,
   And then to give the Spirit forth;
   The two as one with us should be.

7 Lord, may Thy Word in me become
   The Spirit as my life supply,
   And may Thy Spirit in Thy Word
   My true expression be thereby.

816*

8.7.8.7.D.

1 God's own Word must not be taken
　　Just as knowledge but as life,
Not alone God's thought conveying,
　　But Himself to us as life;
Not alone God's mind revealing,
　　But His Christ as life within,
Not alone the teaching giving,
　　But experience of Him.

2 It is only knowledge to us
　　If we in the letter read,
But when reading in the spirit
　　It is truly life indeed.
All the knowledge in the letter
　　Only brings us into death,
But the Word in spirit taken
　　Gives to us the quickening breath.

3 If we miss the Lord in Scripture,
　　It is just as knowledge vain;
But when Christ we touch within it,
　　Then His life we may obtain.
When we read, the Lord not touching,
　　'Tis but mental stimulus;
But when Christ we touch by reading,
　　It becometh life in us.

4 All the knowledge of the Scriptures
    Into life must be transformed,
All the mental understanding
    In the spirit must be formed;
All the Scriptural understanding
    Must become the life received,
All the knowledge of the letters
    In the spirit be conceived.

5 Just to touch the Word for knowledge
    Is to take the very way
By which Eve was lured by Satan
    And by knowledge led astray;
But as life to take the Scripture
    Is the tree of life to eat;
Thus the Word we must be taking
    In the spirit as our meat.

STUDY OF THE WORD —
LIGHT AND TRUTH UNLIMITED

817

8.6.8.6.D.

1 We limit not the truth of God
    To our poor reach of mind,
By notions of our day and sect,
    Crude, partial and confined.
Now let a new and better hope
    Within our hearts be stirred:
The Lord hath yet more light and truth
    To break forth from His Word.

continued

2 Who dares to bind by his dull sense
   The oracles of heaven,
For all the nations, tongues and climes
   And all the ages given!
The universe how much unknown!
   That ocean unexplored!
The Lord hath yet more light and truth
   To break forth from His Word.

3 Darkling our great forefathers went
   The first steps of the way;
'Twas but the dawning yet to grow
   Into the perfect day;
And grow it shall, our glorious Sun
   More fervid rays afford:
The Lord hath yet more light and truth
   To break forth from His Word.

4 The valleys past, ascending still,
   Our souls would higher climb,
And look down from supernal heights,
   On all the bygone times;
Upward we press, the air is clear,
   And the sphere-music heard!
The Lord hath yet more light and truth
   To break forth from His Word.

5 O Father, Son and Spirit, send
   Us increase from above;
Enlarge, expand all Christian hearts
   To comprehend Thy love;
And make us all go on to know
   With nobler powers conferred:
The Lord hath yet more light and truth
   To break forth from His Word.

8.8.8.8.

1 Christ is the mystery of God;
 God is invisible, unshown,
 His image man hath never seen,
 But Christ the Son hath made Him known.

2 Christ is the very Word of God,
 He is God's explanation true;
 God's full embodiment is He
 And God's own image brings to view.

3 Image of God invisible,
 Effulgence of God's glory fair;
 God's fulness ever dwells in Him,
 God's testimony He doth bear.

4 The Church the myst'ry is of Christ,
 For He is now to man unshown;
 No man on earth may see Him now,
 But thru the Church He is made known.

5 The Church is Christ's expression full,
 In her Christ dwelleth bodily;
 She is His duplication true,
 And man in her Himself may see.

6 The Church the image has of Christ,
 She is His increase and His spread;
 Christ's very self is found in her,
 The Body, she, to Christ the Head.

7 Thus, in the Son the Father is,
 And now the Spirit is the Son;
 The Spirit of the triune God
 Is in the Church and with her one.

819*

8.5.8.5.

1   As the body is the fulness
    To express our life,
So to Christ the Church, His Body,
    Doth express His life.

2   E'en as Eve is part of Adam
    Taken out of him,
So the Church is Christ's own increase
    With Himself within.

3   As from out the buried kernel
    Many grains are formed,
As the grains together blended
    To a loaf are formed;

4   So the Church, of many Christians,
    Christ doth multiply,
Him expressing as one Body,
    God to glorify.

5   As the branches of the grapevine
    Are its outward spread,
With it one, abiding, bearing
    Clusters in its stead;

6   So the Church's many members
    Christ's enlargement are,
One with Him in life and living,
    Spreading Him afar.

7   Fulness, increase, duplication,
    His expression full,
Growth and spread, continuation,
    Surplus plentiful,

8 Is the Church to Christ, and thereby
    God in Christ may be
  Glorified thru His redeemed ones
    To eternity.

9 Thus the Church and Christ together,
    God's great mystery,
  Is the mingling of the Godhead
    With humanity.

THE CHURCH — THE FULNESS OF CHRIST

8.8.8.8.   **820***

1 Riches of Christ we should enjoy
  And then His fulness we will be;
  Partaking of His very self,
  His testimony men will see.

2 Riches of Christ are what He is
  To us who are His members true;
  His fulness is what we become
  As body doth to man accrue.

3 Riches of Christ are typified
  By Canaan's produce rich and sweet,
  With which the temple great was built,
  The Church's greatest type replete.

4 As Eve to Adam fulness was,
  So is the Church to Christ her Head;
  As Eve from Adam's being came,
  The Church by Christ's own life is bred.

5 Christ's riches are Himself within,
  His fulness is the Church without,
  As His expression, full of Him;
  The Church with Christ is built throughout.

821*   8.8.8.8.

1 The Church the vessel is to Christ,
   Him to contain and Him express,
   Just as the human body doth
   Man's life show forth, his life possess.

2 As was the temple to the ark,
   Receptacle and resting-place;
   So Christ the Church's content is,
   And in the Church, Christ's dwelling-place.

3 As Christ is God's true mystery,
   God to explain and God express;
   So is the Church Christ's mystery,
   Christ to explain and manifest.

4 The members of the Church of Christ
   Are all primarily of clay;
   They need to be transformed and made
   Transparent, precious day by day.

5 By transformation they are built,
   A vessel they to Christ afford;
   His all-inclusiveness they hold;
   Transparent, they express the Lord.

6 Thru all the transformation work
   The triune God performs in them,
   The Church a corporate vessel is
   And like the new Jerusalem.

7 How precious she in each respect,
   Transparent too in every phase;
   Christ with God's fulness she contains,
   Christ with God's glory she displays.

8 With Christ as life, with God as light,
   And with the Spirit's living flow,
   The triune God she manifests
   For all the universe to know.

8.8.8.8.

822*

1　The Church the lampstand is to Christ,
　　Christ is the lamp with God as light;
　　The light divine from Christ doth shine,
　　The Church upholds its glory bright.

2　The light which shines within the lamp
　　Is God as life, unique, divine;
　　The stand must therefore be of gold
　　To match the glory which doth shine.

3　Amid the darkness of this age
　　The light of life divine doth beam
　　In many centers of mankind
　　Where Jesus' testimony's seen.

4　To be this testimony pure
　　"First love" to Christ the Church must keep;
　　Then from the "tree of life" she may
　　The overcomer's portion reap.

5　She must the persecution bear
　　That she the "crown of life" may gain;
　　Adult'ry spiritual o'ercome,
　　The "hidden manna" to obtain.

6　The deeds of "Jezebel" desert,
　　That she may rule the earth with might;
　　Defiling deadness overcome
　　To be arrayed in "garments white."

7　Like 'Philadelphia" she must be
　　To keep Christ's word, confess His Name;
　　All "lukewarm" pride she must o'ercome
　　To feast with Him who overcame.

8　Thus will the Church be purified
　　To be the lampstand of pure gold,
　　To match the testimony pure,
　　The life of Jesus fit to hold.

continued

9 The local churches here on earth
   The lampstands in this age should be;
   The glorious new Jerusalem
   The lampstand in eternity.

10 That city as pure gold will be,
    The final lampstand consummate;
    Christ as the lamp she e'er will hold
    And God's full light will radiate.

THE CHURCH — HER GENERAL DEFINITION

823*

8.7.8.7.D.

1 God before the world's foundation
   Chose the Church in Christ the Son,
   That the Church might share the sonship,
   Holy, blameless, with Him one;
   That the Church be His possession
   With the Spirit as the seal,
   Of our heritage the earnest
   While His Son He does reveal.

2 To the throne Christ has ascended,
   Far above all rule and power;
   God has made Him Head o'er all things
   To the Church, His Body here.
   All in all He ever filleth,
   And His fulness is expressed
   Through the Church, which is His Body
   And His image manifests.

3 We, once dead in our offences,
   Walking in the worldly course,
   Lusts of flesh and mind fulfilling,
   Satan and his hosts their source,
   God with Christ has resurrected,
   Seated in the heavenlies;
   We, His masterpiece, created
   In Christ Jesus, Him to please.

4 Jews and Gentiles are one body —
    God His myst'ry has made known —
  On apostles, prophets founded,
    Jesus Christ the cornerstone;
  We in Him are built together
    For God's dwelling manifest,
  Fitly framed by God the Spirit
    For His pleasure and His rest.

5 In eternal ages purposed
    That His wisdom be made known,
  Was the Church, His hidden myst'ry,
    Where the Son could make His home;
  That the saints may all in spirit
    Apprehend His boundlessness,
  Know His love which passes knowledge,
    All God's fulness to possess.

6 One in body, hope, and Spirit,
    One in faith, one Lord, the Son,
  One baptizing, with one Father,
    That the Church may thus be one;
  Christ to know in all His fulness,
    Unto manhood be matured,
  Ne'er by winds of doctrine carried,
    Nor by cunning men allured.

7 Many gifts the Lord has given,
    That His Body He may build,
  That the saints may be perfected
    And their ministry fulfilled.
  Thus we must put off the old man
    That we may put on the new;
  Thus, renewed in mind and spirit,
    We will bear God's image true.

continued

8 Christ in love Himself has given
      That the Church be sanctified,
   Without blemish, spot, or wrinkle,
      To become His glorious bride.
   He does nourish her and cherish
      As a man his body treats;
   He and she become one body —
      Thus the myst'ry very great.

9 Body, house, new man the Church is,
      Bride, and temple, and yet more:
   She's the army too which fighteth
      All God's foe to triumph o'er.
   She is clothed with all God's armor,
      In His mighty strength is strong,
   Standing in the Lord, resisting,
      With all prayers she fighteth on.

824* 7.6.7.6.D.

1 The Church is Christ's own Body,
      The Father's dwelling-place,
   The gathering of the called ones,
      God blended with man's race;
   Elect before creation,
      Redeemed by Calv'ry's death,
   Her character and standing
      Of heaven, not of earth.

2 New man of new creation,
      Born through her risen Lord,
   Baptized in God the Spirit,
      Made holy by His Word;
   Christ is her life and content,
      Himself her glorious Head;
   She has ascended with Him
      O'er all her foes to tread.

3 Christ is her one foundation,
    None other man may lay;
  All that she has, as Christ, is
    Divine in every way;
  Her members through the Spirit
    Their death on Calv'ry own;
  They're built in resurrection —
    Gold, silver, precious stone.

4 One God, one Lord, one Spirit —
    Her elements all one —
  One faith, one hope, one baptism,
    One Body in the Son;
  The triune God is in her,
    One Body members own,
  By faith they are united,
    In hope of glory shown.

5 From every tribe and nation
    Do all the members come,
  Regardless of their classes
    United to be one.
  No high there is, nor lowly,
    No Jew, nor Gentile clan,
  No free, nor slave, nor master,
    But Christ, the "one new man."

6 One Body universal,
    One in each place expressed;
  Locality of dwelling
    Her only ground possessed;
  Administration local,
    Each answ'ring to the Lord;
  Communion universal,
    Upheld in one accord.

continued

7 Her local gatherings model
    The New Jerusalem;
  Its aspects and its details
    Must show in all of them.
  Christ is the Lamp that shineth,
    With God within, the Light;
  They are the lampstands bearing
    His glorious Image bright.

825   8.7.8.7.D.

1 Church of God, beloved and chosen,
    Church of Christ for whom He died,
  Claim thy gifts and praise the Giver,
    Ye are washed and sanctified.
  Sanctified by God the Father,
    And by Jesus Christ His Son,
  And by God the Holy Spirit,
    Holy, Holy, Three in One.

2 By His will He sanctifieth,
    By the Spirit's power within;
  By the loving hand that chasteneth
    Fruits of righteousness to win;
  By His truth and by His promise,
    By the Word, His gift unpriced,
  By His own blood, and by union
    With the risen life of Christ.

3 Holiness by faith in Jesus,
    Not by effort of thine own,
  Sin's dominion crushed and broken
    By the power of grace alone,
  Christ, the holiness within thee,
    His own beauty on thy brow:
  This shall be thy pilgrim brightness,
    This thy blessed portion now.

4 He will sanctify thee wholly;
   Body, spirit, soul shall be
   Blameless till thy Savior's coming
   In His glorious majesty!
   He hath perfected forever
   Those whom He hath sanctified;
   Spotless, glorious, and holy,
   Is the Church, His chosen Bride.

826

10.10.10.10.

1 I saw great throngs — each was a brother dear,
  Linked with each other in one Body here;
  Each in close union with the living Head,
  The witness-folk, by Jesus' Spirit led.

2 At every time, in every clime I found
  Those, not with words to Christ, but Spirit bound.
  He strengthens them with might each day, each hour;
  Through them true works divine are wrought in power.

3 This is the Church the Spirit hath begot,
  Elect from every people, Christ their lot.
  They follow where His shepherd-staff doth lead;
  The members of this host are blessed indeed.

4 And when on earth they meet His death to show,
  To Him their vows of love they oft renew.
  Some little flock will gather there or here;
  Christ, Head of all, to every soul most near.

5 This is the temple which our Lord approves,
  The Church which truly honors Him and loves,
  Whose sacrifice is on the altar bound;
  She soon in glory will His throne surround.

827   11.11.11.11.(T)

1 I have found life's Giver, and the Prince of Life;
   He has quenched my thirst, and vanquished all my
   He, my living bread, became my daily meat;   [strife.
   Death has died in me, Life's triumph is complete.

2 In the Church, what glory! Far horizons glow!
   And His Name all radiant on each brow doth show.
   Christ doth breathe upon her, He's her living Rock,
   Shepherd of His sheep all gathered in one flock.

3 There one holy flame doth burn within each breast;
   By one blood redeemed, in Christ they find their rest.
   All their thirst He quenches from one living stream;
   They in adoration lowly worship Him.

4 There as Bread of life faint souls He ever feeds;
   There each hungry soul may take whate'er he needs.
   Lovingly He draws each soul that truly lives,
   And in bread and wine Himself to them He gives.

5 Gone is all the earth-taint thru abounding grace;
   Hear the song of triumph from the ransomed race.
   All in glory shining, glory not their own,
   Blended into oneness, they approach the throne.

828   10.10.10.10.10.10.

1 The "churches" here below, so narrow bound,
   Reach not the hungry throngs which us surround;
   They run partway with truth, but miss the goal.
   Earth-vision blurred and dim, their eyes doth hold —
   But broken gleams have they of radiance gold;
   Too dazzling is the splendor of the whole.

2 Brothers with brothers have not all one heart,
   In wrath they turn away and walk apart,
   Who from one stream of life had common birth.

What fight for forms! O'er doctrines what vain strife!
Instead together sharing God's one life,
Who worshipped is by heaven and by earth.

3 "Where is the truth?" I asked; for this I longed:
None answered right 'mid all the answering throng;
For ever side by side lay light and shade.
"Where is," I cried, "the one communion pure?
Where is the Church in which, clear-traced and sure,
The Spirit's very likeness is portrayed?"

4 So sought I long, and hopeless was my quest;
These eyes grew dim and blind and found no rest,
Till God's touch opened them, and I was freed.
I found the Spirit's Church in souls made one
In this, that they in troth to Christ had come —
His Bride, to follow where the cross may lead.

5 Thus when I see this small world's narrow thought,
Behold the brother not with brother brought,
Yet serving Christ — as each one deemeth right —
Ah, then a voice from realms of glory calls,
Where the last veil is rent and earthward falls,
And where God's love, eternal, burneth bright.

6 No more we put that query without end,
To which self-chosen church our feet did trend —
What doctrines we believed, what sacred rites.
In Christ we were in bonds that nought could break;
Who, by His cross and death, do all forsake,
Such as were far asunder He unites.

7 No longer does one heed mere formal phrase,
Or seek for others' creeds through winding maze,
For in Himself was truth made manifest.
And out of every tongue and every land
He formed one Church to meet His own demand —
His Body, where His fulness is expressed.

829*

10.10.10.10.

1 The Church's seed is nought but Christ Himself
Sown into human hearts as life, thereby
Growing as wheat, producing flour fine
For bread both God and man to satisfy.

2 But Satan hath the false believers sown
Among the saints as tares among the wheat,
To bring confusion and to hinder growth
That they may not fulfill God's plan complete.

3 The Church's life just as the herb must be,
Grown out of Christ, who is the mustard seed;
Hidden and transient, little on the earth,
But good for food the hungry ones to feed.

4 But Satan came and made the little herb
To change its nature and to change its form,
That fully grown it did a tree become
Where many evil ones may lodge and swarm.

5 Satan has also used the fallen "church"
Evil and heathen practice to include,
As leaven mingled with the meal of wheat,
Thus to corrupt its purity as food.

6 But Christ as life would so transform the saints
That they may be as pearl and precious stone,
As the materials suitable to build
Into His Church to make His Kingdom known.

7 Such an assembly grown in Christ as life,
Transformed and built with Christ in them annealed,
Is as the goodly pearl for preciousness
And as the treasure hidden in the field.

8 Lord, separate us from the devil's "tares,"
Each one deliver from the monstrous "tree,"
From all the "leaven" may Thou purify,
That we may be as food to man and Thee.

9   Cause us to grow in life divine each day
     That we may be transformed and built by Thee
     Into a body to express Thyself,
     That Thou in us Thy Church and Kingdom see.

THE CHURCH — HER FAITH

830

8.8.8.8.8.8.

1   Faith of our fathers, living still
     In spite of dungeon, fire and sword,
     O how our hearts beat high with joy
     Whene'er we hear that glorious word!
     Faith of our fathers! holy faith!
     We will be true to thee till death!

2   Our fathers, chained in prisons dark,
     Were still in heart and conscience free;
     And blest would be their children's fate,
     If they, like them should die for thee:
     Faith of our fathers! holy faith!
     We will be true to thee till death!

3   Faith of our fathers, we will strive
     To win all nations unto thee;
     And through the truth that comes from God
     Mankind shall then indeed be free.
     Faith of our fathers! holy faith!
     We will be true to thee till death!

4   Faith of our fathers, we will love
     Both friend and foe in all our strife,
     And preach thee, too, as love knows how
     By kindly words and virtuous life.
     Faith of our fathers! holy faith!
     We will be true to thee till death!

831*

8.7.8.7.D.(I)

1 The unity of Church is but
    The saints in oneness living;
The Spirit which indwelleth them
    This oneness ever giving.
Thus it is realized and called
    The unity of Spirit;
'Tis based upon the common faith
    Which all the saints inherit.

2 This precious faith of all the saints,
    Is constituted solely
Of Christ and His redemptive work,
    Which are unique and holy.
In this the saints are truly one,
    Together all agreeing,
And it is from this common faith
    The Church came into being.

3 The Church within the universe
    Is one as Christ's possession;
The Church must therefore locally
    Be one in her expression;
For all her elements are one —
    One God, one Lord, one Spirit,
One faith, baptism, Body too,
    One hope all saints inherit.

4 This oneness is the Church's ground,
    The ground of common standing,
The only ground of unity
    The Spirit is demanding.
The Church in actual practise thus
    May keep her vital union,
And her expressions locally
    Be built up in communion.

5   Lord, help us ever strive to keep
This unity by taking
The Church's ground of unity,
The Body-life partaking,
That all Thy heart's profound desire
May fully be effected,
And God's eternal purpose may
Completely be perfected.

11.11.11.11.(T)

832*

1   Christ the Son of God and His redemptive deed
Are the saving faith which is our only creed.
All the other doctrines do not faith comprise;
Christ, His work and person, only qualifies.

2   All the other teachings used improperly
Are the "winds of doctrine," spoiling unity:
Blowing saints away from Christ who is the Head,
Building not the Body, tearing down instead.

3   Thus we must relinquish doctrines of all kinds,
Only keep the faith that oneness we may find.
In the Lord the Spirit we are one indeed;
Just to keep this oneness is our only need.

4   Truth we must be holding, which is Christ Himself,
That we be delivered from the sects of self,
That in all things growing into Christ the Head,
Built will be the Body and to fulness led.

5   To the "unity of faith" we must attain,
All the "winds of doctrine" evermore disdain;
Holding Christ the Spirit, our reality,
For the Body's growing in its unity.

833

7.6.7.6.D.

1 The Church's one foundation
    Is Jesus Christ her Lord;
She is His new creation
    By water and the Word:
From heav'n He came and sought her
    To be His holy Bride;
With His own blood He bought her,
    And for her life He died.

2 Elect from every nation,
    Yet one o'er all the earth,
Her charter of salvation,
    One Lord, one faith, one birth;
One holy Name she blesses,
    Partakes one holy food,
And to one hope she presses,
    With every grace endued.

3 'Mid toil and tribulation,
    And tumult of her war,
She waits the consummation
    Of peace for evermore;
Till, with the vision glorious,
    Her longing eyes are blest,
And the great Church victorious
    Shall be the Church at rest.

4 Yet she on earth hath union
    With God the Three in One,
And mystic sweet communion
    With those whose rest is won:
O happy ones and holy!
    Lord, give us grace that we,
Like them, the meek and lowly,
    In love may dwell with Thee.

8.7.8.7.D.

1 The chief Cornerstone Thou art, Lord,
   Jewish builders did despise;
  God by resurrection placed Thee,
   Thou art precious in His eyes.
  Through Thee we receive salvation,
   And, together built by Thee,
  Jews and Gentiles are Thy dwelling,
   One new man, in harmony.

2 Thou too art the smitten Rock, Lord,
   That man's thirst by Thee be filled,
  That frail man may stand upon Thee,
   But e'en more, God's house to build.
  The Foundation Stone in Zion,
   Tested and secure, Thou art;
  And the Rock, the Church supporting,
   Her foundation to impart.

3 On Thyself the Church is builded,
   And though many storms assail,
  Still it stands erect, for 'gainst it
   Gates of hell cannot prevail.
  Thine authority possessing,
   It doth bind and loose in Thee,
  Bringing men into Thy kingdom,
   Satan's captives setting free.

4 Living Stone of life art Thou, Lord,
   Precious, chosen thus to be;
  Living stones Thou too hast made us,
   One in character with Thee.
  Built together as a temple
   That our God may dwell therein,
  Thus we are a holy priesthood,
   Offering sacrifice to Him.

continued

834*

5 Lord, Thou art the Son of David
   That God's temple Thou may build;
King and Priest Thou art together,
   That Thy calling be fulfilled.
As the King, for God Thou rulest,
   Making men submit to Him;
As the Priest before God's presence,
   Bringing men to enter in.

6 Thine authority doth issue
   From the throne to render peace;
Fellowship is in the river
   To supply and give increase.
When these, balanced, go together,
   Then God's purpose is fulfilled;
King and Priest in Thee combining,
   Thou God's dwelling place dost build.

7 Thou art God, yet flesh becamest,
   God with man in Thee doth dwell;
Thou, the Temple for His glory,
   God in Thee Himself doth tell.
Thus the Church too is the mingling
   Into one of God and man;
So it is with every member
   For the building of God's plan.

8 Thou, the everlasting Dwelling,
   In all ages art our home;
We in Thee enjoy protection,
   Living in Thyself alone.
Thou our Sanctuary art, Lord,
   We and God abide in Thee;
Thou, God's presence art within us,
   Where we worship ceaselessly.

9 Cornerstone, Foundation, Topstone,
  Rock, and Church, and Living Stone,
Dwelling-place, and Sanctuary,
  Builder too art Thou, we own.
Praise we give for what Thou art, Lord,
  As Thy wondrousness we see!
Grant that we may be built up, Lord,
  As the living stones in Thee.

8.8.8.8. **835**

1 On Christ, salvation rests secure;
  The Rock of Ages must endure;
  Nor can that faith be overthrown
  Which rests upon the "Living Stone."

2 No other hope shall intervene;
  To Him we look, on Him we lean;
  Other foundations we disown,
  And build on Christ, the "Living Stone."

3 In Him it is ordained to raise
  A temple to Jehovah's praise,
  Composed of all His saints, who own
  No Savior but the "Living Stone."

4 View the vast building, see it rise:
  The work how great! the plan how wise!
  O wondrous fabric! pow'r unknown:
  That rests it on the "Living Stone."

5 But most adore His precious name:
  His glory and His grace proclaim!
  For us, the lost, condemned, undone,
  He gave Himself, the "Living Stone."

THE CHURCH — HER FOUNDATION

836

8.7.8.7.8.7.

1 Christ is made the sure foundation,
   Christ the head and cornerstone,
Chosen of the Lord and precious,
   Binding all the Church in one;
Holy Zion's help forever,
   And her confidence alone.

2 Founded on the Lord victorious,
   Christ the everlasting Rock,
Stands the Church in heav'nly places,
   Dreading not the storm or shock;
Built with life divine she ever
   Stands against attack and mock.

3 Though the gates of hades frustrate,
   Yet the Church still stands for God,
Overcoming evil spirits
   By her Lord's victorious blood;
And at Christ's return in triumph
   All her foes will then be trod.

THE CHURCH — HER BUILDING

837*

8.8.8.8.

1 We praise Thee, Lord, for Thy great plan
That we Thy dwelling-place may be;
Thou live in us, we filled with Thee,
Thou in the Son expressed might be.

2 Though in Thine image made by Thee
And given Thine authority,
Yet we are only made of clay
Without a trace of divinity.

3 When we receive Thee as our life,
Thy nature we thru grace possess;
Mingled together, we with Thee
One Body glorious will express.

4   When flows Thy life thru all our souls,
     Filling, renewing every part,
     We will be pearls and precious stones,
     Changed to Thine image, as Thou art.

5   But, Lord, we fully realize
     These are not wrought men's praise to rouse,
     But as material to be built
     Together for Thy glorious house.

6   Here, Lord, we give ourselves to Thee;
     Receive us into Thy wise hands;
     Bend, break, and build together in Thee
     To be the house to meet Thy demands.

7   Break all the natural life for us,
     Deal Thou with each peculiar way,
     That we no more independent be
     But with all saints are one for aye.

8   Then we shall be Thy Bride beloved,
     Together in Thy chamber abide,
     Enjoy the fulness of Thy love.
     How Thou wilt then be satisfied!

8.8.8.8.   **838***

1   Thy blueprint, Lord, I treasure dear,
     It shows Thy tabernacle real,
     It tells how Thou wouldst have it built,
     How Thou Thy glory wouldst reveal.

2   The ark's the center of the tent,
     The tent is but its resting-place:
     In it the ten commandments are,
     And in the tent it ever stays.

continued

838*

3 The ark the God-man, Christ, displays —
   God mixed with man, as gold, wood meet;
   The law is God's expression full,
   Which dwells in Christ the Son complete.

4 Thus Christ's the center of the Church,
   Which is to Him a resting-place;
   In Christ the Father ever dwells,
   And in the Church, Christ's dwelling-place.

5 The tent's the increase of the ark,
   Both are of wood with gold o'erlaid;
   The Church the increase is of Christ,
   God blent with man here too displayed.

6 The boards when joined support the tent
   On silver sockets standing sure;
   Gold overlaid, with golden rings
   And interlocking bars, secure.

7 The Church is thus the gathered saints,
   On Christ's redemption standing sure;
   In life divine, by Spirit bound,
   Together built and framed secure.

8 The tent's four-layered cover shows
   The Christ of God in every phase;
   God's glory thus is signified,
   Covering His holy dwelling-place.

9 Covered by such a glorious Christ,
   All saints together knit may be;
   Enjoying all He is for them,
   In Him they're builded gloriously.

10 The law is placed within the ark,
   The ark within the tent doth rest;
   So God in Christ within the Church
   His wondrous glory manifests.

7.7.7.7.D.

1 Lord, Thou art a potter skilled
   And a glorious builder too,
   Molding for Thy vessel great,
   Building with Thy house in view.
   I am both a man of clay
   And a new-made living stone,
   That Thy vessel I may be
   And the temple Thou wouldst own.

2 Though of clay Thou madest us,
   Thou wouldst have us be transformed;
   With Thy life as purest gold,
   Unto precious stones conformed.
   We shall, through Thy building work,
   Then become Thy loving Bride,
   In one Body joined to Thee,
   That Thy heart be satisfied.

3 What Thy heart desires and loves
   Are not precious stones alone,
   But together these to build
   For Thy glory, for Thy home.
   Thou, the all-inclusive Christ,
   Dost a builded Church require,
   That Thy glorious riches may
   Radiate their light entire.

4 Not the person spiritual
   In an individual way,
   But the corporate life expressed
   Will Thy heart's desire display.
   Members separate and detached
   Ne'er express Thee perfectly,
   But Thy Body tempered, built,
   Ever shall Thy fulness be.

continued

5   Build me, Lord, with other saints,
     Independence ne'er allow,
     But according to Thy plan
     Fitly frame and join me now.
     In experience not my boast,
     Nor in gifts would be my pride;
     For Thy building I give all,
     That Thou may be glorified.

840*   8.7.8.7.D.

1   Freed from self and Adam's nature,
     Lord, I would be built by Thee
     With the saints into Thy temple,
     Where Thy glory we shall see.
     From peculiar traits deliver,
     From my independent ways,
     That a dwelling place for Thee, Lord,
     We will be thru all our days.

2   By Thy life and by its flowing
     I can grow and be transformed,
     With the saints coordinated,
     Builded up, to Thee conformed;
     Keep the order in the Body,
     There to function in Thy will,
     Ever serving, helping others,
     All Thy purpose to fulfill.

3   In my knowledge and experience
     I would not exalted be,
     But submitting and accepting
     Let the Body balance me;
     Holding fast the Head, and growing
     With His increase, in His way,
     By the joints and bands supplying,
     Knit together day by day.

4 By Thy Spirit daily strengthened
  In the inner man with might,
I would know Thy love surpassing,
  Know Thy breadth and length and height:
Ever of Thy riches taking,
  Unto all Thy fulness filled,
Ever growing into manhood,
  That Thy Body Thou may build.

5 In God's house and in Thy Body
  Builded up I long to be,
That within this corporate vessel
  All shall then Thy glory see;
That Thy Bride, the glorious city,
  May appear upon the earth,
As a lampstand brightly beaming
  To express to all Thy worth.

6.5.6.5.D.

841*

1 Thou art all my life,
    Lord,
  In me Thou dost live;
With Thee all God's fulness
  Thou to me dost give.
By Thy holy nature
  I am sanctified,
By Thy resurrection,
  Vict'ry is supplied.

2 Now Thy flowing life,
    Lord,
  Doth enlighten me,
Bringing in the spirit
  Fellowship with Thee;
All my need supplying,
  Making Thy demand,
Leading me to cleansing
  And in Thee to stand.

3 Thy anointing Spirit
  Me shall permeate,
All my soul and spirit
  Thou wouldst saturate;
Every part transforming
  Till conformed to Thee,
Till Thy life shall bring me
  To maturity. *continued*

775

4 Lord, Thy life abundant,
  Flowing, rich and free,
Constantly refreshes
  And empowers me.
Death by life is swallowed,
  Weakness is made strong,
All my bonds are broken,
  Gloom is turned to song.

5 I would give myself, Lord,
  Fully unto Thee,
That Thy heart's desire
  Be fulfilled in me.
I no more would struggle
  To myself reform,
Thus in me to hinder
  What Thou wouldst perform.

6 I would cease completely
  From my efforts vain,
Let Thy life transform me,
  Full release to gain;
Build me up with others
  Till in us Thou see
Thy complete expression
  Glorifying Thee.

842*   6.6.8.6.

1 Breathe Thou, O Lord, on me,
  My drooping spirit raise;
Deliver me from fear and death
  Into Thy life of praise.

2 Breathe Thou, O Lord, on me,
  Strength to my spirit bring,
That running, walking, fainting not,
  I'll mount on eagles' wings.

3   Breathe Thou, O Lord, on me
That I may enter rest,
That heart and spirit joyful be
By leaning on Thy breast.

4   Breathe Thou, O Lord, on me
Till filled with Thee, I plead,
No longer I that live, but Christ
In thought, and word, and deed.

5   Breathe Thou on me and touch
My independency,
That in Thy Body I'll be built
With all the saints in Thee.

9.8.9.8.   **843***

1   Lord, breathe Thy breath of life upon me,
I'm as a bone disjoined and dry;
O may Thou quicken and restore me
And with Thy Body unify.

2   Lord, breathe Thy breath of life upon me,
My spirit is so bound and slow;
O break my shackles and release me,
To mingle in Thy Body's flow.

3   Lord, breathe Thy breath of life upon me,
My burdened spirit cannot rise;
May Thou encourage and revive me
To share Thy Body's full supplies.

4   Lord, breathe Thy breath of life upon me,
My barren spirit has no joy;
O may Thou satisfy and bless me,
Thy Body's riches to enjoy.

5   Lord, breathe Thy breath of life upon me,
To me a true dependence give;
Deal with my death and isolation,
That in Thy Body I may live.

844*

8.8.8.7.

1 Lord, speak Thy Word, upon us breathe;
Behold, dry bones fill all the earth
In graves and scattered 'round in death;
   Lord, speak and breathe upon us!

2 Lord, speak Thy Word, upon us breathe,
Revive the bones with quickening breath,
That we may leave our graves, our death;
   Lord, speak and breathe upon us!

3 Lord, speak Thy Word, upon us breathe,
Thy people all to make alive,
A mighty host, the foe to drive;
   Lord, speak and breathe upon us!

4 Lord, speak Thy Word, upon us breathe,
That all Thy people may be one,
Led by the headship of the Son;
   Lord, speak and breathe upon us!

5 Lord, speak Thy Word, upon us breathe,
Thy people fitly frame with grace
To be Thy rest, Thy dwelling-place;
   Lord, speak and breathe upon us!

6 Lord, speak to me, upon me breathe,
Revive me, in Thy Body build,
No more secluded and self-willed;
   Breathe now, O Lord, upon me!

7 Lord, speak to me, upon me breathe
That with Thy saints the foe I'll fight,
That in Thy house Thou may delight,
   Breathe now, O Lord, upon me!

THE CHURCH — HER BUILDING

10.10.10.10.

845*

1 Release my spirit! This is what I need:
O may my spirit with the saints' be knit;
No more in private ways Thyself to seek,
But freed from self and for Thy building fit.

2 Release my spirit! This is what I ask,
That self-confined or closed I may not be;
How deep within myself I long have been,
If Thou deliver not, I'll ne'er be free.

3 Release my spirit! 'Tis for this I pray,
That from myself I fully may come forth;
Thy Spirit then through me may freely flow,
And Thou Thy presence fully may show forth.

4 Release my spirit! This is what I want,
That I from my seclusion may depart;
My private seeking poverty has brought,
Now save from self, Thy wealth to me impart.

5 Release my spirit! This is what I seek,
That prisoned in my self no more I'll be;
By Satan's cunning cheated nevermore,
But loosed from self to Thine infinity.

6 Release my spirit! 'Tis for this I yearn,
That self may bind my spirit nevermore;
With all the saints I'd mingle in Thy life,
And all Thou art enjoy forevermore.

6.4.6.4.6.6.6.4.

846*

1 Oh, may my spirit flow,
Oh, may it flow!
Now I beseech Thee, Lord,
Oh, may it flow!
My past I would forsake,
The iron walls would break,
My spirit free would make;
Oh, may it flow!

continued

779

2 Oh, may my spirit flow,
   Oh, may it flow!
Now I implore Thee, Lord,
   Oh, may it flow!
No more self-satisfied,
No more in self-bound pride,
No more my spirit tied;
   Oh, may it flow!

3 Oh, may my spirit flow,
   Oh, may it flow!
For this I plead with Thee,
   Oh, may it flow!
High-minded not to be,
Pride shall not prison me,
I'd flow unceasingly,
   In spirit flow.

4 Oh, may my spirit flow,
   Oh, may it flow!
For this I seek Thee, Lord,
   Oh, may it flow!
No more to isolate,
Nor self to perfect make,
My spirit nought abate,
   Deeply to flow.

5 Oh, may my spirit flow,
   Oh, may it flow!
I ask Thee, gracious Lord,
   Oh, may it flow!
My trust in self o'erthrow,
Down from self's throne I'll go,
That living water flow
   In spirit, Lord.

6 Oh, may my spirit flow,
   Oh, may it flow!
Answer my prayer, dear Lord,
   Oh, may it flow!
Not just commune with Thee,
I long to builded be,
Mingle with others free
   In spirit, Lord.

9.8.9.8.   **847***

1 I long for fellowship in spirit,
  That mingled with the saints I'll be,
  Long to be saved from independence
  And to be built with saints in Thee.

2 I long for fellowship in spirit,
  That opened shall my spirit be,
  Long to be rescued from seclusion,
  And with the saints to worship Thee.

3 I long for fellowship in spirit,
  Long that my spirit forth may come,
  Long to be saved from self-deception,
  And every hindrance overcome.

4 I long for fellowship in spirit,
  With saints in spirit thus to pray,
  Long for deliv'rance from pretention,
  Long for true fellowship today.

5 I long for fellowship in spirit,
  Long thus to know authority;
  Long for true fellowship in service,
  Coordinated thus to be.

6 O Lord, fulfill our heart's deep longing,
  Saints for such fellowship inspire,
  That we may realize Thy building
  And soon fulfill Thy heart's desire.

848*

8.7.8.7.D.

1 What a blessing, what a priv'lege!
    Called of God a royal priest,
That this glorious, holy office
    I should bear, though last and least.

    All the building of the Body
        On the priesthood doth depend;
    Ever praying in the spirit
        I this office would attend.

2 If I keep this royal calling
    Under Thine authority,
Priestly duty thus fulfilling,
    Then the church will builded be.

3 Now the church is but the priesthood;
    Thus the priesthood formed we need;
When the priests are knit together,
    Then the church is built indeed.

4 Through the church's degradation,
    Saints this office desolate;
Through the weakness of their spirits
    Preaching doth predominate.

5 Most are leaning on the message
    And the preaching emphasize,
Yet neglect the priestly praying
    And their spirits' exercise.

6 Deal with me and make me balanced,
    As in preaching, so in prayer;
Leading others oft in praying,
    As Thy Word I too declare.

7 Only serving by our praying
    Will our spirits mingled be;
Stressing prayer as much as preaching —
    Thus the church is built for Thee.

1 Holy priests are living stones
    For God's building work today;
    If these stones would builded be
    All the priests must learn to pray.

      To the holiest often come,
      In the spirit touch the throne,
      Let the Lord flow thru in prayer,
      Thus the building work is done.

2 All the saints must serve as priests,
    That the living stones they be;
    Each must priestly work perform,
    Then their functions we will see.

3 Tent and priests of olden times
    Always did together go;
    When the priests served in the tent,
    Into one the two did flow.

4 Now the building spiritual
    And the priesthood all are one;
    Now the building of the house
    By the priestly work is done.

5 In the priests the substance is
    Of the building work replete;
    When the priests their work discharge,
    Then God's house will be complete.

6 Building God and man in one
    Is their work before the Lord;
    In this fellowship divine
    Saints are built in one accord.

7 When in prayer our spirits blend,
    Then together built are we,
    Then a priesthood we become,
    Off'ring sacrifice to Thee.   *continued*

THE CHURCH — HER BUILDING

8 Grant us grace, O Lord, that we
Treasure dear the priestly call;
In the spirit serve and pray,
That Thy church be built withal.

THE CHURCH — HER ATTRACTION

850
9.8.9.8.D.

1 O Lord, we have loved her fair beauty,
The house Thou hast chosen for Thee,
The courts where Thy gladness rejoiceth,
And where Thou delightest to be.
We love to be made the fair dwelling
Where God in His grace may abide;
We'd cast forth whatever may grieve Thee,
And welcome none other beside.

2 O blessed the grace that has made us
The home of the gladness of God,
The dwelling wherein Thou delightest,
The house Thou hast bought with Thy blood.
'Tis there that Thy joy overfloweth,
We feel it, we take of it there;
By all that Thou workest within us,
Thy temple is holy and fair.

3 The secret of that inner chamber,
Thy place is of heavenly rest;
The stillness of thoughts that adore Thee,
The shrine that Thou lovest the best.
The temple where Christ hath His dwelling,
The souls He hath ransomed, forgiv'n;
The temple where I have my dwelling,
Is Christ in the glory of heav'n.

8.8.8.8.

1 How lovely is Thy dwelling-place!
  Within Thy courts I long to be;
  Thy presence, Lord, my spirit craves,
  For this my heart cries out to Thee.

2 At Thy burnt-offering altar, Lord,
  And at Thine incense altar blest,
  Even the sparrow finds a home,
  And swallow there prepares her nest.

3 Men, as the sparrow, frail and small,
  When living in Thy house find rest,
  Relying on the altar's blood,
  Enjoying there the incense blest.

4 How blessed are those men indeed!
  Trusting in Thee they are made strong;
  Highways to Zion in their hearts,
  The way they care not, rough or long.

5 Passing the weeping valley they
  Make it a place of springing wells;
  The rain with blessings covers it
  And in the way God's mercy tells.

6 From strength to strength they go, and all
  Before the Lord in Zion meet;
  Thus ever seeking Thine own self,
  They need Thy care and grace replete.

7 Better a day within Thy courts
  Than days a thousand I would tell;
  I'd rather at Thy threshold stand
  Than in the wicked's tents to dwell.

continued

8   Thou art a sun, Thou art a shield,
    Thou grace and glory wilt supply;
    Thy presence and Thy very self
    My need in fulness satisfy.

9   Not one good thing wilt Thou withhold
    From those who walk in uprightness;
    Bless'd is the man that trusts in Thee
    With grace and glory measureless.

852*
    8.6.8.6.

1   Thy dwelling-place, O Lord, I love;
    It is Thy Church so blessed,
    It is Thy joy and heart's delight
    And where Thy heart finds rest.

2   For her, Thyself Thou gavest, Lord,
    That she be Thine, complete;
    For her, I too my body give,
    Thy heart's desire to meet.

3   For her, Thou hast become my life,
    That she my living be;
    For her, I would forsake myself,
    That she be filled with Thee.

4   The Church is Thy beloved Bride,
    Thou in Thy Body seen;
    She is my joy and heart's desire,
    The one on whom I lean.

5   In her, Thy full supply, O Lord,
    Thou dost to me impart;
    In her am I possessed by Thee
    To satisfy Thy heart.

6 Thy dwelling-place, O Lord, I love;
It is Thy Church, Thy home;
In it I would forever live
And never longer roam.

6.6.8.6.　　　　　　　　**853**

1　I love Thy kingdom, Lord,
The house of Thine abode,
The Church our blest Redeemer bought
With His own precious blood.

2　I love the Church, O God!
Her walls before Thee stand,
Dear as the apple of Thine eye
And graven on Thy hand.

3　For her my tears shall fall,
For her my prayers ascend;
To her my cares and toils be given
Till toils and cares shall end.

4　Beyond my highest joy
I prize her heavenly ways,
Her sweet communion, solemn vows,
Her hymns of love and praise.

5　Sure as Thy truth shall last,
To Zion shall be given
The brightest glories earth can yield,
And brighter bliss of heaven.

854*

6.5.6.5.

1 All the saints of Christ are
   Members every one;
   All coordinating
   Into oneness come.

2 Though the gifts are many,
   Yet the Spirit one;
   Many too the functions,
   But one Lord, the Son.

3 Each, the others needing,
   Must impartial be;
   Each his place possesses
   And utility.

4 By our grace are measured
   Gifts both large and small;
   Each with sober judgment
   Takes his place with all.

5 Each fulfills his duty,
   Shows his usefulness,
   Fervent in the spirit,
   Girt with faithfulness.

6 Knitting and supplying,
   Bearing much in grace;
   Not a trace of discord,
   Christ is giv'n His place.

7 We, the Church, His Body,
   He, the Head, the Son;
   By the Spirit's flowing,
   We are joined in one.

8.6.8.6.D.

Behold, how good, how pleasant 'tis
  When brethren dwell in one!
'Tis like the oil on Aaron's head,
  Which to his skirts did run;
As dew of Hermon that descends
  On Zion's mountains o'er;
The Lord His blessing there commands,
  E'en life forevermore.

8.6.8.6.   **856**

1 How pleasant and how good it is
     When brethren in the Lord
   In one another's joy delight
     And dwell in sweet accord.

2 Such oneness, like anointing oil
     On head to body poured;
   Such oneness, like the morning dew,
     With sweet refreshment stored.

3 To those who dwell in brotherhood
     The Lord His blessing sends,
   He crowns them with the bliss of life,
     Of life that never ends.

Psa. 133. From THE PSALTER 1912.

857

8.6.8.6.

1 How sweet, how heav'nly is the sight,
    When those who love the Lord
In one another's peace delight,
    And so fulfill His Word;

2 When each can feel his brother's sigh,
    And with him bear a part;
When sorrow flows from eye to eye,
    And joy from heart to heart;

3 When, free from envy, scorn and pride
    Our wishes all above,
Each can his brother's failings hide,
    And show a brother's love;

4 When love, in one delightful stream,
    Through every bosom flows;
When union sweet, and dear esteem,
    In every action glows.

5 Love is the golden chain that binds;
    The saints Thy grace thus prove.
And he is glory's heir that finds
    His bosom glow with love.

8.6.8.6. with repeat.

1 All praise to our redeeming Lord,
  Who joins us by His grace,
And bids us, each to each restored,
  Together seek His face,
  Together seek His face.

2 He bids us build each other up;
  And, gathered into one,
To our high calling's glorious hope,
  We hand in hand go on,
  We hand in hand go on.

3 The gift which He on one bestows,
  We all delight to prove;
The grace through every vessel flows,
  In purest streams of love,
  In purest streams of love.

4 We all partake the joy of one;
  The common peace we feel;
A peace to worldly minds unknown,
  A joy unspeakable,
  A joy unspeakable.

5 And if our fellowship below
  In Christ yet be so sweet,
What height of rapture shall we know,
  When round His throne we meet,
  When round His throne we meet!

859   6.6.8.6.

1   Let party names no more
        The Christian world o'erspread;
    Gentile and Jew, and bond and free,
        Are one in Christ, their Head.

2   Among the saints on earth
        Let mutual love be found;
    Heirs of the same inheritance,
        With mutual blessings crowned.

3   Let envy, child of hell!
        Be banished far away:
    Those in sweet fellowship should dwell,
        Who the same Lord obey.

4   Thus will the Church below
        God's purpose ever prove;
    Where streams of endless pleasure flow,
        And every heart is love.

860   6.6.8.6.

1   Blest be the tie that binds
        Our hearts in Christian love;
    The fellowship our spirit finds
        Is like to that above.

2   Before our Father's throne,
        We pour our ardent prayers;
    Our fears, our hopes, our aims are one —
        Our comforts and our cares.

3   We share our mutual woes;
        Our mutual burdens bear;
    And often for each other flows
        The sympathizing tear.

4   When we asunder part,
     It gives us inward pain;
     But we shall still be joined in heart,
     And hope to meet again.

5   From sorrow, toil, and pain,
     And sin we shall be free;
     And perfect love and oneness reign
     Through all eternity.

9.8.8.9. with chorus.   **861**

1 God be with you till we meet again;
   By His counsels guide, uphold you,
   With His sheep in love enfold you;
   God be with you till we meet again.

     Till we meet, till we meet,
     Till we meet at Jesus' feet;
     Till we meet, till we meet,
     God be with you till we meet again.

2 God be with you till we meet again!
   'Neath His wings protecting hide you,
   Daily manna still provide you;
   God be with you till we meet again!

3 God be with you till we meet again!
   When life's perils thick confound you,
   Put His arms unfailing round you;
   God be with you till we meet again!

4 God be with you till we meet again!
   Keep love's banner floating o'er you,
   Smite death's threatening wave before you;
   God be with you till we meet again!

862

8.8.8.8.

1 Jesus, where'er Thy people meet,
  There they behold Thy mercy-seat;
  Where'er they seek Thee, Thou art found,
  With grace and mercy to abound.

2 For Thou, within no walls confined,
  Inhabitest the humble mind;
  Such ever bring Thee where they come,
  And going, take Thee to their home.

3 Dear Shepherd of Thy chosen few,
  Thy former mercies here renew;
  Here, to our waiting hearts, proclaim
  The sweetness of Thy saving Name.

4 Here may we prove the power of prayer
  To strengthen faith and sweeten care;
  To teach our faint desires to rise,
  And bring Thy light before our eyes.

5 Lord, we are few, but Thou art near;
  Nor short Thine arm, nor deaf Thine ear;
  Oh, rend the heavens, come quickly down,
  And make our waiting hearts Thine own.

6 Command Thy blessing in this hour;
  And as the Spirit full of pow'r
  With life and vision fill this place,
  That all Thy purpose we may trace.

7 O Thou, our Head, our Life, our Guide,
  May nought in life or death divide
  The saints in Thy communion blessed,
  That all Thy fulness be expressed.

10.10.10.10.

1   In daily walk and in our meetings too,
      Christ is the center, Christ is everything;
      'Tis not for form nor doctrine good and true,
      But 'tis for Christ alone we're gathering.

2   Christ is the way and Christ the light of life,
      In Him we walk and by Him we are led;
      Christ is the living water and the food;
      Of Him we drink and we with Him are fed.

3   Christ is the truth, 'tis Him we testify,
      Christ is the life, 'tis Him we minister;
      Christ is the Lord, 'tis Him we magnify,
      Christ is the Head, and we exalt Him here.

4   Christ is the All in all to God and man —
      With Him both we and God are satisfied;
      Christ, the reality within the Church —
      By Him are life and numbers multiplied.

5   By all the hymns and prayers we offer here,
      Christ the reality we would express;
      All the activities in fellowship —
      Christ thus in operation manifest.

6   'Tis in His Name we meet, in Spirit act,
      With nothing in our mind to formalize;
      'Tis by His pow'r we pray, in unction praise,
      And with Himself in spirit exercise.

7   All things forgetting, cleaving unto Christ,
      Applying Him until maturity;
      Let us count everything but loss for Him,
      For Him, our All in all, eternally.

864*

8.8.8.6. with chorus.

1 Whene'er we meet with Christ endued,
   The surplus of His plenitude
We offer unto God as food,
   And thus exhibit Christ.

> Let us exhibit Christ,
> Let us exhibit Christ;
> We'll bring His surplus to the church
> And thus exhibit Christ.

2 In Christ we live, by Christ we fight,
   On Christ we labor day and night,
And with His surplus we unite
   To thus exhibit Christ.

3 Our life and all we are and do
   Is Christ Himself, the substance true,
That every time we meet anew
   We may exhibit Christ.

4 In meetings Christ to God we bear
   And Christ with one another share,
And Christ with God enjoying there,
   We thus exhibit Christ.

5 The risen Christ to God we bring,
   And Christ ascended offering,
God's satisfaction answering,
   We thus exhibit Christ.

6 The center and reality,
   The atmosphere and ministry,
Of all our meetings is that we
   May thus exhibit Christ.

7 The testimony and the prayer,
   And all the fellowship we share,
The exercise of gifts, whate'er,
   Should just exhibit Christ.

8   The Father we would glorify,
       Exalting Christ the Son, thereby
    The meeting's purpose satisfy
       That we exhibit Christ.

MEETINGS — WORSHIPING GOD

8.6.8.6.   **865***

1   In spirit and in truth, O Lord,
       We meet to worship here;
    As taught by Christ, the Son of God,
       We now in Him draw near.

2   Thank God, He is a Spirit true,
       So near, so dear to us;
    That we may contact Him in life,
       In truth to worship thus.

3   A spirit God has made for us
       That we may worship Him,
    Not striving, serving outwardly,
       But seeking from within.

4   Regenerated by the Lord,
       Renewed in mind and heart,
    He dwells within us as our life
       True worship to impart.

5   We worship here according to
       The inner consciousness,
    Anointed by His Spirit now
       His fulness we express.

6   In truth we serve and worship too,
       In shadows nevermore,
    In Christ, the one reality,
       The Father we adore.

continued

7   To God we offer Christ the Lord
    Whom we experience;
    With God we too delight in Him,
    His light and sweetness sense.

8   In spirit and reality
    Together here we meet,
    To worship, praise, and fellowship
    Around the mercy-seat.

MEETINGS — EXERCISING THE SPIRIT

866*

6.5.6.5.

1 Exercise the spirit!
  Human thought reject;
  Meet with one another,
  Body life respect.

2 Exercise the spirit!
  All the forms forsake;
  Share with one another,
  Each of Christ partake.

3 Exercise the spirit!
  Natural sense renounce;
  Serve with one another,
  Christ the Lord announce.

4 Exercise the spirit!
  Soulish life deny;
  Helping one another,
  On the Lord rely.

5 Freed within the spirit
  From self-righteousness,
  From self-condemnation
  And self-consciousness.

6 Freed within the spirit
  From self-will and pride,
  From self-love and glory,
  All to override.

7 Exercise the spirit,
  Victory to claim
  By the blood which cleanses
  And the mighty Name.

8 Exercise the spirit
  Thus to touch the Lord;
  Ever by the spirit
  Take Him thru His Word.

9 It is by the spirit
  Christ is testified;
  It is by the spirit
  Man is satisfied.

10 Exercise the spirit!
   This is what we need!
   Exercise the spirit!
   May the Lord so lead!

7.6.7.6.D.

1 As members of the Body
     Christ we would manifest,
  Each learning how to function
     His fulness to express;
  We would not be spectators
     But each as members move,
  None bringing death or damage
     But each our profit prove.

2 As in a team we'd never
     Act independently,
  But in coordination,
     Each would dependent be;
  Not acting by our choosing
     But following the flow,
  Distraction never bringing,
     The Spirit's way we'd know.

3 On Christ we here would focus,
     No other center make;
  With Christ in sweet communion
     His riches to partake.
  He is our Head and content,
     His Body we express;
  Whate'er we do while meeting
     Himself must manifest.

4 Built up in love together,
     Not one would criticize;
  To perfect one another,
     We all would exercise.
  Each one from self delivered,
     The natural life forsakes;
  In grace each trained in spirit
     The Body-life partakes.

868*

10.10.10.10.

1 Ere from our gathering we're dismissed, dear Lord,
We sing again to thank Thee from our heart,
For Thy dear presence and refreshing grace,
Which Thou so richly didst to us impart.

2 Though now the meeting's over, in Thy grace,
Thy presence never will from us depart;
But as the Spirit Thy sustaining strength
Thou wouldst in love unceasingly impart.

3 Lord, may Thy presence go with us, we pray,
To bear with us the burden on our heart,
That every moment we Thyself enjoy,
Till in the coming meeting we take part.

869*

10.10.10.10.

1 Ere we depart, we praise Thee, Lord, again
For Thy dear presence and Thy living word;
We are attracted by Thy preciousness,
Our hearts incline to Thee through what we've heard.

2 Thy word is spirit and is life to us,
By it we're nourished, growing, Lord, in Thee;
Thus to Thine image we may be transformed,
With Thy full measure to maturity.

3 Impart Thyself to us, Lord, more and more,
And make us in the spirit walk and move,
That we be kept in fellowship with Thee,
Until we meet again, Thy grace to prove.

7.6.7.6.D. with chorus.

1 Stand up! stand up for Jesus!
   Ye soldiers of the cross;
Lift high His royal banner,
   It must not suffer loss:
From vict'ry unto vict'ry
   His army shall He lead,
Till every foe is vanquished
   And Christ is Lord indeed.

   Stand up for Jesus
   Ye soldiers of the cross;
   Lift high His royal banner,
   It must not, it must not suffer loss.

2 Stand up! stand up for Jesus!
   The trumpet call obey;
Forth to the mighty conflict
   In this His glorious day.
Ye that are men, now serve Him
   Against unnumbered foes;
Let courage rise with danger,
   And strength to strength oppose.

3 Stand up! stand up for Jesus!
   Stand in His strength alone;
The arm of flesh will fail you;
   Ye dare not trust your own.
Put on the Gospel armor,
   And, watching unto prayer,
Where duty calls, or danger,
   Be never wanting there.

continued

SPIRITUAL WARFARE — STANDING UP

4   Stand up! stand up for Jesus!
        The strife will not be long:
    This day the noise of battle,
        The next the victor's song;
    To him that overcometh
        A crown of life shall be;
    He, with the King of glory,
        Shall reign eternally.

SPIRITUAL WARFARE — MARCHING ON

871

6.5.6.5.D. with chorus.

1   Onward Christian soldiers!
        Marching as to war,
    With the cross of Jesus
        Going on before.
    Christ, the royal Master,
        Leads against the foe;
    Forward into battle,
        See, His banners go!

    Onward, Christian soldiers!
        Marching as to war,
    With the cross of Jesus,
        Going on before.

2   At the name of Jesus
        Satan's host doth flee;
    On then, Christian soldiers,
        On to victory!
    Hell's foundations quiver
        At the shout of praise:
    Brothers, lift your voices,
        Loud your anthems raise!

3 Like a mighty army
      Moves the Church of God:
   Brothers, we are treading
      Where the saints have trod;
   We are not divided,
      All one Body we —
   One in faith and Spirit,
      One eternally.

4 Crowns and thrones may perish,
      Kingdoms rise and wane;
   But the Church of Jesus
      Constant will remain.
   Gates of hell can never
      'Gainst the Church prevail;
   We have Christ's own promise,
      Which can never fail.

5 Onward, then, ye people!
      Join our happy throng;
   Blend with ours your voices
      In the triumph song.
   Glory, laud and honor
      Unto Christ, the King;
   This through countless ages
      Men and angels sing.

Used by permission of J. Curwen & Sons, Ltd.
Verse 3, lines 7 and 8 altered by permission.

SPIRITUAL WARFARE — FIGHTING ON

8.8.8.8.   **872**

1 Fight the good fight with all thy might!
   Christ is thy strength, and Christ thy right;
   Lay hold on life, and it shall be
   Thy joy and crown eternally.

continued

2 Run the straight race through God's good grace,
Lift up thine eyes, and seek His face;
Life with its way before us lies,
Christ is the path, and Christ the prize.

3 Cast care aside, lean on thy Guide;
His boundless mercy will provide;
Trust, and thy trusting soul shall prove
Christ is its life, and Christ its love.

4 Faint not nor fear, His arms are near,
He changeth not, and thou art dear;
Only believe, and thou shalt see
That Christ is all in all to thee.

SPIRITUAL WARFARE — CHARGING THROUGH

873†   7.6.7.6.D.

1 Charge, soldiers, charge in battle!
The conflict has begun;
Thy battle song triumphant —
"The victory is won!"
Hell's power must be vanquished
And Satan's forces strewn;
The Captain of the Army
Will come and triumph soon.

2 Charge, soldiers, charge in battle!
And gaze upon thy Lord;
If thou wilt fight His battle,
The throne is thy reward.
This war is of the spirit,
Not fought on earthly ground;
The Lord well knows the foe is near,
Encircling us around.

3 Charge, soldiers, charge in battle!
  Christ's throne awaiteth thee;
His resurrection power
  Will lift thy spirit free.
Through Him thou wilt have power,
  The foe to battle down;
Through Him thou wilt the triumph sing,
  And wear the victor's crown.

4 Charge, soldiers, charge in battle!
  Thou shalt ascend the throne;
A feast He is preparing,
  How happy thou to own.
With Him we're resurrected
  Above the battle din;
Transcending all that binds us,
  We're far above in Him.

5 Charge, soldiers, charge in battle!
  Thou art the royal heir;
The Lord from dust did choose thee,
  That thou His kingdom share.
Thou hast no part in darkness,
  Thy future, O how bright;
With Christ to dwell forever
  And in His love delight.

6 With joyful shouts charge forward!
  The kingdom is before;
Upon the peak of Zion
  We'll sing, the battle o'er.
The Lamb has won the victory!
  The Lamb is on the throne!
With shouts of joy we praise Him,
  For He must overcome.

874

7.7.7.5.

1 Standing in the evil day,
Heeding not what men may say,
Fearing not the face of clay,
Christian soldier, stand.

2 Standing for the Word of God,
Standing for the precious blood,
Following where the saints have trod,
Christian soldier, stand.

3 Stand 'mid Satan's every wile,
Stand 'mid pleasure's wanton smile,
Stand when error would beguile;
Christian soldier, stand.

4 Stand till ends life's little day,
Stand for Jesus, come what may,
Stand and fight and watch and pray;
Christian soldier, stand.

SPIRITUAL WARFARE — BY PRAISING

875

7.6.7.6.D.

1 'Tis easy when the morning
Appears at last to view
To praise thy strong Redeemer
Who burst the bondage through,
But 'tis the praise at midnight
That gives the foe alarm,
That glorifies thy Savior,
And bares His strong right arm.

2 If thou wouldst be a conqueror,
    Yea, more than conqueror thou,
If thou wilt shout in triumph
    And claim the victory now;
The prison-doors will open,
    The dungeon gleam with light,
And sin-chained souls around thee
    Shall see thy Lord's great might.

6.4.6.4.   **876**[†]

1 When war is hot and fierce,
    And Satan strong,
Then firmly trust God's Word
    And sing faith's song.

2 You need to shout but once,
    And you will win;
Oh, do not shut your mouth
    And lose therein.

3 If pressed your spirit is
    And powerless,
Pray thru the precious blood,
    Victorious.

4 The foe though fierce, you can
    Still fight with him;
If you will keep your stand,
    You soon will win.

5 Therefore you must declare
    Christ's victory;
The situation dark
    Soon changed will be.

877

7.6.7.6.D. with chorus.

1 I dare not be defeated
With Calvary in view,
Where Jesus conquered Satan,
Where all His foes He slew;
Come, Lord, and give the vision
To nerve me for the fight,
Make me an overcomer
Clothed with Thy Spirit's might.

A victor, a victor!
Because of Calvary.
Make me an overcomer,
A conqu'ror, a conqu'ror, Lord, in Thee.

2 I dare not be defeated
Since Christ, my conquering King
Has called me to the battle
Which He did surely win.
Come, Lord, and give me courage,
Thy conquering Spirit give,
Make me an overcomer,
In power within me live.

3 I dare not be defeated,
When Jesus leads me on
To press through hellish regions
To share with Him His Throne;
Come, Lord, and give Thy soldier
The power to wield the sword,
Make me an overcomer
Through Thine inerrant Word.

4 I dare not be defeated,
Just at the set of sun,
When Jesus waits to whisper,
"Well done, beloved, well done";

SPIRITUAL WARFARE — BECAUSE OF CALVARY

Come, Lord, bend from the Glory,
On me Thy Spirit cast,
Make me an overcomer,
A victor to the last.

SPIRITUAL WARFARE — BY FAITHFULNESS

9.7.9.7.8.7.8.7. with chorus.

878

1 Conquering now and still to conquer,
   Rideth a King in His might,
Leading the host of all the faithful
   Into the midst of the fight;
See them with courage advancing,
   Clad in their brilliant array,
Shouting the name of their Leader,
   Hear them exultingly say:

   "Not to the strong is the battle,
      Not to the swift is the race;
   Yet to the true and the faithful
      Vict'ry is promised through grace."

2 Conquering now and still to conquer,
   Who is this wonderful King?
Whence are the armies which He leadeth
   While of His glory they sing?
He is our Lord and Redeemer,
   Savior and Monarch divine;
They are the stars that forever
   Bright in His kingdom will shine.

3 Conquering now and still to conquer,
   Jesus, Thou Ruler of all,
Thrones and their scepters all shall perish,
   Crowns and their splendor shall fall,
Yet shall the armies Thou leadest
   Faithful and true to the last,
Find in Thy kingdom eternal
   Rest, when their warfare is past.

SPIRITUAL WARFARE — BY WATCHFULNESS

879

6.5.6.5.D.

1 Christian, dost thou see them
   On the holy ground,
How the powers of darkness
   Compass thee around?
Christian, up and smite them,
   Counting gain but loss;
Smite them by the merit
   Of the holy cross.

2 Christian, dost thou feel them,
   How they work within,
Striving, tempting, luring,
   Goading into sin?
Christian, never tremble,
   Never be downcast;
Gird thee for the conflict;
   Watch, and pray, and fast.

3 Christian, dost thou hear them,
   How they speak thee fair?
"Always fast and vigil,
   Always watch and prayer?"
Christian, answer boldly,
   "While I breathe I pray";
Peace shall follow battle,
   Night shall end in day.

SPIRITUAL WARFARE — BY OBEDIENCE

880 †

8.7.8.7.D.

1 To the foe my word is always, "No,"
   To the Father it is "Yes,"
That His plan and all His counsel
   Be accomplished with success;
When Thine orders I'm obeying,
   Grant me, Lord, authority
To fulfill Thy plan eternal
   Thru the Spirit's power in me.

SPIRITUAL WARFARE — BY OBEDIENCE

2 To the foe my word is always, "No,"
   To the Father it is, "Yes";
  'Tis my attitude eternal;
   May the Lord protect and bless,
 Lest while walking in obedience
   Satan undermine the way;
 When I'm list'ning to Thine orders,
   Grant me mercy, Lord, I pray.

3 To the foe my word is always, "No,"
   To the Father it is, "Yes";
 I completely would obey Him,
   Though deep suff'ring may oppress.
 If the Lord will save and keep me,
   As I forward press with Him,
 Then no trials shall prevent me,
   Nor will opposition grim.

SPIRITUAL WARFARE — IN FAITH

11.10.11.10.
   881

1 We rest on Thee, our Shield and our Defender;
   We go not forth alone against the foe;
 Strong in Thy strength, safe in Thy keeping tender,
   We rest on Thee, and in Thy Name we go.

2 Yea, in Thy Name, O Captain of salvation!
   In Thy dear Name, all other names above;
 Jesus our Righteousness, our sure Foundation,
   Our Prince of glory and our King of love.

3 We go in faith, our own great weakness feeling,
   And needing more each day Thy grace to know:
 Yet from our hearts a song of triumph pealing;
   We rest on Thee, and in Thy Name we go.

continued

SPIRITUAL WARFARE — IN FAITH

4 We rest on Thee, our Shield and our Defender:
   Thine is the battle, Thine shall be the praise
When reigning in the Kingdom of Thy splendor,
   Victors, we rest with Thee, through endless days.

Used and altered by permission of Marshall, Morgan & Scott, Ltd.

882   8.6.8.6.D. with chorus.

1 Encamped along the hills of light,
   Ye Christian soldiers rise,
And press the battle ere the night
   Shall veil the glowing skies;
Against the foe in vales below
   Let all our strength be hurled;
Faith is the victory, we know,
   That overcomes the world.

   Faith is the victory!
   Faith is the victory!
   O glorious victory,
   That overcomes the world.

2 His banner over us is love,
   Our sword the Word of God;
We tread the road the saints before
   With shouts of triumph trod.
By faith, they like a whirlwind's breath,
   Swept on o'er every field;
The faith by which they conquered death
   Is still our shining shield.

3 On every hand the foe we find
   Drawn up in dread array;
Let tents of ease be left behind,
   And onward to the fray.

SPIRITUAL WARFARE — IN FAITH

Salvation's helmet on each head,
　　With truth all girt about,
The earth shall tremble 'neath our tread,
　　And echo with our shout.

4 To him that overcomes the foe,
　　White raiment shall be giv'n;
Before the angels he shall know
　　His name confessed in heav'n;
Then onward from the hills of light,
　　Our hearts with love aflame,
We'll vanquish all the hosts of night,
　　In Jesus' conqu'ring name.

SPIRITUAL WARFARE — IN THE LORD'S NAME

7.7.7.7.

883

1 In the Overcomer's Name
　Be an overcomer too!
　Stand and put the foe to shame
　All the livelong battle through!

2 Jesus is the Name to sound,
　Name to rally fainting hearts!
　To recapture "forfeit" ground,
　Lost awhile through Satan's arts.

3 Backward drive the Evil One!
　Force him out of every hold;
　Smite until the sinking sun
　Sets upon the warrior bold!

4 In the Overcomer's Name
　Be an overcomer too!
　Stand and put the foe to shame
　All the livelong battle through!

884

8.6.8.6.D.

1 The Son of God goes forth to war,
   A kingly crown to gain;
His blood-red banner streams afar:
   Who follows in His train?
Who best can drink his cup of woe,
   Triumphant over pain,
Who patient bears his cross below,
   He follows in His train.

2 The martyr first, whose eagle eye
   Could pierce beyond the grave,
Who saw his Master in the sky,
   And called to Him to save:
Like Him, with pardon on his tongue,
   In midst of mortal pain,
He prayed for them that did the wrong:
   Who follows in his train?

3 A glorious band, the chosen few
   On whom the Spirit came,
Twelve valiant saints, their hope they knew,
   And mocked the cross and flame.
They met the tyrant's brandished steel,
   The lion's gory mane,
They bowed their necks, the death to feel:
   Who follows in their train?

4 A noble army, men and boys,
   The matron and the maid,
Around the Savior's throne rejoice,
   In robes of light arrayed.
They climbed by strength divine from heaven,
   Through peril, toil, and pain:
O God, to us may grace be given
   To follow in their train.

1   Fight the battle in the Body,
     Never fight it on your own;
With the Body to the Head joined,
     Fight the battle on the throne.

     Fight the battle in the Body!
       By the virtue of the Head;
     Standing firmly with the Body,
       Into vict'ry you'll be led.

2   For the Body is God's armor,
     Not for anyone alone;
When you wrestle in the Body,
     All its benefits you own.

3   'Tis the Church on Christ established
     Satan shall not overpow'r;
'Tis the Body built together
     Which resists the evil pow'r.

4   In the Body, by the Headship,
     Sitting in the heavenlies,
Struggle with the wicked spirits
     And the principalities.

5   As a member of the Body,
     With the brethren stand for God;
Praying always in the Spirit,
     Claim the vict'ry through the Blood.

6   In the heav'nlies more than conqu'ror,
     In the power of His might,
As a soldier in the army,
     In the Lord the battle fight.

7   Keep on wrestling in the Body,
     Mighty vict'ry you will see,
Bind and loose, God's will fulfilling,
     And the foes your food will be.

886

Peculiar Meter.

1 A mighty Fortress is our God,
A Bulwark never failing;
Our Helper He amid the flood
Of mortal ills prevailing:
For still our ancient foe
Doth seek to work us woe;
His craft and power are great,
And, armed with cruel hate,
On earth is not his equal.

2 Did we in our own strength confide,
Our striving would be losing;
Were not the right Man on our side,
The Man of God's own choosing:
Dost ask who that may be?
Christ Jesus, it is He;
Lord Sabaoth His Name,
From age to age the same,
And He must win the battle.

3 And though this world, with devils filled,
Should threaten to undo us,
We will not fear, for God hath willed
His truth to triumph through us:
The Prince of Darkness grim,
We tremble not for him;
His rage we can endure,
For lo! his doom is sure,
One little word shall fell him.

4 That word above all earthly powers,
No thanks to them, abideth;
The Spirit and the gifts are ours
Through Him who with us sideth:

SPIRITUAL WARFARE — BY GOD AS FORTRESS

Let goods and kindred go,
This mortal life also;
The body they may kill:
God's truth abideth still,
His Kingdom is forever.

SPIRITUAL WARFARE — WITH GOD'S ARMOR

8.6.8.6.D.

887 †

1 The name of Jesus is our stand,
  It is our victory;
Not on ourselves do we rely,
  But, mighty Lord, on Thee.
Our weapons are not arms of flesh,
  But ours the Spirit's sword,
And God's whole armor putting on,
  We battle in the Lord.

2 Behold, the foe doth meet and plot,
  Stand firm in one accord!
Though war be fierce and darkness thick,
  Resist him in the Lord!
If one thru fear should backward turn,
  He undermines the rest.
Oh, do not let your brothers down,
  Nor by you be distressed.

3 The devil knows his time is short,
  He is the more enraged,
And by his wiles would weaken us
  Before the battle's waged.
The trials now more numerous are,
  The suff'ring e'en more sore,
The force of hell opposing us
  More dreadful than before.

continued

4 What should our posture be today
   In such a desperate hour?
Should we our ease and pleasure seek
   And let the foe devour?
Or with increasing conflict strong,
   Courageous to endure?
'Tis here that life or death is won!
   Who will God's praise secure?

5 For Christ the Lord we then would stand,
   He is the Conqueror!
For Him we would endure the pain
   Until the fight is o'er.
The hour of triumph soon we'll see —
   The Lord will come again;
If now we suffer for His sake,
   Then we with Him shall reign.

888
                  6.6.8.6.D.

1 Soldiers of Christ, arise,
   And put your armor on,
Strong in the strength which God supplies,
   Through His eternal Son;
Strong in the Lord of Hosts,
   And in His mighty pow'r,
Who in the strength of Jesus trusts
   Is more than conqueror.

2 Stand then in His great might,
   With all His strength endued;
And take, to arm you for the fight,
   The panoply of God,

That, having all things done,
And all your conflicts past,
Ye may o'ercome through Christ alone,
And stand complete at last.

3   Leave no unguarded place,
No weakness of the soul,
Take every virtue, every grace,
And fortify the whole.
To keep your armor bright
Attend with constant care,
Still walking in your Captain's sight
And watching unto prayer.

4   Pray, without ceasing pray,
Your Captain gives the word;
His summons cheerfully obey,
And call upon the Lord:
To God your every want
In instant prayer display;
Pray always; pray, and never faint;
Pray, without ceasing pray.

5   From strength to strength go on;
Wrestle, and fight, and pray;
Tread all the powers of darkness down,
And win the well-fought day:
Still let the Spirit cry
In all His soldiers, "Come!"
Till Christ the Lord descend from high,
And take the conquerors home.

889*

8.7.8.7.D.

1 By the blood of Christ the Victor
   Overcome the enemy;
   By its virtue and its power
   You will win the victory.

   By the blood of Christ the Victor
   Overcome the enemy;
   By its virtue and its power
   You will win the victory.

2 By the blood of Christ the Victor
   Counter him who doth accuse;
   By the blood for you defending
   All the sland'rer's blame refuse.

3 By the blood of Christ the Victor
   God's sure faithfulness believe;
   Thru the blood of your Redeemer
   God's forgiveness now receive.

4 By the blood of Christ the Victor
   Your position now declare;
   Thru the blood, prevailing ever,
   All His vict'ry fully share.

5 By the blood of Christ the Victor
   Claim His full authority;
   Just apply the blood of Jesus
   And defeat the enemy.

6 By the blood of Christ the Victor
   Standing in the heavenlies;
   In the pow'r of Christ ascended,
   Tread the principalities.

SPIRITUAL WARFARE — BY THE LORD'S VICTORY

8.5.8.5.D.

890

1 Hallelujah! Christ is Victor,
Tell with every breath,
That the Savior still is conqu'ror
Over sin and death.

Hallelujah! Christ is Victor,
Tell where'er you go,
That the Lord is still the conqu'ror,
Over every foe.

2 Hallelujah! Christ is Victor,
Pain and sickness flee,
When we plead the mighty victory
Won on Calvary.

3 Hallelujah! Christ is Victor,
Therefore do and dare;
Go wherever Jesus sends you
In prevailing prayer.

4 Hallelujah! Christ is Victor,
No defeat nor fear
Evermore must dim thy vision!
Christ the way will clear.

5 Hallelujah! Christ is Victor,
Soon His voice shall ring,
"Come ye conquerors, come up hither,
Join thy conquering King."

SPIRITUAL WARFARE — BY THE LORD'S EMPOWERING

Peculiar Meter.

891

1 O Lord, to conflict new
You daily call your servant;
With joy and spirits fervent
We rise to follow You.
Lead us to battle too,
We are Your soldiers true.

continued

SPIRITUAL WARFARE — BY THE LORD'S EMPOWERING

Chorus:

Our hands empow'r,
Our hearts enflame!
We'll overcome in Jesus' name,
We'll overcome in Jesus' name!
Our hands empow'r, our hearts enflame!

2 Fully equip us, Lord,
With faith and perseverance,
With wisdom and adherence,
With zeal and love outpoured;
Set us on fire, O Lord,
To win the great reward.

3 We lift up firm and high
The Cross, our banner glorious.
The enemy notorious
By Blood we dare defy.
To self the Cross apply,
On Christ alone rely.

4 Wrestle, suffer and pray!
The end shall be victorious.
The promised crown all-glorious
We shall receive one day.
Wrestle, suffer and pray!
We'll reign with Christ for aye.

SPIRITUAL WARFARE — BY THE LORD'S AUTHORITY

892†   8.8.8.8.

1 With all the pow'r in heav'n and earth
Our resurrected Lord's endued;
If we unite and live by Him,
The enemy will be subdued.

SPIRITUAL WARFARE — BY THE LORD'S AUTHORITY

2 In Jesus' name we must declare
That we shall overcome the foe;
We draw authority from Him
The serpent's head to crush below.

3 No matter what, thou mountain high,
In heav'n or earth, where'er thou art,
At any cost we'll level thee,
In Jesus' name thou must depart!

4 Faith orders thee "Remove from here,
And be thou cast into the sea!"
We should, we must, we can, we will,
Fulfill God's purpose faithfully.

SPIRITUAL WARFARE — BY THE LORD'S COMING

6.6.8.6.D.

893 †

1 Conflict today is fierce,
The strength of Satan more;
The cry of battle calling now
Is louder than before.
The rebel voice of hell
E'en stronger now becomes;
But list, the midnight cry resounds,
Behold, I quickly come!

2 Trials more bitter grow,
The fighting doth enlarge;
Hell's forces rally all their pow'rs
And gather for the charge.
Yet while we wait and watch
And feel the war severe,
We hear the joyful song ring out,
Jesus, the Lord, is near!

continued

3   'Tis harder at the end
      The word to testify,
For Satan fights with all his pow'r
      Our witness to defy.
      Much greater strength we need
      The foe to overcome;
How happy when the Lord we see
      And all our sighing's done!

4   Who then will forward go
      Strong in His mighty power?
Who then will firmly trust the Lord
      Until the vict'ry hour;
      Till with the conqu'rors blest,
      The triumph song's begun?
That man will then rejoice to hear,
      Behold, I quickly come!

5   Who then will choose God's best,
      And take the narrow track,
Though passing thru the wildest storms,
      Yet never turning back?
      Who now will dare press on,
      Enduring pain and fear?
All such will then rejoice to see
      Jesus, the Lord, is near!

6   Though deep the darkness be
      We still would onward go,
Till we the day of rapture greet
      And glory 'round shall glow.
      'Tis there we'll see the Lord,
      And Satan overcome;
The overcomers will rejoice,
      Jesus, the Lord, has come!

8.5.8.5.D.

894*

1 Will you be an overcomer?
   Christ is calling now!
Will you then be such a follower,
   Though you know not how?

   Will you be an overcomer?
      Will you make this choice?
   Christ is calling, Christ is calling,
      Listen to His voice!

2 Will you be an overcomer?
   To the Lord be drawn!
Keep the "first love," never leave it,
   Till the break of dawn.

3 Will you be an overcomer?
   On His life depend!
Dare to suffer persecution,
   Faithful to the end.

4 Will you be an overcomer?
   Testimony bear!
Keep away from false religion,
   "Hidden manna" share.

5 Will you be an overcomer,
   Simple, real, and pure?
Overcome all evil mixture,
   Ruling pow'r secure.

6 Will you be an overcomer?
   Trust the living Lord!
Keep your "garments" from the deadness,
   Win the life-reward.

7 Will you be an overcomer?
   Never lukewarm be,
Ne'er content with what you've gotten,
   More you need to see.

continued

8 Will you be an overcomer?
   Christ is calling still!
   Will you now be loyal to Him,
   His demand fulfill.

SERVICE — TO THE WORK

895   12.12.12.12. with chorus.

1 To the work! to the work! we are servants of God,
   Let us follow the path that our Master has trod;
   With the might of His power our strength to renew,
   Let us do by His grace what He calls us to do.

   Work for Him by His grace;
   Work thru Him for His praise;
   Work with Him all the days;
   And work in Him in many ways.

2 To the work! to the work! let the hungry be fed;
   To the fountain of life let the thirsty be led;
   In the cross and its vict'ry our glory shall be,
   While we herald the tidings, "Salvation is free!"

3 To the work! to the work! in the strength of the Lord,
   By the pow'r of His Name, with the light of His Word,
   All the slaves of the darkness of Satan set free
   And His riches of grace in His glory we'll see.

896   8.8.8.8.

1 Go, labor on; spend, and be spent;
   Thy joy to do the Father's will;
   It is the way the Master went;
   Should not the servant tread it still?

2 Go, labor on: 'tis not for nought;
　　Thy earthly loss is heav'nly gain;
　Men heed thee, love thee, praise thee not;
　　The Master praises, what are men?

3 Go, labor on; your hands are weak,
　　Your knees are faint, your souls cast down;
　Yet falter not; the prize you seek
　　Is near, a kingdom and a crown.

4 Go, labor on while it is day,
　　The world's dark night is hastening on;
　Speed, speed thy work, cast sloth away,
　　It is not thus that souls are won.

5 Men die in darkness at your side,
　　Without a hope to cheer the tomb;
　Take up the torch and wave it wide,
　　The torch that lights time's thickest gloom.

6 Press on, faint not, keep watch and pray;
　　Be wise the erring soul to win;
　Go forth into the world's highway,
　　Compel the wanderer to come in.

7 Press on, and in thy work rejoice;
　　For work comes rest, the prize thus won;
　Soon shalt thou hear the Master's voice,
　　The midnight cry, Behold, I come!

7.6.7.6.D. **897**

1 Work, for the Day is coming,
　　Day in the Word foretold,
　When, 'mid the scenes triumphant,
　　Longed for by saints of old,
　He, who on earth a stranger
　　Traversed its paths of pain,
　Jesus, the Prince, the Savior,
　　Comes evermore to reign. *continued*

2 Work, for the Day is coming,
  Darkness will soon be gone;
Then o'er the night of weeping
  Day without end shall dawn.
What now we sow in sadness
  Then we shall reap in joy;
Hope will be changed to gladness,
  Praise be our blest employ.

3 Work, for the Day is coming,
  Made for the saints of light;
Off with the garments dreary,
  On with the armor bright:
Soon will the strife be ended,
  Soon all our toils below;
Not to the dark we're tending,
  But to the Day we go.

4 Work, for the Lord is coming,
  Children of light are we;
From Jesus' bright appearing
  Powers of darkness flee.
Out of the mist, at His bidding,
  Souls like the dew are born:
O'er all the East are spreading
  Tints of the rosy morn.

5 Work, then, the Day is coming,
  No time for sighing now;
Prize for the race awaits thee,
  Wreaths for the victor's brow.
Now morning Light is breaking,
  Soon will the Day appear;
Night shades appall no longer,
  Jesus, our Lord, is near.

7.6.7.6.D.

1   The love of Christ constraineth;
     Oh, let the watchword ring
  Till all the world adoring
     To Jesus' feet it bring.
  Till north and south the kingdoms
     Shall own His glorious sway,
  And east and west the nations
     Rejoice to see His Day.

2   The love of Christ constraineth;
     At home, abroad, where'er
  By sea or shore abiding
     His Name and mark we bear.
  We ask not that our service
     Or great or small may be,
  If only Thou wilt own it,
     Dear Lord, as unto Thee.

3   The love of Christ constraineth;
     And we who trust His Word,
  Who know and feel its power
     To gladder service stirred,
  Shall neither faint nor falter,
     Though dark the night and long,
  And weak our hands that labor;
     His strength shall make us strong.

4   The love of Christ constraineth,
     Then let us work and pray,
  And watch the glad appearing
     Of that triumphant day,
  When Father, Son, and Spirit,
     By every tongue confessed,
  All earth His broad dominion
     In His dear love shall rest.

899

Peculiar Meter.

1 The work is Thine, O Christ our Lord,
  The cause for which we stand;
And being Thine, 'twill overcome
  Its foes on every hand.
Yet grains of wheat, before they grow,
Are buried in the earth below;
All that is old doth perish there
To form a life both new and fair:
So too are we from self and sin made free.

2 Through suff'ring Thou, O Christ, didst go
  Unto Thy throne above,
And leadest now the selfsame way
  Those true in faith and love;
So lead us, then, though suff'rings wait,
To share Thy kingdom's heav'nly state;
Thy death has broken Satan's might,
And leads the faithful to the light;
Eternal light, from darkness into light.

3 Thou hast, O Savior, led the way
  Through agony and death;
O give, we pray, yet more and more
  Thy Spirit's living breath!
Send messengers o'er land and sea
To bring Thy children all to Thee;
Thy name can save, Thy name makes free;
We consecrate ourselves to Thee
As servants true, as warriors brave and true.

Peculiar Meter.

1 Oh, to be nothing, nothing!
Only to lie at His feet,
A broken and emptied vessel —
For the Master's use made meet!
Emptied that He might fill me
As forth to His service I go;
Broken, that so unhindered,
His life through me might flow.

Oh, to be nothing, nothing!
Only to lie at His feet,
A broken and emptied vessel —
For the Master's use made meet!

2 Oh, to be nothing, nothing!
Only as led by His hand —
A messenger at His gateway,
Only waiting for His command;
Only an instrument ready
His praises to sound at His will —
Willing, should He not require me,
In silence to wait on Him still.

3 Oh, to be nothing, nothing!
Painful the humbling may be!
Yet low in the dust I'd lay me
That the world might my Savior see!
Rather be nothing, nothing!
To Him let their voices be raised!
He is the fountain of blessing,
He only is meet to be praised!

901   9.8.9.8.8.

1 Lord, how can man e'er preach Thy Word?
 He is a brittle, crazy glass;
Yet in Thy temple is conferred
 This glorious and transcendent place,
 To be a window through Thy grace.

2 But when Thou dost anneal Thy story
 In glass, Thy life to shine within
The holy preachers, light of glory
 More radiant grows and more doth win,
 Which else shows waterish, bleak, and thin.

3 The life and doctrine blent in one
 As light and color mingled, bring
A strong regard; but speech alone
 Doth vanish like a flaring thing,
 And in the ear, not spirit ring.

902   6.6.6.6.D.

1 Shine Thou upon us, Lord,
 True Light of men, today,
 And through the written Word
 Thy very self display;
 That so from hearts which burn
 With gazing on Thy face,
 Thy little ones may learn
 The wonders of Thy grace.

2 Breathe Thou upon us, Lord,
 Thy Spirit's living flame,
 That so with one accord
 Our lips may tell Thy name;
 Give Thou the hearing ear,
 Fix Thou the wandering thought,
 That those we teach may hear
 The great things Thou hast wrought.

3   Speak Thou for us, O Lord,
In all we say of Thee;
According to Thy Word
Let all our teaching be;
That so Thy lambs may know
Their own true Shepherd's voice,
Where'er He leads them go,
And in His love rejoice.

4   Live Thou within us, Lord;
Thy mind and will be ours;
Be Thou beloved, adored,
And served with all our powers;
That so our lives may teach
Thy children what Thou art,
And plead, by more than speech,
For Thee with every heart.

8.8.8.8.   **903**

1   Lord, speak to me, that I may speak
In living echoes of Thy tone;
As Thou hast sought, so let me seek
Thy erring children lost and lone.

2   O lead me, Lord, that I may lead
The wandering and the wavering feet;
O feed me, Lord, that I may feed
Thy hungering ones with manna sweet.

3   O strengthen me, that while I stand
Firm on the rock, and strong in Thee,
I may stretch out a loving hand
To wrestlers with the troubled sea.

continued

4   O teach me, Lord, that I may teach
The precious things Thou dost impart;
And wing my words, that they may reach
The hidden depths of many a heart.

5   O give Thine own sweet rest to me,
That I may speak with soothing power
A word in season, as from Thee
To weary ones in needful hour.

6   O fill me with Thy fulness, Lord,
Until my very heart o'erflow
In kindling thought and glowing word,
Thy love to tell, Thy praise to show.

7   O use me, Lord, use even me,
Just as Thou wilt, and when, and where,
Until Thy blessed face I see,
Thy rest, Thy joy, Thy glory share!

SERVICE — BY DWELLING WITH THE LORD

904   8.8.8.8.D.(A)

1   We have a most glorious King;
The heavens, He says, are His throne;
All worlds are His mighty domain,
All kingdoms His scepter shall own.
He dwells with His people below,
He loves in their trials to share;
We dwell with the King for His work,
His burden we willingly bear.

2 I'm dwelling with Jesus my King;
   I've found where He dwells with His own;
   I've opened the door of my heart;
   He's made it His temple and throne.
   Like Mary I sit at His feet,
   Like John I recline on His breast;
   His presence is fulness of joy,
   His bosom is infinite rest.

3 I dwell with the King for His work,
   I've part in His glorious plan
   To bring in His kingdom to earth
   And tell His salvation to man.
   The world has its work and rewards,
   I count them but folly and loss;
   My business is only His work,
   My message is only His cross.

4 I dwell with the King for His work,
   The work, it is His and not mine;
   He plans and prepares it for me
   And fills me with power divine.
   So duty is changed to delight,
   And prayer into praise as I sing;
   I dwell with my King for His work
   And work in the strength of my King.

5 We'll dwell with the King for His work
   And work thru each day of the year.
   Perhaps ere it passes, the King
   In glory Himself shall appear.
   Oh, then in some closer embrace,
   Oh, then in some nobler employ
   We'll dwell with the King for His work
   In endless, ineffable joy!

905

8.8.8.8.

1 O Master, let me walk with Thee
In lowly paths of service free;
Tell me Thy secret, help me bear
The strain of toil, the fret of care.

2 Help me the slow of heart to move
By some clear, winning word of love;
Teach me the wayward feet to stay,
And guide them in the Godward way.

3 Teach me Thy patience; still with Thee
In closer, dearer company,
In work that keeps faith sweet and strong,
In trust that triumphs over wrong.

4 In hope that sends a shining ray
Far down the future's broad'ning way,
In peace that only Thou canst give,
With Thee, O Master, let me live.

SERVICE — BY THE LORD WITHIN

906

9.8.9.9.8.

1 How much can we do for our Savior?
How much for our dear fellow man?
The way to do more than we're able
Is Jesus within to enable;
Thus we can do more than we can.

2 How much can we be for our Savior
In life with its brief, fleeting span?
If Jesus within us is dwelling
Our life and our actions infilling,
We all can do more than we can.

3 How much can we bear for our Savior?
How much for our dear fellow man?

SERVICE — BY THE LORD WITHIN

If in us His love is constraining,
If 'neath us His arms are sustaining,
　We all can do more than we can.

4 How much can we give for our Savior?
　To succor our dear fellow man?
If from us His love is o'erflowing,
Our life will be ever outgoing;
　We'll always do more than we can.

SERVICE — BY THE LORD'S LEADING

7.7.7.7.

907

1 Not where we elect to go,
　But where Jesus leads the way,
　There the living waters flow,
　There our darkness turns to day.

2 Not our self-appointed task
　Will the Lord's approval win,
　But the work we did not ask,
　Finished humbly, just for Him.

3 Not the prayer we long to plead
　When we bend before the Throne,
　But the touching deeper need
　Of the Spirit's wordless groan.

4 Not the gift we proudly lay
　On His altar will He heed,
　If our hearts have said Him, "Nay,"
　When He whispered, "I have need."

5 Thus we die, and dying live
　In the heavenlies with the Lord;
　Thus we serve, and pray, and give,
　Christ Himself our great Reward.

908* 8.7.8.7.D.

1 Not of letters, but of spirit,
   The New Testamental way;
For 'tis life the spirit giveth,
   But the letters always slay.
Outward work God never reckons,
   But what's from the inmost part;
It is not to serve in letter,
   But life's newness to impart.

2 Not just by the outward teachings,
   But by His anointing moved;
Not just by the outward pattern,
   But by inward vision proved.
Not by human rules or rituals,
   But by heaven's rule within;
Not by human-made decisions,
   But by guidance giv'n of Him.

3 Not a dead religion serving,
   But in Christ as life to live;
Not theology dispensing,
   But a living Christ to give.
Not the knowledge of mere doctrine,
   But the message Christ should be;
Not the gifts, the forms, the teachings,
   But God's Christ — reality.

4 Not objectively to worship,
   But to serve Him inwardly;
Not to preach a Christ objective,
   But Himself subjectively.
Not just by the Scripture serving,
   But in spirit and in life;
Not by flesh, but by the Spirit
   Filling, freeing from all strife.

12.12.12.12. with chorus.

1   In the stream! in the stream! let us work
          for the Lord,
       By His mind, in His way, as revealed in
          His Word;
    In the flow of His life let us work with His
          pow'r
       For His Kingdom and Church in the time
          of His hour.

       In the stream! in the stream!
       Let us work in the stream!
       In the stream! in the stream!
       We'll work as in the heav'nly team!

2   In the stream! in the stream! let us work
          with the Lord
       In the flow of the Spirit, as taught by
          His Word;
    Never working by self, independent and
          free,
       But in service related in full harmony.

3   In the stream! in the stream! let us work
          in the Lord,
       With the Church, with the saints, in the
          light of His Word;
    Give the Word, life supply to the people
          in need,
       Thus fulfilling God's plan, in His flow
          we'll proceed.

910*

8.7.8.7.D.(I)

1 The overflow of life is work,
   The work should be our living!
What we experience e'er should be
   The message we are giving.
When living and the work are one,
   The work will be effectual;
When message and the life are one,
   The word will be successful.

2 The work must be the fruit of life,
   Born thru the Spirit's flowing;
As branches of the Lord, the vine,
   Fruit bearing, life bestowing.
'Tis Christ Himself thru us to work,
   Himself as life expressing,
And all the riches of His life
   To others manifesting.

3 'Tis not a movement borne of man,
   But by His power moving;
'Tis not the deeds done outwardly,
   But inward action proving.
'Tis not the work of enterprise,
   But 'tis His life confessing;
'Tis not to toil for our success,
   But 'tis Himself expressing.

4 Our plans, our aims, our energy
   We must abandon wholly,
That He may work His plan thru us,
   His aim and object solely.
Ourselves, with all we are and have,
   To death we must surrender,
That Christ may live Himself thru us
   With riches and with splendor.

8.7.8.7.D.

1 O how blessed is the priest's life,
　　Christ to him is all in all:
All His clothing, food, and dwelling,
　　And His portion therewithal.

O how blessed is the priest's life,
　　Christ to him is all in all:
All his clothing, food, and dwelling,
　　And his portion therewithal.

2 All the clothing of his service
　　Is the beauty of the Lord;
Glorious splendor do his garments,
　　Breast and shoulder-piece afford.

3 When in sacrifice he offers
　　Christ to God as God has willed,
Then as food he doth enjoy Him
　　And is with His riches filled.

4 Putting on the Lord as clothing,
　　Christ without he doth express;
Eating, drinking, with Him mingled,
　　Christ within doth him possess.

5 Holy, glorious is their dwelling,
　　'Tis the increase of the Lord;
Here the priests built up together
　　Unto God a house afford.

6 All his portion, all his living,
　　Everything the priests possess —
All is Christ and Christ forever,
　　In His all-inclusiveness.

912*

8.7.8.7.D.

1 Christ to minister is service
　　Both to God and others too,
　Christ, the surplus, e'er supplying,
　　Off'ring Him as service true.

　Christ to minister is service
　　Both to God and others too,
　Christ, the surplus, e'er supplying,
　　Off'ring Him as service true.

2 As the Israelites did offer
　　From the surplus of their land,
　Thus some produce reaped of Jesus
　　Must be in our serving hand.

3 We on Christ, as land, must labor,
　　Harvest Him for all our fare;
　Tasting Him to overflowing,
　　Christ with others we may share.

4 Holding Christ, as members growing,
　　Each his function must observe;
　Christ receiving, Christ partaking,
　　To His Body Christ we serve.

5 Fellowship and testimony,
　　Ministry and worship too,
　In all helps and ministrations
　　Christ is all our service true.

SERVICE — IN THE BODY

913*

8.7.8.7.D.

1 Serve and work within the Body,
　　This the Lord doth signify;
　For His purpose is the Body,
　　And with it we must comply.

SERVICE — IN THE BODY

Chorus:

Serve and work within the Body,
Never independently;
As the members of the Body,
Functioning relatedly.

2 As the members we've been quickened
Not as individuals free;
We must always serve together,
All related mutually.

3 Living stones, we're built together
And a house for God must be,
As the holy priesthood serving,
In a blessed harmony.

4 Thus we must be built together,
In position minister;
For the basis of our service
Is the body character.

5 In our ministry and service,
From the Body, our supply;
If detached and isolated,
Out of function we will die.

6 'Tis by serving in the Body
Riches of the Head we share;
'Tis by functioning as members
Christ's full measure we will bear.

7 To the Head fast holding ever,
That we may together grow,
From the Head supplies incoming
Thru us to the Body flow.

8 Lord, anew we give our bodies;
May we be transformed to prove
All Thy will, to know Thy Body,
And therein to serve and move.

914*

8.7.8.7.D.

1 For the Church should be our service,
  'Tis the perfect will of God;
'Tis the only way of working
  Which the Lord's apostles trod.

  For the Church should be our service,
    Not our aims to satisfy;
  This, the perfect will of God is,
    And with it we must comply.

2 For 'tis God's eternal purpose
  That the Church His vessel be;
He intends that all our service
  Build His Church continually.

3 All the gifted persons given
  To the Body by the Head
Are to aid the Church's building,
  That to fulness she be led.

4 All the gifts and all the functions,
  All the spirit's power shown,
All the ministries are given
  For the Church and that alone.

5 All the preaching of the Gospel,
  All the teaching ministry,
Every other kind of service
  For the Church alone should be.

6 Ministry is for the Churches,
  Not the Church for ministry;
All the lampstands are the Churches,
  Not a form of ministry.

7 This will keep the Church's oneness,
    Saving us from every sect;
  This will ever test our motives,
    And our aim will thus correct.

8 Lord, deliver us from our work,
    From the work of any sect;
  For Thy Church alone we'd labor
    And its building up effect.

PREACHING OF THE GOSPEL — THE NATIONS' CALL

915

7.6.7.6.D.

1 From Greenland's icy mountains,
    From India's coral strand,
  Where Afric's sunny fountains
    Roll down their golden sand;
  From many an ancient river,
    From many a palmy plain,
  They call us to deliver
    Their land from error's chain.

2 What though the spicy breezes
    Blow soft on Ceylon's isle;
  Though every prospect pleases,
    And only man is vile;
  In vain with lavish kindness
    The gifts of God are strown;
  The heathen, in his blindness,
    Bows down to wood and stone.

3 Can we, whose souls are lighted
    With wisdom from on high;
  Can we to men benighted
    The lamp of life deny?

continued

Salvation! O salvation!
  The joyful sound proclaim,
Till each remotest nation
  Has learned Messiah's name.

4 Waft, waft, ye winds, His story;
     And you, ye waters, roll,
   Till, like a sea of glory,
     It spreads from pole to pole;
   Till o'er our ransomed nature,
     The Lamb for sinners slain,
   Redeemer, King, Creator,
     In bliss returns to reign.

916   7.7.7.7.

1 Now the Lord our souls has fed,
   With Himself, the Living Bread;
   Fed us, sitting at His feet,
   With the finest of the wheat.

2 We have endless treasure found;
   We have all things and abound;
   Rich abundance and to spare;
   Shall we not the blessing share?

3 For, while we are feasting here,
   Starving millions, far and near,
   Call us with the bitter cry:
   Come and help us, or we die.

4 In this day of full increase,
   Shall we, can we, hold our peace?
   Staying here we do not well;
   Now then, let us go and tell:

5 Tell how He hath set us free,
How He leads triumphantly;
How He satisfies our need;
How His rest is rest indeed.

6 Speak, for we, Thy servants, hear;
Thou hast taught us not to fear;
And whate'er Thy word shall be,
We can do it, Lord, in Thee.

PREACHING OF THE GOSPEL — "GO YE!"

11.10.11.10 with chorus.   **917**

1 Far, far away, in heathen darkness dwelling,
Millions of souls forever may be lost;
Who, who will go, salvation's story telling,
Looking to Jesus, counting not the cost?

"All pow'r is given unto me,
All pow'r is given unto me,
Go ye into all the world and preach
the gospel,
And lo, I am with you alway."

2 See o'er the world, wide open doors inviting:
Soldiers of Christ, arise and enter in!
Christians, awake! your forces all uniting,
Send forth the Gospel, break the chains of sin.

3 "Why will ye die?" the voice of God is calling,
"Why will ye die?" re-echo in His name:
Jesus hath died to save from death appalling,
Life and salvation therefore go proclaim.

918

11.10.11.10. with chorus.

1 Christians, make haste, your mission high fulfilling,
    To tell to all the world that God is Light,
That He who made all nations is not willing
    One soul should perish, lost in shades of night.

    Publish glad tidings, tidings of peace;
    Tidings of Jesus, redemption and release.

2 Behold how many thousands still are lying,
    Bound in the darksome prison-house of sin,
With none to tell them of the Savior's dying
    Or of the life He died for them to win.

3 'Tis yours to save from peril of perdition
    The soul for whom the Lord His life laid down;
Beware lest, slothful to fulfill your mission,
    You lose one jewel that should deck His crown.

4 Proclaim to every people, tongue, and nation
    That God, in whom they move and live, is love;
Tell how He stooped to save His lost creation,
    And died on earth that men He might approve.

5 Give of your sons to bear the message glorious;
    Give of your wealth to speed them on their way;
Pour out your soul for them in prayer victorious,
    And all you spend our Savior will repay.

6 He comes again; O brothers, ere you meet Him,
    Make known to every heart His saving grace;
Let none whom He hath ransomed fail to greet Him,
    Through your neglect unfit to see His face.

7.7.7.7.7.7.

1 He shall reign o'er all the earth,
He who wore the crown of thorn,
Whom they deemed of little worth,
Whom they met with hate and scorn;
Send the tidings forth, that all
Humbly at His feet may fall.

2 Long His heritage hath lain
'Neath the false usurper's sway;
He will claim it back again,
Rout the foes and win the day.
Send the tidings forth, that all
Humbly at His feet may fall.

3 Then, beneath His rule of peace
Heaven shall smile, and earth shall sing,
Ever yielding rich increase
To the honor of her King.
Send the tidings forth, that all
Humbly at His feet may fall.

4 Hasten, Lord, the wondrous hour,
Bid it strike from shore to shore,
Thine the kingdom and the power,
Thine the glory evermore.
Bow each rebel heart, that all
At Thy feet adoring fall.

920

6.4.6.4.6.6.6.4.

1 Sound ye the trumpet-call;
   Heralds proclaim
Jesus as Lord of all,
   Sound forth His fame;
Tell of His great renown,
Lift high the kingly crown,
Let every knee bow down
   At His blest name.

2 Who will go forth for Him?
   Who will arise?
Though eyes with tears are dim,
   Severed love's ties:
Counting all things but loss,
Earth's highest gain but dross,
And glorying in the cross,
   Who will arise?

3 Go, for the crowning day
   Draws ever near;
Time will soon pass away,
   Jesus be here:
Raise ye the cross where now
Nations to idols bow;
Dawn o'er the mountain's brow
   Tells He is near.

4 Hark to the trumpet-blast!
   Jesus is King!
He comes to reign at last,
   All conquering:
Then the wide world shall own,
Bending before His throne,
Jesus is King alone,
   Jesus is King!

Peculiar Meter.

1 Rescue the perishing,
   Care for the dying,
Snatch them in pity from sin and the grave;
   Weep o'er the erring one,
   Lift up the fallen,
Tell them of Jesus the mighty to save.

   Rescue the perishing,
      Care for the dying;
   Jesus is merciful,
      Jesus will save.

2 Though they are slighting Him,
   Still He is waiting,
Waiting the penitent child to receive;
   Plead with them earnestly,
   Plead with them gently;
He will forgive if they only believe.

3 Down in the human heart,
   Crushed by the tempter,
Feelings lie buried that grace can restore;
   Touched by a loving heart,
   Wakened by kindness,
Chords that are broken will vibrate once more.

4 Rescue the perishing,
   Duty demands it;
Strength for thy labor the Lord will provide;
   Back to the narrow way
   Patiently win them;
Tell the poor wand'rer a Savior has died.

922*   8.7.8.7.D.

1 To the lost world minister Christ,
     Not just by word, but by life,
   Imparting Christ by living deeds
     To the poor souls living in strife.

   To the lost world minister Christ,
     By daily walk making Him known;
   Imparting Christ by whom you live,
     Share with all men what you own.

2 To the lost world minister Christ,
     The precious One you possess,
   Imparting Christ to those you love
     As all their gain and success.

3 To the lost world minister Christ,
     The very Christ you enjoy,
   Imparting Christ to all your friends
     As all their boast and their joy.

4 To the lost world minister Christ,
     Who is your life and your all,
   Imparting Christ to all you meet,
     All fallen ones, great or small.

PREACHING OF THE GOSPEL —
COLLECTING MATERIALS

923*   10.10.10.10.

1 Go to collect materials for the House,
   Go to convince dear souls and bring them in;
   Bring in the very souls whom God has made,
   Bring in the souls usurped by every sin.

2 Go to collect materials for the House,
   Go to deliver people from the world,
   From all Satanic darkness and deceit,
   From the allurements Satan has unfurled.

3   Go to collect materials for the House,
     Go to win souls to glorify the Lord;
     Go to defeat the enemy of God,
     Go, sinners to release, with one accord.

4   Go to collect materials for the House,
     Go, Christ proclaiming, on the Body ground;
     Go thus in oneness with the faithful saints,
     And let the trumpet of the gospel sound.

PREACHING OF THE GOSPEL — FEEDING PEOPLE

924

8.6.8.6.D. with chorus.

1   Along the shores of Galilee,
     When Christ five thousand fed,
  Not one was omitted
     In the breaking of the bread.
  Today they die in heathen lands,
     They die in want and dread,
  For they have been omitted
     In the breaking of the Bread.

     Lord, I would give them the Bread of Life,
       The Living Water too;
     My heart cries out, "Oh, here am I,
       Ready, Thy will to do."

2   Long years have passed and few have heard
     That Jesus Christ has bled,
  That they might feed on Him who died
     To be that Living Bread.
  To gods of stone and wood they cry,
     Yet they are never fed,
  For they have been omitted
     In the breaking of the Bread.

continued

3 Great God, who gave Thine only Son,
   Help us, now Spirit-led,
To tell the story of Thy love
   To those who ask for bread.
Then gladly will we go or send,
   Till this blest news has spread,
And they have been included
   In the breaking of the Bread.

PREACHING OF THE GOSPEL —
BY THE FLOW OF LIFE

925*

8.7.8.7.D.

1 Outreach of the glorious gospel
   Is the flow of life within;
It is by our testimony
   That lost sinners we may win.

Grant us, Lord, the living outflow,
   May Thy life through us be seen;
Through us as Thy living vessels
   Quicken people from within.

2 It is by the life convincing
   That the people may believe;
It is by the life imparting
   That the souls may life receive.

3 Always in the Lord abiding,
   As the branches fruit to bear;
By the inner life out-flowing
   Christ with others we may share.

4 May our living be the preaching,
   Making Christ to others known;
Not the word of doctrine-preaching,
   But the seed of life be sown.

8.8.8.6.

1 Send Thou, O Lord, to every place
Swift messengers before Thy face,
The heralds of Thy wondrous grace,
  Where Thou Thyself wilt come.

2 Send men whose eyes have seen the King!
Men in whose ears His sweet words ring;
Send such Thy lost ones home to bring;
  Send them where Thou wilt come.

3 To bring good news to souls in sin;
The bruised and broken hearts to win;
In every place to bring them in,
  Where Thou Thyself wilt come.

4 Gird each one with the Spirit's sword,
The sword of Thine own deathless word;
And make them conquerors, conquering Lord,
  Where Thou Thyself wilt come.

5 Raise up, O Lord the Holy Ghost,
From this broad land a mighty host,
Their war-cry, We will seek the lost,
  Where Thou, O Christ, wilt come!

927

8.8.8.8.

1 O God of burning altar fire,
   O God of love's consuming flame,
Make pure the flame of our desire
   To win the lost to seek Thy Name.

2 There is no coldness, Lord, in Thee,
   Oh, keep us kindled lest we bring
To our dear Lord of Calvary,
   Dead ashes for our offering.

3 Dead ashes, husk of corn for wheat
   Lord of our consecration vow,
We gather round Thy wounded feet,
   We see the thorn about Thy brow.

4 Oh, by Thy cross and passion, Lord,
   Grant us this plea, this sovereign plea,
Save us from choosing peace for sword,
   And give us souls to give to Thee.

Used by permission of the Dohnavur Fellowship.

PREACHING OF THE GOSPEL —
A CHANNEL OF BLESSING

928

9.9.10.9. with chorus.

1 Is your life a channel of blessing?
Is the love of God flowing through you?
Are you telling the lost of the Savior?
Are you ready His service to do?

   Make me a channel of blessing today,
   Make me a channel of blessing, I pray;
   My life possessing, my service blessing,
   Make me a channel of blessing today.

PREACHING OF THE GOSPEL —
A CHANNEL OF BLESSING

2 Is your life a channel of blessing?
　Are you burdened for those that are lost?
　Have you urged upon those who are straying,
　The Savior who died on the cross?

3 We cannot be channels of blessing
　If our lives are not free from all sin;
　We will barriers be and a hindrance
　To those we are trying to win.

929

10.7.10.7. with chorus.

1 Out in the highways and byways of life,
　Many are weary and sad;
　Carry the sunshine where darkness is rife,
　Making the sorrowing glad.

　　Make me a blessing, make me a blessing,
　　Out of my life may Jesus shine;
　　Make me a blessing, O Savior, I pray,
　　Make me a blessing to someone today.

2 Tell the sweet story of Christ and His love,
　Tell of His pow'r to forgive;
　Others will trust Him if only you prove
　True, every moment you live.

3 Give as 'twas given to you in your need,
　Love as the Master loved you;
　Be to the helpless a helper indeed,
　Unto your mission be true.

930   8.7.8.7.D.

1 "Must I go, and empty-handed,"
   Thus my dear Redeemer meet?
   Not one day of service give Him,
   Lay no trophy at His feet?

     "Must I go, and empty-handed?"
       Must I meet my Savior so?
     Not one soul with which to greet Him:
       Must I empty-handed go?

2 Not at death I shrink nor falter,
   For my Savior saves me now;
   But to meet Him empty-handed,
   Thought of that now clouds my brow.

3 O the years in sinning wasted;
   Could I but recall them now,
   I would give them to my Savior,
   To His will I'd gladly bow.

4 O ye saints, arouse, be earnest,
   Up and work while yet 'tis day;
   Ere the night of death o'ertake thee,
   Strive for souls while still you may.

PREACHING OF THE GOSPEL — LOVE FOR SOULS

931   5.4.5.4.D.

1 Out in the darkness,
    Shadowed by sin,
  Souls are in bondage,
    Souls we would win.
  How can we win them?
    How show the way?
  "Love never faileth,"
    Love is the way.

2 Think how the Savior
　　Came from above
　Suffered on Calvary,
　　Breathing out love;
　Think how He loves us,
　　E'en when we stray:
　We must love others,
　　Love is His way.

3 See, they are waiting,
　　Looking at you,
　Silently watching
　　All that you do;

Seeming so careless,
　Hardened and lost:
"Love never faileth,"
　Count not the cost.

4 "Love never faileth,"
　　Love is pure gold:
　Love is what Jesus
　　Came to unfold;
　Love these souls thru us,
　　Savior, we pray;
　Thy love ne'er faileth,
　　Love is Thy way.

8.6.8.6.D.　　　　　　　**932**

1　Lord, lay some soul upon my heart,
　　　And love that soul through me;
　　And may I bravely do my part
　　　To win that soul for Thee.

　　　Some soul for Thee, some soul for Thee,
　　　　This is my earnest plea;
　　　Help me each day, on life's highway,
　　　　To win some soul for Thee.

2　Lord, lead me to some soul in sin,
　　　And grant that I may be
　　Endued with power and love to win
　　　That soul, dear Lord, for Thee.

3　To win that soul for Thee, my Lord,
　　　Will be my constant prayer;
　　That when I've won Thy full reward
　　　I'll with that dear one share.

933

11.11.12.11. with chorus.

1   I have a Savior, He's pleading in glory,
    A dear loving Savior, though earth-friends be few;
    And now He is watching in tenderness o'er me,
    But oh, that my Savior were your Savior too!

        For you I am praying,
        For you I am praying,
        For you I am praying,
        I'm praying for you.

2   I have a Father: to me He has given
    A hope for eternity, blessed and true;
    He'll call me one day to the kingdom of heaven,
    But oh, that He'd let me bring you with me too!

3   I have a peace: it is calm as a river,
    A peace that the friends of this world never knew;
    My Savior alone is its Author and Giver,
    And oh, could I know it was given to you!

PREACHING OF THE GOSPEL — MYRIADS WON

934

11.10.11.10.11.10.11.12.

1 I cannot tell why He, whom angels worship,
    Should set His love upon the sons of men,
  Or why, as Shepherd, He should seek the wand'rers,
    To bring them back, they know not how or when.
  But this I know, that He was born of Mary,
    When Bethl'hem's manger was His only home,
  And that He lived at Nazareth and labored,
    And so the Savior, Savior of the world, is come.

2 I cannot tell how silently He suffered,
　As with His peace He graced this place of tears,
Or how His heart upon the Cross was broken,
　The crown of pain to three and thirty years.
But this I know, He heals the broken-hearted,
　And stays our sin, and calms our lurking fear,
And lifts the burden from the heavy laden,
　For yet the Savior, Savior of the world, is here.

3 I cannot tell how He will win the nations,
　How He will claim His earthly heritage,
How satisfy the needs and aspirations
　Of east and west, of sinner and of sage.
But this I know, all flesh shall see His glory,
　And He shall reap the harvest He has sown,
And some glad day His sun shall shine in splendor
　When He the Savior, Savior of the world, is known.

4 I cannot tell how all the lands shall worship,
　When, at His bidding, every storm is stilled,
Or who can say how great the jubilation
　When all the hearts of men with love are filled.
But this I know, the skies will thrill with rapture,
　And myriad, myriad human voices sing,
And earth to heaven, and heaven to earth, will answer:
　At last the Savior, Savior of the world, is King.

Used by permission of The Carey Kingsgate Press Ltd.

935

7.6.7.6.D.

1 Around Thy grave, Lord Jesus,
In spirit here we stand,
With hearts all full of praises,
To keep Thy blest command:
Our souls by faith rejoicing,
To trace Thy path of love,
Down through death's angry billows,
Up to the throne above.

2 Lord Jesus! we remember
The travail of Thy soul,
When through Thy love's deep pity,
The waves did o'er Thee roll;
Baptized in death's dark waters,
For us Thy blood was shed;
For us Thou, Lord of Glory,
Wast numbered with the dead.

3 O Lord! Thou now art risen,
Thy travail all is o'er;
For sin Thou once hast suffered,
Thou liv'st to die no more;
Sin, death and hell are vanquished
By Thee, the Church's Head;
And lo! we share Thy triumphs,
Thou first-born from the dead.

4 Unto Thy death baptizèd,
We own with Thee we died;
With Thee, our Life, we're risen,
And shall be glorified.
From sin, the world, and Satan,
We're ransomed by Thy blood,
And here would walk as strangers,
Alive with Thee to God.

BAPTISM — BURIED AND RISEN

936*

In death's waters I am buried,
For with Christ my Savior, I have died;
Now the world cannot pursue me,
For its power here is nullified.
I with Christ have risen too,
Out of death with Him I walk and live;
Now the Spirit life supplies
And His strength exhaustless unto me doth give.

937*

8.6.8.6.

1 Lord, when by baptism we confess
    Our oneness in Thy death,
  Oh, by Thy mercy and Thy grace,
    May Thou reveal its worth.

2 By baptism in Thy death we're one
    And buried too with Thee;
  Thus we're forever dead to sin
    And from its bondage free.

3 By baptism in Thy death we're one
    And buried too with Thee;
  Thus to the world we bid farewell,
    From Satan's slavery free.

4 We're resurrected with Thee too,
    From death's great pow'r set free;
  Now fruit of holiness we bear
    In our new life with Thee.

5 We're baptized unto Thy dear name,
    No more our own are we;
  Thy steps we'd follow, for Thee live,
    And e'er be one with Thee.

BAPTISM — NO LONGER I

938* 8.7.8.7.

1 Already dead! And buried too!
   With the old man I am through!
   Already dead! And buried too!
   With the old man I am through!

2 No longer I! No longer I!
   Christ in me I'll testify!
   No longer I! No longer I!
   Christ in me I'll testify!

THE LORD'S DAY — DAY OF RESURRECTION

939 7.6.7.6.D.

1 O day of resurrection,
   O day of joy and light,
   O seal of our redemption,
   Most beautiful, most bright:
   On thee the high and lowly,
   Bending before the throne,
   Sing "Holy, holy, holy,"
   To the great Three in One.

2 On thee at the creation
   The light first had its birth;
   On thee, for our salvation,
   Christ rose from depths of earth;
   On thee, our Lord, victorious,
   The Spirit sent from heaven;
   And thus on thee, most glorious,
   A triple light was given.

3 Today on weary nations
   The heavenly manna falls!
   To holy convocations
   The silver trumpet calls,

Where gospel light is glowing
With pure and radiant beams,
And living water flowing
With soul-refreshing streams.

4 New graces ever gaining
From this of days the best,
We reach the rest remaining
For people who are blest;
To Holy Ghost be praises,
To Father and to Son;
The Church her voice upraises
To Thee, blest Three in One.

THE LORD'S DAY — BEST OF THE WEEK

940

7.7.7.7.D.

1 Passing through another week,
God has granted us His aid;
Let us now a blessing seek,
On the day the Lord hath made;
Day of all the week the best,
Emblem of eternal rest.

2 While we pray for pard'ning grace,
Through the dear Redeemer's name,
Show Thy reconcilèd face;
Take away our sin and shame:
From our worldly cares set free,
May we rest this day in Thee.

(Repeat the last two lines of each stanza)

continued

3   Here we come Thy name to praise,
     Let us feel Thy presence near;
  May Thy glory meet our eyes,
     While we in Thy house appear:
  Here afford us, Lord, a taste
     Of our everlasting feast.

4   May Thy gospel's joyful sound
     Conquer sinners, comfort saints;
  Make the fruits of grace abound,
     Bring relief for all complaints:
  Thus may all our Lord's Days prove,
     Till we meet the Lord above.

THE KINGDOM — ITS MEANING

941*   7.6.7.6.D.

1   God's kingdom is God's reigning,
     His glory to maintain;
  It is His sovereign ruling,
     His order to sustain.
  He exercises fully
     His own authority
  Within His kingdom ever
     And to eternity.

2   Upon the throne, the center
     Of government divine,
  God reigns, and with His purpose
     Brings everything in line.
  God's headship and His lordship
     He only can maintain
  As King within His kingdom,
     O'er everything to reign.

3　By reigning in His kingdom
　　　God worketh all His will,
　　And under His dominion
　　　His purpose doth fulfill.
　　'Tis only in God's kingdom
　　　His blessing we may know;
　　'Tis from His throne almighty
　　　The stream of life doth flow.

4　Submitted to God's ruling,
　　　All virtue thus will win;
　　Rebellion to His Headship
　　　Is but the root of sin.
　　The evil aim of Satan —
　　　God's throne to overthrow;
　　Our aim and goal is ever
　　　His rule to fully know.

5　Within God's sovereign kingdom
　　　His Christ is magnified;
　　When Christ in life is reigning,
　　　The Father's glorified.
　　When God is in dominion,
　　　All things are truly blessed;
　　When Christ for God is reigning,
　　　God's glory is expressed.

6　In fulness of the seasons
　　　God's Christ will head up all,
　　Then all will own His reigning
　　　And worship, great and small.
　　Such reign in life and glory
　　　The Church e'en now foretastes,
　　And to His rule submitting
　　　Unto His kingdom hastes.

942*

8.8.8.8.

1 God's Kingdom on the earth is now
His sovereign government within;
'Tis Christ Himself in us to live
As Lord and King to rule and reign.

2 His life with His authority
Enthrones Him now within our hearts
To govern all our words and deeds
And regulate our inward parts.

3 The Lord enthroned within our hearts
His Kingdom doth establish there,
Assuring His full right to reign
And for God's purpose to prepare.

4 'Tis by His reign within our hearts
That life to us He e'er supplies;
When taking Him as Lord and King,
His wealth our being satisfies.

5 'Tis by His ruling from within
His fulness vast is testified;
'Tis when His inner kingdom rules
His Body's blessed and edified.

6 'Tis by His heav'nly rule within
As heav'nly citizens we live;
'Tis by submission to His rule
Expression of His reign we give.

7 Here in this heav'nly realm we live,
And with this heav'nly pow'r possessed
We walk and fight in heav'nly light
Until the Kingdom's manifest.

8.8.8.8.

1 Requirements of the Kingdom are
Much stricter than the law's decrees;
No other requisite of God
Has ever higher been than these.

2 "Repent, the Kingdom has come near,"
This is the Kingdom's first demand;
A change of mind we all must have
And on God's side must firmly stand.

3 That we the Kingdom enter in,
Surpassing righteousness we need,
Exceeding that which is of law;
From life alone it must proceed.

4 That we the Kingdom enter in,
We need to do the Father's will,
Not by our choice to work or act
But His one purpose to fulfill.

5 That we the Kingdom enter in,
A simple child we must become —
Adjustable, obedient, meek —
And everything of self o'ercome.

6 The Heav'nly Kingdom e'en requires
That we as God should perfect be;
This standard we must fully meet
That we may share its ecstasy.

7 The Kingdom is the reign of God;
To match His nature is required;
'Tis only by the life of God
The Kingdom's entry is acquired.

8 The Kingdom is the rule of heav'n;
With heaven's state we must accord;
'Tis only by the life of heav'n
That we may share it with the Lord.

944*

8.8.8.8.

1 The essence of the Kingdom is
A life that's under heaven's rule,
A life whose nature is divine
With Christ experienced in full.

2 Such is this life: in spirit poor,
With heart repentant, mourning, meek,
Which is to others merciful
And purely God Himself doth seek;

3 As sons of God the peace to make,
For righteousness e'en suffering pain;
Reviled and hurt for Jesus' sake,
Exceeding joyfulness to gain;

4 As salt to kill corruption rife,
In darkness shining as the light,
In heart and action right and true,
In perfect love to claim no right.

5 This life self-glory doth renounce
And ever for God's kingdom prays;
It trusts in God for every need
And seeks His kingdom first always.

6 'Tis strict with self, with others kind,
And always dealing with the Lord;
It ever does the Father's will
And acts according to His word.

7 To Satan it does not give ground,
Nor to the world, or self, or sin,
But seeks beneath the heaven's rule
God's full authority to win.

8 'Tis such a life which subjugates
All things with pow'r to God's behest;
The time it hastens when the Lord
Will here His kingdom manifest.

945*

8.8.8.8.

1 The Son of God has come to sow
Himself, the seed of life, in man,
That thru Himself God's Kingdom grow
And thus fulfill th' eternal plan.

2 He was the only grain of wheat
Whence many grains have been produced
To be the Kingdom's children meet,
Thru whom God's reign is introduced.

3 But Satan, enemy of God,
Sowed many tares among the wheat,
The Kingdom's children to confuse,
And awful damage to create.

4 'Tis by this subtle work of his,
The mixing of the tares with wheat,
The Kingdom in appearance is
Abnormal and grotesquely great.

5 The Kingdom should as mustard be,
A little herb, yet good for food,
But it has changed into a "tree,"
A system of great magnitude.

6 Instead of being good for food,
A lodge of "birds" it has become;
'Tis now a place where evil men
And evil spirits make their home.

7 A great religion of the world
Its outward form to us reveals,
Including pagan, evil things,
As leaven mingled with the meal.

8 A system of the world as such,
It thus has changed in outward form;
By evil things which it imbibes,
Corruption inwardly doth swarm.

continued

9 But something hidden God doth seek,
As "pearl" and "treasure in the field";
As such the Lord would us transform
That pearl and treasure be revealed.

10 'Tis hidden from vast Christendom
And from the Kingdom's great facade,
Yet in its full reality
'Tis transformed like to Christ and God.

11 Lord, separate us from the "tares,"
And save us from the monstrous "tree";
From all the "leaven" purge us now
That we may purely be of Thee.

12 May Thou in life transform our souls
That we as precious stones may be,
Meet for Thy house to build and in
Thy Kindgom's full reality.

THE KINGDOM — ITS MANIFESTATION

946*   8.7.8.7.D.

1 Lo, the glory! Lo, the splendor!
Heaven's Kingdom manifest!
And its glorious King, our Master,
Is by God's appointment blest.
Once in flesh He came so lowly,
Hated and despised by man;
Now He comes again in glory
To fulfill the Kingdom plan.

2 Going to receive the Kingdom
From His God, the Ancient of Days,
Now He cometh with the Kingdom
And its glorious, ruling rays.
He's "the Stone" which breaks the nations
Into pieces lowliest,
Which "a mountain great" becometh
As the Kingdom manifest.

3 Lo, the earth, all lands and kingdoms,
    By the Lord and Christ possessed;
  Earth beneath their sovereign ruling
    Will be full of peace and rest.
  No more war and no more hatred
    'Twixt the nations will there be;
  But God's knowledge shall suffuse them
    As the waters fill the sea.

4 All the Christian overcomers
    Shall with Christ in glory reign,
  And the remnant saved of Israel
    Then God's priesthood shall obtain.
  As God's people shall the nations
    'Neath their rule and teaching be,
  And a glorious restoration
    All creation then shall see.

5 Satan will be bound and banished;
    From his rule will earth be freed;
  With Christ's sovereign reign and headship
    Earth will then be blessed indeed.
  All to Christ will then be subject,
    To His pow'r and to His will;
  As the Head and Center glorious,
    He God's purpose will fulfill.

THE KINGDOM — AS AN EXERCISE AND A REWARD

11.12.12.12.   **947***

1 God's Kingdom today is a real exercise,
  But when Christ comes to reign it will be a great prize;
  It is wisdom divine that we now may be trained
  That His plan be fulfilled and His justice maintained.

2 God's children, we're born to be kings with His Son,
  And we need to be trained that we may overcome
  And to know how to rule in His kingdom as kings,
  That His kingship thru us be expressed o'er all things.

    continued

3 Today we must learn to submit to His throne,
How to have a strict life and His government own;
His authority then we'll be able to share,
O'er the nations to rule with God's Son as the heir.

4 With a life strict to self we must righteousness hold,
Kind to others in peace, and with God joyful, bold;
In the Kingdom's reality e'er to remain,
For its manifestation prepared thus to reign.

5 Then Christ when He comes with the kingdom
from God
Will to us grant His kingship to share as reward;
Thus the Lord will His righteousness thru us maintain
And His wisdom to heavenly powers make plain.

6 For this the Apostle pressed on at all cost,
For the Kingdom assured that he would not be lost;
'Tis for this he charged others, Be true to the Lord,
That the Kingdom might be unto them a reward.

7 O Lord, give us grace for Thy Kingdom to live,
To be trained that Thou may the reward to us give;
Make the Kingdom's reality our exercise,
That its manifestation may be our great prize.

HOPE OF GLORY — CHRIST IN ME

948*   11.9.11.9. with chorus.

1 Myst'ry hid from ages now revealed to me,
'Tis the Christ of God's reality.
He embodies God, and He is life to me,
And the glory of my hope He'll be.

Glory, glory, Christ is life in me!
Glory, glory, what a hope is He!
Now within my spirit He's the mystery!
Then the glory He will be to me.

2 In my spirit He regenerated me,
   In my soul He's now transforming me.
   He will change my body like unto His own,
   Wholly making me the same as He.

3 Now in life and nature He is one with me;
   Then in Him, the glory, I will be;
   I'll enjoy His presence for eternity
   With Him in complete conformity.

HOPE OF GLORY — CHRIST AS THE GLORIFICATION

Peculiar Meter.   **949***

1 Christ is the hope of glory, my very life is He,
He has regenerated and saturated me;
He comes to change my body by His subduing might
Like to His glorious body in glory bright!

   He comes, He comes, Christ comes to glorify me!
   My body He'll transfigure, like His own it then
     will be.
   He comes, He comes, redemption to apply!
   As Hope of glory He will come, His saints to glorify.

2 Christ is the hope of glory, He is God's mystery;
He shares with me God's fulness and brings God
     into me.
He comes to make me blended with God in every way,
That I may share His glory with Him for aye.

3 Christ is the hope of glory, redemption full is He:
Redemption to my body, from death to set it free,
He comes to make my body a glorious one to be
And swallow death forever in victory.

4 Christ is the hope of glory, He is my history:
His life is my experience, for He is one with me;
He comes to bring me into His glorious liberty,
That one with Him completely I'll ever be.

HOPE OF GLORY — BLESSED LIKENESS

950   10.10.10.10.

1   And is it so! I shall be like Thy Son?
    Is this the grace which He for me has won?
    Father of glory — thought beyond all thought! —
    In glory, to His own blest likeness brought!

2   Oh, Jesus, Lord, who loved me like to Thee?
    Fruit of Thy work, with Thee, too, there to see
    Thy glory, Lord, while endless ages roll,
    Myself the prize and travail of Thy soul.

3   Yet it must be: Thy love had not its rest
    Were Thy redeemed not with Thee fully blest;
    That love that gives not as the world, but shares
    All it possesses with its loved co-heirs.

4   Nor I alone; Thy loved ones, all complete
    In glory, round Thee there with joy shall meet;
    All like Thee, for Thy glory like Thee, Lord,
    Object supreme of all, by all adored.

HOPE OF GLORY — BLESSED HOPE

951   8.7.8.7.8.7.

1   Christ is coming! let creation
    From her groans and travail cease,
    Let the glorious proclamation
    Hope restore, and faith increase.
    Christ is coming! Christ is coming!
    Come, Thou blessed Prince of Peace.

2   Earth can now but tell the story
    Of Thy bitter cross and pain;
    She shall yet behold Thy glory
    When Thou comest back to reign.
    Christ is coming! Christ is coming!
    Let each heart repeat the strain.

3   Long Thy people have been pining
For Thy peace and rest, and Thee,
Soon, in heav'nly glory shining,
Their Restorer shall they see.
Christ is coming! Christ is coming!
Haste the joyous jubilee.

4   With that blessed hope before us,
Let no harp remain unstrung;
Let the mighty advent chorus
Onward roll on every tongue.
Christ is coming! Christ is coming!
Come, Lord Jesus, quickly come.

Peculiar Meter.   **952**

1 A lamp in the night, a song in time of sorrow,
   A great glad hope which faith can ever borrow
To gild the passing day with the glory of the morrow,
   Is the hope of the coming of the Lord.

Blessed hope, blessed hope,
Blessed hope of the coming of the Lord;
  How the aching heart it cheers;
  How it glistens through our tears,
Blessed hope of the coming of the Lord.

2 A star in the sky, a beacon bright to guide us;
   An anchor sure to hold when storms betide us;
A refuge for the soul, where in quiet we may hide us,
   Is the hope of the coming of the Lord.

3 A call of command, like trumpet clearly sounding,
   To make us bold when evil is surrounding;
To stir the sluggish heart, and to keep in good
    abounding,
   Is the hope of the coming of the Lord.

continued

4 A word from the One to all our hearts the dearest,
   A parting word to make Him aye the nearest;
Of all His precious words, the sweetest, brightest, clearest,
   Is the hope of the coming of the Lord.

HOPE OF GLORY — THE CROWNING DAY

953   Peculiar Meter.

1 Our Lord is now rejected,
     And by the world disowned,
   By the many still neglected,
     And by the few enthroned;
   But soon He'll come in glory!
     The hour is drawing nigh,
   For the crowning day is coming
       By-and-by.

     O the crowning day is coming,
       Is coming by-and-by,
     When our Lord shall come in power
       And glory from on high.
     O the glorious sight will gladden
       Each waiting, watchful eye,
     In the crowning day that's coming
         By-and-by.

2 The heavens shall glow with splendor,
     But brighter far than they,
   The saints shall shine in glory,
     As Christ shall them array.
   The beauty of the Savior
     Shall dazzle every eye,
   In the crowning day that's coming
       By-and-by.

3 Our pain shall then be over,
   We'll sin and sigh no more,
Behind us all of sorrow,
   And naught but joy before,
A joy in our Redeemer,
   As we to Him are nigh,
In the crowning day that's coming
   By-and-by.

4 Let all that look for hasten
   The coming joyful day,
By earnest consecration,
   To walk the narrow way;
By gathering in the lost ones,
   For whom our Lord did die,
For the crowning day that's coming
   By-and-by.

954

8.7.8.7.D.

1 There's a light upon the mountains,
      and the day is at the spring,
When our eyes shall see the beauty
      and the glory of the King;
Weary was our heart with waiting, and
      the night-watch seemed so long,
But His triumph-day is breaking, and
      we hail it with a song.

continued

2 In the fading of the starlight we can
   see the coming morn;
And the lights of men are paling in
   the splendors of the dawn;
For the eastern skies are glowing as
   with lights of hidden fire,
And the hearts of men are stirring
   with the throb of deep desire.

3 There's a hush of expectation, and
   a quiet in the air;
And the breath of God is moving in
   the fervent breath of prayer;
For the suffering, dying Jesus is the
   Christ upon the throne,
And the travail of our spirit is the
   travail of His own.

4 He is breaking down the barriers,
   He is casting up the way;
He is calling for His angels to build
   up the gates of day;
But His angels here are human, not
   the shining hosts above,
For the drum-beats of His army are
   the heart-beats of our love.

5 Hark! we hear a distant music, and
   it comes with fuller swell;
'Tis the triumph song of Jesus, of
   our King Emmanuel;
Zion, go ye forth to meet Him,
   and my soul, be swift to bring
All thy sweetest and thy dearest for
   the triumph of our King.

8.7.8.7.

1 In the advent light, O Savior,
   I am living day by day;
   Waiting, working, watching ever,
   Knowing Thou art on Thy way.

2 Separated unto Jesus,
   Loosed from all the world beside;
   Blinded by the advent glory,
   Hour by hour would I abide.

3 So from glory unto glory,
   Gladdened by the advent ray;
   All the path is growing brighter,
   Shining unto perfect day.

4 In the advent light to witness
   To a dark and dying world;
   This the holy ordination;
   May His banner be unfurled.

5 In the advent light rejoicing;
   Songs of praise along the road
   Seem to make the journey shorter,
   Mounting upward to our God.

6 He is coming! He is coming!
   Pass the heavenly watchword on:
   Go ye forth to meet the Bridegroom,
   Hail! to God's anointed Son.

7 See the advent glory breaking;
   Faith will soon be lost in sight;
   Face to face I shall behold Him,
   Bathed in His eternal light.

956*   11.9.11.9. with chorus.

1 Soon our Lord will come, the day is drawing nigh,
    Sound of His approaching we can hear.
Watchful we must be and always on alert
    That the Lord our hearts with rapture cheer.

    Glory! glory! Christ will come again!
    Glory! glory! We with Him shall reign!
    With a glorious body, ever with the Lord,
    Singing all His praise with glad accord.

2 Soon our Lord will come, the Morning Star appear;
    Night is deep, and soon will dawn the day.
Never with the current of the age we go,
    That from trials we'll be kept away.

3 Soon our Lord will come His servants to reward;
    Those who love Him then the crown will share.
Watchful we must be and treasure not the world,
    Love and serve the Lord, His burden bear.

4 Soon our Lord will come and in His kingdom reign;
    Satan will be bound, the world subdued.
We must fight the battle, overcome the foe,
    On His throne He then will us include.

957   Peculiar Meter.

1 Watch! for the morning is breaking,
    A moment, and He will be here!
The mists and the shadows are fleeing,
    The darkness will soon disappear;
And He, for whom ages have waited,
    The Lord Who has tarried so long,
Will come in an outburst of glory,
    A moment, and we shall be gone.

HOPE OF GLORY — WAITING AND WATCHING

2 Watch! for the morning is breaking,
    A moment, the crown will be won!
  A moment, and we shall be with Him,
    A moment, the journey is done!
  Lord, keep us each moment unsleeping,
    And count us all worthy to be
  In that noble band of Thy watchers,
    Whose life is a vigil with Thee.

HOPE OF GLORY — LONGING AND PRAYING

11.10.11.10.11.10.11.12.   **958**†

1 Since long ago at Bethany we parted,
  Within my heart there is a ceaseless void;
  How can I take my harp down from the willow?
  How can my songs without Thee be enjoyed?
  And when at night I'm keeping lonely vigil —
  Grown numb alike to sorrow and to cheer —
  Then I recall the promise of Thy coming,
  But sigh: O Lord, why, why Thou dost not yet appear?

2 Thy manger wakes the thought: I too am homeless;
  Thy cross strips earthly pleasures from my soul;
  Thy coming bids me seek a better country,
  For Thou Thyself art now my final goal.
  Since Thou art gone my joy has lost its flavor,
  My song the sweetness I would fain convey.
  Since Thou art gone the sense of void o'erwhelms me.
  Oh, how I long that Thou wilt come and not delay.

3 Though even now I know Thy loving presence,
  Yet in my heart there's still a sense of lack.
  Enlightening and tenderest sustaining
  Can no more satisfy: I want Thee back.
  Despite Thy peace within, I still feel lonely;
  Despite Thy joy there still remains a sigh;
  When I feel most content, the silent yearning
  To see Thee face to face becomes an uttered cry.

continued

958[†]

4 What exile cannot but desire his homeland
  And long his people once again to greet?
  What soul on alien soil forgets his kindred?
  What parted lovers never yearn to meet?
  O Lord, how can these earthly loves and pleasures
  With all the joy of Thy return compare?
  Then, if I cannot here behold Thy countenance,
  What can I do but sigh till Thou, my Lord, appear?

5 Could'st Thou, O Lord, forget Thy word of promise
  Soon to return and take me unto Thee?
  Yet day by day and year by year I've waited
  And still I wait, and no return I see!
  Remember, Lord, the years I have been waiting
  While Thy dear footsteps linger far away.
  How long? How long? Oh! must I wait still longer
  Till Thou shalt come again in glorious array?

6 From generation unto generation
  Thy saints have come and gone, but have not seen
  Thy glorious promise pass into fulfilment.
  How long, how very long the time has been!
  Why cannot we, dear Lord, discern Thy footsteps?
  Why are the heavens still so closely sealed?
  Oh! must our waiting be prolonged still further
  Before Thou in Thy matchless splendor art revealed?

7 Lord, I recall the many years I've waited
  For Thy return — yet, Lord, not I alone,
  But Thy dear saints through many generations —
  Beseeching Thee to come back for Thine own.
  To countless tears and countless fervent pleadings,
  By Thine appearing haste to make reply.
  Oh, may Thou come, the echo of the ages,
  Come, come and answer now this mighty corp'rate cry!

11.10.11.10. with chorus. **959**†

1 Since Thy departure from Olivet's Mountain,
  Why is Thy coming again so delayed?
Thru the long years we have longed for Thy coming;
  Hast Thou not heard all the prayers that
      we've prayed?

   Come Thou, come now;
   Lord, for Thy coming we yearn;
   All our desire is Thy promised returning,
   Oh, may Thou quickly return.

2 Beloved Lord, since the year Thou ascended
  Everything here has been tasteless and dry;
Often in praying and often in watching,
  In every movement, for Thee, Lord, we sigh.

3 Scenes although lovely, yet when will we meet Thee?
  Birds and the flowers fair beauty embrace;
All are delightsome, but none satisfy me,
  For I am longing for Thy loving face.

4 Lord, we're impatient awaiting Thy coming,
  We do not know how much longer 'twill be;
From every sunrise to every bright sunset
  Hope we each moment Thy coming to see.

5 Whene'er 'tis raining, or strong winds are blowing,
  Whene'er the moon shines, or rises the sea,
We ever hope to discover Thy coming;
  How disappointed when no sign of Thee!

6 If it were not for the bidding Thou gav'st us,
  We'd be discouraged, Thy service we'd shirk;
But Thou dost want us while waiting Thy coming,
  For Thee to live and in diligence work.

7 Oh Lord, remember the days have been lengthened
  Since Thou hast promised ere going away;
We hope and hope and are endlessly hoping,
  That Thou wilt come. Canst Thou come e'en today?

960†

8.6.8.6.D.

1 My King will soon come back again,
   The sky be filled with Him;
   The universe to be redeemed
   Will see His light therein.
   The Lord will soon fulfill His plan,
   His footsteps now I hear;
   His glorious frame I faintly see
   Beginning to appear.

2 I'm longing for His presence blest
   And dare not slothful be
   While waiting for my Lord's return,
   His own dear self to see.
   My only hope — that He may come
   And change my faith to sight;
   There is no other joy on earth
   Which gives my heart delight.

3 My heart is always with Himself,
   My eyes are heavenward,
   My lips would utter nothing else
   Than meeting with my Lord.
   The coming of the Lord draws nigh,
   His coming is for me;
   His promise ever standeth firm
   And soon fulfilled I'll see.

4 My Savior, all Thy holy words
   Can never doubted be;
   With them encouraged day by day,
   I'm faithful unto Thee.
   Oh, may Thy glory soon appear,
   The foe be overthrown;
   Thy promises be realized,
   And we brought to Thy throne.

5 Thy saving arm a refuge is,
    My Savior God, to me;
Thou as the Father keepeth them
    Who put their trust in Thee.
The sheep and shepherd are of one,
    The head and body same;
None e'er can pluck from out Thy hand
    The child who trusts Thy Name.

6 A thousand hands won't hinder me,
    Nor will ten thousand eyes;
The thorns upon the road but help
    Me onward to the prize.
Arise, my spirit and my heart,
    And let the world go by;
The Lord of life will take me soon
    To be with Him on high.

7 Thou healing sun! Thou hope of man!
    I really love Thy ray.
Oh, righteous Lord! oh, glorious King!
    I bow to Thee and pray:
Oh, may Thou soon ascend Thy throne
    And quickly show Thy face;
Thy heav'nly kingdom may Thou found
    And grant all men Thy grace.

8 The truth should triumph and be king,
    And freedom should be queen;
But falsehood, which has rampant run,
    Head of the world is seen.
We ask Thee, Truth, to quickly come
    And bring Thy light from heav'n;
The foe be crushed and all Thy sons
    Into Thy bosom giv'n.

6.6.8.6.D.

1 The Church has waited long,
  Her absent Lord to see,
And still in loneliness she waits,
  A friendless stranger she.
  Age after age has gone,
  Sun after sun has set,
And still in weeds of widowhood,
  She weeps a mourner yet.

2 Saint after saint on earth
  Has lived, and loved, and died;
And as they left us one by one,
  We laid them side by side;
  We laid them down to sleep,
  But not in hope forlorn;
We laid them but to ripen there,
  Till the last glorious morn.

3 The serpent's brood increase,
  The powers of hell grow bold,
The conflict thickens, faith is low,
  And love is waxing cold.
  How long, O Lord our God,
  Holy, and true, and good,
Wilt Thou not judge Thy suffering Church,
  Her sighs, and tears, and blood?

4   We long to hear Thy voice,
    To see Thee face to face,
To share Thy crown and glory then,
    As now we share Thy grace.
    Should not the loving bride
    Her absent bridegroom mourn?
Should she not wear the signs of grief
    Until her Lord return?

5   The whole creation groans,
    And waits to hear that voice
That shall her beauteousness restore,
    And make her wastes rejoice.
    Come, Lord, and wipe away
    The curse, the sin, the stain,
And make this blighted world of ours
    Thine own fair world again.

Peculiar Meter.   **962***

Oh, how long before my Lord comes back,
    My heart desires to see Thy face,
That the song of triumph I may sing
    And behold my Beloved, full of grace.
Come quickly, Lord, and tarry not!
    Oh, when wilt Thou return to comfort me;
Come quickly, Lord, and tarry not!
    My heart desires to be with Thee.

963

8.7.8.7.D.

1 Face to face with Christ, my Savior,
Face to face — what will it be?
When with rapture I behold Him,
Jesus Christ who died for me.

Face to face I shall behold Him,
Far beyond the starry sky;
Face to face in all His glory,
I shall see Him by and by!

2 Only faintly now, I see Him,
With the darkling veil between,
But a blessed day is coming,
When His glory shall be seen.

3 What rejoicing in His presence,
When are banished grief and pain;
When the crooked ways are straightened,
And the dark things shall be plain.

4 Face to face! O blissful moment!
Face to face — to see and know;
Face to face with my Redeemer,
Jesus Christ who loves me so.

8.5.8.5.D.

1 'Midst the darkness, storm, and sorrow,
    One bright gleam I see;
  Well I know the blessed morrow
    Christ will come for me.
  'Midst the peace, the joy, the glory
    And the light, God's own,
  Christ for me is watching, waiting,
    Waiting 'til I come.

2 Long the blessed Guide has led me,
    By the desert road;
  Now I see the coming splendor,
    Splendor of my God.
  There amidst the love and glory
    He is waiting yet;
  On His hands a name is graven
    He can ne'er forget.

3 Who is this, who comes to meet me,
    On the desert way,
  As the Morning Star foretelling
    God's unclouded day?
  He it is who came to win me,
    On the cross of shame;
  In His glory well I know Him,
    Evermore the same.

4 O the blessed joy of meeting,
    All the desert past;
  O the wondrous words of greeting,
    He shall speak at last!
  He and I together ent'ring
    The fair realm above;
  He and I together sharing
    All the Father's love.

continued

5 Where no shade nor stain can enter,
  Nor the gold be dim,
In His holiness unsullied,
  I shall walk with Him.
Meet companion then for Jesus,
  From Him, for Him, made —
Glory of God's grace forever
  There in me displayed.

6 He who in His hour of sorrow
  Bore the curse alone;
I who through the lonely desert
  Trod where He had gone;
He and I, in that bright glory,
  One deep joy shall share —
Mine, to be forever with Him;
  His, that I am there.

965†   8.8.8.4. with repeat.

1 When my blest Lord will come again,
I will be saved from all my pain,
With all the saints I'll follow Him,
  O praise the Lord!
O praise the Lord! O praise the Lord!
With all the saints I'll follow Him,
  O praise the Lord!

2 When I shall see Him face to face,
And dwell with Him thru endless days,
I will rejoice and sing His grace,
  O praise the Lord!
O praise the Lord! O praise the Lord!
I will rejoice and sing His grace,
  O praise the Lord!

3 When I meet Him before the Throne,
   My suff'rings then will all be gone,
   The joy of vict'ry will be won,
       O praise the Lord!
   O praise the Lord! O praise the Lord!
   The joy of vict'ry will be won,
       O praise the Lord!

4 In that day I will testify
   That nothing with Christ's life can vie,
   What glorious rapture to the sky,
       O praise the Lord!
   O praise the Lord! O praise the Lord!
   What glorious rapture to the sky,
       O praise the Lord!

5 May we in our Lord's side e'er hide,
   Be always one and ne'er divide,
   That His heart may be satisfied,
       O praise the Lord!
   O praise the Lord! O praise the Lord!
   That His heart may be satisfied,
       O praise the Lord!

6 O come, our King, O come, dear Lord!
   Receive us by Thy promised word,
   And give the victors Thy reward,
       O praise the Lord!
   O praise the Lord! O praise the Lord!
   And give the victors Thy reward,
       O praise the Lord!

966* 10.10.10.10. with chorus.

1 O hope of glory, our Christ will return!
　　We will be raptured, with glory transformed;
　Glorified with Him, Himself to enjoy,
　　In His full likeness we then will be formed.

　　Glorious hope! Christ will return!
　　Glorious hope! Christ will return!
　　We will be raptured, with glory transformed;
　　O hope of glory, our Christ will return!

2 O hope of glory, our Christ will return!
　　The old creation will vanish away,
　No more we'll groan, but have full liberty,
　　Enjoy salvation in its utmost way.

3 O hope of glory, our Christ will return!
　　Over the nations with Him we will reign,
　Priests we will be in His presence to serve,
　　Thus His salvation in fulness we'll gain.

4 O hope of glory, our Christ will return!
　　Waiting and watching, we faithfully serve,
　Running the race, pressing on toward the goal
　　That we the Kingdom's reward might deserve.

HOPE OF GLORY — CHRIST COMING TO REIGN

967 Peculiar Meter.

1 Thou art coming, O my Savior,
　　Thou art coming, O my King,
　In Thy beauty all resplendent,
　In Thy glory all transcendent;
　　Well may we rejoice and sing;
　　Coming! In the opening east,
　　Herald brightness slowly swells:
　　Coming! O my glorious Priest,
　　Hear we not Thy golden bells?

2   Thou art coming, Thou art coming;
      We shall meet Thee on Thy way;
   We shall see Thee, we shall know Thee,
   We shall bless Thee, we shall show Thee
      All our hearts could never say:
      What an anthem that will be,
      Ringing out our love to Thee,
      Pouring out our rapture sweet
      At Thine own all-glorious feet.

3   Thou art coming, at Thy Table
      We are witnesses for this;
   While rememb'ring hearts Thou meetest
   In communion clearest, sweetest,
      Earnest of our coming bliss,
      Showing not Thy death alone,
      And Thy love exceeding great,
      But Thy coming and Thy throne,
      All for which we long and wait.

4   Oh, the joy to see Thee reigning,
      Thee, my own beloved Lord!
   Every tongue Thy Name confessing,
   Worship, honor, glory, blessing,
      Brought to Thee with one accord;
      Thee, my Master and my Friend,
      Vindicated and enthroned,
      Unto earth's remotest end
      Glorified, adored, and owned!

968

7.6.7.6.D.

1 Hail to the Lord's Anointed,
   Great David's greater Son!
Hail, in the time appointed,
   His reign on earth begun!
He comes to break oppression,
   To set the captive free;
To take away transgression,
   And rule in equity.

2 He shall come down like showers
   Upon the fruitful earth;
And love, joy, hope, like flowers,
   Spring in His path to birth:
Before Him on the mountains
   Shall peace, the herald, go;
And righteousness, in fountains,
   From hill to valley flow.

3 Kings shall fall down before Him,
   And gold and incense bring;
All nations shall adore Him,
   His praise all people sing;
For He shall have dominion
   O'er river, sea, and shore,
Far as the eagle's pinion,
   Or dove's light wing can soar.

4 To Him shall prayer unceasing
   And daily vows ascend;
His kingdom still increasing,
   A kingdom without end.
The mountain dews shall nourish
   A seed in weakness sown,
Whose fruit shall spread and flourish,
   And shake like Lebanon.

5   O'er every foe victorious
      He on His throne shall rest,
   From age to age more glorious,
      All-blessing and all-blest.
   The tide of time shall never
      His covenant remove;
   His Name shall stand forever,
      His changeless Name of Love.

HOPE OF GLORY — CHRIST AS THE END

969

11.10.11.10.

1   Hark what a sound, and too divine for hearing,
      Stirs on the earth and trembles in the air;
   Is it the thunder of the Lord's appearing?
      Is it the music of His people's prayer?

2   Surely He cometh, and a thousand voices
      Shout to the saints, and to the deaf and dumb;
   Surely He cometh, and the earth rejoices,
      Glad in His coming who hath sworn: I come!

3   This hath He done, and shall we not adore Him?
      This shall He do, and can we still despair?
   Come, let us quickly fling ourselves before Him,
      Cast at His feet the burden of our care.

4   Thru life and death, thru sorrow and thru sinning
      He shall suffice me, for He hath sufficed:
   Christ is the end, for Christ was the beginning,
      Christ the beginning, for the end is Christ.

HOPE OF GLORY — THE MANIFESTATION OF THE SONS OF GOD

970*

8.7.8.7.

1 For the glorious revelation
    Of the sons of God to come,
All the creatures wait, expecting,
    That they all may free become.

2 All creation groans together,
    Subject now to vanity,
Looking for their full deliv'rance
    From corruption's slavery.

3 Even we ourselves are groaning,
    Till we reach maturity;
We are growing to adoption,
    With Christ in conformity.

4 'Tis for this the Spirit groaneth,
    That to Christ we be conformed;
All things also work together,
    That in life we be transformed.

5 God will bring us into glory,
    We will then be glorified;
Fully saturated with Him,
    We'll be wholly sanctified.

6 To the freedom of this glory,
    All creation will be freed;
With the kid shall lie the leopard,
    And the cow with bear shall feed.

7 Heirs with Christ in full adoption,
    We'll His heritage possess,
Glorified with Him as brethren,
    God's full glory we'll express.

1 God's eternal purpose
   Is to join with man,
Causing man, His vessel,
   To be born again,
His own life imparting,
   Filling to the brim;
Man may thus express Him,
   And be one with Him.

2 God in His own image
   Hath created man,
That he may be able
   To fulfill His plan;
That he may receive Him
   As the tree of life
To become His fulness
   As to man the wife.

3 In His life's rich flowing
   Man will be transformed
Into precious substance
   And to Him conformed.
Thus will man be builded
   As His counterpart,
Thus to be His dwelling,
   Satisfy His heart.

4 'Tis the holy city,
   New Jerusalem;
With His saints God mingles,
   Makes His home with them.
He becomes their content,
   His expression they;
They shall share His glory,
   One with Him for aye.

continued

ULTIMATE MANIFESTATION —
GOD'S ETERNAL PURPOSE

5   He's the very center,
     Ruling on the throne;
By His life the power,
     Saints are kept in one.
By His light of glory,
     They are kept in light,
Harmony enjoying
     In divine delight.

6   He's their living water,
     And their food supply;
All their thirst and hunger
     He doth satisfy.
He's for them the temple,
     In Himself they live,
In His constant presence
     Worship ever give.

ULTIMATE MANIFESTATION —
GOD'S CENTRAL THOUGHT

972*

7.7.7.7.

1   Lo, the central thought of God
Is that He be one with man;
He to man is everything
That He might fulfill His plan.

2   Earthen vessel man was made —
Body, soul, and spirit too,
God as life that he may take
And with Him have oneness true.

3   By the flow of life divine,
    Man becomes a precious stone
    Fit for building God's abode,
    That His glory might be known.

4   'Tis the city God hath built,
    'Tis the dwelling God requires,
    'Tis the new Jerusalem
    Which fulfills His heart's desires.

5   'Tis the building of the saints,
    'Tis the blend of God and man,
    Purposed by the Father's will
    Long before the world began.

6   In its center, as its pow'r,
    Is the throne of Christ and God,
    Whence doth flow the stream of life
    As the Spirit's living flood.

7   Christ, the tree of life, is there
    In the flowing of the stream,
    Yielding fruit of life divine
    As the food of life supreme.

8   God in Christ, the glorious light,
    Thru the city brightly shines,
    Scattering all the deathly night
    With its light of life divine.

9   God in man and man in God
    Mutual dwelling thus possess;
    God the content is to man,
    And the man doth God express.

973

10.10.10.10. with repeat.

1 Our goal — the holy city with the Lord,
It is our portion, 'tis where He's adored;
Although our bodies still are living here,
Our spirits with our glorious Lord are there;
Our spirits with our glorious Lord are there.

2 Our goal divine — the new Jerusalem —
That holy city made for God with men;
For all redeemed, who have Thy pathway trod,
Shall have the right to share the bliss with God,
Shall have the right to share the bliss with God.

3 And every time we toward that city gaze,
Then every time we long to see Thy face;
We long to hear the shout that calls to Thee,
With Thee to share Thy God eternally,
With Thee to share Thy God eternally.

4 Our heart's desire is not the peace so sweet,
Our longed for hope is not the joy we'll meet;
But Thou Thyself, Thou art "our hope," O Lord,
For 'tis Thyself that will be our reward,
For 'tis Thyself that will be our reward.

5 O Jesus, Lord, we pray Thee hear our cry,
Come! Bring us to that city from on high!
That in that glory we may share with Thee,
Thy loving Self partake eternally,
Thy loving Self partake eternally.

6 O Lord, Thou sayest, "I make all things new,"
New heav'ns, new earth, and all within them too!
Our God Himself our portion then shall be;
O Lord, come quickly! Take us up with Thee,
O Lord, come quickly! Take us up with Thee.

11.11.11.11. with chorus.

1 He looked for a city and lived in a tent,
A pilgrim to glory right onward he went;
God's promise his solace, so royal his birth,
No wonder he sought not the glories of earth.

City! O city fair!
God's dwelling with man to eternity is there.

2 He looked for a city, his God should prepare;
No mansion on earth, could he covet or share,
For had not God told him, that royal abode
Awaited His pilgrims on ending the road.

3 He looked for a city; if sometimes he sighed
To be trudging the road, all earth's glory denied,
The thought of that city changed sighing to song,
For the road might be rough, but it could not be long.

4 He looked for a city, his goal, Lord, we share
And know that bright city, which Thou dost prepare
Is ever our portion, since willing to be
Just pilgrims with Jesus, our roof a tent tree.

10.10.10.10.

1 It was a garden in the primal age,
But at the end it is a city square;
Creation's center in the garden was,
God's building issues in the city fair.

2 Both in the garden and the city fair
A river and the tree of life are seen,
Christ typifying as the life supply,
The Spirit showing as the living stream.

3 Both in the garden and the city bright
Three kinds of precious substances are found;
There are the gold, the pearls, and precious stones
Which for the building work of God abound.

4 But in the garden all these precious things
Are just materials lying in the earth,
Yet in the city all are builded up
And form that dwelling of transcendent worth.

5 Man in the garden of the clay was formed,
In nature as the Lord created him;
The tree of life was then without the man,
Not having yet become his life within.

6 But in the city glorious the tree
Within the corporate "man" doth grow, thereby
Revealing Christ Himself as life divine
Being to man his inward life supply.

7 'Tis for the city man is wrought upon,
   Therefore regenerated and transformed
   To purest gold, to pearls and precious stones,
   As Christ's own Body, to Himself conformed.

8 Within the garden also was a bride,
   Who was to Adam as his counterpart;
   Lastly, the city is itself the bride
   As Christ's own fulness, precious to His heart.

9 The city is God's building work replete,
   A composition of the justified;
   A habitation it affords to God
   And is to Christ His own beloved bride.

10 'Tis God's expression, ultimate and full,
    Corporate and universal, marvelous;
    God's glory it completely manifests,
    And is Christ's counterpart most glorious.

976*

8.7.8.7.D. with chorus.

1 O Lord Jesus, Thy redeemed ones
     Are Thy Body and Thy Bride;
   As Thy fulness, Thine expression,
     In her Thou art glorified.
   Thou, her all in all forever,
     She Thy riches doth declare;
   Thou dost fully saturate her
     And Thy glory with her share.

continued

Chorus:

Lo, the holy city,
Full of God's bright glory!
It is God's complete expression
In humanity.

2   God with man completely blended,
Mystery of godliness,
God in glory, full, resplendent,
Man, His dwelling, doth express.
'Tis a vessel universal
All God's fulness to express;
All His beauty manifesting,
Mingled with His holiness.

3   'Tis a living composition
Of the saints He hath transformed;
As the pearls and stones most precious,
To His image they're conformed:
From the throne of God, its center,
Flows the living water free;
Christ the tree of life doth flourish,
Bearing fruit abundantly.

4   'Tis th' eternal golden lampstand,
Holding Christ, the lamp of light;
God in Christ the light of glory
As the Spirit shineth bright!
'Tis the ultimate expression —
Man in God and God in man;
'Tis their mutual habitation,
Goal of God's eternal plan.

8.7.8.7.D.

1 Glorious things of thee are spoken,
  Holy city of our God;
He whose word cannot be broken
  Formed thee for His own abode;
On the Rock of Ages founded,
  What can shake thy sure repose?
With salvation's walls surrounded,
  Thou may'st smile at all thy foes.

2 See the streams of living waters,
  Springing from eternal love,
Well supply thy blessed members,
  And all fear of want remove;
Who can faint, when such a river
  Ever flows their thirst t' assuage?
Grace which, like the Lord, the giver,
  Never fails from age to age.

3 Blest constituents of Zion,
  Washed in the Redeemer's blood;
Jesus, whom their souls rely on,
  Makes them kings and priests to God.
'Tis His love His people raises
  Over self to reign as kings:
And as priests, His worthy praises,
  Each his thankful offering brings.

4 Savior, if of Zion's city
  I, through grace, a member am,
Let the world deride or pity —
  I will glory in Thy name.
Fading is the worldling's pleasure,
  All his boasted pomp and show;
Solid joys and lasting treasure
  None but Zion's members know.

ULTIMATE MANIFESTATION —
THE NEW JERUSALEM

7.6.7.6. with chorus.

1 In new heaven and new earth
New Jerusalem lies;
Out of God it has its birth,
With God's radiance thrice.

Lo, God's image it doth bear,
And God's glory it doth share!
And the Lord Himself is there
In that city of God.

2 All the gates are pearls assigned
In the city of gold,
And the street is gold refined
With foundations twelvefold.

3 There life's crystal river flows
With abundant supplies,
And the tree of life there grows
And all need satisfies.

4 God is there the great I AM
In that city of light;
God's the light within the Lamb,
And there never is night.

8.8.8.8.

1 How glorious, how bright it shines,
The holy, new Jerusalem;
It is God's dwelling place with man,
The spotless bride of Christ, the Lamb.

2 Saints of the Old and of the New,
Heirs of the promise God bestowed,
Components of the city are,
Together built for God's abode.

3 Perfectly square the city lies,
All sides are equal — length, width, height;
No measurement more long or short,
No part oblique, it stands upright.

4 The city with its street pure gold
As clear as glass transparent is,
Showing that God's transcendent life
Its quality and nature is.

5 Twelve city gates are each one pearl;
Thus man is through redemption shown
Reborn and as a pearl transformed,
Entering to a realm God's own.

6 The twelve foundations of its wall
Are with twelve precious stones adorned;
Through fire and pressure recomposed
And with eternal value formed.

7 The wall of jasper, crystal clear,
God's glory by it fully shown;
His glorious light through it does shine,
And He appears as jasper stone.

8 The wall a separation makes,
Excluding all that is unclean;
Gold, pearls, and precious stones alone
The holy city has within.

9 God and the Lamb the Temple are!
We shall behold His glorious face;
His presence never will depart,
We'll worship Him thru endless days.

continued

10 The city needs no sun nor moon
For God's own glory is its light;
The Lamb's the lamp the city bears,
In all directions blazing bright.

11 Out from the throne of God and the Lamb
Flows midst the street a living stream,
And on its banks, on either side,
The tree of life is thriving seen.

12 This signifies the life of God
Not just for food or water flows,
But carries God's authority
As it throughout the city goes.

13 The street of purest gold therein
God's nature as the way doth show;
A river in it flows for drink
And fruits of life abundant grow.

14 The number twelve means government,
Perfection which eternal is;
God blent with man it also tells —
Three multiplied by four shows this.

15 Darkness and death shall be no more,
Sorrow and pain shall pass away,
Old will be gone and all be new,
God will abide with man for aye.

16 The city has God's image full,
It rules for Him, the sovereign King,
Fulfilling His eternal plan,
Complete content to Him to bring.

8.8.8.8.

1 Throughout the whole of Holy Writ
The saints in type are manifest
As like a bride, God's heart to please,
And as a building for His rest.

2 The types and figures of the Church
In the Old Testament are these:
A building meet for life and rule,
A bride the man to match and please.

3 God's people in the ancient times
Were called by God His very spouse;
Among them and with them were built
God's ruling city and God's house.

4 Incarnate God, the God-man, Christ,
As Bridegroom for the Bride has come;
With His own life He quickened her,
That she His counterpart become.

5 In resurrection Christ doth now,
As David's Son, God's temple build,
That God may have a resting place
And there accomplish all He willed.

6 The Church is thus the Bride of Christ,
In whom His full delight doth rest;
It is a dwelling place to God
Where He may live and be expressed.

continued

7 The new Jerusalem will be
The full perfection ultimate
Of all the types of house and bride,
Th' eternal plan to consummate.

8 It is the Bride which matches Christ,
Thru whom He may Himself express;
It is God's tabernacle too
In which our God can rule and rest.

9 The ultimate completion 'tis
Of God's work in humanity,
His full expression glorious
Thru His redeemed eternally.

CHRIST HEADING UP ALL THINGS

981*

8.7.8.7.

1 In His Christ to head up all things
Is our God's economy;
Taking Christ as Head and Center,
All is one in harmony.

2 Christ as Head will be the Center;
God within will be the Light;
Christ enthroned, with God, His substance,
Will fulfill His heart's delight.

3 Christ as life will be the content,
Heading up all things in light;
All the saints will be the vessel,
To express His glory bright.

4   Satan hath himself injected
      Into man all things to spoil,
      Bringing darkness and corruption
      God's eternal plan to foil.

5   Christ has come, Himself imparting
      Into man as life to save,
      That the pow'r of death and darkness
      May no more all things enslave.

6   Thru the Church which is His Body
      Christ as Head will sum up all;
      All will fitly join together,
      All things either great or small.

7   Under Christ, by His full headship,
      All in union will subsist;
      In the light the Church expresses
      All in oneness will exist.

8   Owning Christ as Head and Center,
      All will be in harmony;
      Thru the shining of His Body
      All will share His liberty.

9   No more darkness and corruption,
      No more death and vanity;
      All will be released from bondage
      Throughout all eternity.

10.10.10.10.10.10.

1 How true it is no heart may comprehend
 The glory God prepareth for His own,
 And what will happen when this age shall end;
 But yet in vision Jesus hath made known
 How fair and holy shall the Church descend,
 Lit up with light of precious jasper stone.

2 And He shall make His Church all heavenly fair,
 With gold and pearls, and every radiant stone,
 And reign in holiness and glory there,
 And shine as suns and stars have never shone;
 And He shall lead His Bride, His joy and care,
 With blissful singing to His Father's throne.

3 And then the blest communion shall have come,
 Of God's dear children meeting from afar;
 Within His burning love they blend as one,
 Yet each, according as His counsels are,
 Shall have peculiar glory of his own,
 As one star differeth from another star.

4 And God is all in all in that great day,
 And He is their exceeding great Reward;
 Their stream of life, their beautiful array,
 Their food, their joy, their radiance, Christ the Lord;
 The music of their wondrous song shall say,
 How great the joy that passeth thought or word.

5 And this is that eternal life of heaven,
 Laid up with Christ in God, the mystery
 Of resurrection life which He hath given:
 A fount of living waters full and free;
 A life by which the gates of death are riven,
 A life which on the throne of Christ shall be.

6   And here in this waste wilderness begun,
    So soon as we believe in Christ aright,
    And quickened by the Spirit of the Son,
    Receive Him as our only life and light,
    As all the branches in the vine are one,
    So we are one forever in His sight.

7   Now come, Lord Jesus, quickly from above,
    Do Thou sustain us on the desert road,
    And draw us after Thee by might of love,
    Our Fatherland art Thou, O love of God;
    Once safe in Thee, no more shall we remove,
    O Thou our everlasting sure abode.

ULTIMATE MANIFESTATION — LIFE IN ETERNITY

983

8.6.8.6.D.

1   There is a stream which issues forth
    From God's eternal throne
   And from the Lamb, a living stream,
    Clear as the crystal stone.
   In it doth grow the tree of life,
    It makes the ransomed sing:
   Its living draught revives the heart;
    Hence all the joys do spring

2   Such joys as are unspeakable,
    And full of glory too;
   Such splendid riches, meat and drink,
    As worldlings do not know.
   Eye hath not seen, nor ear hath heard,
    For fancy 'tis concealed,
   What Thou, Lord, hast laid up for Thine
    And hast to me revealed.

continued

3   I feel Thy touch, I hear Thy voice,
    I taste Thy sweetest grace;
My soul doth leap: but, oh, that I
    May see Thee face to face!
Then with the saints my soul shall feast
    On joys that always last:
Blest be my God, the God of joy,
    That gives here such a taste!

984*

8.7.8.7. with chorus.

1   River of living water,
    River that flows from the throne,
Fellowship giving and making
    God's own authority known.

    River of living water,
    Fellowship freely bestows;
    Bringing authority with it,
    Through every place where it flows.

2   Water of life is the Spirit,
    God as the life in it flows;
Carrying with it His Lordship,
    Through every place where it goes.

3   Midst the gold street it floweth,
    Thus showing to us the way;
As in God's nature it floweth,
    So in His way we will stay.

4   The tree of life by the river,
    Shows to us God as our food;
We by the river's full flowing
    Take of the tree's plenitude.

7.6.7.6.

1 No more in earthen vessels
  God's treasure then shall be,
But in unclouded beauty
  Thou, Lord, wilt shine thru me.

2 Afar thru that gold vessel
  God's glory shineth bright;
There'll be no need of sunshine,
  For God will be the light.

3 With Christ, the Stone most precious,
  God's city shall be fair;
And He shall shine as jasper
  In cloudless glory there:

4 Undimmed in that great vessel,
  The glory of that light,
Illum'ning with its fulness
  The earth in radiance bright.

5 All in His new creation
  God's glory there shall see;
The vessel for that shining
  The Lamb's own Bride shall be:

6 A golden vessel glorious,
  That all who see adore
God in the Lamb in glory
  Expressed forevermore.

986

8.7.8.7. with chorus.

1 Christ has a full redemption made:
  What a wonderful Savior!
We are redeemed! the price is paid:
  What a wonderful Savior!

  What a wonderful Savior is Jesus,
    my Savior;
  What a wonderful Savior is Jesus,
    my Lord!

2 I praise Him for the cleansing blood,
  What a wonderful Savior!
That reconciled my soul to God,
  What a wonderful Savior!

3 He cleanses me from all my sin:
  What a wonderful Savior!
And now He reigns and rules within;
  What a wonderful Savior!

4 He dwells within me day by day,
  What a wonderful Savior!
And keeps me faithful all the way,
  What a wonderful Savior!

5 He gives me overcoming power,
  What a wonderful Savior!
And triumph in each conflict hour,
  What a wonderful Savior!

6 To Him I've given all my heart,
  What a wonderful Savior!
The world shall never share a part,
  What a wonderful Savior!

ONE DAY

987

J. Wilbur Chapman   11.10.11.10. with chorus.

1 One day when heaven was filled with His praises,
   One day when sin was as black as could be,
Jesus came forth to be born of a virgin —
   Dwelt among men, my example is He!

     Living, He loved me; dying, He saved me;
        Buried, He carried my sins far away;
     Rising, He justified freely forever:
        One day He's coming — O glorious day!

2 One day they led Him up Calvary's mountain,
   One day they nailed Him to die on the tree;
Suffering anguish, despised and rejected;
   Bearing our sins, my Redeemer is He.

3 One day they left Him alone in the garden,
   One day He rested, from suffering free;
Angels came down o'er His tomb to keep vigil;
   Hope of the hopeless, my Savior is He.

4 One day the grave could conceal Him no longer,
   One day the stone rolled away from the door;
Then He arose, over death He had conquered;
   Now is ascended, my Lord evermore.

5 One day the trumpet will sound for His coming,
   One day the skies with His glory will shine;
Wonderful day, my beloved ones bringing;
   Glorious Savior, this Jesus is mine!

988†

6.5.6.5.D.

Merciful and loving,
    Suff'ring pain and loss,
All for us, the sinners,
    Going to the cross;
Tasting death for all men,
    Dying for our sins;
This is Christ the Savior,
    What will you do with Him?

989

10.10.10.6. with chorus.

1 Jesus, my Savior, to Bethlehem came,
Laid in a manger to sorrow and shame;
O it was wonderful, blest be His name,
    Seeking for me, for me:
    Seeking for me, for me,
    Seeking for me, for me;
O it was wonderful, blest be His name,
    Seeking for me, for me.

2 Jesus, my Savior, on Calvary's tree
Paid the great debt, and my soul He set free;
O it was wonderful — how could it be?
    Dying for me, for me!
    Dying for me, for me,
    Dying for me, for me;
O it was wonderful — how could it be?
    Dying for me, for me!

3 Jesus, my Savior, the same as of old,
While I was wand'ring in darkness and cold,
Gently and long did He plead with my soul,
    Calling for me, for me!
    Calling for me, for me,
    Calling for me, for me;
Gently and long did He plead with my soul,
    Calling for me, for me!

4 Jesus, my Savior, shall come from on high.
  Sweet is the promise as weary years fly:
  O I shall see Him descend from the sky,
    Coming for me, for me!
  Coming for me, for me,
  Coming for me, for me;
  O I shall see Him descend from the sky,
    Coming for me, for me!

8.7.8.7. with chorus. **990**

1 The Great Physician now is near,
    The sympathizing Jesus;
  He speaks the drooping heart to cheer,
    Oh, hear the voice of Jesus!

  Sweetest note in seraph song;
  Sweetest name on mortal tongue;
  Sweetest carol ever sung:
    Jesus, blessed Jesus!

2 Your many sins are all forgiv'n,
    Oh, hear the voice of Jesus;
  The veil 'twixt you and God is riven,
    Redemption wrought by Jesus.

3 All glory to the dying Lamb!
    I now believe in Jesus;
  I love the blessed Savior's name,
    I love the name of Jesus.

4 His name dispels my guilt and fear,
    No other name but Jesus;
  Oh, how my soul delights to hear
    The precious name of Jesus!

991

Peculiar Meter.

1 We have heard the joyful sound:
   Jesus saves! Jesus saves!
Spread the tidings all around:
   Jesus saves! Jesus saves!
Bear the news to every land,
Climb the steeps and cross the waves;
Onward! — 'tis our Lord's command;
   Jesus saves! Jesus saves!

2 Waft it on the rolling tide,
   Jesus saves, Jesus saves;
Tell to sinners far and wide,
   Jesus saves, Jesus saves;
Sing, ye islands of the sea,
Echo back, ye ocean caves;
Earth shall keep her jubilee,
   Jesus saves, Jesus saves.

3 Sing above the battle's strife,
   Jesus saves, Jesus saves;
By His death and endless life,
   Jesus saves, Jesus saves;
Sing it softly thru the gloom,
When the heart for mercy craves,
Sing in triumph o'er the tomb,
   Jesus saves, Jesus saves.

4 Give the winds a mighty voice,
   Jesus saves, Jesus saves;
Let the nations now rejoice.
   Jesus saves, Jesus saves;
Shout salvation full and free,
Highest hills and deepest caves,
This our song of victory,
   Jesus saves, Jesus saves.

10.6.10.6. with chorus.

1 There's not a Friend like the lowly Jesus:
    No, not one! no, not one!
None else could heal all our souls' diseases:
    No, not one! no, not one!

    Jesus knows all about our struggles;
        He will guide till the day is done:
    There's not a Friend like the lowly Jesus:
        No, not one! no, not one!

2 No friend like Him is so high and holy,
    No, not one! no, not one!
And yet no friend is so meek and lowly,
    No, not one! no, not one!

3 There's not an hour that He is not near us,
    No, not one! no, not one!
No night so dark, but His love can cheer us,
    No, not one! no, not one!

4 Did ever saint find this Friend forsake him?
    No, not one! no, not one!
Or sinner find that He would not take him?
    No, not one! no, not one!

5 Was e'er a gift like the Savior given?
    No, not one! no, not one!
Will He refuse us the bliss of heaven?
    No, not one! no, not one!

993

8.5.8.5.D. with chorus.

1 O how sweet the glorious message,
   Simple faith may claim;
Yesterday, today, forever,
   Jesus is the same.
Still He loves to save the sinful,
   Heal the sick and lame;
Cheer the mourner, still the tempest;
   Glory to His name!

   Yesterday, today, forever,
      Jesus is the same,
   All may change, but Jesus never!
      Glory to His name,
      Glory to His name,
      Glory to His name;
   All may change, but Jesus never!
      Glory to His name.

2 He who was the friend of sinners,
   Seeks thee, lost one, now;
Sinner, come, and at His footstool,
   Penitently bow.
He who said, "I'll not condemn thee,
   Go and sin no more,"
Speaks to thee that word of pardon,
   As in days of yore.

3 Oft on earth He healed the suff'rer,
   By His mighty hand;
Still our sicknesses and sorrows,
   Go at His command.
He who gave His healing virtue,
   To a woman's touch;
To the faith that claims His fulness,
   Still will give as much.

4 As of old He walked to Emmaus,
   With them to abide;
So through all life's way He walketh,
   Ever near our side.
Soon again we shall behold Him,
   Hasten, Lord, the day!
But 'twill still be "this same Jesus,"
   As He went away.

GOSPEL — REDEMPTION

994

11.9.11.9. with chorus.

1 Oh, how dark the night that wrapt my spirit round!
Oh, how deep the woe my Savior found
When He walked across the waters of my soul,
Bade my night disperse and made me whole!

All the way to Calvary He went for me,
   He went for me, He went for me;
All the way to Calvary He went for me,
   He died to set me free.

2 Tremblingly a sinner bowed before His face,
Naught I knew of pardon, God's free grace;
Heard a voice so melting, "Cease thy wild regret,
Jesus bought thy pardon, paid thy debt."

3 O 'twas wondrous love the Savior showed for me!
When He left His throne for Calvary,
When He bore my trespass, bore it all alone;
Praise His Name forever, make it known.

995

8.6.8.6.D.

1 There is a green hill far away,
   Without a city wall,
Where the dear Lord was crucified,
   Who died to save us all.

   Oh, dearly, dearly has He loved,
      And died our sins to bear;
   We trust in His redeeming blood,
      And life eternal share.

2 We may not know, we cannot tell,
   What pains He had to bear;
But we believe it was for us
   He hung and suffered there.

3 He died that we might be forgiven,
   He died to make us good,
That we might from our sins be freed,
   Saved by His precious blood.

4 There was no other good enough
   To pay the price of sin,
He only could divine life give
   And dwell Himself within.

7.7.7.7.

1 Jesus, Savior, Son of God,
Bearer of the sinner's load,
Breaker of the captive's chain,
Cleanser of the guilty's stain,

2 Thou the sinner's death hast died,
Thou for us wast crucified;
For our sins Thy flesh was torn,
Thou our penalty hast borne.

3 Savior, Surety, Lamb of God,
Thou hast bought us with Thy blood;
Thou hast wiped the debt away,
Nothing left for us to pay;

4 Nothing left for us to bear,
Nothing left for us to share
But the pardon and the bliss,
But the love, the light, the peace.

5 I to Thee will look and live,
And, in looking, praises give;
Looking lightens, looking heals,
Looking all the gladness seals.

6 Jesus, Savior, Son of God,
Bearer of the sinner's load,
I would rise to Thee above,
I would look, and praise, and love.

997

6.6.6.6. with chorus.

1 I hear the Savior say,
   "Thy strength indeed is small,
   Child of weakness, watch and pray,
   Find in Me thine all in all."

   Jesus paid it all,
   All to Him I owe;
   Sin had left a crimson stain,
   He washed it white as snow.

2 Lord, now indeed I find
   Thy pow'r, and Thine alone,
   Can change the leper's spots,
   And melt the heart of stone.

3 For nothing good have I
   Whereby Thy grace to claim —
   I'll wash my garments white
   In the blood of Calv'ry's Lamb.

4 And when, before the throne,
   I stand in Him complete,
   "Jesus died my soul to save,"
   My lips shall still repeat.

998*

8.8.8.8. with chorus.

Christ has become one with sinners,
Sharing in all of our living;
Crucified even for sinners,
Glorious life to us giving.

   Christ Jesus came for us,
   Christ Jesus died for us;
   O yes, for us, for us, for us.
   Christ came and died for us.

8.6.8.6. with chorus.

1 Alas, and did my Savior bleed?
And did my Sovereign die?
Would He devote that sacred head
For such a worm as I?

At the cross, at the cross where
I first saw the light,
And the burden of my heart
rolled away,
It was there by faith I received
my sight,
And now I am happy all the day!

2 Was it for sins that I had done
He groaned upon the tree?
Amazing pity! grace unknown!
And love beyond degree!

3 Well might the sun in darkness hide,
And shut His glories in,
When Christ, the mighty Maker, died
For man, His creature's sin.

4 Thus might I hide my blushing face
While His dear cross appears.
Dissolve my heart in thankfulness,
And melt mine eyes to tears.

5 But drops of grief can ne'er repay
The debt of love I owe;
Here, Lord, I give myself away,
'Tis all that I can do.

1000

Peculiar Meter.

1 Working will not save me;
Purest deeds that I can do,
Holiest thoughts and feelings too,
Cannot form my soul anew;
Working will not save me.

Jesus wept and died for me;
Jesus suffered on the tree;
Jesus waits to make me free,
He alone can save me.

2 Weeping will not save me;
Though my face were bathed in tears,
That could not allay my fears,
Could not wash the sins of years;
Weeping will not save me.

3 Waiting will not save me;
Helpless, guilty, lost I lie,
In my ear is mercy's cry;
If I wait I can but die:
Waiting will not save me.

4 Praying will not save me;
All the prayers that I could say
Could not wash my sins away,
All I owe could never pay:
Praying will not save me.

5 Faith in Christ will save me;
Let me trust Thy gracious Son,
Trust the work that He has done,
To His arms, Lord, help me run;
Faith in Christ will save me.

1001

Peculiar Meter.

1 Free from the law — oh, happy condition!
Jesus hath bled, and there is remission;
Cursed by the law and bruised by the fall,
Christ hath redeemed us once for all.

Once for all — oh, sinner, receive it;
Once for all — oh, doubter, believe it;
Cling to the cross, the burden will fall,
Christ hath redeemed us once for all.

2 There on the cross your burden upbearing,
Thorns on His brow your Savior is wearing;
Never again your sin need appall,
You have been pardoned once for all.

3 Now we are free — there's no condemnation;
Jesus provides a perfect salvation:
"Come unto Me," oh, hear His sweet call,
Come, and He saves us once for all.

4 Children of man — oh, glorious calling,
Surely His grace will keep us from falling;
Passing from death to life at His call,
Blessed salvation once for all.

1002

7.5.7.5.D.

1 Nothing either great or small —
   Nothing, sinner, no;
   Jesus did it, did it all,
   Long, long ago.

   "It is finished!" yes, indeed,
   Finished every jot:
   Sinner, this is all you need —
   Tell me, is it not?

2 When He, from His lofty throne,
   Stooped to do and die,
   Everything was fully done;
   Hearken to His cry:

3 Weary, working, burdened one,
   Wherefore toil you so?
   Cease your doing; all was done
   Long, long ago.

4 Till to Jesus' work you cling
   By a simple faith,
   "Doing" is a deadly thing —
   "Doing" ends in death.

5 Cast your deadly "doing" down —
   Down at Jesus' feet;
   Stand in Him, in Him alone,
   Gloriously complete.

8.8.6.8.8.6.

1 Why should I worry, doubt and fear?
Has God not caused His Son to bear
  My sins upon the tree?
The debt that Christ for me has paid,
Would God another mind have made
  To claim again from me?

2 Redemption full the Lord has made,
And all my debts has fully paid,
  From law to set me free.
I fear not for the wrath of God,
For I've been sprinkled with His blood,
  It wholly covers me.

3 For me forgiveness He has gained,
And full acquittal was obtained,
  All debts of sin are paid;
God would not have His claim on two,
First on His Son, my Surety true,
  And then upon me laid.

4 So now I have full peace and rest,
My Savior Christ hath done the best
  And set me wholly free;
By His all-efficacious blood
I ne'er could be condemned by God,
  For He has died for me!

1004

8.5.8.3.D.

1 Precious, precious blood of Jesus,
  Shed on Calvary;
Shed for rebels, shed for sinners,
  Shed for thee.

  Precious, precious blood of Jesus
    Ever flowing free;
  Oh, believe it; oh, receive it,
    'Tis for thee.

2 Precious, precious blood of Jesus,
  Let it make thee whole;
Let it flow in mighty cleansing,
  O'er thy soul.

3 Though thy sins are red like crimson,
  Deep in scarlet glow,
Jesus' precious blood shall wash thee,
  White as snow.

4 Precious blood that hath redeemed us!
  All the price is paid;
Perfect pardon now is offered,
  Peace is made.

5 Now the holiest with boldness
  We may enter in;
For the open fountain cleanseth
  From all sin.

6 Precious blood, by this we conquer
  In the fiercest fight,
Sin and Satan overcoming
  By its might.

7 Precious blood whose full redemption
    Makes us nigh to God;
Precious blood, our way of glory,
    Praise and laud.

1005

9.9.9.9. with chorus.

1 Christ our Redeemer died on the cross,
    Died for the sinner, paid all his due;
Sprinkle your soul with the blood of the Lamb,
    "And I will pass, will pass over you."

"When I see the blood,
When I see the blood,
When I see the blood,
I will pass, I will pass over you."

2 Chiefest of sinners, Jesus will save;
    All He has promised, that will He do;
Wash in the fountain opened for sin,
    "And I will pass, will pass over you."

3 Judgment is coming, all will be there,
    Each one receiving justly his due;
Hide in the saving, sin-cleansing blood,
    "And I will pass, will pass over you."

4 O great compassion! O boundless love!
    O loving kindness, faithful and true!
Find peace and shelter under the blood,
    "And I will pass, will pass over you."

1006

8.6.8.6. with repeat.

1 There is a fountain filled with blood
   Drawn from Immanuel's veins;
And sinners, plunged beneath that flood,
   Lose all their guilty stains:
   Lose all their guilty stains,
   Lose all their guilty stains;
And sinners, plunged beneath that flood,
   Lose all their guilty stains.

2 The dying thief rejoiced to see
   That fountain in his day;
And there may I, though vile as he,
   Wash all my sins away:
   Wash all my sins away,
   Wash all my sins away;
And there may I, though vile as he,
   Wash all my sins away.

3 Dear dying Lamb, Thy precious blood
   Shall never lose its power,
Till all the ransomed ones of God
   Be saved, to sin no more:
   Be saved, to sin no more,
   Be saved, to sin no more;
Till all the ransomed ones of God,
   Be saved to sin no more.

4 E'er since by faith I saw the stream
   Thy flowing wounds supply,
Redeeming love has been my theme,
   And shall be till I die:
   And shall be till I die,
   And shall be till I die;
Redeeming love has been my theme,
   And shall be till I die.

5   When this poor lisping, stammering tongue
      Lies silent in the grave,
  Then in a nobler, sweeter song,
      I'll sing Thy power to save:
      I'll sing Thy power to save,
      I'll sing Thy power to save;
  Then in a nobler, sweeter song,
      I'll sing Thy power to save.

1007

11.9.11.9. with chorus.

1 Have you been to Jesus for the cleansing pow'r?
  Are you washed in the blood of the Lamb?
  Are you fully trusting in His grace this hour?
  Are you washed in the blood of the Lamb?

    Are you washed in the blood,
    In the soul-cleansing blood of the Lamb?
    Are your garments spotless? Are they white as snow?
    Are you washed in the blood of the Lamb?

2 Are you walking daily by the Savior's side?
  Are you washed in the blood of the Lamb?
  Do you rest each moment in the Crucified?
  Are you washed in the blood of the Lamb?

3 When the Bridegroom cometh will your robes be white?
  Are you washed in the blood of the Lamb?
  Will your soul be ready for His presence bright,
  And be washed in the blood of the Lamb?

4 Lay aside the garments that are stained with sin,
  And be washed in the blood of the Lamb;
  There's a fountain flowing for the soul unclean,
  O be washed in the blood of the Lamb.

1008

Peculiar Meter.

1 What can wash away my sin?
Nothing but the blood of Jesus;
What can make me whole again?
Nothing but the blood of Jesus.

> Oh! precious is the flow
> That makes me white as snow;
> No other fount I know,
> Nothing but the blood of Jesus.

2 For my cleansing this I see —
Nothing but the blood of Jesus!
For my pardon this my plea —
Nothing but the blood of Jesus!

3 Nothing can my sin erase —
Nothing but the blood of Jesus!
Naught of works, 'tis all of grace —
Nothing but the blood of Jesus!

4 This is all my hope and peace —
Nothing but the blood of Jesus!
This is all my righteousness —
Nothing but the blood of Jesus!

1009

10.9.10.8. with chorus.

1 Would you be free from your burden of sin?
There's power in the blood, power in the blood;
Would you o'er evil a victory win?
There's wonderful power in the blood.

> There is power, power, wonder-working power,
> In the blood of the Lamb;
> There is power, power, wonder-working power,
> In the precious blood of the Lamb.

2 Would you be free from your passion and pride?
  There's power in the blood, power in the blood;
Come for a cleansing to Calvary's tide,
  There's wonderful power in the blood.

3 Would you be whiter, much whiter than snow?
  There's power in the blood, power in the blood;
Sin-stains are lost in its life-giving flow,
  There's wonderful power in the blood.

4 Would you do service for Jesus your King?
  There's power in the blood, power in the blood;
Would you live daily His praises to sing?
  There's wonderful power in the blood.

1010

8.6.8.6. with chorus.

1   O now I see the cleansing wave!
      The fountain deep and wide;
    Jesus, my Lord, mighty to save,
      Points to His wounded side.

    The cleansing stream I see, I see;
    I plunge, and O it cleanseth me!
    O praise the Lord it cleanseth me!
    It cleanseth me, yes, cleanseth me.

2   I see the dear Redeemer raised,
      I hear the speaking blood;
    It speaks! My spirit is amazed!
      And quickened by its flood.

3   I rise to walk in God's own light
      Above the world and sin,
    With heart renewed and garments white
      And Christ enthroned within.

1011

8.4.8.4.8.8.8.4.

1 One there is above all others,
    Oh, how He loves!
His is love beyond a brother's,
    Oh, how He loves!
Earthly friends may fail or leave us,
One day soothe, the next day grieve us;
But this Friend will ne'er deceive us:
    Oh, how He loves!

2 'Tis eternal life to know Him,
    Oh, how He loves!
Think, oh, think how much we owe Him,
    Oh, how He loves!
With His precious blood He bought us,
In the wilderness He sought us,
To His flock He safely brought us:
    Oh, how He loves!

3 Blessed Jesus! would you know Him?
    Oh, how He loves!
Give yourselves entirely to Him,
    Oh, how He loves!
Think no longer of the morrow,
From the past new courage borrow,
Jesus carries all your sorrow:
    Oh, how He loves!

4 All your sins shall be forgiven,
    Oh, how He loves!
Backward shall your foes be driven,
    Oh, how He loves!
Best of blessings He'll provide you,
Nought but good shall e'er betide you,
Safe to glory He will guide you:
    Oh, how He loves!

10.6.10.6. with chorus.

1   There is no love like the love of Jesus,
     Never to fade or fall,
  Till into the rest of the house of God
     He has gathered us all.

     Jesus' love, precious love,
       Boundless, and pure, and free;
     Oh, turn to that love, weary wand'ring soul;
       Jesus pleadeth for thee.

2   There is no heart like the heart of Jesus,
     Filled with a tender love;
  No throb nor throe that our hearts can know,
     But He feels it above.

3   There is no eye like the eye of Jesus,
     Piercing so far away;
  Ne'er out of the sight of its tender light
     Can the wanderer stray.

4   There is no voice like the voice of Jesus,
     Tender and sweet its chime;
  Like musical ring of a flowing spring
     In the bright summertime.

5   Oh, let us hark to the voice of Jesus!
     Then we shall never roam;
  And we shall rest on His loving breast,
     And with Him we'll be one!

1013*

13.8.13.8. with chorus.

1 What can keep the wanderers from going
    all astray?
  Nothing but the love of Jesus!
What can turn the fallen people from
    their sinful way?
  Nothing but the love of Jesus!

    Nothing but the love of Jesus
        can constrain!
    Nothing but the love of Jesus
        can sustain!
    Nothing both in heav'n and earth can
        sinners gain,
      Nothing but the love of Jesus!

2 What can chase the bitterness from all
    the suffering ones?
  Nothing but the love of Jesus!
What can wipe away the tears of all
    the weeping ones?
  Nothing but the love of Jesus!

3 What as ointment to the wound can heal
    the wounded hearts?
  Nothing but the love of Jesus!
What as showers to the drought can cheer
    despairing hearts?
  Nothing but the love of Jesus!

4 What can satisfy the human life
    of vanity?
  Nothing but the love of Jesus!
What can swallow up the taste of
    all mortality?
  Nothing but the love of Jesus!

1014

10.10.10.6. with chorus.

1 Oh, what a Savior that He died for me!
From condemnation He hath made me free;
"He that believeth on the Son" saith He,
"Hath everlasting life."

"Verily, verily, I say unto you;"
"Verily, verily," message ever new!
"He that believeth on the Son" — 'tis true! —
"Hath everlasting life!"

2 All my iniquities on Him were laid,
All my indebtedness by Him was paid;
All who believe on Him, the Lord hath said,
"Hath everlasting life."

3 Though poor and needy, I can trust my Lord;
Though weak and sinful, I believe His word;
Oh, glad message; every child of God
"Hath everlasting life."

4 Though all unworthy, yet I will not doubt;
For him that cometh He will not cast out:
"He that believeth" — oh, the good news shout!
"Hath everlasting life."

1015*

8.6.8.6. with repeat.

O glory, glory, what a life
I have received today!
All darkness, death and pow'r of sin
Have now been chased away!
Have now been chased away!
Have now, have now been chased away!

1016   9.8.9.8. with chorus.

1   Under the burdens of guilt and care,
      Many a spirit is grieving,
    Who in the joy of the Lord might share,
      Life everlasting receiving.

          Life! life! eternal life!
          Jesus alone is the Giver:
          Life! life! abundant life!
          Glory to Jesus forever!

2   Burdened one, why will you longer bear
      Sorrows from which He releases?
    Open your heart, and rejoicing, share
      Life more abundant in Jesus.

3   Leaving the mountain, the streamlet grows,
      Flooding the vale with a river;
    So, from the hill of the Cross, there flows
      Life more abundant forever.

4   Oh, for the flood on the thirsty land!
      Oh, for a mighty revival!
    Oh, for a sanctified, fearless band,
      Ready to hail its arrival!

1017*   15.15.15.6. with chorus.

Christ has put on human nature and become
      a man like me,
He has died upon the cross that I from Adam
      might be free,
He has risen and as Spirit He has come
      to live in me
    That He might be my life.

First chorus:
   Glory! glory! Hallelujah!
   Glory! glory! Hallelujah!
   Glory! glory! Hallelujah!
   For Christ is now my life!

Second chorus:
   Vict'ry! vict'ry! Hallelujah!
   Vict'ry! vict'ry! Hallelujah!
   Vict'ry! vict'ry! Hallelujah!
   For Christ is now my all!

GOSPEL — LIGHT

11.8.11.8. with chorus.

1018

1 The whole world was lost in the darkness of sin;
   The light of the world is Jesus;
Like sunshine at noonday His glory shone in,
   The light of the world is Jesus.

   Come to the light, 'tis shining for thee;
   Sweetly the light has dawned upon me;
   Once I was blind, but now I can see;
   The light of the world is Jesus.

2 No darkness have we who in Jesus abide,
   The light of the world is Jesus;
We walk in the light when we follow our Guide,
   The light of the world is Jesus.

3 Ye dwellers in darkness with sin-blinded eyes,
   The light of the world is Jesus;
Go, wash, at His bidding, and light will arise;
   The light of the world is Jesus.

1019

11.11.11.6. with chorus.

1 A ruler once came to Jesus by night,
To ask Him the way of salvation and light;
The Master made answer in words true and plain,
"Ye must be born again!"

"Ye must be born again!"
"Ye must be born again!"
"I verily, verily say unto thee,
Ye must be born again!"

2 Ye children of men, attend to the word
So solemnly uttered by Jesus, the Lord,
And let not this message to you be in vain,
"Ye must be born again."

3 Oh, ye who would enter that glorious rest,
And sing with the ransomed the song of the blest;
The life everlasting if ye would obtain,
"Ye must be born again."

GOSPEL — FREEDOM

1020†

Peculiar Meter.

Who can set us free from sin?
Only Christ! only Christ!
Who can be our life within?
Only Christ!
Only Christ! Only Christ!
Only Christ can set us free,
Only Christ!

GOSPEL — FREEDOM

8.6.8.6.D.

1021*

All sinners are the slaves of sin,
  All poisoned by death's sting;
Christ only can from sin and death
  A full deliverance bring.
He is the Everlasting One,
  Who longs to set us free;
If we do not believe in Him,
  We'll die in misery.

GOSPEL — NEED OF CHRIST

1022

8.8.8.7.

1 I've tried in vain a thousand ways
  My fears to quell, my hopes to raise;
  But what I need, the Bible says,
    Is ever, only Jesus.

2 My soul is night, my heart is steel —
  I cannot see, I cannot feel;
  For light, for life I must appeal
    In simple faith to Jesus.

3 He died, He lives, He reigns, He pleads;
  There's love in all His words and deeds;
  There's all a guilty sinner needs
    Forevermore in Jesus.

4 Though some should sneer, and some
      should blame,
  I'll go with all my guilt and shame;
  I'll go to Him because His name,
    Above all names, is Jesus.

1023

7.6.7.6.D.

1 I need Thee, precious Jesus!
   For I am full of sin;
My soul is dark and guilty,
   My spirit dead within:
I need the cleansing fountain,
   Where I can always flee:
The blood of Christ most precious,
   The sinner's perfect plea.

2 I need Thee, precious Jesus!
   For I am very poor;
A stranger and a pilgrim,
   I have no earthly store:
I need the love of Jesus,
   To cheer me on my way,
To guide my doubting footsteps,
   To be my strength and stay.

3 I need Thee, precious Jesus!
   I need a friend like Thee;
A friend to soothe and comfort,
   A friend to care for me:
I need the heart of Jesus,
   To feel each anxious care,
To bear my every burden,
   And all my sorrow share.

4 I need Thee, precious Jesus!
   I need Thee day by day,
To fill me with Thy fulness,
   To lead me on my way;
I need Thy Holy Spirit,
   To teach me what I am;
To show me more of Jesus,
   To point me to the Lamb.

5 I need Thee, precious Jesus!
    And hope to see Thee soon,
    Encircled with Thy glory,
    And seated on Thy throne;
    There with Thy blood-bought people,
    My joy shall ever be
    To praise Thee, precious Jesus,
    To gaze, my Lord, on Thee.

1024*

Peculiar Meter.

1 Christ the Savior is just the One you need,
   He's God incarnate, as a man indeed;
   In His body He suffered every pain
   And died to cleanse your every stain,
       So you need Jesus!

       You need Jesus! You need Jesus!
           Men and women all need Him!
       For redemption you need Him,
       For salvation you need Him!
       And for everlasting life,
           Yes, you need Jesus!

2 He has risen and gone up into heav'n,
   That life eternal might be fully giv'n;
   Just receive Him, believing in your heart,
   Then all you need He will impart,
       So you need Jesus!

3 He'll enlighten your darkened heart with light,
   Forgive your sins and rescue you with might;
   He will cleanse you from all stains with His blood,
   And give to you the life of God,
       So you need Jesus!

continued

4 In your living there is a lack you sense,
And thru the years it grows the more intense;
Only Jesus this need can satisfy;
All vanity He will defy,
  So you need Jesus!

    You need Jesus! You need Jesus!
      Men and women all need Him!
    To escape from vanity,
    To obtain reality,
    To make life significant,
      Yes, you need Jesus!

5 All this world now is rife with toil and pain,
In troubled times there's nothing to sustain;
All is empty, on what can you rely?
All things reveal and testify
  That you need Jesus!

1025*

8.7.8.7.D.

1 Give up the world, Christ to obtain,
  He is your heart's very need;
  What else can you desire or seek?
  All things are empty indeed!

    He is so rich, He is so full,
      He can fulfill all your needs!
    He is so good, He is so sweet,
      All your desire He exceeds!

2 Give up the world, Christ to obtain,
  He is the One you require;
  Once you receive this glorious Christ,
  Never the rest you'll desire.

3 Though very great is all the world,
 And very small is your heart,
 Yet the great world with all its wealth
 Never can fill your small heart.

4 If you have Christ, you have all joys;
 Without this Christ, only pains;
 Where there is Christ there morning is;
 Where He is not, night remains.

GOSPEL — THE LORD'S CALLING

1026

6.4.6.4.

1 Today the Savior calls;
 Ye wand'rers come:
 O ye benighted souls!
 Why longer roam?

2 Today the Savior calls;
 O hear Him now!
 Before your day is gone,
 To Jesus bow.

3 Today the Savior calls;
 For refuge fly;
 The storm of vengeance falls,
 And death is nigh.

4 The Spirit calls today;
 Yield to His pow'r;
 O grieve Him not away,
 'Tis mercy's hour!

1027

11.7.11.7. with chorus.

1 Softly and tenderly Jesus is calling —
    Calling for you and for me;
  Patiently Jesus is waiting and watching —
    Watching for you and for me!

      Come home! come home!
        Ye who are weary, come home!
      Earnestly, tenderly, Jesus is calling,
        Calling, O sinner, come home!

2 Why should we tarry when Jesus is pleading —
    Pleading for you and for me?
  Why should we linger and heed not His mercies —
    Mercies for you and for me?

3 Time is now fleeting, the moments are passing —
    Passing from you and from me;
  Shadows are gathering, death-beds are coming —
    Coming for you and for me!

4 Oh, for the wonderful love He has promised —
    Promised for you and for me!
  Though we have sinned, He has mercy and pardon —
    Pardon for you and for me!

10.8.10.7. with chorus.

1   Jesus is tenderly calling thee home —
      Calling today, calling today!
  Why from the sunshine of love wilt thou roam,
      Farther and farther away?

      Calling today! calling today!
      Jesus is calling, is tenderly calling today!

2   Jesus is calling the weary to rest,
      Calling today! calling today!
  Bring Him thy burden and thou shalt be blest:
      He will not turn thee away.

3   Jesus is waiting, O come to Him now!
      Waiting today! waiting today!
  Come with thy sins, at His feet lowly bow;
      Come, and no longer delay.

4   Jesus is pleading, O list to His voice!
      Hear Him today! hear Him today!
  They who believe on His name shall rejoice:
      Quickly arise, come away!

1029

8.8.8.8. with chorus.

1 Christ calling yet! shall I not hear?
Earth's pleasures shall I still hold dear?
Shall life's swift passing years all fly,
And still my soul in slumber lie?

    Calling yet, oh, hear Him!
    Calling yet, oh, hear Him!
    Christ is calling yet; oh! hear
       Him calling, calling!
    Calling yet, oh, hear Him!
    Calling yet, oh, hear Him!
    Christ is calling yet; oh, hear
       Him calling yet!

2 Christ calling yet! shall I not rise?
Can I His loving voice despise,
And basely His kind care repay?
He calls me still; can I delay?

3 Christ calling yet! and shall He knock,
And I my heart the closer lock?
He still is waiting to receive;
And shall I dare His Spirit grieve?

4 Christ calling yet! and shall I give
No heed, but still in bondage live?
I wait, but He does not forsake:
He calls me still; my heart, awake!

5 Christ calling yet! I cannot stay;
My heart I yield without delay;
Vain world, farewell! from thee I part;
The voice of Christ has reached my heart.

8.9.8.9.D.

1 I hear my risen Savior say:
"Follow me, follow me, follow me";
His voice is calling all the day,
"Follow me, follow me, follow me;
For thee I trod the bitter way,
For thee I gave my life away,
And drank the gall thy debt to pay,
Follow me, follow me, follow me."

2 "I know thy life of guilt and pain;
Follow me, follow me, follow me!
I know each ache of heart and brain;
Follow me, follow me, follow me!
How often I have called in vain,
And offered pardon in my name,
And now I plead yet once again!
Follow me, follow me, follow me!"

3 "Though thou hast sinned I'll pardon thee;
Follow me, follow me, follow me!
From every sin I'll set thee free;
Follow me, follow me, follow me!
In all thy changing life I'll be
Thy God, thy guide on land and sea,
Thy bliss through all eternity,
Follow me, follow me, follow me!"

4 "Come, cast on Me thine every care;
Follow me, follow me, follow me!
Thy heavy load I will upbear;
Follow me, follow me, follow me!
Come, look to Me — dismiss thy fears;
And trust Me through eternal years;
My hand shall wipe away thy tears;
Follow me, follow me, follow me!"

continued

5 Dear Lord, I yield to Thee my will;
   I'll follow Thee, follow Thee, follow Thee!
   Oh, bid my struggling soul be still;
   I'll follow Thee, follow Thee, follow Thee!
   Lord, cleanse me, with Thy Spirit fill,
   And keep me safe from every ill;
   And all Thy Word in me fulfill;
   I'll follow Thee, follow Thee, follow Thee!

GOSPEL — PERSUASION

1031

8.6.8.6. with chorus.

1 Come, every soul by sin oppressed,
   There's mercy with the Lord;
   And He will surely give you rest
   By trusting in His Word.

   Only trust Him! Only trust Him!
   Only trust Him now!
   He will save you! He will save you!
   He will save you now!

2 For Jesus shed His precious blood
   Rich blessings to bestow;
   Plunge now into the crimson flood
   That washeth white as snow.

3 Yes, Jesus is the Truth, the Way,
   That leads you into rest;
   Believe in Him without delay,
   And you are fully blest.

4 Come then, and join the holy band,
   And on to glory go;
   In Christ's redemption take your stand,
   And all His goodness know.

8.7.8.7.8.7.

Come, ye sinners, poor and wretched,
Weak and wounded, sick and sore;
Jesus ready waits to save you,
Full of pity, love and pow'r:
He is able, He is able,
He is willing, doubt no more.

2 Come, ye needy, come and welcome;
God's free bounty glorify;
True belief and true repentance,
Every grace that brings us nigh,
Without money, without money,
Come to Jesus Christ and buy.

3 Let not conscience make you linger,
Nor of fitness fondly dream;
All the fitness He requireth
Is to feel your need of Him:
This He gives you, this He gives you,
'Tis the Spirit's rising beam.

4 Come, ye weary, heavy laden,
Lost and ruined by the fall;
If you tarry till you're better,
You will never come at all:
Not the righteous, not the righteous,
Sinners Jesus came to call.

5 Agonizing in the garden,
Your Redeemer prostrate lies;
On the bloody tree behold Him!
Hear Him cry, before He dies,
"It is finished!" "It is finished!"
Sinner, will not this suffice?

continued

6 Lo! th' incarnate God, ascended,
  Pleads the merit of His blood;
Venture on Him, venture wholly;
  Let no other trust intrude:
None but Jesus, none but Jesus,
  Can do helpless sinners good.

1033

10.6.10.6. with chorus.

1 Ye who are troubled and burdened by sin,
    Come just as you are;
  Come to the Savior, a new life begin,
    Oh, come just as you are.

    Come just as you are,
      Oh, come just as you are;
    Give up your sin, let the Savior come in,
      And come just as you are.

2 Deep in your heart sin has written its scar,
    Come just as you are;
  Though from the Father you've wandered afar,
    Oh, come just as you are.

3 Sinful and guilty, heart broken and lost,
    Come just as you are;
  Think what your ransom on Calvary cost!
    Oh, come just as you are.

GOSPEL — PERSUASION

4 Naught of your goodness God's favor can win,
  Come just as you are;
Trust in the blood which was shed for your sin,
  And come just as you are.

5 Come with your heartache, your sorrow and pain,
  Come just as you are;
No one has come to the Savior in vain,
  Oh, come just as you are.

1034

11.11.11.7. with chorus.

1 "Whosoever heareth!" shout, shout the sound!
Send the blessed tidings all the world around;
Spread the joyful news wherever man is found:
  "Whosoever will may come!"

  "Whosoever will! whosoever will!"
  Send the proclamation over vale and hill;
  'Tis a loving Father calls the wand'rer home:
    "Whosoever will may come!"

2 "Whosoever cometh" need not delay,
Now the door is open, enter while you may;
Jesus is the true, the only Living Way:
  "Whosoever will may come!"

3 "Whosoever will!" the promise is secure;
"Whosoever will," forever must endure;
"Whosoever will!" 'tis life forevermore;
  "Whosoever will may come."

1035

11.9.11.9. with chorus.

1 There is life for a look at the Crucified One,
   There is life at this moment for thee;
  Then look, sinner, look unto Him and be saved,
   Unto Him who was nailed to the tree.

   Look! look! look and live!
   There is life for a look at the Crucified One,
   There is life at this moment for thee.

2 Oh, why was He there as the Bearer of sin,
   If on Jesus thy guilt was not laid?
  Oh, why from His side flowed the sin-cleansing blood,
   If His dying thy debt has not paid?

3 It is not thy tears of repentance or prayers,
   But the blood, that redeemeth the soul;
  On Him, then, who shed it, thou mayest at once
   Thy weight of iniquities roll.

4 Then doubt not thy welcome, since God has declared
   There remaineth no more to be done;
  That once in the end of the world He appeared,
   And completed the work He begun.

5 Then take with rejoicing from Jesus at once
   The life everlasting He gives;
  And know with assurance, thou never canst die
   Since Jesus, thy Righteousness, lives.

7.6.7.3.D. with chorus.

1   Look to Jesus, weary one,
     Look and live! look and live!
  Look at what the Lord has done,
     Look and live!
  See Him lifted on the tree,
     Look and live! look and live!
  Hear Him say, "Look unto Me!"
     Look and live!

     Look! the Lord is lifted high,
     Look to Him, He's ever nigh;
     Look and live! why will ye die?
     Look and live!

2   Though unworthy, vile, unclean,
     Look and live! look and live!
  Look away from self and sin,
     Look and live!
  Long by Satan's power enslaved,
     Look and live! look and live!
  Look to Me, ye shall be saved,
     Look and live!

3   Though you've wandered far away,
     Look and live! look and live!
  Harden not your heart today,
     Look and live!
  'Tis thy Father calls thee home,
     Look and live! look and live!
  Whosoever will may come,
     Look and live!

Peculiar Meter.

1 "Though your sins be as scarlet,
   They shall be as white as snow;
Though your sins be as scarlet,
   They shall be as white as snow;
Though they be red as crimson,
   They shall be as wool;"
"Though your sins be as scarlet,
Though your sins be as scarlet,
   They shall be as white as snow,
   They shall be as white as snow."

2 Hear the voice that entreats you,
   O return ye unto God!
Hear the voice that entreats you,
   O return ye unto God!
He is of great compassion,
   And of wondrous love;
Hear the voice that entreats you,
Hear the voice that entreats you,
   O return ye unto God!
   O return ye unto God!

3 He'll forgive your transgressions,
   And remember them no more;
He'll forgive your transgressions,
   And remember them no more;
"Look unto Me, ye people,"
   Saith the Lord your God!
He'll forgive your transgressions,
He'll forgive your transgressions,
   And remember them no more,
   And remember them no more.

10.8.10.8. with chorus.

1038

1   If you are tired of the load of your sin,
        Let Jesus come into your heart;
    If you desire a new life to begin,
        Let Jesus come into your heart.

>   Just now, your doubtings give o'er;
>   Just now, reject Him no more;
>   Just now, throw open the door;
>   Let Jesus come into your heart.

2   If 'tis for purity now that you sigh,
        Let Jesus come into your heart;
    Fountains for cleansing are flowing near by,
        Let Jesus come into your heart.

3   If there's a tempest your voice cannot still,
        Let Jesus come into your heart;
    If there's a void this world never can fill,
        Let Jesus come into your heart.

Peculiar Meter.

1039

1   There's a Stranger at the door,
        Let Him in;
    He has been there oft before,
        Let Him in;
    Let Him in, ere He is gone,
    Let Him in, the Holy One,
    Jesus Christ, the Father's Son,
        Let Him in.

2   Open now to Him your heart,
        Let Him in;
    If you wait He will depart,
        Let Him in;
    Let Him in, He is your Friend,
    He your soul will sure defend,
    He will keep you to the end,
        Let Him in.

continued

3 Hear you now His loving voice?
   Let Him in;
Now, oh, now make Him your choice,
   Let Him in;
He is standing at your door,
Joy to you He will restore,
And His name you will adore,
   Let Him in.

4 Now admit the heav'nly Guest,
   Let Him in;
He will make for you a feast,
   Let Him in;
He will speak your sins forgiv'n.
And when earth ties all are riv'n,
Comfort, rest, you will be giv'n,
   Let Him in.

1040†   Peculiar Meter.

1 Hark, the Savior's knocking, knocking,
   Knocking at your heart!
Oh, do not be hardened, hardened,
   Lest He should depart.
Rise and open up your heart,
   Quickly let Him in;
Life divine He'll give you, give you,
   And forgive your sin.

   Let Him in! Let Him in!
   He's knocking at your heart;
   Let Him in! Oh, let Him in!
   Let Him in your heart.

2 Why should you still tarry, tarry,
   Keep Him waiting there?
He is kind and gracious, gracious,
   Merciful and dear.

Listen to His tender voice,
Do not grieve His heart;
Won't you let Him enter, enter,
And His grace impart.

1041

9.9.9.7. with chorus.

1 Jesus is standing in Pilate's hall —
Friendless, forsaken, betrayed by all:
Hearken! what meaneth the sudden call?
What will you do with Jesus?

What will you do with Jesus?
Neutral you cannot be;
Some day your heart will be asking,
"What will He do with me?"

2 Jesus is standing on trial still,
You can be false to Him if you will,
You can be faithful through good or ill:
What will you do with Jesus?

3 Will you evade Him as Pilate tried?
Or will you choose Him, whate'er betide?
Vainly you struggle from Him to hide:
What will you do with Jesus?

4 Will you, like Peter, your Lord deny?
Or will you scorn from His foes to fly,
Daring for Jesus to live or die?
What will you do with Jesus?

5 "Jesus, I give Thee my heart today!
Jesus, I'll follow Thee all the way,
Gladly obeying Thee!" will you say:
"This will I do with Jesus!"

1042

7.7.7.7. with chorus.

1 While we pray and while we plead,
While you see your soul's deep need,
While our Father calls you home,
Will you not to Jesus come?

Why not now? Why not now?
Why not come to Jesus now?
Why not now? Why not now?
Why not come to Jesus now?

2 You have wandered far away;
Do not risk another day;
Do not turn from God thy face,
But today accept His grace.

3 In the world you've failed to find
Aught of peace for troubled mind;
Come to Christ, on Him believe,
Peace and joy you shall receive.

4 Come to Christ, confession make;
Come to Christ, and pardon take;
Trust in Him from day to day,
He will keep you all the way.

1043

7.7.7.3. with chorus.

1 Life at best is very brief,
Like the falling of a leaf,
Like the binding of a sheaf,
Be in time!
Fleeting days are telling fast
That the die will soon be cast,
And the fatal line be passed,
Be in time!

Chorus:

Be in time! Be in time!
While the voice of Jesus calls you,
    Be in time!
If in sin you longer wait,
You may find no open gate,
And your cry be just too late:
    Be in time!

2 Fairest flowers soon decay,
Youth and beauty pass away;
O you have not long to stay,
    Be in time!
While God's Spirit bids you come,
Sinner, do not longer roam,
Lest you seal your hopeless doom,
    Be in time!

3 Time is gliding swiftly by,
Death and judgment draweth nigh,
To the arms of Jesus fly,
    Be in time!
O I pray you count the cost!
Ere the fatal line be crossed,
And your soul in hell be lost,
    Be in time!

4 Sinner, heed the warning voice,
Make the Lord your final choice,
Then all heaven will rejoice,
    Be in time!
Come from darkness into light;
Come, let Jesus make you right;
Come, receive His life tonight,
    Be in time!

1044*

Peculiar Meter.

Are you ready God to meet?
Are you ready God to meet?
Are you ready God to meet,
Ready God to meet?
Are you ready, are you ready,
Ready God to meet?

1045

8.8.8.5. with chorus.

1 O do not let the Word depart,
And close thine eyes against the light:
Poor sinner, harden not your heart,
Be saved, O tonight.

O why not tonight?
O why not tonight?
Wilt thou be saved?
Then why not tonight?

2 Tomorrow's sun may never rise
To bless thy long-deluded sight;
This is the time, O then be wise,
Be saved, O tonight.

3 Our Lord in pity lingers still,
And wilt thou thus His love requite?
Renounce at once thy stubborn will,
Be saved, O tonight.

4 Our blessed Lord refuses none
Who would to Him their souls unite;
Believe on Him, the work is done.
Be saved, O tonight.

Peculiar Meter.

1 "Almost persuaded" now to believe;
"Almost persuaded" Christ to receive;
  Seems now some soul to say,
  "Go, Spirit, go Thy way,
  Some more convenient day
    On Thee I'll call."

2 "Almost persuaded," come, come today;
"Almost persuaded," turn not away;
  Jesus invites you here,
  Angels are ling'ring near,
  Prayers rise from hearts so dear;
    O wand'rer, come!

3 Oh, be persuaded! Christ never fails —
Oh, be persuaded! His blood avails —
  Can save from every sin,
  Cleanse you without, within —
  Will you not let Him in?
    Open the door!

4 "Almost persuaded," harvest is past!
"Almost persuaded," doom comes at last;
  "Almost" cannot avail;
  "Almost" is but to fail!
  Sad, sad that bitter wail —
    "Almost — but lost!"

5 Be now persuaded, oh, sinner, hear!
Be now persuaded, Jesus is near;
  His voice is pleading still,
  Turn now with heart and will,
  Peace will your spirit fill —
    Oh, turn today!

1047

8.8.8.8.8.8.

1   Eternity! Eternity!
How will you spend Eternity?
This question comes to you and me!
How will you spend Eternity?
Tell me, what shall your answer be —
How will you spend Eternity?

2   Eternity! Eternity!
How will you spend Eternity?
Many are choosing Christ today,
Turning from all their sins away;
Christ shall their blessed portion be:
How will you spend Eternity?

3   Eternity! Eternity!
How will you spend Eternity?
Leaving the strait and narrow way,
Going the downward road today,
What shall the final ending be —
How will you spend Eternity?

4   Eternity! Eternity!
How will you spend Eternity?
Turn, and believe this very hour,
Trust in the Savior's grace and power:
Then shall your joyous answer be,
Saved through a long Eternity!

8.8.8.8.

1 Just as I am, without one plea,
But that Thy blood was shed for me,
And that Thou bid'st me come to Thee,
O Lamb of God, I come! I come!

2 Just as I am, and waiting not
To rid my soul of one dark blot;
To Thee whose blood can cleanse each spot,
O Lamb of God, I come, I come!

3 Just as I am, though tossed about
With many a conflict, many a doubt;
Fightings within, and fears without,
O Lamb of God, I come, I come!

4 Just as I am, poor, wretched, blind;
Sight, riches, healing of the mind;
Yes, all I need, in Thee to find,
O Lamb of God, I come, I come!

5 Just as I am, Thou wilt receive,
Wilt welcome, pardon, cleanse, relieve;
Because Thy promise I believe,
O Lamb of God, I come, I come!

6 Just as I am, Thy love unknown
Has broken every barrier down;
Now, to be Thine, yea, Thine alone,
O Lamb of God, I come, I come!

1049

8.8.8.6.

1 Drawn to the Cross which Thou hast blest,
With healing gifts for souls distrest,
To find in Thee my Life, my Rest,
Christ crucified, I come.

2 Stained with the sins which I have wrought
In word and deed and secret thought;
For pardon which Thy Blood hath bought,
Christ crucified, I come.

3 Weary of selfishness and pride,
False pleasures gone, vain hopes denied,
Deep in Thy wounds my shame to hide,
Christ crucified, I come.

4 Thou knowest all my griefs and fears,
Thy grace abused, my misspent years;
Yet now to Thee, for cleansing tears,
Christ crucified, I come.

5 I would not, if I could, conceal
The ills which only Thou canst heal;
So to the Cross, where sinners kneel,
Christ crucified, I come.

6 Wash me, and take away each stain,
Let nothing of my sin remain;
For cleansing, though it be through pain,
Christ crucified, I come.

7 To share with Thee Thy life divine,
Thy very likeness to be mine,
Since Thou hast made my nature Thine,
Christ crucified, I come.

8 To be what Thou wouldst have me be,
Accepted, sanctified in Thee,
Through what Thy grace shall work in me,
Christ crucified, I come.

Peculiar Meter.

1 Out of my bondage, sorrow, and night,
    Jesus, I come! Jesus, I come!
Into Thy freedom, gladness, and light,
    Jesus, I come to Thee!
Out of my sickness into Thy health,
Out of my want and into Thy wealth,
Out of my sin and into Thyself,
    Jesus, I come to Thee!

2 Out of my shameful failure and loss,
    Jesus, I come! Jesus, I come!
Into the glorious gain of Thy cross,
    Jesus, I come to Thee!
Out of earth's sorrows into Thy balm,
Out of life's storm and into Thy calm,
Out of distress to jubilant psalm,
    Jesus, I come to Thee!

3 Out of unrest and arrogant pride,
    Jesus, I come! Jesus, I come!
Into Thy blessed will to abide,
    Jesus, I come to Thee!
Out of myself to dwell in Thy love,
Out of despair into raptures above,
Upward for aye on wings like a dove,
    Jesus, I come to Thee!

4 Out of the fear and dread of the tomb,
    Jesus, I come! Jesus, I come!
Into the joy and pleasure, Thine own,
    Jesus, I come to Thee!
Out of the depths of ruin untold,
Into the flock Thy love doth enfold,
Ever Thy glorious face to behold,
    Jesus, I come to Thee!

1051

6.6.8.6. with chorus.

1   I hear Thy welcome voice,
That calls me, Lord, to Thee,
For cleansing in Thy precious blood
That flowed on Calvary.

I am coming, Lord,
Coming now to Thee:
Wash me, cleanse me in the blood
That flowed on Calvary.

2   Though coming weak and vile,
Thou dost my strength assure;
Thou dost my vileness fully cleanse,
Till spotless all, and pure.

3   'Tis Jesus who confirms
The blessed work within,
By adding grace to welcomed grace,
Where reigned the power of sin.

4   And He the witness gives
To loyal hearts and free,
That every promise is fulfilled,
If faith but brings the plea.

5   All hail, redeeming blood!
All hail, life-giving grace!
All hail, the gift of Christ our Lord,
Our strength and righteousness.

GOSPEL — COMING TO THE LORD

1052

8.5.8.5. with chorus.

1 I've wandered far away from God,
   Now I'm coming home;
The paths of sin too long I've trod,
   Lord, I'm coming home.

   Coming home, coming home,
     Nevermore to roam;
   Open wide Thine arms of love;
     Lord, I'm coming home.

2 I've wasted many precious years,
   Now I'm coming home;
I now repent with bitter tears,
   Lord, I'm coming home.

3 I'm tired of sin and straying, Lord,
   Now I'm coming home;
I'll trust Thy love, believe Thy word;
   Lord, I'm coming home.

4 My soul is sick, my heart is sore,
   Now I'm coming home;
My strength renew, my hope restore:
   Lord, I'm coming home.

5 My only hope, my only plea,
   Now I'm coming home;
That Jesus died, and died for me;
   Lord, I'm coming home.

6 I need His cleansing blood, I know,
   Now I'm coming home;
O wash me whiter than the snow;
   Lord, I'm coming home.

1053

8.8.8.8.

1 With broken heart and contrite sigh,
A trembling sinner, Lord, I cry;
Thy pard'ning grace is rich and free:
O God, be merciful to me!

2 I smite upon my troubled breast,
With deep and conscious guilt oppressed;
Christ and His cross my only plea:
O God, be merciful to me!

3 Far off I stand with tearful eyes,
Nor dare uplift them to the skies;
But Thou dost all my anguish see,
O God, be merciful to me!

4 With alms, or deeds that I have done,
Not one sin's pardon can be won;
To Calvary alone I flee;
O God, be merciful to me!

5 And when redeemed from sin and hell,
With all the ransomed throng I dwell,
My raptured song shall ever be,
God has been merciful to me!

8.5.8.5. with chorus.

1 Pass me not, O gentle Savior,
    Hear my humble cry;
While on others Thou art calling,
    Do not pass me by.

    Savior, Savior,
        Hear my humble cry;
    While on others Thou art calling,
        Do not pass me by.

2 Let me at Thy throne of mercy
    Find a sweet relief;
Kneeling there in deep contrition,
    Help my unbelief.

3 Trusting only in Thy merit,
    Would I seek Thy face;
Heal my wounded, broken spirit,
    Save me by Thy grace.

4 Thou the spring of all my comfort,
    More than life to me;
Whom have I on earth beside Thee?
    Whom in heaven but Thee?

1055*

8.7.8.7. with chorus.

I am sinful, I am helpless,
  Humbly at Thy feet I bow;
Full of problems, I am hopeless,
  Oh, dear Savior, save me now!
Save me now! save me now!
  Oh, dear Savior, save me now!
Save me now from all my problems,
  Oh, dear Savior, save me now!

1056

8.8.8.6. with chorus.

1 Jesus, my Lord, to Thee I cry;
  Unless Thou save me, I must die:
  Oh, bring Thy free salvation nigh,
    And take me as I am!

      And take me as I am!
      And take me as I am!
    My only plea — Christ died for me!
      Oh, take me as I am!

2 Helpless I am, and full of guilt;
  But yet for me Thy blood was spilt,
  And Thou canst make me what Thou wilt,
    And take me as I am.

3 No preparation can I make,
  My best resolves I only break,
  Yet save me for Thine own Name's sake,
    And take me as I am.

4 Behold me, Savior, at Thy feet,
  Deal with me as Thou seest meet;
  Thy work begin, Thy work complete,
    But take me as I am.

7.7.7.7.D.

1   Jesus, lover of my soul,
    Let me to Thy bosom fly,
    While the nearer waters roll,
    While the tempest still is high:
    Hide me, O my Savior, hide,
    Till the storm of life is past;
    Safe into the haven guide;
    O receive my soul at last.

2   Other refuge have I none,
    Hangs my helpless soul on Thee;
    Leave, oh, leave me not alone,
    Still support and comfort me.
    All my trust on Thee is stayed,
    All my help from Thee I bring;
    Cover my defenseless head
    With the shadow of Thy wing.

3   Thou, O Christ, art all I want;
    More than all in Thee I find;
    Raise the fallen, cheer the faint,
    Heal the sick and lead the blind.
    Just and holy is Thy name,
    I am all unrighteousness;
    Vile and full of sin I am,
    Thou art full of truth and grace.

4   Plenteous grace with Thee is found,
    Grace to cover all my sin;
    Let the healing streams abound;
    Make and keep me pure within.
    Thou of life the fountain art,
    Freely let me take of Thee;
    Spring Thou up within my heart,
    Rise to all eternity.

1058

7.7.7.7.7.7.

1 Rock of Ages, cleft for me,
   Let me hide myself in Thee;
   Let the water and the blood,
   From Thy riven side which flowed,
   Be of sin the double cure,
   Save me from its guilt and power.

2 Not the labor of my hands
   Can fulfill Thy law's demands;
   Could my zeal no respite know,
   Could my tears forever flow,
   All could never sin erase,
   Thou must save, and save by grace.

3 Nothing in my hands I bring,
   Simply to Thy cross I cling;
   Naked, come to Thee for dress,
   Helpless, look to Thee for grace:
   Foul, I to the fountain fly,
   Wash me, Savior, or I die.

4 While I draw this fleeting breath,
   When mine eyes shall close in death,
   When I soar to worlds unknown,
   See Thee on Thy judgment throne,
   Rock of Ages, cleft for me,
   Let me hide myself in Thee.

7.6.7.6. with chorus.

1 Jesus, keep me near the cross,
  There a precious fountain,
  Free to all — a healing stream,
  Flows from Calv'ry's mountain.

  In the cross, in the cross,
    Be my glory ever;
  From the cross my ransomed soul
  Nothing then shall sever.

2 Near the cross, a trembling soul,
  Love and mercy found me;
  There the Bright and Morning Star
  Sheds its beams around me.

3 Near the cross! O Lamb of God,
  Bring its scenes before me;
  Help me walk from day to day,
  With its shadow o'er me.

4 Near the cross I'll watch and wait,
  Hoping, trusting ever,
  Till I see my Savior's face,
  Leave His presence never.

1060

Peculiar Meter.

1 Thou didst leave Thy throne and Thy kingly crown,
   When Thou camest to earth for me;
But in Bethlehem's home was there found no room
   For Thy holy nativity:

   Oh, come to my heart, Lord Jesus!
   There is room in my heart for Thee;
   Oh, come to my heart, Lord Jesus, come,
   There is room in my heart for Thee.

2 Heaven's arches rang when the angels sang,
   Proclaiming Thy royal degree;
But of lowly birth cam'st Thou, Lord, on earth,
   And in great humility:

3 The foxes found rest, and the birds had their nest
   In the shade of the forest tree;
But Thy couch was the sod, O Thou Son of God,
   In the deserts of Galilee:

4 Thou camest, O Lord, with the living Word
   That should set Thy people free;
But with mocking scorn, and with crown of thorn,
   They bore Thee to Calvary:

   Oh, come to my heart, Lord Jesus!
   Thy cross is my only plea;
   Oh, come to my heart, Lord Jesus, come,
   Thy cross is my only plea.

5 When heaven's arches shall ring, and her choirs
    shall sing
  At Thy coming to victory,
Let Thy voice call me up, saying, "Yet there
    is room,
  There is room at My side for thee!"

And my heart shall rejoice, Lord Jesus!
When Thou comest and callest for me;
And my heart shall rejoice, Lord Jesus!
When Thou comest and callest for me.

1061

9.7.9.7. with chorus.

1   Come into my heart, O Lord Jesus,
    Come into my heart, I pray;
    My soul is so troubled and weary,
    Come into my heart, today.

      Into my heart, into my heart,
      Come into my heart, Lord Jesus;
      Come in today, come in to stay,
      Come into my heart, Lord Jesus.

2   Come into my heart, O Lord Jesus,
    I need Thee through life's dreary way;
    The burden of sin is so heavy,
    Come into my heart to stay.

3   Come into my heart, O Lord Jesus,
    Now cleanse and illumine my soul;
    Fill me with Thy wonderful Spirit,
    Come in and take full control.

1062

7.7.7.7. with chorus.

1 I am coming to the cross;
 I am poor, and weak, and blind;
 I am counting all but dross;
 I shall full salvation find.

  I am trusting, Lord, in Thee,
  Blessed Lamb of Calvary;
  Humbly at Thy cross I bow,
  Save me, Jesus, save me now.

2 Long my heart has sighed for Thee;
 Long has evil dwelt within;
 Jesus sweetly speaks to me,
 "I will cleanse you from all sin."

3 Here I give my all to Thee —
 Friends and time and earthly store,
 Soul and body Thine to be —
 Wholly Thine forevermore.

4 In the promises I trust;
 Now I feel the blood applied;
 I am prostrate in the dust;
 I with Christ am crucified.

1063

6.5.6.5.D. with chorus.

1 Jesus, I will trust Thee,
  Trust Thee with my soul,
 Guilty, lost and helpless,
  Thou canst make me whole:
 There is none in heaven
  Or on earth like Thee:
 Thou hast died for sinners,
  Therefore, Lord, for me.

Chorus:

> Jesus, I will trust Thee,
>> Trust Thee with my soul,
> Guilty, lost and helpless,
>> Thou canst make me whole.

2 Jesus, I must trust Thee,
>> Pondering Thy ways;
> Full of love and mercy
>> All Thine earthly days:
> Sinners gathered round Thee,
>> Lepers sought Thy face:
> None too vile or loathsome
>> For a Savior's grace.

3 Jesus, I can trust Thee,
>> Trust Thy written Word,
> Though Thy voice of pity
>> I have never heard:
> When Thy Spirit teacheth,
>> To my taste how sweet!
> Only may I hearken,
>> Sitting at Thy feet.

4 Jesus, I do trust Thee,
>> *Trust* without a doubt;
> Whosoever cometh
>> Thou wilt not cast out:
> Faithful is Thy promise,
>> Precious is Thy blood:
> These my soul's salvation,
>> Thou my Savior God!

1064

7.6.7.6.D. with chorus.

1 I love to tell the story
   Of unseen things above,
Of Jesus and His glory,
   Of Jesus and His love.
I love to tell the story,
   Because I know 'tis true;
It satisfies my longings
   As nothing else can do.

   I love to tell the story,
   'Twill be my theme in glory
   To tell the old, old story
   Of Jesus and His love.

2 I love to tell the story;
   More wonderful it seems
Than all the golden fancies
   Of all my golden dreams,
I love to tell the story,
   It did so much for me;
And that is just the reason
   I tell it now to thee.

3 I love to tell the story;
   'Tis pleasant to repeat
What seems each time I tell it,
   More wonderfully sweet.
I love to tell the story;
   For some have never heard
The message of salvation
   From God's own holy Word.

4   I love to tell the story;
      For those who know it best
    Seem hungering and thirsting
      To hear it like the rest.
    And when, in scenes of glory,
      I sing the new, new song,
    'Twill be the old, old story,
      That I have loved so long.

1065

7.7.7.5.D.

1   O how great His salvation!
    O how great His salvation!
    O how great His salvation!
      Jesus saves me now!

    Jesus breaks every fetter!
    Jesus breaks every fetter!
    Jesus breaks every fetter!
      Jesus sets me free!

2   All my sins are forgiven!
    All my fetters are riven!
    I enjoy peace of heaven!
      Jesus saves me now!

3   Neither sin nor temptation,
    Neither Satan's vexation,
    Nor the world's best elation
      Can enslave me now!

4   I will sing Hallelujah!
    I will sing Hallelujah!
    I will sing Hallelujah!
      Jesus saves me now!

1066

9.9.9.5. with chorus.

1 Down at the cross where my Savior died,
Down where for cleansing from sin I cried,
There to my sin was the blood applied;
    Glory to His name!

Glory to His name,
Glory to His name;
There to my sin was the blood applied;
    Glory to His name!

2 I am so wondrously saved from sin,
Jesus so sweetly abides within;
There at the cross where He took me in;
    Glory to His name.

3 Oh, precious fountain that saves from sin,
I am so glad I have entered in;
There Jesus saves me and keeps me clean;
    Glory to His name.

4 Come to this fountain so rich and sweet;
Cast thy poor soul at the Savior's feet;
Plunge in today, and be made complete;
    Glory to His name.

12.9.12.9. with chorus.

1 There was One who was willing to die
in my stead,
That a soul so unworthy might live,
And the path to the cross He was willing
to tread,
All the sins of my life to forgive.

They were borne on the cross,
They were borne on the cross,
O how much He was willing
to bear!
With what anguish and loss,
Jesus went to the cross!
But He carried my sins with
Him there.

2 He is tender and loving and patient
with me,
While He cleanses my heart of its
dross;
But "there's no condemnation," I
know I am free,
For my sins were all borne on
the cross.

3 I will cling to my Savior and never
depart —
I will joyfully journey each day,
With a song on my lips and a song in
my heart,
That my sins have been taken away.

1068

Peculiar Meter.

1 In tenderness He sought me,
   Weary and sick with sin,
And on His shoulders brought me
   Into His flock again.
While angels in His presence sang
Until the courts of heaven rang.

     Oh, the love that sought me!
     Oh, the blood that bought me!
  Oh, the grace that brought me to the
     flock,
     Wondrous grace that brought me to
     the flock!

2 He washed the bleeding sin-wounds,
   And poured in oil and wine;
He whispered to assure me,
   "I've found thee, thou art Mine:"
I never heard a sweeter voice,
It made my aching heart rejoice.

3 He pointed to the nail-prints,
   For me His blood was shed;
A mocking crown so thorny,
   Was placed upon His head:
I wondered what He saw in me,
To suffer such deep agony.

4 I'm sitting in His presence,
    The sunshine of His face,
While with adoring wonder
    His blessings I retrace.
It seems as if eternal days
Are far too short to sound His praise.

5 So while the hours are passing,
    All now is perfect rest;
I'm waiting for the morning,
    The brightest and the best,
When He will call us to His side,
To be with Him, His spotless Bride.

1069

8.8.8.8. with chorus.

We're feeding on the living Bread,
We're drinking at the fountainhead;
And whoso drinketh, Jesus said,
Shall never, never thirst again.

    What! never thirst again?
    No, never thirst again!
    What! never thirst again?
    No, never thirst again!
    And whoso drinketh, Jesus said,
    Shall never, never thirst again!

1070

Peculiar Meter.

1 I was sinking deep in sin,
   Far from the peaceful shore,
Very deeply stained within,
   Sinking to rise no more;
But the Master of the sea
   Heard my despairing cry,
From the waters lifted me,
   Now safe am I.

     Love lifted me!
     Love lifted me!
   When nothing else could help,
     Love lifted me.

2 All my heart to Him I give,
   Ever to Him I'll cling,
In His blessed presence live,
   Ever His praises sing.
Love so mighty and so true
   Merits my soul's best songs;
Faithful, loving service, too,
   To Him belongs.

3 Souls in danger, look above,
   Jesus completely saves;
He will lift you by His love
   Out of the angry waves.
He's the Master of the sea,
   Billows His will obey;
He your Savior wants to be —
   Be saved today.

7.7.7.7.D.   **1071**

1 Sinners Jesus will receive;
    Sound this word of grace to all
Who the heavenly pathway leave,
    All who linger, all who fall.

    Sing it o'er and o'er again;
    Christ receiveth sinful men;
    Make the message clear and plain:
    Christ receiveth sinful men.

2 Come, and He will give you rest;
    Trust Him for His word is plain;
He will take the sinfulest;
    Christ receiveth sinful men.

3 Now my heart condemns me not,
    Pure before the law I stand;
He who cleansed me from all spot,
    Satisfied its last demand.

4 Christ receiveth sinful men,
    Even me with all my sin;
Purged from every spot and stain,
    Glory I shall enter in.

10.6.10.6. with chorus.   **1072**

1 She only touched the hem of His garment
    As to His side she stole,
Amid the crowd that gathered around Him;
    And straightway she was whole.

    Oh, touch the hem of His garment!
    And thou, too, shalt be free!
    His saving power this very hour
    Shall give new life to thee!   *continued*

2   He's pow'rful, present, real and gracious;
    Thou too canst touch Him now!
    Just come and touch while He is still passing,
    His power thou shalt know.

3   Just touch in faith and touch Him in spirit,
    And He will make thee whole;
    And peace that passeth all understanding
    With joy will fill thy soul.

GOSPEL — MYSTERY

1073*

8.8.8.6.D.

Hark, here is a hidden myst'ry,
Hidden from the human hist'ry!
Hark and take this glorious myst'ry,
    Christ will be one with you!
Glory, glory, hallelujah!
Glory, glory, hallelujah!
Hark and take this glorious myst'ry,
    Christ will be one with you!

1074*

Peculiar Meter.

O what a mystery, the Savior
    With me is one!
O what a marvelous salvation
    God gives me in His Son!
Hallelujah! Hallelujah!
    Glorious mystery!
Nothing in heav'n or earth can sever
Jesus my Lord from me!

7.6.7.6. with chorus.

1   Tell me the old, old story,
     Of unseen things above,
  Of Jesus and His glory,
     Of Jesus and His love;
  Tell me the story simply,
     As to a little child,
  For I am weak and weary,
     And helpless and defiled.

     Tell me the old, old story,
     Tell me the old, old story,
     Tell me the old, old story,
       Of Jesus and His love.

2   Tell me the story slowly,
     That I may take it in —
  That wonderful redemption,
     God's remedy for sin;
  Tell me the story often,
     For I forget so soon,
  The "early dew" of morning
     Has passed away at noon.

3   Tell me the story softly,
     With earnest tones and grave;
  Remember I'm the sinner
     Whom Jesus came to save;
  Tell me the story always,
     If you would really be,
  In any time of trouble,
     A comforter to me.

continued

4 Tell me the same old story,
      When you have cause to fear
   That this world's empty glory
      Is costing me too dear;
   And when the Lord's bright glory
      Is dawning on my soul,
   Tell me the old, old story:
      "Christ Jesus makes thee whole."

1076

7.6.7.6.D.

1 O teach me what it meaneth:
      That Cross uplifted high,
   With One, the Man of Sorrows,
      Condemned to bleed and die.
   O teach me what it cost Thee
      To make a sinner whole;
   And teach me, Savior, teach me
      The value of a soul.

2 O teach me what it meaneth:
      That sacred crimson tide,
   The blood and water flowing
      From Thine own wounded side.
   Teach me that if none other
      *Had sinned, but I alone,
   Yet still, Thy blood, O Jesus,
      Thine only, must atone.

*The Compilers prefer that the following three lines be used
in place of the last three lines in verse 2.

Had sinned but only I,
Yet still, O blessed Savior,
   Thou on the cross must die.

3 O teach me what it meaneth:
    Thy love beyond compare,
  The love that reacheth deeper
    Than depths of self-despair!
  Yea, teach me, till there gloweth
    In this cold heart of mine
  Some feeble, pale reflection
    Of that pure love of Thine.

4 O teach me what it meaneth,
    For I am full of sin;
  And grace alone can reach me,
    And love alone can win.
  O teach me, for I need Thee,
    I have no hope beside,
  The chief of all the sinners
    For whom the Savior died.

5 O teach me what it meaneth:
    The rest which Thou dost give
  To all the heavy-laden
    Who look to Thee and live.
  Because I am a rebel
    Thy pardon I receive:
  Because Thou dost command me,
    I can, I do believe.

6 O infinite Redeemer,
    I bring no other plea;
  Because Thou dost invite me
    I cast myself on Thee.
  Because Thou dost accept me
    I love and I adore;
  Because Thy love constraineth,
    I'll praise Thee evermore.

Used by permission of Robert Behnett.

1077

Peculiar Meter.

1 There were ninety and nine that safely lay
   In the shelter of the flock,
But one was out on the hills away,
   Far off in the cold and dark;
Away on the mountains wild and bare,
Away from the tender Shepherd's care.

2 "Lord, Thou hast here Thy ninety and nine;
   Are they not enough for Thee?"
But the Shepherd made answer: "This of Mine
   Has wandered away from Me;
And although the road be rough and steep,
I go to the desert to find My sheep."

3 But none of the ransomed ever knew
   How deep were the waters crossed;
Nor how dark was the night which the Lord
     passed through
   Ere He found His sheep that was lost.
Out in the bleak desert He heard its cry —
All bleeding and helpless, and ready to die.

4 "Lord, whence are those blood-drops all the way
   That mark out the mountain's track?"
"They were shed for one who had gone astray
   Ere the Shepherd could bring him back."
"Lord, whence are Thy hands so rent and torn?"
"They're pierced tonight by many a thorn."

5 And all through the mountains, thunder-riven,
   And up from the rocky steep,
There arose a cry to the gate of heaven,
   "Rejoice! I have found My sheep!"
And the angels echoed around the throne,
"Rejoice, for the Lord brings back His own!"

(Repeat the last line of each stanza)

THEN JESUS CAME

1078

Oswald J. Smith   11.10.11.10.D.

1   One sat alone beside the highway begging,
    His eyes were blind, the light he could not see;
    He clutched his rags and shivered in the shadows,
    Then Jesus came and bade his darkness flee.

    When Jesus comes the tempter's pow'r is broken;
    When Jesus comes the tears are wiped away.
    He takes the gloom and fills the life with glory,
    For all is changed when Jesus comes to stay.

2   From home and friends the evil spirits drove him,
    Among the tombs he dwelt in misery;
    He cut himself as demon pow'rs possessed him,
    Then Jesus came and set the captive free.

3   "Unclean! unclean!" the leper cried in torment,
    The deaf, the dumb, in helplessness stood near;
    The fever raged, disease had gripped its victim,
    Then Jesus came and cast out every fear.

4   Their hearts were sad as in the tomb they laid him,
    For death had come and taken him away;
    Their night was dark and bitter tears were falling,
    Then Jesus came and night was turned to day.

5   So men today have found the Savior able,
    They could not conquer passion, lust and sin;
    Their broken hearts had left them sad and lonely,
    Then Jesus came and dwelt, Himself, within.

1079

10.9.10.9.D.

1 If I gained the world, but lost the Savior,
Were my life worth living for a day?
Could my yearning heart find rest and comfort
In the things that soon must pass away?
If I gained the world, but lost the Savior,
Would my gain be worth the lifelong strife?
Are all earthly pleasures worth comparing
For a moment with a Christ-filled life?

2 Had I wealth and love in fullest measure,
And a name revered both far and near,
Yet no hope beyond, no harbor waiting,
Where my storm-tossed vessel I could steer;
If I gained the world, but lost the Savior,
Who endured the cross and died for me,
Could then all the world afford a refuge,
Whither, in my anguish, I might flee?

3 O what emptiness! — without the Savior
'Mid the sins and sorrows here below!
And eternity, how dark without Him!
Only night and tears and endless woe!
What, though I might live without the Savior,
When I come to die, how would it be?
O to face the valley's gloom without Him!
And without Him all eternity!

4 O the joy of having all in Jesus!
What a balm the broken heart to heal!
Ne'er a sin so great, but He'll forgive it,
Nor a sorrow that He does not feel!
If I have but Jesus, only Jesus,
Nothing else in all the world beside —
O then everything is mine in Jesus;
For my needs and more He will provide.

8.8.8.5. with chorus.

1 What profit all the labor here?
There's nothing new for you and me!
Remember not the former things,
They're all vanity!

Vanity! Vanity!
Vanity! Vanity!
'Tis chasing the wind,
It's all vanity!

2 Man's life is full of grief and pain:
Much wisdom bringeth misery!
Increasing knowledge addeth woe!
It's all vanity!

3 What good our pleasure and our wealth?
Though joys we have and family,
We'll have our worries just the same!
It's all vanity!

4 Days of toil to gain and restless nights:
Though gained without calamity,
When death comes it is gone for aye!
It's all vanity!

5 Remember God in days of youth!
Fear Him, and such will be your gain!
With Him you will be satisfied,
For He is not vain!

Christ without, all is vain!
Christ within, all is gain!
All things are vain,
Christ only is gain!

John 17

(Tune: #861)
9.8.8.9. with chorus.

1 Father God, Thou art the source of life.
We, Thy sons, are Thine expression;
In Thy name, our dear possession.
Father God, Thou art the source of life.

> In Thy life, in Thy life,
> We have oneness in Thy life.
> In Thy life, in Thy life,
> In Thy life, O Father, we are one.

2 How we thank Thee that Thy holy Word
With Thy nature, saturates us;
From the world it separates us.
Thank Thee, Father, for Thy holy Word.

> Through Thy Word, through Thy Word,
> We have oneness through Thy Word.
> Through Thy Word, through Thy Word,
> Through Thy holy Word we're all made one.

3 Oh, the glory of the Triune God!
We're His sons, oh, what a blessing!
We His glory are expressing —
Oh, the glory of the Triune God!

> In Thy glory, in Thy glory,
> In Thy glory we are one.
> In Thy glory, in Thy glory,
> In Thy glory we are all made one!

1082

Psalm 16

(Tune: #278)
11.11.11.11.

1 The living of Christ when He sojourned on earth,
The sixteenth Psalm shows us, was wholly of worth.
His attitudes, choices, and interests all tell
The man who in God's tabernacle may dwell.

2 "Preserve me, O God, for in Thee I confide" —
In God He took refuge whate'er did betide.
"O Thou art my Lord, I've no good beyond Thee" —
He spoke in Himself unto God constantly.

3 "As for all the saints who are dwelling on earth,"
To Him they're the people of excellent worth.
Of them He has said He has all His delight —
In proving this all the four Gospels unite.

4 "The Lord is my portion, the Lord is my cup" —
For everything He to the Father looked up.
"The Lord I will bless who my counsel doth give" —
Himself He denied and by God's word did live.

5 His heart thus was glad and His spirit rejoiced,
And e'en in His death praise to God could be voiced;
His soul God would never abandon to hell,
But in resurrection His body would dwell.

6 God raised Him, and He with God's glory
    was crowned;
Then fulness of joy in God's presence He found.
E'en now at the Father's right hand is His seat,
Where flowing forever are pleasures complete.

1 O how nigh the Lord is unto all who call on Him!
  When we call, His very presence strengthens us within.
  Seeking Jesus, He is found, and calling, He is near —
  O what a comfort to our hearts to call His name
    so dear!

    Jesus! O what a name!
    O Lord Jesus! Life-giving name!
    Name victorious, name all-glorious,
      Name exalted — O what a name!
    Jesus! Strengthening name!
    O Lord Jesus! Comforting name!
    Name to breathe in prayer, calling everywhere,
      "O Lord Jesus!" O what a name!

2 Call upon the name of Jesus, and you will be saved,
  O Lord Jesus, hallelujah, nevermore enslaved!
  We may take salvation's cup by calling on the Lord;
  Salvation from a host of things does His dear
    name afford.

3 To the Lord, the Jew, the Greek and everyone's
    the same;
  He is rich unto all men that call upon His name.
  O Lord Jesus, what a joy to call and really live;
  When breathing in Thy name, what pleasure Thou
    to us dost give.

4 In the God of our salvation we may take delight, [blight.
  Calling on His name at all times, though in bliss or
  I will call upon His name as long as I shall live, [give.
  Because He has inclined His ear, and grace so full does

5 We will call upon the Lord, who's worthy of our praise;
  Thus our grateful hearts in worship we to Him may raise.
  We are those who call upon His name in every place
  With all the saints who from a pure heart call and taste
    His grace.

1084

8.8.8.8.

1 Thy name is as ointment poured forth:
  Jesus, Jesus, Jesus, Jesus!
  Thy name is as ointment poured forth,
  Thy name is as ointment poured forth.

2 Therefore do the virgins love Thee:
  Jesus, Jesus, Jesus, Jesus!
  Therefore do the virgins love Thee,
  Therefore do the virgins love Thee.

3 Thy love is much better than wine:
  Jesus, Jesus, Jesus, Jesus!
  Thy love is much better than wine,
  Thy love is much better than wine.

4 Draw me, we will run after Thee:
  Jesus, Jesus, Jesus, Jesus!
  Draw me, we will run after Thee,
  Draw me, we will run after Thee.

5 Behold, Thou art fair, my Beloved:
  Jesus, Jesus, Jesus, Jesus!
  Behold, Thou art fair, my Beloved,
  Behold, Thou art fair, my Beloved.

6 I found Him whom my soul doth love:
  Jesus, Jesus, Jesus, Jesus!
  I found Him whom my soul doth love,
  I found Him whom my soul doth love.

7 I held Him and would not let go:
  Jesus, Jesus, Jesus, Jesus!
  I held Him and would not let go,
  I held Him and would not let go.

8 Make haste, my Beloved, to come:
  Jesus, Jesus, Jesus, Jesus!
  Make haste, my Beloved, to come,
  Make haste, my Beloved, to come.

9 We love Thee with all of our heart:
   Jesus, Jesus, Jesus, Jesus!
   We love Thee with all of our heart,
   We love Thee with all of our heart.

Peculiar Meter.   **1085**

His Name is Wonderful;
His Name is Counselor;
His Name The Mighty God,
   Jesus my Lord.

A Child and Son is He;
Eternal Father He;
The Prince of Peace to me,
   Jesus my Lord.

Praise the Creator,
Jesus our Savior,
Life-giving Spirit now.
In spirit worship Him,
Love and adore Him;
His Name is Wonderful,
   Jesus my Lord.

Peculiar Meter.   **1086**

How we love the glorious name,
   The name of Jesus!
'Tis the name above all names —
   On earth or in heav'n.
As we breathe this precious name,
   Darkness and death cannot remain;
For we *call* and get the Person of that name!

Dear Lord Jesus, with our tongues —
   We gladly confess Thy name,
To the glory of the Father God above.
   For to us to speak Thy praise,
Is the enjoyment of our days;
   Calling JESUS is to call the One we love!

1087

(Tune: #1015)
Peculiar Meter.

1 Oh, hallelujah, what a death
    Christ died upon the cross!
  Not only was He dying there
  But everything that death did share:
    God was included too,
    All men with me and you —
  Oh, hallelujah, for such a cross!

2 Oh, praise the Lord, man died in God
    And to an end was brought!
  Now from this man I'm wholly free
  For God has terminated me!
    Oh, what a wondrous death,
    Oh, what a wondrous death;
  Oh, hallelujah, for such a death!

3 Oh, praise the Lord, God died in man,
    In man to be released.
  The grain of wheat fell to the ground,
  And now a multitude is found
    Filled with the life of God,
    Filled with the life of God;
  Oh, hallelujah, for such a life!

4 Lord, how we praise You for Your cross,
    Your all-inclusive death!
  The center of the universe,
  It has untold, eternal worth!
    Lord, how we love Your cross,
    Lord, how we love Your cross;
  Oh, hallelujah, for such a cross!

(Tune: #889)
Peculiar Meter.

1088

1 God was born a human being
  As the Babe of Bethlehem,
Passed He then through human living,
  Perfect blend of God with men.
God, according to His plan,
  Lived a mingled life with man.
Hallelujah, Hallelujah,
  Hallelujah, Amen!

2 Then with God this man was blended
  On the altar as He died;
God and man and all creation
  On the cross were crucified.
Man and all of God's creation,
  Sunk in total termination.
Hallelujah, Hallelujah,
  Hallelujah, Amen!

3 Everything we are was ended,
  Terminated on the cross,
Only man in God ascended,
  Man in Adam suffered loss.
Hallelujah, we're elated,
  Our old man was terminated.
Hallelujah, Hallelujah,
  Hallelujah, Amen!

4 Like the grain of wheat that's buried
  In the earth to be increased,
God's own life the death must suffer,
  Thus in man to be released.
Oh, the Lord of all be praised;
  God released in man is raised!
Hallelujah, Hallelujah,
  Hallelujah, Amen!

1089

John 1:29; 3:14; 12:24
(Tune: #33)
8.7.8.7.8.7. with repeat.

1 Lamb of God so pure and spotless,
Lamb of God for sinners slain.
Thy shed blood has wrought redemption,
Cleansing us from every stain.
Lamb redeeming, Lamb redeeming,
Bearing all our sins away,
Bearing all our sins away!

2 Brazen serpent, to Thee looking,
Son of Man, uplifted high.
Thou didst bear the flesh of sin in
Likeness on the cross to die.
Old creation's termination;
Finished, Satan and the world,
Finished, Satan and the world!

3 Grain of wheat, so small and lowly,
Without death abides alone;
Life divine enclosed within it,
Into death it must be sown.
Life releasing, Christ increasing,
Many grains to birth to bring,
Many grains to birth to bring!

4 Lamb of God — our sin's redemption,
Brazen serpent — Satan's end,
Grain of wheat — life's reproduction,
Now with many grains we blend.
Hallelujah! Hallelujah!
What an all-inclusive death,
What an all-inclusive death!

(Tune: #852)
8.6.8.6.

1 Dear Lord, how precious is Thy blood,
    Of the New Testament!
  By it God's blessings we receive,
    And we with Him are blent.

2 'Tis by Thy blood we've been redeemed,
    And by it sanctified.
  Now is our conscience free from sin,
    From dead works purified.

3 Better than Abel's, now Thy blood
    Speaks unto God for us.
  Perfect redemption it provides,
    Meeting God's righteousness.

4 Through the eternal Spirit, Thou
    Offeredst Thyself to God.
  This sacrifice can ne'er grow old;
    Timeless is Thy dear blood.

5 'Tis by Thy blood we boldly come
    Unto the throne of grace,
  Unto our God, the cov'nant new,
    And to the Holiest Place.

6 Lord, by Thy blood, God is obliged
    His very Self to give;
  He must receive us to Himself,
    And He in us must live.

7 Dear Lord, how precious is Thy blood
    Of the New Testament!
  By it God's blessings we receive,
    And we with Him are blent.

1091

(Tune: #680)
10.10.10.10.10.10.

1 We praise Thee, O Lord Jesus, Thou didst come,
The way into God's presence to reveal.
We worship Thee that Thou didst leave
  Thy throne,
To come as our High Priest with sin to deal.
Lord Jesus, Thou hast offered Thine own blood,
And settled once for all our peace with God.

2 Thy blood has now been sprinkled on the throne
In full redemption for Thy people's sin.
The sweetness of the love that Thou hast shown
Has ris'n to fill the holiest place within.
And by the blood once offered in that place
God flows to us in mercy and in grace.

3 Yet, Lord, Thou camest not just to atone,
But Thou didst come and bear our sins away.
We, with a conscience purged, approach
  the throne,
For all our sins were laid on Thee that day.
Thou, separated from the Father's face,
Didst pay the awful price for us in grace.

4 The way into God's presence thus is cleared,
For ransomed sinners who have heard Thy call.
Thou, Lord, hast taken all that we had feared
When Thou didst shed Thy blood and give
  Thine all;
Our heart in grateful praise to Thee we bind,
And now our life in Thee alone we find.

1 The saints throughout the centuries
   Have praised the Lord that He,
   The Lamb of God, has saved us,
   From sin has set us free;
   Yet scarcely for the Lion
   Have we yet sounded praise,
   Though oft for our redemption
   We've all our voices raised.

2 John wept as he considered
   That none the right did own
   The scroll to take and open,
   God's myst'ry to make known;
   No, none on earth nor heaven,
   Nor universe around —
   And we, too, would be weeping
   If none were worthy found.

3 The universe, mysterious,
   Would be in darkness still,
   Could none break through to open
   The scroll, to show God's will;
   But, lo, the worthy Lion
   Of Judah hath prevailed
   The seven seals to open,
   And have the scroll unveiled.

4 No longer now in darkness
   God's secret is enclosed,
   But to our inner vision
   It's open, full, disclosed;
   Our hearts are for this purpose,
   Our lives are for His plan;
   And for this revelation
   We praise the Lion-Lamb!

continued

5   The four-and-twenty elders
All fall before that sight.
The living creatures praise Him,
Who rest not, day nor night.
So let us join their praises
To Him who loosed God's plan;
We'll lift with theirs our voices
To praise the Lion-Lamb!

1093

Revelation 5
(Tune: #295)
8.8.8.8.

1   Through countless ages, many men
Have longed and sought and tried to see
The secret of the universe,
So vast, so great a mystery.

2   Yet not through struggling could frail man
The secret of this myst'ry find;
Nor chance, by stumbling, come upon
Such hidden things — to these he's blind.

3   Behold in heav'n a throne is set,
And One upon the throne revealed;
And held in His right hand a scroll —
The mystery is tightly sealed.

4   Through all the universe, a cry —
'Can one be found of such great worth
The scroll to take?' . . . yet no reply,
From heav'n, below, or on the earth.

5   Were it a matter now for man
By chance, or some ability,
Then surely one would now step forth
To open God's economy.

6   Yet sad and solemn was that sight.
John wept as then he looked around;
And we, too, still might weeping be
If none at all were worthy found.

7   But then the angel said, 'Weep not!
Behold, the Lion has prevailed
To take the scroll and loose its seals;
He has the mystery now unveiled!'

8   So, John looked up the Lion to see,
But, lo, he then beheld a Lamb;
Christ both o'ercame the enemy,
And wrought redemption's work for man.

9   The angels fall before His throne,
Four living creatures offer praise,
All glory to the Lion-Lamb;
Let us with theirs our voices raise!

PRAISE OF THE LORD —
HIS VICTORY AND EXALTATION

1094

Psalm 2
(Tune: #203)
8.7.8.7.D.

1   Lo, the nations all assemble
    And imagine vanity,
Kings and princes plot together
    'Gainst the Lord in unity.
"Let us break their bonds asunder,
    Cast away their cords from us."
'Gainst the Lord and His Anointed
    Worldly rulers counsel thus.

continued

2 He who sitteth in the heavens
   In contempt will laugh at them,
Vex them in His fierce displeasure,
   Terrifying all such men.
Yet upon the hill of Zion
   God has His anointed King —
This is God's own declaration,
   All the kings admonishing.

3 Now 'tis Christ, 'tis God's Anointed,
   Who declares the Lord's decree:
"Thou'rt my Son (in resurrection),
   This day I've begotten Thee.
All the nations I will give Thee
   For Thine own inheritance.
Thou shalt dash them into pieces
   In Thy kingly excellence."

4 Now be wise, O be instructed,
   All ye rulers of the earth,
Fear the Lord, rejoice with trembling,
   Serve the only One of worth.
Kiss the Son, lest He be angry
   And ye perish in the way.
"All who trust in Him are blessed,"
   All who trust in Him will say.

5 Lord, we praise Thee, we have seen Him —
   Thy unique Anointed One —
And from vanity repenting,
   We in love have kissed Thy Son.
"All who trust in Him are blessed" —
   Not "all those who keep the law."
In that risen One believing,
   We are blest forevermore.

(Tune: #380)
7.6.7.6.D.

1 The Lord shall get the glory
   If we will sing His praise,
   And angel hosts will listen
   When we our voices raise;
   The world around will hear us
   Give glory unto God,
   And Satan's hosts will tremble
   And flee our conqu'ring rod.

2 Our mouth shut up defeats us
   And wins the Devil's smile;
   So why not open battle
   And chase him all the while.
   By "sacrifice of praises"
   And shouts of victory —
   'Twill cost us but our faces
   God's chosen fools to be!

3 The world has never helped us
   To shout our Savior's praise,
   Nor given Him the glory
   Nor lent one thankful phrase;
   So need we ask permission
   To praise th' ascended Lord?
   Cry out! Release your spirit!
   Much grace He does afford!

4 O brothers, be not silent!
   O sisters, cry aloud!
   The sound shall tell God's triumph
   And blessings far abroad.
   Now is the time to praise Him,
   Yes now, at any cost!
   O joy in your salvation,
   And in His mercy boast!

PRAISE OF THE LORD —
HIS VICTORY AND EXALTATION

(Tune: #181 Second tune)
8.4.8.4.8.8.8.4.

1 'Tis the local church proclaiming,
    Jesus is Lord!
  All the saints with joy are naming
    Jesus as Lord.
  All His work He has completed,
  Satan and his hosts defeated;
  On the throne of glory seated,
    Jesus is Lord!

2 Jesus is the living Spirit,
    Jesus is Lord!
  He is here, all people, hear it:
    Jesus is Lord!
  Be no more a poor lamenter;
  Call on Him, and He will enter
  And become your glorious center —
    Jesus is Lord!

3 He will transform all your living,
    Jesus, the Lord!
  All His riches to you giving,
    Jesus, the Lord!
  He'll forever satisfy you,
  Everyday real life supply you,
  And with God will unify you,
    Jesus, the Lord!

4 In His mercy He received us,
    Jesus, the Lord!
  He will never, never leave us,
    Jesus, the Lord!
  All the fullness of His being
  In His Body we are seeing,
  And the enemy is fleeing —
    Jesus is Lord!

Psalm 8

(Tune: #522)

8.6.8.6.D.

1 O Lord, our Lord, how excellent
   Thy name in all the earth!
Let every people, tribe, and tongue
   Proclaim its boundless worth.
Out of the mouth of little ones
   Thou hast established praise,
That Thou may still Thine enemy
   And swiftly end his days.

2 When we the universe behold,
   The work of Thy great hand —
The sun, the moon, and all the stars
   By lofty wisdom planned;
O what is man that Thou should'st care
   That Thou should'st mindful be?
The son of man Thou visitest
   In Thine economy.

3 O Jesus Lord, Thou art that man,
   The One who joined our race,
Who put upon Himself the flesh
   And took a lower place.
But now with glory Thou art crowned,
   With sovereignty complete.
Now through Thy Body Thou dost rule
   With all beneath Thy feet.

4 Thine incarnation, rising too,
   And Thy transcendency,
Thy Lordship, Headship, kingdom full,
   And Body here we see.
By all these steps of work divine
   Thou hast established praise.
With overflowing hearts to Thee
   Our joyful voice we raise.   *continued*

5 Oh, soon that blessed day shall come —
All tongues these words shall peal!
But in the local churches now
We have a foretaste real.
O Lord, our Lord, how excellent
Thy name in all the earth!
Let every people, tribe, and tongue
Proclaim its boundless worth.

1098

Psalm 45 — Part 1
(Tune: #15)
7.6.7.6.D.

1 Our hearts are overflowing
To speak a goodly thing —
To tell what we've experienced
Of our exalted King.
Our tongues as pens are ready,
We've volumes here to "write" —
The glories of our Bridegroom,
Our Lord and our delight.

2 Lord Jesus, Thou art fairer
Than all the sons of men;
Thy goodness is transcendent —
Hallelujah! Amen!
Upon Thy lips most holy
Abundant grace is poured;
Forever God has blessed Thee,
Our gracious, glorious Lord!

3 Thou art the mighty Warrior
   Who rides to victory;
In Thy majestic glory
   Ride on triumphantly!
The peoples fall beneath Thee —
   The conquering One Thou art.
Thine arrows in their sharpness
   Have entered Satan's heart!

4 Thy throne, O God, forever
   And ever shall endure;
The sceptre of Thy kingdom
   Upon the earth is sure.
'Tis with the oil of gladness
   God has anointed Thee
Above all Thy companions —
   How worthy there to be!

5 Of aloes, myrrh, and cassia
   Do all Thy garments smell:
Thy death and resurrection
   Do all Thy deeds forthtell.
Out of the local churches
   Shall praises make Thee glad,
And praises upon praises
   Thy joyful saints shall add.

1099

Psalm 45 — Part 2

(Tune: #15)

7.6.7.6.D.

1 The queen in gold of Ophir
  At Thy right hand doth stand;
King's daughters are the women
  Who fill Thy honored band.
The church in all her glory
  Shall match her glorious King,
And all the saints, the women,
  Thy likeness there shall bring.

2 O daughter, now consider,
  E'en now incline thine ear:
Remember not thy people
  And all thine own things here.
Thy beauty then shall blossom —
  'Twill be the King's desire;
For He thy worthy Lord is,
  Thy worship to inspire.

3 The daughter's glorious garments
  Are made of inwrought gold —
Within the inner palace,
  How wondrous to behold!
The glory of God's nature
  Is given her to wear,
That all His holy being
  She may in life declare.

4 In clothing too embroidered
    She'll to the King be led,
In that fine linen garment
    To be exhibited.
'Tis by the Spirit's stitching
    That Christ in us is wrought,
And with this glorious garment
    We'll to the King be brought.

5 What gladness and rejoicing
    When we the King shall see!
We'll shout His worthy praises
    Through all eternity.
And though the King we worship
    Or glory in the Queen,
In all this blest enjoyment
    The glory goes to Him.

1100

Psalm 68
(Tune: #149)
8.7.8.7.7.7.8.7.

1 God shall rise, His foes be scattered,
    All that hate Him flee away.
As the wax before the fire,
    All the wicked He shall slay.
But the righteous shall rejoice
    With a loud, triumphant voice,
Singing praises, singing praises,
    Singing praises unto God!

continued

2 He is riding through the deserts,
   Bringing in His saints in need.
He's a Father to the orphans
   And a refuge tried indeed
In His holy habitation —
   What a wonderful salvation!
Hallelujah, hallelujah,
   Hallelujah, Amen!

3 Here the lone have found a family,
   Here the desolate a home;
Prisoners are brought from bondage
   To prosperity unknown.
For the flock — what wondrous grace —
   God prepared this dwelling place:
Hallelujah, hallelujah,
   Hallelujah, Amen!

4 Now the Lord in mighty triumph
   Sends the news of victory;
We the "women" spread the tidings —
   "Kings of armies flee, they flee!"
No more sweat and dreary toil;
   We at home divide the spoil!
Hallelujah, hallelujah,
   Hallelujah, Amen!

5 Lo, on high Christ hath ascended,
   Leading captives in His train;
These as gifts He has perfected
   That the Lord may dwell with them.
Brothers, sisters, we are those,
   We're those transformed, vanquished foes!
Hallelujah, hallelujah,
   Hallelujah, Amen!

6 Blessed be the Lord forever:
   Day by day He loads with good,
E'en the God of our salvation —
   Spread His worthy praise abroad.
His the goings forth from death,
   Every foe He conquereth!
Hallelujah, hallelujah,
   Hallelujah, Amen!

7 They have seen, O God, Thy goings
   In Thy holy dwelling place,
Thy triumphal, high processions
   Midst a mighty voice of praise.
See the singers go before,
   Praising, praising o'er and o'er:
Hallelujah, hallelujah,
   Hallelujah, Amen!

8 Little Benjamin is leading,
   Then great Judah's company:
Son of sorrow at God's right hand,
   Lion with the scepter see.
Zebulun and Naphtali
   Make the joyful tidings fly:
Hallelujah, hallelujah,
   Hallelujah, Amen!

9 Saints, thy strength has been commanded
   From the temple glorious;
Still we pray that God may strengthen
   All that He has wrought for us.
Higher yet our praise shall rise
   Till the utmost earth replies:
Hallelujah, hallelujah,
   Hallelujah, Amen!

Revelation 12, 18-21
(Tune: #1017)
15.15.15.6. with chorus.

1 Lo, the kingdom of the world is now
   the kingdom of the Lord!
   O what joy to all the saints does His
   eternal reign afford!
   Let us swell the mighty chorus of His
   praise in one accord —
      The victory is won!

      Vict'ry, vict'ry, Hallelujah!
      Vict'ry, vict'ry, Hallelujah!
      Vict'ry, vict'ry, Hallelujah!
         The victory is won!

2 That great dragon, the old serpent called
   the devil, down is cast;
   Satan and his fallen angels' long deceiving
   days are past!
   Now our praises like a thunder through the
   universe shall blast —
      The victory is won!

3 Now is come salvation, power, and the
   kingdom of our God;
   The accuser of the brethren underneath
   our feet is trod!
   The authority of Christ is now the church's
   ruling rod —
      The victory is won!

4 By the Lamb's redeeming blood th' accuser
   we have overcome;
   By our word of testimony, all declaring,
   "It is done!"

Unto death, our souls not loving — all the
glory to the Son!
The victory is won!

5 Oh, but brothers, sisters, listen to another
mighty voice,
"Babylon is fallen, fallen" — what a reason
to rejoice!
O how blest that coming out from her was
our eternal choice —
The victory is won!

6 She's the mother of the harlots, Myst'ry,
Babylon the Great!
O how all her evil fornication we have learned
to hate!
But our God has doubly judged her — this our
spirits doth elate.
The victory is won!

7 Hallelujah! Glory, power to the Lord our
God belong!
True and righteous are His judgments on
the harlot for her wrong!
See, her smoke is rising! Echo hallelujah
in your song —
The victory is won!

8 "Praise our God now, all ye servants, small
and great," His voice constrains.
As the sound of many waters, we will thunder
our refrains:
Hallelujah, hallelujah, for the Lord Almighty
reigns!
The victory is won!

continued

9 Now rejoice and be exceeding glad! What
    glory is displayed!
  For the marriage of the Lamb, the wife all
    ready now is made!
  In fine linen, bright and pure, 'twas granted
    her to be arrayed —
      The victory is won!

10 Now the devil's in the lake of fire, for John
    has seen him there;
  Hallelujah, never more need we his provo-
    cations bear!
  What a triumph for the saints his judgment
    boldly to declare —
      The victory is won!

11 Now behold the greatest wonder — New
    Jerusalem descend!
  She's the building of the Triune God with
    man — a perfect blend!
  She's the Bride, prepared, adorned for Christ —
    of all God's work, the end!
      The victory is won!

12 It's the tabernacle of our God, His dwelling
    place with men;
  In His holiness and glory He's expressed
    through all of them.
  "It is done!" O brothers, see it! See the
    New Jerusalem!
      The victory is won!

    Hallelujah, hallelujah!
    Hallelujah, hallelujah!
    Hallelujah, hallelujah!
      The victory is won!

PRAISE OF THE LORD —
HIS VICTORY AND EXALTATION

Psalm 110

(Tune: #873)

7.6.7.6.D.

1 The Lord said unto my Lord,
"Sit Thou at My right hand;
Thy foes shall be Thy footstool,
Upon them Thou shalt stand."
The sceptre of Thy strength shall
The Lord from Zion send
To rule o'er all the nations
Forever 'til the end.

2 A voluntary offering,
The young ones are to Thee;
In consecration's splendor
How beautiful to see!
For as the dew of morning
Refreshes all the land —
The young ones given to Thee
Are precious in Thy hand.

3 The Lord hath sworn forever
And never will turn back,
"Thou art a priest forever,
As was Melchizedek."
Oh, Thou hast no beginning
Of days; of life: no end!
And on Thine intercession
We ever do depend.

4 The Lord is at Thy right hand
And in His day of wrath
He'll strike through rulers, judging
The nations in His path.
While riding on to triumph
He'll drink of us, the stream,
His head uplifted, strengthened,
The whole earth to redeem. *continued*

1029

5   Oh Lord, Thou art ascended
To God's right hand to sit;
As Head o'er all things, to Thee
God doth Thy foes commit.
Our King — for us Thou reignest,
Our Priest — we are supplied,
Our all we give unto Thee,
Thou Conqueror glorified.

PRAISE OF THE LORD — HIS ALL-INCLUSIVENESS

1103

Peculiar Meter.

1   What He is: He's the Father.
He's the everlasting Father.
He's the firstborn of creation.
He's the One who lives inside of me.
He's the Father! Wonderful!

2   What He is: He's the river.
He's the mighty flowing river.
He waters me in a desert land.
He's my hiding place; He is our man.
He's the river! Wonderful!

3   What He is: He's the vine tree.
He's the branch, the root of Jesse.
He's the tree of life: we have the right
To eat of Him and have His life.
He's the vine tree! Wonderful!

4   What He is: He's the Shepherd.
He's the lamb of God, the he-goat.
We rest and feed in the pasture land.
We strike the blood and eat the lamb.
He's the Shepherd! Wonderful!

5   What He is: He's the Spirit.
He's the all-inclusive Spirit.
He's our everything; He's our all in all.
He gives life to us whene'er we call.
He's the Spirit! Wonderful!

6   What He is: He's a Person.
He's a real and living Person.
He is living now inside of us.
This Person is so glorious.
He's a Person! Wonderful!

7   What He is: He's the Body;
He's the fulness of the Godhead;
He's the center of the Father's plan,
Christ and the church, the one new man.
He is wonderful, wonderful.

He is wonderful, wonderful.
He is wonderful, wonderful.

PRAISE OF THE LORD — AS OUR PEACE OFFERING

1104

Leviticus 3; 7:11-38

(Tune: #239)

7.6.7.6.D. with chorus.

1 Lord, Thou art our peace offering;
   We lay our hands on Thee.
 We're one with Thee, Lord Jesus,
   In fact and practically.
 Here in the tent of meeting
   We offer Thee to God
 And with the Father feasting
   Enjoy Thee as our food.

   Christ is our peace! Christ is our peace!
     We praise Thee, blessed Lord!
   Our peace with God, our peace with man
     Have fully been restored.

2 O what a peace it gives us
   To see the sprinkled blood.
 The blood of our peace offering
   Has brought us peace with God.
 With boldness we're proclaiming —
   Now hear this, enemy —
 "Peace by the blood of Jesus!"
   This is our victory.

3 Based on the burnt oblation
   And the meal offering too,
 We now may offer Jesus
   As our peace offering true.
 The more we eat and drink Him
   In His humanity,
 The more we may enjoy Him
   While feasting corporately.

   What fellowship, what fellowship
     With God and man we share!
   O what a joy, O what a feast
     With all God's people here.

4   Here God enjoys His portion —
     'Tis inward, hidden, sweet —
  And all the priestly family
     May here the wave breast eat.
  The offering priest — how precious —
     May of the best partake:
  He gets the right heave shoulder
     And one unleavened cake.

5   How sweet to eat the wave breast,
     The all-embracing love
  Of Christ in resurrection!
     It sets us all above.
  What strength to eat the shoulder
     Of the ascended One
  And with the cake be nourished
     To walk as He has done.

6   With all the cleansed ones feasting,
     How rich the Christ we eat!
  Oh, this is true communion,
     The only way to meet.
  We bring our full thanksgiving
     And e'en would make a vow —
  We're for the Lord's recovery
     As He is for us now.

PRAISE OF THE LORD — REMEMBRANCE OF HIM

(Tune: #196)   **1105**
8.7.8.7.D.

1   Lo, the table spread before us
     With the bread and with the wine:
  Lo, the Savior waiting for us,
     Bidding us to come and dine.

continued

"Come and dine," the Lord is calling,
"Sup with Me and I with thee";
He's prepared for us this table —
Let us feast abundantly.

2 We are feasting with our Savior,
He with us and we with Him;
Hallelujah, hallelujah!
Feast of feasts that ne'er will end!
Eating, drinking with Thyself, Lord,
We are wholly satisfied.
Taste we of that glorious banquet
Thou wilt share with us, Thy Bride.

1106

12.11.12.12.

1 We gather together to eat the Lord's supper:
By eating and drinking, our oneness we show.
His presence possessing, our oneness confessing,
'Tis *thus* we eat and drink, and His blessing we know.

2 We're eating the bread of His body once broken
As now we're enjoying His Body made one:
One loaf on the table — one Body, we're able
To testify to all that the Lord's made us one.

3 We also are drinking the cup of His blessing,
The church's true fellowship of the Lord's blood;
Redeemed by believing, all saints we're receiving,
All those who through redemption have come unto God.

4 Oh, what can we say now except "Hallelujah!"
For such a reality given to us.
Thy blood we're employing, Thy Body enjoying;
Thus Thou wilt have the church for Thyself glorious.

(Tune: #608)
11.10.11.10. with chorus.

1   We're gathered here, O Lord, as Thy one Body:
    Though we be many, yet we all are one.
    We share Thy life and own that we are members,
    And thus within, in life we all are one.

        There is one Body in this universe,
        And we express it here on earth;
        We stand as one in each locality
        For all to see, for all to see.

2   There is one loaf, the symbol of Thy body:
    'Twas broken so that all the saints may share.
    We eat this bread and, as we are partaking,
    Our actual oneness with all saints declare.

3   One bread, one cup are now upon the table,
    Showing that we can be naught else but one.
    Christ has redeemed us, made us His own Body:
    What can we say but, "Amen, Lord, we're one!"

4   We stand as one, and cannot be divided,
    Because our oneness is of Christ alone.
    We eat as one: one loaf, one cup partaking,
    And thus our oneness visibly is shown.

5   Oh, what a joy to have this blessed oneness!
    We sense that Thou, O Lord, art satisfied;
    And we too share this blissful satisfaction —
    Sweet foretaste of the Bridegroom with His Bride.

1108   9.9.9.9. with chorus.

1 Eat the bread, ye people of the Lord:
Praise His name, for He has made us one.
Now we come to eat in one accord
As the church which He has made His own.

Eat the bread and drink the wine, ye saints!
We are one in Him fore'er.
Stand in oneness on the local ground,
Eat and drink in oneness there!

2 Drink the wine, ye people of the Lord:
We're the church His precious blood has bought.
We're redeemed to be in one accord —
This the goal for which He long has sought.

3 Stand as one, ye people of the Lord:
Not as individual grains are we —
We are one, we're blent in one accord
As a loaf in each locality.

4 We are one as people of the Lord;
We declare that we are really one!
Not just word, but life in one accord
Testify what God in us hath done.

5 Eat the bread, ye people of the Lord:
Praise His name, for He has made us one.
Now we come to eat in one accord
As the church which He has made His own.

(Do not repeat chorus after last verse)

1109   (Tune: #300 Second tune)
6.6.6.6.8.8.8.

1 Take, drink this cup, His blood,
Redemption of our God.
The peace which Christ has made,
Is in this cup displayed.

We fellowship now with the Son:
On Calvary the work was done:
The way is clear, now all can come!

2 Take, drink this cup, each one,
His death show till He come.
Eat, drink, display this feast:
God in the Lamb released!
Around the table, sup and dine;
We eat the bread and drink the wine.
All blessing in this cup we find.

3 No blood of cow or goat
Could give us any hope.
Our sins would all remain
Still year by year the same.
A God-man, sinless, He must find —
No other offering of His kind,
A spotless lamb for all mankind.

4 Come! Now enjoy His blood.
What access this to God!
Here wondrous cleansing power
Flows to us, hour by hour.
One sacrifice for all was made,
And peace our conscience does pervade.
Redemption's price is fully paid!

5 Redeemer! Savior! King!
Of Thy dear blood we sing,
For in it now we see
Thy mercy, boundless, free.
This cup, our portion blessed of God,
Is of the cov'nant in Thy blood —
Dear, precious, precious, priceless blood!

1110

(Tune: #17)
11.10.11.10. with chorus.

1 O Jesus Lord, when present at Thy table,
  And on the bread and on the wine we gaze;
  We praise Thee, Lord, that Thou as food art able
  To be enjoyed by man in many ways.

    So all our being sings in praise to Thee,
    How small Thou art, how small Thou art!
    And Thee we'll eat through all eternity;
    How small Thou art, how small Thou art!

2 O what a shame — when Christ with all His riches,
  Has come into the world, life to supply —
  That man would live, not by Him, but by teachings,
  So powerless these riches to apply.

    But all we need to do is eat the Lord;
    He's marvelous, He's wonderful!
    And as we eat, we're inwardly restored;
    Christ grows in us, grows to the full.

3 O Jesus Christ, Thou camest not to mankind
  To be a king, to rule us outwardly.
  But Thou hast come as food to satisfy us,
  And by Thy life to guide us inwardly.

    (First chorus)

4 We praise Thee, Lord, for all Thy glorious grandeur,
  For all Thy strength and majesty replete;
  And yet, O Lord, what special thanks we give Thee,
  That all Thou art is small enough to eat.

    (First chorus)

Genesis 14:17-20

1111

(Tune: #223)

7.7.7.7.D.

1 Gathered at Thy table, Lord;
Here the bread and wine are spread.
Thou, our High Priest, present here;
We, by Thee, are richly fed.
Thou, Lord, our Melchisedec —
We, the ones You come to feed;
God to us to minister,
Rich supply to us indeed.

2 From the slaughter of the kings
Abram did return one night,
O'er the foe victorious,
With the spoils of the fight.
On the way this One he met,
Who for him did intercede;
King of Righteousness and Peace
Meeting Abram in his need.

3 We too, Lord, the kings have fought
In the battle all day long;
By Thine intercession, Lord,
We are now victorious, strong.
Round this table here we meet,
We Thy church victorious,
To enjoy the ministering
Of the processed God to us.

4 We're not sinners, miserable;
All our sins are history!
Now to us, the fighters true,
Is Thy priestly ministry.
Gathered in thanksgiving, Lord,
Now our hearts to Thee we raise;
To our great Melchisedec,
Render we our highest praise!

1112

(Tune: #861)
9.8.8.9. with chorus.

1　Oh, how glorious is Thy table, Lord,
　　Thou, the man, our Host, presiding,
　　In Thy house, Thy home, abiding;
　　Oh, how glorious is Thy table, Lord!

　　　Hallelujah! Hallelujah!
　　　Hallelujah for this feast!
　　　Hallelujah! Hallelujah!
　　　Oh, how glorious is Thy table, Lord!

2　How enjoyable Thy table, Lord,
　　As we fellowship around it,
　　Hallelujah, we have found it,
　　How enjoyable Thy table, Lord!

3　Oh, how precious is Thy table, Lord —
　　Bread and wine Thy death announcing;
　　Here our soul-life we're renouncing,
　　By partaking of Thy table, Lord.

4　How significant Thy table, Lord —
　　We Thy Body in the loaf seen,
　　Object of Thy love bespeaking;
　　How significant Thy table, Lord!

5　How refreshing is Thy table, Lord —
　　So completely satisfying,
　　Day by day our need supplying;
　　How refreshing is Thy table, Lord.

6　How encouraging Thy table, Lord —
　　"Till He come," its promise giving
　　Hope, to fill our daily living;
　　How encouraging Thy table, Lord!

FULLNESS OF THE SPIRIT —
AS THE INDWELLING SPIRIT

11.9.11.9. with chorus.

1 Now the Triune God has come to dwell within
    As the wonderful Spirit in us.
  We are mingled with the Lord, we're one with Him
    As the life-giving Spirit in us.

    Oh, He's the wonderful Spirit in us,
    He's the wonderful Spirit in us!
    God is in the Son, the Son's the Spirit now —
    He's the wonderful Spirit in us!

2 "Abba Father" is the cry from deep within
    From the wonderful Spirit in us.
  'Tis the Spirit of the Son who cries to Him
    As the life-giving Spirit in us.

3 Jesus Christ the Lord is living now in us
    As the wonderful Spirit within.
  He has been transfigured, we enjoy Him thus,
    As the life-giving Spirit within.

4 Now the Spirit of reality is here
    As the wonderful Spirit within.
  Now the things of Christ are all so real and clear
    By the life-giving Spirit within.

5 We will all stir up this gift that's deep within
    As the wonderful Spirit in us.
  When we call "Lord Jesus" how our spirits spring
    With this life-giving Spirit in us!

FULLNESS OF THE SPIRIT — AS THE BREATH

1114
(Tune: #278)
11.11.11.11.

1 The Spirit today is the air that we breathe;
Our spirits rejoice in this living inflow.
For just as our body the breath does receive,
So also in spirit to live it is so.

2 The Spirit today is the air that we breathe;
What thing more important than breathing to do?
For breathing each moment, new life we receive,
And God's living freshness is constant and new.

3 For God has been processed, as air now, He's free;
This life-giving pneuma is all that we need.
He's rich and abundant, so plentiful, He,
In spirit to walk is to breathe Him indeed.

4 O, say, aren't you glad that the Spirit's outpoured
And God, fully processed, is flowing in us?
So freely we're breathing this life-giving Lord,
And breathing, receiving His life, glorious!

FULLNESS OF THE SPIRIT — AS THE LIVING WATER

1115
Ezekiel 47:1-12
11.11.11.11.

1 We have come, we have come to the house of God;
We have come to the house, whence outflows the flood.
On the right, day and night, constant is its flow,
Watering us and causing fruits of life to grow.

2 From the house, from the house flows this living stream,
From the house, to the earth, with the life supreme.
Yet more deep, Lord, we seek that the flow may be;
Thus we must be measured and possessed by Thee.

3 Measure us, measure us, measure every day;
   Measure us, measure more, measure all the way,
   Till we know that the flow is a mighty flood,
   Sweeping over all the earth for Christ the Lord.

4 Take us through, take us through, take us through
      the flow;
   Take us through, through and through, everywhere
      we go.
   Flow increase, never cease, till we swim in Thee,
   Till we are immersed in God eternally.

5 All shall live, all shall live where the river comes;
   All shall live, really live, everywhere it runs.
   Let the fount from this mount life abundant bring,
   Till the deserts of the earth with churches spring!

AS THE COMPOUND SPIRIT

Exodus 30:22-25, 34-36   **1116**
(Tune: #1085)
Peculiar Meter.

1 Pure myrrh and cinnamon,
   Calamus and cassia —
   These are Thy elements,
      Jesus my Lord!
   In olive oil they're blent
   In wondrous measurement —
   O what an ointment this,
      Anointing us!

   Four-in-one mingled,
   Compounded Spirit,
   Sweet with Christ's suffering death,
   Full of the fragrance
   Of resurrection —
   O what an ointment flows
      In spirit, Lord!   *continued*

1043

2   Stacte and onycha,
    Galbanum and frankincense —
    These are Thy elements,
        Jesus my Lord!
    Stacte doth sons produce,
    Onycha from sin doth loose,
    Galbanum all death repels,
        In spirit, Lord.

    Equal proportion,
    In resurrection;
    Seasoned with salt are they.
    Ground into powder fine,
    Consumed with fire divine —
    O what an incense this,
        Jesus my Lord!

3   Ointment is Christ for us,
    Exceeding glorious!
    Incense is Christ for God,
        Wholly for Him.
    Ointment flows down to us,
    Christ is our portion thus;
    Incense ascends to God,
        Fragrant to Him.

    'Tis by th' anointing
    Christ we experience
    And then the incense burn.
    Christ in our prayer and praise —
    O what a Christ we raise
    From our experience,
        Precious to God.

FULLNESS OF THE SPIRIT —
AS THE CONFORMING SPIRIT

(Tune: #40)
Peculiar Meter.

1 We praise Thee, O God,
For the Spirit of Christ
Who has come to indwell us
And be all our life.
Hallelujah! What a Spirit!
Hallelujah! Within!
Hallelujah! Life abundant
That never shall end!

2 In spirit we sing
Of the One who has come
As the life-giving Spirit
With us to be one.
Hallelujah! This is Jesus,
Hallelujah! Still more,
Hallelujah! He's the Spirit,
Our life evermore.

3 In spirit reborn,
We're being transformed,
And to God's Son completely
We'll soon be conformed.
Hallelujah! Life imparting,
Hallelujah! Transformed,
Hallelujah! Soon transfigured
And to Him conformed!

4 Conformed we will be
As in spirit we feed
On the life of the One
Who knows all that we need.
Hallelujah! Full salvation!
Hallelujah! Our prize!
Hallelujah! So sufficient
For all of our lives.

12.10.12.10. with chorus.

1 Th' anointing's here! The Lord is moving now
   in us;
   The ointment dear to us has been applied.
   His blood prevails! It gives to us the fellowship,
   And now we have the living flow of life.

   (Sisters sing)
   Th' anointing's here! O Christian brothers,
   Th' anointing's here! We have believed.
   Within our spirit, the Spirit's moving,
   And this from Him we have received.

   (Brothers sing)
   Th' anointing's here! O Christian sisters,
   The flow within will never cease.
   As He anoints us, we are abiding —
   O Hallelujah! Life and peace!

2 Th' anointing's here! 'Tis God Himself that
   blends with us,
   And now the two are mingled into one.
   And hour by hour we live, and move, and have
   our life
   In God Himself — the Spirit through the Son.

3 Th' anointing's here! It teaches us in everything;
   The sense of life we always have within.
   Obey this sense, and you will know what you
   must *do*,
   And live by Life — Yes, clear in everything.

8.7.8.7. with chorus.

1 In the Word of God I found it,
  Wonderful this Word to me;
  I need not man's natural teaching,
  The anointing lives in me!

> Yes, in my spirit now He is moving!
> Yes, I have the anointing!
> God in me is flowing!
> Thank God, I see it!
> His Word revealed it!
> I will apply it ever!
> The anointing lives in me!

2 Making Christ experiential,
  God at His pure Word I take;
  As the Spirit joined unto me,
  He cannot His promise break.

3 Based upon the blood that cleanses
  So that nothing stands between,
  Christ, the ointment, moves within me!
  For His move I'm made so clean.

4 God in Christ as life in Spirit
  Into my own spirit came!
  He the Holy One anoints me
  Till in spirit we're the same.

5 God in Spirit; I can touch Him;
  In my spirit He's the flow.
  Deeper, wider, richer, fuller —
  Oh, the very God I know!

6 As I heed "that same anointing"
  Ever to "abide in Him,"
  He is teaching, He is reaching,
  Even all my heart to win.

FULLNESS OF THE SPIRIT —
THE ANOINTING, SEALING, AND PLEDGING

(Tune: #244)
8.8.8.8.

1 The Holy Spirit is the seal,
   The foretaste, earnest, and the pledge.
   He designates us as God's own
   And guarantees our heritage.

2 'Twas after we believed in Christ,
   The word of truth, the gospel, heard,
   The Holy Spirit us did seal
   To show that we belong to God.

3 This Spirit as the living seal,
   To us God's image now imparts;
   Conforming us unto the Son,
   He stamps His image in our hearts.

4 This Spirit also is the pledge,
   Our earnest and our foretaste true.
   He witnesses that we are sons,
   With God's inheritance in view.

5 'Tis by this Spirit God does spread
   Into our mind, emotion, will;
   By sealing every inward part,
   He will our very being fill.

6 Oh Lord, we would cooperate
   With all Thy Spirit's inward move;
   That we'd become Thy masterpiece,
   Th' eternal purpose thus to prove.

(Tune: #73 or #776)
8.7.8.7.

1 Praise the Lord, who firmly joined us
   Unto the Anointed One.
  Thus we all have been anointed
   With th' anointing of the Son.

2 Now in Christ, in the anointing,
   We are the anointed ones.
  Oh, how blessed is this ointment
   Poured upon the many sons!

3 Hallelujah, the anointing
   Unto us God's essence brings;
  It is now abiding in us,
   And it teaches us all things.

4 We're the Lord's peculiar treasure,
   Purchased by His precious blood.
  He has put His seal upon us,
   We are those marked out by God.

5 Day by day we're under sealing,
   That we may His likeness share.
  By the impress of His Person
   We will Jesus' image bear.

6 Now we have the pledge, the foretaste,
   Of the Christ we soon will see.
  We are longing for the full taste —
   God, our feast eternally.

7 God has wrought us for this purpose,
   Giving us the earnest here,
  Guarantee of full enjoyment
   Of our Lord Himself, so dear.

8 The anointing, seal, and earnest —
   In our spirit are all three.
  Such a wondrous, blest deposit
   God has given you and me.

1122

Revelation 1:4; 4:5; 5:6
(Tune: #262)
7.7.7.7. with chorus.

1 "Seven Spirits" of our God —
Lo, the age has now been turned
To the Spirit with the Son.
For the churches He's concerned.

Come, O seven Spirits, come,
Thy recovery work be done!
Burn and search us thoroughly,
All the churches are for Thee.
Burn us, search us,
All the churches are for Thee!

2 Sevenfold the Spirit is
For the deadness of the church,
That the saints may turn and live,
That the Lord may burn and search.

3 Now the Spirit of our God
Has become intensified:
'Tis not one but sevenfold
That the church may be supplied!

4 Now the seven Spirits are
Seven lamps of burning fire,
Not to teach us, but to burn,
Satisfying God's desire.

5 See the seven Spirits now —
Seven piercing, searching eyes.
In the church exposing us,
All the church He purifies.

6 Seven Spirits doth the Lord
For the churches now employ;
All those in the local church
May this Spirit now enjoy.

1 Of the Spirit, born of Spirit —
     This the source of Jesus is;
   Filled with Spirit, all of Spirit —
     This the essence truly His.
   In the Spirit, with the Spirit,
     As the Spirit Jesus came;
   Now the Lord is just that Spirit
     And in spirit we're the same.

2 Baptized in the Holy Spirit,
     In the Spirit we're immersed;
   All the church is born of Spirit,
     All religion is dispersed.
   In the Spirit, in the Spirit —
     Brothers, this is all we need.
   Now the church must be in Spirit,
     Not in teaching, form, or creed.

3 The communion of the Spirit
     Is the fellowship we share;
   All the brothers, all the sisters
     Only for the Spirit care.
   Now the Spirit in the churches
     Speaks to those who have an ear.
   Seven Spirits for the churches
     Are our blessed portion here.

4 "Come and drink the living water,"
     Say the Spirit and the Bride —
   Church and Spirit speak together,
     Utterly identified.
   Just according to the Spirit
     Must be our reality;
   Just the Spirit in the churches
     Is the Lord's recovery.

1124

(Tune: #548, First tune)

7.7.7.7.

1 What! Not sing of blood divine?
   What! Not tell to all mankind?
   What! Not speak to hearts unclean
   Of the precious living stream.

2 By this blood, God's life released,
   Blood surpassing any beast's;
   Perfect, spotless Lamb of God,
   Incorruptible His blood.

3 Voice it has, this holy blood;
   Pow'r possessed to speak with God;
   Speaks it for us at the throne
   With its glorious virtue shown.

4 Failure on our conscience is —
   Conscience means a "knowing this" —
   Causing us much grief and pain,
   Telling us of every stain.

5 All the while we're unaware
   Of the blood's effectual prayer.
   Jesus' blood speaks of our case,
   That we might receive His grace!

6 We need not dead works to bring,
   Nor another offering.
   Nothing else could please our God,
   Heav'n is listening for His blood.

7 In His blood forgiveness shines;
   Oh, 'tis glorious to find!
   Israel just atonement knew,
   We have that and cleansing too.

8 Heart and mind are now at peace
   Rest! Our conscience has been reached.
   Never more we blush in shame,
   We are washed from every stain.

9 Hallelujah! Fathomless!
All that's in His blood for us!
Sing we will, and sing we must;
In His blood is all our trust!

1125

(Tune: #1066)
9.9.9.5. with chorus.

1 Down at the cross where my Savior died,
God's righteous nature was satisfied;
There to my sin was the blood applied,
  Glory to His name!

  Glory to His name,
  Glory to His name;
There to my sin was the blood applied,
  Glory to His name!

2 Saved from our sin at this fountain, we
Fully enjoy our redemption free;
This we'll enjoy for eternity,
  Glory to His name!

3 Oh, precious fact, when my Savior died,
Not only sin's debt was satisfied;
Life's flowing fountain was opened wide!
  Glory to His name!

  Glory to His name,
  Glory to His name;
Life's flowing fountain was opened wide,
  Glory to His name!

4 Now both redemption and life we share,
Cleansed in His blood, we're abiding there
Drinking the water of life fore'er;
  Glory to His name!

1126

(Tune: #116)
8.6.8.6.D.

1 O Jesus Lord, we come to Thee,
   Thy presence to enjoy;
   Our entrance now with boldness is,
   As we Thy blood employ.
   Not by our merit do we stand,
   Nor in our righteousness,
   Thy blood and righteousness we need;
   Their worth we now confess.

2 Thy judgments, Lord, we must admit,
   Are holy, righteous, fair.
   We own our sins as crimson are,
   We've no excuse to bear.
   We have no argument, no plea;
   No veil our sin can hide.
   But, praise Thee, Lord, Thy precious blood
   Is to our sin applied!

3 God has not overlooked our sin,
   But judged it once for all;
   His righteous fury, not on us,
   But on His Lamb did fall.
   A new and living way is made —
   We stand on legal ground;
   Our Surety and our Substitute
   Has pardon for us found.

4 O Jesus Lord, we worship Thee,
   Redemption now enjoy;
   Thy precious blood again we see,
   Its virtue now employ.
   Dear Lord, Thy mercy is so vast,
   Unlimited and free.
   Oh, Lamb of God, we'll sing Thy praise,
   Through all eternity!

7.8.7.8. with chorus.

1 God has saved me from the world;
  I'll never go back anymore.
 God has saved me from the world;
  I'll never go back anymore.

 No, no, no, no, no,
  I'll never go back anymore;
 No, no, no, no, no,
  I'll never go back anymore.

2 I've come out from Babylon;
  I'll never go back anymore.
 I've come out from Babylon;
  I'll never go back anymore.

3 Since I found the local church,
  I'll never go back anymore.
 Since I found the local church,
  I'll never go back anymore.

4 Since I've touched the Lord within,
  I'll never go back anymore.
 Since I've touched the Lord within,
  I'll never go back anymore.

5 Christ is everything to me;
  I'll never go back anymore.
 Christ is everything to me;
  I'll never go back anymore.

6 Praise the Lord, I'm home at last;
  I'll never go back anymore.
 Praise the Lord, I'm home at last;
  I'll never go back anymore.

7 I'm for God's recovery;
  I'll never go back anymore.
 I'm for God's recovery;
  I'll never go back anymore.

1128

Exodus 15:1-22

(Tune: #41)

13.8.13.8. with chorus.

1 We were held in bondage, toiling down
  in Egypt land,
    Glory to God, Hallelujah!
  But the God of Hebrews rescued us
    from Pharaoh's hand,
    Glory to God, Hallelujah!

  We will sing unto the Lord
    for His mighty victory,
  For the rider and the horse
    He has cast into the sea.
  Now the dwelling place of God
    on the earth will builded be,
    Glory to God, Hallelujah!

2 Now we're on the other side, we'll go
    back nevermore!
    Glory to God, Hallelujah!
  Look! Th' Egyptians all are lying dead
    upon the shore!
    Glory to God, Hallelujah!

3 Brothers, sisters — Hallelujah! Through
    the sea we've crossed,
    Glory to God, Hallelujah!
  All the things that used to hold us
    are forever lost!
    Glory to God, Hallelujah!

4 We're the Hebrews, now we're standing
    on the sea of glass,
    Glory to God, Hallelujah!
  And we sing the song of Moses,
    everything we've passed,
    Glory to God, Hallelujah!

Hebrews 2:3

(Tune: #339 Second tune)

11.11.11.11.

1 "So great a salvation," ye saints of the Lord,
To us is revealed in His marvelous Word!
Since all that He is and has done is for us,
We'll give earnest heed to this word glorious.

2 What He is of God and of Man as the Son,
We now may enjoy since with Him we are one;
Our High Priest and Captain — salvation is He!
He'll cause us to grow in His glory to be.

3 He's washed all our sins, purified them fore'er;
Tasted death on the cross, ended slavery there.
He took on our nature, the devil has slain,
And put you and I in His glorious train.

4 So great the extent of salvation to us —
We're partners of Christ in His plan glorious.
He'll bring us to glory and we'll rule with Him,
To the uttermost saved by His working within.

5 To such a salvation our heed we must give,
Lest drifting away or neglecting we live.
Christ now as our life, future ruling with Him,
We'll miss if we miss this salvation within.

6 "So great a salvation" is given to us
That we may be made like our Lord glorious!
By all that He is and by all He has done
We're brought into glory with God's firstborn Son.

1130

Hebrews 7

8.7.8.7.8.8.7.

1 Sing praise to Christ Who lives in us,
The God of our salvation;
Who saves us by His life divine,
And not by regulation;
After we've worked — done all we can,
His life has power to change a man:
His life divine can change us.

2 He saves us to the uttermost
By His life-giving power;
Transfusing Himself into us,
He saves us hour by hour.
He saved the lost by coming in,
He's saving now from more than sin:
He's saving us to glory!

3 Our Lord was constituted priest
To be a real life-giver;
Life is the nature of this One
Who can from self deliver:
His life is indestructible,
By it He saves us to the full:
Praise God, He's fully able!

4 His life is fully qualified
To bring us through to glory;
Were it not for His tested life,
'Twould be another story:

His life was fully tried on earth,
To crucifixion from His birth:
He passed through death and Hades.

5 He's pledged to save us to the full,
His life is operating;
He's doing everything for us
'Tis all for our perfecting;
Our life's a failure at its best,
Only His life can stand the test:
His life brings full salvation!

6 He's living now to intercede,
Continuing forever;
He undertakes into the age,
His priesthood changes never;
He always lives to intercede,
Such a High Priest is what we need:
He's higher than the heavens.

7 Come forward now to God through Him,
Ne'er shrink back to destruction;
Come forward now to get the life,
Which brings the proper function;
Come forward now the life to take,
By life His people us He'll make,
And swallow death forever.

Romans 5:1-11
Peculiar Meter.

1 In a low dungeon, hope we had none;
Tried to believe, but faith didn't come;
God, our sky clearing, Jesus appearing,
We by God were transfused!
We by God were transfused!

Propitiation made by the blood,
Jesus' redemption bought us for God!
No condemnation, justification!
We have peace toward God!
We have peace toward God!

2 Born into Adam, dying we were;
We had a sickness no one could cure.
God, His Son sending, old Adam ending;
He is dead, we are free!
He is dead, we are free!

3 Now we're rejoicing, standing in grace,
Oh hallelujah! Sin is erased!
God, in us flowing, in our hearts growing,
We are saved in His life!
We are saved in His life!

Peculiar Meter.

1 Lord, teach us how to pray,
  Not as the nations do in vain,
  But turn us from our way,
  And cause us, Lord, to call on You each day —
    Lord Jesus, grow in us.

2 Lord, You're the seed of life;
  You've sown Yourself into our heart,
  And now You have a start;
  So day by day more life to us impart —
    Lord Jesus, grow in us.

3 Lord Jesus, soften us;
  You know the source from which we came.
  By calling on Your name,
  Lord, let no earth unturned nor rocks remain —
    Lord Jesus, grow in us.

4 Lord, how Your light makes clear
  That we could not but e'er fail You;
  Yet there's a message true,
  The seed of life within us will break through —
    Lord Jesus, grow in us.

5 Make us in spirit poor;
  Lord, take whate'er we think we know.
  We'll open to life's flow,
  And thus take in the life that makes us grow —
    Lord Jesus, grow in us.

6 Lord, make us pure in heart;
  For we'll be not content until
  You all our being fill,
  O Lord, renew our mind, emotion, will —
    Lord Jesus, grow in us.

continued

7   Yes, Lord, impress our heart
    That we must take You in each day;
    The seed will have its way;
    Your growing brings the kingdom here to stay —
        Lord Jesus, grow in us.

8   Amen! — The growth in life!
    There's nothing that Your life can't do;
    Our every part renew.
    We'll make it, we'll make it just by You.
        Lord Jesus, grow in us.
        Lord Jesus, grow in us.

LONGINGS — FOR REVELATION OF CHRIST

1133

Ephesians 1:17-23
(Tune: #278)
11.11.11.11.

1 O Father of glory, now grant unto me
    A spirit of wisdom, a spirit to see;
    O give unto me the full knowledge of Him,
    Enlight'ning the eyes of my heart deep within.

2 O show me that Christ is the hope of Thy call —
    O glorious hope, Christ will fill all in all!
    Reveal Him — the riches of glory in us —
    As God's own inheritance. How glorious!

3 O God of our Lord Jesus, let me perceive
    Th' exceeding great pow'r unto us who believe,
    The power that raised Christ, Thy Son, from the dead
    And made Him o'er all, to His Body, the Head.

4 O God, Thou hast wrought all this pow'r into Christ,
    Who now lives in me as my Person, my life.
    O grant revelation, dear Father, to see
    This transcending pow'r is a Person in me.

5 O Christ is the hope, He's the glory and power;
So Christ I must take as my Person each hour.
Then in me such power will be exercised,
My hope and God's glory will be realized.

LONGINGS — FOR SANCTIFICATION

1134

Ephesians 3:17-20
9.7.9.7. with chorus.

1 Oh, strengthen my spirit, Lord Jesus,
Oh, strengthen my spirit, I pray;
Oh, strengthen my spirit with power
And spread to my heart today.

Into my heart, into my heart,
Spread into my heart, Lord Jesus;
Make home today and have Your way
In all of my heart, Lord Jesus.

2 Spread into my heart, O Lord Jesus,
Spread into my heart, I pray;
Spread into my heart from my spirit,
Spread into my heart today.

3 Make home in my heart, O Lord Jesus,
Make home in my heart, I pray;
That we may be filled with Your fullness,
Make home in my heart today.

4 To Him who is able to do it
Above all we think or say,
We open our hearts wide and welcome
Him into our heart today.

1135

Ephesians 5:26-29
(Tune: #256)
12.12.12.8. with chorus.

1   Oh, sanctify us, Lord; now add Thyself to us,
    In our experience, Thy Person spread in us,
    That in reality the church be glorious,
    O Lord, do add Thyself, we pray.

      Oh, sanctify us, Lord, today;
      Lord Jesus, You're the only way.
      We take Your Person, Lord;
      Oh, spread Yourself abroad.
      Oh, sanctify us, Lord, today.

2   Oh, purify us, Lord, by speaking in our heart;
    Thy living, spoken word this washing will impart.
    Increase Thy speaking, Lord, and cleanse our
        every part.
    Oh, purify us, Lord, we pray.

      Oh, purify us, Lord, today;
      Wash all our natural life away.
      Speak now Thy words in us,
      And make us glorious.
      O Lord, do speak in us today.

3   O Lord, do nourish us; You are the food we need;
    As we are eating You, we'll be transformed indeed;
    We're fully satisfied as on Yourself we feed,
    So nourish us, O Lord, we pray.

O Lord, do nourish us today
As all our self You wash away.
Not only purify,
But fill and satisfy;
O Lord, do nourish us today.

4 O Lord, do cherish us, as on Thyself we feed;
Warm us so tenderly and meet our every need.
Our hardness soften, Lord, till we are Yours indeed;
Oh, cherish us, dear Lord, we pray.

O Lord, do cherish us today,
Until our coldness flees away.
Oh, hold us close to Thee
And cherish tenderly;
O Lord, do cherish us today.

5 Lord, make us glorious, by all Your inner work,
Not glory for ourselves, but glory for the church;
That You may have Your Bride, thus ending all
    Your search.
O Lord, do work on us, we pray.

O Lord, do work on us today!
To form the church Your glorious way.
Oh, spread Yourself in us
Till we are glorious;
Oh, make us glorious, Lord, today.

1136
(Tune: #589)
8.7.8.7.D.

1 Oh, Lord, grant us revelation,
   Grant us light and sight to see
That as life, within our spirit,
   Thou art our reality;
And that from within our spirit,
   Now You must possess each part
Spreading out to all our being,
   Making home in all our heart.

2 It is not the outward action —
   Pure behavior, conduct good,
Proper poise and perfect manners,
   Doing what we think we should;
But it's Christ, a living Person,
   Mingled thus with us within,
Spreading into all our being,
   So that we might live by Him.

3 Oh, Lord, let our every action,
   Everything we do and say,
Come from Thee alone, experienced
   In a real and inner way.
We reject the empty teachings,
   Leave the methods and the strife.
Let our only way of living
   Be the overflow of life!

4 Following the inner feeling,
   Living in the overflow,
Moving in the rich anointing,
   Not by what we think or know,
Nothing through intent or motive,
   Or with purpose duly done,
But just following this feeling,
   Living by the living One!

5   Thus we're sanctified completely,
Saturated thoroughly;
Not the old religious concept:
Separated doctrinally.
But 'tis Christ Himself within us,
Added to our every part,
All supplying, satisfying,
Making home in all our heart.

LONGINGS — FOR FELLOWSHIP OF CHRIST'S SUFFERINGS

(Tune: #334)
11.8.11.8.D. with repeat.

1137

1 His countenance angels can often behold,
But ne'er taste His love in His grace;
His saints, though they know of His pure,
boundless love,
Have never yet once seen His face.
His saints will before long His visage behold,
E'en in His bright glory will share;
But Mary, beholding His tears as He wept,
Could touch His heart's agony there.
Could touch His heart's agony there.

2 We'll soon see the Lord, as He is, face to face,
We'll know Him as never before;
But that touch today, healing our broken heart,
In that day will be felt no more.
That day, though our lips offer unceasing praise,
No tears, then, nor prayers fervent burn;
Nor is there the comfort received through much pain,
Nor trust gained through trials to learn,
Nor trust gained through trials to learn.

continued

1137

3 Exceeding in glory, that day we'll be crowned,
  Yet there'll be no cross to obey;
  The sweet fellowship of His suff'rings for us
  We only can share in today.
  Once we've that rest entered, no weariness then,
  Nor chance will remain to partake
  The trials nor the hardships, nor happiness lost,
  Nor suffering borne for His sake,
  Nor suffering borne for His sake.

4 Oh, chances to suffer for Him are so few,
  His shame and derision to bear;
  Such blest opportunities soon pass away,
  That He in our troubles may share.
  All loneliness, misunderstandings and scorn
  Despisings and sorrows will flee;
  I treasure these blessings, for through them, O Lord,
  I enter sweet oneness with Thee,
  I enter sweet oneness with Thee.

5 I long to behold, Lord, Thy countenance soon,
  What rapture with Thee, Lord, to meet.
  But neither seek I all these trials to avoid;
  Such times, Lord, are too rare and sweet.
  Have mercy on me, fill me with Thy great love,
  For Thee, Lord, to live at all cost;
  Lest Thy servant, hoping for that blessed day,
  That day, regret chances were lost,
  That day, regret chances were lost.

(Tune: #319)
8.7.8.7.D.

1138

1   Lord, Thou art our consecration,
       Thou the consecrated One;
    Thou hast satisfied the Father —
       Consecration thus was done.
    When on earth Thou hadst no pleasure,
       Save to do the Father's will;
    Now Thou livest here within us,
       Consecration to fulfill.

2   Lord, we praise Thee for the picture:
       Consecration's ram we see,
    Burnt for God's full satisfaction,
       Eaten and enjoyed to be.
    Thou art now our ram, Lord Jesus,
       Offered for the will of God;
    By Thy consecration, faultless,
       We may walk where Thou hast trod.

3   As we eat Thyself, Lord Jesus,
       Consecrated we become;
    By Thy wondrous life within us,
       Thy obedience is our own.
    No more need we strive and struggle,
       Consecrated try to be;
    Consecration dwells within us —
       Now our part to eat of Thee.

4   Lord, we praise Thee, consecration
       Is nought else but Thee as food:
    As we eat Thee and enjoy Thee,
       We are all made one with God;
    One in will and one in purpose
       We become by eating Thee:
    As we take and eat Thyself, Lord,
       Consecrated we will be.

Song of Songs 4:6
(Tune: #7)
8.7.8.7. with chorus.

1 I will get me to the mountain,
    I will get me to the hill;
In Thy death and resurrection,
    Jesus, take me deeper still.

I will get me to the mountain,
Willingly would get me there.
All my self fore'er forsaking,
One with Thee, O Lord,
    Thy death to share.

2 Still at times I sense the shadows
    Of my nature, untransformed;
Lord, I'll go unto the mountain,
    To Thy death to be conformed.

3 On the mountain till the daybreak,
    Linger I, Lord, thus with Thee,
May Thy all-transforming Spirit
    Saturate me thoroughly.

4 Mingled with Thee on the mountain,
    Soon my sun begins to shine;
Death has worked her deep impression,
    Now my nature's one with Thine.

Romans 7
(Tune: #154)
10.10.10.10.4.

1 Our old man has been crucified with Christ;
Yes, all we are in oldness He sufficed
To bring to naught upon the cross that He
Himself as our new Husband fully be
    Enjoyed by us.

2 Yes, all our strength of independence died,
For we with Christ were fully crucified.
Now we're so glad to be His proper wife,
Dependently enjoying Him as life
    Forevermore.

3 Our dying was not such a sad affair,
The new man was rejoicing to be there;
The old man dead and buried, we were free
To marry Christ, and live eternally,
    His wife, fore'er.

4 Now as the new, regenerated man,
We do two things, according to God's plan:
Bear fruit to God and serve in spirit new
So God becomes the fruit of all we do,
    And all we are.

5 There are three laws in Romans seven, see —
The law of God; the mind, the good old me;
The sinful law indwelling bodily;
Yet from these all the Lord has set us free,
    To live by Him.

6 In Romans eight the law of Spirit is,
Where we're in Christ, and we are fully His,
The law of life has set us wholly free
And Christ becomes our life eternally,
    Hallelujah!

1141

10.9.10.9.

1 We will sing to the Lord with our spirit,
We will sing to the Lord from within,
We will sing hallelujah to Jesus;
And be blent into oneness with Him.

2 We have been many years in religion,
We have been many years in our mind,
We have been many years in emotions,
Always seeking, but never to find.

3 Now we're learning to turn to our spirit,
Now we're learning to take Christ as life;
Now we're learning to feed upon Jesus
And be freed from all struggling and strife.

4 Hallelujah for life in the Spirit,
Hallelujah for newness within.
When we turn from our mind to our spirit,
We enjoy all the riches of Him.

EXPERIENCE OF CHRIST — AS THE SPIRIT

1142

(Tune: #890)
8.5.8.5. with chorus.

1 Jesus is the living Spirit,
   Our reality;
We enjoy Him just by calling
   In simplicity.

Jesus is the living Spirit,
We must now proclaim;
He is rich unto all men
That call upon His name.

2 *He* is living now within us,
   Giving liberty;
He is good and He is gracious
As we taste and see.

3 Jesus is the living Spirit
And the living Word;
When we touch Him by pray-reading
We receive this Lord.

4 Jesus is the living Spirit
Who among us flows;
Fellowship of life in spirit
Unity bestows.

5 Jesus is the living Spirit,
He is our rich feast;
As the Body now enjoys Him,
Praises are released.

EXPERIENCE OF CHRIST — AS FOOD AND DRINK

(Tune: #313)
8.6.8.6.

1143

1 The tree of life, how sweet the fruit,
With God as life complete.
I once was dead, but now I live,
Was starved, but now I eat.

2 'Twas God that brought me to the tree,
With Christ Himself as meat;
How precious did that tree become
When I began to eat.

3 The Lord Himself is food to me,
He is my life supply;
He will my pure enjoyment be,
None else can satisfy.

4 I freely eat this living tree,
For eating is the way
To put God's life inside of me,
To live by Him today.

EXPERIENCE OF CHRIST — AS FOOD AND DRINK

1144

(Tune: #276)
10.9.10.9. with chorus.

1 In the Word of old, we are clearly told,
  In His image God created man.
To express His worth, to subdue the earth,
  Have dominion and fulfill His plan.

> Image, image,
> In His image He created man.
> Image, image,
> For dominion, to fulfill His plan.

2 Yet no rules He gave, no instructions, save:
  "Every tree shall be to thee for meat."
But one tree, He said, surely makes you dead;
  Fruit of knowledge isn't good to eat.

> Knowledge, knowledge,
> Fruit of knowledge wasn't meant for meat.
> Knowledge, knowledge,
> Fruit of knowledge isn't good to eat.

3 Midst the garden fair, see the life tree there —
  God Himself the tree of life does show.
But the enemy, somehow subtly,
  Tempted man the other tree to know.

> Fallen, fallen,
> Man has eaten of the deadly tree.
> Fallen, fallen,
> Man requires a full recovery.

4 Then came Jesus Christ as the tree of life,
  Satisfying all that God required.
He redeemed the earth, giving man new birth,
  And became the food that man desired.

> Jesus, Jesus,
> Jesus Christ is really good to eat.
> Jesus, Jesus,
> He is real drink and real meat.

5 Jesus ne'er designed e'er to feed our mind;
    All good knowledge only puffeth up.
But He came, He said, as a feast instead,
    Not to analyze, but only sup.

> Take Him, take Him,
> Wholly satisfying, glorious.
> Take Him, take Him,
> Jesus is the tree of life to us.

6 As we eat the Lord, growth He does afford,
    Life and numbers soon will be increased.
We must clearly see God's recovery —
    Christ is not religion, but a feast.

> Eat Him, eat Him,
> Christ as life is all the food we need.
> Eat Him, eat Him,
> He who eateth Him shall live indeed.

7 Eating is the way to live Christ today,
    Of the eating there should be no lack.
As the churches eat, they become complete,
    Eating Christ will bring the Bridegroom back.

> Eating, eating,
> Of our eating there must be no lack.
> Eating, eating,
> Eating Christ will bring the Bridegroom back.

1145

(Tune: #864)
8.8.8.6. with chorus.

1 God gave His Son to man to be
   The tree of life so rich and free,
   That every man may taste and see
      That God is good for food.
         Yes, God is good for food!
         Yes, God is good for food!
         We've tasted and we testify
         That God is good for food!

2 We eat this feast and take God in,
   And as we eat we live by Him,
   For all the elements within
      This feast are God Himself.
         Yes, Jesus is our feast!
         Yes, Jesus is our feast!
         We eat this feast and live by Him,
         For Jesus is our feast!

3 Christ Jesus is the food we eat;
   He is our bread, He is our meat;
   He is our life-supply complete;
      We daily eat of Him.
         We daily eat of Him,
         We daily eat of Him.
         He is our life-supply complete;
         We daily eat of Him.

4 This feast is so enjoyable;
   To men it's so available,
   For God said whosoever will
      May come and freely eat.
         Yes, come and freely eat;
         Yes, come and freely eat.
         For God said whosoever will
         May come and freely eat.

(Tune: #382)
8.8.8.8. with chorus.

1 Let us eat Jesus every day,
  Eating His flesh in such a way
  That in the trials great or small
  He as a Man will be our all.

    Eat, eat more of Jesus!
    Eat, eat more of Jesus!
    Why should we undernourished be
    When we have His humanity?

2 Let us drink Jesus till we see
  That we are human, Jesusly!
  Till rivers flood the barren ground
  And quench the thirst of all around.

    Drink, drink more of Jesus!
    Drink, drink more of Jesus!
    Why should we ever thirsty be
    When we have His humanity?

3 We must eat Jesus till God can
  Have the fulfillment of His plan —
  One man expressed for all to see,
  One church in each locality.

    We'll masticate Jesus!
    We'll masticate Jesus!
    Then to the tent of meeting bring
    Jesus, our real meal offering.

1147

Exodus 16
(Tune: #411)
6.6.8.6.

1 Christ is our manna true,
Our bread of life indeed;
He's our supply of nourishment,
As on Him now we feed.

2 From Egypt Israel fled
Into a desert land;
Egyptian food they left behind,
And wandering began.

3 One day, the manna fell,
Oh, what a wondrous feat;
This was the bread the Lord had giv'n
For Israel to eat.

4 Unique this manna is,
It comes with morning dew;
The visit of God's grace it is,
Forever fresh and new.

5 God is majestic, high,
And greater than us all;
But that we may partake of Him,
In Christ, He's fine and small.

6 Though ground, or beat, or baked,
He's so available;
As bread and cakes and wafers fresh,
We eat Him to the full.

7 Manna shows Him to be
The germ of life, the seed;
'Tis God Himself sown into us,
The source of all we need.

8 Between the morning dew
And cold of winter snow,
This manna too is frost which kills
Things negative below.

9 How pure and white and clean;
   In type our Christ we see;
   As we digest His element,
   He washes inwardly.

10 Manna with honey is;
   Two lives this type does show;
   One for the Lord's redemptive work,
   And one His life to grow.

11 By eating more of Christ
   We'll be the less opaque;
   We'll then appear as bdellium,
   Transparent us to make.

12 Lord, as we're eating here
   And in the manna see
   The riches of this glorious Christ,
   We're filled with praise to Thee.

1148

Peculiar Meter.

1 "Come and dine," the Lord is calling,
   "Come and dine" —
   We can eat and drink of Jesus all the time!
   He's our daily food supply,
   Only He can satisfy.
   "Come and dine," the Lord is calling,
   "Come and dine."

2 "Come and dine," the Lord is calling,
   "Come and dine."
   When we eat and drink of Jesus all the time,
   He becomes our life within,
   And He fills us to the brim.
   "Come and dine," the Lord is calling,
   "Come and dine."

1149   Peculiar Meter.

1   Of Him whence grace and truth did spring,
    We're at the fountain drinking;
    This Christ we'll ever praise and sing,
    Here in the church, His home!

      Glory to God! We're at the fountain
        drinking!
      Glory to God! We're in the church,
        our home!

2   Ask but His grace, and lo, 'tis giv'n,
    We're at the fountain drinking;
    Seek but Himself, the heaven of heaven,
    And find Him here at home!

3   Though Satan fights with all his power,
    We're at the fountain drinking;
    He'll not prevail, not one short hour,
    Against the church, our home!

4   Athirst we to this spring do fly,
    We're at the fountain drinking;
    Drink deep, this well will not run dry!
    It's in the church, our home!

1150   (Tune: #1069)
                       8.8.8.8. with chorus.

1   We're feeding on the living bread,
    We're drinking at the fountainhead;
    And whoso drinketh, Jesus said,
    Shall never, never thirst again.
    What, never thirst again? No, never thirst again!
    What, never thirst again? No, never thirst again!
    And whoso drinketh, Jesus said,
    Shall never, never thirst again!

2 We are feeding on the living bread,
  Eating of the feast our Lord has spread,
  And whoso eateth, Jesus said,
  Shall hunger nevermore.
  What, hunger nevermore? Yes, hunger nevermore!
  What, hunger nevermore? Yes, hunger nevermore!
  And whoso eateth, Jesus said,
  Shall hunger nevermore.

3 We are breathing in the living air,
  Breathing in the One whose life we share,
  And whoso breatheth — now, fore'er —
  Shall have the life of God.
  What, have the life of God? Yes, have the life of God!
  What, have the life of God? Yes, have the life of God!
  And whoso breatheth — now, fore'er —
  Shall have the life of God.

4 We are tasting of the living wine,
  In spirit tasting life divine,
  And whoso tasteth, everytime
  Shall have the joy of God.
  What, have the joy of God? Yes, have the joy of God!
  What, have the joy of God? Yes, have the joy of God!
  And whoso tasteth, everytime
  Shall have the joy of God.

5 Christ is the resurrected King,
  Who died and rose, our life to bring,
  If you receive Him you will sing,
  And live forevermore.
  What, live forevermore? Yes, live forevermore!
  What, live forevermore? Yes, live forevermore!
  If you receive Him you will sing,
  And live forevermore.

1151

Revelation 22
Peculiar Meter.

1 Drink! A river pure and clear that's flowing from
   the throne;
Eat! The tree of life with fruits abundant, richly
   grown;
Look! No need of lamp nor sun nor moon to keep it
   bright, for
Here there is no night!

Do come, oh, do come,
Says Spirit and the Bride:
Do come, oh, do come,
Let him that heareth, cry.
Do come, oh, do come,
Let him who thirsts and will
Take freely the water of life!

2 Christ, our river, Christ, our water, springing
   from within;
Christ, our tree, and Christ, the fruits, to be
   enjoyed therein,
Christ, our day, and Christ, our light, and Christ,
   our morning star:
Christ, our everything!

3 We are washing all our robes the tree of life to eat;
"O Lord, Amen, Hallelujah!" — Jesus is so sweet!
We our spirits exercise, and thus experience Christ.
What a Christ have we!

4 Now we have a home so bright that outshines the sun,
Where the brothers all unite and truly are one.
Jesus gets us all together, Him we now display
In the local church.

14.14.14.14. with chorus.

1 To Jesus every day we find our hearts are closer drawn;
  He's fairer than the sons of men and fresher than
    the morn;
  He's all that we can say of Him in fairest words
    and more,
  And every day He's dearer than He was the day before.

    The half cannot be fancied of such a treasure-store,
    And every day He's dearer than He ever was before!

2 His glory broke upon us when we saw Him in
    the church,
  For here are all His riches, here we've given up
    our search;
  'Tis here He satisfies our longing spirits o'er and o'er,
  And every day He's dearer than He was the
    day before.

3 Now He's the living Spirit who within our
    spirit dwells,
  And by His sweet anointing, how His life within
    us swells!
  As with the saints we're meeting, full released our
    spirits soar,
  For now our Lord is dearer than He ever was before.

4 The Lord has made us one with Him for His recovery:
  The riches of this Christ, the church His fullness, men
    must see.
  Yes, all we have and all we are, we every day outpour
  For His tremendous purpose, ever dearer than before.

1153

9.7.9.7. with chorus.

1 We have found the Christ who's all in all;
    He is everything to us;
  O how blest upon His name to call,
    How divine, how glorious!

  It is joy unspeakable and full of glory,
    Full of glory, full of glory;
  It is joy unspeakable and full of glory,
    And the half has never yet been told!

2 We have found that Christ the Spirit is
    Who within our spirit dwells;
  How available, how near He is,
    And His sweetness all excels.

3 We have found the way to live by Christ —
    Pray His Word and call His name!
  This — the eating, drinking — has sufficed
    And its worth we now proclaim.

4 We have found the local church, our home;
    We are home and home indeed!
  Nevermore in Babylon we roam;
    In the church is all we need.

5 We have found that meeting with the saints
    Is the greatest joy on earth;
  'Tis by this our spirit never faints
    And our lives are filled with worth.

Song of Songs
Peculiar Meter.

1 I love Thee, Jesus,
   And Thy love to me
   Draws me, ever to seek Thee
     And run after Thee,
   Draws me, ever to seek Thee
     And run after Thee.
       Thou art beloved,
       Yea! Altogether lovely,
       The One in whom my heart delighteth.

2 Thy love, Lord Jesus,
   Is sweeter than wine,
   And Thy fragrance of ointments
     My heart doth entwine,
   And Thy fragrance of ointments
     My heart doth entwine.
       A fount in gardens,
       A well of living waters,
       Which streams and flows from Lebanon's
         mountains.

3 O come Beloved,
   On my garden blow,
   That the odor of spices
     May break forth and flow,
   That the odor of spices
     May break forth and flow.
       My spouse, My sister,
       I'm come into My garden
       To feast upon wine, milk and honey.

(Repeat the last three lines of each stanza)

continued

4 Set me, Lord Jesus,
    As seal on Thine heart;
Jealousy's cruel as Sheol,
    And love's strong as death,
Jealousy's cruel as Sheol,
    And love's strong as death.
        Much water cannot
        Quench love, nor do floods drown it.
        All man could give for love is contemned.

1155   Song of Songs
            (Tune: with chorus, #268; without chorus, #466)
                        8.7.8.7.D.

1 How I love Thee, precious Jesus,
    That Thy love laid hold of me;
Thou hast drawn and wooed and kissed me
    That a lover I may be!

    Our Beloved, how we love Him,
        So attractive, our delight.
    We are captivated wholly
        And are comely in His sight.

2 As a company of horses,
    Thou, O Lord, has likened me,
Strong and swift, with Pharaoh's chariots,
    Full of natural energy.

3 Just a lover with the dove's eyes
    Fixed on Him and Him alone;
Changed are all my natural concepts,
    Oh, the Lord in me has grown!

4 Now a lily of the valley,
    Standing out among the thorns,
In the Lord alone I'm trusting,
    Of my self-strength I've been shorn.

5   Make us doves that hide in Thee, Lord;
      Bring us to the secret place.
    There You find our voices sweet, Lord,
      And desire to see our face.

6   Make us then, Lord, smoking pillars,
      Coming from the wilderness.
    By Thy death and resurrection
      All our natural will suppress.

7   You desire a couch to rest on —
      We become a rest to Thee;
    Thou the Person in our being,
      Gone our personality.

8   Now a palanquin You're making —
      Nothing natural You'll allow.
    For Your move and Your expression
      Start this work within us now!

9   You supply the wood and pillars
      For the structure and support,
    Bottom gold and seat of purple
      For our King of royal court.

10 Only this, O Lord, we offer
      For Thy palanquin so fine:
    Just our love, so pure and fitted,
      The interior design.

11 What a sight when our Beloved
      Wears a crown upon His brow;
    Christ, the Church, are now united —
      Boast and glory to Him now!

1156

Song of Songs
(Tune: #7)
8.7.8.7. with chorus.

1 To the Lord we're as a garden,
 Out from which the spices flow;
All the precious fruits of Jesus
 Freely in this garden grow.

  Spikenard, saffron, henna flower,
  Cinnamon and calamus,
  Frankincense and myrrh and aloes;
  O Lord, we would ever grow Thee thus.

2 O Lord, come into Thy garden,
 Come, Beloved, come and eat
Freely for Thy satisfaction
 Of Thy fruit, abundant, sweet.

  "Yea," Thou answerest, "I am eating
  Honeycomb with honey pure."
  All sweet spices from Thy garden,
  Doth Thy satisfaction, Lord, secure.

3 All the produce of the garden
 Is with resurrection filled
That the Lord may have a city,
 Fruits of resurrection build.

  From the garden to the city,
  Growth transformed to precious stone;
  Christ is thus expressed, reflected —
  God in all His glory fully shown.

4 Now the city, fair and comely,
 As the dawn, triumphantly,
Is an army strong and mighty
 Marching forth in victory.

  Lo, the city and the army —
  Saints transformed in one accord.
  What a terror to the devil,
  And so beautiful unto the Lord!

Song of Songs 2:3-4
Peculiar Meter.

1157

1 His banner over me is love,
His banner over me is love;
He brought me into His banqueting house,
And His banner over me is love.

Is love! Is love!
His banner over me is love;
He brought me into His banqueting house,
And His banner over me is love.

2 His fruit is sweet unto my taste,
His fruit is sweet unto my taste;
I'm feasting here in His banqueting house,
And His fruit is sweet unto my taste.

How sweet! How sweet!
His fruit is sweet unto my taste;
I'm feasting here in His banqueting house,
And His fruit is sweet unto my taste.

Peculiar Meter.

1158

1 Dear Lord Jesus, precious Jesus,
Thou hast won each love from me;
Who like Thee — so fair and comely?
Who like Thee — so sweet and lovely?
Matchless One, unrivaled beauty,
None can e'er compete with Thee!

2 Dear Lord Jesus, precious Jesus,
Gladly will I hear Thy call;
Since Thy voice my heart hath entered,
I from all things could but sever;
Void are all my other seekings,
Every pride hath disappeared.

continued

1158

3 Dear Lord Jesus, precious Jesus,
    How can I still stubborn be?
  At Thy feet cast all my hard'nings,
    And return with songs and singings;
  'Tis my love to be Thy bondslave,
    'Tis my joy to Thee obey.

4 Dear Lord Jesus, precious Jesus,
    Thy way only will I choose;
  Though in tears while I'm obeying,
    Yet I would not change my standing;
  All I long for is Thy pleasure,
    And the peace Thy love would bring.

5 Dear Lord Jesus, precious Jesus,
    When Thy presence does depart,
  Seems the dawn has lost its traces,
    Hidden are my smiling faces;
  All I yearn for is Thy coming
    And Thy presence' sweet embrace.

6 Dear Lord Jesus, precious Jesus,
    Can I tell it all to Thee?
  Thou my love and satisfaction,
    Thou my everlasting portion;
  Thou art all that I desire,
    Nothing else I would pursue.

7 Dear Lord Jesus, precious Jesus,
    All I have I give to Thee;
  Who like Thee — so fair and comely?
    Who like Thee — so sweet and lovely?
  Matchless One, unrivaled beauty,
    None can e'er compete with Thee!

1 Jesus Lord, I'm captured by Thy beauty,
   All my heart to Thee I open wide;
Now set free from all religious duty,
   Only let me in Thyself abide.
As I'm gazing here upon Thy glory,
   Fill my heart with radiancy divine;
Saturate me, Lord, I now implore Thee,
   Mingle now Thy Spirit, Lord, with mine.

2 Shining One — how clear the sky above me!
   Son of Man, I see Thee on the throne!
Holy One, the flames of God consume me,
   Till my being glows with Thee alone.
Lord, when first I saw Thee in Thy splendor,
   All self-love and glory sank in shame;
Now my heart its love and praises render,
   Tasting all the sweetness of Thy name.

3 Precious Lord, my flask of alabaster
   Gladly now I break in love for Thee;
I anoint Thy head, Beloved Master;
   Lord, behold, I've saved the best for Thee.
Dearest Lord, I waste myself upon Thee;
   Loving Thee, I'm deeply satisfied.
Love outpoured from hidden depths within me,
   Costly oil, dear Lord, I would provide.

4 My Beloved, come on spices' mountain;
   How I yearn to see Thee face to face.
Drink, dear Lord, from my heart's flowing fountain,
   Till I rest fore'er in Thine embrace.
Not alone, O Lord, do I adore Thee,
   But with all the saints as Thy dear Bride;
Quickly come, our love is waiting for Thee;
   Jesus Lord, Thou wilt be satisfied.

1160

(Tune: #542)
8.7.8.7.D.

1 Jesus is our lovely Bridegroom,
And our Bridegroom is with us!
Now our praying's turned to praising
In His presence glorious.

O our Bridegroom! O our Bridegroom!
Lord, Thou art our Bridegroom sweet!
How we treasure Thy dear presence —
O what bliss and joy complete!

2 We are fellows of the Bridegroom
And our fasting days have ceased.
With the Bridegroom in His chamber,
Joyfully we keep the feast.

3 We as virgins may enjoy Him,
Virgins simple, single, chaste.
Going forth to meet the Bridegroom,
Out from all the world we haste.

4 We are guests by God invited
To His Son's great wedding feast.
Brothers, sisters, hallelujah,
From religion we're released!

5 Now rejoice with joy excelling,
Joy of joys, all else beside —
Not just fellows, guests, or virgins,
Hallelujah, we're the Bride!

Hallelujah! Hallelujah!
Lord, Thou art our Bridegroom sweet!
Hallelujah! Hallelujah!
O what bliss and joy complete!

Song of Songs
(Tune: #246 or 268)
8.7.8.7. with chorus.

1161

1 Christ will make His seeking lover
    Pillar, couch, and palanquin,
E'en a crown, His boast and glory;
    He will do it all! Amen!

    His beloved — how He loves her,
      So attractive, His delight.
    He is captivated wholly;
      She is comely in His sight.

2 But there still remains a shadow;
    Christ is still not satisfied.
He must have a growing garden
    To become His loving Bride!

3 Paradise of pomegranates,
    Pleasant fruits, and henna flowers,
Spikenard, saffron, myrrh, and aloes:
    His enjoyment now — not ours.

4 He has come into His garden,
    Gathered myrrh and spices there,
Eaten honeycomb and honey;
    Wine and milk He'll drink fore'er.

5 From the garden comes the city,
    All materials thus supplied;
God is satisfied completely,
    And the foe is terrified.

6 "Thou art fair, my love, as Tirzah,
    Comely as Jerusalem."
O Lord Jesus, Hallelujah,
    Thou wilt do it all! Amen!

1162

John 15

Peculiar Meter.

1 We've found the secret of living,
We've seen the vision divine:
We are of God in Christ Jesus,
We're abiding, abiding in the vine.

Abiding in the vine,
Abiding in the vine,
All the riches of God's life are mine!
Praise God, He put us here,
Never to leave; oh, we're —
Abiding, abiding in the vine.

2 No more in vain need we struggle,
Trying the way in to find.
Praise God — we're in Him already,
Hallelujah, abiding in the vine.

3 In us, the ointment is moving,
'Tis the anointing divine;
God's precious essence bestowing,
While abiding, abiding in the vine.

4 Now in the life-flow we're living,
O how the light in us shines!
Both God and man are at home now
By the mutual abiding in the vine.

John 15

1163

(Tune: #474)

8.7.8.7. with chorus.

1 He's the vine and we're the branches,
   We should e'er abide in Him,
   And let Him abide within us
   As the flow of life within.

     In the vine, in the vine,
     In the vine, in the vine,
     We would know Thee, Lord,
       more deeply,
     E'er abiding in the vine.

2 As we hear His instant speaking,
   He's the rich indwelling Word;
   To abide we must be faithful
   To the speaking that we've heard.

3 For 'tis here we know abiding
   In the real and deepest way;
   If we love our Lord completely,
   We would do whate'er He'd say.

4 Then His love abides within us,
   And in love abiding, we
   Know the joy of life-communion,
   Full and perfect harmony.

5 Oh, how precious this abiding,
   Oh, how intimate and sweet;
   As the fruit of life is added,
   And our joy is made complete.

1164

Deuteronomy 8:7-10
(Tune: #530)
Peculiar Meter.

1 Jesus, the all-inclusive land,
      Is everything to me:
   A Christ of brooks, of depths and streams,
      And fountains bubbling free.
   Springing from valleys and from hills,
   Flowing till every part He fills,
   He waters us — how glorious —
      By His life!

2 Jesus is now the land of wheat —
      Incarnate, crucified.
   But resurrection life is He
      By barley signified.
   He is a land of figs and vines —
   Blood of the grape, the cheering wine.
   With such supplies He satisfies —
      Christ our land!

3 O what a rich, abundant Christ:
      Our pomegranate true,
   The olive tree whose oil is now
      Anointing us anew.
   Rich milk and honey He doth bring,
   Sweet, satisfying, nourishing.
   Our Christ is such; He is so much!
      What a Christ!

4 In our good land we eat the bread —
      There is no scarcity.
   We never lack one thing in Him,
      So rich, so full is He.
   He is a land so vast, immense;
   He is complete in every sense.
   How He expands — land of all lands —
      In our heart!

5 Christ is a land of iron stones,
    Whence comes authority.
  We must dig out this solid Christ
    To bind His enemy.
  Then we must through the sufferings pass
  To be refined as burnished brass.
  With iron bind, as brass refined,
    Is our need.

6 Lord, how we bless Thee for this land,
    The all-inclusive Christ!
  We've eaten Him, we're filled with Him,
    O how He has sufficed!
  Teach us to labor constantly
  Upon this vast reality;
  This is our joy, this our employ —
    Christ our land!

8.8.8.8. with chorus.   **1165**

1 We're in the land, we're in the land!
  O Hallelujah! In the land!
  Christ is the land, Christ is the land,
  O praise the Lord, He is the land!

    He is the milk and honey, too;
    The grain, the oil, the wine so new.
    We're in the land! We're in the land!
    O Hallelujah! In the land!

2 This land includes so many things:
  Wheat, barley, vines, deep-flowing springs,
  Fig trees and never-failing bread —
  O what a land before us spread!

    To have the produce and abound
    We daily labor on the ground;
    Then to the meetings we will bring
    The topmost Christ, our offering!

1166

Deuteronomy 8:7-10
(Tune: #149)
8.7.8.7.7.7. with chorus.

1   God has set the land before us,
    And the land we will possess.
    God has finally found a people
    Tired of the wilderness.
    Down with every weight and sin;
    Let's go up and enter in.

      Hallelujah, Hallelujah,
      Hallelujah, Amen.

2   God has cleared the way before us
    Through the victory of His Son;
    Raised the Victor's banner o'er us,
    All the battles He has won.
    All that's left for us to do
    Is by faith to follow through.

3   It's a land of hills and valleys,
    Brooks of water flowing free;
    Fountains rich with living water,
    Streams that flow abundantly.
    Brothers, joyfully we stand
    In His promise, Christ the land.

4   God has made the fruit to grow here,
    Filled the land with produce sweet:
    Olive oil and pomegranates,
    Fig trees, honey, vines and wheat.
    We need nothing else besides,
    All we need the land provides.

5   We have eaten unto fullness,
    And with joy we bless the Lord,
    For the good land He has given;
    Faithful to His promised Word.
    Here we find there is no lack —
    Never, never we'll go back!

6 All we need to do is labor,
   Working on the land each day;
   Not expecting 'manna' blessing,
   Working in a normal way.
   God and man cooperating
   While for harvest we are waiting.

7 Labor thus will bring the increase
   Of the land with all its worth,
   And the Lord will have the harvest,
   When He comes to reap the earth.
   To provide the Lord the way,
   We must labor day by day.

1167

Peculiar Meter.

1 Laboring on the good land, laboring in the morning,
   Laboring through the noontime to the early eve,
   Laboring for a harvest, reaping all the produce,
   Coming to the meeting, bringing in the sheaves.

   Bringing in the sheaves, bringing in the sheaves,
   Here we are rejoicing, bringing in the sheaves!
   Bringing in the sheaves, bringing in the sheaves,
   Here we are rejoicing, bringing in the sheaves!

2 Reaping wheat and barley, death and resurrection,
   Though the loss sustained our old man often grieves;
   But in life abundant, life in resurrection,
   Coming to the meeting, bringing in the sheaves.

3 Grain and wine and oil — bringing in the surplus
   Of the wheat and barley, vine and olive trees:
   Wine to cause rejoicing, oil to give anointing,
   Bringing in the top tenth, bringing in the sheaves.

1168

10.10.10.10. with chorus.

1 Laboring on Jesus, the good land so real,
  Plowing and planting and watering the field.
  He yields the produce of reality,
  God reaps a harvest of Jesus in me.

> O Jesus! You're God's good land
> For me to labor on!
> I'll bit by bit possess You
> Until the whole is won!
> With Canaan is God's purpose,
> The labor He will bless;
> Lord Jesus, here I gain Yourself,
> Your Person to possess.

2 Laboring on Jesus! My heart has been set,
  Labor's begun, and I have no regret,
  For with my labor God's sending the rain,
  And all my labor on Christ yields much gain.

3 Laboring on Jesus this practical way —
  Praying His Word in the spirit each day,
  Foll'wing His living anointing within,
  Built up with others, the church life to win.

4 Laboring on Jesus yields reality,
  Meetings of fullness for all men to see;
  There God and man are indeed satisfied,
  And there God's presence cannot be denied.

5 Labor on Jesus to have Him increased!
  Then seek God's dwelling and come to the feast!
  There bring and offer your surplus to God,
  There eat the riches, rejoice in the Lord!

(Tune: #903)

1169

8.8.8.8.

1 Our worship in reality
Is typified in Moses' law:
With Canaan's produce, rich and sweet,
All Israel came and worshipped God.

2 'Tis thus that we must come today
To worship in reality:
When we bring Christ as produce sweet
God fully satisfied will be.

3 The worship that God so desired
Was not with manna sent from heav'n,
But from their labor on the land
The people's gifts to God were giv'n.

4 Thus, what God so desires today
Are not the miracles so grand,
But daily, normal life in Christ,
As worship, produce of the land.

5 The manna came from God alone;
The produce, from man's work on Him.
So all our worship now must come
From mingling with the Lord within.

6 As day by day we live in Christ,
And take Him as our everything,
The produce of the land comes forth
And worship true to God we'll bring.

7 The manna, Lord, no more we'll seek,
But Christ in all we will apply;
Then we will have some produce sweet,
Thine own dear heart to satisfy.

1170

Psalm 23
Peculiar Meter.

1 The Lord is my Shepherd forever,
    He maketh me down to lie,
He leads me beside the still waters
    O how He does satisfy!

    Surely goodness and mercy shall follow me
        All the days, all the days of my life;
    Surely goodness and mercy shall follow me
        All the days, all the days of my life.
    And I shall dwell in the house of the Lord
        forever,
    And I shall feast at the table spread for me;
    Surely goodness and mercy shall follow me
        All the days, all the days of my life.

2 My Shepherd Himself is my pasture,
    My Shepherd, the waters of rest;
I eat of His riches in spirit,
    I drink, and O how I am blest!

3 My Shepherd my soul is restoring,
    My will, and emotion, and mind;
And though through the valley I'm walking,
    O what a Companion I find!

4 A table prepared by my Shepherd
    I feast on and Satan destroy;
My head is anointed with oil,
    My cup runneth over with joy!

5 And now in His house I am dwelling
    Enjoying the goodness of God;
My pleasure is far beyond telling,
    My pleasure is Jesus my Lord!

(Tune: Just a Closer Walk With Thee)
Peculiar Meter.

1 In the Testament of old
See th' acacia wood with gold;
Such humanity behold!
Praise the Lord, praise the Lord,
praise the Lord!

2 Jesus is th' acacia wood —
What a man, so fine and good!
All corruption He withstood —
Praise the Lord, praise the Lord,
praise the Lord!

3 Jesus, wisdom of God's plan,
Son of God and Son of Man;
A new manhood He began —
Praise the Lord, praise the Lord,
praise the Lord!

4 For since by the one came death,
By this man came living breath;
Man the Lord recovereth —
Praise the Lord, praise the Lord,
praise the Lord!

5 Types and shadows to us show
Jesus is the man to know.
Now this man in us must grow —
Amen, Lord! Amen, Lord! Amen, Lord!

6 Lord, may Thy humanity
Permeate us thoroughly,
Drawing many men to Thee —
Amen, Lord! Amen, Lord! Amen, Lord!

1172

Peculiar Meter.

1 Lo, the conflict of the ages
   Is upon us today,
And the forces of rebellion
   Are in total array.
The humanity of Jesus
   Now the saints must possess,
His true image and dominion
   On the earth to express.

   Let us stand up in Jesus
      In His full human life,
   Human virtues prevailing
      'Gainst corruption so rife;
   In this wickedness concerted,
   In this age perverse, perverted,
   The humanity of Jesus
      Must the church now display.

2 Lo, how Satan came to damage
   Human life on the earth;
But the Lord in all this ruin
   Raised a man full of worth!
From the seed of the woman
   God incarnate became
The man Jesus — the last Adam —
   To destroy Satan's aim!

3 It's by calling, drinking, eating
   The man Jesus today,
His humanity enjoying
   Bruises Satan each day.
To the Lord we must be turning,
   All our soul life deny,
To destroy all Satan's working
   And the new man supply.

4 See the ruin of a nation
    Going downward in sin;
    All humanity is fallen
    And corrupted within.
    But as children of the kingdom
    We are salting the earth;
    His humanity preserves us
    In the midst of such dearth.

1173

(Tune: #807)
8.8.9.8. with chorus.

1 Grant us the vision clear to see
    We need a new humanity;
    From all our nature, we must be free;
    Eating of Jesus is the key!

    Breathing this man within the Word,
       Calling with them who call "O Lord";
    Eating this man in one accord —
       Breathe, call and eat!

2 Our flesh for building is no good;
    God's house must have acacia wood!
    Christ's human life is balanced and fine,
    And it's adorned with gold divine.

    We want to stand as boards so strong,
       Held by the bars where we belong;
    To be the church for which You long —
       One full-grown man!

3 Satan's one aim: to ruin man,
    Man, who's the center of God's plan!
    But man will rule the earth utterly,
    Conquering every enemy.

    Each time we turn and eat this man
       We put an end to Satan's plan.
    Jesus through His humanity
       Has conquered all!

1174

(Tune: #602)
8.7.8.7.8.7.

1 What a victory! What a triumph!
God Himself became a man,
Clothed Himself in human nature
To fulfill His mighty plan.
He through death destroyed the devil;
Risen now, the Son of Man!

2 Jesus by His human virtues
Did the subtle one arrest;
He as man withstood the tempter,
Fully passed through every test.
Now in spirit I can take Him,
All His virtues to possess.

3 In the Spirit of this Jesus
Is His human life so fine.
Human virtues have been added
To the Spirit all divine.
What abundance in this Spirit,
Rich supply for all mankind!

4 How mysterious! Yet how real!
Such a man now lives in me.
Into all my heart He's spreading —
He, my human life, to be.
Hallelujah! Hallelujah!
I will praise unceasingly.

5 Oh, what wonder! Oh, how glorious!
God in flesh is manifest.
We the members of His Body
His humanity express.
For the building of God's dwelling
We His human life possess.

EXPERIENCE OF CHRIST —
THE POWER OF HIS RESURRECTION

Ephesians 1:19-23
(Tune: #1009)
10.9.10.8. with chorus.

1175

1 Power, exceeding great pow'r is to us,
   To us who believe, us who receive!
   Power that raised Christ, yes, pow'r glorious
   Is giv'n to His Body, the church!

> There is pow'r, pow'r, resurrection pow'r,
>   To the church, to the church!
> There is pow'r, pow'r, resurrection pow'r,
>   Given to His Body, the church!

2 Power that set Christ at God's own right hand,
   This pow'r is to us — yes, even us!
   Power above every name that is named
   Is giv'n to His Body, the church!

> There is pow'r, pow'r, all-transcending pow'r,
>   To the church, to the church!
> There is pow'r, pow'r, all-transcending pow'r,
>   Given to His Body, the church!

3 Power that put all things under His feet
   Is ours here and now — right here and now!
   Power subjecting all, power complete,
   Is giv'n to His Body, the church!

> There is pow'r, pow'r, all-subduing pow'r,
>   To the church, to the church!
> There is pow'r, pow'r, all-subduing pow'r,
>   Given to His Body, the church!

4 Power that made Him o'er all things the Head
   Is now to the church, now to the church!
   Power, such pow'r, will be exhibited
   O'er all through His Body, the church!

> There is pow'r, pow'r, overruling pow'r,
>   To the church, to the church!
> There is pow'r, pow'r, overruling pow'r,
>   Given to His Body, the church!

1176

1 Pow'r exceeding great God did demonstrate
When He raised His Son from the dead.
May this pow'r we see, with it strengthened be,
And in resurrection life be led.

Power, power, resurrection power,
Energize us mightily within!
Power, power, resurrection power,
Energize us in the inner man!

2 Pow'r exceeding high God did magnify
When He raised His Son far above all.
Principalities, pow'rs, and majesties
At the name of Jesus Christ must fall.

Power, power, all-transcending power,
Elevate us mightily within!
Power, power, all-transcending power,
Elevate us in the inner man!

3 Pow'r surpassing too, all things to subdue
Has been given to Christ, pow'r complete.
We His Body are; so, hallelujah,
Everything must be beneath our feet!

Power, power, all-subduing power,
All-subjecting mightily within!
Power, power, all-subduing power,
All-subjecting to the inner man!

4 And the best of all, overruling all,
O'er all to the church Christ is Head.
Pow'r so glorious over all's *to us*;
To the highest place the church is led.

Power, power overruling power,
Ruling over all, without, within!
Power, power, overruling power,
Ruling, reigning, through the inner man!

Peculiar Meter.

1 Oh, Christ in all His glory put on humanity
So He could be my Person, and live instead of me.
A man in life and being, He fully fits my case,
So all His glorious Person can me replace.

> O Lord, O Lord, You are the man for me!
> I take You as my Person, as my full identity.
> O Lord, O Lord, subdue my every part,
> And every moment, every place, make home in all
>   my heart.

2 Oh, Christ became the Spirit to speak inside of me,
And as the speaking Spirit He speaks unceasingly.
His speaking is the water that washes me within,
Discharging all my oldness, imparting Him.

> O Lord, O Lord, speak all You want to me.
> Your speaking is Your presence — I must have it
>   constantly.
> O Lord, O Lord, speak-wash my every part
> And by this metabolic change, make home in all
>   my heart.

3 Oh, Christ will come, the Bridegroom, for us,
    His glorious Bride,
By coming from within us the church is glorified.
His Person is the glory expanding now in us;
This glory is our Person — how glorious!

> O Lord, O Lord, by Your economy
> So flood us with Your glory, saturate us
>   thoroughly.
> Come out, come out, break forth in glory here,
> And from the church, O glorious One, in glory
>   soon appear.

1178

Peculiar Meter.

1 We have seen Christ is reality:
But it's not sufficient just to see:
He in our experience must be
    Everything to us.
We in prayer behold Him face to face,
In the Word and meetings know His grace;
But in daily life, in every place,
    What is He to us?

    Hallelujah! By His light we see
    Oh, how real, how full our Lord will be
    If we'll only turn to Him at every time,
        in every day,
    Every thing, in every way and —
    Be specific for reality!
    And be done with generality!
    If we'll just apply Him, we will see
        He's everything to us.

2 Life is full of opportunities
Ordered by our Father's hand: we see
Everything's the best that it could be,
    So let's gain Christ!
Christ our content and reality
To shine out from us unceasingly:
He must have a way in you and me,
    He must have a way.

    Hallelujah! In the body we
    Bear the death of Christ continually:
    Thus His life comes forth for all to see as
    The outer man is broken down,
    The inner man is shining so that —
    In these earthen vessels men can see
    There's the treasure of reality!
    Thus the gospel's glorious light will be
        Shining out from us.

Not just doctrines and theology,
But the content of reality:
Christ as everything in you and me,
He's everything to us!

(Tune: #154)
10.10.10.10.4.

1179

1 My old man has been crucified with Him,
With all its foul corruption deep within;
And buried too its nature serpentine,
Completely finished — this great fact is mine,
   I hold it fast.

2 But there's a Person in my spirit now,
Born as a babe so small, so weak, so low;
Who by the Word's pure milk will grow to be
The overcoming inner man in me
   To gain my heart.

3 Christ as my Person must possess my heart
And be preeminent in every part.
The former owner died but haunts it still.
O Lord, move in; my mind, emotion, will
   Now welcome Thee.

4 In spirit mingled, we are one, O Lord,
The human and divine in one accord;
Yet Thou must have a proper faculty
That all Thy glorious personality
   May be expressed.

5 So, Lord, I give my heart to Thee today,
That it may be Thy home in every way,
A place for Thee to come and settle down,
And all Thy grand recovery work to crown
   In one new man.

1180

1 My old person has been nullified;
With my Lord upon the cross he died;
Now in nothing shall he be applied;
    He's dead to me.
My new Person in my spirit dwells;
Springing in me as a bubbling well;
Flowing out until each part He fills
    With abundant life.

    Christ, my Person, in my spirit lives;
    And my heart to Him I'd daily give;
    That my inner man could have a home
    And a place to settle down, yes,
    A place to call His own, and —
    There be my complete reality,
    There expressing all He is to me,
    Living in my heart abundantly
        As my Person real.

2 By this Person being formed in me,
I'll a member of His Body be,
No more acting individually,
    But with the saints.
More and more our Person He must be;
That our natural personality
Be eliminated thoroughly
    Till Christ is all.

    Only Christ, our Person, must remain;
    From our aims, our goals we must refrain,
    Till the church be only Christ Himself
    Built up as the one new man,
    Thus fulfilling God's great plan of —
    Mingling fully with the human race
    To obtain a proper dwelling place,
    'Stablishing His kingdom's rule and grace;
        Over all the earth.

Not Himself just individually,
But the church together corporately,
Taking Christ as all in all, to be
The full-grown, perfect man.

(Tune: #221)
8.7.8.7.D. with chorus.

1181

1 Lord, to know Thee as our Person,
    Earnestly we seek and pray;
To experience Thy fulness
    In a constant inner way.
Never longer only outward
    Or with soulish thoughts obsessed,
But, O Lord, in realest contact
    We by Thee would be possessed.

Lord, Thou art our Person,
    In our inmost being,
May we constantly experience
    This reality.

2 All the world is under darkness,
    Driven by the fallen soul,
And the enemy designing
    Does the soulish life control.
Such we were till God, through mercy,
    Caused His Son to dwell in us;
Now we fully come to know Him
    In His church so glorious.

3 Once we walked a soulish person,
    Wandering in the wilderness,
Never knowing that our spirit
    Craved God's fullness to express;
At the moment Jesus entered
    Instantly the whole was changed.
Now we're people spirit-centered!
    Hallelujah! Rearranged!

continued

1113

4　Now our spirit is our person —
　　What a glorious fact is this!
　　Christ Himself in us expressing
　　　God's intent and holiness.
　　Not the soul-life's vain delusion,
　　　But the spirit strengthened is;
　　Christ Himself is now our Person —
　　　He is ours and we are His.

1182　　　　　　　　　　　(Tune: #18)
　　　　　　　　　　　　　　8.6.8.6.D.

1　In spirit and reality
　　We meet to worship Thee,
　　And every principality
　　Must fall down or must flee.
　　　Reality, reality,
　　　O what a joy to see,
　　　That Christ may be enjoyed by us
　　　As our reality.

2　A Person, Thou hast come in us,
　　Into our spirit now,
　　And quickened us until we know
　　Our inner man art Thou.
　　　O praise Thee, Lord, we sense Thee thus,
　　　Forever inwardly;
　　　Thy Person in each one of us
　　　Is our reality.

3　And now the corporate life we live —
　　Christ in His Body known;
　　Where every portion adds more Christ,
　　Until the whole is shown.
　　　O Hallelujah, one new man!
　　　Our portions blend as one;
　　　In one accord, express the Lord,
　　　And He will quickly come.

EXPERIENCE OF CHRIST —
AS THE SON OF MAN AMIDST THE LAMPSTANDS

Revelation 1:9-20

(Tune: #977)

8.7.8.7.D.

1 On the Lord's day, John, in spirit,
Heard a voice and turned and saw
Seven lampstands brightly shining;
Of pure gold, divine, they were.
In the midst of them, appearing,
He beheld the Son of Man,
Ever for the churches caring,
Tending God's eternal plan.

2 His appearance, lo, how different
From the One John knew before.
Now He's girt in golden raiment,
Not the robe which then He wore.
Girt about the breasts and serving,
He the priesthood fully bears;
Cherishing the lampstands dearly,
He for all the churches cares.

3 Ancient One He is, yet fresher
Than the newly driven snow;
Eyes are as a flaming fire,
Feet as burnished brass aglow.
Tender eyes that gazed at Peter,
Now are as a burning flame;
And the voice that whispered, "Mary,"
Many waters now became.

4 John, once formerly reclining
On His breast, now fell as dead,
When he saw Him thus in spirit,
As He is, exhibited.
Lo, the Christ of Revelation!
See Him, thus intensified,
That the lampstands, His expression,
May be strengthened and supplied.

Revelation 1

(Tune: #835)

8.8.8.8.

1 In Revelation chapter one
   God gives a vision of the Son,
   Of Him who was and is to come;
   Oh, let us to this One now come.

2 In spirit hear His trumpet voice;
   We must be turned to see His choice —
   The seven lampstands golden fair;
   The Son of Man is walking there.

3 The great high priestly robe He wears,
   For every church He fully cares:
   He trims the lamp, the oil supplies;
   He makes them burn, flames in His eyes.

4 A golden girdle on His breast —
   His work is done, and from His rest
   He unto all the churches pours
   Himself in love, the treasure store.

5 His head, His hair is white as wool —
   The ancient One with youth is full.
   His face is shining as the sun
   To burn and lighten every one.

6 Oh, when this living One we see,
   We'll fall as dead, we'll finished be.
   But then the Lord His comfort gives —
   He once was dead, but now He lives.

7 Let every church just love Him more —
   His riches then He will outpour.
   All other loves now lay aside;
   Let's take this Jesus, none beside.

John 5:1-9

1185

(Tune: #628)

8.7.8.7.D.

1 In the multitude he lay there
With a sickness many years;
Impotent and lying helpless,
Ever fraught with many fears.
Waiting for the water's moving,
Waiting for the angel's stir;
Powerless to move, however,
Helpless, hopeless, lying there.

2 At this pool how clear the picture
Of the hopeless case of all
Who are seeking self-perfection
To recover from the fall.
Though the law is good and holy,
Flesh, to keep the law, is dead;
What we need is not religion,
But the Word of life instead.

3 Though it's feast day, he's not happy,
Though the Sabbath, there's no rest;
Lying in his poor condition,
Miserable and sore depressed.
At that moment Jesus saw him,
Knowing he was thus so long.
"Will you be made whole?" He asked him,
"Healed and walking, well and strong?"

4 Though he told his hopeless story,
Scarce believing what he'd heard,
Yet, soon to his feet arising,
He received the living word.
This is all our situation,
We — like him — were lying there
In the sheep-fold of religion,
Under law's prevailing care. *continued*

5 While we yet were weak and helpless,
    Christ the Son of God did come.
  By His word we're now enlivened;
    He's the life-imparting One!
  Hallelujah for this Jesus,
    He's the Word of life to men;
  From law's bondage He releases,
    Death is turned to life again!

EXPERIENCE OF CHRIST — VERSUS RELIGION

1186

John 1:19-36
(Tune: #887)
8.6.8.6.D.

1 The scribes and Pharisees all thought
    A leader great would come.
  So they to John the Baptist came
    To ask if he's the One.
  "Art thou the Coming One?" they asked,
    To which he made reply:
  "I'm not the Christ — I am not He —
    A voice, that's all, am I."

2 And on the morrow, John stood there
    And spoke to two or three.
  And as he lifted up his eyes,
    He then did Jesus see.
  He said, "Behold the Lamb of God,
    'Tis He Who walks this way.
  He's here to take the sins of all
    And bear them all away!"

3　Yet poor religion counted not
　　These things of any worth,
　　But seeking for a leader great
　　It lingered on in dearth;
　　And looking for a movement strong,
　　Continued in its strife.
　　Preoccupied with all these things,
　　They missed the Lord of LIFE!

4　Religion is Christ's enemy,
　　It's even so today.
　　For though they name Him, should
　　　He come,
　　They'd put the Lord away.
　　They did it then, they'd do it now,
　　They'd miss the Lord again.
　　So let us seek the Lord Himself,
　　The lamb, the dove obtain.

5　Now in the Lord's recovery
　　We're drawn to Christ alone.
　　The Spirit as the gentle dove
　　Has found in us a home.
　　Let all religion turn away
　　To movements wide and great;
　　This testimony of Himself
　　Our Lord will vindicate!

Hebrews 8
(Tune: #146)
6.6.6.6.8.8.

1 Your ministry, O Lord,
     How excellent it is;
   A better covenant,
     And better promises;
   Enacted on a better law.
   Of such You are Executor.

2 A better covenant,
     And better promises;
   A better law of life
     And sacrifice this is.
   Redemption's work, done long ago,
   A better blood has made it so.

3 In Hebrews eight we see
     The way to make us whole;
   Life planted deep within,
     Which spreads into the soul.
   The law of life, imparted, still
   Inscribed in mind, emotion, will.

4 The law of letters leave,
     The law of life pursue;
   The one is old and dead,
     The other fresh and new.
   Dead teachings cannot help the seed;
   The law of life is what we need.

5 The law of life in us,
     In function now we see,
   Works not by will and thought
     But automatically.
   It saturates, conforms to Him;
   The standard model spreads within.

6   Our sins are all forgiv'n,
     His life imparted too;
God is our God today,
     And we're His people true.
We know Him in an inward way:
These blessings four have come to stay.

7   We're being sonized now;
     The life within will do
The deep transforming work
     Of making us anew.
In ages past, the work was done —
Now prayer is over — praise the Son!

Hebrews 8   **1188**
(Tune: #330)
8.6.8.6.D.

1   Upon the throne of Jesus Christ
     We've taken up our seat.
The world and Satan, sin and self
     Are all beneath our feet!
Christ's finished work did put us here,
     When once for all He died;
No more are we the sinners poor,
     We're fully glorified.

2   We're dwelling in the house of God,
     The church life glorious.
The shrinking-back, low Christian life,
     Is not the life for us!
We're passing through the Holy Place
     Of mind, emotion, will;
We're dwelling in the Holiest
     Where God our being fills.

continued

3 We're under the New Covenant,
   With glorious items, three:
The law of life, spontaneous,
   Transforming utterly;
We are His people, He's our God —
   Oh, bless'd reality;
We all are fully able now
   To know God inwardly.

4 A supplement God added then;
   This item we must know:
Christ Jesus did put sin away
   Two thousand years ago.
No memory of sin at all,
   It's hist'ry, done and gone;
In spirit now the law of life
   Will take us swiftly on.

5 Two things accomplished by our Lord
   On Calvary's cross, we see:
The law of life, the end of sin!
   Our God's economy.
Since all His work was finished there,
   He entered into rest;
Now on the throne He prays that we
   Will take our full bequest.

6 We'll drop our former concepts, Lord,
   To take this finished way;
Appropriating each bequest,
   We'll praise You more each day.
We'll heed our High Priest's inward call —
   "Come forward!" to the end —
Until we reach the final goal;
   The New Jerusalem!

(Tune: #1115)
11.11.11.11.

1 Son of Man, Son of Man on the throne today;
Son of Man, Pioneer, He has led the way;
Following, how we sing, Jesus leads us on;
We are marching with the Victor to the throne.

2 On we go, on we go to the throne with Him;
On we go through this age, age so dark and grim;
Then shall we — formerly, Satan's captured ones —
Be exalted with the Lord upon His throne.

3 Called as sons, called as sons, destined to be kings;
Called as sons we've no time for the worldly things:
Yet we know, it is so — we don't qualify!
Thus the Lord must search and burn and purify.

4 Search and burn, search and burn all our
    inward parts;
Search and burn, thoroughly, to refine our hearts;
We'll not fear, but be clear — burning, searching thus
Is the gracious visit of the Lord to us.

5 With the Man, with the Man is a rainbow fair;
Glorious bow, 'round the throne, faithfulness declares:
We deserved to be served with God's judgment sore,
But we have been spared to praise Him more
    and more.

1190

Genesis 12
(Tune: #256)
12.12.12.8. with chorus.

1 O Lord, You've called to us, and Canaan we would win,
To be Your corporate man and dwell with You therein;
But how the darkness of this world does hold us in —
  O Lord, appear to us, we pray.

    O Lord, appear to us today;
    We see this is the only way.
    The idols to forsake
    And Canaan land partake,
    O Lord, appear to us today.

2 O God of glory, shine; draw and we'll follow You.
Our strength and motive be, it's nothing we could do.
Your light attracts us, Lord, 'til all else fades from
    view —
  O Lord, do shine on us, we pray.

    O Lord, do shine on us today;
    Till all our background fades away,
    Till You alone we see,
    Shining so gloriously —
    O Lord, do shine on us today.

3 In Your appearing, Lord, we have Your speaking clear;
Your word empowers us and drives away all fear.
So, Lord, keep calling us, Your voice we need to hear.
  O Lord, do speak to us, we pray.

    O Lord, do speak in us today;
    You know the words You need to say.
    To open all our heart,
    Your very Self impart.
    O Lord, do speak in us today.

4 O Lord, it's not of us, we've seen it's all of You;
   You are the calling One, Originator too!
   We can receive this call by our beholding You —
   O God of glory, come, we pray.

   O God of glory, come today;
   We've seen this is the only way
   To answer Your dear call
   That You might be our all —
   O God of glory, come today.

EXPERIENCE OF GOD — AS LIFE

1191

12.8.12.8. with chorus.

1 From my spirit within flows a fountain of life —
   The Triune God flowing in me;
   God the Father's the source, Christ the Son is
      the course,
   And the Spirit imparts life to me.

   Lord, I treasure the sweet flow of life,
   And my soul-life at last I lay down;
   O Lord, deepen the pure flow of life;
   At Your coming may life be my crown.

2 In the fresh, tender grass Jesus makes me lie down;
   He leads me by waters of rest;
   No more struggle and strain; all self-effort is vain;
   In the flow I am perfectly blessed.

3 Jesus called me one day to the Holiest Place,
   To live in His presence divine;
   Hallelujah, I've heard an encouraging word:
   "Abide — you're a branch in the vine."

1192

Genesis 1
(Tune: #495)
7.7.7.7.

1 Chapter one of Genesis:
   Life is God's one emphasis,
   Showing Christ subjectively,
   Step by step He grows in me.

2 Just as earth became a waste,
   Death and darkness once I faced.
   God had judged, no light did shine;
   Hollowness and void were mine.

3 Satan's fall had filled the seas
   With corruption, sin, disease.
   Yet the Spirit brooded o'er
   The abyss: chaos no more!

4 God then spoke: the air was cleared!
   Darkness which I once had feared
   Was dispelled by God's own light.
   A new day! No longer night!

5 As the light began to shine
   His discernment became mine.
   I began to see aright;
   God divided dark from light.

6 Then the waters He did split;
   An expanse between them fit,
   Earthly things from heavenly,
   Separated hence they'd be.

7 On the third day God designed
   That the waters be confined.
   In our lives dry land must be;
   No more death and no more sea!

8 God commands: death's water halt!
Christ, the good land, we exalt!
Separated from all strife
We enjoy Christ as our life.

9 Growing in us inwardly;
Grass, then herb, then fruitful tree.
We begin as but a blade;
Soon our being He'll pervade.

10 Then the fourth day lights He set;
Bearers these, more definite.
Richer light to radiate,
Higher life to generate.

11 Sun, the greater light we see
Ruling day triumphantly;
Yet when darkness fills the skies,
Waxing moon is on the rise!

12 'Tis the Church she typifies;
For her light on Christ relies.
In His image meant to be,
She reflects Christ perfectly.

13 Lastly, precious stars He placed,
Strong in spirit, full of grace;
Shining when the moon seems faint,
These are overcoming saints.

14 What a glorious picture here:
Sun and moon and stars appear!
Lord, our prayer is that we'd be
Full of light and life in Thee.

EXPERIENCE OF GOD — AS LIFE

1193

Peculiar Meter.

1 Life is God the Father in Christ Jesus
  As the Spirit flowing into us.
  How enjoyable, this Person wonderful!
  He's our life so rich and bountiful.

2 We experienced regeneration
  When we opened to this living One.
  We were born again; another life came in.
  Now it floods us till we're full of Him.

3 He within us is the living Spirit
  In our spirit, flowing out of it
  Into all our heart, transforming every part
  By the life which He Himself imparts.

4 Now He must have our cooperation.
  We must set our mind upon the Son.
  We must turn away from all that leads astray,
  Till our mind is set on Him each day.

5 Lord, our human spirit now contains You.
  Still Your purpose in us You would do;
  If our wandering mind would leave old
      thoughts behind,
  Then Your life and peace in it we'll find.

6 Lord, we would our every thought be captured
  By the rich enjoyment in Your Word.
  In it we're supplied, our mind there will abide,
  Till our thoughts are wholly sanctified.

7 Let's keep practicing the application
  Of this life by minding just the Son.
  Praise Him for the way to live by Him today!
  Lord, on You our minds will ever stay.

Peculiar Meter.

1 There are two lines to live by in our living today —
One the life line to bring us into Christ all the way.
But the other is knowledge which will make us die;
We must be very careful on which line we abide.

Oh, we'll stay on God's life line, never
turning aside.
We don't care for vain knowledge, which
will cause us to die.
Lord, we'll touch You by calling on Your
name each day;
Living in Your appearing, in Your
presence we'll stay.

2 Lord, we would be as Abel, fully contacting You;
Not by knowledge or concept, but by life fresh
and new.
Just as Enosh began to call upon Your name,
And as Enoch who walked with You, we'll do just
the same.

Keep us living and walking as did old Abraham;
In Your holy appearing to be transfused like him.
As did Isaac and Jacob, Moses lived this way —
So dependent upon Your presence with him each day.

Full enjoyment had David, ate the life-giving tree.
Daniel prayed to his God and lived by Him constantly.
Jesus lived by the Father to be life complete;
Now as His living Body of the life tree we'll eat.

1195

(Tune: #549)
10.10.10.10.

1 Life is mysterious, life is God Himself,
   Whose whole intention focuses on man.
   God made him to take in the tree of life,
   To have a man of life for His own plan.

2 But man was tempted and seduced to sin,
   By taking knowledge from the other source.
   This man then fell as knowledge entered in
   And dominated him with all its force.

3 This knowledge has developed in the man
   Into the human culture on the earth.
   So man, created to fulfill God's plan,
   Became a failure full of Satan's dearth.

4 Then God came in the Person of the Son;
   Lived He on earth, Christ Jesus was His name —
   A living model so that everyone
   Could live by life, God's fullness to obtain.

5 This God-man, Christ, went to the cross and died,
   By death He ended knowledge, the old man.
   Things negative forever crucified,
   Death He subdued, a new life He began!

6 From death He resurrected and became
   The living Spirit to give life to us.
   When we believe and call upon His name;
   This living Spirit comes to dwell in us.

7 By this the very Triune God is now
   The living Spirit mingling deep within.
   Our spirit joins in oneness; this is how
   We are one spirit evermore with Him.

8 'Tis by this Spirit that we walk and act,
   We have our being, think, and see all things;
   We're now within this Spirit! What a fact!
   This Spirit to us all God's fullness brings!

9 So now we have to set our mind on Him;
  Each day, each hour, our mind on Him must be;
  That by this Spirit we'd be saved within
  By life and reign in life eternally.

10 'Tis by this Spirit that we shall be freed
  From Sin whose law inside us death would bring.
  Our mortal bodies will have life indeed;
  Thus sanctified we'll be in everything.

11 This Spirit shall transform our natural life,
  Save us from self, build us in one new man,
  Till we're conformed to be like Jesus Christ,
  Thus finishing our God's eternal plan.

12 Life is our God and life is Christ our Lord.
  Life is the Spirit. Life's the only way —
  Till we're transfigured and redeemed to God.
  We're waiting, looking forward to that day!

Peculiar Meter.   **1196**

1 Our God is living — say, Hallelujah!
  He's living in us — say, Hallelujah!
    We taste His riches,
    He is our portion.
  Just say 'O Lord' to taste and see.

2 We come together — there's nothing better —
  For in the Spirit we are His family,
    His living Body!
    We just express Him.
  Jesus is our reality.

3 In all the churches we're being filled now
  For the saturation throughout the nation,
    To spread our Jesus
    To every city —
  This land will see the living Christ.

EXPERIENCE OF GOD — AS LIGHT

1197

1 John 1:5-7
Peculiar Meter.

God is light, and in Him there is no darkness at all!
Oh, how we love within His presence to dwell!
In this light we enjoy a constant cleansing within —
From every sin!

Sisters:	In the light,
Brothers:	We are walking —
Sisters:	Fellowship,
Brothers:	We're enjoying;
Sisters:	And the blood
Brothers:	Of God's Son
Everyone:	Is cleansing us from sin.

Sisters:	We confess,
Brothers:	He is faithful
Sisters:	To forgive —
Brothers:	He is righteous.
Sisters:	What a joy!
Brothers:	We are cleansed
Everyone:	From every sin!

EXPERIENCE OF GOD — HIS DISPENSATION

1198

(Tune: #886)
Peculiar Meter.

1 A mighty flowing-out is God,
   He flows throughout the ages.
   And so to flow Himself to man
   He is in many stages;
   Yet still one God is He,
   One flow eternally;
   His stages pave the way
   To flow through man today,
   And now He flows within us!

2   In the beginning we can see,
    God as a flowing river,
    The river to convey the tree,
    Himself as life deliver.
    And at the end the same,
    The river doth remain,
    God in the Lamb doth flow,
    The tree prevails to grow,
    And God flows on forever.

3   God flowed Himself into a man,
    The man we call Christ Jesus.
    He gave up His own life for man
    And God's own life releases.
    Though Satan did his best
    To put God's flow to rest —
    He had Him crucified
    And cruelly pierced His side —
    But out came blood and water!

4   The blood and water flowed from Him,
    In streams of pure salvation.
    The blood brings cleansing from all sin;
    Water, regeneration.
    And now the Spirit flows,
    Brings God where'er He goes.
    All he could do, the foe,
    Was just release the flow.
    And God just keeps on flowing.

1199

(Tune: #1017)
15.15.15.6. with chorus.

1 God's intention in this universe is with humanity, [be.
So the Lord became the Spirit just with man to mingled
We rejoice that we can all partake of His economy.
    Yes, mingling is the way.

        Mingle, mingle, hallelujah,
        Mingle, mingle, hallelujah,
        Mingle, mingle, hallelujah,
        Yes, mingling is the way!

2 In the center of our being, past our mind, emotion, will,
Is a certain spot created to contain the Lord until
By His flowing and His flooding He will all our being fill;
    Yes, mingling is the way.

3 Now within the Lord's recov'ry, we're so glad to find
    the way
To experience the Triune God and live by Him today —
Get into the mingled spirit, and within the spirit stay;
    Yes, mingling is the way.

4 In the midst of seven lampstands, now the Son of Man
    we see;
Eyes ablaze and feet a'burning, He's for God's recovery.
God's intention He's accomplishing — a corporate entity;
    Yes, mingling is the way.

5 In our daily life and all we are and do and think and
    say,   [each day;
How we need a deeper mingling just to gain the Lord
Lord, we give ourselves completely just to take the
    mingled way.
    Yes, mingling is the way.

6 From the fruit of daily living, New Jerusalem we'll see,
It's the ultimate in mingling — it's divine humanity.
And what joy that we can share it all, and share it
    corporately.
    Yes, mingling is the way.

Ezekiel 1:4
Peculiar Meter.

1 There's a stormy wind a-blowing from the north;
    Let it blow! Let it blow!
God as our exp'rience will the wind bring forth;
    Let it blow! Let it blow!

> Let it blow! the rushing mighty wind;
>   Let it blow us into life!
> Let it blow! the gracious wind of God;
>   Let it blow us into Christ!

2 There's a hov'ring cloud a-following the wind,
    Covering us! Covering us!
And the presence of the Lord the cloud does bring,
    Covering us! Covering us!

> Covering us, God's overshadowing cloud —
>   God has come to stay with us.
> Covering us, the gracious cloud of God —
>   Strength and comfort glorious!

3 With the cloud continually a fire does flash
    Burning us! Burning us!
It exposes sin, the soul life, and the flesh,
    Burning us! Burning us!

> Let it burn! the jealous flame of God;
>   Let it burn continually!
> Let it burn! this all-consuming flame;
>   Let it burn us thoroughly!

4 Then from out the fire does the electrum glow,
    Shining forth! Shining forth!
The redeeming God does our experience show,
    Shining forth! Shining forth!

continued

Let Him shine! This gold and silver One;
Let Him shine for all to see!
'Tis the Lamb-God who has now become
Our enjoyment inwardly.

5 Let the wind, cloud, fire and th' electrum be
Wrought in us, o'er and o'er;
Let this cycle be repeated constantly
More and more, more and more!

Blow and hover, burn and shine forth, Lord,
All our being to possess,
That we all may gain Thee constantly
All Thy likeness to express.

1201
Ezekiel 1:4-10
(Tune: #325)
8.7.8.7.D.

1 From the north where God is dwelling
Comes a rushing, stormy gale.
Now the mighty Spirit blowing
All our being does assail.
We are stirred to our foundations —
How this wind awakens us!
Thus we're open for God's dealings,
And the cloud descends on us.

2 With the cloud we have His presence
Sweetly hov'ring over us;
So enveloped by His nearness;
In the Lord we put our trust.
But the cloud brings with it fire
To consume our selfish lusts;
That as ashes something higher
May be added into us.

3 Then from out the flashing fire
   Comes th' electrum glowing bright.
   God as gold and man as silver
   Now are mingled. What a sight!
   This bright metal, O Lord Jesus,
   Is Thyself, Lamb-God sublime.
   O Lord, work Thyself within us
   Till th' electrum in us shines.

4 By our passing through this cycle,
   Living creatures we become
   To express the life of Jesus;
   He with whom we've been made one.
   We express Him as a human,
   As a man so good and fine;
   Balanced, normal, never striving;
   Fully human, yet divine.

5 We express Him as a lion
   Conquering every enemy;
   As an ox obedient, lowly,
   Faithful in His ministry.
   We express Him as an eagle,
   So transcendent, soaring high;
   Never held by fear or flatter,
   He above it all does fly.

6 Hallelujah! What a figure
   Of the way God deals with us!
   From the wind, cloud, fire, electrum,
   To the creatures glorious:
   As the man, the ox and lion,
   As the eagle — all the four
   Will be our complete expression
   As we eat Him more and more.

EXPERIENCE OF GOD —
HIS PURPOSE IN JUSTIFICATION
(Tune: #431 First tune)
10.10.10.10.

1 God in His justifying has a plan,
A deeper purpose for a corporate man.
When we were called, this mighty Lord of all
Appeared to us to save us from the fall.

2 We walked as strangers unaware of Him,
But in His glory God shined deep within,
Infusing His own element in us;
This precious essence was our Lord Jesus.

3 What glory! How attractive was this light!
How we appreciated such a sight!
Our first reaction was belief in Him —
This precious God has placed Himself within.

4 Our first reflection of this element
Reflected Jesus back to God, Who sent
His own response to count as righteousness
Our faith in Him Who was infused in us.

5 But we would hold to this reality,
Our Jesus Christ in us our all to be,
Enjoying all He is abundantly,
Content to have this One eternally.

6 Thus God could never be so satisfied;
Knowing that we cared only to abide
In our experiences of His Son,
Not caring for His goal to make us one.

7 Still He would seek those faithful saints
who'd hear
His call to give up everything so dear,
To offer up their individual Christ;
To come together for the Body life.

EXPERIENCE OF GOD —
HIS RIGHTEOUSNESS, HOLINESS, AND GLORY
Romans
1203
(Tune: #977)
8.7.8.7.D.

1 God is righteous in His doings,
　　He is perfect in His ways;
　　Just is He in all His actions,
　　And He well deserves our praise.
　　Righteous was His condemnation,
　　Righteous His requirement;
　　For the law had deemed us sinners,
　　And for judgment we were meant.

2 Oh, how blest the love that spared us,
　　For the law had judged us dead.
　　God, to meet the righteous judgment,
　　Passed it on His Son instead.
　　Hallelujah! Our Redeemer,
　　Christ, to God has purchased us;
　　Now enjoying His redemption,
　　We become God's righteousness.

3 God is holy in His nature,
　　Holiness is what He is.
　　In this way He sanctified us,
　　Makes our nature one with His.
　　Spreading from our quickened spirit,
　　He renews each inward part,
　　Moving into all our being,
　　Making home in all our heart.

4 Oh, how blessed is this process!
　　It's the Lord's life-saving way.
　　It's our constant, real experience;
　　It's our life from day to day.
　　As we're minding just the spirit,
　　Then the mind is life to us,
　　And the Lord in us is gaining
　　Transformation marvelous!

continued

5   Glory is God's true expression,
All He is, in full, expressed;
Final stage of our redemption,
Bodily made manifest.
Glory is the consummation
Of this life which sanctifies;
Our complete transfiguration
Is the goal which life supplies.

6   'Tis for this we wait, expecting
To be raptured, glorified.
Then the earth will see God's fullness;
Christ completely testified.
We fore'er will just express Him,
Nature will rejoice to see
All the sons of God in glory
Manifested finally.

7   By His mercy, we're selected,
Ours a glorious destiny.
Not by running, nor by willing,
But through God's own sovereignty.
Once we were wild olive branches,
Now the root and fat partake,
Grafted in, rejoice together,
Growing for the kingdom's sake.

8   As we're daily in this process
And by life are sanctified,
How we thank Him for the blessing
Of the church life He's supplied.
Here God is our full enjoyment,
Practical and real to us;
Sons we are, and heirs together,
In the church life, glorious!

(Tune: #620)
Peculiar Meter.

1 The cross — we all were there,
   Hallelujah! hallelujah!
For all that death did share!
   Hallelujah! hallelujah!
God there upon it died,
And man and all beside
Were wholly crucified —
   Hallelujah for the cross!

      Hallelujah! hallelujah!
      Hallelujah for the cross!
      Hallelujah! hallelujah!
      It shall never suffer loss!

2 The cross, it holdeth fast,
   Hallelujah! hallelujah!
All things upon it cast,
   Hallelujah! hallelujah!
Two arms extended strong
Hold those who there belong;
We're through with self — our song:
   Hallelujah for the cross!

3 'Tis there man died in God,
   Hallelujah! hallelujah!
There ceased this human clod,
   Hallelujah! hallelujah!
With joy we all declare,
We're terminated there!
We'll sing now and fore'er,
   Hallelujah for the cross!

continued

4 'Tis there man died in God,
  Hallelujah! hallelujah!
Fulfilling thus His plan,
  Hallelujah! hallelujah!
Through death He was released
And now He has increased;
His life is our rich feast —
  Hallelujah for the cross!

Hallelujah! hallelujah!
God has been released in us!
Hallelujah! hallelujah!
Hallelujah for the cross!

ENCOURAGEMENT — FOR PRESSING ON

1205   Philippians 3:10-14
              8.6.8.6. with chorus.

1 Press on, press on toward the goal —
  The all-inclusive Christ.
To gain the prize of God's high call,
  Press on, press on to Christ!

Pressing on! Pressing on!
Pressing on! Hallelujah for the prize
We're pressing on! On and on!
To gain the Christ of God!

2 Press on, press on, count all things loss,
  All that is gain to us,
To win the prize, the Christ of God,
  Is far more glorious!

3 Press on, press on to know the Lord
  And resurrection power —
Oh, this is our supreme reward,
  E'en in the suffering hour!

ENCOURAGEMENT — FOR PRESSING ON

4 Press on, press on, this one thing do,
   Forget the things behind;
   Press onward to the Christ before,
   Press onward with this mind!

ENCOURAGEMENT — FOR RUNNING THE RACE

Hebrews 12:1-2

1206

11.9.11.9. with chorus.

1 There's a race for us to run — Hallelujah,
   And a way for us the race to win.
   To all those who have begun — Hallelujah,
   God has spoken, "Look away to Him!"

   Look away! O look away!
   Look to Jesus now today!
   Look away from everything unto Jesus,
   Look away from everything to Him!

2 Look away from all around — Hallelujah,
   Look away from all the strife and din;
   Look away where peace is found — Hallelujah,
   Look away from everything to Him.

3 Look away from fickle soul — Hallelujah,
   Look away from failing self within;
   Look away toward the goal — Hallelujah,
   Look away from everything to Him.

4 Look away from all the past — Hallelujah,
   Look away from both the good and sin;
   To the living One hold fast — Hallelujah,
   Look away from everything to Him.

5 Look away into His face — Hallelujah,
   He who'll finish what He did begin.
   O what grace to run the race — Hallelujah —
   We obtain by looking off to Him!

1207

Hebrews 12:1-2
(Tune: #1200)
Peculiar Meter.

1 There's a way before us and a race to run —
    Christ our way, Christ our way!
   Turn away from everything distracting us —
    Run the race, run the race!
   From the altar through the Holy Place,
    Through the veil into our God,
   To the law of life within the ark;
    'Tis the goal, our great reward.

2 There's a cloud of witnesses surrounding us,
    Urging us, forward come!
   There is Abel, Enoch, Jacob, Abraham,
    Moses, David, Solomon.
   John the Baptist greater than them all,
    Even he bids forward come! ·
   These all died in faith, receiving not
    Promises that were to come.

3 The Old Testament believers give the call,
    "Forward come, forward come!"
   For complete perfection they depend on us
    Going on! Going on!
   We are at the consummation now
    Of our God's economy;
   Better things we are experiencing.
    Praise the Lord — reality!

4 E'en the least of us is greater than their great.
    We're not small, we're not small!
   They are waiting, watching, and expecting us.
    "Forward come!" hear their call!
   They have run the race and for their sakes
    We'll obey the law of life.
   Till the day we'll all be joined in one
    To express God's glorious Christ.

ENCOURAGEMENT —
FOR ENTERING THE HOLY OF HOLIES
(Tune: #342)
9.9.9.4. with chorus.

1208

1 Years I spent in sorrow 'round the cross,
 Still repenting over sins and dross.
 Then at last the river I did cross,
   To touch the throne.

   Mercy now is flowing, oh, the grace —
   That I find of Him to run the race!
   Boldly now I come again to taste
     My glorious Lord.

2 In my Christian life I'd daily fall,
 So I answered every altar-call,
 Till I left the altar, left it all,
   To touch the throne.

3 Brothers, to the Holiest forward come;
 Leave your sins behind, the race now run.
 Hallelujah! All the work is done —
   The veil is gone!

4 Now within the veil, enjoying God,
 Manna, law of life, and budding rod;
 Christ Himself, the ark, is our abode —
   Hallelujah!

(Tune: #300 Second tune)   **1209**
6.6.6.6.8.8.

1   Praise God for tidings glad —
     We're at the throne of grace;
     Our gospel's not so low,
     We're in the highest place.
   We're meeting here around the throne,
   Enjoying God with all His own.

2   Start in the outer court,
     But aim to get inside;
     The Holy Place is good,
     But do not there abide.
   Leave sin behind — it's put away;
   We're in the veil with God to stay.
continued

ENCOURAGEMENT —
FOR ENTERING THE HOLY OF HOLIES

3   To rise from earth to heav'n,
     A deeper turn we need;
     To be where Christ is now
     Upon the throne indeed.
   We're gathered at the throne of grace,
   Beholding Jesus face to face.

4   We're being turned as one,
     Not individually;
     Not private Christians now,
     But Body Christians we.
   As members here in one accord,
   We are the Body of the Lord.

5   As Body Christians now
     We have a higher word.
     Foundation's word we see,
     'Tis altar, cross, and blood.
   Perfection's word is little known,
   'Tis fellowship around the throne.

6   Christ is objective too,
     But subjective are we
     In our experience;
     Our spirit is the key.
   God, throne, and holiest — we see
   Our spirit now contains all three.

7   Leviticus is past,
     And Aaron's work is o'er;
     Melchisedec is here,
     High Priest forevermore;
   His ministry is now so fine:
   He comes to feed us bread and wine.

Romans 8:17-39   **1210**
(Tune: #713)
10.9.10.9.D.

1 Through God's word, my hope at His returning
  Is that all my being be redeemed;
  Yet in times of grief and tribulation,
  Doubt and fear arise, no hope is seen.
  In those hours, when prayer cannot be uttered,
  Only groaning from my breast is heard.
  Then the Spirit, in like manner, helps me,
  Praying in my weakness unto God.

2 Lord, my prayer is not for deeper suffering,
  But that from each trial I'd be free.
  Let the cup of bitterness be taken;
  Yet, Thy will, not mine, dear Lord, must be.
  Even now, though trials sore surround me,
  Still within my heart there is a peace,
  For the love of God outpoured within me
  Floods my heart and bids my doubting cease.

3 Blest assurance! God has fully ordered
  Every matter by His sovereign hand;
  Every person (though we see so dimly),
  Every thing's according to His plan.
  Every trial is but the Father's answer
  To the groaning of the Spirit's prayer;
  May He gain in every tribulation,
  Until we Christ's glory fully share.

4 How could God from all His dealings spare us,
  After He spared not His only Son?
  Could the Potter's hand upon the vessel
  Ever leave the shaping work undone?
  For the center of God's heart's desire
  Is that many brethren we will be
  Unto Christ, His precious First-begotten,
  And to Him, conformed we'll fully be. *continued*

5   Heirs of God! Joint-heirs with our Lord Jesus!
    What a hope of glory this for us!
    Though the suff'rings presently seem grievous,
    Greater far the glory then for us!
    Yea, in all these things we more than conquer,
    Through the One whose love has us possessed;
    Soon the day for which waits all creation,
    When the sons of God are manifest!

VARIOUS ASPECTS OF THE INNER LIFE
THE GROWTH IN LIFE

1211
2 Peter 1:3-11
(Tune: #1115)
11.11.11.11.

1 Given us, given us, God has given us
   Precious faith, power divine, greatest promises.
   We believed, we received, now we have all three;
   By these we may grow unto maturity.

2 Precious faith in each saint, precious equally,
   Precious faith holding us, holding ceaselessly.
   Disagree or agree, still it holds us fast,
   Day by day, eternally this faith shall last.

3 Power divine wrought in us is the source so great;
   Power divine is in us now to operate.
   Hence will spring everything for our life within
   And for godliness without, expressing Him.

4 Promises, promises, all God's called ones share;
  Promises, given us, great and precious are.
  These we take to partake of God's nature true,
  Having thus escaped the world's corruption too.

5 Christ within, as the pow'r, in our spirit lives;
  Christ without is the Word — all God's promises.
  Now the key is that we daily contact both,
  Calling, praying, reading to produce the growth.

6 Faith and pow'r, promises — these our full supply.
  Diligence, diligence, let us now apply;
  For if we, to these three, full attention show
  From the seed of faith the fruit of love will grow.

7 In the growth from the seed many items come;
  By this growth in the Lord fruitful we become.
  For this we need to see what the Lord's begun,
  Ne'er forgetful be nor blind to what He's done.

8 Diligence day by day will this growth insure;
  Diligence thus will make our election sure.
  When indeed with this seed we cooperate,
  We're supplied the kingdom's entrance, rich and great.

9 For this growth, for this growth, Lord, ourselves we give,
  By the faith, promises, and the pow'r to live.
  Nothing more, nothing less, will our basis be
  By Thy grace we will cooperate with Thee.

1212

8.6.8.6.D.

1 The Lord of all has shown His plan
    Unto each faithful one,
Who leaves behind the worldly things
    As virgins for His Son.
To be His Bride we must match Him,
    Within and outwardly;
To be this one who matches Him,
    Enjoy Him constantly.

2 Like virgins who so single are,
    They love the Groom so much,
They in His presence ever stay —
    Lord Jesus, make us such.
Lord, make us those who are so wise,
    Who gain You every day,
The wise ones who enjoy the feast,
    Who all the price will pay.

3 The virgins are mature in life,
    They grow so normally.
They daily eat and drink the Lord,
    Their lot eternally.
Our need today is growth in life,
    Christ's inward work indeed;
Not knowledge, teachings, gifts, nor pow'r —
    But life is all we need.

4 Lord, as the seed of life within,
    Grow more in us each day;
By spreading from our deepest part,
    Gain us in every way.
Lord, strengthen Thou our inner man;
    Make home in all our heart.
Fill us completely with Thyself
    In every inward part.

1213

10.6.10.6. with chorus.

1 If from your nat'ral man you would be free,
   Amen the law of life!
This law works in us automatically,
   Amen the law of life!

   Amen the law of life!
   Amen the law of life!
This law transforms us, to Christ conforms us —
   Amen the law of life!

2 From life divine it does originate,
   Amen the law of life!
Its function, working, power are innate,
   Amen the law of life!

   Amen the law of life!
   Amen the law of life!
Stop all your trying, on life relying,
   Amen the law of life!

3 The law of life fulfills our God's desire,
   Amen the law of life!
Our self-improvement He does not require,
   Amen the law of life!

   Amen the law of life!
   Amen the law of life!
God's plan fulfilling; Yes, Lord, we're willing,
   Amen the law of life!

4 This law transforms us metabolically,
   Amen the law of life!
'Til we are permeated corporately,
   Amen the law of life!

   Amen the law of life!
   Amen the law of life!
Old man denying, God's life supplying,
   Amen the law of life!

continued

VARIOUS ASPECTS OF THE INNER LIFE
THE LAW OF LIFE

5 This law's inscribing Christ upon our hearts,
   Amen the law of life!
'Til He is written in our inward parts,
   Amen the law of life!

   Amen the law of life!
   Amen the law of life!
Christ's form engraving, not mere behaving,
   Amen the law of life!

DEALING WITH THE HEART

1214

9.10.9.10. with chorus.

1 Dig away, dig away, dig away,
   Condemnation in my heart dig away!
Dig away, dig away, dig away,
   Condemnation in my heart dig away!

   All the guilt has to go
   That His life may flow . . . Hallelujah!
   Dig away, dig away, dig away,
   Condemnation in my heart dig away!

2 Dig away, dig away, dig away,
   All my vain imaginations dig away!
Dig away, dig away, dig away,
   All my vain imaginations dig away!

   All my dreams have to go
   That His life may flow . . . Hallelujah!
   Dig away, dig away, dig away,
   All my vain imaginations dig away!

3 Dig away, dig away, dig away,
   All my troublesome emotions dig away!
Dig away, dig away, dig away,
   All my troublesome emotions dig away!

All self love has to go
That His life may flow . . . Hallelujah!
Dig away, dig away, dig away,
All my troublesome emotions dig away!

4 Dig away, dig away, dig away,
All resistance in my will dig away!
Dig away, dig away, dig away,
All resistance in my will dig away!

All self will has to go
That His life may flow . . . Hallelujah!
Dig away, dig away, dig away,
All resistance in my will dig away!

5 Dig away, dig away, dig away,
All self seeking in my heart dig away!
Dig away, dig away, dig away,
All self seeking in my heart dig away!

All my hopes have to go
That His life may flow . . . Hallelujah!
Dig away, dig away. dig away,
All self seeking in my heart dig away!

6 Life can flow, praise the Lord, life can flow!
From the fountain in my heart life can flow!
Life can flow, praise the Lord, life can flow!
From the fountain in my heart life can flow!

When my heart's wholly free,
Christ can flow through me . . . Hallelujah!
Life can flow, praise the Lord, life can flow!
From the fountain in my heart life can flow!

1215

2 Timothy 1:7
(Tune: #1009)
10.9.10.8. with chorus.

1 God has not giv'n us a spirit of fear —
   There's pow'r deep within, pow'r deep within!
   We have His Word — brothers, sisters, let's hear —
   That pow'r deep within may flow out.

   O there's pow'r, pow'r, overcoming pow'r,
   Deep within, deep within;
   O there's pow'r, pow'r, normal Christian pow'r
   In the spirit God's given us!

2 God has not giv'n us a wavering will —
   There's pow'r deep within, pow'r deep within!
   But one our spirit will strengthen and fill —
   There's wonderful pow'r deep within!

3 God has not giv'n us emotions so weak —
   There's pow'r deep within, pow'r deep within!
   Open our hearts and in love let us speak —
   There's wonderful pow'r deep within!

4 God has not giv'n us a mind that is bound —
   There's pow'r deep within, pow'r deep within!
   But one that's healthy and perfectly sound —
   There's wonderful pow'r deep within!

VARIOUS ASPECTS OF THE INNER LIFE
INNER LIFE, DAILY LIFE, MEETING LIFE

Peculiar Meter.

1 We have an inner life; that's for our daily life;
  That's for the meeting life — just Christ!
  We'll live the inner life; we'll have the daily life;
  We'll see the meeting life — that's just the church.

2 Christ is our inner life; He's in our spirit now;
  Not far away from us — He's right inside!
  And as we turn to Him and take Him as our all
  He will become in us our inner life.

3 Out from our inner life will come our daily life,
  And all our living be filled up with Christ.
  Then as we live by Him, He lives His life in us,
  And He becomes to us our daily life.

4 The real experience of Christ in daily life,
  Will fill the meeting life with Christ Himself.
  Not empty forms and such, but *Christ* will be
    so much;
  And we will see Him here as the meeting life.

5 Without the inner life there is no daily life,
  There is no meeting life, there is no church!
  Christ as our inner life, Christ in our daily life
  Will make the meeting life new and glorious!

1217

(Tune: #559)
8.7.8.7.D.

1 Lord, we've heard the call, "Come forward,"
   Unto the most Holy Place,
   To behold shekinah glory
   Shining from Your blessed face.

   Coming forward to the Holiest,
   Through the incense altar's prayer;
   No more veil of separation,
   We may boldly enter there.

2 We come forward by a new way,
   Freshly cut and freshly slain,
   To the Holiest of Holies;
   Glorious access we obtain.

3 We come forward unto our God,
   Who is sitting on the throne;
   He has paved the way to glory
   By His blood and cross alone.

4 We come forward to the new age,
   With assured heart, true and bold.
   To enjoy th' eternal purpose,
   Ne'er to shrink back to the old.

5 Praise You, Lord, we've all come forward.
   Now within the Holiest,
   You're our God and we're Your people;
   Here we dwell forever blest.

1 If from the world you're longing to be free,
   Amen the Word of God!
If you would live in all reality,
   Amen the Word of God!

   Amen the Word of God!
   Amen the Word of God!
His Word receiving, His Word believing,
   Amen the Word of God!

2 If with your sin and self you would be through,
   Amen the Word of God!
If you would let the Lord your mind renew,
   Amen the Word of God!

   Amen the Word of God!
   Amen the Word of God!
His Word is living, life-power giving —
   Amen the Word of God!

3 Christ as the land of Canaan is our lot —
   Amen the Word of God!
If you would enter, harden not your heart —
   Amen the Word of God!

   Amen the Word of God!
   Amen the Word of God!
His Word discerns us, all that concerns us —
   Amen the Word of God!

4 Jesus is coming, now He's on His way —
   Amen the Word of God!
Would you be ready if He comes today —
   Amen the Word of God!

   Amen the Word of God!
   Amen the Word of God!
His Word prepares us, to Jesus bears us —
   Amen the Word of God!

1219

12.8.12.8. with chorus.

1 What a wonderful change in my living is wrought
  By saying Amen to God's Word.
  More of Christ into me at each instance is brought
  By saying Amen to His Word.

  By saying Amen to His Word,
  By saying Amen to His Word,   [part,
  Thus the Lord takes my heart, and transforms every
  By saying Amen to His Word.

2 What I never could do God is doing in me,
  By saying Amen to His Word.
  And the change is so real all the brothers can see,
  By saying Amen to God's Word.

3 I have ceased from my wandering and going astray
  By saying Amen to God's Word.
  And my old inclinations are passing away
  By saying Amen to His Word.

4 Now the secret of faith in the Lord I can see —
  It's saying Amen to His Word.
  He is more real and precious than all things to me
  By saying Amen to His Word.

5 Now my love for the brothers abounds more and more
  By saying Amen to God's Word.
  And I'm being related as never before
  By saying Amen to His Word.

6 Now my hope in the Lord's soon return groweth bright
  By saying Amen to His Word.
  I am ready to see Him, my Lord, my delight,
  By saying Amen to His Word.

  Lord Jesus, Amen to Your Word,
  Lord Jesus, Amen to Your Word.
  You are coming again — all my heart says Amen!
  Lord Jesus, Amen to Your Word!

(Tune: #66)
8.6.8.6. with repeat.

1 Remove the veils, Lord, from my heart;
True revelation grant to me;
A vision clear, O Lord, impart
Of Thy recovery.

2 By revelation I perceive
The power that raised Christ from the dead;
When I by faith this power receive,
I to the church am led.

3 Thy mighty power has set me free
From all the world's distracting things;
An entrance to the local church
This mighty power brings.

4 Once in the local church, I need
To take Thee as my person, Lord;
My outward man each day recede,
My heart is for the Lord.

5 I take Thee as my person, Lord;
I have been crucified with Thee.
My inner man has been restored;
I'm now indwelt by Thee.

6 When all Thy members self forsake,
Thy glorious Body, Lord, is known;
When of Thy Person we partake,
The one new man is shown.

7 The church life is the one new man
In every local church expressed;
Thy Body is a corporate man,
One Person manifest.

(Repeat the last two lines of each stanza)

1221

John 10
(Tune: #260)
8.7.8.7. with chorus.

1 Jesus, our wonderful Shepherd
    Brought us right out of the fold
Into His pasture so plenteous,
    Into His riches untold.

    Glorious church life,
    Feasting from such a rich store!
    Here where we're dwelling in oneness
    God commands life evermore.

2 In the divisions He sought us,
    Weary and famished for food;
Into the good land He brought us,
    Oh, to our spirit how good!

3 Jesus Himself is our pasture,
    He is the food that we eat;
We as His sheep are fed richly
    Each time, whenever we meet.

4 Dwell we here on a high mountain,
    Wet with the morning-fresh dew,
Slaking our thirst at the fountain,
    Water so living and new.

5 Christ is our rest and enjoyment,
    Here we have nothing to fear;
Here all the sheep dwell securely,
    Kept by His presence so dear.

11.10.11.10. with chorus.

1 Sing aloud your praises to the Lord of all,
Now He is dwelling in Jerusalem.
Tell among us all His doings great and small,
His throne, the heavens, yet He walks with men.
  Oh, the salvation out of Zion comes;
  He brought us back from our captivity.
  Now we rejoice and are exceeding glad;
  Now we rejoice and are exceeding glad!

2 In the Holy City with His own He dwells;
O Lord, our Lord, how excellent Thy name!
He's enthroned upon the praises of His saints;
All His delight in Zion does remain.
  The local churches are His move today —
  He is our portion, we are satisfied.
  Oh, what a goodly heritage have we;
  Oh, what a goodly heritage have we!

3 Who shall in His holy tabernacle dwell,
Who shall ascend to His most holy hill?
Those who seek for Him and purify their heart;
This generation now that seeks His face.
  Oh, seek His face, ye children of the earth,
  Open your heart, and let the King come in.
  He will come in, and He shall live and reign;
  He will come in, and He shall live and reign!

4 Look! God's tabernacle now is with the saints;
Emmanuel — God with us, we proclaim.
Everything is done, so let His children come;
Christ and the church — where God and man
      are one!
  Lift up your heads, ye cities of the earth;
  Open your gates, and let the King come in.
  Shout to His praise — He's coming in to reign!
  Shout to His praise — He's coming in to reign!

1223

Psalm 48

9.7.9.7. with repeat.

1 O walk about, walk about Zion,
   Go round about her in love.
   O walk about, walk about Zion
   And count the towers thereof.

2 O set your heart on her bulwarks,
   O set your heart on her walls,
   O set your heart on her bulwarks,
   Consider her palaces.

3 In elevation how beauteous,
   The joy of all the earth!
   In elevation how beauteous
   Is Zion, that city of worth!

4 O there is a river in Zion
   That flows so deep and so broad.
   O how the streams of that river
   Make glad the city of God!

5 Praise waiteth for Thee, Lord, in Zion,
   Praise waiteth, O God, for Thee,
   Praise waiteth for Thee, Lord, in Zion,
   For Zion is filled with Thee.

6 How great the Lord is in Zion,
   How greatly to be praised,
   How great He is in that city
   Which over the earth is raised.

7 O bless the Lord out of Zion,
   O let His praises swell,
   O bless the Lord out of Zion,
   Ye who in Jerusalem dwell.

8　The Lord bless thee out of Zion,
　　The Lord bless thee o'er and o'er!
　　The Lord bless thee out of Zion
　　　With life for evermore!

9　Behold how good and how pleasant
　　With all the brethren to be!
　　Behold how good and how pleasant
　　　To dwell in unity!

10　O tell it to all generations,
　　O tell it to all who will come,
　　O tell it to all generations,
　　　The Spirit and Bride say, "Come!"

(Tune: #864)
8.8.8.6. with chorus.

1224

1　We from the law to Christ have turned;
　　To trust in Him by grace we've learned.
　　And since His glory we've discerned
　　　We only care for Christ!

　　We only care for Christ!
　　We only care for Christ!
　　And since His glory we've discerned
　　　We only care for Christ!

2　Christ brings us to God's house to dwell,
　　Where all day long His praises swell.
　　O hallelujah! None can tell
　　　How lovely is God's house!

　　How lovely is God's house!
　　How lovely is God's house!
　　O hallelujah! None can tell
　　　How lovely is God's house!

continued

1224

3 The house enlarged the city is;
The joy of all the nations 'tis,
The place for God to rule is this
    On Zion's holy hill.

On Zion's holy hill,
On Zion's holy hill,
The place for God to rule is this
On Zion's holy hill.

4 From Zion Christ will take the earth
And reign and fill its souls with mirth.
All nations will proclaim His worth,
    Break forth and sing for joy.

Break forth and sing for joy,
Break forth and sing for joy,
All nations will proclaim His worth,
Break forth and sing for joy.

5 Christ — house — the city — earth, we see;
Thus God's great plan fulfilled will be.
O brothers, let us utterly
    Be one with Him for this.

Be one with Him for this,
Be one with Him for this,
O brothers, let us utterly
Be one with Him for this.

THE CHURCH — AS CHRIST'S BODY

(Tune: #552)
8.7.8.7.D.

1225

1 Lord, to know Thee as the Body,
Is my desperate need today,
Oh, to see Thee in Thy members,
'Tis for this I long and pray.
No more just to know Thy headship,
In an individual way,
But to see Thee incarnated,
As the Body-Christ, I pray.

2 Through the years, Thy saints have
  sought Thee,
Longing for reality;
Gazing upward, searching inward,
Thirsting for the sight of Thee.
Now reveal that Christ in heaven,
Is the Body manifest;
And the Christ who dwells within us
As the Body is expressed.

3 Prone to be misled, I know it,
By my lofty thoughts of Thee,
Easy 'tis for self to seek Thee,
Yet not touch reality,
Oh, how much I need to find Thee,
In Thy members here below.
God eternal dwells among us,
Manifest in flesh to know.

4 Limit, Lord, my independence,
Let me to Thy Body turn;
Not just seeking light from heaven,
But the church's sense to learn.
May we be the stones for building,
Not the formless, useless clay,
Gain in us Thy heart's desire,
Corporately Thyself display.

1226

15.11.15.11. with chorus.

1   Oh, the church of Christ is glorious, and we are
      part of it —
  We're so happy that the Lord has made us one!
There's a Body in the universe and we belong to it —
  Hallelujah, for the Lord has made us one!

     Hallelujah for the Body!
     We are members of the Body!
     We are wholly for the Body!
     Hallelujah, for the Lord has made us one!

2   Not the individual Christians, but a corporate
      entity —
  God must have it for His full expression now;
Not just individual churches but the Body
      corporately —
  Hallelujah, we are in the Body now!

     Hallelujah for the Body!
     Satan trembles at the Body!
     We're victorious in the Body!
     Hallelujah, we are in the Body now!

3   There are seven golden lampstands in the nature
      all divine —
  Nothing natural does the Body life allow.
When we're one and share God's nature, how the
      lampstand then does shine —
  Hallelujah, it is brightly shining now!

     Hallelujah for the Body!
     For the lampstands of the Body!
     For the golden, shining Body!
     Hallelujah, it is brightly shining now!

4   How may we express such oneness, be divine
        and shining too?
     Hallelujah, eating Jesus is the way!
   He's the tree of life, the manna, and the feast
        that's ever new —
     Hallelujah, we may eat Him every day!

        We are one by eating Jesus!
        We're divine by eating Jesus!
        How we shine by eating Jesus!
        Hallelujah, eating Jesus is the way!

THE CHURCH — AS CHRIST'S BRIDE

(Tune: #67)
8.8.8.7. with chorus.

1227

1   Our Lord, that One of peerless worth
     Came first to die to give new birth;
     He comes again to have on earth
        A glorious Bride forever.

        Jesus! Oh, You're coming soon,
        Jesus! as our dear Bridegroom;
        Jesus! may our hearts make room
        To be Your Bride forever.

2   What our dear Lord desires the most,
     Is not to just redeem the lost;
     But that some saints would pay the cost,
        To be His Bride forever.

3   As virgins we must single be,
     No other husband could have we,
     That when He comes we'll then be free
        To be His Bride forever.

4   How could we love this fading world,
     When Christ desires that one great pearl;
     To Him we must our love unfurl
        To bring Him back forever.

1228

8.6.8.6. with chorus.

1 The Bible is the Word of God,
　　Its message is but one —
　Christ and the church, His holy Bride,
　　The two becoming one.

　　　Oh, what a miracle that we could be His Bride!
　　　　Oh, what a miracle! All else we lay aside
　　　That we may now prepare to meet Him in the air
　　　And ever in our Bridegroom's love abide.

2 The Father is the mighty God,
　　His purpose is but one —
　To find a Bride for Christ the Lord
　　And give her to His Son.

3 The Son is Jesus Christ the Lord,
　　His heart desire's but one —
　To have a loving counterpart,
　　A Bride He's wooed and won.

4 The Spirit is but Christ Himself,
　　He is the Lord applied
　To generate the men of earth,
　　Transform them as His Bride.

5 The living Word is Jesus too,
　　God-breathed as life to us,
　That we be wholly sanctified,
　　A Bride all-glorious.

1229

(Tune: #824)
7.6.7.6.D.

1 The church is Christ's deep longing
　　And His good pleasure too.
　His every word and action
　　Is made with her in view.
　His heart's love is established,
　　And nought can Him deter;
　Before the earth's foundation
　　His thoughts were filled with her.

2 The eve of all creation
  He mused on His delight,
And pondered every feature,
  Well-pleasing in His sight.
Creation sprang to being,
  But deep in Him did hide
A heart of depth unfathomed
  Fixed on a glorious Bride.

3 And thus His will was 'stablished
  His counterpart to gain:
This blessed, firm intention,
  Eternally the same.
Though sin should e'en beguile man,
  Then mock his helpless state,
He never could forsake her,
  His yearning ne'er abate.

4 Then mercy richly flourished,
  And love was, oh, so vast,
As graciously He sought her
  With wisdom unsurpassed.
The love He gave to win her
  God only comprehends!
His life laid down, an offering
  Whose fragrance yet ascends.

5 And now in resurrection
  To her He draws most near,
And with untold affection
  In glory does appear.
As she beholds her Bridegroom,
  His glory floods her heart,
'Til she, His Bride, is raptured,
  His longed-for counterpart.

1230

Peculiar Meter.

1 One new man is the Father's plan;
   He redeemed us from the sons of men.
   Every kindred, tribe and tongue,
   In Himself He called us to be one.
   God's expression on the earth
   Now reveals His glorious worth.
   One new man is the Father's plan;
   He redeemed us from the sons of men.

2 On the cross ordinances slain,
   That He might form just one of twain.
   Reconciling us to God,
   Thus on the serpent's head He trod.
   He breaks down the middle wall
   As upon His name we call;
   On the cross ordinances slain,
   That He might form just one of twain.

3 For this cause Your Person, Lord,
   We take and stand in one accord;
   All the members self forsake,
   And of the Body-Christ partake.
   We in Christ as one new man
   Now come forth to take this land.
   For this cause Your Person, Lord,
   We take and stand in one accord.

(Tune: #1015)

Peculiar Meter.

1 O praise the Lord, God has a plan —
That's why He formed a man;
To exercise authority,
Subdue the earth entirely.
O what a joy to be
In His recovery,
O praise God He made me a V.I.P.

2 O hallelujah, Christ became
A man to die for me.
And dying once my life to be,
In spirit now He lives in me.
The man supreme is He,
My all He came to be;
O hallelujah, He lives in me!

3 O hallelujah, I'm a man,
The center of God's plan.
I'm God's own image made to be,
Expressing His authority.
It's great to be a man,
O praise God, I'm a man,
O hallelujah, I am a man!

4 O hallelujah, one new man,
The building of God's plan!
God's plan throughout eternity —
Not man, but men built corporately.
This man cannot be beat,
All things beneath his feet,
Christ and the church one man complete.

1232

Ephesians 2-3
Peculiar Meter.

1 Once by nature we were dead in sin,
In a world of utter discord;
But together God has quickened us,
Raised us up to sit together with the Lord.

　Jesus is getting us together,
　Come and see the saints in one accord.
　His love is knitting us together,
　To the stature of the fullness of the Lord.

2 Thus with all saints we can apprehend,
All the vast dimensions of God.
Knowing Christ's love passes all we know,
We're together filled to fullness with our God.

3 Now we know the purpose of our God,
Visible the mystery became:
Christ, the church, together now we see,
And together put the enemy to shame.

4 For this cause we pray the Father God —
Strengthen Thou with might our inner man;
Make Yourself at home in all our hearts,
Root us, ground us in Your love and for Your plan.

5 In the Body we'll be fitly framed
As the many members Christ supply;
Working in the measure of each part,
All by growth in love the Body edify.

6 Now we're one His purpose to fulfill,
As the one new man of His plan.
Unto Him be glory in the church,
And in Jesus Christ forevermore — Amen!

Peculiar Meter.

1   O home in the church,
     Where we've ended our search
With the brothers rejoicing all day;
    Where Christ is our life,
    And we're through with all strife,
Now we're home, hallelujah, to stay!

    Home, home in the church;
    Yes, it's here that we've ended our search;
      And through all our days
       We will shout to His praise,
    "Hallelujah for Christ and the church!"

2   Here God is at rest,
     Of His treasures the best —
How His heart is rejoicing all day!
    His home is our heart,
    Ne'er for Satan a part,
Here His glory He'll fully display.

    God's home is the church;
    Yes, it's here that He ended His search;
      And through all our days
       We will shout to His praise,
    "Hallelujah for Christ and the church!"

1234
12.10.12.10. with chorus.

1 I thirsted in the barren land of Babylon
And nothing satisfying there I found;
But to the blessed local church one day I came,
Where springs of living water do abound.

Drinking at the springs of living water,
Happy now am I,
My heart they satisfy;
Drinking at the springs of living water,
O wonderful and bountiful supply!

2 How sweet the living water from the hills of God,
It's flowing in and flowing out of me;
O now I've found the place for which I long had sought,
Where there is life and life abundantly.

3 O brother, won't you gather in the local church?
A fountain here is flowing deep and wide.
The Shepherd now would bring you to the local church,
Where thirsty spirits can be satisfied.

1235
(Tune: #1205)
8.6.8.6. with chorus.

1 Oh, listen to the wanderer
In whom there was a lack;
Then hearken to the song he sings
And follow in his track.

Praise the Lord, praise the Lord,
Praise the Lord, Hallelujah! Hallelujah!
Praise the Lord, praise the Lord,
I'll never be the same!

2 A wanderer within the world
   For pleasure ever seeks;
   Be it in body or in mind,
   With vanity it reeks.

3 For self I labored day and night,
   My castles built in sand;
   But, praise the Lord, He wrecked them all —
   Much better things He planned.

4 Once all for self — confused, alone,
   How could I bear the shame?
   But now within the local church
   I'll never be the same.

5 I am a happy member now
   Within the local church.
   A wanderer has found his home
   And ended all his search.

6 I was an individualist,
   An island in myself;
   But now the Lord is building me
   With others in Himself.

7 I'm drawn together with His own
   In fellowship so sweet.
   I've learned from others to receive
   Of Christ whene'er we meet.

8 My wanderings have really ceased —
   I've found the church, God's best!
   The secret of my happiness —
   Enjoying God's own rest!

1236

(Tune: #324)
Peculiar Meter.

1 In the church the sound of life upon our ear is falling,
Then we see the joy of Christ expressed on every hand;
Babylon and things of earth in vain to us are calling.
  We are home forever in Christ our land.

  We're churching in the Spirit
  On the church's local ground;
  We're churching with our brothers,
  Our family we have found.
  Oh, yes, we're churching with the churches, and
      we'll make the earth resound
    With hallelujahs for Christ our land!

2 Far away our background seems with all its gifts
      and teaching,
Farther still, the worldly things with all their foul
      demand;
As the love of Jesus Christ our inmost heart is
      reaching,
  Not a thing can move us from Christ our land.

3 "I will build My church upon this rock," said the
      Lord Jesus,
And we see the building of His purpose and His plan;
Setting members in the Body as Himself it pleases,
  Building us together in Christ our land.

4 Now the Lord's recovery is everywhere proceeding,
All the churches join in one to give the Lord
      command:
"Speed the day when all the earth will echo with
      pray-reading
  And with hallelujahs for Christ our land."

15.11.15.11. with chorus.

1 Splendid church life! His green garden! He has
    brought us, praise the Lord,
      To experience the Christ Who's growing here!
  He is full of rich enjoyment to His saints in
    one accord;
      He is new and fresh, available and dear.

  I'm so happy in this lovely place,
  In the garden growing in His grace!
    There is no finer pleasure than to eat
      the living tree
    And to get the living water into me.

2 It is not a school or fact'ry or a chapel in the air;
    But a garden where our Lord can plant and sow.
  So He's placed us all here corporately to be
    His garden fair,
      Where He's free to cultivate and make us grow.

3 Thus within the church-life garden there's a
    fruit-producing tree
      Full of life and so available to eat.
  So be simple, don't be hardened, drop your
    concepts — eat that tree!
      Take in Jesus every moment — He's so sweet!

4 With the tree there is the water, flowing God
    in Christ to us,
      Quenching all our dryness, ending all our strife.
  Hallelujah! In His garden Jesus flows Himself to us,
    As the full supply for us to grow in life.

5 Aren't you satisfied and thankful that our Lord
    has brought you in
      Where His pleasures and His riches flow so free?
  So be happy and be joyful, in the spirit feast on Him,
    So God's garden can bear fruit abundantly.

1238

(Tune: #1071)
7.7.7.7.D.

1 Never did I dream before,
Such a place could e'er be found,
Where the tears of sorrow cease,
Songs of endless joy abound.
One who seldom ever sang,
Now delights his voice to raise;
Singing hymns with all the saints,
Echoing the ceaseless praise.

2 Day by day the world goes on,
Just as it has gone before.
Millions grasp and clutch at life,
Wond'ring if there could be more;
Such was I and would be, yet
Mercy found me out somehow;
With what gratefulness I say,
"I'm in God's own family now."

3 How delightful 'tis to know;
How subjective, real, and sweet
Is this inward joy of grace
We experience when we meet;
Life abundant Jesus gives
As my full reality;
Praise You, Lord, it's really true,
I'm in Your own family.

4 At the closing of this age,
Just before Your kingdom's dawn,
May You gain a people, Lord,
For Your dwelling place, Your home.
Since for me You gave Your all,
Everything I lay aside;
For Your church my all I'd give,
That You would be satisfied.

(Tune: #495)
7.7.7.7.

1 In this age we're being turned
    To the Spirit to be burned;
    Now in spirit we can see
    Christ, the church, our unity!

2 In the spirit we can taste
    All the riches of Thy grace;
    All Thy fullness, blessed Lord
    Is for those in one accord!

3 In the spirit, on the ground —
    Here is where Thy life is found.
    Dwelling thus in unity,
    We enjoy reality!

4 Out of death and into life,
    Done with all divisive strife!
    Free indeed to love but Thee,
    Growing to maturity!

5 "Amen, Jesus," is our prayer
    To the purging work, whate'er;
    Now Thy church must desperate be
    More the growth in life to see.

6 O Lord, make Thy home our heart,
    Our true inner man Thou art;
    God and man are mingled thus —
    Christ, the church, all glorious!

1240

10.5.10.5. with chorus.

1 Deeper, deeper, in the cross of Jesus;
　　Deeper let me go;
　Death and life, they always go together;
　　Deepen, Lord, the flow.
　　　Oh, deeper yet we pray,
　　　Do work in us each day;
　　　Go deeper, through and through,
　　　Till in Thee we're wholly new.

2 Higher, higher, in the life of Jesus;
　　Lord, we are so low.
　By Thy life we all can go much higher —
　　Higher let us go.
　　　Oh, higher yet we pray —
　　　Transform us every day —
　　　And richer in the flow;
　　　May Thy life be all we know.

3 Growing, growing, in us He is growing,
　　More and more each day.
　Into all our living He is flowing —
　　This is now His way.
　　　For growth, O Lord, we pray;
　　　Increase in us each day.
　　　It's not enough to know;
　　　Now Thy life in us must grow.

4 Living, living, Christ is all our living,
　　He's so practical:
　Small things, big things, anything and
　　　all things —
　　He's involved in all.
　　　Live Christ in every way;
　　　Oh, live Him out today.
　　　His name you now must call,
　　　And give Him your all for all.

5 Person, Person, Jesus is our Person,
  Living now in us.
He's our tastes, our attitudes and actions;
  Oh, how glorious!
      Our Person, Lord, Thou art;
      Make home in all our heart.
      As life in every way
      Be our Person, Lord, each day.

6 Churches, churches, in the local churches
  We all find the flow:
Deeper, higher, Christ as all our living,
  For the church we grow.
      The churches are today
      Just Christ in every way.
      For this, from self we cease,
      For Thy Body, Thine increase.

7 Building, building, we will see the building
  Of the church this way:
Christ experienced will produce the building —
  He's the only way.
      Oh, build us, Lord, we pray,
      By growth of life each day.
      Oh, make us now such men
      For the new Jerusalem.

8 Coming, coming, Jesus soon is coming
  For His chosen Bride.
In the churches we are all preparing
  To be glorified.
      Lord Jesus, come again —
      This cry is deep within.
      We'll praise Thee to the end,
      Oh, come back! Come back! Amen!

1241

Song of Songs
(Tune: #858)
8.6.8.6. with repeat.

1 God's life and building can be seen
    Within the Song of Songs;
  He shows by types His seeking ones,
    The Bride for whom Christ longs!

2 She, as a team of horses shows
    A love, so swift and strong!
  But this is love that's natural —
    It pulls the world along!

3 As time goes by, her concepts change,
    With dove's eyes she can see
  That naught can with her love compare —
    There's none so dear as He!

4 A lily she is now to Him
    (For still the Lord draws on),
  Her faith is not in earthly toil,
    But in the wondrous Son.

5 She's next a dove who hides herself
    Within the cloven rock;
  Now in her Lord's ascended life
    Is love which knows no shock!

6 Of smoke, a pillar she's become,
    And now, as wand'ring ends,
  Her wills to His will are subdued,
    What fragrance sweet ascends!

7 *Behold His* couch . . . (O, can this be?)
    E'en midst the fearsome night . . .
  She now affords her Lord such rest,
    The foe is put to flight!

8 A vessel to contain the King!
    (This type is full of worth.)
  A palanquin He's made Himself
    For His move on the earth!

9 Of wood this vessel is composed:
    Christ's ris'n humanity.
  Its silver pillars for support
    And floor of gold we see!

10 The seat of purple signifies
    Christ is of kings the King.
  To Him, as fittings for within,
    Their love His dear ones bring!

11 The day will come — ('tis surely soon)
    And glad will be Thy heart —
  What boast and glory to Thyself;
    Thy crown, Thy counterpart!

12 A garden fair, enclosed is she
    With spices, fragrant, sweet.
  She now brings forth materials
    The building to complete!

13 A city pleasant, comely, too;
    No greater building, this!
  So beautiful, yet to the foe
    A conq'ring army 'tis!

14 As we eat Jesus, praise the Lord,
    The transformation's done,
  Until at last, the work's complete —
    Christ and His Bride are one!

1242

(Tune: #1152)
14.14.14.14. with chorus.

1   The Lord, the seed of life, has sown
      Himself into our heart
  To grow up into fullness and become
      His counterpart.
  The seed requires no rules or forms,
      for water is its need —
  By this the all-inclusive seed will grow
      in us indeed!

    The seed is simply Jesus!
      Oh, Jesus lives in me!
    And by His growth this seed
      in us will reach maturity.

2   The growth of Christ, the seed, in us
      will soon produce the wheat,
  The life within break forth — yet work
      divine is not complete;
  For wheat alone can never be the seed's
      expression true;
  So all the grains must blend together
      into something new.

    The seed is simply Jesus;
      now wheat is Jesus too!
    The grains of wheat must blend
      together into something new.

3 The individual grains of wheat no longer
  must be free,
But crushed together, ground to powder,
  every grain must be,
Until the wheat becomes the meal from
  which the loaf is formed
Till all the saints will blend and to His
  Body be conformed.

 We all must take the grinding
  until the Christ within
 Can mold into His Body all the
  individual grains.

4 The seed is planted, wheat is grown
  and meal is the sum
Of all the growth upon God's farm,
  where Christians grow as one;
But all the growth in life is for the
  building of the church,
That God and man may have a home
  and both may end their search.

 The farm is for the building,
  for God and man a home,
 Where both may dwell among
  His people gathered into one.

continued

5 God's building is produced by silver,
    precious stones, and gold —
From meal through transformation,
    pressure, heat, and pain untold.
The meal must not be satisfied to stay
    as meal alone,
But must submit to transformation
    into precrous stone.

    The meal must pass through suffering
        that precious stones be formed;
    Then built into God's building, to His
        purpose full conformed.

6 From fullest growth and transformation
    comes a pearl of worth;
This simple, precious, all-inclusive gem
    will then come forth.
Conceived in death and formed in life
    by that all-glorious One,
The church, His Bride, the fruit of all the
    work that He has done.

    The pearl is what He's after,
        the Bride to please His heart,
    So single, pure and precious,
        and His very counterpart.

7   The growth in life begins when planted
on God's farm we're found;
The growing seed becomes the wheat
from which the meal is ground.
But building work proceeds when meal
submits to be transformed;
Then gold and silver, precious stones
for building will be formed.

The farm is for the building,
built up by precious stones,
From which the priceless pearl comes
forth to be His Bride, His own.

8   Lord, keep us poor in spirit, pure in heart
that we may be
Good ground in which the seed of life
may grow abundantly,
Until the final stage is reached and
You are satisfied
And have Your priceless, chosen pearl,
Your joy complete, Your Bride.

Lord, keep us poor in spirit
and purified in heart,
That growing up in us You may
bring forth Your counterpart.

1243

Peculiar Meter.

1 We are one in the spirit, by His life we are one,
We have left all divisions, Body-life has begun,
For the Lord broke all barriers, proclaiming,
  "It is done."

> *Brothers:*
> In the church we are brothers,
> Praise the Lord, praise the Lord!
>
> *Sisters:*
> In the church we are sisters,
> Praise the Lord, praise the Lord!
>   (Praise the Lord!)
>
> *Everyone:*
> And we praise Him that our unity
> has now been restored.

2 We are one in the spirit, yet it goes deeper still,
For this oneness is spreading to our mind,
  emotion, will,
As we all stand together that His purpose
  He fulfill.

3 We are one in the spirit, we are one actually,
Not in talk nor in theory, but in fact, practically,
In the churches we're all enjoying this reality.

4 We are one in the spirit in each locality,
For the Lord's own intention we would
  consecrated be,
That the oneness He's given us the whole world
  may see.

Psalm 133

1244

(Tune: #300 Second tune)

6.6.6.6.8.8.

1 Behold how good a thing
It is to dwell in peace;
How pleasing to our King,
This fruit of righteousness;
When brethren all in one agree,
They know the joy of unity!

2 When all are sweetly joined
(True followers of the Lamb),
They're one in heart and mind,
They think and speak the same;
When all in love together dwell;
The comfort is unspeakable!

3 Where unity takes place,
The joys of heav'n we prove;
This is the gospel grace,
The unction from above;
The Spirit on all saints is shed,
Descending swift from Christ the Head.

4 Where unity is found,
The sweet anointing grace
Extends to all around,
And shines from every face;
To every praising saint it comes,
And fills him with divine perfumes.

5 On all His chosen ones
The precious oil comes down:
Anointing as it runs,
Anointing on and on.
E'en to His skirts (the meanest name
That longs to love the bleeding Lamb).

1189   *continued*

6 From Aaron's beard it rolls,
(Those nearest to His face),
The humble, trembling souls
Who know abundant grace;
The grace, the grace for all is free,
For, lo, it reaches now to me!

THE CHURCH — FOLLOWING

1245

1 Thessalonians 1:6; Philippians 3:17
(Tune: #703)
8.7.8.7.D.

1 When the brothers are in order,
And you sense Christ is their life,
Follow them and watch for Jesus,
Ending thus your thought and strife.

Follow brothers, follow sisters,
When you sense Christ is their life,
Follow brothers, follow sisters,
Help prepare the Bride for Christ.

2 When you follow, as you follow,
Take the blood, and call His name;
Much assurance He will give you,
And the enemy you'll shame.

3 When they speak, as they are speaking,
Open wide your heart to them,
Thus the Word of God receiving,
Word of God, and not of men.

4 Now the Word of God is running,
Running fast, and running free.
This is how the Lord is moving,
In His own recovery.

5 *O be glad*, rejoice, dear brothers,
For the coming wedding day.
Then the Bride will be made ready —
Those who followed all the way.

10.6.10.6. with chorus.

1 We give ourselves to follow the churches,
    Oneness in Christ display;
Follow His move in all of the churches,
    Stand fast as one this way.

    We must follow the Spirit
      In all simplicity.
    In our spirit is Jesus —
      He follows perfectly!

2 We give ourselves to follow the followers,
    By this we truly learn;
Never desiring to be the leaders,
    But to the Spirit turn.

3 We give ourselves the flock's steps to follow,
    Knowing the Shepherd's care.
Now in the churches Jesus is leading
    And He is speaking there.

4 We give ourselves to Thee, O Lord Jesus,
    Never to turn aside;
Where'er the Lamb goes, there we would follow,
    Follow whate'er betide.

5 We give ourselves to enter the kingdom,
    That marriage feast, with Him;
Come persecution, suffering, and trials,
    Still we will enter in.

6 Christ wants some followers here in the churches,
    Followers of whom to say:
"These saw My purpose, followed Me wholly" —
    May we be those today!

1247

(Tune: #268)
8.7.8.7.D.

1 If our hearts would be established;
   If in spirit we would be;
   If we would be overcomers;
   Follow Jesus constantly.

     Follow Jesus in the spirit;
     Be the overcomers true;
     Follow Jesus every moment —
     Jesus, help us follow You.

2 If we would be built together;
   If related we would be;
   To be fitly framed together;
   Follow brothers constantly.

     Follow brothers for the building;
     Never independent be;
     Follow brothers, be in order,
     Functioning in harmony.

3 If we're for the Lord's recovery;
   If the earth the Lord's would be;
   If we would bring in the kingdom;
   Follow churches constantly.

     Follow all the local churches;
     Thus, the kingdom we will see.
     Follow in the churches' flowing
     For the Lord's recovery.

4 We would all be better followers,
   Taking in with joy the Word;
   It enables us to follow
   Brothers, churches, and our Lord.

     Follow Jesus; follow brothers;
     Follow churches in the flow;
     By the Word of God amening
     We can all attain this goal.

Peculiar Meter.

1248

1 Recall how David swore,
"I'll not come into my house,
Nor go up to my bed,
Give slumber to mine eyelids,
Until I find a place for Thee,
A place, O Lord, for Thee."
Our mighty God desires a home
Where all His own may come.

2 How blinded we have been,
Shut in with what concerns us;
While God's house lieth waste —
Lord, break through, overturn us;
We'll go up to the mountain,
Bring wood and build the house;
We'll never say, "Another day!"
It's time! We'll come and build!

3 O Lord, against these days,
Inspire some for Your building,
Just as in David's day —
A remnant who are willing
To come and work in Your house,
Oh, what a blessed charge!
Your heart's desire, is our desire —
We come, O Lord, to build.

4 Within those whom You'd call
Put such a restless caring
For building to give all —
These times are for preparing;
The gates of hell cannot prevail
Against the builded Church!
The hours are few, the builders too —
Lord, build, O build in us!

(Repeat the last four lines)

1249

(Tune: #288)
8.7.8.7.D.(I)

1 How oft believers through the years
Have sought the will of Jesus,
And would have offered everything
To walk as Him it pleases.
If you should seek the will of God,
Don't waste another minute;
The church life is His glorious will,
And you too must get in it.

2 "What is the will of God for me?"
How oft you've asked this question.
It is the church life, corporately,
Where God finds His expression.
Don't watch the church life from afar,
Or erringly construe it;
Come gaze upon it from within —
You'll give your whole life to it.

3 The church life here is realized,
'Tis all the Lord intended;
And in this rich experience
All further seeking's ended.
The church life is His glorious will —
Now for yourself begin it.
The surest way to know His will
Is simply to get in it.

4 So let us give our all for this,
And hold ourselves not dearly;
The church life is the will of God,
Let's take our standing clearly.
Oh, we have found the will of God;
Christ died and rose to win it.
The church life is His glorious will,
And, praise the Lord, we're in it!

Psalm 132

1250

(Tune: #522)

8.6.8.6.D.

1 O surely I will not come in
    Within my house to stay,
Nor yet give sleep unto my eyes,
    Till Jesus has His way.
Upon the earth, the Lord desires
    A place where He may live;
For this, Thy habitation, Lord,
    Myself I fully give.

2 We heard of it while yet far off,
    We found it in the way;
We then came up into her courts,
    And here we'll ever stay.
Arise, O Lord, into Thy rest,
    Thou and Thy ark so strong.
Thy priests are clothed with righteousness;
    Thy saints with joy and song.

3 The Lord has sworn in truth to us,
    He will not turn away —
His Seed shall sit with Him enthroned,
    And reign with Him for aye.
The Lord hath found a place to dwell,
    Hath chosen Zion fair;
His habitation it will be,
    It is His rest fore'er.

4 Her food abundant He will bless,
    Her needy, satisfy;
And with salvation clothe her priests,
    And all her want supply.
The horn of David's budding here,
    A lamp for earth's dark night.
His enemies are clothed with shame,
    His saints with crowns of light.

continued

5 And now within these latter days,
  Amidst earth's dark unrest,
God's house is being built again
  And all His people blessed.
Secure within the local church,
  With saints in one accord
We meet to just release our praise,
  And thus enjoy the Lord.

THE CHURCH — THE LORD'S RECOVERY

1251

Ezra 1-3
(Tune: #551)
Peculiar Meter.

1 To Jerusalem we've come,
  We are through with Babylon,
  We have gathered to be one,
    O glory be to God!
  Of the teachings we're bereft,
  All opinions we have left,
  Spirit from the soul is cleft,
    In the local churches now.

  Hallelujah! Hallelujah!
  We are all in one accord
  For the building of the Lord.
  Hallelujah! Hallelujah!
  We are living in the local
    churches now!

2   That recovery may proceed
Real priests are what we need —
Those who live in Christ indeed,
  O glory be to God!
Saturated with the Lord,
They have Christ as their reward.
These the building work afford
  In the local churches now.

3   And the kingship we must see
With divine authority —
To this rule we'll all agree,
  O glory be to God!
To the Spirit we'll submit
For the church's benefit —
This is His prerequisite
  In the local churches now.

4   We the altar must obtain,
Have our all upon it lain.
The burnt-offering must be slain,
  O glory be to God!
This we never should dispute,
For the church be absolute,
All that's otherwise uproot
  In the local churches now.

5   The foundation now is laid —
O what glory doth pervade!
We are all with joy arrayed,
  O glory be to God!
Let us raise a mighty shout —
They will hear us far without,
And the enemy we'll rout
  In the local churches now.

1252

Ezra 1

(Tune: #276)

10.9.10.9. with chorus.

1 Down in Babylon, in captivity,
  Oh, the Lord has stirred our spirit up!
Scattered everywhere, without unity,
  Oh, the Lord has stirred our spirit up!
    Stirred up! Stirred up!
    Oh, the Lord has stirred our spirit up!

2 Up from Babylon, where the sects abound,
  From division we must all rise up!
Brothers, Babylon's not the proper ground;
  From division we must all rise up!
    Rise up! Rise up!
    From division we must all rise up!

3 To Jerusalem, from captivity,
  God is with us, let us all go up!
To the one unique ground of unity,
  God is with us, let us all go up!
    Go up! Go up!
    God is with us, let us all go up!

4 Platters full of Christ, bowls with Spirit filled —
  All the vessels of the Lord bring up!
Bring them to the church as the Lord has willed —
  All the vessels of the Lord bring up!
    Bring up! Bring up!
    All the vessels of the Lord bring up!

5 In Jerusalem, chosen of the Lord,
  Now the temple of the Lord build up!
Serve with all the saints, share in one accord,
  Now the temple of the Lord build up!
    Build up! Build up!
    Now the temple of the Lord build up!

(Tune: #203)
8.7.8.7.D.

1 Lord, Thy word of old to David
We have heard and hear it now:
"On Thy throne will sit forever
Thine own seed — this is My vow."
This has been fulfilled in Jesus
Seated on the throne on high,
Sitting on the throne of David
Resurrected, ne'er to die.

2 Then another promise followed
David's seed upon the throne:
"I'll rebuild His tabernacle
And by this I will be known."
Lord, we thank Thee, Thou art faithful
To perform Thy promised word.
David's tabernacle, ruined,
Soon by Thee will be restored.

3 Lord, we are that tabernacle,
Thy rebuilding work on earth;
Lord, restore Thyself a dwelling
Where is seen Thy boundless worth.
Thus shall all of mankind seek Thee,
And the Gentiles call Thy name.
From Thy holy tabernacle
All the earth shall know Thy fame.

4 Hasten, Lord, Thy work upon us
To restore and build us now.
For this work we give ourselves, Lord;
Here to Thee we make a vow:
"Though our strength is weak and feeble,
Yet our hearts would ever be
From this day, Lord, for Thy building,
Now and for eternity."

1254

Haggai 1
Peculiar Meter.

1 This is the time for building the temple of the Lord
That all the local churches may fully be restored.
'Tis not the time for our house while God's house
  lieth waste —
O brothers, for God's building, rise up, make haste!

  Be strong, be strong, God's dwelling place to build!
  The Lord of hosts is with us, with His glory 'twill
    be filled!
  Be strong, be strong, and work in one accord,
  That all the nations may behold the temple of
    the Lord.

2 O hear, the Lord is speaking: Consider now your
    ways,
Ye sow and bring in little, for lacking is My praise.
Go up into the mountain, material to provide,
And build My house that I may be glorified.

3 Ye who are priests, ye remnant of Christians now
    obey —
The Lord Himself is with us, whatever men may
    say,
With spirits stirred and burning, now let us come
    to work;
May none his part with others in building shirk.

4 I'll fill this house with glory, the Lord of hosts
    has said,
And the desire of nations will be exhibited.
Its glory will be greater than all that's gone before,
And we will share this glory forevermore.

1255

Peculiar Meter.

We are for the Lord's recovery
  Of the local church;
We are for the Lord's recovery
  Of the city and the earth.
Standing on the ground of oneness,
  Oneness in the Lord,
We are building up the temple
  Of our glorious Lord.

  We are for the Lord's,
  We are for the Lord's,
We are for the Lord's recovery!
  We are for the Lord's,
  We are for the Lord's,
We are for the Lord's recovery!

We are for the Lord's recovery,
  To our hearts so dear;
When we exercise our spirit,
  Our vision is so clear.
Babylon the Great is fallen,
  Satan is cast down,
And the local church is builded
  On the local ground.

1256

Peculiar Meter.

Praise the Lord, we're in the Lord's recovery —
  Home at last, here in the church.
Praise the Lord, we're in the new creation —
  One new man, the end of our search.
With the saints, builded, coordinated;
  No more I, forever "we."
We are one in the Son, standing here till He comes;
Yes, nothing can stop our God till He's done!

1257

8.7.8.7. with chorus.

1 Do you see them in the cities,
　　Meeting on the local ground?
They're the local, golden lampstands,
　　Where the Lord His home has found.

　　'Tis the local church, the church God
　　　　has chosen,
　　　　Where all the saints dwell as one!
　　'Tis the local church, the church God
　　　　has chosen,
　　　　Where all the saints dwell as one!

2 Do you see them in the meetings,
　　Lifting up their voice on high,
Every brother, sister sharing,
　　Christ the Lord to magnify?

3 Do you hear them all pray-reading,
　　Breathing in the living Word?
Praying, praising, drinking, feeding,
　　How they all enjoy the Lord!

4 Do you hear them call, "Lord Jesus"?
　　How they love that blessed name!
All the more their joy increases
　　As His Lordship they proclaim.

5 Have you heard their hallelujahs,
　　Like a mighty thunder blast?
Hallelujah! Hallelujah!
　　Down the enemy is cast!

6 Do you see the saints migrating?
　　Praise the Lord the move is on
For the church in every city
　　That our blessed Lord may come!

7 Do you see the Lord is coming
   For the church for whom He died?
   In the churches He's preparing
   Now His holy, chosen Bride.

   'Tis a glorious church without spot or wrinkle,
     Filled with the glory of the Lord!
   'Tis a glorious church without spot or wrinkle,
     Filled with the glory of the Lord!

Psalm 84   **1258**

(Tune: #114)

8.7.8.7.D.

1 Oh, how lovable, how precious
   Are Thy local churches, Lord!
   My soul longeth, even fainteth
   For the courts of Thine abode;
   'Tis my heart's deep thirst and longing
   And my spirit deeply sighs;
   Fellowship among the churches —
   For this my whole being cries.

2 Blessed is the man whose heart, to
   Zion, is an open way;
   He's the one whose strength is in Thee;
   He will praise Thee all the day.
   In communion with the churches,
   Trusting Thee, Thy praise he sings;
   Passing through the weeping valley,
   It becomes a place of springs.

3 One day spent among Thy churches,
   Better than a thousand is!
   Even to the lowest member,
   Sun and shield Jehovah is.
   Grace and glory, every good thing,
   On us now He doth outpour;
   Blessed is that man who dwelleth
   In the churches evermore.

1259

(Tune: #871)
6.5.6.5.D. with chorus.

1 See the local churches,
  'Midst the earth's dark night;
  Jesus' testimony,
  Bearing Him as light.
  Formed by Him, unmeasured,
  In the Spirit's mold —
  All are one in nature,
  One pure work of gold.

  See the local churches,
  'Midst the earth's dark night;
  Burning in the Spirit,
  Shining forth with Christ.

2 God in Christ, embodied,
  As God's lampstand, He
  Has become the Spirit,
  The reality.
  Spirit as the lampstand
  Has been multiplied;
  Many local churches,
  Now are realized!

3 Caring for the churches
  Is the Son of Man:
  Voice of many waters,
  Stars in His right hand;
  Eyes aflame; His face is
  Shining as the sun;
  Churches — fear no trial,
  He's the living One!

4   What can quench the lampstands?
    Who can them defy?
    More the opposition —
    More they multiply!
    Deeper darkness 'round them,
    Brighter do they shine.
    They are constituted
    With the life divine.

5   Soon the local churches
    Shall the Bride become,
    Bringing in that city —
    New Jerusalem.
    Then the many lampstands
    Shall one lampstand be;
    Triune God expressing,
    Universally.

      Lo, from heav'n descending,
      All the earth shall see
      God's complete expression,
      For eternity.

1260

Peculiar Meter.

We're in the local church,
    God's chosen ground;
Here we have Christ as life
    And blessings all abound.
"In spirit, on the ground" —
    Our battle cry;
And we will overcome the enemy
    To bring the kingdom nigh.

1261

(Tune: #273)
Peculiar Meter.

1 In Chicago* land we must take our stand
   To meet Thy demand in these days.
   Lord, Thy purpose great doth our heart elate,
   As Thy name we now exalt and praise.

   Purpose, purpose, Thine eternal purpose;
   Show forth Christ and shame the enemy;
   Purpose, purpose, Thine eternal purpose
   In Chicago realized must be.

2 All things we forsake for Thy Body's sake,
   Soul-life for us break in Thy way.
   We've been wrecked by Thee, since Thy plan we see;
   On Thine altar everything we lay.

   Break us! Break us! For Thy purpose break us.
   Grant our spirits, Lord, a full release;
   Break us! Break us! For Thy purpose break us;
   In Chicago, Jesus must increase.

3 With this vision clear and Thy presence dear,
   Our hearts have no fear — forth we go.
   Lord, Thy heart's desire has set us afire;
   To Thy chosen ones this vision show:

   Lampstand, lampstand, see the golden lampstand,
   Shining with the glory of the Lord.
   Lampstand, lampstand, see the golden lampstand,
   In Chicago, Jesus Christ is Lord.

   *The name of the city may be replaced
   with any 3-syllable name; or in the place
   of "in Chicago," "here in Akron," or
   "here in Houston" may be sung.

(Tune: #116)
8.6.8.6.D.

1 It's by our mingled spirit, Lord,
      That we can shine with Thee,
   And be a golden lampstand now
      For all the world to see.
   It's not by forms or rituals,
      Mere Christianity;
   It's by our Christ enjoyed as life
      We all can shine with Thee.

2 The burning Christ has feet as brass
      Which in the furnace burns,
   His eyes are as a flame of fire —
      'Tis to this Christ we turn!
   How could we ever lukewarm be
      When on His face we gaze?
   O Lord, we give ourselves to You
      To set us all ablaze!

3 The seven golden lampstands in
      The seven cities see,
   So burning, shining with this Christ,
      It's God's economy!
   We're absolute that this become
      Our full reality
   Upon the earth, within the church
      In each locality.

1263

(Tune: #977)
8.7.8.7.D.

1 There's a church in New York City*,
   Standing on the local ground;
   There's a lampstand brightly beaming,
   Shining out to millions 'round.
   We were raised from every nation,
   Every people, tribe, and tongue —
   With us God has gained a dwelling,
   'Tis where all His own may come.

2 In your midst, O New York City,
   Little do you realize —
   Fallen is a seed within you,
   'Midst corruption it shall rise;
   Rising up in resurrection,
   With an increase many fold,
   It shall blossom, manifesting
   Riches of God's life untold.

3 For the church in New York City
   Faithfully the saints have prayed.
   'Gainst the church in New York City
   How the devil is enraged!
   For behold, within the center
   Of his kingdom, dark and grim,
   God has gained a testimony,
   Moving, fighting on for Him.

*The name of the city may be replaced with
other names that fit the meter: e.g. San Diego,
San Francisco. Or, the first line of each verse
may be sung as follows: There's a living church
in Dallas, Houston, Cleveland, etc.

4 There's a church in New York City
  Who the gospel does proclaim,
  To the hungry, poor, and weary,
  Sick, imprisoned, and the lame.
  Now this gospel of the kingdom
  Shall be preached until the end;
  Till the Lord who with the kingdom
  Of the heavens does descend.

5 There's a church in New York City,
  Honoring the risen Christ;
  Caring for the other churches —
  Following in truth and light;
  With them in coordination,
  We the kingdom will possess;
  Fighting as one mighty army,
  Till the kingdom's manifest.

Peculiar Meter.

1264

In the age of Revelation,
Out from all denomination,
We are in the local churches,
  In spirit one.
Nothing old or religious binds,
Everyone's a star that shines;
Every church a golden lampstand,
  Burning with Christ.

  Christ and a burning church,
  Christ and a burning church,
  Christ and the church with the saints,
    all shining stars!
  Hallelujah, hallelujah,
  Lord, we've given our all to Thee
  To be burning in the spirit, to be
    shining forth with Christ.

1265

(Tune: #877)
7.6.7.6.D. with chorus.

1 The churches are the Body
  Of Christ on earth today.
They are His testimony,
  That He may have a way.
They are the golden lampstands
  In cities far and wide.
They are His fighting army,
  And His beloved Bride.

> The churches, the churches,
>   Upon the earth today;
> Lord, stir our hearts for Thy desire,
> And build us, oh, build us, Lord,
>   we pray.

2 Oh, how we need the churches,
  All of them, great or small!
We need their many portions
  To profit us withal.
Yes, Lord, enlarge the churches;
  We love their needs to bear.
Enlarge our hearts, Lord Jesus,
  In fellowship and prayer.

3 The Lord's eyes o'er the whole earth
  Are running to and fro;
Those seven, burning, searching,
  Our heart's desire to know.
His purpose — many churches,
  Built up in one accord;
This golden testimony
  Will thus express the Lord.

4 And soon will be the coming
  Of our triumphant King!
  He's coming for the churches
  Where His sweet praises ring.
  Come, Lord, come reap the firstfruits,
  As draws the harvest nigh,
  And to Thy throne do take us,
  To reign with Thee on high.

(Tune: #1264)
Peculiar Meter.

1266

1 Burning, burning, we are burning,
  Ever to our spirits turning,
  One for Thine eternal purpose,
      in spirit one;
  On the ground of locality,
  We express our unity —
  Many members, but one Body,
      Christ as our Head.

  Christ and the local church,
  Christ and the local church,
  Christ and the church, our reality
      and life,
  Hallelujah! Hallelujah!
  Lord, we've given our lives to You,
  For the building of Your Body,
  For our building up in love.

2 Breathing, breathing, we are breathing,
  With each breath new life receiving,
  What a transformation from the old
      to the new;
  Breathing out the old life from us,
  Breathing in new life and oneness,
  We are breathing in of Jesus, we are
      breathing in of life.

1267

(Tune: #132)
8.7.8.7.

1 We are for the great migration,
And, O Lord, we seek Thy face.
Who? and when? and where? Lord Jesus,
Grant us now Thy blessed grace.

2 This is for Thy house and city,
This is for Thy kingdom, Lord;
To subdue the earth before us
We are all in one accord.

3 Of the Father, through Christ Jesus,
By the Spirit's flowing free;
In our spirit, on the church-ground —
This the way of victory.

4 Burden us with Thy great plan, Lord;
Consecrated we would be.
To fulfill Thy holy purpose
Saturate us thoroughly.

5 Build, O build us all together,
Let us here our lessons learn,
Send us forth to many cities
For the church-life there to burn.

6 Many places need a beachhead
To bring in Thy reign and rule.
Lord, build up the local churches
That Thy kingdom come in full!

7 Then the earth will give Thee glory
And the devil get the shame.
For Thy kingdom's rule and reigning
All will praise Thy glorious name.

8 Blessed days are quickly coming;
We rejoice and give Thee praise
For the glorious consummation
And Thy royal ruling days.

9 Hallelujah to the Father,
Hallelujah to the Son,
Hallelujah to the Spirit —
Hallelujah, it is done!

10 Hallelujah for the churches,
Hallelujah for the saints,
Hallelujah for the meetings
And their holy, sweet constraints!

11 Hallelujah, hallelujah,
Hallelujah we will sing;
Hallelujah, hallelujah,
Hallelujah to our King!

THE CHURCH — AS THE ARK OF NOAH

Genesis 6-8   **1268**
(Tune: #1152)
14.14.14.14. with chorus.

1 When Noah worked upon the ark as God to
him decreed,
So many others watched, yet to his words they
gave no heed.
But Noah heard the voice of God and did His
word obey;
His business was to build the ark; he couldn't
waste a day.

Now Jesus' testimony, we in the churches see,
The ark of testimony built in each locality.

2 The generation at that time was evil and perverse;
The wickedness upon the earth was waxing worse
and worse.
But Noah stood against the age and ne'er the
vision lost.
The ark of testimony must be built at any cost.

continued

1268

3 There were at that time many men who said
     they worshipped God;
  They served Him and they sacrificed and yet
     'twas very odd,
  The very thing that God desired they mocked
     and ridiculed.
  Their heart was set upon this age and by the
     devil ruled.

4 One day the ark was finished and eight souls
     were led aboard.
  God shut the door and then the heavens opened
     and outpoured.
  It rained, but Noah took no thought for he was
     safe inside.
  When all the earth was flooded, he above it all
     did ride.

5 The ark was just God's testimony on the earth
     that time.
  For God had found a corporate man through
     whom His light could shine.
  He needed something built through which He'd
     fully be expressed,
  And now it is the local church where God is
     manifest.

6 Be careful lest this age would lead you from God's
     heart's desire.
  For Jesus' testimony must set all our hearts afire.
  The local churches are the ark, God's testimony
     true.
  For this we leave the age behind and give our
     hearts anew.

(Tune: #871)
11.11.11.11. with chorus.

1 There in old Chaldea, product of man's fall,
God appeared to Abram — called him from it all.
"Get thee from thy country, from thy father's clan,
Get thee from thy kindred to another land."

Our Lord God Jehovah called a corporate man,
One that would express Him and fulfill His plan.

2 Through the Lord's infusion, Abraham became
Father of the faithful — life had changed his name.
Though the Lord's appearing, brought him
     to the land,
Still he needed Isaac to fulfill God's plan.

3 Isaac from his father did inherit all:
Sonship's full enjoyment, blessing of God's call.
Though all things receiving, incomplete was he;
Lacking transformation and maturity.

4 In his father's footsteps, Jacob then became
Prince of God, a wrestler, Israel his name;
By the Spirit's dealing, fully grown, he reigned;
O'er the earth, through Joseph, ruling pow'r
     obtained.

5 Thus do Jacob, Isaac, Abraham portray
Path that we, God's called ones, must walk
     in today:
Members of the Body, as a corporate man,
We complete His calling and fulfill His plan.

1270

(Tune: #1205)
8.6.8.6. with chorus.

1   We are the Hebrews! Praise the Lord!
    We're from the other side.
    Throughout our hist'ry we have passed
    Through rivers deep and wide.

        Praise the Lord! Praise the Lord!
        He has brought
        All us river-crossing Hebrews
        To the land, to build up
        The temple of our God.

2   Old Noah's age was so corrupt,
    In deep depravity;
    So Noah passed across the flood —
    That separating sea.

        Praise the Lord! He has brought
        From the old
        To a new recovered region
        Where he built in this land
        An altar for his God.

3   Then Abraham was called apart,
    For God to take a stand;
    So through the river he was led
    Into a new, good land.

        Step by step he was led
        From Chaldee
        Through the river into Canaan,
        That good land, there to be
        The servant of his God.

4   The Israelites in bondage were
    To Pharaoh's choking hand.
    The God of Hebrews made a way
    For them to leave that land.

        Through the sea, they all passed;
        Egypt fell,
        Hallelujah! In the good land
        They built up God's own house
        To satisfy His heart.

5   Then wand'ring through the wilderness,
    The land they could not find;
    Till through the Jordan they did pass
    To leave themselves behind.

        Praise the Lord! In the land
        They built up
        God's own temple. Hallelujah!
        Praise the Lord! There they dwelt,
        His people and their God.

6   But then religion conquered all,
    So John the Baptist came
    And buried all beneath that flood.
    The Jews were not the same.

        Buried all! Buried all!
        Buried all!
        Underneath the Jordan River
        Buried all to become
        The Hebrews passing through.

continued

7   Now in the church life, we have left
The world, religion too;
Now we're the river-crossing ones,
Enjoying Christ so new!

    Praise the Lord! Praise the Lord!
We have passed
From the oldness, Hallelujah,
Into Christ — one new man.
And now we're one with Him!

8   O Lord, You've taken us across
The fiery sea of glass,
With all the worldly things beneath;
Across the sea we've passed.

    Praise the Lord! Praise the Lord!
Now we stand
As the Hebrews, Hallelujah,
On the sea! Praise the Lord!
We've passed through everything!

1271

(Tune: #1222)
11.10.11.10. with chorus.

1   We're the river-crossers, Hebrews is our name;
Crossed the Euphrates, idols all are slain.
Entered into Canaan, left the other side;
Seeking a city, which shall e'er abide.
    We are the Hebrews, that's our real name;
We've crossed the river, we are not the same.
    Building God's house that He may dwell on earth,
Building God's house that He may dwell on earth.

2 We were bound in Egypt, building for the foe;
God of the Hebrews said, "Let My people go!"
We have crossed the Red Sea, reached the other side;
Pharaoh, his army, perished in the tide.
  God of the Hebrews, speak again today;
  God of the Hebrews, lead us all the way.
  Save all Your people from this crooked age,
  Save all Your people from this crooked age.

3 We're released, and now we build the house of God;
His tabernacle is our true abode.
Forty years of oldness left in Jordan's tide,
Fight we for Canaan on the kingdom side.
  Salvation's Captain sounds the trump of war;
  City by city, take we more and more,
  To gain His kingdom, enter into rest,
  To gain His kingdom, enter into rest.

4 What was once God-given soon a form became;
Then John the Baptist did God's word proclaim —
Make another crossing, God is going on;
Judaism's over; listen to My Son!
  Turn from the prophets, turn unto the Son;
  He's My Beloved, He and I are one;
  His Word will save you to the uttermost,
  His Word will save you to the uttermost.

5 Now we're overcomers on the sea of glass;
This final crossing will forever last.
Sing the song of Moses, make the praise complete,
Look! All our enemies beneath our feet.
  We're overcomers, that's our real name.
  God has His city; Satan gets the shame.
  God is our portion for eternity,
  God is our portion for eternity.

1272

(Tune: #892)
8.8.8.8.

1   The birthright God has giv'n to us
    Must be our goal, our highest prize,
    For we're the church of the first-born —
    Let us our portion realize!

2   A double portion of the land
    Was Joseph's birthright — and 'tis ours
    If we our garments keep from sin,
    And stay pure in temptation's hour.

3   The priesthood was to Levi giv'n
    As his inheritance — for he
    Did count his family ties but loss
    And owned God's things supreme to be.

4   The kingship, Judah did receive
    For tending to young Joseph's need;
    Through Benjamin's adversity,
    He was his comforter indeed.

5   The double portion we would seek,
    The priesthood and the kingship too;
    Make us so desperate, Lord, for Thee
    That Thee, our birthright, we'd pursue.

6   We would be those who pay the price,
    Deny the soul, reject the self;
    Ambitious for the birthright thus
    We'd gain Thee, Lord, above all else.

7   The promise, Lord, 'twas giv'n to us,
    Oh, let us ne'er this right despise;
    Enflame us, Lord, to gain Thyself,
    And Thee, our birthright realize.

(Tune: #1043)
7.7.7.3.D. with chorus.

1   Christ has called us once to Him,
    But He calls us once again.
    To His call we say Amen!
      Overcome!
    For the church has fallen low,
    Thinking everything they know,
    But the life is missing; so,
      Overcome!

      Overcome! Overcome!
      Overcome degraded Christianity!
      All your working lay aside,
      All the teachings that divide;
      Eat the Lord whate'er betide —
        Overcome!

2   Eating is man's destiny
    And the Lord's recovery;
    This defeats the enemy —
      Overcome!
    Come enjoy the tree of life,
    Leave the doctrines, leave the strife!
    Overcome by eating Christ —
      Overcome!

3   Teachings ne'er transform the soul,
    Teachings never reach God's goal,
    Eating Christ will do it all —
      Overcome!
    We must overcome to eat,
    By ourselves and when we meet,
    Eat Him as the feast complete —
      Overcome!

continued

THE CHURCH — THE OVERCOMERS

4   Eating gives the manchild birth,
Eating brings the Lord to earth;
Eat Him now midst all the dearth —
   Overcome!
Be the manchild Christ requires,
Thus the church that He desires,
Then the Bride that He admires —
   Overcome!

THE CHURCH — HER COURSE

1274

Revelation 2-3
(Tune: #892)
8.8.8.8.

1   In Revelation two and three,
The seven local churches see:
The lessons there for you and me
Are for the Lord's recovery.

2   The words to them are words to us,
So that the church be glorious,
And all their warnings we must heed
So that the Lord can meet His need.

3   To Ephesus, the word is clear:
"To your first love you're not so near;
You've left to work so far away;
Repent, return to Him today."

4   Thus, we must all turn back to Him,
Leave other loves, for these are sin.
Oh, let us hearken to His call —
If we miss this, we've missed it all!

5   Then unto Smyrna, suffering, sore —
"You have been tried, but something more —
Be faithful unto death," we're told
(Not just of body but of soul).

6 Be faithful 'til what's natural dies;
Your circumstances don't despise;
The Lord has sent them all to you
To prove that your first love is true.

7 From Pergamos we clearly see
The world has wed Christianity!
And faithful Antipas did fall —
He dared to stand against it all.

8 To wed the world we all must fear:
His spoken word will save us here —
If to His speaking we give heed,
We'll separated be indeed.

9 Then Thyatira comes at length:
Her mixture with the world her strength.
Fine flour leavened by the yeast,
A harlot riding on a beast.

10 Lord, we are mixed but hardly know;
To us this mixture fully show.
Each added thing we will refute
Until we're wholly absolute.

11 And then from Sardis, we can know
Life is the way that we must go!
She says she's living, but she's dead;
She needs to touch the Lord instead.

12 Lord, take us all the way to life
To overcome the deadness rife.
Away from deadness we would flee
That full of life we'll always be.

continued

13 Now Philadelphia comes at last;
That which she has she should hold fast —
The brothers' love, the name, the word;
This church has satisfied the Lord.

14 We as the brothers all are one;
We're one by life, and life alone.
If we His word and name do keep
A glorious building God will reap.

15 Laodicea warns us all:
From Philadelphia some will fall.
By saying, "I am rich," it's then
The Lord is outside wanting in.

16 Lukewarmness we must ever spurn
And in the spirit always burn,
The inward life experience gain,
And pay the price with Him to reign.

17 Lord, shine Your light on us today
That we may fully go Your way;
Anoint our eyes and let us see
So You can have recovery.

1275

THE CHURCH — PHILADELPHIA
Revelation 3:7-13
(Tune: #977)
8.7.8.7.D.

1 Glorious things to thee are spoken,
    Philadelphia, church of love.
These things saith the One who's holy,
    He who's real speaks from above;
He that has the key of David,
    Who the kingdom's entrance won,
"I will open, no man shutteth" —
    He has spoken; it is done.

2   Hallelujah, Philadelphia,
     Thine are works that please the Lord.
  Strength thou hast, though just a little
  And hast kept His living Word.
  Thou His holy name denied not,
     But confessed it here below —
  Lo, a door is set before thee,
     Through which none but thee can go.

3   Thou, beloved Philadelphia,
     Dost His Word of patience keep.
  From the hour of trial He'll save thee,
     Which o'er all the world shall sweep.
  Troublers too shall know He loves thee;
     They to thee must then bow down.
  "Hold thou fast, for I come quickly,
     That no man may take thy crown."

4   Hallelujah, overcomers,
     "In the temple of My God,
  I will build them in as pillars,
     Nevermore to go abroad."
  God's own name is written on them
  And the new name of the Lord.
  With the triune God they're blended;
     They're the city of our God.

5   Hallelujah, out of heaven,
     Comes the New Jerusalem:
  Gates of pearl and walls of jasper,
     Mingled with each precious gem.
  Philadelphia, Philadelphia,
     Has become His Bride so dear.
  Now the Spirit in the churches
     Speaks to all who have an ear.

1276

Revelation 3:7-13
(Tune: #73)
8.7.8.7.

1 Oh, the Lord is quickly coming,
He has spoken in His Word;
And confirmed it by the churches,
For His Spirit we have heard.

2 Not to all the seven churches
Did the Lord speak in this way;
To the church in Philadelphia
Did He choose these words to say.

3 Philadelphia, Philadelphia,
Church so full of brotherly love,
You're the church to bring the Bridegroom
Back to earth from heav'n above.

4 He that hath the key of David,
He that shuts and opens too,
Knows thy works, O Philadelphia;
That's why you're His Bride so true.

5 Not so strong by worldly standards,
Hidden from religion's fame;
Jesus loves you, Philadelphia,
For you're faithful to His name.

6 By His Word you're overcoming —
How the Amen does resound!
Just hold fast to what you've gotten,
That no man may take your crown.

7 You have kept His Word of patience;
He will keep you from that hour
Which upon the whole world cometh
When the Lord comes in His power.

8 "I come quickly," Philadelphia,
Speaks the Lord to none but you;
"Amen! Quickly come, Lord Jesus,"
Answer back His faithful few.

(Tune: #181 Second tune)
8.4.8.4.8.8.8.4.

1   Now in all the churches flowing,
      Brotherly love.
    Light and life and love bestowing,
      Brotherly love.
    In the oneness all believing,
    Fellowship with all receiving,
    Nevermore the Spirit grieving,
      Brotherly love.

2   To maintain the sweet communion,
      Brotherly love;
    Fellowship and healing union,
      Brotherly love.
    Love believing for the brothers,
    Hoping all things for the others,
    Suffering all with one another,
      Brotherly love.

3   For the issue of fruit bearing,
      Brotherly love.
    Fellowship in oneness sharing,
      Brotherly love.
    Here our soul life we're forsaking,
    And the Spirit's way we're taking,
    Now from death to life we're breaking,
      Brotherly love.

4   Oh, this perfect way of gladness,
      Brotherly love!
    No more fear, imparting sadness,
      Brotherly love!
    Now is our sure affirmation,
    Life and Spirit our foundation,
    Building up, the consummation —
      Brotherly love.

continued

5 Seed of life within us growing,
Brotherly love.
Philadelphia now is flowing,
Brotherly love.
To this love God has restored us;
Everything will fall before us;
Love is over all victorious,
Brotherly love!

THE CHURCH — GENERAL

1278 11.11.11.11.

1 In the church of Jesus there is love for you,
Love most pure and tender, love most deep and true;
Why should you be lonely, why for friendship sigh,
When the church of Jesus has a full supply?

2 In the church of Jesus there is life for you,
Warm as summer sunshine, sweet as morning dew;
Why should you be fearful, why take anxious thought,
Since the church of Jesus cares for those He bought?

3 In the church of Jesus there is work for you;
Such as even angels might rejoice to do;
Why stand idly sighing for some life work grand,
While the church of Jesus seeks your reaping hand?

4 In the church of Jesus there's a place for you;
Glorious, bright, and joyous, right and peaceful too;
Why then like a wand'rer, roam with weary pace,
If the church of Jesus holds for you a place.

(Tune: #1103)
Peculiar Meter.

1 What we are, we're His image;
   We're created in His image,
   To express the Christ, subdue the earth,
   The purpose of our second birth,
   We're His image, glorious!

2 What we are, we're the called ones,
   We've been called into the purpose.
   No longer low in Adam's fall,
   God's glory is our holy call.
   We're the called ones, glorious!

3 What we are, we're the joint-heirs;
   We inherit full salvation.
   We overcome and share His throne.
   All things today we fully own.
   We're the joint-heirs, glorious!

4 What we are, we're Christ's partners:
   We share the same anointing.
   No longer we're just serving Him;
   His riches we may all share in.
   We're His partners, glorious!

5 What we are, we're the brothers.
   We are all the holy brothers.
   The life of Christ we did obtain,
   For holiness the gold we gain.
   Holy brothers, glorious!

6 What we are, we're the lampstand;
   We're the shining forth of Jesus.
   In this world's darkness, sin, and strife,
   We're holding Christ, the light of life.
   We're the lampstand, glorious.

1280

8.7.8.7. with chorus.

1 We've become the Lord's dear brothers
   Through His resurrection pow'r;
   He desires many brothers
   Sharing in His triumph hour!

> Jesus is our Elder Brother,
> First-born of God's sons is He;
> He came forth in resurrection,
> From religion He is free!
> As His church we come together;
> Oldness, form, and self deny;
> Just to meet with our Big Brother,
> Him alone to glorify!

2 In our Brother's resurrection
   Resurrected we must meet,
   Never in our natural standing —
   This will make His joy complete!

3 Every day we must see Jesus
   As we're eating of the Word;
   Then we'll run to all the meetings
   Burning, bubbling with the Lord!

4 In the meetings we are feasting
   On the food unlimited.
   Jesus always satisfies us,
   Feeding us the living bread!

5 We would satisfy our Brother,
   Even though our portion's small.
   Every one must share his "new dish"
   For the benefit of all!

6 Not for message or for speaker,
   But to meet the Lord we're here;
   Caring only for His presence,
   We would see our Brother dear!

MEETINGS — IN RESURRECTION

1 All the meetings Christ appointed
 And attended here on earth
Were apart from all religion,
 All its rituals, forms, and dearth.
Resurrection, not religion,
 Must be our reality;
Let us meet in resurrection,
 From all dead religion free.

2 When the Lord was resurrected,
 All religious things were through;
Christ is now our living temple,
 Christ is all our offerings too.
With our Lord in resurrection,
 Hallelujah, we're released!
Pity all the old religion —
 All our meetings are a feast!

3 Yet religion — oh, how subtle —
 In our blood is hiding out;
God must give us revelation,
 All that unseen monster rout.
Lord, we still are too religious —
 Down with our religious soul!
We would all release our spirit,
 Let each meeting reach the goal.

4 In the meetings, in the meetings,
 On the mountain, at the shore,
Jesus, Jesus, living Jesus,
 He is here — what want we more?
Bury all the old religion,
 Even Christianity —
Jesus, Jesus, we have Jesus,
 He is our reality!

SPIRITUAL WARFARE — MARCHING ON

1282

Peculiar Meter.

Marching on, marching on, in the Spirit
    marching on;
  Hallelujah! the churches march on.
Marching on, marching on, in the Spirit
    marching on;
  Hallelujah! the churches march on.
    In the church we see
    The Lord's recovery
And for it the Spirit seven-strong.
    The world will know,
    Wherever we shall go,
That in our age the Lord's marching on!

SPIRITUAL WARFARE — FIGHTING ON

1283

Peculiar Meter.

Fight, saints, for Jesus our Lord!
Take in His life, stand in one accord!
Never fear God's enemy;
Tread on his head triumphantly!
Pray that the daily church life be strong,
That all the saints in spirit press on,
Fighting as the one new man,
Fulfilling our Lord's great plan!
    (Glory! Hallelujah!)

(Tune: #877)
7.6.7.6.D. with chorus.

1 Our eyes have seen the vision:
The goal is now in view,
Christ has defeated Satan,
And sin and death are through.
The way is cut and open,
The paths are all made straight;
We've heard the call: Come forward!
We've laid aside each weight.

Come forward! Come forward!
Our Christ is on the throne.
His ministry, so heavenly,
Brings all — brings all the fighters home.

2 Our eyes have seen the vision
Since Christ our conquering King
Has called us to the battle,
Which He did surely win.
The vict'ry He bequested
Two thousand years ago
To all the glorious fighters
Who'll forward with Him go.

3 Our eyes have seen the vision.
Our Captain leads us on.
To press into our spirit,
To share with Him the throne.
Lord, Thou hast giv'n Thy soldiers
The pow'r to wield the sword,
And made us glorious fighters
Through Spirit, church, and Word.

1285

(Tune: #333)
8.6.8.6. with chorus.

1 The faith which once for all was giv'n
 Unto the saints of old,
Has been committed unto us
 To guard, defend, and hold.

  And we know whom we have believèd
  And are persuaded that He is able
  To guard, through the Holy Spirit,
  Our deposit to that day.

2 This good deposit is the mark
 Of God's economy,
Without it we will miss the aim
 Of His recovery.

3 The myst'ry of the common faith,
 A conscience pure requires;
A holy, separated life
 For us the Lord desires.

4 This outline of the healthy words,
 In faith and love we'll hold;
All different teaching, fruitless talk,
 Reject with spirit bold.

5 Oh, healthful teaching, wholesome words:
 The truth of godliness!
Oh, good deposit, common faith,
 And life of holiness!

6 Lord, make us now those faithful men
 Who pass on what we've heard;
Make us examples of the saints
 In spirit, faith, and word.

(Tune: Loyalty to Christ)
6.6.12.6.6.12. with chorus.

1286

1   The Lord has shown the way
     Within the church today —
It's laboring, laboring, laboring on Christ.
     Christ is the Canaan land;
     In Him we boldly stand,
While laboring, laboring, laboring on Christ.

     On to victory! On to victory!
     Cries our great Commander — On!
       We'll move at His command
       And now possess the land
     Through laboring, laboring, laboring on Christ.

2   The way that God has planned
     To labor on the land
Is "Amen, Lord! Amen, Lord! Amen to Your Word!"
     Whene'er He speaks today,
     Whatever He may say,
It's "Amen, Lord! Amen, Lord! Amen to Your Word!"

     On to victory! On to victory!
     Cries our great Commander — On!
       We'll move at His command
       And now possess the land
     By "Amen, Lord! Amen, Lord! Amen to Your Word!"

3   The Lord has also shown
     The land we'll fully own
By following, following, following the church.
     Where'er the Body goes,
     Howe'er the Spirit flows,
It's following, following, following the church.

     On to victory! On to victory!
     Cries our great Commander — On!
       We'll move at His command
       And now possess the land
     By following, following, following the church.

1287
(Tune: #1118)
12.10.12.10. with chorus.

1 Let's take the land! The land that God has given us;
In all our living, Christ can be so much:
To take this land, we have th' equipment that
    we need —
The blood, the Word, the Spirit, and the church.

(Sisters sing)
Let's take the land! O Christian brothers,
The land that God has given us.
Be strong and take it, for we can make it
And gain this land so glorious!

(Brothers sing)
Let's take the land! O Christian sisters,
And to these things give earnest heed.
The Lord implores us; He's gone before us
And given everything we need!

2 We have the blood! Christ is our spotless offering,
Who gave Himself, our God to satisfy;
And so we come with boldness to the throne of grace,
And all day long, the precious blood apply.

3 We have the Word! The written Word's our daily food;
We mix this Word with faith and say "Amen!"
Then thro' the day, the spoken Word will speak to us
And regulate our living from within.

4 The Spirit's ours! The Spirit of reality,
He's independent of the way we feel;
He dwells in us, and teaches us to dwell in Him,
And guides us into everything that's real.

5 We have the church! All saints are needed to possess
The fullness of this vast reality;
Together we will gain this all-inclusive Christ,
And He to us our everything will be.

(Tune: #886)
Peculiar Meter.

1 In Eden's garden, Satan thought
   He'd wreck the Lord's intention.
   And so, conspiring, then, he wrought
   His subtle intervention.
   To man he entered in,
   Became indwelling sin,
   And by this deed so bad
   He really thought he had
   Undone the Lord completely.

2 'Twas all according to God's plan
   To trap the Devil, Satan.
   His sphere of moving narrowed now,
   Man's flesh his habitation;
   Though brilliant was his plan
   To enter into man,
   This man became instead
   The means to bruise his head,
   And finish him forever.

3 So Christ put on our human flesh —
   An act of wisdom purely.
   And on the cross did thus enmesh
   His foe held so securely.
   Though desperate Satan's plight —
   He fought with all his might;
   But when the morning came
   Christ was alive again,
   And Satan crushed forever.

1289

(Tune: #1118)
12.10.12.10. with chorus.

1 The vict'ry's won! The Lord has triumphed
    o'er the foe!
  The vict'ry shout is heard afar and near!
  His blood prevails! It giveth us the victory!
  And soon the mighty Victor will appear.

> *(Sisters sing)*
> The vict'ry's won! O Christian brothers,
> The vict'ry's won! This shout we raise!
> In Zion's city, proclaim His vict'ry
> Till all the earth is filled with praise.

> *(Brothers sing)*
> The vict'ry's won! O Christian sisters,
> The mighty work of Christ is done!
> The Lord victorious has conquered for us —
> Eternal joys have now begun.

2 The vict'ry's won! We've overcome the enemy.
  The Word of God we boldly testify.
  God speaks His Word — in it there's life and
    liberty —
  And by the Word the devil we defy.

3 The vict'ry's won! Beneath our feet the enemy,
  For we love not our soul life unto death;
  And so we shout, "O Lord, You are our victory!"
  And praise our God with all our spirit's breath.

(Tune: #36)

13.13.13.13.

1   O Lord, we've seen Your purpose to bring the
        many sons
    To share in Your full glory and see Your kingdom
        come.
    We praise You, Lord, this glory is You, Yourself
        within,
    Spread out in all Your people to shine in all of them.

2   Since we received Your life, Lord, a seed's been
        growing there:
    The seed of inward glory, the glory we will share!
    By growing 'til the blossom of glory blooms in full,
    We'll thus enjoy Your increase and glory bountiful.

3   Hail! Captain of Salvation! Our heav'nly Pioneer!
    Our praises, midst the battle and tumult, You will
        hear.
    We're following our Captain all through the mighty
        fray.
    Our glorious, faithful Captain sustains us all the way.

4   Lord, fighting on to glory, You now have gone before;
    Now fighting in Your footsteps we'll conquer o'er
        and o'er.
    From glory unto glory, we'll fight until we see
    The glory from within us shall manifested be.

5   Then, Lord, at last the fighting and battle cry
        will cease,
    And we'll appear in glory, Your kingdom and increase.
    That day we'll be completed, that day Your face
        we'll see,
    For in that blessed day, Lord, we'll in the glory be!

1291

Luke 22:31-32
(Tune: #1194)
13.13.13.13.D.

1 At the end of Luke's gospel, chapter twenty
    and two,
The Lord says to Peter, "Satan wants to sift you,"
But the Lord's interceding and His prayer is true,
Hallelujah! He's prayed for us, we'll never
    sift through!

    Though there's all kinds of battles in our
        living each day,
    And we always face trials, life is ordered
        that way,
    Still, in all situations, as He intercedes,
    He in all things supplies us and meets all
        of our needs.

2 Just a Christian alone, however strong he may be
Cannot withstand the sifting of the Lord's enemy;
Though he might sift one only, yet he'll ne'er
    sift two,
Hallelujah! Together we're too big to sift through!

3 What a wonderful purpose God has purposed for us,
To be transformed and reigning with His Son,
    glorious;
So it just doesn't matter what the foe might do —
Hallelujah! The church is much too big to sift
    through!

(Tune: #904)
8.8.8.8.D.(A)

1   An uplifted gospel have we,
    One we're not ashamed to proclaim.
    Our gospel's the highest of all,
    For it is God's goal and God's aim.
    No longer so lowly and poor,
    We've found that we're God's holy sons.
    No more will we preach as before;
    Now each man on earth can be won.

2   Our Brother's inherited all
    God made Him to rule His affairs
    Appointed — this office He fills
    And shares it with us, His joint-heirs.
    Elected before earth was formed,
    We've found that we are qualified
    To share all His glory and worth.
    How could men but for Christ decide?

3   Yes, we're holy brothers with Christ,
    No higher could any man be.
    This highest of all gospels is;
    This gospel each human must see.
    Partakers of this heavenly call,
    Could any this gospel reject?
    With Christ sitting far above all —
    This highest of all gospels yet!

1293

Peculiar Meter.

1 O I'm a man —
 I'm the meaning of the universe;
 Yes, I'm a man —
 I'm the meaning of the universe.
   God made me such,
   I am so much;
 I'm the center and the meaning of the universe.

2 Christ lives in me —
 He's the meaning of my human life;
 Christ lives in me —
 He's the meaning of my human life.
   Yes, He's in me
   My all to be;
 He's the meaning and reality of my human life.

3 The church is Christ —
 His expression on the earth today;
 The church is Christ —
 His expression on the earth today.
   This corporate man
   Fulfills God's plan,
 That this man may have dominion over all the earth.

4 The local church —
 It's the new and real family life;
 The local church —
 It's the new and real family life.
   We have the way
   To live today —
 Eating, drinking Christ we're built up as the
     local church.

5   What shall we do?
      We should go and tell the world of this.
    What shall we do?
      We should go and tell the world of this.
          Disciple all —
          This is our call.
    Let us go and spread the news abroad to every land.

PREACHING OF THE GOSPEL —
SPEAKING THE WORD
(Tune: #1293)
Peculiar Meter.

1294

1   Come let us speak till the kingdom of the
          Lord comes down.
    Yes, let us speak till the kingdom of the
          Lord comes down.
          Why hold your peace?
          The Word release.
    Let us speak until the kingdom of the Lord
          comes down.

2   Oh, loose the Word! It shall not return
          unto Him void.
    Yes, loose the Word! It shall not return
          unto Him void.
          Let's sow the seed,
          This is our need;
    Loose the Word, and it shall not return
          unto Him void!

continued

3 It's gospel time! Let us spread the gospel
    all around.
  Yes, gospel time! We will never fear the
    people's frown!
  God's done His work;
  Let us not shirk;
  We're but pilgrims here, and we'll not fear
    the people's frown!

4 If we will speak, Christ will witness in the
    hearts of men.
  If we will speak, Christ will witness in the
    hearts of men.
  Tell every man,
  Win all we can.
  Through our speaking, Christ is speaking
    in the hearts of men!

5 The harvest's ripe! We are preaching the
    full gospel now!
  The fields are white! We are preaching the
    full gospel now!
  For this men search —
  Christ and the church!
  Let us reap the harvest, preaching the
    full gospel now!

Philippians 1
10.6.10.6.D.

1 Ours is a fellowship in the gospel
  Since we received the Lord;
We're for the furtherance of the gospel,
  Spreading to all His Word.
For its defense and strong confirmation
  We all partake of grace —
He who began this work will perfect it
  Till we shall see His face.

2 May all the things that come to us daily
  Unto the gospel turn,
That all may see we're bound for the gospel
  And of the Lord may learn.
May we be bold and fearless in spirit,
  Speaking the Word of God,
Do it in love and do it in power,
  While living in the Lord.

3 Lord, we're expecting that we'll be given
  Boldness with every breath.
Christ must be magnified in our body
  Whether by life or death.
We hope in nothing to be ashamed,
  For us to live is Christ —
He is the Person in all our living,
  Our everything, our life.

4 May all our lives be worthy the gospel
  Whatever may betide,
All standing fast in oneness of spirit,
  All striving side by side.
Let us proclaim the gospel in fullness
  To satisfy the Lord:
Christ is the life, the church His expression,
  Sound everywhere abroad.

THE KINGDOM — ITS COURSE

(Tune: #884)

8.6.8.6.D.

1 The universe of God consists
   Of heaven, earth, and air.
The enemy of God resists
   His purpose everywhere.
At first the mighty rebel one
   The earth from God obtained;
Then from the Lord the air had won,
   Establishing his reign.

2 So God's intention was to gain
   His kingdom on the earth,
The place where He could fully reign
   And show to all His worth.
Thus He began in Genesis
   To forward His great plan.
Out of this darkened, lost abyss
   Our God created man.

3 But Satan caused the man to fall
   From God's eternal grace.
Then Abraham received the call
   To head the chosen race.
The Jews were led from Pharaoh's hand
   Through sea and wilderness
Into the promised Canaan land,
   God's kingdom to express.

4 The Israelites refused God's reign,
   Desired an earthly king;
The kingdom then was lost again
   Till David was to bring
God's kingdom back to earth once more
   For God to rule through him;
But Israel failed as once before
   God's kingdom to bring in.

5 Such was the situation when
   Our God became a man,

Declaring to all men,"Repent!
  The kingdom is at hand."
A perfect model of God's rule,
  The King, full qualified!
But Satan as a desperate fool
  Had Jesus crucified.

6 This Jesus went into the grave
  And death He overcame.
Now resurrected He will save
  The earth from Satan's reign.
He as the Spirit enters man
  To fill him with His life.
These men, the church, fulfill His plan
  To save the earth from strife.

7 Now on the earth the church we see,
  God's kingdom here expressed,
Where He has full authority
  His rule to manifest.
The place where Satan has to flee
  Our mighty conquering rod,
The kingdom through the church will be
  Brought to the earth for God.

ITS INNER REIGN
Peculiar Meter.

1297

From the beachhead in our spirit
  To our mind, emotion, will.
Christ will spread through all our being
  And our vessel wholly fill.
He will cast out all rebellion,
  Change our darkness into light.
Satan's kingdom will be swallowed,
  And Christ will reign with might.
This is the Lord's recovery,
  This is His very best!
Brothers, give the Lord the ground in you
  Till His kingdom's manifest.

1298

(Tune: #295)
8.8.8.8.

1 Chosen by God in ages past,
   Our God will never let us go;
  Salvation is assured fore'er;
   'Tis such security we know.

2 "I give to them eternal life,
   They shall not perish," is His word;
  "No one shall snatch them from Our hands,"
   This is the promise of the Lord.

3 Yet there's a word for God's own sons,
   Which is a warning from the Lord:
  For those not ready when He comes,
   "Worse punishment" and not "reward."

4 Reward is not eternal life,
   It's based on how we run the race;
  It all depends on what we build,
   It's not a matter, here, of grace.

5 'Tis for God's kingdom we press on,
   Like Moses, we are for the Lord;
  We suffer with God's people here
   And look away to the reward.

6 Richer by far, reproach of Christ,
   Than Egypt's treasures, which are sin;
  By faith we leave Egyptian land,
   Avoiding next age discipline.

7 Our soul gained for the kingdom's age —
   For this we lose our soul life here;
  If we lay down our soul life now,
   We'll save it for Christ's kingdom there.

8 We all must learn to pay the price,
   Christ must be worked into our soul;
  'Tis thus our soul is gained by Him,
   This is our aim and this our goal.

(Tune: #125)
8.7.8.7.D.

1 Man's Creator has a purpose
   For our being here on earth.
   In His image we're created,
   To express His rule on earth.
   But man fell to Satan's tempting;
   Thus God's goal was hid from view.
   Still our God will have His kingdom,
   For His Son will see it through.

2 Jesus Christ will get His kingdom
   Notwithstanding Satan's plans;
   He's obtaining something real by
   Growing in the hearts of man.
   Nothing like religion teaches:
   "You must wait until you die" —
   For the kingdom Christ is building,
   Is on earth before our eyes.

3 His Son, Jesus, is our Savior.
   Once in human form He came.
   Now as Spirit He can enter
   As the breath of life to man.
   As a seed within our spirit
   Christ takes root and starts to grow,
   Spreading in our inmost being
   Till His life we come to know.

4 Time is short, oh, brothers, hear it,
   Christ is longing for His Bride.
   We can hasten His returning
   Simply by the growth in life.
   No more struggling, no more striving,
   Simply turn to Christ within.
   See the seed begin to blossom,
   Growing fully into Him.

continued

5 Jesus Christ will get His kingdom
Just by growth — the normal way.
Not an instant transformation;
Growth goes on from day to day.
This life-seed is all-inclusive —
Everything we'll ever need;
Yes, our God's eternal purpose
Is within this precious seed.

1300

(Tune: #396)
8.8.8.8.D.

1 The Lord has been revealed in us,
The kingdom-seed so glorious;
He's planted deeper than our heart,
And from us He will ne'er depart.
This seed is never satisfied
Just in our spirits to abide;
He wants to grow and spread today
To live in us in every way.

2 We're like a glove, an empty man,
So meaningless without a hand;
Lord, saturate each inward part
And form Yourself in all our heart.
The Lord must spread into our mind,
Our natural thoughts and concepts bind;
Imaginations, dreams be gone,
The kingdom-seed in us is sown!

3 In our emotions He must grow;
Raw, fragile feelings overthrow;
Our love, our hatred, must be His —
Lord, we agree with You for this.
Another part the Lord must fill —
Our hard, unbending, stubborn will;
Lord, our resistance quickly break,
Subdue us for Thy kingdom's sake.

4 Our conscience too the Lord must clear,
That we may walk in godly fear;
Our conscience must be keen today,
Else we cannot the Lord obey.
'Tis by His growing, spreading thus,
The Lord will have His home in us;
A place on earth where He is Lord,
Full rights to Him we will afford.

(Tune: #151)
10.10.10.10. with chorus.

1301

1 Jesus the kingdom has come into us,
Reigning and shining He's all glorious,
Christ as the seed is the King who has come,
Into our spirit His kingdom He's sown.

O let Him grow, O let Him grow;
His kingdom life be all we know.
Jesus, the kingdom is sown into us;
Jesus, the kingdom, O how glorious!

2 We must repent for the kingdom's at hand;
All that we do, think, or feel, or have planned
Must be abandoned and changed in our mind;
Leave all the world and self-seeking behind.

3 All of religion has missed it again,
Teaching for doctrines the concepts of men;
They vainly wait for the kingdom to be.
A dispensation they're hoping to see.

4 But now the kingdom to us has been shown,
It is no less than our Jesus alone.
It is the Person of Christ in us all,
And it begins as a seed when we call.

1302

Matthew 25:1-13
7.7.7.7. with chorus.

1 All the signs point to the end,
Christ soon will be here again;
We must be ready for Him —
Jesus is coming again!

Coming again, coming again,
Time is swiftly passing by,
Soon we may hear the midnight cry!
Coming again, coming again,
As the wise virgins we must be prepared!
Jesus is coming again!

2 From soul and self turn away,
Look unto Jesus today;
There is no time to delay —
Jesus is coming again!

3 Foolish ones never will turn;
When the Lord comes they will learn
There is no oil left to burn —
Jesus is coming again!

4 Wise virgins buy up the time;
Never drunk with the world's wine,
Filled in the spirit they shine —
Jesus is coming again!

5 Let us go forth unto Him,
Not only with our lamps trimmed,
Buy the oil now lest they dim —
Jesus is coming again!

6 Jesus is now on His way,
Watch, for you know not the day;
Ever in His presence stay —
Jesus is coming again!

Matthew 25:1-13   **1303**
(Tune: #904)
8.8.8.8.D.(A)

1 The kingdom of God is at hand:
   Ten virgins with lamps lit arise
   To go forth to meet the Bridegroom,
   But only five virgins are wise.
   The wise have abundance of oil,
   The foolish are empty instead;
   The wise used their time to buy oil,
   The others their chance forfeited.

2 Lord Jesus, Thy message is clear:
   You're coming for those who are wise,
   Who buy up their oil today,
   Who deal with all hindering ties.
   Those virgins whose souls are transformed,
   Whose vessels much oil contain,
   Who love not their lives unto death —
   They in Thy great kingdom shall reign.

3 Our lamps to shine forth must be trimmed
   By calling on Thee every day.
   In spirit we must exercise
   To burn all the oldness away.
   But there is a much deeper need:
   Reality in us must grow,
   Until it makes home in our hearts,
   Till oil in our vessels o'erflows.

4 We see how this age is so dark,
   We know that blest hour is near.
   Our Lord may return anytime —
   Lord, strike in us this holy fear,
   That we may each moment redeem
   By taking Thy Word in·by prayer,
   By learning each lesson You give,
   And thus for that hour prepare.   *continued*

5   Lord Jesus, how blest to be those
Who bring in Thy kingdom to earth,
Affording Thee rule over all
And showing to all Thy great worth!
How blest to be those at the feast,
Where Thou wilt be one with Thy Bride!
Lord, make us wise virgins for Thee,
Who e'er in Thy presence abide.

1304   Matthew 25; Revelation 14
(Tune: #1043)
7.7.7.3.D. with chorus.

1   Christ comes quickly for His Bride,
Wedding feast He will provide,
Garments bright and pure supplied —
    Dress in time!
Taking Christ as life she's dressed,
By much suffering stitched and pressed;
Righteous acts are thus possessed —
    Dress in time!

    Be in time! Be in time!
    For the marriage feast of Jesus
        Be in time!
    If your soul life you deny
    And the Spirit you apply,
    Then you'll fully qualify —
        Be in time!

2   Virgins Christ comes quickly for,
Those with oil an extra store,
Not the fools who oil ignore —
    Buy in time!
For the oil a price we pay,
Deal with self without delay,
Fill your vessels every day —
    Buy in time!

3 For His servants Christ will come
   And reward each faithful one;
   Slothful ones will be undone —
       Serve in time!
   Make your single talent count,
   All self's problems now surmount,
   Serve with Christ, the living fount —
       Serve in time!

4 Christ comes quickly for His grain,
   Ripened firstfruits to obtain;
   Unripe harvest will remain —
       Ripen now!
   From earth's water grain must dry,
   From the world your soul deny;
   To mature the self must die —
       Ripen now!

5 Overcomers Christ will take,
   Those who all for Him forsake,
   Those who of first love partake —
       Win in time!
   All the deadness overcome,
   With the living Christ be one,
   Toward the goal now swiftly run —
       Win in time!

6 Christ comes for His kingdom too;
   Heav'nly reign we must pursue,
   Let His rule our self subdue —
       Yield in time!
   Rebel self must be dethroned,
   Lessons must not be postponed,
   Quickly yield to Christ enthroned —
       Yield in time!

1305

12.12.12.12. with chorus.

1 Our faith to God-ward must in these days spread
    abroad
To show we've turned from idols to the living God.
We'll mix His Word with faith by answering "Amen!"
And to Christ in the Word turn again and again.

Our work of faith must grow exceedingly,
The labor of our love increase abundantly,
His sanctifying work in us go on and on,
While in patience of hope we will watch till
    He come.

2 The love for all the brothers, in our midst is found,
But in these days our love must increase and abound.
The Lord direct our hearts into the love of God
And prepare us in full for the day of the Lord.

3 Our spirit, soul, and body wholly sanctified —
Our faithful Lord will do it to prepare His Bride,
While we amen His voice in matters great or small,
That we all may be ready to hear Jesus' call.

4 The Lord Himself shall come, and we shall be
    with Him —
Oh, what a glorious hope! Come quickly, Lord,
    Amen.
We'd ever watchful be to see Thee in the air
And as sons of the day for that meeting prepare.

(Tune: #853)
6.6.8.6.

1 We love Thy coming, Lord!
   We know not when 'twill be,
   But turn from all distracting things
   Thine own dear face to see.

2 We serve the living God
   And wait His Son to see;
   For this we need faith, love, and hope,
   Increasing constantly.

3 In Thy dear presence, Lord,
   We hope we all may be
   A crown of glory and a joy
   To those we then shall see.

4 We love Thy coming, Lord;
   The time is very nigh.
   Our hearts unblameable must be
   To greet Thee from on high.

5 The Lord Himself shall come
   With loud assembling word,
   And all the saints in Christ shall be
   Forever with the Lord.

6 We're children of the day,
   We're children of the light;
   That day should never come to us
   As does a thief at night.

7 Lord, wholly sanctify
   And blameless let us be
   In spirit, soul, and body too
   For that blest day with Thee.

1307

11.10.11.10.D.

1 The day approaches; Jesus soon is coming.
Redeem the time; it must not slip away.
Lord, make us ready for the cry: "Behold Him!"
By using every moment of each day.

When Jesus comes, will we go in to meet Him?
When Jesus comes, will we from self have ceased?
He's coming soon to take the wise ones with Him.
Oh, let us not be left outside the feast.

2 Lord, help us to redeem these golden moments;
Our vessels fill with ointment from above;
Help us amen each trial and tribulation;
Increase in us; make us abound in love.

He's coming soon — these moments are so precious.
The oil is here — Oh, let us buy the more.
Amen the trials and welcome tribulations —
The kingdom's ours through these afflictions sore.

3 Lord, ever turn us from our soulish pleasures
To gaze upon Thy tender, loving face.
Oh, keep us running forth to meet the Bridegroom
And patiently attending to the race.

When Jesus comes, will we be in His presence?
When Jesus comes, will we His face behold?
Oh, let us not return to sloth and folly,
But jealously His loving presence hold.

4 As His dear Bride, let us go forth to meet Him,
Our lamps well-trimmed, our fires burning bright,
Our vessels filled, our eyes set on His glory,
To be with Him completely satisfied.

Yes, satisfied — Christ and His Bride together.
Yes, satisfied — throughout eternity.
Oh, what a rest, what joy, what love, what favor
To be His Bride when He comes to His feast!

Matthew 25:1-13   **1308**
10.8.10.9. with chorus.

1 We have oil in our lamps — we are burning!
  We have oil in our lamps today!
 To the spirit, O Lord, keep us turning,
  Keep us turning, turning all the way!

  O Lord! Amen! Hallelujah!
  We are burning, burning every day!
  O Lord! Amen! Hallelujah!
  Turning, turning all the way!

2 But our vessels need oil for Thy coming;
  We must gain a reserve supply.
 So our vessels we give for the filling
  That our lamps may never, never die.

  Fill us, Jesus! Fill us, Jesus!
  Every moment give us more of Thee!
  Fill us, Jesus! Fill us, Jesus!
  Fill us with reality!

3 Then we'll burn till the Lord comes to meet us,
  Then we'll burn till He comes that day.
 Then we'll go in with Him to the wedding
  And be brightly burning all the way.

  Come, Lord Jesus! Come, Lord Jesus!
  Come and find us filled and burning bright!
  Come, Lord Jesus! Come, Lord Jesus!
  Come and in Thy Bride delight.

1309

11.7.11.7. with chorus.

1 Who can tell how soon the Bride may hear the cry,
   "Behold, the Bridegroom cometh!"
   Hear the shout of triumph ringing in the sky,
   "Behold, the Bridegroom cometh!"

   We can almost see His glory in the sky;
   It must be the dawning of that day is nigh.
   How our hearts would leap if we should hear
       the cry,
       "Behold, the Bridegroom cometh!"

2 Who will have their lamps all trimmed and burning
       bright?
   "Behold, the Bridegroom cometh!"
   Extra oil have ready should you hear tonight,
   "Behold, the Bridegroom cometh!"

3 Who will now be washed by water in the Word?
   "Behold, the Bridegroom cometh!"
   Spots and wrinkles cleanse before the shout is heard,
   "Behold, the Bridegroom cometh!"

4 Who will be the counterpart to Christ today?
   "Behold, the Bridegroom cometh!"
   Ready be to match Him now without delay,
   "Behold, the Bridegroom cometh!"

5 Who will now be clothed in linen bright and pure?
   "Behold, the Bridegroom cometh!"
   Acts of righteousness will make her rapture sure,
   "Behold, the Bridegroom cometh!"

6 Hark! As one the Spirit and the Bride doth say,
   "Behold, the Bridegroom cometh!"
   Brothers, sisters, this may be the wedding day!
   "Behold, the Bridegroom cometh!"

(Tune: #852)
8.6.8.6.

1 The Lord is longing for His Bride,
   All glorious within.
   His heart will then be satisfied
   When she is fit for Him.

2 'Tis by the Word the church is made
   Holy and pure as He;
   All spots and wrinkles it removes
   That she His Bride may be.

3 We must redeem these golden days,
   Eating the Word in prayer,
   Amening every line and phrase,
   And thus for Him prepare.

4 Oh, how the Word doth penetrate,
   Spirit and soul divide,
   Revealing every hidden weight
   For us to lay aside.

5 Lord, how we thank Thee for Thy Word,
   Living and operative.
   Oh, for Thy coming, we are stirred
   Ever by it to live!

6 Lord, make us those who bring Thee back,
   Who satisfy Thy heart.
   Now by Thy Word supply our lack,
   Make us Thy counterpart.

1311

14.12.14.12. with chorus.

1 The local churches are preparing for
    the Lord's return —
  We know the time is near for our
    Bridegroom so dear.
He's coming back to claim the Bride
    for which His heart doth yearn,
  That with Him we may be through
    all eternity.

  The Christ we love is coming soon,
  And He will come as our Bridegroom.
  We'll wait for Him, we'll watch and pray —
  It may be today, it may be today!

2 How we must give Him all our heart
    and from all idols turn!
  Oh, who else could there be who
    loves so tenderly?
Lord Jesus, You're the only One who
    makes our heart to burn —
  O please do not delay! Come quickly,
    e'en today!

3 A glorious Bride He is preparing for
    His wedding day;
  She'll be so bright and pure, fine
    linen covering her.
O Lord, work in Thy righteousness,
    this is the only way;
  And blessed we will be to join that
    feast with Thee.

12.12.12.8. with chorus.

1 It may be at morn as the day we are greeting;
  It may be the time when the saints all are meeting;
  But one thing we know, for the Spirit bears witness,
    That Jesus will come very soon!

      O Lord Jesus, Amen!
      The church soon will see Thee again!
      "Thou art coming! Hallelujah!
      Hallelujah, Amen!
      Hallelujah, Amen!"

2 The days hasten by — there's no time for delaying;
  So grasping each moment by watching and praying
  And in everything giving thanks and rejoicing,
    We'll welcome our Lord's return.

3 An instant, a twinkling, and Jesus descending
  Will come for His saints in His glory transcending.
  He'll come as the Bridegroom — as such we'll behold
    Him —
    To take to Himself His Bride!

4 What joy, what delight, when we finally meet Him!
  The One whom we love — O what rapture to greet
    Him!
  Our Lord and our life, our Beloved, our Bridegroom
    Will take to Himself His Bride!

1313

15.11.15.11. with chorus.

1 In that bright and golden moment when the
   Christ we love shall come,
   And the radiance of His glory we shall see;
When the Bride shall meet the Bridegroom and
   His loving wife become,
   What a meeting, what a meeting that will be!

   What a meeting, what a meeting,
   What a meeting with our Lover, with
   our Bridegroom in the air!
   What a meeting, what a meeting,
   What a meeting any moment we will share!

2 When to all who love His coming He shall speak
   the word, "Arise!"
   Oh, how blessed for that summons to be free!
With what rapture we shall greet Him as we
   join Him in the skies —
   What a meeting, what a meeting that will be!

3 Now in all the local churches we are meeting
   day by day
   And expecting any moment Christ to see,
But when Jesus comes the meeting starts that
   ne'er will pass away —
   What a meeting, what a meeting that will be!

4 Even now while we are meeting, Lord, we hope
   to see Thy face
   And forever without ceasing be with Thee.
Then we'll just go right on meeting in another
   meeting place —
   What a meeting, what a meeting this will be!

(Tune: #175)
Peculiar Meter.

1   Lord, Thou wilt soon appear,
      Thy day is almost here.
Oh, how we love Thy coming soon!
      We have no other
      Lord, life, or lover
Than Thou, Lord Jesus, our Bridegroom!

2   The hour is drawing nigh,
      Soon we shall hear Thy cry
And see Thee in the clouds descend.
      Oh what an hour sweet
      When Bride and Bridegroom meet
And love surpassing comprehend.

3   The moments fly apace,
      Soon we shall see Thy face!
Amen, Lord Jesus! Quickly come!
      We long Thyself to see
      And with Thee ever be,
Thou who our inmost heart hath won.

4   'Tis but a moment now;
      Thou, our Lord Bridegroom, Thou
Soon wilt return to claim Thy Bride.
      O Hallelujah!
      'Tis this we long for,
And Thou too wilt be satisfied.

1315

Matthew 25:1-13
9.7.9.7. with chorus.

1 Rejoice! Rejoice! Our Bridegroom's coming,
   And the time will not be long
Before we hail that wedding morning
   And lift up the glad new song.

      Oh, wondrous day! Oh, glorious morning,
         When the Christ we love shall come:
      With vessels filled and lamps all burning
         Let us welcome His return.
      Rejoice! Rejoice! Our Bridegroom's coming
         And the time will not be long
      Before we hail that wedding morning
         And lift up the glad new song.

2 Oh, let us now redeem each moment,
   More the precious oil to buy,
And have our vessels filled with ointment
   Ere we hear the midnight cry.

3 Oh, what a joy it is preparing
   For our wedding with the Lord,
E'en in the tribulations sharing
   For the bliss of such reward!

4 Oh, with what rapture and rejoicing
   Shall the wedding day begin;
And then a thousand years of dining
   At the marriage feast with Him!

HOPE OF GLORY — THE WEDDING DAY

(Tune: #953)
Peculiar Meter.

1316

1 Our Bridegroom soon is coming
   To claim His holy Bride,
The ones whom He has wooed, won,
   And wholly sanctified.
O Lord, we would be ready
   And get our hearts in tune
For the wedding day that's coming
      Very soon.

   Oh, the wedding day is coming,
      Is coming very soon,
   When the Bride shall be prepared
      And shall marry her Bridegroom.
   Oh, what love and consecration
      Should all our hearts attune
   For that wedding day that's coming
         Very soon.

2 Oh, that fine linen garment
   Which on that day we'll wear
E'en now, Lord, work within us
   And stitch by stitch prepare.
For this we would redeem
   Every moment opportune
For the wedding day that's coming
      Very soon.

3 Lord, may Your portion in us
   Continually increase
That we may be invited
   Unto that wedding feast.
And keep us always watching —
   At morning, night, or noon —
For the wedding day that's coming
      Very soon.

HOPE OF GLORY — THE WEDDING DAY

1317

(Tune: My Savior First of All)
14.11.14.11. with chorus.

1 When our Lord comes in glory and we're raptured to
    His side,
  When that bright and glorious moment we shall see,
  We shall know our dear Bridegroom as He comes to
    take His Bride,
  And He'll know the Bride He's loved so tenderly.

> We shall know Him! We shall know Him!
> When we see Him, our Bridegroom glorified!
> He shall know us! He shall know us!
> We're His church, His beloved, and His Bride!

2 Even now in the Spirit He reveals Himself to us,
  And His Person dear we've learned to recognize.
  But our eyes shall behold Him — O what rapture
    glorious
  When we gaze on Him unveiled in the skies!

3 In the Word we have seen Him shining forth in truth
    and grace,
  O how blessed to behold His features thus!
  But the day soon is coming when we'll see Him face
    to face,
  He, the living Word, in full revealed to us.

4 In the brothers and sisters, O how blest to see the Lord,
  In their attitudes and actions Christ expressed!
  But the day soon is coming when in rapturous accord
  We shall see His Person fully manifest.

5 In the meetings of the churches He's unveiled
    increasingly —
  O the joy unspeakable and glory too!
  As the meetings grow higher we're expecting soon
    to see
  The full glory of our Lord come into view.

HOPE OF GLORY — THE WEDDING DAY

Genesis 24
(Tune: #1237)
8.7.11.8.7.11. with chorus.

1318

1 'Twas a day in early springtime,
By an ancient wayside well,
Eliezer paused to rest his camel train.
He had found a bride for Isaac
Ere the evening shadows fell,
For his weary journey had not been in vain.

> Oh, get ready! Evening shadows fall.
> Don't you hear the Eliezer call?
> There's going to be a wedding,
> And our joy will soon begin,
> In the evening when the camel train comes in.

2 So he took the fair Rebekah,
Dressed in jewels rich and rare,
Quickly to her waiting bridegroom far away.
Where Rebekah loved her Isaac,
And he loved Rebekah fair;
Oh, it must have been a happy wedding day.

3 Now the blessed Holy Spirit,
From our Father God above,
Has come down to earth to find a worthy Bride.
For our Isaac over yonder
Has prepared His tents of love,
And He wants His fair Rebekah by His side.

4 We have left our kinfolk gladly;
We have bade the world goodbye.
We've been called to be His pure and spotless Bride;
Where we'll soon behold our Jesus
In that blest eternity —
What a happy, happy wedding that will be!

1319

(Tune: #333)
8.6.8.6. with chorus.

1 That which for long the prophets sought,
  The righteous yearned to see,
  Has in these last of days appeared
  In its reality.

    And we're now in the final stages,
    'Tis the completion of all the ages.
    All those who believed the promise
    Are perfected now in us.

2 Oh, blessed are our eyes that see,
  Our ears, how blessed to hear;
  Things angels ne'er could look into
  Are now to us made clear.

3 Our sense is corporate, bold and strong,
  His grace, how free to take;
  Encouraging the others on,
  Run for the kingdom's sake.

4 We're weary not this race to run,
  It makes our joy complete;
  For this we know, around the bend,
  The Lord we'll surely meet.

1320

(Tune: #1257)
8.7.8.7. with chorus.

1 We have seen the Lord is coming
  For the church for whom He died;
  We are in the age of ages,
  When the Lord will take His Bride!

    'Tis a glorious age, the age of the ages,
    Now, in this age, Christ will come!
    So prepare ye now the church for the marriage,
    Christ and the church will be one!

2 Praise God, in this age we're living,
   Age of God's recovery.
   We are in the local churches,
   Where the Bride prepared may be.

3 Unreservedly we're giving
   All, that He be satisfied;
   For the life and for the building
   Of His holy, chosen Bride.

    'Tis a glorious age, the age of the ages,
    Now in this age Christ will come!
    We're preparing now the church for
      the marriage,
    Christ and the church will be one!

THE MANIFESTATION OF THE SONS OF GOD

(Tune: #960)
8.6.8.6.D.

1321

1 The grace which God bestows on us
   Is just His Son in full;
   The rich enjoyment of this Christ
   Is plenteous, bountiful.
   'Tis far too great to comprehend,
   Too wondrous to contain:
   How we, once children of despair,
   God's masterpiece became.

2 The whole creation now beneath
   The weight of bondage sore,
   In seeing God's sons manifest
   Is freed forevermore.
   Th' eternal purpose of our God
   Will be full manifest;
   The hope of glory now concealed
   Is then to all expressed.

continued

3 The briars will be myrtle trees,
  The thorn will be no more,
  And peace will reign where war did rage,
  The curse will then be o'er.
  'Tis then the trees shall clap their hands,
  And all the hills shall sing;
  This glorious freedom shall God's sons
  Thus manifested bring.

4 God's deepest work of grace goes on
  Each day, though hidden, small,
  Until that day, when manifest,
  It is revealed to all.
  By then God's wrought His finished work:
  Himself dispensed to us;
  And all creation 'round admires
  His product, glorious.

5 The angels that before our God
  In brightest splendor stand,
  Will join the universal praise
  To Him for all He's planned.
  And of the devil, of his end . . . ?
  We'll praise the Lord for how
  Just distant smoke is all that's left
  Of all that troubles now.

6 So shall we not delight to give
  Ourselves in every way,
  And let the Lord dispense Himself
  Into us more each day;
  The grace that we receive each day,
  Though hidden oft, and small,
  Is God Himself wrought into us,
  That day to shine o'er all.

1 In spirit, in the church we see
   The high estate we're destined for.
   It's higher, vaster, more profound
   Than anything we've seen before.

2 It's not a view in doctrine bare
   But an unveiling of the Christ.
   He's marvelous and far beyond
   Our mental thought or power to share.

3 He's rich, unlimited, profound,
   Immeasurable, and marvelous.
   Yet 'tis a greater wonder still
   He needs heirs of salvation — us.

4 God has accomplished many things —
   He's planned, created, and brought forth.
   The Son is now appointed Heir,
   Administrator of God's worth.

5 But in th' economy of God
   There is not one, but many sons.
   One is the firstborn Son of God
   With many other living ones.

6 Christ will inherit all God's things,
   And we're the heirs of God with Christ.
   We're growing now to be matured;
   As heirs we'll soon be legalized.

7 We're joint-heirs with the firstborn Son,
   Inheriting the universe.
   We're in this corporation vast —
   All partners of Christ and the church.

8 In spirit, in the church, we see
   Our calling of unrivaled worth.
   We're destined, not to go to heaven.
   We're destined to be kings on earth.

continued

9 We're paupers, yet we're glorious kings.
   Inheriting the kingdom vast,
   The earth, God's throne, and e'en all things
   And all the Father is and has.

HOPE OF GLORY — GENERAL

1323
Song of Songs 2:8-17
(Tune: #206)
7.6.7.6.D.

1 The voice of my Beloved,
   Behold, He quickly comes;
   He leaps upon the mountains,
   And o'er the hills He runs.
   The signs of His appearing
   Are seen on every side;
   The Bridegroom soon is coming
   To claim His loving Bride.

2 How real that He is coming —
   Come quickly, Lord, again!
   We watch for His appearing,
   His precious Word amen.
   Oh, don't delay His coming,
   Pray without ceasing, pray;
   He's eagerly awaiting
   That coming wedding day.

3 He longs to hear our voices,
   He longs to see our face —
   Our voices filled with sweetness,
   Our countenance with grace.
   "Arise, My love, My fair one,"
   We long to hear Him say.
   The voice of our Beloved —
   "Arise and come away!"

4   The winter rain is over,
    The flowers appear on earth;
    The rising sun of Jesus
    Fills all our hearts with mirth.
    It is the time of singing,
    The turtle dove is heard;
    For our Beloved's coming
    The sweetest chords are stirred.

5   Oh, let us take the foxes
    That spoil the blooming vine;
    Our vineyards are in blossom,
    And all, Beloved, is Thine.
    The day is quickly dawning,
    The shadows flee away;
    Upon the mount of spices
    Our Lord may come today.

ULTIMATE MANIFESTATION — GOD'S ETERNAL PURPOSE

(Tune: Joyful, Joyful We Adore Thee)
8.7.8.7.D.

1324

1   Our God is a God of purpose,
    What He plans, He will fulfill!
    Genesis to Revelation
    Shows His full and glorious will.
    What He's after is a building.
    In creation He began
    With a simple garden planted —
    This, the setting for His plan.

continued

2   Man was made, the first step God took
    To achieve His final goal,
    As a vessel, a container,
    Three parts — body, spirit, soul.
    God, of dust, a body formed him,
    Breath of life into him breathed —
    This part is man's human spirit
    By which God may be received.

3   In the garden God had planted
    Every tree He made to grow,
    Good for food, to sight most pleasing,
    And the tree of life also!
    Second, then, in God's intention
    Was that man should freely eat
    Of the life-tree in the center
    To obtain His life complete.

4   Third, we see a river flowing,
    Out of Eden coming forth,
    With its flow in four directions —
    East and west and south and north.
    As on Christ our life we're feeding,
    Living water in us flows.
    Hallelujah for this river
    And the watering it bestows!

5   In the flowing of the river
    Gold, pearl, onyx stone we see;
    Three materials, raw yet precious,
    For God's building meant to be.
    Look, these elements are shining!
    How can we, then, shine as they?
    Simply by the Lord, the Spirit,
    Us transforming every day.

6 God the Father (in this fourth step),
   Source of life, is gold divine;
   Christ the Son was wounded by us
   To produce the pearl so fine.
   God the Spirit brings the stones forth —
   Transformation of the clay.
   By the flowing of the Spirit
   Changed we'll be from day to day.

7 Insufficient are materials
   Precious though they be and best;
   These must be built up together
   That God's house they may express.
   Fifth step: We ourselves hand over
   To the building that we be
   Built into God's house, His dwelling,
   One in each locality.

8 Finally, in Revelation,
   Is the picture of Christ's Bride —
   Consummation of God's purpose;
   He is fully satisfied.
   New Jerusalem, a city,
   Is the Bridegroom's counterpart —
   So the church built up together
   Forms the Bride for Christ's own heart.

9 How can we, as those who truly
   Long to see God reach His goal,
   Be united and related?
   By denial of our soul!
   As we contact Christ in spirit,
   Feed on Him as life to us,
   Then His life will flow, transform us
   To His Bride, all glorious!

ULTIMATE MANIFESTATION —
GOD'S ETERNAL PURPOSE

1325

(Tune: #589)
8.7.8.7.D.

1 God eternal has a purpose,
   Formed in His eternal past,
Spreading to eternal future;
   'Twixt these ends all time is cast.
For with time there is the process,
   Time for His accomplishment;
And in time we're merely travelers —
   For eternity we're meant.

2 God would have a group of people
   Built together in His plan,
Blended, knit, coordinated
   As His vessel — one new man.
God would come into this vessel
   With His nature, life and ways,
Mingling Spirit with our spirits
   For His joy and to His praise.

3 God has worked in three directions
   For His plan so marvelous:
As the Father, Son, and Spirit
   To dispense Himself to us!
All creation gives the setting —
   Heav'n and earth are for this plan;
'Tis for this God made a body,
   Soul and spirit — three-part man.

4 As the center, as the kernel,
   Of God's plan our spirit is;
Calling on the name of Jesus
   Makes our spirit one with His.
From the center to circumference
   God would saturate each part;
Feeling, mind, and will renewing,
   Making home in all our heart.

5   Thus in life we're built together,
    Then in love we're knit as one;
    God is now His plan fulfilling,
    Finishing what He's begun.
    Lord, increase Thyself within us
    That we might be built by Thee
    Into that great corporate vessel
    Filled with God exclusively.

6   As the product, the fulfillment,
    Will the church in glory stand,
    Consummation of the purpose
    In eternal ages planned.
    God will have His corporate vessel,
    All His glory to contain;
    Lord, we're wholly for Thy purpose
    All Thy goal in us attain.

GOSPEL — GENERAL

7.7.7.7.D.   **1326**

What is living all about,
Where's the answer? Let's find out!

Call, "Lord Jesus!" Taste and see!
Christ becomes reality,
Life He gives abundantly
As a river flowing free.
With a new life we begin,
Joy is springing from within,
Love — He fills us to the brim!
And it's all because of Him! (Hallelujah)

8.8.8.8. with chorus.

1327

1 Once I thirsted for a fountain,
   Something deep that would satisfy,
   But the fountain that I'd drink from,
   Left me searching and still so dry.
      Then one day I found Him,
      He satisfied my thirst,
      Became in me a deeper source
      Whence living waters burst.
         Now I drink Him!
      Jesus, Jesus is my life now,
      Jesus, Jesus is my life;
      I'm fully satisfied now,
      Jesus, Jesus is my life.

2 After tasting such a fountain,
   Longed my heart for a place of springs;
   Caught a vision on a mountain,
   In Jerusalem's a gathering.
      Then one day He found me,
      He brought me to the church,
      Pleasures here abound fore'er
      I've given up my search.
         Hallelujah!
      Jesus, Jesus is my life now,
      Jesus, Jesus is my life;
      I'm fully satisfied now,
      Jesus, Jesus is my life.

3 Empty wanderer drop the striving —
   Isn't worth all the troublin';
   Open up your heart believing,
   Call "Lord Jesus" and He'll come in!
      Then today you'll find Him,
      And calling on His name,
      You're joined to Him, you're one with Him —
      You'll never be the same.
         You won't want to!

Jesus, Jesus is my life now,
Jesus, Jesus is my life;
I'm fully satisfied now,
Jesus, Jesus is my life.

Peculiar Meter. **1328**

My wandering days grew increasingly empty
As I searched for the way,
Just to fill this gap inside me —
Found my seeking vain.

Though all this dark earth would convince me
    life's worthwhile,
Inside all my mirth
Was a cry for something real.
Don't you lie to me, world!

For my heart tells me different
When I hear of contentment
Deep within a lack knew better
Why not be honest, world.

A flood of strong doubt as I heard the old story
Of a man they called Lord;
Yet my heart ne'er ceased to wonder,
Is He really Lord?

A search in His Word found my hardened
    heart softened,
And earth's vanities faded.
In the brightness of His presence
Jesus came into me.

Now we're always together
Growing into God's fullness.
O Lord Jesus, how I love You!
You brought life into me.

1329

John 2 - 11

11.10.11.10.D.

1 The wedding feast, the peak of man's enjoyment
Was full of pleasure till the wine ran dry.
The human life, like wine, is soon exhausted,
Till Jesus comes, divine life to supply.

> When Jesus comes, new wine is made from water,
> When Jesus comes, the darkness turns to light.
> He touches death — it's turned to life eternal,
> Weakness to strength and blindness into sight.

2 One night a moral righteous man, a ruler
To Jesus came, more teaching to pursue;
But teachings ne'er could change the fallen nature,
So Jesus said, "You must be born anew."

3 "I have no husband," sighed the thirsty sinner.
Indeed her many husbands left her dry.
Daily she came to draw the failing water
Till Jesus came, her thirst to satisfy.

4 A man among the multitude lay helpless,
So weak while waiting till the water stirred.
Religion of the law could never heal him;
Then Jesus came and spoke the living word.

5 Within the tomb, four days and nights he lay there,
Death's grip had come; they 'round the grave did weep.
Silent he lay, all bound and wrapped in grave clothes;
Then Jesus came, and woke him from his sleep.

6 And still today, this Jesus is so living,
Able to save from death in any form.
Now open up your heart and call upon Him;
To you He'll come, in spirit you'll be born.

Peculiar Meter.

1 "All things are ready," come to the feast!
Come for the table now is spread;
Ye famishing, ye weary, come,
And thou shalt be richly fed.

Hear the invitation,
Come, whosoever will;
Praise God for full salvation
For whosoever will.

2 "All things are ready," come to the feast!
Come, for the door is open wide;
A place of honor is reserved
For you at the Master's side.

3 "All things are ready," come to the feast!
Come, while He waits to welcome thee;
Delay not while this day is thine,
Tomorrow may never be.

4 "All things are ready," come to the feast!
Leave every care and worldly strife;
Come, feast upon the Christ of God
And drink everlasting life.

1331

Peculiar Meter.

1 Just taste and see that the Lord is good;
Just taste and see that the Lord is good.
He's good for you, as He is for me;
So whatever you do, just taste and see.

2 Just call O Lord — He'll change your life;
Just call O Lord — He'll change your life.
Amazing grace He will afford;
If in every place you call O Lord.

3 You'll feel real love coming into your heart;
You'll feel real love coming into your heart.
You'll sense a flow from God above;
And you will know you've found real love.

4 So praise the Lord for His life in you;
Yes, praise the Lord for His life in you.
Something of Christ He has outpoured
Into *your* life; so praise the Lord!

1332

(Tune: #789)
8.7.8.7.D.

1 Do you know that you were chosen
Long before the world began;
That by God you were selected
And appointed for His plan?
Something in your inmost being
Tells you this is surely true;
That's why you are in this meeting,
And *you* feel the way you do.

2 All the sins you've e'er committed,
 Everything you've ever done,
 All by God has been forgiven,
 Taken care of by God's Son.
 Struggle not, no; just believe this,
 For His word assures it's true;
 All you need to do is thank Him
 For all that He's done for you.

3 Did you know that all the Bible
 Is a will, a testament?
 Everything that Christ accomplished
 Is for all God's children meant.
 As His child you are included,
 For His word stands fast and true;
 So by faith you now inherit
 All that He has done for you.

4 Did you know God has a family?
 Yes, He does, in fact, it's us.
 That's why we are here enjoying
 All He is, so marvelous.
 He's our God and we're His people,
 Day by day we love Him more;
 We're so happy and so thankful,
 We just praise Him o'er and o'er.

5 All we know is that we love Him,
 We're so glad for what He's done;
 We are brought to Him, and we all
 Know the joy of being one.
 We're so glad that we're included,
 What a fellowship have we!
 So we'd like to welcome you, friend,
 Into God's own family.

1333

Peculiar Meter.

1 What a happy day
When I no more could turn away,
When Jesus took my heart
from the black of night
Into the kingdom of His light.

2 Now my life's begun,
The "really life" that's in the Son.
No more am I enthralled by
earth's empty dreams;
Deep in me flows a living stream.

3 As I turn to Him
He fills me with His life within.
His life becomes my life in reality;
Oh, hallelujah, He's in me!

4 I just love You, Lord,
With other loves, You break the cord.
You'll be my life for all eternity;
You are the only One for me.

SCRIPTURES FOR SINGING

1334

Thou hast turned my mourning into dancing for me;
  Thou hast put off my sackcloth;
Thou hast turned my mourning into dancing for me,
  And girded me with gladness;
To the end my glory may sing praise unto Thee,
  And not be silent.
O Lord my God, I will give thanks unto Thee forever.

Psalm 48:1-2 **1335**

Great is the Lord, and greatly to be praised,
  In the city of our God,
  In the mountain of His holiness.
Beautiful in elevation, the joy of the whole earth,
  Is Mount Zion, on the sides of the north,
    The city of the great King.
  Is Mount Zion, on the sides of the north,
    The city of the great King.

Psalm 116:12-13 **1336**

What shall I give unto the Lord
For all, for all, for all He's done for me?
I'll take the cup of salvation,
And call, and call, and call upon the name
  of the Lord.

SCRIPTURES FOR SINGING

1337

Psalm 126:1-6

1 When the Lord turned again the captivity of Zion,
We were like them that dream,
We were like them that dream.

2 Then was our mouth filled with laughter,
And our tongue with singing:
Then said they among the nations,
The Lord hath done great things,
The Lord hath done great things for them.

    The Lord hath done great things for us;
    Whereof we are glad.
    The Lord hath done great things for us;
    Whereof we are glad.

3 Turn again our captivity, O Lord, as the streams,
As the streams in the south,
As the streams in the south.

4 They that sow in tears shall reap in joy,
They that sow in tears shall reap in joy.

5 He that goeth forth and weepeth,
Bearing precious seed, shall doubtless,
Come again with rejoicing,
Come again with rejoicing,
Bringing his sheaves with him.

    The Lord hath done great things for us;
    Whereof we are glad.
    The Lord hath done great things for us;
    Whereof we are glad.

6 When the Lord turned again the captivity of Zion,
We were like them that dream,
We were like them that dream.

SCRIPTURES FOR SINGING

Psalm 132:13-16

This is My rest forever;
  Here will I dwell,
For the Lord hath chosen Zion,
He hath desired it for His habitation.

He will abundantly bless her provision:
He will satisfy her poor with bread.
He will clothe her priests with salvation,
And her saints shall shout aloud for joy.

Psalm 133

1 Behold how good and how pleasant it is,
  For brethren to dwell together in unity!
  Behold how good and how pleasant it is,
  For brethren to dwell together in unity!

  It is like the precious ointment upon the head,
  That ran down upon the beard,
  Even Aaron's beard:
  That went down to the skirts of his garments.

2 Behold how good and how pleasant it is,
  For brethren to dwell together in unity!

  It is like the precious ointment upon the head,
  That ran down upon the beard,
  Even Aaron's beard:
  That went down to the skirts of his garments.

3 As the dew of Hermon,
  And as the dew that descended
  Upon the mountains of Zion:
  For there the Lord commanded the blessing,
  Even life for evermore.

SCRIPTURES FOR SINGING

1340   Isaiah 12:3-4, 6

> Therefore with joy shall ye draw water
>   Out of the wells of salvation.
> And in that day shall ye say,
>   Praise the Lord.

         (Repeat the above four lines)

> Call upon His name, declare His doings
>   among the people,
> Make mention that His name is exalted.
> Cry out and shout, thou inhabitant of Zion:
> For great is the Holy One of Israel in the
>   midst of thee.

1341   Isaiah 51:11

> Therefore the redeemed of the Lord shall return,
> And come with singing unto Zion;
> And everlasting joy shall be upon their head.
> Therefore the redeemed of the Lord shall return,
> And come with singing unto Zion;
> And everlasting joy shall be upon their head.

> They shall obtain gladness and joy;
> And sorrow and mourning shall flee away.

         (Repeat the first three lines)

1342   Jeremiah 31:12

> Therefore, they shall come and sing in the height of Zion,
> And shall flow together to the goodness of the Lord,
> For wheat, and for wine, and for oil, and for the young,
>   for the young of the flock and of the herd:
> And their soul shall be as a watered garden;
> And they shall not sorrow any more at all.

John 13:34-35 **1343**

A new commandment
I give unto you
That you love one another
As I have loved you,
That you love one another
As I have loved you.
　By this shall all men
　Know you are My disciples
　If you have love one to another.
(Repeat the last three lines)

Romans 11:33-37 **1344**

Oh, the depth of the riches and the
　wisdom and knowledge of God;
How unsearchable are His judgments;
How untraceable are His paths.
For who has known the mind of the Lord,
　Or who has been His counselor?
Or who has first given to Him,
And it will be repaid to Him?
Because out of Him and through Him
　And to Him are all things.
To Him be the glory forever. Amen.

2 Corinthians 3:16-17 **1345**

Whenever the heart shall turn to the Lord,
　The veil shall be taken away.
So turn your heart to the Lord all the day,
　And the veil shall be taken away.
　Now the Lord is that Spirit,
　And where the Spirit of the Lord is,
　There is liberty — such liberty!
Whenever the heart shall turn to the Lord,
　The veil shall be taken away.

SCRIPTURES FOR SINGING

1346 1 Timothy 1:17

Now unto the King eternal, immortal, invisible,
The only wise God, the only wise God,
Be honor and glory forever and ever. Amen. Amen.
Be honor and glory forever and ever. Amen.

1347 Revelation 12:10-12

Now is come salvation and strength
And the kingdom of our God
And the authority of His Christ:
For the accuser of our brethren is cast down
Which accused them before our God day and night.

And they overcame him by the blood of the Lamb,
And by the word of their testimony
And they loved not their soul lives unto death.
Therefore rejoice, rejoice, rejoice!

1348 Revelation 21:3-5

Behold, the tabernacle of God is with men,
And He will dwell with them, and they shall be
His people,
And God Himself shall be with them and be their God.
Behold, the tabernacle of God is with men,
And God shall wipe away all tears from their eyes;
And there shall be no more death, neither sorrow,
nor crying, neither shall there be any more pain,
For the former things are passed away.
Behold, I make all things new.

INDEX OF FIRST LINES
AND CHORUSES

HYMNS 1-1080

First lines are in lower case type; choruses in small caps.

1293

INDEX OF FIRST LINES AND CHORUSES
HYMNS 1-1080

INDEX OF FIRST LINES
AND CHORUSES
HYMNS 1081-1348

First lines are in lower case type; choruses in small caps.

SCRIPTURE REFERENCE INDEX
HYMNS 1081-1348

ISBN 0-7363-1122-X

9 790736 311228 >

Printed in the Netherlands

Printed in the Netherlands